THE PSYCHIATRIC WRITINGS FROM ALIENATION AND FREEDOM

ALSO AVAILABLE FROM BLOOMSBURY

THE PSYCHIATRIC WRITINGS FROM ALIENATION AND FREEDOM

Frantz Fanon

Edited by Jean Khalfa and Robert J.C. Young
Translated by Steven Corcoran

BLOOMSBURY ACADEMIC
LONDON • NEW YORK • OXFORD • NEW DELHI • SYDNEY

BLOOMSBURY ACADEMIC
Bloomsbury Publishing Plc
50 Bedford Square, London, WC1B 3DP, UK
1385 Broadway, New York, NY 10018, USA
29 Earlsfort Terrace, Dublin 2, Ireland

BLOOMSBURY, BLOOMSBURY ACADEMIC and the Diana logo
are trademarks of Bloomsbury Publishing Plc

First published in *Ecrits sur L'Alienation et La Liberte* in France © Editions LA
DÉCOUVERTE, Paris, France, 2015
Reprinted 2019

First published in English in *Alienation and Freedom*, Great Britain, 2018

Paperback edition first published in Great Britain, 2021
Reprinted in 2022, 2023, 2024

Copyright to the collection and editorial material © Jean Khalfa and
Robert J. C. Young, 2018, 2021
Copyright to the English translation © Steven Corcoran, 2018, 2021

For legal purposes the Acknowledgements on pp. xvi-xviii constitute
an extension of this copyright page.

Cover design by Charlotte Daniels

All rights reserved. No part of this publication may be reproduced or transmitted
in any form or by any means, electronic or mechanical, including photocopying,
recording, or any information storage or retrieval system, without prior
permission in writing from the publishers.

Bloomsbury Publishing Plc does not have any control over, or responsibility for,
any third-party websites referred to or in this book. All internet addresses given
in this book were correct at the time of going to press. The author and publisher
regret any inconvenience caused if addresses have changed or sites have ceased
to exist, but can accept no responsibility for any such changes.

A catalogue record for this book is available from the British Library.

A catalog record for this book is available from the Library of Congress.

ISBN: PB: 978-1-3501-2591-9
          ePDF: 978-1-3501-2592-6
          eBook: 978-1-3501-2593-3

Typeset by Integra Software Services Pvt. Ltd.
Printed and bound in Great Britain

To find out more about our authors and books visit www.bloomsbury.com
and sign up for our newsletters.

CONTENTS

ILLUSTRATIONS

Figures

Graphs in "Day hospitalization in psychiatry: value and limits", 1959

FRANTZ FANON: WORKS CITED

Peau noire, masques blancs, Seuil, 1952. English translation, *Black Skin, White Masks*, trans. Richard Philcox, New York: Grove Press, 2008.

L'An V de la révolution algérienne, Maspero, 1959. English translation, *A Dying Colonialism*, trans. Haakon Chevalier, New York: Grove Press, 1965.

Les Damnés de la terre, Maspero, 1961. English translation, *The Wretched of the Earth*, trans. Richard Philcox, New York: Grove Press, 2004.

Pour la révolution africaine, Écrits politiques, Maspero, 1964. English translation, *Toward the African Revolution*, trans. Haakon Chevalier, New York: Grove Press, 1967.

Œuvres, Paris: La Découverte, 2011.

EDITORS' PREFACE

Jean Khalfa and Robert J.C.Young

n 2015 we published an edition of Frantz Fanon's uncollected and unpublished writings *Écrits sur l'alienation et la liberté* (Paris: La Découverte), translated into English in 2018 as *Alienation and Freedom* (London: Bloomsbury). For this paperback English edition, the publisher suggested that given the size of the original it would make sense to break it up into three books. *Alienation and Freedom* was in fact already divided into three main sections, plays, psychiatry and politics, and these form the basis of the division of the material for the paperbacks: *The Plays from Alienation and Freedom*, *The Psychiatric Writings from Alienation and Freedom* and *The Political Writings from Alienation and Freedom*.

During his lifetime, Fanon published three books: *Black Skin, White Masks* (1952), *A Dying Colonialism* (1958), and *The Wretched of the Earth* (1961). After his death in 1961, his publisher François Maspero collected up some of Fanon's political writings in the volume translated as *Toward the African Revolution* (1964). As he announced in the Preface to that volume, Maspero intended to follow it with a further collection that would bring together Fanon's psychiatric writings. For a variety of reasons, this was never published. Maspero and Fanon's friend Giovanni Pirelli had intended if possible to publish all Fanon's unpublished or uncollected work that was available to them: in putting together *Alienation and Freedom*, we have been able to complete their task, some fifty years later. With the passage of time, some of the original material has disappeared, while new material has been found.

Fanon has always been celebrated for his passionate language, but his early writing for theatre was long thought to be lost. In *The Plays from Alienation and Freedom* we print two remarkable plays that he wrote during his medical studies in Lyon. Never before published, they throw a striking philosophical light on the texts published during his lifetime. These first texts are steeped in the poetry of Césaire and the theatre of Claudel and of Sartre. In them, however, we can also glimpse passages which foreground the unbearable, raw light that one must risk preferring to the reassuring choice of an obscurity in which conflict is avoided; the relation of words to action; the desire to accept the event as such rather than the comfort of the known, a comfort akin to death – a Nietzschean conception of the tragic that informed Fanon's political thinking on disalienation and independence. In Sartre, the thinker he probably admired most, he had already discerned the thought of the present that would be developed in *Critique de la raison dialectique*, about which he later gave seminars to officers of the Algerian National Liberation Army.

The Psychiatric Writings from Alienation and Freedom completes the plan for the collection of Fanon's psychiatric work first announced by Maspero in 1964:

> Since becoming a psychiatrist at Blida Hospital [in Algeria], and even more so after the outbreak of the [November 1954] insurrection, Fanon also came to be a militant in the Algerian revolutionary organization. At the same time, he carried on a remarkable medical activity, innovating at many levels, deeply, viscerally close to his patients, whom he regarded as primarily victims of the system he was fighting. He collected clinical notes and developed analyses of phenomena of colonialist alienation as seen through mental illnesses. He explored local traditions and their relations to colonization. This essential material remains untouched, but it is too scattered, and we hope to be able to assemble it and present it in a separate volume.[1]

In the current collection of psychiatric texts, the reader will find not only Fanon's dissertation in psychiatry (defended viva voce in November 1951) and the scientific articles, both single-authored and collaborative, that he published throughout the 1950s, but also manuscripts and fragments that we have discovered. We have reprinted editorial texts that were originally published in the ward

---

[1]Frantz Fanon, *Toward the African Revolution*, 1967, p. viii (translation modified – SC).

newspaper of Saint-Alban Hospital, where, in 1951 and 1952, Fanon was an intern of the revolutionary psychiatrist François Tosquelles, and further editorials from the newspaper that he set up at Blida-Joinville Hospital (today the Frantz-Fanon Hospital, Blida, Algeria), which formed an essential element of the 'socialtherapy' he helped to pioneer. Many of these texts that he wrote between 1954 and 1956 were long forgotten, ignored, or, for some manuscripts, unknown.

The wealth and impact of his political oeuvre are such that, given his short life (of only thirty-six years),[2] it was no doubt difficult to think that Fanon could have produced psychiatric research of any importance alongside it. On occasion, this psychiatric work was perhaps somewhat obscured or played down when seemingly out of sync with later fashions. But it would have been surprising had someone of Fanon's rigour been satisfied with a slapdash philosophy. As the reader shall see, the political work is in fact grounded on an astonishingly lucid epistemology and innovative scientific work and clinical practice. The dissertation in psychiatry aimed to establish a scientific distinction between the psychiatric and the neurological, by underlining the importance of the body and movement, of social and spatial relations, in structuring consciousness, or else in the alienation of consciousness when the aforementioned are hindered. The scientific articles explore and unfold the consequences of this intuition, in particular as part of a critique of the biologism of colonial ethnopsychiatry, and enable him to revisit culture in its relation both to the body and to history. Such work clearly underlies the famous talk on 'National Culture' that he delivered at the Second Congress of Black Artists and Writers, held in Rome in 1959. This psychiatric work also leads toward the overall mental health programme that he implemented while in Tunis, where he founded the Neuropsychiatric Day Centre of Charles-Nicolle Hospital, which he headed from 1957 to 1959 and which was one of the first open psychiatric clinics in the Francophone world. Moreover, some psychiatrists whose practice, it seems, he shook up, could not stop themselves, albeit much later, from claiming his heritage.[3]

---

[2]Some key dates are to be found in the Chronology at the end of each volume.
[3]On this point, see the Introduction to the *Psychiatric Writings*, vol. II, p. 35, footnote 75.

Tunisian sociologist Lilia Ben Salem has entrusted us with the notes she took of Fanon's lectures on society and psychiatry at the Institut des Hautes Études in Tunis: the lectures synthesize and broaden the meaning of his works, and tell us about the books and films that excited him at the time. But leafing through the editorials of Saint-Alban and Blida, which Fanon compared to the pages of a logbook, we already see some of the structuring themes of his thinking: vigilance as the essence of being human, a theme he presents when remarking upon the difference between wakefulness and insomnia; his constant reminders to the orderlies that he was training to inquire into the meaning of all their actions; and the distrust of institutionalization that, in his last writings, informs the critique of the neocolonial elites that emerged in many countries after winning independence.

The Political Writings from Alienation and Freedom focuses on Fanon's political writings, where we reprint articles originally published in *El Moudjahid* from 1958 on. These texts were not collected in *Toward the African Revolution*, but, on the basis of precise contemporary testimonies and crosschecking done by his editors immediately after his death, it seems to us that Fanon's thinking at least strongly influences them, even if they were perhaps only partly authored by Fanon himself.[4] Along with a previously untranslated speech offering a justification for the FLN use of violence, the reader will also find here two previously unpublished texts dealing with important issues: a propaganda pamphlet published in Accra, Ghana, where Fanon was the ambassador of the Provisional Government of the Algerian Republic – the pamphlet develops an acerbic critique of some new African elites, whom he calls 'stooges of imperialism', and of neocolonialism more generally; and, in a letter to Iranian philosopher Ali Shariati, kindly provided to us by Dr Sara Shariati, we find his reflections and doubts on the role of religion in a revolutionary process. However, much of Fanon's political correspondence remains undiscovered.

---

[4] Anonymity was the rule at *El Moudjahid*. The articles retained in 1964 were done so 'under the control of Mme F. Fanon'. The editor stipulated that he had conserved only 'those of which we had irrefutable certainty that Frantz Fanon had written them. His contribution, naturally, was not limited to these precise texts. But, as in every team, and particularly in this revolution in full ferment, there was constant osmosis, interaction, mutual stimulation' (x; translation modified – SC). We provide the reasons for our selections in the introduction to the articles we have selected.

We have also consulted the family library[5] and provide in each paperback a list of the works from the collection that most probably belonged to Fanon himself, reproducing his marks and annotations whenever significant.

Finding and assembling these texts was not a simple process. In this task, Fanon's Italian editors, Giovanni Pirelli and Giulio Einaudi, of course preceded us, as did François Maspero, who drew up the first inventory of Fanon's writings. The essential part of the correspondence containing this inventory is presented in the third volume in the section titled 'Publishing Fanon'. Retracing the work of these pioneers, who radicalized publishing with a view to creating a new society, we saw that the works that we now take as fixed, Fanon rather viewed as elements of shifting arrangements. Their plans to publish Fanon's complete works, which they arranged in a somewhat different fashion from what we consider today as the Fanon corpus, nevertheless did not come about. For over a decade now, we have sought to tackle this corpus anew.

There is no substantive archive of Fanon's work that contains all his original typescripts, drafts or letters in the manner of those preserved for many eminent European writers. Fanon does not seem to have been too concerned with conserving his writings or his preparatory works (even if he was proud of the plays he wrote in his youth). Moreover, he did not exactly write, but, for the most part, dictated, without notes, as is still the practice for many doctors. The texts gathered in these volumes were therefore assembled over a considerable period of time by putting together disparate material drawn from a multiplicity of sources from four continents. We were first required to engage in painstaking work to identify everything that he had written – in Algeria, in France and in Martinique – whether published or not. Through our works and persistence, we eventually won the trust of Fanon's descendants and of others who were in possession of documents, which were sometimes discovered following our encounters. In some cases, we had to restore texts that were too damaged to be immediately

---

[5]In 2013 the family library was given to the Centre National de Recherches Préhistoriques, Anthropologiques et Historiques (CNRPAH) in Algiers (see http://www.cnrpah.org/index.php/fondset- catalogues).

legible.[6] We warmly thank all those who placed their trust in us and helped us in our editorial work.

Alienation and Freedom is based on the surmise that an author of this magnitude cannot genuinely be understood without knowing all his work, in its continuities as much as in its transformations. In approaching it, the two of us took a different point of departure: one of us, Jean Khalfa, set out from the history of psychiatry and a longstanding interest in Francophone writings from the Antilles and the Maghreb, the other, Robert J.C. Young, from the history of colonialism and decolonization, in particular in the Anglophone and Francophone regions. We were both similarly dissatisfied with reductive interpretations of Fanon, interpretations that eliminate either the historical/political dimension or the philosophical/psychological dimension, depending on the social imperatives of the moment. By turning him into a political icon, his well-argued and very lucid critiques of the possible despotic future of postcolonial societies get buried. By seeing him as the thinker of contemporary identity issues, his essential aim is forgotten: namely, to think and construct freedom as disalienation within a necessarily historical and political process. Even Fanon's most technical psychiatric writings seem to us to add depth to an understanding of his other texts, which are already known the world over. Through editorial notes, we have endeavoured to indicate how this is so. Everything in this thinker's work has its intelligibility. Fanon had a very precise idea of what mattered to him and made use of anything that could enrich his perspective (he devoured in equal measure literature, philosophy, psychiatry, history, politics, sociology and ethnology). We also talked at length with many people who knew Fanon well and who kindly provided information on the detail of his work methods and on his own understanding of his work's significance. In retrospect, this collection has far exceeded our original hopes, something for which we are very glad. The persistence and talents of our French publisher, François Gèze, in mediating between all the interested parties, was extraordinary. He

---

[6]For these documents, restored on the basis of poor quality manuscripts or typescripts (as in the case of the two plays), we have indicated in brackets the words that remained unclear.

belongs to the tradition of those aforementioned great publishers. But we also view this edition as only one stage along the road and as an appeal to the future. Other texts by Fanon, in particular from his correspondence as well as his Blida and Tunis case notes, and his seminars for officers of the Algerian National Liberation Army remain unavailable. The interest of what we present in this edition will, we hope, give rise to further enrichments.

Note to the paperback edition

We have taken the opportunity of the reprinting of the English edition in three paperback volumes to correct errors present in the original hardback. This edition should be considered the definitive English text.

ACKNOWLEDGEMENTS

In our work to prepare this edition of the Plays, Psychiatric work and Political writings of Fanon, we have received help from numerous parties. We are especially indebted to the British Academy, the Leverhulme Trust, New York University, Trinity College, Cambridge and Wadham College, Oxford, all of which helped make this research possible. The role of Mireille Fanon-Mendès France (president of the Fondation Frantz-Fanon, which was established in Paris and in Montréal in 2007 and boasts an international network) was decisive. In 2001, she took the initiative, along with her brother Olivier, to deliver to the Institut Mémoires de l'édition contemporaine (IMEC, Paris and Caen), a Fanon Collection that includes a large part of the documents on which we worked and to which she gave us access, something for which we are deeply thankful. We owe a special debt of gratitude to the IMEC archivists, who always willingly facilitated our work there. Olivier Fanon (president of the National Association Frantz-Fanon, created in Algiers in 2012) authorized us to consult the documents that he had also deposited at IMEC, and permitted us, along with Professor Slimane Hachi, to consult and arrange the Frantz Fanon Collection that he set up at the *Centre national de recherches préhistoriques, anthropologiques et historiques in Algiers* (CNRPAH).

Jacques Azoulay's family kindly passed onto us the complete text of his PhD dissertation and Numa Murard gave us access to the transcription of the interviews he conducted with Jacques Azoulay. Charles Geronimi replied at length to our questions and gave us access to his beautiful text on Fanon at Blida. Marie-Jeanne Manuellan – who was Fanon's assistant in Tunis – was generous in providing us with many indications and clarifications about Fanon's method of writing, his clinical practice and his life and encounters. We are especially grateful to Neelam Srivastava, who located the Fanon-Pirelli correspondence and has introduced it here, as well as to Sara Shariati, who did the same for Fanon's correspondence with her father. Mireille Gauzy and association SACPI (Saint-Alban arts culture psychothérapie institutionnelle) provided us with copies of the Saint-Alban hospital ward newspaper containing editorials by Fanon. Amina Bekkat provided us with a considerable number of copies of the Blida hospital ward newspaper and Paul Marquis kindly gave us a number of the issues we were still missing, issues he discovered during his research. For their help with our research, we thank Norman Ajari, A. James Arnold, Margaret Atack, Levanah Benke, Elina Caire, J. Michael Dash, Olysia Dmitracova, Louise Dorignon, Jessica Galliver, Lucy Graham, Azzedine Haddour, Joshua Heath, Ellen Iredale, Andrew Lanham, Nicholas Mirzoeff, Mélina Reynaud, Weimin Tang, Daniel Wunderlich and Heather Zuber. James Kirwan from the Wren Library restored the illegible parts of the plays typescripts. Mélanie Heydari offered considerable editorial support throughout the preparation of this volume, in particular with translation issues. We are very grateful to Gabriel Quigley for assistance in copy-editing the volumes for this paperback edition.

INTRODUCTION: FANON, REVOLUTIONARY PSYCHIATRIST

Jean Khalfa

Commenting on the passages in his books where Frantz Fanon describes the psychopathology that colonization brings about, critics sometimes mention his psychiatric writings; however, these texts, written during his professional career as a neuro-psychiatrist between 1951 and 1960, in parallel to his political œuvre, are hardly ever studied for themselves or for what they show about the evolution of his thought. Reasons for this include: their technical nature; Fanon's sustained interest in now discredited therapies like electroshocks or insulin coma therapy (methods that he used and on which he wrote scientific articles); or his experimentation with first-generation neuroleptics. Some commentators also find it troubling that, when considering psychoanalysis from a clinical viewpoint, he subordinated it to a more general neuro-psychiatric approach.

Yet Fanon regarded himself essentially as a psychiatrist and practiced and researched psychiatry almost continuously, whether in France, Algeria or Tunisia. Had he regarded psychiatry a merely professional activity outside his main interests, he would most likely have opened one of those private practices that flourished at the time.[1] Instead, he opted for hospital-based clinical practice, conducted original research, which

---

[1] Charles Geronimi, one of Fanon's interns, made this remark in the interview I conducted with him on 24 May 2014.

he presented at professional congresses and had published, supervised clinical dissertations, and considerably impacted the vocation and careers of the many interns and nursing staff that he attracted very early on thanks to his reputation as a doctor committed to revolutionizing mainstream psychiatric practice. Read systematically, his psychiatric writings quickly reveal that they bear on the most interesting debates in the field, at a time during which the discipline was in a period of feverish redefinition. Furthermore, as François Maspero notes in his preface to *Pour la révolution africaine*, these writings are also worth studying for an understanding of his thought as a whole.[2]

Fanon's scientific work sets out from a fundamental discussion of psychiatry's specificity with respect to neurology, the topic on which he wrote his medical doctorate (see *below*, p. 39 sq.). After completing it, he published articles on his experiments with neuropsychiatric treatments and their limits, before proceeding to adopt a sociotherapeutic approach, the difficulties of which soon led him to study the essential role of culture in the development of mental illness. From the outset he refused all forms of naturalization of mental illness, and soon violently rejected the forms that colonial ethnopsychiatry, essentially a racist biologism, had invented and integrated into the very structure of modern colonial hospitals, in particular the Blida-Joinville Hospital. Along the way, Fanon experimented with approaches that would make him one of the pioneers of modern ethnopsychiatry. He would ultimately distance himself from social therapy (*socialthérapie*),[3] or institutional therapy, and create a mental health clinic that operated

---

[2]For an overall view of Fanon's psychiatric practice and his writings, the reader ought first to consult the remarkable biographies that have been written on him by Alice Cherki and David Macey. Several special issues of journals have been devoted to these writings, including: *L'Information psychiatrique*, vol. 51, no. 10, 1975; *History of Psychiatry*, vol. 7, no. 28, 1996; *Sud/Nord*, vol. 14, no. 1, 2001, and vol. 22, no. 1, 2007; *Tumultes*, vol. 31, 2008; *L'Autre*, vol. 13, no. 3, 2012. See also: Hussein Abdilahi Buhlan, *Frantz Fanon and the Psychology of Oppression*, New York, NY: Plenum Press, 1985; Jock McCulloch, *Black Soul White Artifact: Fanon's Clinical Psychology and Social Theory*, Cambridge: Cambridge University Press, 1983; Jock McCulloch, *Colonial Psychiatry and the 'African Mind'*, Cambridge: Cambridge University Press, 1995; Richard Keller, *Colonial Madness: Psychiatry in French North Africa*, Chicago, IL: University of Chicago Press, 2007.

[3]Fanon speaks most often about '*socialthérapie*', a term used by Tosquelles. Daumezon used '*sociothérapie*'. In general, the term used herein is 'social therapy', except for the few passages where Fanon uses '*sociothérapie*', duly translated as 'sociotherapy'. For more on social therapy, the reader may consult the important 'Symposium on collective psychotherapy', organized by Henri Ey in September 1951, of which the papers and ensuing discussions were published in *L'Évolution psychiatrique* (no. 3, 1952). In it, we

outside of the psychiatric hospital system, thus advancing a model for future mental health institutions.

The founding medical dissertation on 'Mental Alterations' (1951)

Fanon's dissertation, which he defended in Lyon in November 1951 as part of his qualification for a medical doctorate, was his first major text. He was twenty-six years old at the time.[4] This dissertation has often been presented as a technical work, hastily produced in order to obtain a qualification and submitted in lieu of *Peau noire, masques blancs*, itself deemed unacceptable as a medical dissertation because of the overly subjective viewpoint from which it is written.[5] Fanon's account differs:

> When I began this book, having completed my medical studies, I thought of submitting it as my dissertation. And then the dialectic required a redoubling of my positions. Although in one way or another I had tackled the psychic alienation of the black man, I could not ignore certain elements that, however psychological they may be, generate consequences that fall within the remit of other sciences.[6]

---

find the first critiques of social therapy, in particular by the communist psychiatrist Louis Le Guillant, to whom Tosquelles replied sharply. Fanon's last psychiatric articles bear traces of this debate. This issue also contains an article by Ey, 'À propos d'une réalisation d'assistance psychiatrique à Saint-Alban (http://psychiatrie.histoire.free.fr/hp/documents/stalban.htm). In it, Ey employs the term 'socialthérapie'.
[4]Frantz Fanon, *Mental alterations, character modifications, psychic disorders and intellectual deficit in spinocerebellar heredodegeneration: a case of Friedreich's ataxia with delusions of possession*, doctoral dissertation defended at the Faculty of Medicine and Pharmacy in Lyon, 29 November 1951. We refer to this text, in the present editions, as: Fanon, Mental alterations, p. x. One of its chapters, 'Mental disorder and neurological disturbance', was republished in *L'Information psychiatrique*, vol. 51, no. 10, 1975, pp. 1079–90.
[5]See, for example, Claudine Razanajao and Jacques Postel, 'La vie et l'œuvre psychiatrique de Frantz Fanon', *Sud/Nord*, no. 22, 2007, https://doi.org/10.3917/sn.022.0147, pp. 147–74: 149.
[6]Frantz Fanon, *Black Skin, White Masks*, p. 30 (translation modified – SC). Fanon's university file reveals that the doctoral project he had submitted in November 1950, 'Contribution to the study of Psychological Mechanisms likely to hinder a healthy understanding among the various members of the French Community', was not refused on grounds of scientific content. Both Jean Dechaume, Fanon's supervisor, and the Dean of the Faculty of Medicine in Lyon, stress that they see in it an interesting

This dialectic is one of psychiatry and sociology, of subjectivity and history, and Fanon underlines as much in his introduction:

> Reacting against the constitutionalist tendency of the late nineteenth century, Freud insisted that the individual factor be taken into account through psychoanalysis. He substituted an ontogenetic perspective for a phylogenetic theory. It will be seen that the Black's alienation is not an individual question. Beside phylogeny and ontogeny stands sociogeny.[7]

Fanon did not hesitate to set himself in a lineage of illustrious predecessors and was cognizant from the start about what would comprise the strength and modernity of his future political thought: his constructing a strong notion of alienation that articulates all three of these dimensions. But to do so, alienation had first to be shown to be irreducible to disturbances in the organic constitution, or in an individual's history taken in isolation from social relations. This is precisely the subject matter of the psychiatric dissertation. There are several reasons why this text must be taken seriously, both in itself and in its essential link with his other works.

First, the illness at the heart of the dissertation, a hereditary neurological illness that is often but not always accompanied by psychiatric symptoms, which are themselves variable. Fanon studied it in a patient that he closely and carefully observed over a long period, and working in a department oriented towards neurology, he was well placed to examine the relations between neurological and psychiatric causality. Conjecturing that this illness would provide him with a key to the problem, he examined all the recent cases in nearby clinics and those published in the medical literature since

---

project in social psychology. But they think that this study of affective shocks linked to manifestations of racism could be used politically against its very aims, and elicit precisely the sort of misunderstandings between members of the French Union that should be erased. Fanon is thus encouraged to apply for a grant for fieldwork in Martinique to pursue a separate study and focus on a purely medical subject for his doctoral research. (Archives de l'Université Claude Bernard-Lyon1, dossier des étudiants, dossier Franz Fanon. File hand-inscribed "colonial". Information kindly provided by Prof. Michelle Zancarini-Fournel.)

[7]Fanon, *Black Skin, White Masks*, p. xv. 'Constitutionalist' here designates a theory that identifies mental illnesses with disorders in the biological constitution of the individual. Later on Fanon uses the term to refer to colonial ethnopsychiatry, which sees the 'native' as constitutionally 'primitive'.

the nineteenth century, with the explicit aim of empirically proving the inadequacy of the organicist reductionism that continued to dominate pre-war psychiatry. Solving this initial problem was in effect a theoretical precondition to his works on the impact of social and cultural factors on the development of mental illnesses and, therefore, to his later thinking on alienation.

Second, at several important points in his dissertation Fanon indicates the future orientation that his own professional and intellectual career would take. On the nature of neuropsychiatry and the respective functions of the neurologist and the psychiatrist, he declares: 'Far from proposing a solution – I believe that a lifetime of study and observation is required – [...].'[8] In the section devoted to the refusal of atomism and cerebral localizations by *Gestalt theory* psychologists, noting the insistence of Swiss psychiatrist Constantin von Monakow (1853–1930) on the importance of the time factor in the development of mental illnesses – in contrast to the spatial localization of cerebral lesions – the dissertation announces a future work, probably *Peau noire, masques blancs*, which was to be published shortly afterward:

> The occasion will arise, in a work that I have been undertaking for a long time, to tackle the problem of history from the psychoanalytic and ontological angles. In it, I will show that history is only the systematic valorization of collective complexes.[9]

Fanon was an attentive reader of the psychoanalyst Jacques Lacan, probably under the influence of the philosopher Maurice Merleau-Ponty, whose lectures he attended.[10] Devoting a section of his

---

[8]Fanon, *Mental alterations*, p. 84.
[9]Fanon, *Mental alterations*, p. 94.
[10]See Maurice Merleau-Ponty, *Psychologie et pédagogie de l'enfant. Cours de Sorbonne, 1949–1952*, Lagrasse: Verdier, 2001 (*Child Psychology and Pedagogy: The Sorbonne Lectures, 1949–52*, trans. Tania Welsh, Evanston, IL: Northwestern University Press, 2010); in particular, the lecture on Lacan titled 'Les stades du développement enfantin' (pp. 108–16) ('Stages of Child Development', pp. 84–92). It is likely that between 1949 and 1952, Merleau-Ponty gave at least some of his Sorbonne lectures on child psychology and pedagogy also in Lyon, where he held a chair in psychology. Several aspects of Fanon's argument suggest this is so, such as the fact that the same references to Lacan can be found in the lectures, that these references are explained in the same way, and that Fanon takes as given some ideas on which Merleau-Ponty focused, such as the importance of the complex, not just in its pathological dimension but above

dissertation to the Lacanian theory of the pure psychogenesis of madness (which he contrasted to the tempered organogenesis of the great psychiatrist of the period, Henri Ey), he underlines Lacan's insistence on the social constitution of personality ('he envisages madness within an intersubjectivist perspective') and adds, in an interesting *praeteritio*:

> 'Madness', he says, 'is lived within the register of meaning.' ... I would have liked to have written at length here about the Lacanian theory of language,[11] but this would risk taking us further away from the topic. Nevertheless, upon reflection, we ought to recognize that every delusional phenomenon is ultimately expressed, that is to say, spoken.[12]

Fanon himself thus saw in his research on this group of mental illnesses which are irreducible to their neurological origin, the occasion to undertake some in-depth theoretical reflection and indicates that this reflection leads to works, some involving completely different domains, that he intended to pursue later.

Third, we have no reason to underestimate Fanon's continued interest in the biological aspects of clinical psychiatry. Maurice Despinoy, under whom Fanon did his internship at Saint-Alban hospital, remarked that his own experiments on lithium salts were looked upon with great interest by Fanon. Despinoy, a pioneer in

---

all as the form that social relations give to the personality. Moreover, several lesser known authors, amply cited in *Peau noire, masques blancs* and in later works by Fanon, such as Germaine Guex, Jacob Moreno and Kurt Lewin, are also studied in these lectures. Fanon's library contained copies of *Sens et non-sens* (*Sense and Non-Sense*, trans. Hubert Dreyfus and Patricia Allen Dreyfus, Evanston, IL: Northwestern University Press, 1964) and *La Structure du comportement* (*The Structure of Behaviour*, trans. Alden L. Fisher, London: Methuen, 1965) as well as issues of journals to which Merleau-Ponty had contributed. *Peau noire, masques blancs* also makes reference to *Phenoménologie de la perception* (*Phenomenology of Perception*, trans. Donald A. Landes, New York, NY: Routledge, 2012).

[11] Lacan's text continues with a reflection on language.

[12] Fanon, *Mental alterations*, p. 105. In *Peau noire, masques blancs*, Fanon recalls the importance in his view of the Lacanian critique of the idea of constitutional morbidity (p. 65). The quote appears in Lacan's intervention at the 1946 Bonneval colloquium: Lucien Bonnafé, Henri Ey, Sven Follin, Jacques Lacan and Julien Rouart, *Le Problème de la psychogenèse des névroses et des psychoses*, Paris: Desclée de Brouwer, 1950, p. 34 (reprint in 'Bibliothèque des introuvables', Paris: C. Tchou, 2004).

this domain, surmised that had Fanon remained at Saint-Alban, he 'would have done his dissertation in biochemistry'.[13]

Fourth, we know that Fanon worked quickly, dictating his books without using notes and rarely correcting himself.[14] The writing of this dissertation thus took him perhaps as much time, if not more, than that of his books: the catalogue of pertinent cases and the bibliography are extensive; the references supplied are illuminating; and the (generally correct) citations reveal a close reading of the literature. His analyses, moreover, go to the heart of the key problems of the period. It is true that the dissertation is fairly short, largely due to the small number of cases summarized or directly studied, and only minimally compliant with bibliographical conventions. However, it does go straight to the significant problem and we see clearly how it establishes Fanon's style of thinking.

Last, as a work that mixes first- and third-person analyses, *Peau noire, masques blancs* (whose original title was *Essay on the Disalienation of the Black*) may well have been defendable then as a doctoral dissertation, had Fanon wanted to submit it. Under the influence of, among others, Ey and Merleau-Ponty, both of whom were serious readers of Jaspers (as was Fanon himself), the necessity of taking a phenomenological approach to mental illness was central to psychiatric thought at the time. A psychiatry dissertation of this sort would probably be less acceptable today than it would have been then. David Macey pointed out that *Peau noire, masques blancs* which Fanon began to write before embarking on his psychiatric studies, could not have initially been conceived as a doctoral dissertation in medicine.[15]

---

[13]Jacques Tosquellas, 'Entretien avec Maurice Despinoy', *Sud/Nord*, vol. 22, 2007, pp. 105–14 (p. 107). At the end of 1952, Despinoy left Saint-Alban to head the *Centre Hospitalier de Colson*, the psychiatric hospital of Martinique. He remained in contact with Fanon, who, for his part, continued to perform experiments using lithium salts. As Charles Geronimi relates: 'More interesting [than the fruitless attempts at producing shocks with acetylcholine] were the therapeutic tests using lithium salts, for which Fanon showed a real enthusiasm; curiously, he used them in treating agitation and not depression, as became classic. As their use involved a strict control of lithium levels, Fanon obtained the purchase of a photometer from the hospital pharmacist' (*Fanon à Blida*, unpublished manuscript, kindly given to us by the author).

[14]Marie-Jeanne Manuellan, to whom Fanon dictated a good part of *L'An V* and *Les Damnés de la terre*, and who typed them up, described Fanon's work method to me during the many conversations we had between 2014 and 2015. I am deeply indebted to her for her time and generosity.

[15]David Macey, *Frantz Fanon: A Life*, London: Verso, 2012, p. 127.

But the fundamental point is that both works have very different points of departure: the dissertation establishes the ontological foundation of the book by showing that even when a mental illness has clearly its origin in neurological disorders, it generally develops in a socially determined relational space which in turn explains the form it takes. As for the book itself, it is a particular psycho-socio-historical study of alienation in a group of colonies of the *Ancien Régime*, the French Caribbean, where internalized dependence on the metropole is absolute, whether in the form of an identification with it or in the invention of an opposing identity (such as negritude). The book thus goes far beyond the limits of a psychiatric dissertation however much Fanon's dissertation defines its conditions of possibility.

Fanon certainly could have included the two most 'psychological' chapters of *Peau noire, masques blancs* in his dissertation, one of which is more subjective, namely 'The Lived Experience of the Black' (already published in the May 1951 issue of *Esprit*), the other more objective, namely 'The Negro and Psychopathology'. But a medical dissertation on the psychopathology of the 'Negro' that was detached from the concrete socio-cultural and historical contexts that comprise the essential object of the analyses of *Peau noire, masques blancs* would have risked pandering to the essentialism that Fanon had already roundly denounced in 'Le "syndrome nord-africain"',[16] which he wrote around the same time. From Fanon's point

---

[16]This article was first published in *Esprit* in February 1952 and reprinted in 1964 in *Pour la révolution africaine*, pp. 13–25 (*Toward the African Revolution*, pp. 3–16). In it we read the genealogy of a racist attitude based on the assumption that every symptom presupposes a lesion: 'In the face of this pain without lesion, this illness spread in and right throughout the body, this continuous suffering, the easiest attitude and the one to which one is more or less rapidly led, is the negation of all morbidity. In the extreme, the North African is a simulator, a liar, a malingerer, a sluggard, a thief. ... The medical staff discovers the existence of a North African syndrome. Not experimentally, but following an oral tradition. The North African takes place in this asymptomatic syndrome and is automatically situated as undisciplined (cf. medical discipline), inconsequential (with reference to this tenet of faith: every symptom presumes a lesion), and insincere (he says he is suffering when we know there are no *reasons* for suffering). There is a floating idea that is present here, at the limit of my bad faith, and when the Arab unveils himself through his language: "Doctor, I'm going to die", this idea, after having passed through a number of twists and turns, will impose itself, will impress me. No, you certainly can't take these fellows seriously' (*Toward the African Revolution*, pp. 7 and 10. Translation modified – SC). As always, Fanon thinks at once historically and epistemologically, and this paper goes on to propose a radically different model

of view, then, this book also had to be a critique of the idea that the pathological constructions attributed to a 'race' could have sources other than history.

To maintain that mental illnesses are not natural 'entities' while recognizing the possibility of their organic origin was therefore an important stance to take in the medical debates of the time. Fanon defended this stance all the more vigorously as it would enable him to undermine the foundations of colonial ethnopsychiatry. He was preoccupied by the relations between the organic and the mental, but just as passionate about those between history and alienation. It is precisely because he worked in a neurologically oriented research environment, that he saw in his psychiatric dissertation an opportunity to solve the philosophical problem that was the horizon of his thought: providing an empirical proof of the irreducible distinction between the neurological and the psychiatric would open a space for freedom and history.[17]

---

of medical thought, one based on what he suggests calling a neo-hippocratism, where the diagnostic is based on functions more than on organs. 'Series D' of chapter 5 of *Les Damnés de la terre* furthers this early reflection on 'psychosomatic disorders'. In it Fanon uses the materialist 'cortico-visceral' terminology of Soviet psychosomatic medicine that developed on the basis of Pavlov's works. Pavlov, who thereinafter dominated the thinking of communist psychiatrists, viewed the brain as the 'matrix in which the psyche is elaborated'. Fanon nonetheless hastens to temper this terminology by a critique of ethnopsychiatric essentialism: in the colonial context, psychosomatic disorder is not a natural property of the native's mind, but a physiological adaptation to a particular historical situation.

[17]In her remarkable biography, Alice Cherki may have simplified the thinking of Jean Dechaume, then director of the department at which Fanon was studying and a member of his dissertation jury, in writing that 'Dechaume was interested solely in psycho-surgery, and he viewed things through a neuropsychiatric lens that attributed all psychiatric conditions to organic origins – every symptom has a corresponding therapeutic drug and confinement was a given in any and all therapies' (*Frantz Fanon: A Portrait*, trans. Nadia Benabid, Ithaca, NY, and London: Cornell University Press, 2006, p. 17). In his dissertation, Fanon twice cites the chapter that Jean Dechaume wrote in vol. 16 of the major *Traité de médecine*, edited by André Lemierre et al., Paris: Masson & Cie, 1949, pp. 1063–75. There Dechaume vigorously defends the viewpoint of psychosomatic medicine: 'the most localized visceral illnesses can have a psychic impact' (passage cited by Fanon), but conversely the mental disturbance can have a visceral effect. Fanon was probably citing Dechaume under obligation, but he was deeply interested in psychosomatic medicine. The body always appeared to him a crucial element in the complex explanation of the human reality he was studying. Though Dechaume ignored the social dimension, it is perhaps owing to this interest in the psychosomatic dimension that, as Cherki notes, Fanon nonetheless decided to complete his training with him.

The organogenesis and psychogenesis of mental illness

Fanon's dissertation examines a hereditary neuro-degenerative illness, 'Friedreich's ataxia',[18] in order to question the limits of reducing the mental to the neurological. It ends up asserting the relational (interpersonal and by extension social) dimension of the development of mental illness and the forms that it takes, on experimental grounds: it is true that the majority of serious cases have their origin in a neurological pathology that necessitates one or several organic treatments, according to the means available at a given time. However, these treatments do not suffice to cure the mental illness. A mental illness is therefore not reducible to its occasional cause; such an illness has its own dynamic and requires a treatment of an entirely different order. But if there is no pure organogenesis of mental illness, neither is there any pure psychogenesis. For Fanon, the opposition is obsolete, since the forms that mental illnesses take are determined by the structure of relationships in which the individual is able or unable to participate, and therefore by 'external' factors: neither organic nor psychic ones, but institutional and social ones. Henceforth, the neurological disorder will not be conceived as a cause except to the extent that the 'dissolution' of specific higher functions (such as those controlling movements or learning) alters the possibility and the *structure* of social relations and, as a result, the personality. Over time, the mind reacts and reconstructs the personality by utilizing what remains of it after the dissolution. The diverse possible forms of this reconstitution are classified as so many types of mental illness.

From the outset, the dissertation's foreword announces this epistemological dimension of the inquiry: between 1861 and 1931, by being clustered into a family of hereditary degenerative neurological disturbances, 'some clinical symptom clusters sought to reach the dignity of the entity'.[19] Yet this long and complex history shows that, in these cases, neurological symptoms and psychiatric symptoms 'obey

---

[18]This relatively rare genetic illness (which affects one person in 50,000 in Europe and in the United States) has gone by this name ever since the German doctor and neurologist Nikolaus Friedreich (1825–1882) first identified it in 1861.
[19]Frantz Fanon, *Mental alterations*, p. 40.

an absolute polymorphism.[20] In other words, while it was possible to unify the neurological diseases, this task proved impossible for their psychiatric correlates. It is well known that the famous 'general paralysis of the insane', described in 1822 by the French alienist Antoine Laurent Bayle (1799–1858), had seemed so clearly linked to a specific mental syndrome (megalomaniacal delirium and progressive dementia) that psychiatrist Jacques-Joseph Moreau de Tours (1804–1884), followed by nineteenth-century medical positivism, used it as proof of the organic substratum of all mental illness and as the foundation of an organogenetic conception of madness.[21] But from the moment the field of study of madness was broadened to the family of hereditary neurodegenerative diseases such as Friedreich's ataxia, it became clear that, if mental illnesses accompanied a proportion of them, such disorders were rarely identical. This lack of identity thus seemed to call into question the rigid distinctions and simplicity of 'mechanistic and causal explanations'. Fanon saw in it an occasion to refound the domain:

> At a time when neurologists and psychiatrists are striving to define their disciplines as pure sciences, that is to say a pure neurology and a pure psychiatry, it is good practice to set among the debate a group of neurological illnesses that are also accompanied by psychic disorders, and to ask the legitimate question about the essence of these disorders.[22]

And, in an important section of 'general considerations', he explains:

> I do not believe that a neurological disorder, even when inscribed in an individual's germplasm, can give rise to a determinate psychiatric symptom cluster. Instead, my aim is to show that all neurological impairment damages the personality in some way. And that this open crack within the ego becomes all the more perceptible as the neurological disorder takes the form of a rigorous and irreversible semiology. ... We think in terms of organs and focal lesions when we ought to be thinking in terms of functions and disintegrations. Our medical view is spatial, where it ought to become more and more temporal.[23]

---

[20]Fanon, *Mental alterations*, p. 42.
[21]On the history of 'general paralysis', see Jacques Postel and Claude Quetel, *Nouvelle Histoire de la psychiatrie*, Paris: Dunod, 2012, pp. 203–14.
[22]Fanon, *Mental alterations*, p. 42.
[23]Ibid., pp. 50–1.

This epistemological concern is to be found all throughout Fanon's works: a classification may be convenient, but by no means does it prove an ontology. We ought always to be able to think in terms of processes rather than in terms of entities. Such rigour of thought comes at once from phenomenology and from a reflection on the main debates of the previous decade in French psychiatry, in particular those that set Henri Ey against Jacques Lacan, on the one hand, and against the neurologists Julian de Ajuriaguerra and Henri Hécaen, on the other.[24] The same concern informs the works of Gaston Bachelard and Georges Canguilhem, as well as Michel Foucault's early writings.[25] Fanon would come to denounce the vacuity of the fundamental concepts of colonial ethnopsychiatry, but

---

[24]Fanon read and cited the proceedings of the famous encounters that Ey organized at Bonneval (Eure-et-Loir) in 1943. See Henri Ey, Julian de Ajuriaguerra and Henri Hécaen, *Neurologie et psychiatrie* [proceedings of the 1943 meetings], Paris: Hermann, 1947; and Lucien Bonnafé et al., *Le problème de la psychogenèse des névroses et des psychoses* [proceedings of the 1946 meetings], Paris: Desclée de Brouwer, 1950. Fanon's library contained the first two volumes of Ey's *Études psychiatriques: 1. Historique, méthodologie, psychopathologie générale*, 2nd edition, Paris: Desclée de Brouwer, 1952; *2. Aspects séméiologiques*, Paris: Desclée de Brouwer, 1950. Fanon was especially interested in those *Études* linked to the somatogenesis of mental illness, such as the third, in which Ey remarks: 'Is it not nevertheless possible to ask whether the notion of "psychosis" is not precisely contradictory with the idea of "entity" and what is more by analysing simply the pathology of general paralysis', vol. 1, p. 44; new edition, Perpignan: Cercle de Recherche et d'édition Henri Ey [CREHEY], 2006, p. 63). In a note in his dissertation, Fanon, who had a strong interest in psychosomatic perspectives, mentions the title of the fourth volume of *Études psychiatriques* (announced in the preceding volumes but never published): 'Generative somatic processes' (Fanon, *Mental alterations*, p. 92, note 99).
[25]Fanon's library contains Gaston Bachelard's *Nouvel esprit scientifique* (Paris: PUF, 1949 [1934] *The New Scientific Spirit*, trans. Arthur Goldhammer, Boston, MA: Beacon Press, 1984), a book that advances an insubstantialist view of epistemology. In his copy, Fanon underlined several sections that pertain to the importance of incorporating temporal parameters into research, such as the following passage: 'The most obscure metaphysical enigma resides at the intersection of spatial properties and temporal properties. This enigma is difficult to state, precisely because our language is materialist, because we believe to be able, for example, to root the nature of a substance in a placid matter, indifferent to duration. No doubt the language of space-time is more appropriate to studying the nature-law synthesis, but this language has not yet found enough images to attract the philosophers' (p. 63).
Foucault, who was also influenced by phenomenology as much as by Ey's teaching, argued at that time for a position close to Fanon's: 'These problems [the contrast between the organogenesis and the psychogenesis of mental illness] have been discussed ad nauseam, and it would be quite pointless to go over once more the debates to which they have given rise. But one might ask oneself whether the difficulty does not

within the scope of his dissertation this scepticism led him essentially to adopt a structural approach to mental illness.

'A psychiatric desert' is one description that has been given of the University of Lyon during Fanon's time there.[26] Any student resolved on undertaking research of that significance there would therefore have had to demonstrate remarkable lucidity and an astonishing ability to engage on his own in the most interesting debates of the period. It is likely, however, that Fanon came across these psychiatric debates, which Ey had already amply documented, at the university, through Merleau-Ponty's lectures, and through his published works. Moreover, outside the university, in Lyon Fanon would come across the most progressive current of French psychiatry.[27] Through mutual friends he would meet Paul Balvet, a renowned psychiatrist from Le Vinatier hospital. In September 1947, Balvet had published an important article in *Esprit*, titled 'The Human Value of Madness', that Fanon compares in his dissertation with Lacan's analyses. He had been the director of the clinic in Saint-Alban where Fanon later did his internship under the supervision of Maurice Despinoy and François Tosquelles (Tosquelles himself had been recruited by Balvet). In March 1950, Balvet contributed to a special issue of *Esprit* called *Médecine, quatrième pouvoir: L'intervention psychologique et l'intégrité de la personne*, which contained articles devoted to neurosurgery, shock therapies, narcoanalysis and psychoanalysis.[28] Their discussions likely drew on these

---

spring from the fact that we give the same meaning to the notions of illness, symptoms and etiology in mental pathology and in organic pathology. If it seems so difficult to define psychological illness and health, is this not because one is trying in vain to forcefully apply to them concepts that are also intended for somatic medicine? Does not the difficulty in finding unity in organic disturbances and personality changes lie in the fact that they are presumed to possess the same type of causality? Beyond mental pathology and organic pathology, there is a general, abstract pathology that dominates them both, imposing on them, like so many prejudices, the same concepts, and laying down for them, like so many postulates, the same methods. I would like to show that the root of mental pathology must be sought not in some kind of "metapathology", but in a certain relation, historically situated, of man to the madman and to the true man' (*Mental Illness and Psychology*, trans. Alan Sheridan, with a foreword by Hubert Dreyfus, Berkeley, CA: University of California Press, 1976, pp. 1–2; French original, *Maladie mentale et personnalité*, Paris: PUF, 1954, pp. 1–2).

[26]Razanajao and Postel, 'La vie et l'œuvre psychiatrique de Frantz Fanon', p. 148.
[27]Macey, *Frantz Fanon*, p. 141.
[28]In December 1952 *Esprit* was to publish an important issue devoted to the reform of psychiatric institutions titled *Misère de la psychiatrie*. It included articles by Henri Ey, François Tosquelles, Paul Sivadon and Georges Daumézon, all of whom Fanon came to know personally.

debates, which were at the forefront of intellectual life at the time. Fanon, who was always reading works of philosophy, literature and psychiatry, was informed about these questions and naturally decided to stake out a position and make his mark in this field.

From the outset, then, Fanon's dissertation is part of a comparative perspective between philosophy and psychiatry; one could almost say it lies between the two apparently contradictory epigraphs with which it begins. The first epigraph is from Nietzsche: 'I speak only of *lived* things and do not present cerebral processes.'[29] The second is taken from a presentation by Paul Guiraud and Julian de Ajuriaguerra, given at the *Société medico-psychologique* on 8 February 1934: 'The frequency and the importance of mental disorders in familial nervous diseases does not allow us to consider them as fortuitous accidents.'[30]

Paul Guiraud, a highly renowned neurologist, worked on the link between neurological lesions and psychological disorders, and Julian de Ajuriaguerra was to become a world authority in this domain. At this same meeting of the *Société medico-psychologique*, Guiraud also presented, together with Madeleine Derombies, the study of

---

[29]Fanon attributes the quote to *Thus Spoke Zarathustra*, but in fact it comes from a preparatory manuscript of *Ecce Homo* (Autumn 1884): Ich will das höchste Mißtrauen gegen mich erwecken: ich rede nur von *erlebten* Dingen und präsentire nicht nur Kopf-Vorgänge. (*Kritische Studienausgabe*, no. 14, p. 361). This passage was translated in two works to which Fanon had access: *Introduction à la pensée philosophique allemande depuis Nietzsche* by Bernard Groethuysen (Paris: Stock, 1926, p. 28), one copy of which features in his library and in which the passage in question is translated as follows: 'Je ne parle que de choses vécues, et je ne me borne pas à dire ce qui s'est passé dans ma tête' [I speak only of lived things and do not limit myself to speaking only of what has gone on in my head] (text reprised in Bernard Groethuysen, *Philosophie et Histoire*, Paris: Albin Michel, 1995, p. 100); and in Karl Jaspers' book *Nietzsche, introduction à sa philosophie* (Paris: Gallimard, 1950), one of the first volumes published in the 'Bibliothèque de philosophie' (a series established by Merleau-Ponty and Sartre), in which the passage is rendered thus: 'Je parle seulement de choses vécues et n'expose pas uniquement des événements de tête' [I speak only of lived things and do not solely present events in the head] (p. 387). Jaspers does not italicize 'lived' (*erlebten*) but adds: 'Nietzsche sees in intellectual knowledge the subjectivity of a life …' The quote from Nietzsche concludes Fanon's dedication to his brother Joby. If what is at issue here is the object of the dissertation, the gap between the psychiatric and the neurological, there is perhaps also a nod in Joby's direction, an allusion to the lived things that are examined in the first person in *Peau noire, masques blancs*. My thanks to Mark Chinca and David Midgley for putting me on the trail of this fragment.

[30]Paul Guiraud and Julian de Ajuriaguerra, 'Aréflexie, pieds creux, amyotrophie accentuée, signe d'Argyll et troubles mentaux', *Annales médico-psychologiques*, vol. 92, no. 1, 1934, pp. 229–34: 233.

'Un cas de maladie familiale de Roussy-Lévy avec troubles mentaux' (A hereditary case of Roussy-Levy with mental disorders). This illness was accompanied by a psychological syndrome comprising depression, irritability and impaired muscular sensitivity, all impacting on the synthesis of the personality:

> Muscular activity is no longer appropriated into the personality, the subject has the impression of passively undergoing the movements of walking: as he puts it, he does not walk, he is transported, as if he were in a car. The result of this deficit is a weakening (*fléchissement*) of the notion of the ego, of the personality, to such an extent, says the patient, that if he did not stop, he would lose consciousness.[31]

From the neurological point of view, the young man presented all the muscular and physiological symptoms of Roussy-Levy disease (hereditary areflexive dystasia), as confirmed by the study of his heredity. However, 'outlines of infantile delusions of grandeur' also accompanied this pathology.

While the authors concluded from this that there exists a correlation between a specific mental syndrome and a neurological syndrome, they noted, in a text that perhaps inspired Fanon's dissertation, that such a neuropsychiatric correlation is not simple:

> We deem that, in our case, the still unknown lesion (since the Roussy-Levy disease continues to await its pathological anatomy) is not confined to the marrow, but rather reaches the paths or terminal centres of proprioception, in those very regions where neurological life becomes psychic life. It is indeed amply demonstrated that the simple privation of kinesthesic impressions, or those of any other order, are not enough to provoke disorders such as the ego's failure of appropriation and the feeling of passivity with motor acts. *A fortiori*, something else is necessary to explain character disorders, impulsiveness, depression. By contrast, in Friedreich's disease, mental disorders are well known. Mollaret has carefully studied them in his doctoral dissertation. He points to mood and character disorders, impulsiveness, instability as quite frequently associated with mental debility. But in none of these

---

[31]Paul Guiraud and Madeleine Derombies, 'Un cas de maladie familiale de Roussy-Lévy avec troubles mentaux', *Annales médico-psychologiques*, vol. 92, no. 1, 1934, pp. 224–9: 225.

observations does one find as close a relation as in ours between the neurological syndrome and the mental syndromes.[32]

These considerations of the differences between neuropsychiatric diseases clarify Fanon's undertaking. What is at stake here is the nature of psychic life: Friedreich's ataxia makes it possible, even necessary, to understand the independence of psychic life in relation to neurological life within a scientific approach, i.e. without recourse to a spiritualist dualism. Another case studied by Guiraud at the same meeting of the *Société médico-psychologique*, this time with de Ajuriaguerra, presented a syndrome of 'areflexia, pes cavus, heightened amyotrophy, Argyll Robertson pupils and mental disorders'. Once again, we have a list of neurological disturbances, and they are linked to mental disorders – 'psychological imbalance', 'personality disorders', 'onset of cyclothymia' and sometimes 'originary intellectual impairment' – as part of a syndrome not yet fully defined, though undeniable, and fairly similar to Friedreich's disease. The authors' conclusion contains the sentence that Fanon cites in the second epigraph: these hereditary nervous diseases are accompanied by mental disorders so frequent and so significant that they cannot be considered merely fortuitous.

However, a doubt arose at the heart of these three presentations: are these links, which are not coincidental, enough to explain the form and content of mental disorders? Can one remain content with speaking of 'cerebral processes', as Fanon wrote in paraphrasing Nietzsche's 'goings-on in the head' (*Kopf-Vorgänge*), or ought one also study the 'lived things', the forms and states of consciousness, in themselves? An attentive and detailed analysis of the literature on Friedreich's ataxia, together with a study of the specific case on

---

[32]Guirard and Derombies, 'Un cas de maladie familiale de Roussy-Lévy avec troubles mentaux', pp. 228–9. Mollaret's dissertation, a far more detailed neurology dissertation, one that contained a greater number of observations of cases than Fanon's, nonetheless devotes only two paragraphs to the 'pathogenesis of mental illness' in Friedreich's disease. Mollaret sums up the possible explanations under three categories: pure coincidence between the mental disturbance and the illness; direct cause of pathologies by neurological lesions (in the cerebellum); the third position, which seems more probable to him, is that of Saquet, who states that 'among these patients there exists an evident predisposition, and the lesions of the cerebral cortex results from an associated process'. However, he concludes: 'I will not adopt a position in this discussion. The aim was simply to underscore the rather frequent existence of such symptoms in the illness that I have studied' (see Pierre Mollaret, *La Maladie de Friedreich: Étude physio-clinique*, doctoral dissertation, Paris, 1929, p. 180).

which Fanon relied (a 'case of delusion of possession with hysterical structure', including symptoms such as 'agitation, ecstatic attitudes, talk about mystical or erotic themes'[33]) shows that the extreme variety of these forms must cast doubt on any simple reductionism.

An alternative solution comes in a long section of the dissertation comparing the ideas of Ey, Goldstein[34] (together with von Monakow) and Lacan. Even though Fanon appears closer to Ey's organodynamism and to an understanding of the nature of mental illness as a pathological personality-reconstruction – the work of a consciousness initially affected by underlying neurological problems and reacting to them – he also often emphasizes Lacan's insistence on the social dimension of the complex and its impact on the development of mental illness.[35] In the specific medical case on which Fanon focused, the cerebellar degeneration produced dementia and mental immaturity, but the delirium, hysterical manifestations and mysticism (delusion of possession) had to be explained as the reactional behaviour of an ego deprived of social relationships. The original neurological disorder had inhibited cognitive and affective development by impeding mobility and thus socialization (an idea that may reflect Henri Wallon' influence, via Merleau-Ponty): 'systematized delusions, hysterical manifestations and neurotic behaviours must be considered reactional conducts of an ego at odds with intersocial relations'.[36]

---

[33]Fanon, *Mental alterations*, p. 80.
[34]Kurt Goldstein (1878–1965) was a German neurologist and psychiatrist who elaborated a global theory of the organism based on Gestalt theory.
[35]Fanon notes: 'The social category of human reality, to which I personally attach so much importance, is one to which Lacan has been attentive' (Fanon, *Mental alterations*, p. 103).
[36]Fanon, *Mental alterations*, p. 109. Writing on 'mental debility' in childhood linked with a neurological motor disease, Fanon notes: 'the mental debility of these illnesses is easily explained. The paralysis that occurs along with the clinical developments prohibits school attendance. Hence, intellectual development is naturally made impossible. Indeed, the attempt to connect motor debility with mental debility is an extremely seductive one. The affectivity of these patients is similarly impaired, since they cannot pass through the various stages of the genetics described by psychoanalysis, stages that stand, as is well-known, in a close relation with motor function' (Fanon, *Mental alterations*, p. 178). This conclusion as to the role of the body in psychic development is recurrent in his analysis of the impact of the colonial gaze. But here we also find a reflection on the relation between the destruction of the body schema and mysticism, a theme taken up in many texts. On the importance of physical

Ey famously called 'écart organo-clinique' ('organo-clinical gap'), the space of the 'psychic trajectory' of self-reconstruction by consciousness following a neurological dissolution, resulting in what we see as mental illness.[37] For Fanon, this gap increasingly appeared to be structured by 'external' factors, both social and cultural. This is why his later medical publications and manuscripts on the necessary use of the then-available neuropsychiatric treatments also emphasized the limits of these treatments. And when he was confronted with the social divisions specific to the colonial context, he turned more directly to the role of society and culture in mental illness, and reflected on the advantages and limits of social therapy and psychotherapy as treatments performed in the context of the psychiatric hospital.

Value and limits of neuropsychiatric treatments

Fanon's aim in his dissertation had been to establish the foundation of a properly neuropsychiatric approach to the treatment of mental illness. In the subsequent texts that he published in this domain, Fanon explains that this treatment has two stages: first, an organic treatment aiming to wipe the slate clean of previous reactional constructions, one based either on shock therapies – electroshocks (Bini therapy), insulin comas (Sakel's therapy) or a combination of the two – or on sleep therapy. This preliminary phase is then followed by a long phase of psychotherapeutic work aimed at reconstructing the personality and bringing the patient back to as normal a social

---

movement and the concepts of body schema and its dissolution under the racist gaze in *Peau noire, masques blancs* and *L'An V*, see 'Corps Perdu: A Note on Fanon's *Cogito*', in Jean Khalfa, *Poetics of the Antilles*, Bern and Oxford: Peter Lang, 2017, pp. 183–208. Among Fanon's text conserved at the IMEC, there are several reading notes and fragments on neurotic anxiety, thymopathic vertigo, agoraphobia, Westphal's disease, and hepatolenticular degeneration. These notes often concern clinical disorders of the body's relation to space.

[37]See, for instance, Henri Ey, *Études psychiatriques*, 2 vols, Perpignan: CREHEY, 2006, I, p. 168.

existence as possible.[38] Mental illness is never seen as an extreme form of freedom, but rather as a 'pathology of freedom', a phrase Fanon used in several texts, referring to Ey, who himself borrowed it from an eponymous paper by German essayist Günther Anders (1902–1992).[39] Moreover, he contrasted this conception of madness, as a pathology of freedom, with Lacan's. Lacan, in a certain proximity

---

[38]Neuroleptics were not yet in use and these new shock methods aroused significant hope at the time (the first anti-psychotic effects of the first neuroleptic, chlorpromazine, were not discovered until 1952; in 1955 Jean Delay organized an international colloquium on chlorpromazine and neuroleptic medication, the proceedings of which, published in 1956, can be found in Fanon's library). Later, Fanon helped pioneer experiments on the first neuroleptics, particularly in Tunis. See Frantz Fanon and Lucien Lévy, 'First tests using injectable meprobamate for hypochondriac states', first published in *La Tunisie médicale*, vol. 37, no. 10, 1959, pp. 175–91. For electroshocks, Fanon refers to Paul Delmas-Marsalet, *L'Électro-choc thérapeutique et la dissolution-reconstruction* (Paris: J.-B. Baillière et fils, 1943), in particular chapter VII, 'La théorie de la dissolution-reconstruction', which grounds his description of mental illness in an architectural metaphor, in which mental illness is seen as a defective reorganization of the building blocks of mental functions. If these blocks are all there and if the building plans have been preserved (in other words, provided there has been no major neurological damage), it seems that the shocks restore functions to their place in the initial plan. In its general structure, this conception is similar to that which Ey found in the work of the English neurologist Hughlings Jackson (1835–1911), and of which he gave a psychiatric reinterpretation in what was to become a reference work, *Essai d'application des principes de Jackson à une conception dynamique de la neuropsychiatrie* (Paris: Doin, 1938; reissued by L'Harmattan, 2000). In Fanon's copy the passages concerning the speed of mental dissolution are annotated, and include added references to Jaspers and to Lacan. Concerning 'dissolution' through insulin coma therapy, Fanon refers to the inventor of the method, the American psychiatrist and neurologist Manfred Sakel (1900–1957), and in particular to his presentation at the 1950 *Congrès international de psychiatrie* in Paris, titled 'Insulinotherapy and Shock Therapies: Ascent of Psychiatry from Scholastic Dialecticism to Empirical Medicine', in *Congrès international de psychiatrie*, 6 vols, Paris: Hermann, 1950, IV, pp. 163–232. Among Fanon's papers conserved at IMEC, one long typescript in fact comprises a translation of a passage from this text.

[39]See Günther Anders, 'Pathologie de la liberté: essai sur la non-identification', *Recherches philosophiques*, vol. 6, no. 7, 1936, pp. 2–54. Fanon's library contains the majority of the issues of *Recherches philosophiques*. In this volume, the pages for this article are cut. Fanon refers to this text explicitly in *Peau noire, masques blancs*: 'Some men want to swell the world with their being. A German philosopher had described this process, labelling it a pathology of freedom' (p. 176; translation modified – SC). In this passage, the pathology in question is the essentialism of a certain conception of negritude, one unable to think itself in terms of temporality. For Fanon, in psychiatry and politics alike, disalienation therefore consists in 'refusing to allow oneself to be sealed away in the Tower of the Past'.

to the Surrealists, saw in the possibility of madness an essential dimension of human existence.[40]

After his studies in Lyon and a short stint at the Saint-Ylie psychiatric hospital in Dole (Jura) and then in Martinique, Fanon went to Saint-Alban (Lozère) in April 1952 to work with the revolutionary psychiatrist François Tosquelles, who was an advocate of *socialthérapie* (subsequently termed *psychothérapie institutionnelle*). Shortly afterward he published, with Tosquelles and other colleagues, a series of texts centered on shock therapies. They never present these treatments as cures in themselves, but instead as necessary preparations for psychotherapeutic work proper.

They made several presentations at the 51st session of the *Congrès des médecins aliénistes et neurologues de France et des pays de langue française*, held in Pau from 20 to 26 July 1953: 'On some cases treated by the Bini method'; 'Indications of Bini therapeutics in the framework of institutional therapeutics'; 'On an attempt at re-adaptation by a patient with morpheic epilepsy and serious personality disorders' (all three with Tosquelles); 'A note on sleeping-cure techniques with conditioning and electro-encephalographic control' (with Maurice Despinoy and Walter Zenner, who were also from Saint-Alban). These papers describe cases of patients with severe psychotic disorders. Fanon and Tosquelles recall at length the various debates on the risks and ethics of shock therapies, and note that, apart for a mistaken assimilation with lobotomy, a reason for the reluctance to use them is a naïve belief in the permanence of personality: 'Does this attitude not hide an ignorance about the dynamism of the personality, such as psychoanalysis has revealed it

---

[40]Fanon clearly states his agreement with Ey on this point in his debate with Lacan: 'One must read Ey's *La Psychiatrie devant le surréalisme* to understand how far-reaching is this author's presentation of the limits of freedom and madness. The same fall takes on a different value depending on whether it is free or irreversible. Depending on whether it is a flight or a consequence of the psychological weight of the organism. In the first case, we are dealing with the poet, in the second, the madman' (*Mental alterations*, p. 211). Ey's article, which was originally published in *L'Évolution psychiatrique* (vol. 13, no. 4, 1948, pp. 3–52), was printed as a separate volume by the Centre d'Éditions Psychiatriques in 1948, with a drawing by Frédéric Delanglade, a mutual friend of Breton and Ey. Fanon had a copy of this edition in his library and it is annotated throughout. On Ey and Lacan's differing positions on Surrealism, see Paolo Scopelliti, *L'Influence du surréalisme sur la psychanalyse*, Lausanne: L'Age d'homme, 2002, pp. 85–8.

to us?'[41] The personality that the shocks decompose is not a fixed essence but a pathological construction, built as a reaction to an initial disturbance and 'dissolution'.

Shock therapies, which Fanon continued to use extensively in Blida and in Tunis, were thus the instrument of choice for a second 'dissolution', that of pathological reconstructions. Yet operating this second dissolution was not therapeutic in itself. It was necessary to create special conditions and processes that would then enable the patients to reconstruct their personality. This is where psychotherapy (mostly group therapy) and institutional therapy, as elaborated and implemented at Saint-Alban, came in. Institutional therapy comprised the construction of a microcosm of the 'real world', an opening onto the world from within the hospital, such that throughout the day the patient was made to assume an active role through work and the organization of various other activities. The building of a social structure was therefore a crucial factor in the reconstruction of the personality:

> Treating patients using this approach, we insist, necessitates granting the greatest importance simultaneously to hospital organization, and to illnesses' classification and grouping, as well as to the concomitant establishment of group therapy programs. The coexistence of the workshop, the wards and the entire hospital social life is just as essential as the stage of *active* and interventionist *analysis* preceding the treatment. *Outside the possibility of such therapeutic linkages, the Bini cure appears to us a complete nonsense.*[42]

As has often been said, institutional therapy rests on the idea that the institution itself requires treatment if it is to treat its patients. In many cases, the hospital remained a simple place of internment, and patients whose problems were often minor at the

---

[41]Frantz Fanon and François Tosquelles, 'Indications de la thérapeutique de Bini dans le cadre des thérapeutiques institutionnelles', in *Comptes rendus du Congrès des médecins aliénistes et neurologues de France et des pays de langue française*, Paris: Masson, 1953, pp. 545–52: 547. 'Indications of electroconvulsive therapy within institutional therapies', below, p. 133.

[42]Fanon and Tosquelles, 'Indications de la thérapeutique', p. 549; emphasis in the original. 'Indications of electroconvulsive therapy within institutional therapies', below, p. 135.

start, would react to this environment, generating a cycle of violence that in turn condemned them to perpetual confinement. After the Second World War, the memory of famine in French asylums[43] and reports about concentration camps made the reality of the psychiatric hospital particularly intolerable. However, the idea that the institution itself might, through its very structure, engender mental illnesses in patients bearing little relation to their initial problems was not new; Maximien Parchappe de Vinay (1800–1866) claimed it already in the mid-nineteenth century. Vinay, a general inspector of mental asylums, oversaw the second wave of asylum construction in France and wrote that most mental illnesses were in fact generated by internment itself. Fanon knew these texts thanks to Philippe Paumelle, who was a pioneer of institutional therapy and of *psychiatrie de secteur* (community psychiatry) in Paris.[44] Reforms thus appeared necessary and in France they had their origin partly in the solution that Tosquelles developed in Saint-Alban. Tosquelles aimed to abolish all the structural constraints linked to internment – not just the instruments of restraint but also forced idleness and routine – and to recreate within the hospital and under medical supervision the structures of outside society,

---

[43]See Isabelle von Bueltzingsloewen, *L'Hécatombe des fous: la famine dans les hôpitaux psychiatriques français sous l'Occupation*, Paris: Aubier, 2007.
[44]For an indication of Philippe Paumelle's pioneering work, see his 'Le Mythe de l'agitation des malades mentaux', in Henri Ey (ed.), [1953], *Entretiens psychiatriques*, Paris: L'Arche, 1954, pp. 181–93, and '*Réflexion sur les Principes à suivre dans la fondation et la construction des asiles d'aliénés* de Parchappe, 1853–1953', *L'Information psychiatrique*, vol. 29, no. 10, 1953, pp. 270–7. Here is what Parchappe wrote in 1853, cited by Paumelle in this article: 'At the time when the creation of particular living conditions for the insane became a concern, agitation was considered to be something like the normal state of the insane. And the insane asylum was exclusively or almost exclusively made up of a collation of cells of more or less equal number to that of the patients. But as psychiatry progressed, it was acknowledged that agitation among the insane could be reduced to an increasingly smaller number of occurrences, in proportion to improvements made to the material and medical conditions of palliative and remedial treatment.' On Maximien Parchappe de Vinay's career and the birth of statistical analysis in the management of asylums and penitentiaries, see Frédéric Carbonel, 'L'Asile pour aliénés de Rouen: un laboratoire de statistiques morales de la Restauration à 1848', *Histoire et mesure*, vol. 20, nos. 1–2, 2005, pp. 97–136. Parchappe's *Statistical Research on the Causes of Mental Alienation* of 1839 is available at https://gallica.bnf.fr/ark:/12148/bpt6k76696c.

paying careful attention to the texture of daily life as opposed to the tradition of the doctor's morning visit followed by an empty day. In all its material and social dimensions, the hospital was to be run jointly by the patients and the nurses, with the latter needing complete retraining. Slowly and in controlled fashion, most patients recovered at least to the point of being able to interact with one another. Institutional therapy was one source of the 'antipsychiatry' movement of the 1960s, in particular the experiments of Félix Guattari and Jean Oury at the La Borde clinic; Oury was a former intern at Saint Alban and knew Fanon well.

Social therapy and culture:
Lessons from the Blida experiment

Fanon arrived at the Blida-Joinville psychiatric hospital in November 1953, after having worked for two months at Pontorson in Normandy. Equipped with his organo-dynamic and non-essentialist conception

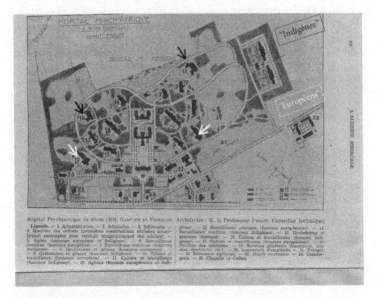

Figure 1 Psychiatric hospital for Blida (Joinville): Draft. From 'L'Assistance psychiatrique en Algérie et le futur Hôpital psychiatrique de Blida' par le Professeur A. Porot. *L'Algérie médicale*, vol. 65, 1933, pp. 86–92.

of mental illness and his experience of institutional therapy, he was thrown into an environment that he quickly transformed into a unique experimental situation and that would have a decisive impact on his thinking. Blida-Joinville was a *deuxième-ligne*, or second-line, hospital, meaning that a good number of its patients had been sent there from Mustapha, a first-line hospital in Algiers, and were considered incurable. As soon as he arrived, Fanon set out to reform the wards under his responsibility. The hospital separated patients along ethnic lines between 'Europeans' and 'natives (*indigènes*)', and Fanon was given two wards, one comprising European women, the other, Algerian men.[45] Social therapy, it so happened, worked wonders with the European women, while it completely failed the Algerian men.

Fanon and his intern, Jacques Azoulay (1927–2011), who had chosen this problem as the topic of his doctoral dissertation, published an important article on this failure and the lessons to be drawn from it.[46] Beyond studying the singularity of the colonial

---

[45]Psychiatry in Algeria had been organized by Antoine Porot, a major figure in colonial ethnopsychiatry who justified the use of segregation as follows: 'We cannot take responsibility for lumping the Europeans and natives together: the hospital community, which is acceptable and in fact established within general hospitals, cannot be introduced here: in disturbed minds, differences of moral or social conception, or latent impulsive tendencies, can disrupt the necessary calm at any moment, can fuel delusions, and trigger or create dangerous reactions in an eminently inflammable milieu'; see A. Porot, 'L'Assistance psychiatrique en Algérie et le futur Hôpital psychiatrique de Blida', *L'Algérie médicale*, vol. 65, 1933, pp. 86–92: 89. See figure 1, map of the project of a psychiatric hospital at Blida (Joinville), designed by Antoine Porot. Jacques Ladsous reported that, in 1954, when he was to take charge of managing the community of children of the Red-Cross in Chréa (very close to Blida), Porot enjoined him not to hire 'indigenous' educators, owing to their mental limitations (interview conducted 10 January 2015). On Fanon's work in this community of children, see Jacques Ladsous, 'Fanon: du soin à l'affranchissement', *Vie sociale et traitements*, vol. 33, no. 89, 2006, pp. 25–9. On the historiography of psychiatry in colonial Algeria, see Richard C. Keller, 'Madness and Colonization: psychiatry in the British and French Empires, 1800–1962', *Journal of Social History*, vol. 35, 2001, pp. 295–326; and *Colonial Madness: Psychiatry in French North Africa*, London and Chicago, IL: The University of Chicago Press, 2007.
[46]Frantz Fanon and Jacques Azoulay, 'La Socialthérapie dans un service d'hommes musulmans: difficultés méthodologiques', *L'Information psychiatrique*, vol. 30, no. 9, 1954, pp. 349–61. See *below*, 'Social therapy in a ward of Muslim men: methodological difficulties', pp. 195–214. This article is a slightly modified version of a section of Azoulay's dissertation. I thank Jacques Azoulay's family for kindly providing me with a copy.

experience, they found here a unique chance to reflect in greater depth upon the process of social therapy itself. For instance, they came to the conclusion that if the film club, the music society and the hospital journal (all of which were run by patients) were able to have a therapeutic function, it was not simply due to the films, music or texts in themselves, but because they were instruments through which the patients could re-learn to impart meaning to the constitutive elements of an environment:

> Film ought not remain a succession of images with sound accompaniment: it must become the unfolding of a life, of a story. Thus, the film committee, by choosing the films, by commenting upon them in a special chronicle of the newspaper, gives to the cinematographic fact its true meaning.[47]

Social therapy worked and soon after, as in Saint-Alban, Fanon could discard the straightjackets and other instruments of restraint in the European ward. But why had these reforms failed with the Algerian men, who remained stuck within their cycle of indifference, withdrawal and agitation, with its correlate of repression? The answer was to be found not in any racial features, but in the fact that the cognitive work of assigning meaning can only be carried out within certain frames of reference, and that these are not universal but culturally determined, something which is sharply revealed in a colonial society.

'Could our judgement have been more impaired than when we proposed to implement a Western-based social therapy program in a ward of mentally ill Muslim men?' ask Fanon and Azoulay. 'How is a structural analysis possible if we bracket out the geographical, historical, cultural and social frameworks?'[48] Charles Geronimi suggests that this failure was deliberate on Fanon's part; it was a necessary stage in the implementation of new therapeutic structures.

---

[47]Fanon and Azoulay, 'Social therapy in a ward of Muslim men', below, p. 198. The therapeutic use of film in psychiatric hospitals was to be the subject of four papers published by André Beley in *L'Information psychiatrique* between 1955 and 1959.
[48]Fanon and Azoulay, 'Social therapy in a ward of Muslim men', p. 204. On the significance of the failure of these reforms, see Alice Cherki, *Frantz Fanon: A Portrait*, p. 69.

It can be legitimately asked whether Fanon had really been 'misguided' in attempting to apply 'European' techniques to a Muslim ward, or whether he deliberately opted for what he knew to be a dead-end from the outset. Azoulay thought that, in his words, 'we had got it totally wrong'. When I expressed my surprise at Fanon's 'impaired judgement', a surprising thing for someone who had just written *Peau noire, masques blancs* and the article published in *Esprit* on 'The North-African syndrome' – works that highlighted the impossibility of an authentic encounter within a colonial framework – he smiled and replied:

You know, you only come to understand things through gut feeling [*on ne comprend qu'avec ses tripes*]. For me, the issue was not to impose methods more or less adapted to the 'indigenous mentality' from the outside. I had to show several things: that Algerian culture carried other values than colonial culture; that these structuring values ought to be taken on board confidently by those who bear them, that is, by Algerian patients or staff. To gain the support of the Algerian personnel, I had to arouse in them a feeling of revolt of the sort: 'We are just as able as the Europeans'. It was up to the Algerian staff to suggest the specific forms of sociability and incorporate them into the process of social therapy. That is what transpired.

And he added: 'Psychiatry must be political.'[49]

So Blida presented Fanon with the ideal experimental situation in which to address the two problems that had haunted him since his dissertation and *Peau noire, masques blancs*, namely those of the links between the neurological and the psychiatric, and between the psychiatric and the social. With his interns (in particular Jacques Azoulay and François Sanchez), he set out to study the ways in which mental illnesses were conceptualized in local cultures.[50] They

---

[49]Charles Geronimi, *Fanon à Blida*.
[50]See Numa Murard, 'Psychiatrie institutionnelle à Blida', *Tumultes*, vol. 23, no. 31, 2008, pp. 31–45, which draws on the author's interview with Jacques Azoulay in October 2007. Here is a key passage from it: 'He [Fanon] sought first to inform himself about the specific culture of Algerian Arabs and then we lived through a particularly picturesque and stimulating period. He was very active, I less so, although he dragged me along to ceremonies for treating hysteria in Kabylian villages, in which women having cathartic fits were chained down for entire nights. And it's striking that he could stay up the whole.

studied and wrote papers on the exorcisms performed by *marabouts* (holy men), which are based on a belief in *Djinns* (forces deemed to have taken over the personality of mentally ill patients), as well as on the impact of colonization on these cultures. From an institutional point of view, the solution for Blida became obvious and a complete reorganization of sociotherapeutic activities followed – the opening of a Moorish café, the celebration of traditional festivals, regular evenings with storytellers and local music groups – all of which soon involved more and more patients. A keen footballer, Fanon also had patients build a football pitch of which he was very proud and on which matches that he organized were played; indeed, it is still in use today. In the article written with Azoulay, these solutions are described only briefly, whereas the problem itself receives a detailed analysis. The point was to lay bare the need for a conceptual shake-up, the success of which would in turn make it possible to undermine the prevalent ethnopsychiatric gaze.[51]

---

night. He was interested in the inner workings of these practices, which were traditional means of responding to certain aspects of mental pathology. Of course, these aspects were limited to hysterical reactions; when nothing worked, as with cases of serious psychosis, people were sent to the hospital at Blida. We also often went to see the *marabouts*, to whom people had recourse whenever an evil eye, malevolent spirits, genies or the transmission of male impotence were concerned (since those who were impotent were supposed to have received a bad spirit from a jealous person), and these *marabouts*, no doubt with satisfactory success, would intervene by writing things, performing ceremonies and managed to clear up a certain part of this pathology, which nowadays would be seen to by a psychiatrist or psychoanalyst. At the time this was common practice and was one of the more common systems of social regulation, dominant in the cultural dimension of mental treatment. So Fanon took an interest in all these aspects and threw himself into Algerian culture. And he sought to transpose that, as best as he could, into his ward for Muslim patients, and it was there that we held get-togethers run by the nurses, who were rooted in the same culture as the patients. I remember that we also organized a Moorish café in the ward, which naturally provoked sarcastic criticisms from the other doctors. He also had storytellers come in, who continued a tradition that had some kind of purchase, storytellers who took up traditional folklore, and at that point a palpable shift occurred in the ward's atmosphere....I don't know if there were many discharges, but in any case there was a remarkable proof of the validity of the spirit of social therapy in the very fact of bringing a ward of a psychiatric hospital to life, and therefore ...I say it with the experience I have accumulated, in allowing those patients who are able to re-engage in an exchange with the world, that it should happen, that it should be made possible.'
[51] A gaze ironically described by Fanon in 'Réflexions sur l'ethnopsychiatrie', *Consciences maghrébines*, vol. 5, 1955, unpaginated (pp. [13]–[14]). This unsigned text was revealed as Fanon's work by the editor of this anticolonialist journal, André Mandouze. See *below*, 'Ethnopsychiatric considerations', pp. 251–4.

Fanon's later psychiatric works, particularly those on mental illness in North Africa, confirm theoretically what this experience had revealed and directly criticize the fundamentally flawed undertaking of pre-war colonial psychiatry, which naturalized mental disorders that were in fact determined by social and cultural factors. If it is true that neurological problems are often at the origin of mental illness, this therapeutic experience also confirms the irreducibility of psychiatric syndromes to the neurological. Scientific reductionism flourished in the colonies, in particular under the authority of Antoine Porot (1876–1965) and his influential 'Algiers school', only because it provided racism with a semblance of scientific foundation.

Speaking at the *Congrès des médecins aliénistes et neurologues* in Nice in September 1955, Fanon and Raymond Lacaton, a colleague from Blida, broached the subject of mental illness in North Africa via a legal problem on which they took an original stance: if most 'European' criminals confess once presented with the evidence against them, the majority of 'indigenous' North Africans deny the facts, even when faced with irrefutable evidence – and they do not try to prove their innocence either. The reaction of the police and public opinion was to naturalize this behaviour by saying that the North African is a liar by constitution. 'Primitivist' psychiatrists gave a subtler explanation. For them, first, criminality is part of the 'mentality' of the 'indigenous' people:

> *Indigenous criminality* has a development, a frequency, a brutality and a savagery that are surprising at first and that are conditioned through that special *impulsiveness* to which one of us has already been able to draw attention.[52] Out of the seventy-five mental assessments of natives one of us has had to perform over the last ten years, sixty-one of them concerned seemingly unmotivated murders or attempted murders.

> In the douars, the only way to shield oneself from such madmen was to burden them with chains: in our modern psychiatric hospitals, it was necessary to increase the number of solitary

---

[52]Antoine Porot and Come Arii, 'L'impulsivité criminelle chez l'indigène algérien. Ses facteurs', *Annales médico-psychologiques*, vol. 90, no. 5. December 1932 [note by Porot and Sutter].

confinement cells, of which there were still not enough to contain the surprising number of 'agitated natives' that we have had to put in there. Indeed, it is again primitivism that provides us with the explanation for this tendency towards agitation. In our opinion, one ought to consider these disordered psychomotor manifestations, in accordance with Kretschmer's idea, as the sudden liberation of preformed 'archaic complexes'; as explosive reactions 'of protest' (fear, panic, defence or flight) in the case of agitation. Whereas the 'evolved' individual still remains, in part, under the domination of higher faculties of control, critique and logic, which inhibit the liberation of his instinctive faculties, as for the primitive, he reacts, beyond a certain threshold, with a total liberation of his instinctive automatisms. We rediscover here the law of all or nothing: the native, in his madness, knows no limits.[53]

As for the tendency towards denying evidence, Antoine Porot and his disciple Jean Sutter (1911–1998) – who began his career with Porot as head of a ward at Blida-Joinville in 1938 – attribute it to a sort of constitutional stubbornness, an inability to integrate the data of experience into a common objectivity, such as when very young children deny the disobedience that they have seen their parents observe in them (with the exception that children have the ability to evolve):

The only intellectual resistance of which they [natives] are capable takes the form of a tenacious and insurmountable *obstinacy*, of a *power of perseveration* that defies all undertakings and that in general is only exercised in a direction determined by interests, instincts or essential beliefs. The wronged native quickly becomes a tenacious and obstinate plaintiff (*revendicateur*). This base of intellectual regression, coupled with gullibility and obstinacy, at first appears to invite comparison between the psychic composition of the native Muslim and that of the child.[54] [This mental puerilism nonetheless differs from that of our children, since it is devoid of

---

[53]Antoine Porot and Jean Sutter, 'Le "primitivisme" des indigènes nord-africains. Ses incidences en pathologie mentale', *Sud médical et chirurgical*, 15 April 1939, Marseille: Imprimerie marseillaise, pp. 11–12. Fanon's library contained a copy of this booklet.
[54]Porot and Jean Sutter, 'Le "primitivisme" des indigènes nord-africains', pp. 4–5.

the curiosity that leads the latter to formulate questions, to pose interminable 'whys', that urges their minds to make unforeseen connections, to make always interesting comparisons, which is the veritable beginning of the scientific mind, which the native lacks entirely.[55]].

The natives were therefore stuck not in a previous stage of ontogenetic development but in a deep phylogenetic difference. Porot and Sutter conclude their essay as follows:

> For primitivism is not a lack of maturity, a pronounced arrest in the development of the individual psyche; ... it is far more deep-seated and we indeed think that it must have its substratum in a particular disposition, if not of the architectonics, then at least of the 'dynamic' hierarchization of the nervous centres.[56]

In a hitherto unpublished typescript, Fanon again wipes the slate clean of presuppositions and sets out from a philosophical reflection on the cultural conditions and legal history of confession, citing Sartre, Bergson, Nabert, Dostoyevsky and, importantly, Hobbes:

> Confession has a moral pole that might be referred to as sincerity. But it also has a civic pole, a position, as is well known, that is dear to Hobbes and philosophers of the social contract. I confess as a man and I am sincere. I also confess as a citizen and I validate the social contract. Certainly, this duplicity is forgotten in everyday existence, but in specific circumstances, it is necessary to know how to lay it bare.[57]

A confession can therefore only make sense within a group that is recognized by the individual and that recognizes the individual. Outside of totalitarian jurisdictions, the role of confession in modern judicial procedures is minimal, since it does not have the status of a

---

[55]Antoine Porot, 'Notes de psychiatrie musulmane', *Annales médico-psychologiques*, May 1918 [Note by Porot and Sutter].
[56]Ibid., p. 18.
[57]Frantz Fanon, 'Conducts of confession in North Africa', unpublished typescript, p. 3 (*below*, p. 263). This text, only signed by Fanon, may be his conference paper or a first draft of the article he subsequently published with Raymond Lacaton. Alice Cherki remarks that during his studies Fanon had a passion for medical jurisprudence. According to his brother, he practiced it during his stay in Martinique in 1952.

proof (confession can be made under duress or in order to exonerate the guilty party). Admission of guilt is therefore better understood as a way of initiating a reintegration within the social group. But this implies the existence of a homogenous group, a reference framework, in which the individual at some point had a place, even if in practice this framework goes unperceived precisely by virtue of its self-evidence and necessity. The published article picks up from this point: no group reinsertion can take place in cases where individuals did not already have a place in a given group. By belonging to another group, with its own ethical-social norms, including a different code of honour, 'indigenous' North Africans cannot legitimize a foreign system through confession. They may well submit fully to the judgement, but will see it only as a decision of God. Fanon never stopped emphasizing that submitting to a power is not the same as accepting it:

> For the criminal, to recognize his act before the judge is to disapprove of this act, to legitimize the irruption of the public into the private. By denying, by retracting, does the North African not refuse this? What we probably see concretized in this way is the total separation between two social groups that co-exist – alas, tragically! – but where the integration of one by the other has not begun. The accused Muslim's refusal to authenticate, by confessing his act, the social contract proposed to him, means that his often profound submission to the powers-that-be (in this instance, the power of the judiciary), which we have noted, cannot be confounded with an acceptance of this power.[58]

The interest of this problem of 'medical jurisprudence' (*médecine légale*) is thus that it reveals that, in colonial society, there is no shared social contract, no subscription by the individual to a social and juridical whole. The legal system shows an irreconcilable contradiction between colonialism and the contractual understanding of the social, even if the former had flagged the latter as one of its justifications. Once again, the idea of assigning mental disorder to a character that is specified by race is just a mask for this contradiction. In the guise of science, the naturalization of mental illness along racial lines was an

---

[58]Fanon and Lacaton, 'Conducts of Confession in North Africa', below, p. 258.

attempt at secretly turning a certain cultural organization, imported from Europe, into a natural norm.[59]

Fanon and Azoulay had noted that the difficulties of applying social therapy to the Algerian men in the ward in Blida stemmed from the fact that 'the biological, the psychological, the sociological were only separated by an aberration of the mind'.[60] In order to explore the real relations between these dimensions and understand the links between individual members of a group and the social whole, Fanon went back to his books, particularly those of sociologists and anthropologists, such as André Leroi-Gourhan,[61] George Gursdorf and Marcel Mauss, from whom he adopted the concept of 'total social fact'.[62] Among the crucial practices that define a society, Fanon placed its attitudes to madness at the intersection of the economy, law, religion, magic and art.

On this matter he wrote several interesting texts, of which the most striking is probably an article co-written with François Sanchez in 1956 titled 'Maghrebi Muslims and their attitudes to madness'. Instead of going back over the tradition of Arab medieval writings on madness as mental illness, Fanon and Sanchez focussed on popular attitudes to mental illness. They studied them by observing *marabouts*' therapeutic procedures and commissioning translations of the treatises on demonology on which these practices are based. Of note, according to Fanon and Sanchez, is that in Europe, even though

---

[59]Fanon criticized neurology in similar fashion during the Algerian war: 'This particular form of pathology (generalized muscular contracture) already caught our attention before the revolution began. But the doctors who described it turned it into a congenital stigma of the "native", an original feature of his nervous system, manifest proof of a predominant extrapyramidal system in the colonized. This contracture is, in actual fact, quite simply the postural accompaniment, the existence in the colonized's muscles of their rigidity, their reluctance, their refusal in the face of colonial authority' (*The Wretched of the Earth*, p. 217; translation modified – SC).

[60]Fanon and Azoulay, 'Social therapy in a ward of Muslim men', *below*, p. 205.

[61]Fanon and Azoulay reproduce long extracts from texts by Leroi-Gourhan almost verbatim, drawing up a table of the demographic, cultural and legal situation of Algeria's 'indigenous' population, but subtly modify them to underscore the colonial nature of this situation (see André Leroi-Gourhan and Jean Poirier, *Ethnologie de l'Union française*, vol. 1, *Afrique*, Paris: PUF, 1953, p. 121). Fanon attended Leroi-Gourhan's lectures at Lyon (Razanajao and Postel, 'La vie et l'œuvre psychiatrique de Frantz Fanon', p. 148).

[62]See Marcel Mauss, 'Essai sur le don', in *Sociologie et anthropologie*, Paris: Presses universitaires de France, 1950, pp. 145–284: 274–5.

madness is now conceptualized in terms of illness and not of evil, social attitudes outside as well as within the hospital are still based on a conception that is moral as opposed to medical. Even trained psychiatric nurses tend to 'punish' the patients who cause trouble, and members of their families feel personally hurt by their attitude:

> In general, the westerner believes that mental illness alienates the person, that the patient's behaviour cannot be understood without taking this illness into account. However, in practice that belief does not always entail a logical attitude and often everything transpires as if the westerner has forgotten about the illness: the mental patient appears to the westerner as indulging in morbidity and taking advantage of it to some extent to exploit those around him.[63]

The North African view of madness differs:

> If one certainty may be established, it is that which the Maghrebi possesses on the topic of madness and its determinism: the mentally ill patient is absolutely alienated, he is not responsible for his disorder; the genies alone bear full responsibility for it.

If you truly believe that the mad are ill because they are ruled by external forces (the *djnoun* or genies), you cannot assign any intentionality, or *a fortiori* any morality, to the behaviour of patients:

> The mother insulted or hit by her ill son will never dream of accusing him of disrespect or murderous desires. She knows that her son would in all liberty be unable to want to do her any harm. There can be no question of attributing to him acts that do not arise from his will, which is itself thoroughly in thrall to the genies.[64]

Fanon thus considers that these societies are more advanced in terms of 'mental hygiene', that is in locally dispensed treatment, than European ones, but not because of some fascination madness itself would inspire (and in this Fanon is rather far from the Foucault

---

[63]Frantz Fanon and François Sanchez, 'Attitudes du musulman maghrébin devant la folie', *Revue pratique de psychologie de la vie sociale et d'hygiène mentale*, vol. 1, 1956, pp. 24–7: 'Maghrebi Muslims and their attitudes to madness', below, pp. 271–2; and also below, pp. 182–9, the remarkable set of editorials of *Our Journal* from November and December 1956).
[64]Fanon and Sanchez, 'Maghrebi Muslims and their attitudes to madness', below, pp. 272–3.

of *Folie et déraison*[65]): 'Madness itself does not command respect, patience, indulgence; instead, it is the human being impaired by madness, by the genies; the human being as such.'[66] Europe has to learn from these attitudes if it is to develop better systems of mental care, but this in no way implies, for Fanon, that one ought to abandon a scientific perspective in psychiatry. The paper closes with a box containing the following proclamation: 'If Europe received from Muslim countries the first rudiments of care for the mentally ill, it has in return contributed to the latter a rational understanding of mental affections!'[67]

Beyond the institution

Fanon's reflection on his experience in Blida confirmed the extent to which social and cultural factors had to be taken into consideration to make the institutional therapy model work. He then wondered whether organizations for mental health other than the institution of the asylum itself could be conceived. In a 1957 paper on the question of agitation (the violence of patients and its relation to the institution), co-authored with one of the interns at Blida, Dr Slimane Asselah, Fanon indicates for the first time a distance with Tosquelles. He questions the idea that the hospital could ever replace the outside world, adding that in such a case external relations of power would also be transposed into it:

---

[65]In his texts on literature, Foucault presents the possibility of madness as a profound and seductive freedom: 'I have the impression, if you will, that very fundamentally, in us, the possibility of speaking, the possibility of being mad, are contemporary, and as twins, that they open, under our steps, the most perilous ones, but perhaps also the most marvelous or the most insistent of our freedoms' (Michel Foucault, *La Grande Étrangère*, Paris: Éditions de l'EHESS, 2013, p. 52). In his dissertation, Fanon mentions the importance of language from the point of view of madness and credited Lacan with this observation, but ultimately argues for Ey's stance. In 1969, *L'Évolution psychiatrique* organized its annual meeting with a focus on 'The ideological conception of Michel Foucault's *L'Histoire de la folie*'. It contains interesting papers by psychiatrists, some of whom Fanon knew. Ey's paper comes down violently on a type of thinking that, according to him, deems 'that Insanity is equal to Reason, that Dream is equal to Existence, that Error is equal to Truth, that Alienation is equal to Freedom.' (*L'Évolution psychiatrique*, vol. 36, no. 2, 1971, p. 257).
[66]Fanon and Sanchez, 'Maghrebi Muslims and their attitudes to madness', below, p. 274.
[67]Ibid., p. 275.

Here, it does not seem useless to recall that understanding the need to organize the ward, to institutionalize it, to make social conducts possible within it, ought not generate any mystification grounded in reference to the outside world. This is how you can understand reflections such as 'the village-hospital', 'the hospital, a reflection of the outside world', 'inside the hospital is like outside', 'the patient should feel at home', and so on. Such expressions, you will surmise, are an attempt to mask the reality beneath falsely psychotherapeutic humanitarian concerns. And Le Guillant is absolutely right to condemn these unreal attitudes.[68]

Thus, as of 1957, during his final years in Tunis, in addition to his work at El Moudjahid and his political activities, Fanon devoted considerable energy to setting up and running a psychiatric day centre attached to a general hospital, Hôpital Charles-Nicolle, in order to replace psychiatric hospitalization. The last of his scientific papers, published in 1959, is a long report on this two-year long experiment. Fanon seems to have been particularly proud of this centre, which he thought was an advanced model for psychiatric

---

[68]Frantz Fanon and Sliman Asselah, 'Le Phénomène de l'agitation en milieu psychiatrique: considérations générales, signification psychopathologique', Maroc médical, vol. 36 no. 380, 1957, pp. 21–4: 24. See, in this volume, 'The phenomenon of agitation in the psychiatric milieu: General considerations, psychopathological meaning', p. 289. This paper is a response to a critique by Tosquelles of Paumelle's denunciation of the 'myth of agitation'; see F. Tosquelles, 'Introduction à la sémiologie de l'agitation', L'Évolution psychiatrique, 1, 1954, pp. 75–97. In their response, Fanon and Asselah stress the importance of the Marxist psychiatrist Louis Le Guillant, who had published a paper in the same issue of L'Évolution psychiatrique titled 'Introduction à une psycho-pathologie sociale' (pp. 1–52). Asking if the desire to readapt and therefore to normalize the patient is linked to a 'desire to penalize', the Our Journal editorial of 15 November 1956 (see below, p. 183–4) clearly expresses such a concern about a repressive bureaucratization within social-therapeutic committees.

In 1959 and 1960, Fanon gave a series of lectures titled 'The meeting between society and psychiatry', at the Institut des Hautes Études in Tunis, as part of a social psychology diploma in the sociology and psychology bachelor programmes. The Tunisian sociologist Lilia Ben Salem, who attended them, noted that Fanon formulated the question thus: 'One says that sociotherapy creates a false society. Can the social milieu be domesticated like the natural milieu?' (see her course notes in the present volume, p. 363). According to her, these lectures drew a very large audience and Fanon's digressions were as interesting as the lectures themselves, as Michel Martini confirms in his memoirs (Chroniques des années algériennes, 1946–1962, Saint-Denis: Bouchène, 2002, p. 369).

treatment able, by virtue of its low cost and considerable therapeutic efficacy, to be developed anywhere, particularly in decolonized societies.[69] The advantage of a day centre over an institution of internment is that social therapy can take place within a patient's normal cultural and social environment. Indeed, the patients at Fanon's day clinic were able to return home each evening after having received an appropriate course of treatment during the day, including, if necessary, an initial course of shock therapy or hypnotherapy, together with a variety of psychotherapies, conducted either individually or in groups.[70]

---

[69]Frantz Fanon, 'L'hospitalisation de jour en psychiatrie, valeur et limites' (in two parts, the second published with Charles Geronimi), *La Tunisie médicale*, vol. 37, no. 10, pp. 698–732. See 'Day hospitalization in psychiatry: Value and limits' (in two parts), *below*, 325–46. Fanon would have been aware of 'open-door' psychiatric clinics from reading G. Boittelle and C. Boittelle-Lentulo, 'Quelques réflexions sur le fonctionnement d'un *open-door*', *L'Information psychiatrique*, vol. 29, no. 1, 1953, pp. 15–18, about an experiment in the psychiatric hospital in Cadillac, and H. Ueberschlag, 'L'Assistance psychiatrique hospitalière en Angleterre', *L'Information psychiatrique*, vol. 31, no. 7, 1955, pp. 332–47, and vol. 31, no. 9, 1955, pp. 476–98, which has a section on Mapperley Hospital in Nottingham and its pioneering director, Duncan Macmillan.
[70]In her aforementioned testimony, Lilia Ben Salem describes the centre as follows: 'He invited some of us, the students of the CES in social psychology, to attend his Thursday morning consultations within the Psychiatric Day Centre at the Charles-Nicolle Hospital in Tunis. Upon his arrival in Tunis, he was first appointed to the La Manouba psychiatric hospital. But faced with his colleagues' reluctance toward his "sociological" interpretation of mental illness, he obtained from the State Secretary for Health and Social Affairs a transfer to the neuro-psychiatric ward at the Charles-Nicolle Hospital. At the Charles-Nicolle Hospital he was freer to adhere to his principles and, with a young team, had the pleasure of establishing a neuropsychiatric day centre there, "Fanon's place in Tunis"'. (On the tensions in the psychiatric ward of La Manouba that would lead Fanon to create the above-mentioned centre, see Alice Cherki, *Frantz Fanon: A Portrait*, p. 115.)

Later on, the Tunisian colleagues whose methods of practice he upended did not hesitate to appropriate his work; see, for example, Sleim Ammar, 'L'assistance psychiatrique en Tunisie: aperçu historique', *L'Information psychiatrique*, vol. 48, no. 7, 1972, pp. 647–57 (the article was reprised and updated in *Journal tunisien de psychiatrie*, vol. 1, no. 1, January 1998, http://psydoc-fr.broca.inserm.fr/bibliothq/revues/jtp/archives/Numero1/APET.htm: 'With the advent of independence in 1956, the succession was to be assured by Tunisian psychiatrists. Vigorously pursuing and emphasizing the work already undertaken, the Tunisian leadership of the establishment (Drs Tahar Ben Soltane and Sleim Ammar), augmented by Fanon's presence from 1958 to 1961, endeavoured to break with all constraints and prohibitions, abolishing straightjackets, caged enclosures and isolation units. In parallel, they contributed to an intensive development of ergotherapy and sociotherapy (a newspaper, excursions, films, theatre performances, as well as musical, sporting and recreational activities of all kinds)'.

In this paper, Fanon, justifying his rejection of confinement, reiterates several times the view inherited from Ey that madness is a pathology of freedom:

In any phenomenology in which the major alterations of consciousness are left aside, mental illness is presented as a veritable pathology of freedom. Illness situates the patient in a world in which his or her freedom, will and desires are constantly broken by obsessions, inhibitions, countermands, anxieties. Classical hospitalization considerably limits the patient's field of activity, prohibits all compensations, all movement, restrains him within the closed field of the hospital and condemns him to exercise his freedom in the unreal world of fantasy. So it is not surprising that the patient feels free only in his opposition to the doctor who has withheld him. … At the day hospital … [t]he institution, in fact, has no hold over the patient's freedom, over his immediate appearing. … The fact that the patients can take things into their own hands, whether through dressing, hairstyling or, above all, the secrecy of an entire part of the day spent outside the hospital setting, reinforces and in any case maintains their personalities, in contrast with the process of dissolutive integration that occurs in a psychiatric hospital and which opens the way to phantasms of bodily fragmentation or the crumbling of the ego.[71]

Fantasies of corporeal fragmentation, a crumbling of the self that the psychiatric institution works only to reinforce instead of transform: in *Peau noire, masques blancs*, Fanon had already made use of these

---

In their study *L'Hôpital Razi de La Manouba et son histoire* (Tunis: Centre de publication universitaire, 2008, p. 79), M. Fakhreddine Haffani and Zied M'Hirsi note that Fanon 'abolished the fences that enclosed the courtyards in the ward of chronically ill patients'. They cite statements collected in Abdelhamid Bouzgarrou's doctoral thesis in medicine (Tunis Medical Faculty), *À propos d'une expérience de transformation institutionnelle au niveau d'un service de psychiatrie*: 'He broke down barriers and provided freedom. Before, we were the trainers and the patients the wild animals. Within this setting, we all lived with an obsessive fear of escape. Fanon worked only a few months at Pinel [paradoxically, the name of one of the isolation wards], but he took a ward of senile and chronic patients and began to make it work like a modern wing. He would say: "It's no big deal if the patient escapes; if he escapes it is because he is doing fine!"'
[71]Fanon, 'Day hospitalization in psychiatry: Value and limits', *below*, pp. 349–50 and 354–5.

notions to describe the alienation produced by the racist gaze and the colonial institution at the very heart of the lived experience of the Black individual. In Fanon's thought, the colonial dissolution is analogous to the neurological dissolution in the genesis of mental illness.[72] But that the world was changing and perpetuating inherently alienating structures within medicine was out of the question. The blueprint of a public mental health programme for a new country, which Fanon presented in his paper about the day centre in Tunis, lays the groundwork for what was to be, under the name of *psychiatrie de secteur* (community psychiatry), a considerable transformation in Europe as well.

Fanon enjoyed the life of a revolutionary, an ambassador and a journalist. But as soon as independence had been won, his intention was to devote the next part of his life to setting up structures able to resolve 'freedom's pathologies'. It is impossible to separate his many lives, which he lived unreservedly, from his scientific and clinical practice.[73]

---

[72]Fanon, *Black Skin, White Masks*, p. 47. The core of this book is the alienation produced by the obsessional consciousness of the body/object induced by the racist gaze upon its surface, the skin. Fanon understands this dissolution as the analogue of the soma/psyche split that results from neurological diseases. The book's chapters can be read as a description of the pathological reconstructions that follow within the historical and sociological context of colonies of the *Ancien Régime*, including even the movement of negritude, perceived in Sartre's terms as a negative moment in the dialectic of a historical phenomenology of the colonized mind (Fanon, *Black Skin, White Masks*, p. 108).

[73]Fanon's texts in this volume are presented and annotated by Jean Khalfa.

1 MENTAL ALTERATIONS, CHARACTER MODIFICATIONS, PSYCHIC DISORDERS AND INTELLECTUAL DEFICIT IN SPINOCEREBELLAR HEREDODEGENERATION: A CASE OF FRIEDREICH'S ATAXIA WITH DELUSIONS OF POSSESSION

Frantz Fanon, November 1951

To my father. He did not have the joy of seeing me complete my medical studies. I've been told that he would have liked to embrace me before he passed on. I piously dedicate this work to his memory.

To my mother. Her ardour for life has always been a marvel to me.

Let her be assured of my profound love.

To my brothers and sisters.

To my brother Joby.

'I speak only of *lived* things and do not simply present cerebral processes.'

Friedrich Nietzsche, *Thus Spoke Zarathustra*.[1]

To my parents.[2]

'The frequency and the importance of mental disorders in familial nervous illnesses does not allow us to regard them as fortuitous accidents.'

Paul Guiraud and Julian De Ajuriaguerra,
paper given at the Société médico-
psychologique,
8 February 1934.

Foreword

Taking certain signs from the syndrome first described by [Nikolaus] Friedreich in 1861, some clinical symptom clusters sought to reach the dignity of the entity. Thirty years after Friedreich's paper in Speyer, Pierre Marie described a new illness that he called cerebellar heredo-ataxia. This individualization appeared justified

---

[1]On the source of this citation, see our introduction, p. 14, note 29.
[2]Doctoral thesis presented to the Joint Faculty of Medicine and Pharmacy in Lyon for the degree of Doctor of Medicine; the viva voce was held before a public audience on 29 November 1951.

As was the custom the thesis is also dedicated to the examiners, as follows: 'To the members of the Jury. Professor Jean Dechaume [president of the Jury], professor of clinical neuropsychiatry at the Faculty of Medicine in Lyon. He has on occasion done me the honour of engaging in detailed fashion with my research, helping me with his advice to avoid numerous errors [*errements*]. His deep sense of humanity has enabled me to grasp better the polymorphism inherent to neuro-psychiatric science. I hereby express my profound gratitude.

Professor J. Bourret, professor of medical jurisprudence at the Faculty of Medicine in Lyon. I am very happy to have him as a dissertation examiner. He taught me medical jurisprudence – that other science of human extremes. And I have been very appreciative of the rigour of his thinking. To him I owe warm admiration.

Professor P. Girard, teaching fellow at the Faculty of Medicine in Lyon. He does me a great honour by examining my dissertation, for which I express my sincere gratitude.

Professor J. de Rougemont, teaching fellow at the Faculty of Medicine in Lyon. In him I have discovered a major philosophical proficiency, philosophy being the risk that the mind takes to assume its dignity. I declare my utmost respect for him.'

and Saquet's dissertation establishes a fairly rigorous semiological distinction of it in a schematic table. Some years later, on 4 February 1926, D. Roussy and Ms Gabrielle Lévy presented to the *Société de neurologie* seven cases of a familial illness characterized by gait and upright stance problems, a generalized tendinous areflexia, the existence of a club foot and a tendency towards big-toe extension. The authors called this syndrome hereditary areflexia dystasia. Bridging these three illnesses is the familial spastic paraplegia of the Strümpell-Lorain type.

In his masterly 1929 physico-clinical study of Friedreich's ataxia, M. Mollaret insisted on the existence of clear-cut boundaries between Friedreich's ataxia and Pierre Marie's cerebellar heredo-ataxia. He made himself the spokesperson of the unitarist theory that, in Raymond, finds its ideal expression in the following phrase: 'All the familial nervous affections form a continuous chain'. However, in his introduction, the author is careful to include a reservation about familial spastic paraplegia. Not until his conclusion does he agree to subsume under the term spinocerebellar hereditary degeneration the overall subject of familial nervous pathology. As he puts it,

> Depending upon the degree of impairment of the spinocerebellar systems, the clinical aspect engendered will sometimes be Friedreich's illness, sometimes cerebellar heredoataxia, sometimes a particular familial paraplegia. We have retained these names but for us they designate no more [than] morbid entities that correspond to a single process of degeneration of a certain area made obligatory by heredity.[3]

In a 1933 article in *La Presse médicale*, M. Mollaret was to return to this question, and in his most recent update, written for the *Encyclopédie médico-chirurgicale*, he definitively includes hereditary areflexic dystasia within the group of spinocerebellar heredodegeneration.

---

[3]Pierre Mollaret, *La Maladie de Friedreich. Étude physio-clinique*, doctoral dissertation, Paris, 1929, p. 265. [The square brackets in notes contain specifications and explanations by the editor of this section of the present volume, Jean Khalfa. The insertions between the square brackets that appear in the text itself correct Fanon's transcription errors. We reprint hereafter the last two paragraphs of Mollaret's dissertation that Fanon's quote condenses: 'Everything leads us to admit that we are dealing with a single

I have insisted on this question of general pathology because it seems, upon consideration, that in the group Mollaret describes neurological symptoms and psychiatric symptoms obey an absolute polymorphism.[4] It was indispensable to unite in a single bundle the scattered givens that constitute familial nervous illnesses. And the psychic side of neurological disorders ought likewise to be described in univocal fashion. We will see that the solution for this latter concern is still far off.

General paralysis, an eminently neurological illness, is almost always accompanied by a given psychiatric symptom cluster. So no shortage of causal or mechanistic explanations have been forthcoming. Now, with spinocerebellar heredodegeneration things are more complicated. It is true that a mental disorder is noted in one tenth of all cases. However, rarely are the same alterations to be found. Hence the impossibility of formulating a law.

So, the point here is to consider the problem of the relations between neurological disorders and psychiatric disorders. At a time when neurologists and psychiatrists are striving to define their disciplines as pure sciences, that is to say a pure neurology and a pure psychiatry, it is good practice to set among the debate a group of neurological diseases that are also accompanied by psychic disorders, and to ask the legitimate question about the essence of these disorders.

I have retained the clinical names under which these disorders appear in the observations to be found in the literature. In this work, however, I deal with the problem of mental disorders in

---

process that strikes the same spinocerebellar systems in a more or less complete manner. Depending upon the extent of the impairment, the clinical aspect formed will sometimes be Friedreich's illness, sometimes cerebellar heredoataxia, sometimes a particular familial paraplegia. I have retained the names, but for me the morbid entities they designate are not distinct. They are only convenient clinical schemas corresponding to a single process of degeneration of a specific domain, which heredity has made necessary. This is why I have retained them, but as subtitles to a more general chapter, which I propose to use one term to name, a name that sums up all the essential characteristics: "spinocerebellar heredodegeneration".]

[4][The notion of polymorphism is important in this dissertation. Fanon uses it in his dedication to Dechaume and he returns to it later concerning the perceptual ambiguities on which tests of cultural perceptions such as the TAT (Thematic Apperception Test) play. The polymorphism of mental illness reveals the gap between the neurological and the psychiatric, a gap that is a condition of possibility of social therapy as well as of psycho-therapies.]

spinocerebellar heredodegeneration. Lastly, it seemed to me of interest to publish a case of psychopathy with a hysterical structure and delusions of possession as part of a Friedreich's illness. The patient that I observed over the course of a year had the advantage of having a higher than average intellectual development (*baccalauréat*). I was unable to find a similar case in the literature, for which reason I had no hesitation in studying it.

History

Friedreich's first description does not indicate the presence of any psychic disorders. On the contrary, he claims that all the cerebral functions remain intact. The problem with mental disorders in spinocerebellar heredodegeneration was first studied in Saquet's dissertation. Before reporting the author's conclusions, an historical reminder seems essential.

In 1879 Seeligmüller became the first person to speak, in parallel to motor ataxia, of an ataxia in the unfolding of thoughts.[5] In 1884, two years after Brousse[6] legitimated the name 'Friedreich's illness' in his dissertation, Musso published a study of six cases and noted some psychic disturbances in them.[7] Longuet and then Soca (in his dissertation) argued the contrary point of view in 1884 and 1888, respectively.[8] For these authors, no intellectual deficit, no mental disturbance, was notable.

In *Nouvelle Iconographie de La Salpêtrière*, Gilles de la Tourette, Blocq and Huet liken Friedreich's illness to multiple sclerosis in terms of psychic integrity.[9] According to them, it involves no impairment to the intelligence. Motor disorders alone explain the fatigue, slowness of ideation and of verbal expression that it involves. In 1890, Auscher

---

[5] [Adolph Seeligmüller, 'Hereditäre Ataxie mit Nystagmus', *European Archives of Psychiatry and Clinical Neuroscience*, vol. 10, no. 1, 1880, pp. 222–42.]
[6] [Auguste Brousse, *De l'ataxie héréditaire*, dissertation, Montpellier, 1882.]
[7] [G. Musso, 'Sulla malattia di Friedreich', *Rivista Clinica*, no. 10, 1884.]
[8] [François-Vincent Soca, *Étude clinique de la maladie de Friedreich*, dissertation, Paris, 1888.]
[9] [*Nouvelle Iconographie de La Salpêtrière. Clinique des maladies du système nerveux*, published under the guidance of Professor Charcot (from the Institute) by Paul Richer (head of the laboratory), Gilles de la Tourette (head of the clinic), Albert Londe (director of the photographic service), Paris: Lecrosnier et Babé, 1888. See, vol. 1, pp. 44–63;

cited a case of late-onset Friedreich's ataxia with mental degeneration in a prostitute.[10]

In his 1891 work on *Le Cervelet et ses fonctions* [The Cerebellum and its Functions], Courmont observed sadness, apathy, indifference and a perturbation of moral sense.[11] Indeed, it has been noted that neurologists have long considered the cerebellum to be the seat of psychic and moral equilibrium. In the same year, Nonne indicated among patients with Pierre-Marie illness the occurrence of carelessness, stupor and gullibility, as did Sanger Brown in 1892.[12]

In 1893, Pierre Marie wrote the following about Friedreich's ataxia in *Semaine médicale*:

> The intelligence is far from being as affected as it might seem initially. … When these patients were carefully interrogated, it could be seen that they were perfectly able to carry out a particular instruction and that their replies attested to a fairly age-appropriate degree of reasoning. It could nonetheless not be claimed that the development of their psychic faculties was totally normal and, in this regard, the difference with normal individuals increased the older they became.[13]

The upshot of this view is clear. Degenerescence that bears on particular neurological sectors does not impair the intellectual

---

pp. 113–18; pp. 155–62; pp. 183–90. 'Speech presents a very manifest problem close to that of multiple sclerosis; it is hesitant, slow, drawling and nasal (*nasonnée*). When made to read, the patient articulated his words poorly; it appeared that he could not master the articulation of syllables and he pronounced his words and syllables by stressing them separately' (p. 48). 'These patients, though their intelligence is sometimes quite developed, forever remain big children; they are unable to take on any serious work, dwell constantly on futile things and, concerning trivial conversations, are prone to fits of extended and silly laughter. There is reason to liken this normal state to the one sometimes observed in multiple sclerosis, striking examples of which we have seen and continue to see in the ward of M. Charcot. Among all these cases there exists a genuinely peculiar mental and physical instability' (p. 115).]

[10][Ernest Auscher, 'Sur un cas de maladie de Friedreich (sclérose névrologique pure), suivi d'autopsie (étude histologique de la moelle épinière des nerfs cutanés)', *Comptes rendus de la Société de biologie*, no. 2, 1890, p. 475. See also: 'Anatomie pathologique de la maladie de Friedreich', *Semaine médicale*, no. 82, July 1890.]

[11][Frédéric Courmont, *Le Cervelet et ses fonctions*, Paris: Félix Alcan, 1891.]

[12][Max Nonne, 'Vier fälle von Elephantiasis congenita hereditaria', *Archiv für Pathologische Anatomie*, no. 125, 1891, pp. 189–96; Sanger Brown, 'On hereditary ataxy, with a series of twenty-one cases', *Brain*, vol. 15, no. 2, 1892, pp. 250–68.]

[13][Pierre Marie, 'Sur l'hérédo-ataxie cérébelleuse', *La Semaine médicale*, no. 50, 1893.]

faculties as selectively. The claim is that disturbances of judgement and affective aberrations appear slowly.[14] Pierre Marie considers that what occurs is an arrest of one's mental development rather than some veritable deviation of psychic faculties.

In 1894 Bouchaud related the case of a brother and a sister, both of whom were affected with Friedreich's ataxia, in which the intellectual weakening first present eventually led to dementia.[15] In 1895, Nolan cites the case of three sisters in whom Friedreich's ataxia evolved with congenital idiocy. In his anatomical, clinical and physiological study on the cerebellum, André Thomas stated that he often encountered mental disturbances coupled with cerebellar syndromes.[16] This notwithstanding, he added, 'the intelligence is usually maintained, the character is sad, attention levels are hardly sustained, and there is a certain degree of intellectual asthenia as there is of physical asthenia'.

Then, in 1898, Raymond identified no cognitive impairment and goes so far as to state, in his *Clinique des maladies du système nerveux*, that the integrity of the psychic faculties was normal.[17] In 1900 [Jules] Vincelet, whose dissertation bore on the pathological anatomy of Friedreich's ataxia, related a case associated with delusion of persecution. In 1902, Gilbert Ballet published his *Traité de pathologie mentale* in which he claims that: 'Among the individuals suffering from Friedreich's ataxia, the intelligence, which is defective from the outset, often continues to weaken further'.[18] In 1904, Pritzche cited a case of two sisters who suffered from Friedreich's ataxia and idiocy with symptoms of dementia. In 1906, Pellizi described a case of familial spastic paraplegia that was linked with dementia praecox. In 1909, Flatau,[19] and then, in 1912, Vogt and Astwazaturow,[20] all

---

[14][This remark heralds Fanon's insistence on the temporal dimension that is specific to psychiatric thinking. See the section on Goldstein in the last part of the dissertation.]

[15][Jean-Baptiste Bouchaud,'Démence progressive et incoordination des mouvements dans les quatre membres, chez deux enfants, le frère et la sœur', *Revue neurologique*, no. 1, 1894, pp. 2–7.]

[16][André Thomas, *Le Cervelet: étude anatomique, clinique et physiologique*, Paris: G. Steinheil, 1897.]

[17][Fulgence Raymond, *Leçons sur les maladies du système nerveux*, Paris: Clinique de la Faculté de médecine de Paris/O. Doin, 1897–1898.]

[18][Gilbert Ballet, *Traité de pathologie mentale*, Paris: O. Doin, 1903.]

[19][Germanus Flatau, 'Klinischer Beitrag zur Kenntnis der hereditären Ataxie', *Deutsche Zeitschrift für Nervenheilkunde*, no. 35, 1908, p. 461.]

[20][Heinrich Vogt and Michail Astwazaturow, 'Über angeborene Kleinhirn Erkrankungen mit Beiträgen zur Entwicklungsgeschichte des Kleinhirns', *Archiv für Psychiatrie und Nervenkrankheit*, vol. 49, no. 1, 1912.]

published cases of either Friedreich's ataxia or Pierre Marie's illness accompanied by idiocy and imbecility. In 1913, Frenkel and Dide reported three cases involving progressive dementia.[21]

In 1919, Saquet's dissertation took stock of the question and added to the number of hitherto published cases, the following: a case of cerebellar heredoataxia involving profound mental debility and instinctive perversions; another of Friedreich's ataxia with mental debility and motor debility; and one of cerebellar heredoataxia with hallucinatory psychosis. A year later, in 1920, Benon and Lerat published a case of cerebellar heredoataxia with delirium in the *Gazette médicale de Nantes*. In 1921, Emmanuel Bergmann emphasized the association between heredoataxia and oligophrenia.[22] Similarly, in 1922, Lamsens and Nyssen made an observation of mental debility.[23] In 1923, de Vries cited two cases of cerebellar heredoataxia accompanied with imbecility.

In 1928, in his report to the congress of alienists and neurologists, Bogaert studied the coexistence of mental disorders in cerebellar atrophies. The following year, he included in his description a variety of olivopontine atrophies, including dementia disorders. Mollaret had his dissertation viva voce in the course of the same year; the author makes twenty-one observations, of which around three-fifths are accompanied by mental disorders.

In 1929, Hiller studied spoken-language disorders and conceptual language disorders in Friedreich's ataxia.[24] He showed the internal relations that exist between these two modalities of verbal expression. Five years later, J.-O. Trelles, in a much-lauded paper, examined anatomopathological lesions and mental disorders in Friedreich's ataxia[25] – later we will have the occasion to return to his observation. That same year, Guiraud and Ms Derombies presented a case of

---

[21][Henri Frenkel, Maurice Dide, 'Rétinite pigmentaire avec atrophie papillaire at ataxie cérébelleuse familiale', *Revue neurologique*, vol. 11, 1913, p. 729.]
[22][Emmanuel Bergmann, *Studies in Heredo-ataxia*, Uppsala: Läkarforenings Förhandlingar, 1921, p. xxvi.]
[23][J. Lamsens and René Nyssen, 'Trois cas d'ataxie familiale cérébello-spasmodique', *Journal belge de neurologie et de psychiatrie*, vol. 22, 1922.]
[24][Friedrich Hiller, 'A study of speech disorders in Friedreich's ataxia', *Archives of Neurology and Psychiatry*, vol. 22, 1929, pp. 75–90.]
[25][Julio-Oscar Trelles, 'À propos d'un cas anatomo-clinique de maladie de Friedreich avec troubles mentaux. Les lésions cérébelleuses dans la maladie de Friedreich, les atrophies cérébelleuses avec troubles mentaux', *Annales médico-psychologiques*, vol. 2, 1934, pp. 760–86.]

Roussy-Lévy illness with mental disorders to the Société médico-psychologique. Again in 1934, Paul Courbon and Louise Mars presented to the Société médico-psychologique the case of a patient who, suffering from multiple phagedenic lesions and mental debility, was slowly sliding into dementia. The coexistence of Friedreich's ataxia seems to me to suggest that the mental disorders were related not to the phagedenism, but instead to Friedreich's ataxia.

In 1935, Pommé presented his second case of Friedreich's ataxia to the Société de médecine in Lyon. (The first case was the topic of a paper delivered in 1931.) In both cases, the author judged the psyche to be intact. In 1936, Klimes and Egedy indicated the presence of affective lability in a case of Friedreich's ataxia.[26] This same thymic characteristic was discovered by Stertz and Geyer in 1937.[27] That same year Van Bogaert and his collaborators reported four cases of Friedreich's ataxia with mental disorders. The authors' conclusions state: (1) that Friedreich's ataxia with mental disorders is not hereditary; (2) that in cases of Friedreich's ataxia with mental disorders, the neurological syndrome precedes the mental evolution by several years; (3) that the mental disorders are usually belated; and (4) that the mental disorders acquired have a certain number of common features.

The onset is marked by manifestations of violence, rage, a state of excitation occurring first in bouts and then becoming continuous. These bouts of excitation sometimes take the character of impulsive irritability, and sometimes of anxiety and anguish. The illnesses' disturbances coincide with paroxysms – the same states in which fugue states arise. During the acute phase of their mental evolution, these patients are difficult, impulsive, negative, noisy, and then brusquely everything returns to order. In these moments, they are not incapable of gentleness and affection towards their own. The mental deficit is not global; owing to their inattention, the patients appear more diminished than they are. Some have managed to keep working at home and even to hold down an occupation for long periods. Their memories are fairly well conserved. Their dotage can be corrected if it is meticulously monitored. Due to their opposition, indifference and inattention, at

---

[26][Karl Klimes and Elemér Egedy, 'Beiträge zur Friedreichschen Ataxie', *Journal of Neurology*, vol. 141, nos. 3–4, 1936, pp. 200–5.]

[27][Georg Stertz and Horst Geyer, 'Zur Erbpathologie der spinalen Ataxie unter besonderer Berücksichtigung des Status dysraphicus', *Zeitschrift für die gesamte Neurologie und Psychiatrie*, vol. 157, no. 1, 1937, pp. 795–806.]

certain moments of their evolution they risk being taken for patients suffering from dementia praecox. But at no moment can any real mental dissociation, cataleptic persistence or stereotypies be observed in them.

That same year in the *Schweizer Archiv für Neurologie und Psychiatrie*, Klein considered psychopathological alterations in a Friedreich family.[28] In 1938, Hempel highlighted a case of Friedreich's ataxia with mental debility. The same year, two Polish Jews, who presented a syndrome of progressive cerebellar ataxia with oligophrenia, were the topic of a publication written by Maere and Muyle for the *Journal belge de neurologie et de psychiatrie*. Again in 1938, Persch studied a case of schizophrenia associated with Friedreich's ataxia.[29] In 1939, Birkmayer described a case of evolving dementia praecox in a patient with a case of Friedreich's ataxia. In 1940, Piton and Tiffeneau reported two cases of Pierre Marie's ataxia with mental disorders displaying retarded ideation.[30]

In 1941, Götze situated the mental disorders in the group of hereditary affections in relation to psychiatric nosology. In 1943, Sjögren's voluminous work, which collates 188 cases of heredoataxia, shows that progressive dementia could be found in half of all cases. The symptoms of this progressive dementia are: a reduction in attention, slowness and difficulty in making associations, and poverty in ideas associated with perseveration, as the functions of judgement and critique are severely impaired.[31] In 1944, Arieff and Kaplan published four cases of cerebellar ataxia associated with mental disorders.[32]

The year of 1946 was rich in publications. First, K. V. Bagh studied a case of Friedreich's ataxia with progressive dementia.[33] Then, in the *Schweizer Archiv für Neurologie und Psychiatrie*, Bleuler and Walder attempted to systematize the problems of mental

---

[28][D. Klein, 'Familienkundliche, körperliche und psychopathologische Untersuchungen über eine Friedreich-Familie', *Schweizer Archiv für Neurologie und Psychiatrie*, vol. 39, 1937, pp. 89–116 and 320–9.]

[29][Reinhold Persch, 'Schizophrenie (Katatonie) und Encephalitis', *Allgemeine Zeitschrift für Psychiatrie*, vol. 107, 1938, p. 246 sq.]

[30][Jean Piton and Robert Tiffeneau, 'Maladie familiale du type de l'hérédo-ataxie', *Revue neurologique*, vol. 72, 1940, pp. 774–7.]

[31][Torsten Sjögren, *Klinische und Erbbiologische Untersuchungen über die Heredoataxien*, *Acta psychiatrica et neurologica*, supplement 27, 1943.]

[32][Alex J. Arieff and Leo A. Kaplan, 'Cerebellar type of ataxia associated with cerebral signs', *The Journal of Nervous and Mental Disease*, vol. 100, no. 2, 1944, pp. 35–141.]

[33][Konrad von Bagh, 'Friedreich's disease with progressive dementia; a typical case', *Annals of Internal Medicine*, 1946, pp. 241–53.]

illness in Friedreich's ataxia. With them the notion of psycho-organic syndrome was born. The authors in fact reveal a kinship between the mental disorders encountered in Friedreich's ataxia and epileptic dementia. This syndrome is characterized by the following: exaggerated sentimentality, especially towards religious ideas;[34] an exaggerated influence of affectivity over reasoning; and vague and imprecise ideas, which are an expression more of some general humour than of any concrete and well-defined content. There is a pronounced poverty of ideation; but what essentially strikes one is the exaggerated sentimentality and imprecision in explanation, along with the tendency towards perseveration. In this work, the authors attempted to delimit the syndrome; but their observations, while they tally with the description, do not enable any law to be drawn. Schneider, who examined two cases of Friedreich's ataxia that same year, substantiates Bleuler and Walder's conclusions.[35] Blöchlinger makes the same observations.[36]

In 1947, in a paper published in the *Journal belge de neurologie et de psychiatrie*, Hans Konrad Knoepfel and Jos Macken revisited the problem from the viewpoint that Bleuler and Walder had adopted. I report both their observations later on. Closer to us, in 1949, Davies presented an analysis of the psychic modifications that arise in Friedreich's ataxia.[37]

As can be seen in the above, no shortage of attention has been paid to the problem of psychic or character alterations in familial nervous illnesses. I have reviewed three cases of spinocerebellar heredodegeneration. The observations that I had before me did not indicate the presence of any psychic disorder. However, upon systematic examination, some disorders, firmly objectified in the Rorschach test, did nonetheless come to light.

---

[34][We will see that Fanon often links religion and mental pathology in his psychiatric work.]

[35][Manfred Bleuler and Hedwig Walder, 'Mental disorders in Friedreich's ataxia and their classification among basic forms of mental diseases' ('Die geistigen Storungen bei der hereditaren Friedreich'schen Ataxie und ihre Einordnung in die Auffassung von Grundformen seelischen Krankseins'), *Schweizer Archiv für Neurologie und Psychiatrie*, vol. 58, 1946, p. 145.]

[36][Kurt Arthur Blöchlinger, *Die psychischen Störungen bei der Friedreichschen Ataxie*, dissertation, University of Zurich, 1946.]

[37][D.L. Davies, 'Psychiatric changes associated with Friedreich's ataxia', *Journal of Neurology, Neurosurgery and Psychiatry*, vol. 12, August 1949, pp. 246–50.]

General considerations

> The most localized visceral diseases may have psychological repercussions.
>
> Jean Dechaume, *Traité de médecine*, vol. 16, p. 1071.[38]

According to Saquet's dissertation, mental disorders can be said to exist in one tenth of cases. Mollaret finds the same proportion in his study. In his report, Friedreich, as we saw, maintains that 'the cerebral functions are not impaired'. It might be asked, however, whether this rate of incidence does not rather conceal the neurologist's systematic disinterest in psychiatric symptoms. The mental state of Vincelet's, or Dupré and Logre's, patients clearly did need to be taken into consideration. However, has the intellectual or mental state of diagnosed cases of spinocerebellar heredodegeneration even been subject to rational interrogation?

My intention is not to discover a clearly structured psychiatric disorder in each case. I do not believe that a neurological disorder, even when inscribed in an individual's germplasm, can give rise to a determinate psychiatric symptom cluster. Instead, my aim is to show that all neurological impairment damages the personality in some way. And that this open crack within the ego becomes all the more perceptible as the neurological disorder takes the form of a rigorous and irreversible semiology.

The most frequently encountered mental disorder seems to be debility. However, this alteration receives a particular meaning, since it moves progressively towards dementia. Saquet even took this to be a law and, as regards development, adopts the same perspective as Fouque, who sees in mental degenerescence the common end of familial nervous diseases .... It being understood, he adds, that the few cases in which psychic integrity remains only work to confirm the rule. In any case, the mental debility of these illnesses is easily explained. The paralysis that comes about owing to the clinical developments prohibits school attendance. Hence, intellectual development is naturally made impossible. For that matter, the attempt to connect motor debility

---

[38] [Jean Dechaume, 'Affections du sympathique', *in* André Lemierre, Charles Lenormant, Philippe Pagniez, Paul Savy, Noël Fiessinger, Lucien de Gennes and André Ravina (eds.), *Traité de médecine*, vol. 16, Paris: Masson & Cie, 1949, pp. 1063–75.]

with mental debility is an extremely seductive one. The affectivity of these patients is similarly impaired, since they cannot pass through the various stages of the genetics described by psychoanalysis, stages that stand, as is well-known, in a close relation with motor function.[39] Character disorders, irritability – so common in the neurological affections of childhood – are bound to appear.

How are we to understand these disorders? Must we see them as the consequence of diencephalic impairment? Must we take a Monakowian perspective and speak of the elliptical repercussion (*diaschisis*) of spatial lesions on personality development, on the forces of *hormè*?[40] Would it not be better to see in them the proof of existence of a ruse of pathology, of what Henri Ey calls the organo-clinical gap? These are so many possibilities of interpretation that nevertheless do not manage to satisfy us. And this dissatisfaction arises from the fact that our thinking is scarcely able to liberate itself from the anatomo-clinical. We think in terms of organs and focal lesions when we ought to be thinking in terms of functions and disintegrations. Our medical view is spatial, where it ought to become more and more temporal.

This is exactly what Monakow and Mourgue express when they argue for a *chronogenous* localization; that is to say, one that grants a major role to the temporal integration of phenomena. And we thereby see emerge, once more, the dispiriting problem of Cartesian dualism. If the body is one thing and the soul another, neurological affections can have no relation with mental disorders, and it becomes necessary to embrace the argument of contingent coincidence. If, by contrast, the person is grasped as a whole, as an indissoluble unity, every attack will contain two aspects: the physical and the mental.

From this point of view, Henri Ey's first 'psychiatric study' is highly significant. It shows clearly the rhythmic alternation between

---

[39][This association of motor and psychological impairment will be a constant of Fanon's work, psychiatric as well as political.]

[40][*Hormè* ('impulsion', 'setting in motion', in Ancient Greek) is a neurological concept forged by von Monakow to designate the 'propulsive tendency of the living being, with all its potentialities acquired through heredity, toward the future'. The *individual hormé* constitutes the synthesis of the two directions of vital phenomena, organo-vegetative (interoceptivity) and the life of relation (exteroceptivity and movement) (see Constantin von Monakow and Raoul Mourgue, *Introduction biologique à l'étude de la neurologie et de la psychopathologie. Intégration et désintégration de la fonction*, Paris: Félix Alcan, 1928, pp. 33 and 40.]

two equally fecund, but essentially incomplete paths of research. Bichat's mistake, for example, was to have tried to found medicine on the plinth of the focal lesion. Such a conception was also due to give us the cerebral localizations. In the extreme, in the domain of interest to us, one argued for the existence of a pathological anatomy of psychoses and neuroses. It is well-known what such premises yielded in the hands of the French mechanistic school of the previous century.[41]

---

[41][Fanon was probably thinking of the second of Ey's *Études psychiatriques*, which bear on the 'Le rythme mécano-dynamiste de l'histoire de la médecine', as well as of the third, 'Le développement "mécaniciste" de la psychiatrie à l'abri du dualisme "cartésien"'. The first study bore on 'La "folie" et les valeurs humaines'.

'"Cartesianism", by making particularly urgent and unavoidable the problem of the relations between the "physical" and the "moral", considered as two juxtaposed substances (the order of thought and the order of extension), certainly served the psychiatric cause, but it led psychiatric science into an impasse' (Henri Ey, *Études psychiatriques*, Étude no. 3, p. 53). Ey adds in a note: 'We say "Cartesianism", in thinking more of Malebranche than of the philosopher of the *Méditations*, whose very lively and concrete speculations have been taken as being at the origin of the phenomenological movement, which presents thought as a mode of existence in and for itself.'

See also pp. 55–6: 'If we have just recalled with these few details the fracas of these great quarrels that have given rhythm to the history of psychiatry since its birth, it is to signal that, raised in these antinomic terms, the problem of the physical and of the moral forever leaves its solution in suspense and lends itself to always impassioned and endless discussions. But "Cartesianism" does not only pose the question poorly, it necessarily commits it to a "mechanistic" solution that rapidly leads to an impasse. In effect, spiritualists and materialists rapidly reach agreement on a formula that ensures the former peace of mind and the latter victory. The mind, in the very perspective that Cartesian dualism lends to the discussion, is either absolute (spiritualists) or else nothing (materialists). This comes more or less down to the same thing, and everyone finds themselves on the same side of the barricade and in agreement to state that psychic phenomena (as "parallel" with the brain or identified with its parts) are nothing else than cerebral atoms for our scientific knowledge. This is how the associationist and sensationist "psychology" and the physiological mechanicism of cerebral localizations collaborated to direct psychiatry's evolution toward the integral mechanism to which by the end of the nineteenth century nearly all psychiatrists rallied. This integral mechanism can be summed up in a few propositions that connect with the anti-Hippocratic arguments of the "mechanism" of general pathology: semiological atomism – the mechanical pathogenesis of symptoms – and the notion of specific entities. Throughout the nineteenth century we see the development of ideas unfold in this triple sense.'

In the seventh *Étude*, Ey thus notes his opposition to Paul Guiraud (whom he considered his teacher): 'Our paths diverge on the following essential point: does the disorder result from the localization of the lesion in psychiatry as it does in neurology? I do not think so. The pathogenesis of mental disorder presupposes an evolutive organization and an energetic disorganization of the whole of psychic life' (p. 168, n. 1). Fanon cites Guiraud at length but, as we will see, hereinafter essentially sides with Ey's viewpoint.]

The mind is strained to such an extent that, in the presence of hypomorality, that is to say of disturbances in an individual's social equilibrium, one does not hesitate to speak of cerebellar atrophies. One tries to find an anatomical localization for the disturbances of consciousness. The matter is, it must be admitted, rather difficult. How many times have we seen, without being able to explain it, mental disorders in conjunction with multiple sclerosis? The patients are often irritable and in one week exhaust the patience of the nursing staff, with their roommates equally complaining about their poor character. The irritability of these patients is often overlooked in favour of the subject's disinterest in his or her paralysis. But after living several days with them, this cheerfulness can be seen to be merely apparent.

Lastly, I had the occasion to examine a case of multiple sclerosis in the neurology ward at Saint-Étienne over the period of a week. The case concerned a former police inspector, who is today a total invalid. After four days, nurses and patients alike complained about his bad faith and his character: 'He wanted by no means to be taken for an idiot'. During the examination, when we asked him if he felt the treatment had done him good, he retorted, rather superbly: 'The great Professor Guillain [the patient had been hospitalized in La Salpêtrière] has understood nothing about my case, so you lot will be unable to grasp it with any clarity. Go on your way'. We wanted to proceed to a complete mental examination but, as the patient demanded he be discharged, we did not have the chance to do so.

Around the same time, in the same ward, but this time with women, a woman with Parkinson's refused to take the Parsidol tablets that the médecin-chef had prescribed her. Persuasion having failed, we explained to her that in case of obstinacy we would be obliged to sign her discharge papers. She literally told us to go to the devil, reminding us that she was at home and that, if we rule the roost, then we only had to return to where we came from, as though it wasn't miserable enough to see genuine French people persecuted by foreigners ... No one, it is true, questions the psychic sensitiveness of people with Parkinson's. Parents of people with Parkinson's are well aware of it and avoid anything liable to set off their psycho-verbal fury. But how are we to understand the mental modifications that come about in such cases? Ought we to describe an affective and character contracture correlative to muscular contracture? Or else ought we to admit, alongside intention tremors, the existence of psychic excitation when in the presence of others?

In any case, it seems to me dangerous to claim that a case of Friedreich's ataxia, or of any other neurological syndrome pertaining to spinocerebellar heredodegeneration, can develop without affecting psychic integrity. Moreover, by taking into account the two aforementioned cases, I would rather say that, in the extreme, every neurological symptom cluster *permits* the emergence of a particular mental state. I elaborate on this problem in the last chapter of the present work.

It seems to me – and in this I am adopting the most recent conclusions of the French school of psychiatry – that all organic disorders that bear on one's system of relationships result in a reworking of one's psychic equilibrium. The last thirty years have proven extremely fruitful in this regard. Gelb and Goldstein's studies,[42] or Monakow and Mourgue's no-less famous ones,[43] have taught us to stop thinking metamerically, and in any case to research in such matters a plan of organization, an architectural level that bears no relation with previous atomist and localizationist theories. This new orientation simply comes down to admitting the genetic method in matters of psychiatry. The anatomical cut is eclipsed by the functional plane. Humanity loses its mechanistic character. It is no longer passively moved. It discovers itself as actor.

In speaking of a tree, it can be said to be on the hill, at the bottom of a valley; of an ashtray, to be on the table. To express a fact is seen to be sufficient. And to be sure, in accordance with the season, the tree will be drab in winter, and heavy and covered with leaves in spring. Yet who does not see that at no point does the idea of relations[44] arise? With a human being, the fact loses all stability. At issue is no longer one fact but a mosaic of facts. A human being always exists in

---

[42][See Adhemar Gelb, Kurt Goldstein and Wilhelm Fuchs, *Psychologische Analysen hirnpathologischer Fälle*, Leipzig: Barth, 1920; and Kurt Goldstein, *Der Aufbau des Organismus*, 1934; English translation: *The Organism*, with an introduction by Oliver Sacks, New York, NY: Zone Books, 2000.]

[43][Von Monakow and Mourgue, *Introduction biologique à l'étude de la neurologie et de la psychopathologie.*]

[44][With the idea of relations, the social, and by extension the political, comes to define human reality. With relations, come temporality and history. In Sartre's phenomenological vocabulary, *Autrui*, the other – clearly present in this paragraph – is constitutive of the self.]

the process of …. He or she is here with other humans and, in this sense, alterity is the reiterated perspective of his or her action. This means that the human being, as an object of study, demands a multi-dimensional investigation.

A key advance of psychoanalysis was precisely to have unveiled this side of the personality, since called the unconscious. From this fact, the three perspectives from which Adler, Jung and Freud considered the drama of ill individuals, far from being limiting, indicates an alternation of primary motivations. For, at the basis of all three, one rediscovers that spasm of affectivity referred to as the *complex*.

The human being ceases to be a phenomenon from the moment that he or she encounters the other's face. For the other reveals me to myself. And psychoanalysis, by proposing to reintegrate the mad individual within the group establishes itself as the science of the collective par excellence. This means that the sane human being is a social human being; or else, that the measure of the sane human being, psychologically speaking, will be his or her more or less perfect integration into the *socius*. May I be forgiven for noting these self-evidences, which have seemingly nothing to do with my subject. But we will see that the four cases of spinocerebellar heredodegeneration reported in this chapter present a partial or total collapse of what we readily call the 'social constants of the personality'.

I said earlier that the human being represents, for his fellow, a latency of action. Whenever we speak of action, we also speak about gesture. And this refers us to gesture's anatomo-physiological conditions, which is to say, that which makes a relationship possible. It is thus difficult to admit that a disruption ending in deficits in the stock of relationships would nonetheless leave a consciousness normal.[45] In other terms, a young man of eighteen, seeing the progressive limitation of his field of action, cannot conserve an intact psyche. I would have liked to show the step-by-step progress of this limitation, which is first biological, then psychic, and lastly metaphysical.[46]

---

[45] [There are many political texts by Fanon in which the body's immobilization, in particular through the internalization of the racist gaze, expresses a deficit of social relations and a form of alienation (see Jean Khalfa, 'Fanon, *corps perdu*', *Les Temps modernes*, vol. 61, nos. 635–6, November–December 2005/January 2006).]
[46] [The first chapter of *Les Damnés de la terre* describes religion as one of the forms of consciousness born from the inability to act. Political action will counteract this metaphysical or pathological shrinkage.]

It would be interesting to show, for example, the profound reason for the mysticism of those who become paralyzed in childhood. Moreover, to state things more truly, we might rather say: belief in occult powers. If this belief dons the guise of mysticism, we ought to see it as only one modality of belief with magical motivation. A paralyzed person, above all, and I believe this to be important, if the cause of this paralysis is not clear (accident, poliomyelitis), this person is, as an individual, biologically, psychically and metaphysically shrunken. Were my arguments to be turned back against me, it might be objected that this psychic limitation is only the result of inadequate intellectual development. I would accept this criticism on condition that I am granted the fact that unexplainable biophysical limitations *permit* the instilment of a tendency to believe[47] in the unexplainable.

I had the occasion to observe a young woman who, from the age of thirteen, suffered from extremely violent migraines. After eliminating the possible aetiologies, I learnt that the patient's mother had the same affection. Equipped with an aetiological diagnostic, the young woman was informed that her migraines were hereditary. She then asked me what 'heredity' meant. And I had the impression that, throughout the explanation, which strived for scientificity, this woman, unable to understand, accepted a fact that flew right by her. Shall I make it explicit? Her attitude was not without resignation.

Heredity for the biologist is not the same as it is for the shopkeeper. For the former, heredity entails the application of a strict law. For the latter, it is a bad deal or bad luck. Similarly, the attitude of the person suffering from familial spastic paraplegia or from Friedreich's ataxia will be fundamentally different to someone who has had both legs amputated. The former never understood what happened to him. The latter *knows* he has had an accident. He has witnessed the surgeon's uncertainty and then the surgeon's striking, at last, a decision. Between the one and the other, there is no common measure.

I now discuss the results of the Rorschach test, to which I submitted some cases of spinocerebellar heredodegeneration.

---

[47] [Here, too, Fanon refuses all mechanistic causality. The point here is rather a deduction of the conditions of possibility of belief. Otherwise put, the content of madness is not the direct product of the neurological disorder, but instead is constituted within an irreducible 'organo-clinical space'.]

Rorschach test of Marie M., spouse J. – Forty-seven years old, hospitalized three years ago in the neurological ward of Hôpital Bellevue (Saint-Étienne) for spastic paraplegia. Maternal grandmother: paraplegic. Mother: paraplegic. Her sister, who died of bronchial pneumonia, similarly presented a paraplegic syndrome. For ten years, the patient has presented disorders typical of the spastic paraplegia series.

I. 1 minute G F– Anim. G F– Anim.	∧ 10″ – A *bat*. – A *butterfly*. – I don't really know, it's from the same family. I would lean more towards the bat.	
II. 1 minute 15″ F F– Anim.	∧>∨/<∧ 1′ – Something like *two bear heads* or else *two large dogs*.	
III. 1 minute 30″ D F– H D F– Anim.	∧ 30′ – I don't grasp this very well. – It has the shape of a *man* or of a *bird*. I don't see it clearly. – A bird, perhaps.	
IV. 1 minute 10″ G F– Anim.	∧>∧/ 10″ – I don't know. – I don't get this very well. Perhaps a *fish*. – The shape of a dab – a flatfish.	dab = a fish
V. 2 minutes 10″ G F+ Anim. G F+ Anim.	∧ 15″ – I see a sort of *butterfly*. – There are two legs, with horns. – It comes close to a *bat*. In the background too.	
VI. 2 minutes D F+ Anim.	∧ 5″ – Well I never! That has a *serpent's head*! >∨/<∧ – I don't see what it is.	
VII. 1 minute 10″	∧<∨>∧ 45″ – Same thing here, I don't see anything at all. – Here, I assure you I don't see anything.	

VIII – 1 minute 30″	∧/∨>/ 1′ – Once more, I've no idea.	
IX. 1 minute 15″ G CK Fire	∧ 15″ – Neither here. – It looks like a *firework*. – I don't see what that represents. – Some sort of drawing.	
X. 2 minutes 5″ D F+ Aim.	∧/<∧ 30″ – Here it looks like *two small rats*, but the rest I don't see.	

T = 19′ – R = 11   G = 7   F+ = 4   Animal = 9

VIII + IX + X = 2   D = 4   F– = 6   Man = 1
    R   11   CK = 1   Fire = 1

Rorschach test of Ms Huguette M. – Eighteen years of age, CEP. The patient went to school until the age of fourteen. She belongs to a family with three children. A brother of eighteen years of age presented some gait disorders for about one year, strongly indicating the possibility of an onset of Friedreich's ataxia.

I. 4 minutes D F– Geo. Ban.	∧2′ – I don't see anything. – I don't know what to tell you … what does that look like (a rather abrupt gesture of irritation). But it looks like a bit of the *map of France*, does it not? – Why do you make me do this?	Lateral detail = Brittany
II. 3 minutes 30″ D F+ D. hum.	∧/>/∧/<∧ 1′30″ – They are *feet*. – I myself don't see anything else. <∧ – Well! I don't see anything there.	Upper red detail
III. 3 minutes 30″ D Fclob. D. hum.	∧ 30″ – That is the *spine*. – I don't see anything. What does that look like? (The patient twists and turns a bit on her chair.)	Median line of the lower part

IV. 45 seconds G F– Anim.	∧ 10″ – It's a *toad*. It looks like a toad. A toad … I don't know. (Manner a little offhand.)	
V. 3 minutes 30″	∧/> </∨∧ 3′15″ – Well! I don't know at all. – Not at all.	
VI. 2 minutes 10″	∧/<∧/∨∧ 2′ – Well! I don't know at all.	
VII. 2 minutes 30″ D F+ Anim.	∧/∨ 2′ – I see an elephant's head there.	Detail D median
VIII. 2 minutes D F+ Anim.	∧<∧< 15″ – What is that, I don't know the name for it. It's an animal, but I don't know the name. It's a … – A wild boar! … Is it not? – Ok! A wild boar! (Offhand manner, wave of the hand.)	
IX. 2 minutes	∧∨∧<∧>∧>∧ 2′ – I don't know. – No!	
X. 1 minute 30″	∧/<∨∧	

T = 35′   R = 6   G = 1   F+ = 3   Animal = 3
likes = IX – I – III   D = 5   F– = 3   Human detail = 2
does not like = VII – III – V   K: C = O: O   Geography = 1

$$\frac{VIII + IX + X = 1}{R \qquad 6}$$

Ban = 1

Extreme poverty in the replies. A complete absence of originality. Such are the conclusions that can be drawn from each of these tests. The third test, on the contrary, illustrated a particular richness in the replies. This shows the impossibility of formulating a law in matters of familial nervous illness. Here we are reminded of Van Bogaert, who said: 'We can only report clinical observations, we cannot go beyond them'.

Rorschach test of J. Maurice. – Twenty-four years of age, typical Friedreich's ataxia, major cerebellar disorders, has had clearly pronounced speech disorders since age nineteen. Pyramidal disorders, club foot. Very summary education. Attended school until ten years of age. Did not continue self-study. Shepherd.

I. 15′	∧>∨	A bat	G	FC	A idole	
	>∨∧	An idol as in China,	D	F	geog	orig
	∧	there in the middle.	D	F		
		Some corner of the				
	∨∧	earth in that part there,	D	F	H	
	∧	as seen from a plane	D	F		
		A sacred statue				
		The body of a man				
		seen from behind up to				
		the belt.				
II. 5′	∧	Two sorts of beasts	G	K	ch	
		fighting, ducks if you will,				
		they have the heads,				
	∨∧	the necks of them.	D	F	ch	
		The white part, you				
	∧>	might call that a	D	F	ch	
	∧	chandelier	D	F	ch	
		An instrument, perhaps				
		a pair of pliers.				
		A compass or dressing				
		forceps.				
III. 3′	∧	A bow tie	D	F	ch An	
	∧	Two species of animal	D	F		
		carrying two baskets.				
IV. 3′	∧	It looks like an x-ray of	D		Anat	orig
	>∨∧	the spine	D	F	An	
		An instrument that				
		looks like a shell.				
V. 4′	∧	A butterfly with	G	F	An An	
	∨>	unfolded wings	G	F		
		I would say that it's a				
		kind of bird.				
VI. 3′	∧	That inspires me: Indian	D	F	ch	orig
	∨	torture poles				
		A wood sculpture (the	D	F	ch	
		black part of the lamp).				
VII. 5′	∧∨	Two sorts of dolls	G	K	H	orig
		whose heads are				
	∨	leaning one against the	D	F		
		other				
		The white part: a				
		bedside lamp on a night				
		table.				

VIII. 5′	∧∨	The two red parts can be seen as a crawling bear	D	K	A	
	∧∨	Rocks in a variety of colours at high altitude.	D	FC	ch	
IX. 7′	∧∨<∧<	The head of a fellow (pink part)	D	F	H	
	<	You might imagine	D	FC		orig
	<	being on a boat on the sea and seeing the inhabited shores.	D	F	An	
	<	A camel head.				
X	∧∨	That part there looks like a pot of flowers; the white part is like vegetation, like that you	Dbl	F		orig
	∧	see in the big parks, on a marble pillar (grey	D	K	An	orig
	∧	part)	D	F	geog	
	∧	The two yellow parts look like lions perched on their front legs	D	F	An	
		The two red part look like Italian soil				
		Two parrots (two grey parts).				

At what point can a neurological disease be suspected of triggering psychic alterations? At what point can it be said that the thought processes are disturbed? At what point can it be claimed that the domain of thought is undergoing a disruption for which a determinate neurological symptom cluster can be held responsible? Upon reflection, it seems that two equally powerful, equally determinant aspects might be able to help with the diagnostic. I have in mind here the ego aspect and the social aspect.

The base semiology of each of these aspects of daily life takes the following form: I *feel* odd; I *find* others odd. This defines the original influence of personality disorders. Both terms will clearly come to have a rhythm inscribed between them. If I feel odd, other people can only confirm me in my mutation, in my difference; and communion will come to be altered by it. If I find others odd, this observation will confirm my difference and my communion will come to be altered by it. Bolstered by these two arguments, child psychiatry is quite quick to diagnose behavioural disorders in adolescents.

It seems to me that every psychiatric examination must ultimately boil down to these two observations: alteration of the ego, alteration of the relations between the ego and the world. The three patients to whom I gave the Rorschach test and with whom I conversed at length unequivocally presented disorders concerning these two constants. A collapse of family relations and an ignorance of affective bonds; or when some affectivity existed, it was found to be extremely labile, resolutely polymorphous.

Ultimately, the mad person is someone who can no longer find his place among people. Either he *feels* superior to them, or he *feels* unworthy of entering the category of the human. In both cases, he *feels* he is different to them.

Some observations

I shall report four cases of spinocerebellar heredodegeneration with mental disorders.[48]

---

[48] [Here Fanon reports on four cases that had been presented and analyzed in the recent medical literature by highly reputed neurologists. He is content merely to cite the passages of interest to him, displaying no major concern for bibliographical accuracy. Such practice was rather commonplace for medical dissertations at the time (we indicate in the notes the passages' contexts and his modifications). He follows them up with a commentary that we indicate as such in a footnote. Following these four observations are two cases that present a similar progression and seem to their authors to plead for a psycho-organic syndrome similar to epileptic dementia: (1) physical degradation; (2) a diminishing ability to be attentive and to discriminate; and (3) a growing affective lability. Lastly, a seventh case is presented, one that Fanon followed. This is the case of 'Friedreich's ataxia with delusions of possession' that is signalled in the subtitle of the dissertation and that comprises its empirical core.

The presentation of these cases might seem today to be rushed and the references allusive. However, it is clear that Fanon saw in the examination of this literature and the questions it raised, as well as in the presentation of the patients that he followed, a decisive moment for treating the questions raised in the preceding section of 'general considerations' on the relations between neurological disorders and mental disorders. This is because all these cases seem to loosen the mechanical causality that had been part of the dominant view, and to require a far more complex understanding, which is the topic of the dissertation's last part.]

1. Friedreich's ataxia ([Julio-Oscar] Trelles[49])

Ad. Jul., aged forty-one, was placed in Sainte-Anne with the following report: 'Ms Ad. Jul., hospitalized at the Paul-Brosse hospice, suffers mental disorders characterized by uncoordinated agitation, cries, insomnia, persistence, and some persecutory-type delusional idea. The patient also has Friedreich's ataxia. As a result, I consider that, being a danger to herself and to others, she ought to be hospitalized in an establishment operating in accordance with the law of 1838'[50] (Villejuif, 8 January 1929. Signed: J. de Dassary).

Immediate assessment, 20 January 1929: 'Is suffering from quadriplegia through Friedreich's ataxia. Muddled ideas of persecution. Confined to bed. Not to be discharged.' (Sainte-Anne Asylum. Signed: Doctor Marie). 15-day assessment: 'Friedreich's ataxia. Character disorders, fits of rage, screams, all of which disturbs the other patients. Resistance to treatments. Not to be discharged'. (Sainte-Anne Asylum. Signed: Doctor Trénel).

The family history provides no indications, as the patient is an only daughter and the mother died young. None of her four maternal uncles and aunts suffer from the affection. The personal history is typical. A normal birth and early childhood. Around six years of age she was treated for kyphoscoliosis and balance disturbances gradually began, emerging clearly only around seventeen years of age, at which time the illness took hold, progressively unfolding the full classical picture of Friedreich's ataxia, hence her admission to Ivry Hospice. Once there, in 1926, M. Charles Foix examined her. He observed a typical quadriplegic form of Friedreich's ataxia, together with cerebellar, pyramidal, sensorial (deep), trophic (club foot, kyphoscoliosis) and psychic disorders. These latter (irritability, fits, tendency to interpretation, agitation) made her intolerable in the ward – and indeed all her neighbours hated her – and accounted, lastly, for her first confinement. Her assessment was as follows:

First entry: 'I, the undersigned, full professor of the Faculty, Doctor of Ivry Hospice, certify that Ms Ad. Jul., forty-one years of age, who

---

[49][Julio-Oscar Trelles, 'À propos d'un cas anatomo-clinique de maladie de Friedreich avec troubles mentaux', *loc. cit.*]

[50][The French law of 30 June 1838, 'Loi des aliénés', organized and governed institutions for the care of mentally ill patients, in particular in terms of sectioning or involuntary commitment. It remained the basis of subsequent legislation until 1990. See https://goo.gl/cTY0KT and https://goo.gl/wGqCua.]

suffers from Friedreich's ataxia, presents a state of psychic and motor excitation characterized by vociferations, by threats that disturb the peace and quiet of the other patients in the room, and that require placement in a special service' (Charles Foix, 6 June 1928). [This was followed by an] immediate assessment[51] on 7 June 1928, according to which, she 'suffers from confused excitation and quadriplegia of the Heine-Médin type (bedridden). Not to be discharged'. (Sainte-Anne Asylum. Signed: Doctor Marie).

The patient was placed at Vaucluse, from which her family took her and had her admitted to Paul-Brousse Hospice, where she was treated in M. Lhermitte's ward. But owing to the mental and character disorders she presented, she could not be kept there and had to be placed in an asylum. The patient remained in M. Trénel's unit for twenty-one months. Her neurological picture only intensified. She never willingly allowed herself to be examined, did not reply to questions, or else hurled insults with vehemence and hostility: 'Leave me, you don't understand anything about my illness, step back, otherwise I'll punch you'. If one insisted, the reply was generally: 'I will not answer you; besides, I'm deaf [not true], I hear nothing. You are only good for nothings, sending me to the madhouse without examination ...' Then she becomes ironic: 'That's a nice report you've done. You can write whatever you like'.

M. Trénel further noted that, as far as one could see, the mental basis was impaired, and self-criticism diminished, but that this patient was remarkable on account of her character disorders, her violent fits of anger, her extreme irritability. She sometimes expressed ideas of persecution: people were annoyed with her, her neighbours hated her, and so on. But these delusional ideas displayed no coherent systematization. Lastly, it is notable that, during her last months, she registered a drop in visual acuity and complained of not seeing well. As we see, the psychiatric semiology properly speaking is thin. The patient has some ideas of persecution; we find no coherent delusion though, and essentially only a confusional state and one of psychomotor excitation.

---

[51] [An assessment attesting an imminent risk, made by a psychiatrist of the establishment within 24 hours of hospitalization.]

2. *Areflexia, high arches, heightened amyotrophy, Argyll*
   Robertson pupil and mental disorders (Paul Guiraud and
   [Julian de] Ajuriaguerra[52]*)*

H. A., forty years of age, was admitted following a suicide attempt. He seems of interest to us on account of the mental disorders he presented.[53] From the mental point of view, H. conforms to the classical type of unbalanced person with character disorders. His intellectual development was normal, and he was a good primary school student until twelve and a half. But early in his childhood, he began to manifest a character disorder. H. got on fairly well with his father, but he always displayed hostility towards his mother and his brother. He would get angry at the slightest vexation and suffered from periods of depression.

At twenty years of age, he was enlisted and mobilized for active army duty; he was ill for some part of the war. After the armistice, he earned a good enough living as a salesman, a trade representative and a mechanic. In 1920, he got married, but quickly fell out with his wife who left him owing to his difficult character. He then started with irregular bouts of drinking, but largely during his periods of depression, akin to dipsomaniacs (as many as fourteen anisettes per day). He employed the usual tricks of the unbalanced person to obtain from his mother the money that he squandered. Irritable, over-excited and with a slight tendency towards ideas of persecution, he was viewed poorly by most of his neighbours.

During other periods, he appeared sad, inactive, pessimistic. During one of these bouts, caused by a sentimental disillusion and under the heavy influence of alcohol, he attempted to commit suicide by drowning. The special orderly's assessment records a state of excitation with logorrhoea, hypertonia, pomposity,

---

[52][Guiraud and de Ajuriaguerra, 'Aréflexie, pieds creux, amyotrophie accentuée, signe d'Argyll et troubles mentaux', pp. 229–34.]
[53][Fanon reproduces here the description made by Guiraud and Ajuriaguerra, but modifies some of its sentences. The original reads as follows: 'He seems interesting to us owing to the association of mental disorders and a complex neurological syndrome' (Guiraud and de Ajuriaguerra, 'Aréflexie, pieds creux, amyotrophie accentuée, signe d'Argyll et troubles mentaux', p. 229).]

instability, hypomoralism and moral degradation.[54] At the asylum, the patient became very docile, but rather under-excited.[55]

It would be of interest, with regard to this patient, to raise the problem of penal responsibility, which is sometimes so difficult to decide. Are the instinctive and anti-social reactions that H. A. presented to be related to his neurological syndrome? Otherwise said, in the case of criminal behaviour, is it laid down that he be considered a 'constitutional pervert' (Xavier and Paul Abely).[56] I think that only the history of the individual and his illness make it possible to decide.

3. Roussy-Lévy syndrome (Guiraud and Derombies[57])

L. R., seventeen years of age, entered the Villejuif asylum on 31 December 1932. His mental disorders were essentially what caught the family's attention. Up to the beginning of 1932, L.'s family thought him to be a timid young man and physically weak, but not ill. After a

---

[54][Original: 'social degradation'.]

[55][Here the original description states: 'More interesting than this mental syndrome, which all in all is rather banal, is the neurological syndrome'. This is followed by a long description in physiological and neurological terms.]

[56][This last paragraph, which underlines the uncertainty of a neurological disorder's causality upon a mental disorder and its implications for the idea of criminal responsibility, is Fanon's commentary on Guiraud and de Ajuriaguerra's considerations. From Xavier and Paul Abély, see: 'The internment of the socially retarded (constitutional perverts)', Annales médico-psychologiques, vol. 92, no. 1, February 1934, pp. 157–83. This instructive article undertakes to distinguish between 'normal delinquents and pathological delinquents', as a better way of pleading for the creation of 'secure psychiatric establishments', as a lock-up for those who are not responsible and cannot be sent to prison, which in any case is unable to 'actually defend society'. 'One sole method would be effective; only one would be desirable for instinctive perverts: a secure asylum facility. Now, the application of such measures demands two conditions: we need specialized establishments and we need special legislation [...] Doubtless when these abnormal individuals are confined, their mental impairments, which receive expression in an anti-social form, will no longer have but rare occasions to manifest themselves. Does this mean that this noxiousness, currently latent, has disappeared? Who would dare support such an opinion? It is like claiming that someone with agraphia is cured when he is not provided with any paper or pen' (p. 177). The concerns of those who fear 'seeing mental medicine, by its committing to a limitless path, coming to encompass all of criminality, if not all of morality', are dismissed as simply due to 'the exaggerations of certain authors'. 'Notions are now more specific and mental medicine has imposed upon itself sound limits in the reality of practice' (p. 160).]

[57][Paul Guiraud and Madeleine Derombies, 'Un cas de maladie familiale de Roussy-Lévy avec troubles mentaux', Annales médico-psychologiques, vol. 92, no. 1, 1934, pp. 224–9.]

bout of flu at the start of the year, he suffered from otitus complicated with mastoiditis, for which he required an operation in April. The following month, he was suddenly overcome with a state of fear including anxiety, and began letting out screams and trembling. He complained of indistinct dizzy spells. In the following days, he remained anxious and tried to escape from his home without being able to provide any explanation. He was taken to the countryside to get some rest, and claimed to be bored in his new lodging, to be suffocating, to its being too hot; he complained that one of his sides was too fat. He was sad, and saw sadness everywhere around him; he was frightened at night, especially when he was alone in his room. From time to time, periods of irritation arose; he complained of not being cared for as he ought to be, and sometimes even pushed his mother and his grandmother.

He was placed at La Salpêtrière, where he has been for two months, but he often has fits of fear with unwarranted agitation and outbursts of anger; once he threw a glass at an orderly's head. That state was the reason for his internment.

The observation and mental examination allow us to single out the following elements.

1) *An almost continuous, depressed state.* Anxiety, pessimism, sadness, feelings of mental and physical weakness. A tendency towards isolation, semi-mutism on and off, cenesthetic disorders with feelings of heat, of suffocation. 'When I am in that state, I do not insist, I just sit down on a bench without a word; I am frightened at nights, as if something is about to happen, as if I am about to pass away'. The tiresome affective state is combined with an almost continual intellectual and psychomotor inhibition.

2) *Excitation, irritability, anger.* The information given above indicates some of these types of incidents. During his stay in the asylum, the patient appeared more docile and apathetic.

3) *Impairment of muscular sensibility and the personality.* As regards the patient's mental syndrome, this element is the most interesting one and it concurs with the physical impairment. Periodically, the psychological notion of the body and especially of the set of active muscles, is severely

disrupted. This imperfection impacts on the patient's psychic personality. Here is how he expresses himself: 'Whenever I walk for some time, I become tired, I no longer feel my legs. It seems to me that I am walking on cotton or on rubber; it becomes necessary to rest, otherwise I would lose consciousness.' On another occasion, he expressed himself more clearly still: 'Whenever I've walked for a long time, I am obliged to stop; it seems that it is not I who walks, I do not feel my legs are walking through my will; I am not moving, I am transported as if I was in a car. I do not feel my personality'.

The first symptom signalled by the patient is a subjective disorder of proprioceptive sensibility, which I had objectively always found to be normal. It is interesting to note the consequences of these subjective disorders of proprioceptive sensibility on the synthesis of the personality: the patient describes it spontaneously with naivety and accuracy; the personality no longer appropriates muscular activity, the individual has the feeling of passively submitting to walking movements; he is not the one who walks, but instead he is, as he says, 'transported as if I was in a car'. The result of this deficit is that the notion of the ego, of the personality, gives out to such a point, the patient says, that if he did not stop, he would lose consciousness.

It is important, within the psychiatric purview, to emphasize this syndrome. On several occasions we said, concerning hebephrenia and chronic delirium that the synthesis of the personality was performed by the combination of kinaesthetic and proprioceptive inputs; here we contribute an example that, from a purely neurological point of departure, moves towards psychic disorder. We must also underscore the missing element of appropriation [into the personality[58]], which, in our view, plays such an important role in the genesis of symptoms of chronic delirium.

4) *First signs of ideas of grandeur of an infantile type.* To the written questionnaire, filled in on the day of admission,

---

[58][These words were omitted from Fanon's transcription of Guiraud and Derombies' text. Neurological disorder produces a flawed motricity that, in turn, disrupts the synthesis of the personality, that is to say, the appropriation of the body by the ego. This relation of identity to the body in movement and self-perception, proven here through its pathological disruption, has many echoes to be found throughout Fanon's œuvre, especially *Peau noir, masques blancs*. It chimes with what he found interesting in Merleau-Ponty's philosophy.]

the patient replied: 'What are your intentions?' Sometimes has ideas of grandeur, the ambition to hold an important position. The day after, he explained: 'On occasion, I have ideas of grandeur, I would like to be a minister, a lawyer, a doctor, but preferably a minister of Post and Telephony and undertake reforms. I am very serious .... I say this, but I am not sure I'm really convinced.' These are imaginary reveries pertaining to childhood and youth that are almost normal, but that are expressed here with infantile naivety.

5) The patient's *mental basis* is barely impaired, his intelligence is normal, his memory is good and his judgement ought to be qualified more as infantile than as defective. He presents neither genuinely delusional ideas nor psycho-sensorial disorders. Added to this mental syndrome is a significant physical syndrome.

Mobility, physical strength: he began to walk at ten months just like other infants. At nine or ten years of age, his family noticed that he could neither walk quickly nor jump. Since that time he has always been muscularly weak, tiring easily, not liking either games or sports. Standing upright, he presents a certain instability with a few oscillations, not of great amplitude. His gait is slow, hesitant, but not uncoordinated; he has no dizziness or steppage gait. We have noted that he is quick to tire.[59]

Guiraud insists on the role of body schema disorders in the genesis of delusion.[60] Over the last twenty years in fact, studies on the notion of one's own body (*corps propre*) have enabled us to understand a great number of psychopathological manifestations.

---

[59][Following this, the original provides a long physiological and neurological description that Fanon does not reiterate.]

[60][To a certain extent he does do this, by putting emphasis on the neurological dimension: The decisive argument that makes us attribute to the same process the neurological syndrome and the mental syndrome is precisely the very form of the mental disorders, which is merely the psychological extension of neurological disorders, as we've shown above. We consider that, in our case, the still unknown lesion (since the Roussy-Lévy syndrome is still awaiting its pathological anatomy) is not confined to the cord but reaches the paths or terminal centres of proprioceptivity in the very regions where the neurological becomes psychological.

(Giraud and Derombies, 'Un cas de maladie familiale de Roussy-Lévy avec troubles mentaux', p. 228).]

Even better, these studies have supported a novel thematization of a philosophical problem: corporeity. Recently, at the International Congress of Philosophy in Geneva,[61] M. Merleau-Ponty observed that the body had, in the wake of multiple studies, recovered its dignity. The wandering mind, ethereal and scornful, discovers a body at its own level.

Here again, we see a combat against spiritualist dualism. In his now classic work, Lhermitte delimited the question.[62] Hécaen envisaged it from a Thomist angle a few years ago.[63] His essay concludes thus: 'What we presented concerning both the repercussions on the personality of symptoms of an anosognosic type and the disruptions of the ego image in the course of neuroses and psychoses does not permit any limits to be fixed between these two modes of facts. ... The feeling of the physical ego cannot be separated from that of the moral ego, as both are profoundly integrated into each other by our affective life, which assures their unity; all that which tends to dissociate the one is reflected in the other. No distinction can be

---

[61][Lecture given at *Rencontres internationales de Genève*, the topic of which was, in 1951, *La Connaissance de l'homme au XXe siècle*. The conference proceedings were published by Éditions de La Baconnière in 1951 and are available on the web site <www.rencontres-int-geneve.ch> (Merleau-Ponty's paper was republished with the title 'Man and adversity' in Maurice Merleau-Ponty, *Signs*, Evanston, IL: Northwestern University Press, 1964 [French Original, 1960]). These proceedings also contain public discussions on the presented papers, in particular a discussion on negritude in relation to ethnologist Marcel Griaule's paper 'Connaissance de l'homme noir', and one on shock therapies and personality in relation to the paper of psychiatrist Henri Baruk.]
[62]Jean Lhermitte, *L'Image de notre corps*, Paris: La Nouvelle Critique, 1939.
[63]Henri Hécaen, '[La notion de] schéma corporel [et ses applications] en psychiatrie', *L'Évolution psychiatrique* [issue 2, 1948, pp. 75–124].
[64][Henri Hécaen, '[La notion de] schéma corporel [et ses applications] en psychiatrie', *L'Évolution psychiatrique* [issue 2, 1948, p. 112]. In that affection the patient is unable to appropriate the paralysed part of his or her body. In the copy of this issue of *L'Évolution psychiatrique* to be found in Fanon's library, this passage is annotated in the margins thus: 'Absolutely'. The passage in question is the first paragraph of the long conclusion of Hécaen's article. In this conclusion, the following sentences, which are crucial for understanding Fanon's later political thought on the relation of the personality with mobility, are marked with a 'good' (*bien*): 'Using a different terminology, R. Mourgue envisages the facts in similar fashion when he writes about the illnesses studied by Minkowski: "In this patient the élan toward the future is inhibited, his prospectivity. [...] If duration no longer flows following a harmonious flux in incessant movement, this is because, as a result of biological phenomena from which we prescind here, the instinctive sphere is troubled and this trouble is reflected in symbolic fashion at the conscious level." Each time this latent propulsive force weakens, a force he recognises as the very essence of duration as Bergson understands it, the synthesis of the personality disaggregates as the static progressively replaces the dynamic'.]

made formally between depersonalization and hemiasomatognosia'.[64] In any case – and Guiraud is right to insist on this – it can henceforth be taken for granted that disorders of the body ego have as much psychopathological weight as character or intellectual disorders.

4. Cerebellar heredoataxia and delusion[65]

Uchai ..., Gaston, thirty years old, a pork butcher, soldier of the nᵒ regiment of colonial infantry, entered the CDP of the XIth region on 27 April 1919. *Family history*: the following information was taken in part from military files and in part gathered by police inquiries among his family and neighbours. The father, who likely had congenital mental retardation, died at fifty-five years of age. The mother, in good health, is mentally fit. An uncle, of weak mind, suffers a nervous affection that has immobilized him and appears to result from cerebellar ataxia. The patient has always been considered as 'a bit' poor in intelligence. In 1908 he volunteered for the nᵒ regiment of the colonial infantry, and was exempted from service for 'idiocy' (?) in Saigon on 18 September 1912 following some accidents that were most likely asthenic and the result of sunstroke. Once cured, he took up the profession of pork butcher up until the start of the war. His intelligence had not weakened to any degree.

History of the illness: enlisted on 28 August 1914, for the duration of the war. He was assigned to nᵒ regiment of colonial infantry and sent immediately to the front. On 9 October 1914, somewhere close to Sainte-Menehould, he was severely wounded and shocked. Assigned to an observation post with one of his colleagues, a shell decapitated his companion and some fragments of it hit him near the right ear and right shoulder. U. took the head of his friend and embraced it saying, 'Goodbye'. He remained at his post, where orderlies came to fetch him. At no time did he lose consciousness. According to him, his ear and shoulder wounds were not 'too serious'. The same day he was evacuated to Sainte-Menehould. He was hospitalized at Troyes for fifteen days. On 24 October 1914, he was exempted on medical grounds for mental problems.

Back home with his mother in X. His mother soon noticed that he had nocturnal urinary incontinence, trembling limbs and problems

---

[65]Raoul Benon and Georges Lerat, 'Hérédo-ataxie cérébelleuse et délire', *L'Encéphale*, vol. 15, 1920, pp. 565–72.

walking; he fell down frequently without losing consciousness. His condition gradually got worse and 'little by little he lost his mind'. At the start of 1918, he became unable to 'eat or dress by himself'. Around March 1919, the patient's mother, given that the disorders were progressing, that his care and observation required constant attention, and surmising that his condition might be a combat stress reaction, asked for medical advice on this issue. One of us, together with another colleague, wrote up a 'consultation' enumerating the observed physical and mental symptoms. The information drawn from a clinical examination, it was concluded, does not of itself admit the existence of a cause-effect relation between these symptoms and combat stress reaction. As a result, investigations within a military setup were necessary. Following action undertaken by the family, the patient entered the Psychiatry Centre of the XIth region on 27 April 1919.

Current state, April 1919: the patient remained in hospital for about a month. He was submitted to repeated examinations. He manifested an as yet undetermined cerebellar syndrome, what is more without any manifest signs of intellectual weakening.[66] Here I study only the mental disorders of particular interest.

The delusional syndrome [syndrome délirant]

The interrogation immediately revealed delusional disorders, which at first glance seemed to be accompanied by psycho-sensorial disorders: illusions or hallucinations. We first describe them and then provide the result of the examination of the psychic functions viewed outside of that which concerns delusion.

a) *Delusional ideas*. The theme of the delusion is the following: the patient declares to all comers that he is married (though he is a bachelor), that he sleeps with his wife every night, that he has voluptuous sensations, etc. Here is how he recounts the facts:

> Since my exemption, I have lived with my mother in X., and every day my wife passes by in front of the house. I stand on the step of my door. She continues her path. We have never spoken a word to each other. She looks at me a little each time: that means that she

---

[66][Benon and Lerat's text (p. 566) differs: 'He presents a clearly characterized cerebellar syndrome, and some specific delusional ideas, but they are of a nature that is difficult to determine, what is more without manifest signs of intellectual weakening. We will study successively the patient's physical state and then the mental disorders'. Following this there is a long section describing 'A. The Cerebellar Syndrome', followed by a section 'B. The Delusional Syndrome', which Fanon takes up.]

loves me. Naturally, I call after her, but she doesn't come. I said that I asked for her hand in marriage, but I have not signed anything. We've never arranged the day or the hour.

He does not recall the exact date of this marriage, which may go back a year and a half. As 'he cannot walk', he never went to the town hall. But it is a genuine marriage: 'My marriage is not all in my head', he said. This woman did not live with him, but she came to see him each night:

She comes to sleep with me, when everyone is asleep. She does not speak to me. She sends me to sleep with chloroform, I feel it nice and strong. She is the one who sends me to sleep. She places herself on top of me, holds me in her arms ... I feel myself falling asleep, it's the chloroform ... She puts me to sleep; it gives me intense physical pleasure ....

On some details variations and contradictions emerge. On one and the same day he said that 'he neither hears nor sees' this woman, and 'that he sees, that he smells her, that her hair is black'. He always states that she has never spoken to him. After the supposed coitus, this woman 'wakes [him] up from the chloroform'. 'At this moment', he says, 'my nerves take over me; they work me over. This puts me in a bad mood and I fall out of my bed'. He presents a nervous breakdown based on annoyance, otherwise put, a hysterical crisis. He had us note that: 'She ought to come and spend the night with me but without putting me to sleep'. He would add that he's had enough of this woman and her hiding, and that he was going to leave her; that being a good-looking boy, he would easily find another: 'Plenty more fish in the sea'.

Asked about this woman's personality, he replied: 'She is twenty years old. She's a marquise.' On another day, he said:

She's a duchess .... An Italian ... I don't know her last name, but her father is a major. She is a millionaire, she's richer than all the countesses put together. She has two small ponies that come from Russia; they are tied to a small car. By marrying her, I have been given the title of baron, because I had nothing. She married me despite my illness, because I'm a good-looking boy .... She's as beautiful as the Holy Virgin. She's the one who makes it rain and could cause stars to fall.

Apart from these ideas of satisfaction including megalomania, he expressed ideas of persecution: 'That woman throws fishes into my face. I still had plenty down my neck a bit earlier …. They are a little like herrings … they pierce my skin. She does it to turn me into an ugly boy; she's jealous of me …'. He also said that a butcher boy from X. follows his wife and dresses up as a demon (he has horns on his head), sometimes throwing himself on his bed and stimulating his nerves with electric wires placed just above his bed, making him fall down on the ground (hysterical crisis).

On another day, he said: 'It's not the butcher, it's my mother who electrifies me to make me insane, out of jealousy of my wife. The electrical current passes through the flooring, then into the feet and into the body'. Doctor: 'Who installed this current?' R.: 'It was installed in my room without me seeing by Doctor N. (present at the questioning and who had seen the patient at X.) … I don't know who installed it here'.

b) *State of psychic functions outside of the delusion.* The patient has a good orientation, and knows that he's been at N. since the month of April 1919. He correctly states his age, his date of birth, the age of his mother, his address in X., where he lived with his mother, his grandmother and his uncle, and so on.

The interrogation was not easy owing to pronounced elocution disorders (the patient speaks spasmodically, in fits and starts, and slowly). Outside of this observation, two facts can be established: voluntary attention is well preserved (he makes an effort to reply exactly to the questions asked); but his comprehension appears rather slow. He declares that his memory has become worse. However, all in all his memory, insofar as old and recent facts are concerned, appears normal (considering the individual's culture and the milieu in which he lived). In sum, there are no noticeable signs of intellectual diminishment or emotional indifference.

Evolution, February 1920: stationary state. Mental faculties are undiminished. Has the same delusional ideas.[67]

---

[67][Here the citing of Benon's and Lerat's article ends. The original goes on to consider the possible explanations of the psychological disorders linked to the illness and notes: 'Just as obscure is the problem of relations between mental illness and organic illness. A developmental parallelism is noticeable, but there seem to be no arguments enabling one to conclude that the mental disorders depend upon the organic state. Are these two associated syndromes, one lesional, cerebellar; the other dynamic, psychological? Are they the expression of different and co-existent individual predispositions? No one knows'. (Benon and Lerat, 'Hérédo-ataxie cérébelleuse et délire', p. 572).]

I now report Konrad Knoepfel and Jos Macken's first two observations. Seizing on Bleuler's conclusions, they tried to turn the psycho-organic syndrome into the mental characteristic of heredoataxias.[68] I will not evaluate the authors' approach, as I am convinced that their efforts have their place in the discussion in the last chapter. In any case, I focus on the intellectual weakness in each of these cases of Friedreich's ataxia.

5. Friedreich's ataxia and psycho-organic syndrome

Jeanne L., born in 1900. *Hereditary antecedents*: a sister suffering from Friedreich's ataxia. The daughter of another sister shows a kyphosis, club hands and a cardiac malformation. *Personal history*: the patient went to school till the age of twelve. Her schooling was poor. She learned her hairdressing job well. At the start of the war of 1914–1918, she set off for England and quit her job. She continued to help her mother with the housework for a few years, doing only the simplest chores, such as washing and cleaning the rooms. She never managed to learn to cook. Her character was calm and docile.

In 1917 (seventeen years old), after a bout of the flu, the patient began to stagger while walking, such that the children of the street took her for a drunkard. At the same time, a sort of weakness came over her legs, before moving gradually to her back and a case of scoliosis appeared. In 1922 (22 years old), she began to present intention tremors, speech disorders and some uncertainty in her gaze. As of 1923, she remained continuously in bed, as standing upright without support and walking had become entirely impossible. In 1927, after about ten years of illness, her sister, who is an intelligent person and a good observer, noted that the patient would start laughing or crying over a trifle, as well as have violent fits of anger for the slightest reason, something that had never been observed before.

From 1936 (after nineteen years of illness), she lost all interest in her family, whereas before she had always wanted to have news of them. From around 1939, her comprehension slowed as did all her psychic reactions. Her affective lability and above all her irritability

---

[68][Hans Konrad Knoepfel and Jos Macken, 'Le syndrome psycho-organique dans les hérédo-ataxies', *Journal belge de neurologie et de psychiatrie*, vol. 47, no. 5, 1947, pp. 314–23.]

became progressively worse. The neurological examination revealed a typical case of Friedreich's ataxia.[69]

Four-month long psychic examination from December 1946 to March 1947: she seemed to have no memory troubles with old or recent events. Only her ability to fix on numbers was slightly diminished, such that she could no longer keep in mind a five-figure number for ten seconds. She had good temporal and spatial orientation, as well as concerning her person. She knew her milieu well. Her understanding had slowed a little, but no other problems were manifest. She understood the questions asked her and performed the things she was asked to. The succession of her thoughts was slow and imprecise. She often lost the topic of a story and obliged the questioner to remind her of the question asked. The intelligence examination revealed a rather clear-cut mental debility. The patient made large errors in calculation (for example: $22 - 15 = 12$; $15 \div 4 = 3$), and was unable to solve only slightly complicated problems (for example: $39 + 49$; $88 + 77$; $42 \div 2$; 7×12). She did not know the provinces of Belgium and believed that Italy is a neighbouring country. She did not know the name of the rivers of her country except Escaut. Her faculty of abstraction was poorly developed: for example, she saw no difference between a dwarf and an infant, believing them to be identical. For her the difference between a tree and a shrub is that the tree is taller, and the soldier differs from the police agent in that the latter likes his job where the former is obliged to do his. For her, a president of state is almost a king, and to have debts means to lend. When we asked her to explain some simple notions, she gave general and imprecise replies, such as, a law: 'It is to uphold the law'; a newspaper: 'it has news in it'.

In addition, her knowledge of everyday life is rather minimal. She does not know how long it takes to walk a kilometre, and sometimes believed that a kilometre comprises one hundred metres and sometimes one metre. She cannot read a clock, but claims that an hour has fifty minutes, and does not know how many seconds are contained in a minute. She is unable to reproduce a simple story (the ass and the load of salt) that has been read to her twice slowly and seems not to have understood the requirements of the Jung test (association). After

---

[69][This sentence sums up a neurological examination performed on 14 March 1947 to which the original devotes two paragraphs.]

fifteen seconds, she repeated the same words that had been said to her and claimed she could not make any sort of association. Her schooling was poor and she had not even learnt to cook.

Alongside this mental debility, she particularly displayed problems in the affective domain, in which she was very unstable. When she was spoken to about her illness, she would start to cry, but recovered right after a gentle word and would then laugh with all her might. When asked why she always turned off the wireless, she began crying, but it was enough to tap her gently on the shoulder to have a blissful smile appear on her face. The various questions of the psychological examination often caused her to burst into laughter, which then demanded a break in the examination. The patient's sister told us that she often cried out of rage when she didn't understand what was being said to her. The nun who has cared for her for two years now also noted that she began to laugh or to cry very easily and for no apparent reason.

But for that affective lability, her rapport with her entourage is good. Her facial expressions, though rare, rather undifferentiated and exaggerated, roughly correspond to the psychological situation. Her activity is extremely diminished and her psychic tendencies reveal major inadequacies. She is no longer interested in her family, whereas previously she had always asked for news of them. When she receives a visit, she replies briefly to the question, but never talked about herself. She spends her day doing nothing, does not concern herself with her illness, and makes no future plans. Also noticeable is her extreme susceptibility to fatigue, which required several interruptions in the examination, and which did not exist prior to the illness.

6. *Friedreich's ataxia with psycho-organic syndrome*[70]

Jeanne P., born in 1894. *Hereditary antecedents*: her mother died at eighty from an unspecified affection; her father, an alcoholic, died at seventy-eight from a neurological illness whose details are unknown. She has four brothers and a sister all in good health. A brother of forty-nine years of age also suffered from heredoataxia.

Personal history: the patient was a full-term baby and learnt to walk and speak normally. She had no illnesses except for the measles. She went to primary school until fourteen years of age and successfully completed an apprenticeship as a seamstress. Then she

---

[70][This is observation 2 of the same article by Knoepfel and Macken.]

found a job as a personal carer and held it down for twenty-two years until the onset of her illness. She was able to earn her own living and enjoyed the respect and consideration of her employers. In her spare time, she liked to busy herself with the flowers in the garden, do small handwork jobs or read good books.

From the age of forty, she began to suffer from walking difficulties, which forced her to give up her work. These walking difficulties became gradually worse, rendering her unable to walk alone without using support. Some years after the onset of her walking disorder, speaking became difficult and she noticed changes to her character. She was not as happy as before her illness and was now quick to anger. Over a trifle, she would become angry and use the crudest swear words. But these crises generally passed in little time and the quicker she was to anger, the quicker she would calm down again. Her brother, her sister-in-law and her niece all confirmed that the patient began to manifest violent fits of anger with the onset of her illness, something she was not prone to before. The type of neurological syndrome is Friedreich's ataxia.[71]

The psychological examination lasted for several months (December 1946– March 1947). Her memory displayed not the least confusion, whether for old events or for recent facts. The patient had good temporal and spatial orientation, as well as concerning her person. She had average intelligence and understood quickly and correctly the questions she was asked throughout the psychological examination. She was interested in good literature and could relate what she had read. Although the psychological functions described above are normal, the succession of her thoughts was palpably confused. She recounted piles of useless details of no relevance to the subject-matter of her thoughts. Asked about her profession, she described the illness of her employers and the flowers in the garden of G., where she had worked.

When recounting the story of her life, she totally lost sight of the issue and gave us a long, richly detailed description of the flowers that she had previously tended to. Her thoughts lost their accuracy and she contented herself with vague and general expressions. To the question, 'What books have you read?', the patient replied: 'Beautiful books' – but it was very difficult to find out which titles. Moreover,

---

[71][This sentence likewise sums up a neurological examination performed on 12 March 1947.]

she showed a slight tendency to perseveration. When asked what she does with her spare time, she literally replied: 'In the flowers, there were many flowers, plant flowers'. Wanting to recite a small poem, she repeated three times: 'It's raining, it's raining, it's raining', before reciting her poem.

But more clear-cut than the problems of coherency in her thinking were the affective alterations. She displayed strong affective lability, which often entailed violent fits of anger. The patient herself told us that she could get angry over a trifle and utter dreadful swear words. These fits ended very quickly. But she could also burst out laughing for the faintest reason and several times she forced us to interrupt the examination of heat/cold sensitivity, because she found it so funny that she laughed ferociously. The Babinski test made her scream out loud and she accompanied her replies in the examination of tactile sensitivity with grimaces. Often she pounded her fist on the table to stress her ideas. Her general humour was euphoric despite the serious illness from which she suffered as well as the major difficulties and restrictions it placed on her life. She claimed to have occasional ideas of suicide, but said that she does not take them seriously.

The medical examination was much to her liking and entertained her. Her affective expression always corresponded to the psychological developments and she could have good affective relations with her entourage. The examination of her psychic tendencies showed nothing abnormal. She took an interest in good books, in newspapers, did the housework and took pleasure in visits from her friends. The Jung test showed a clear deficit of association. Often she merely repeated the test word and in many cases simply gave a translation of it in slang. Her reactions were in general very slow.

Our second patient is a woman of fifty-three years of age suffering from heredoataxia since the age of forty (a form of Friedreich's ataxia with incomplete coronal-radicular predominance). As the illness progressed, different psychic symptoms became manifest, notably a deficit in associations, including an inaccuracy in her ideas and a surfeit of explanation, a tendency to perseveration, an obvious lability with lack of criticism and euphoria.[72]

---

[72][The article ends with two pages in which the authors make a plea to classify these mental disorders under 'the psycho-organic syndrome' and deplore the little study done on this question.]

A case of delusions of possession with hysterical structure

I contribute here the observation of a young woman suffering from Friedreich's ataxia with partially delayed onset, and in whom mental disorders appeared in its wake. These disorders, although weak in appearance, fit the frame of classical hysteria.

C. Odile, thirty-two years old, hospitalized in the free ward of the neuropsychiatric clinic from 18 December 1950 to 22 May 1951, and interned in the county asylum of Le Vinatier since 22 May 1951.[73] Sent to hospital from a house for the disabled due to psychic disorders: agitation, ecstatic attitudes, talk about mystical or erotic themes. Information about the family and the patient's behaviour before entering hospital were obtained from the patient's elder sister, who is a social worker.

Hereditary and family background: the parents died of a non-neuropsychiatric affection. Four sisters in good health, a brother in good health, four deceased brothers, three of whom died from 'progressive paralysis not involving mental problems'. However, the neurological disorders they presented were identical to those of our patient.

Personal history: the patient lived with her grandmother until the age of twelve, then with her aunts for some months, with her father until he died, and then in various religious hospices. Until the age of eighteen, she lived with her brothers and sisters, thus being able to witness the development of the illness of her three brothers. She completed her secondary studies only as far as the baccalauréat. Owing to her illness, she did not attempt a diploma of any sort. She always liked reading and hitherto has sought to keep abreast of modern literature. With her brothers and sisters, she has always shown herself to be rather 'unsociable', and liable to sudden mood swings. Also to be mentioned is an evident sensitiveness.

---

[73][One of the first of France's centres of institutional psychotherapy. Since 1943 it was under the direction of Paul Balvet, who was formerly the director of the psychiatric hospital of Saint-Alban, and whom Fanon knew personally. See our introduction above, p. 13.]

In the various asylums at which she found herself, she got to know young disabled people and, since the start of 1950, has seemed greatly preoccupied with mysticism.[74] The atmosphere in which she lived at the time seems to have played a large role in the later development of her disorder, especially concerning its repercussions on the ego. In February 1950, though she had not presented any distinctive psychic disorder, she wanted to undergo an exorcism at La Salette. It is not known whether the exorcism was really performed. Also to be mentioned is a stay she had in Algeria at around ten years of age, during which the patient came into contact with an old woman from the country who was well-known for her occult talents and who, it was said, practiced witchcraft.

History of the illness: neurological disorders began at the age of twelve. The psychic disorders started towards the end of December 1950. The patient recounts that she had a nervous depression following a failed amorous adventure with her confessor. She had believed that he had fallen in love with her. Certain signs, she said, had given her to understand that the abbot harboured very specific intentions towards her. For reasons unrelated to this adventure, she had to leave the hospital she was in for another asylum, at which she behaved normally for a period of some weeks. The disorders for which the patient was sent to us began after a new placement in an asylum in the Lyon region.

Upon coming to the ward in December 1950, we observed:

1) *Neurological syndrome:* The patient was unable to walk, speech was cerebellar; a kinetic type of cerebellar syndrome; pyramidal syndrome: bilateral Babinski; problems with deep sensitivity, notably in the test of the position of the toes; abolition of tendinous reflexes of the lower limbs; reducible bilateral high arches; slight amyotrophy of the lower limbs; normal fundus of the eye; dissociated bilateral labyrinthine hypoexcitability; normal auditive acuity; EEG: normal; ECG: normal; basal metabolism: normal; LP CSF: normal; serology negative; skull x-ray negative.

2) *Psychic disorders:* On the first day, she stated to the orderly: 'I am possessed by the devil' and had a spectacular fit of agitation

---

[74][On this link between infirmity and mysticism, see *above*, p. 56.]

in front of the other patients in the room. The following day, we were able to ask her questions: easy contact, no problem with confusional series, slight euphoria, and an ironic smile at the start of the examination. Highly changeable facial expression throughout the conversation.

She said that we were able to affect her thought in this room, that we were informed of her entire history, that we saw what she was thinking: 'Why ask me questions, you already know all my history'. Then she declares to have slept with a young girl aged eight and to have had sexual relations with her brother from twelve to fifteen years of age. Recently she was driven towards the abbot. Her words then became ambiguous, she hints that 'many things have happened'. All these phenomena, these perverse acts, very much show, she explained, that she is possessed by the devil, who was making her 'succumb to vice'. She compared these diabolical acts to those described in Bernanos' *Journal d'un curé de campagne*. But, she said, 'diabolical action is more direct, more physical in a way'.

In the following days, the more she was questioned, the richer the symptomatology became: she has visions, she often has orgasms; '*cochons*' [In French, *lit.*, 'pigs'; *fig.*, 'dirty men'] follow her and mistreat her. At the end of a conversation during which the patient's attitude had been equivocal, she told us: 'I am ready', and she confusedly explained that only a marriage would make up for the diabolical acts.

Realizing that the patient multiplied her delusional creations with each interrogation, we decided not to concern ourselves with her for a while. Upon resuming our examination, she admitted, given that our attitude was ironic, that she had made up a lot of the things she had said and that at bottom she did not believe in the story about the devil. She claimed to have invented the story in order to distract herself and to seek refuge in the imaginary. However, she continued to present certain interpretations, notably finding similarities between specific doctors in the ward, her father, her brother and the young abbot.

In April 1951, the patient was placed in a special room because she refused to eat and objected to any interrogations. She lost a lot of weight. She presented some signs of hyposystolia (alterations in the form of ventricular complex on the ECG). On 22 May 1951, the patient was interned; Friedreich's ataxia, psychological compensation syndrome of an hysterical structure, delusion of possession, anorexia, opposition.

24-hour assessment: Friedreich's ataxia, delusional syndrome, agitation, and opposition.

15-day assessment: Friedreich's ataxia; behavioural disorders, negativism, suspicion; notions of influence and of external action. Not to be discharged.

Discussion

Neurological diagnosis: fully developed Friedreich's ataxia, three family cases.

Psychiatric diagnosis: I hesitated for a long time between delusions of influence and psychological manifestations with a hysterical structure. This hesitation is justified within the current tendency of psychiatry, a tendency that involves separating clearly disorders of consciousness from personality disorders. Henri Ey, in line with the conclusions of the Heidelberg school,[75] admits of two modalities for understanding psychopathological life: an impairment to the ego or an impairment of the ego; a disorder of consciousness or a dislocation of the person. Here, we are rather dealing with a disorder of consciousness.

In referring to classical symptomatology, the following must be considered: 1) the plasticity of the delusional ideas depends upon the attitude of the person doing the interrogation (this is literally a matter of 'pithiatic'[76] manifestations; that is what we call the adductive power of hysterical behaviour); 2) the tendency to exhibit defects (Hartenberg[77]) or to make things up (e.g. alleged incestuous relations); 3) a calm or euphoric attitude in the delusions[78] (the patient certainly had fits of agitation but always in the sense of a call; this ambivalent attitude of adherence to the delusion, which could

---

[75][A school of psychiatry whose major representatives were Karl Jaspers (1883–1969) and Kurt Schneider (1887–1967) and which undertook in particular to study schizophrenia.]

[76][That is to say, caused through persuasion.]

[77][Paul Hartenberg (1871–1949), French psychiatrist, author of classic works on neurotic anxieties, timidity and hysteria.]

[78]This third point does not at all entail the support of psychoanalysis, which describes an infrastructure of anxiety in hysteria. [See Henri Ey, *Études psychiatriques*, no. 15, 'Anxiété morbide'.]

be called complacency, is very different from delusions of influence); and 4) a strong sexual charge, which impregnates the attitude and the conversation.

For these reasons, we think that this was a case of delusion, or at least of delusional behaviour with a hysterical structure.

Mental disorder and neurological disturbance

This problem has certainly been one of the thorniest that neuropsychiatrists have had to ponder over the last twenty years. This problem, though foreseen the previous century, had yet to take on its character as a stumbling block of doctrines. The responsibility for this is to be found in today's very powerful urgency towards specialization, and thus towards boundaries. What are the respective limits of neurology and of psychiatry? What is a neurologist? What is a psychiatrist? In such a situation what, then, becomes of the neuropsychiatrist?

Far from proposing a solution – I believe a life of study and observation is required – I would like to relate the most representative positions of current doctrinaires: in France, Henri Ey and Jacques Lacan; and abroad, Kurt Goldstein. It should be added that Ey is situated in the Jacksonian heritage and that Goldstein, who has multiple points in common with Monakow and Mourgue, finds in Ajuriaguerra an exponent worthy of him.

It seemed to me that this clarificatory exercise would not be in vain. First, it can only help us to take a theoretical position as regards the object of neuropsychiatry. Also, this study assumes a value in the particular framework of this work, since it is absolutely unclear to what the psychic disorders encountered in spinocerebellar heredodegeneration are to be related.

Henri Ey's Position

Henri Ey is unquestionably the most powerful of heads of school. His numerous works, his preparatory lectures for the medical exams, and his consultations have made him a real figurehead. I will obviously provide a very systematic [Fanon probably meant to write 'schematic'] overview of his thought. May the author pardon me. However, I will attempt to formulate some clear ideas that are nonetheless not unsuited to the spirit of the doctor from Bonneval.

According to Ey, the nervous system is divided into two 'planes': 1) the plane of elementary or instrumental sensorimotor and psychic functions (reflex apparatuses for the coordination of movements, the regulation of tonus, of walking …); and 2) the plane of higher or energetic psychic functions (e.g. remembering, judging, believing, loving). The instrumental functions are specifically and morphologically inscribed in the brain. The main focus in studying them is the morphological and spatial genesis of nervous functions of relational life, as ordered with respect to the notion of cerebral localization of functional apparatuses. The energetic functions are more personal and plastic modes of activity. The main focus in studying them is the historical and chronological genesis of the psychological levels of relational life set in order by the notion of psychological tension. Concerning the pathological side of things, we rediscover both these planes.

1) *Pathology of the instrumental functional plane* represented by functional or local disintegrations. At this level an extremely important element is situated: the localization of the disorder. We shall see that things are not the same with global dissolutions. The characters of functional disintegrations are as follows: these disintegrations are partial (hemiplegia, aphasia …); and these disintegrations are basal, otherwise put, they leave the overall and higher edifice intact. For, as Ey says, 'aphasia in its most typical forms, chorea, hemitremor, Parkinson's disease, all disturb but do not alter in itself and by themselves the subject's consciousness, judgement or social activity'.[79]

2) *Pathology of the energetic functional plane.* A localization is not possible here, because the disintegrations have an essentially global character. The personality as a whole participates in the disease. Hence, the second notion of dissolutions of an apical nature.

---

[79]This sentence is one that other authors, such as Monakow and Mourgue, and above all Goldstein, utterly denounce.

Ey proposes that we call neurology the science of the instrumental plane, and psychiatry, the science of the energetic plane.

These differing points, which Ey formulated during the colloquium in Bonneval in 1942, continue the doctrinal trajectory of their author.[80] Fifteen years ago, Ey and Rouart laid the first foundations for an organo-dynamist conception of neuropsychiatry. Taking up Hughlings Jackson's theoretical ideas,[81] they laid down the factors behind the mental illnesses so finely studied by the English neurologist.

The different sorts of madness being the proper object of psychiatry, it is important, Jackson says, to distinguish four original factors: a) the different depths of dissolution of the higher cerebral centres; b) the different persons who have suffered this dissolution; c) the different speeds at which the dissolutions occur; and d) the influence of the different bodily states and different external circumstances on the people who have suffered such dissolutions. Next to these, Jackson places local dissolutions, which are the object of neurology. The aim here is not to reprise the Jacksonian account in detail. It is known that the curve of dissolution extends from illusion and abnormal emotional states all the way to dementia; from the dream to schizophrenia via the epileptic fit.

Ey's doctrine retains Jackson's fundamental elements, namely: evolution, hierarchy of functions, dissolution. These three points represent the infrastructure of a key phenomenon: integration. The pathology that introduces disintegration permits the emergence of negative signs (caused by the disease properly speaking) and of positive signs (the remaining personality). Ey ultimately thinks that the distinction between global and partial dissolutions corresponds 'to the only possible distinction between the object of neurology and that of psychiatry'.[82] This phrase is indicative of Ey's thought. Jackson envisaged the dialectic of the human being and world. Ey, through the

---

[80]Henri Ey, Julian de Ajuriaguerra, and Henri Hécaen, *Les Rapports de la neurologie et de la psychiatrie*, Paris: Hermann & Cie, 1947. [New edition 1998. Henri Ey's sentence quoted in the previous note is on page 12.]
[81][John Hughlings Jackson (1835–1911). See Henri Ey, Julien Rouart and Henri Claude, *Des idées de Jackson à un modèle organo-dynamique en psychiatrie*, Paris: Doin, 1938; Toulouse: Privat, 1975; Paris: L'Harmattan, 2000.]
[82][Ey, de Ajuriaguerra and Hécaen, *Les Rapports de la neurologie et de la psychiatrie*, p. 100.]

structural dynamism that he introduces, tries to formulate the major lines of a dialectic of the human being and thought. The neurological consists in that which is localizable, spatial, instrumental, elementary. The psychiatric, in that which is non-localizable, historical, global, synthetic. The psychiatric is not the psychic.[83]

A mental illness admits of no psychic causality. An organic dynamism lies at the basis of psychoses. And, says the author in his catechism of neo-Jacksonism,

> A dynamic conception of mental disorders entirely based on the notion of a dissolution of functions demands the tying of structural levels to organic disorders, which necessarily condition both slight neurotic dissolutions as well as confusional delirious states, dementia [etc.]. The tying of 'states', 'syndromes', 'structural levels' or 'psychoses' to etiological [organic] processes is the ultimate end of that medical science called psychiatry.[84]

The neurological is the partial level. The psychiatric is the global level.

After having determined the lower limits of psychiatry,[85] Ey tries to make its upper limits explicit. What is posed here is the entire problem of psychic causality. Is a mental illness, psychosis or neurosis, of psychic origin, or does it necessarily receive an organic conditioning? In the case of the co-existence of neurological disorders and mental disorders, is it a matter of personal reactions to psychic inflation or must we quite simply admit an extension of lesions in the encephalon?

Mental disorders do not have a psychic causality. Such is Ey's first doctrinal statement. Pre-empting his adversaries, who might be inclined to wave psychically conditioned psycho-neuroses before his eyes, the author takes up the instance of that violent emotion through which the hair turns white: 'This symptom', he says, 'must be related

---

[83] [In the sense that the psychic would constitute a determinate entity.]
[84] [Ey, Rouart and Claude, *Des idées de Jackson*, p. 166.]
[85] The attitude here, as can be seen, is clearly axiological. In it, we re-discover the Jacksonian hierarchy.

not to the emotion, which is the accidental psychogenetic aspect, but to a deeper endocrine disruption.[86]

After dismissing the theory according to which emotion is the basis of pathology, the author successively considers the three other psychogeneticist schools, whose masters are Kretschmer, Freud and Babinski. The former, well studied in Lacan's dissertation,[87] conceives delusion as the reactions of a consciousness that is 'sensitized' to the vital situations into which it is plunged. The Freudian perspective overlaps with the previous one by going beyond it. Where Kretschmer, a psychiatrist, attaches a fundamental importance to predispositions, to the constitution, Freud refutes them. Much later, in the wake of the sometimes malevolent criticisms of his adversaries, the Viennese master recognized the efficiency of heredity and of predispositions.[88] The notion of terrain was born.

Ey reproached Kretschmer for limiting psychic causality through the idea of constitution. Moreover, he finds in the development of schizophrenic dissociations into dementia an argument in favour

---

[86]Lucien Bonnafé et al., *Le Problème de la psychogenèse des névroses et des psychoses*, *op. cit.* [Exact quote, p. 142: 'It is necessary to relate this symptom not to the emotion under its occasional psychogenetic aspect, but to a deeper endocrine disruption'. This sentence of Ey's is in fact cited and criticized by the materialist psychiatrists Sven Follin and Lucien Bonnafé in their 'Étude critique de l'organo-dynamisme de Henri Ey', a paper presented at the third colloquium in Bonneval in 1946. The papers from the colloquium (including Jacques Lacan's 'Propos sur la causalité psychique') comprise this volume, which was published in 1950.]
[87]Jacques Lacan, *De la psychose paranoïaque dans ses rapports avec la personnalité* (*On Paranoid Psychosis and its Relations to the Personality*) [Dissertation, Paris, 1932; Paris: Seuil, 1975.]
[88]Freud, quoted by Ey: 'Psychic causality is a second-degree causality, insofar as the psychic concept only acquires a pathogenic charge on certain terrains.' [Henri Ey, *Études psychiatriques*, Étude no. 6, 'Freud et la psychanalyse', p. 156. This quote is actually taken from Sacha Nacht and is worth resetting in the context of Ey's text. Ey sought to rally psychoanalysts to his point of view: 'This is why all psychoanalysts since Freud himself, as soon as they are pushed or themselves go to the end of their argumentation, do not ever fail to admit that "organic factors", "somatic disorders" or, what amounts to the same, "an alteration of the Ego", play a determining role. We submitted this study to the opinion of S. Nacht. He provided us with some precious advice for our writing and was kind enough to comment upon the text itself. Thus, apropos of "psychic causality", which is to say the properly psychogenetic argument that we take to be the essence of Freudian theory, he wrote a small note that we have taken the liberty of reiterating here: "Psychic causality is a second-degree causality, insofar as the psychic concept only acquires a pathogenic charge on certain terrains." To this extent, to repeat, he seems to agree with most psychoanalysts, who claim not to be purely psychogeneticist … and with us!']

of his criticism. If dementia occurs, it is because an organic lesion must have occurred at some point. As for Babinski, Ey, by turning him into a dualist, denies his doctrine has any value. We know the importance that suggestion takes on in Babinski's system. The plane of the idea characterizes the mental illness, that is, when all is said and done, pithiatism.[89] Whatever does not fit it springs from localizable neurological processes.

This puts the core of Freudian doctrine into question: psychic trauma is merely an outmoded monument, the architecture of which does not indicate the use its workers intended for it .... Infantile regression is presented as a literary cliché. For Ey, 'every geneticist and dynamist theory of psychic activity leads to the notion of normal psychogenesis and repudiates that of pathological psychogenesis'. This means that psychogenetic activity is a normal, free activity.[90] And thus we see the psychiatricide

---

[89][The French neurologist Joseph Babinski (1857–1932) employed the term 'pithiatism' to designate functional disorders appearing to be without any organic cause, which can be reproduced through suggestion and which are supposedly curable through persuasion. In so doing he attempts, according to Ey, 'to delimit with precision the domain of hysteria [...] from that of lesional neurology' (*Manuel de psychiatrie*, 6th edition, updated by Paul Bernard and Charles Brisset, Paris: Masson, 1989, p. 320).]

[90]One must read Ey's *La Psychiatrie devant le surréalisme* to understand how far-reaching is this author's presentation of the limits of freedom and madness. The same fall takes on a different value depending on whether it is free or irreversible. Depending on whether it is a flight or a consequence of the psychic weight of the organism. In the first case, we are dealing with the poet, in the second, the madman.

[Henri Ey, *La Psychiatrie devant le surréalisme*, Paris: Centre d'éditions psychiatriques, Bibliothèque neuropsychiatrique de langue française, 1948. Fanon's library contains a highly annotated copy of this volume. The following sentences of the conclusions are marked in the margin: 'But opposed to this movement of "extrication" ("*dégagement*") by which freedom is defined, and which is the true path of freedom, is the reflux toward the automatic pole of our being, the veritable principle of psychological inertia. When that fall is free, that is to say when it engenders art (and notably that aesthetic form called surrealism), when that fall is also "flight", the "poet" abandons himself to the powerful germination of images which rise in him and that we call inspiration. HE CREATES THE MARVELLOUS. When, on the contrary, that fall – vertiginous, irresistible and irreversible (as in sleep or psychosis) – pertains to the physical weight of our organism, it engenders delusion. That is to say, it is not a sought-for and accepted automatism, but a forced automatism, an automatism of powerlessness. Then, and only then, is man mad, not at all as he has become a machine but because, no longer being free, he tends to become a machine. And then being half-way between being and nothingness, between life and the death of the mind, he becomes what he was only inside of himself, in the reverse of his full reality. Caught in the fantastic existence of images, in their miraculous unreality, HE IS MARVELLOUS.']

dilemma deflated.[91] On the one hand, the psychogeneticist theory, which sees mental illness as an exclusively psychic creation; on the other, the mechanistic theory, which situates mental illness in the localized region of the brain. Delusion is the product of excited nervous cells.

The author rejects both spiritualist dualism and materialist monism: 'We simultaneously repudiate dualism, which separates too much, and monism, which does not separate enough'.[92] Ey's entire position could reside in this petition: 'Between the physical and the moral, there is life'.[93] Ey refuses to choose between the physical and the mental, between mind and body. For him, 'mental life is rooted in organic life, from which it draws nourishment, which it uses, *integrates* and as a result goes beyond'.[94]

---

[91]The expression is Ey's. [Henri Ey, *Études psychiatriques*, Étude no. 4, p. 69. The subject of the study is the following: 'The position of psychiatry in the framework of the medical sciences (the notion of "mental illness")'. In it Ey sums up the dilemma thus: 'Let's try to put ourselves on the very terrain on which these two conceptions are opposed. One pleads for the "purely psychological" origin of the pathological variations studied in psychiatry. The other "purely and simply" identifies psychopathological disorder with a "simply anatomophysiological accident". Supporters of the first theory are known as "psychists", "psychologists" or better "psychogeneticists", for they defend what has come to be known as the psychogenesis of "mental illnesses". The second are known as "organicists" or "somatists" or better "mechanicists", insofar as they defend the "purely physical" character of "mental illnesses".']

[92][Henri Ey, *Études psychiatriques*, Étude no. 7, 'Principes d'une conception organo-dynamiste de la psychiatrie', p. 157. Ey writes: 'But to go beyond all these theories, it is necessary that we reject at once dualism, which separates too much, and monism, which does not separate enough, the psyche from life. We should see in the organism qua form of existence, not merely an architecture but a becoming, a movement, which moves us from the order of "vitality" to that of "humanity"'. We will see that, for Fanon, this temporal gap is the condition of possibility not only of psychiatry as a separate discipline from neurology, but also of social therapy. Thus he writes on 11 August, 1955, in *Notre Journal*: 'For the worst error consists in believing that the work undertaken, if it is abandoned even for a moment, remains intact. It collapses section after section. Man creates himself or undoes himself every day. The task must be conducted with tenacity everyday'. This conviction runs through his radical opposition to the neocolonial bourgeoisies and bureaucracies which hasten to terminate the revolutionary self- creation of an autonomous community as soon as they gain power.]

[93][Henri Ey, *Études psychiatriques*, Étude no. 4, p. 74.]

[94][Bonnafé et al., *Le Problème de la psychogenèse des névroses et des psychoses*, p. 13 sq. Ey adds something on which Fanon comments in the following paragraph: 'This blossoming in the organism of a specific causality constitutes the psyche, which, at its peak, constitutes the spirituality of human nature, *a reality* that is ignored both by dualism, which makes the mind a mind without existence, and materialism, which

Speaking of the psyche, the author, who moreover utilizes the conclusions of diverse schools of thought, writes: 'The structural whole that psychology and psychopathology would come to deal with got built up little by little'. In the psyche, we ought to distinguish between the given and the taken, the passive and the active. We should also bear in mind: both character and affectivity in close relation with the 'instrumental' functions (sensory, mnesic and verbal qualities proper to each individual). Ey calls this part the *psychic trajectory*.[95] In this trajectory, the field to be traversed is precisely the psychic field. The psychic field refers naturally to psychic life, which is by no means endowed with immutability. It 'oscillates between disinterest for the outside world and the present and, in its most attentive and efficient form, supreme adaptation to the present and the real'.[96] This sentence clearly owes a lot to Janet's research.[97] For that matter, Ey acknowledges the influence of the theoretician of psychological tension on the direction of this thought. Psychogenesis is the norm. This position admits a corollary: mental illness involves organogenesis, and psychiatry, refusing any

---

turns the mind into an "epiphenomenon". Indeed, the sphere of this mental causality is a reality so real that it is that of our social interactions, of our properly human, relational life. It is at once determined by the historical progress of our existence, which provides its matrix, and the instrumental functions that serve it as a basis; and indeterminate inasmuch as, with the personality, a specific energetic system is constituted, a centre of autonomous forces, a centre of indetermination, the concrete contents of these concepts of will and freedom, of which one can of course pretend naively to do without although they constitute spiritual *reality*, the substratum of properly human life. The entire play of mental activity is thus to be inscribed between these two coordinates, the "given" and the "taken", the passive and the active, habit and intention, automatism and will'.]

[95][Bonnafé et al., *Le Problème de la psychogenèse des névroses et des psychoses*, p. 12.]
[96][Ibid., p. 13. Fanon summarizes and cites at the same time a long paragraph on the operations of the psychic field in its temporal dimension.]
[97][Pierre Janet (1859–1947), a French philosopher and psychologist, is the inventor of the 'subconscious' as concept. Ey refers here to *La Force et la faiblesse psychologiques* (Paris: Maloine, 1932): 'The fundamental aspect of Pierre Janet's thought is constituted by its hierarchy of functions of the real, subtended by psychological tension. For him, what we call the psychic functions are nothing other than a series of conducts, which bring us more-or-less close to reality. Everything transpires as if the activity of man unfolded on an increasingly complicated and difficult scale of levels of thought, which ultimately arrives at the apprehension of the world of objects'. (*Études psychiatriques*, p. 179). Ey will find it easy thereafter to talk about the dissolution of this hierarchy and to see in Janet a precursor to his organo-dynamism.]

value to the concept of pathological psychogenesis, reserves itself a domain of study with no relation to that of freedom.[98]

But, then, what difference can there be between schizophrenia and general paralysis? An illness, Ey says, if it is always organic in its etiology, is always psychic in its pathogeny: 'It is a mental alteration of organic nature.'[99] What is the master of Bonneval's position in the particular case of interest to us? That the mental disorders found in spinocerebellar heredodegeneration ought not be understood as a reaction of the personality to an inferiorizing situation, any more than they ought to be reduced to a production of a valorizing unconscious. Character modifications and personality disorders occur in relation to the disease in question's organic alterations, at whatever level they are situated.[100]

Goldstein's position

The *hormè*[101] school and the *Gestalt* school bear a point of difference. This difference is that the reflexive act that Monakow and Mourgue held to be a metameric reaction[102] becomes, with Goldstein, a total reaction of the organism. For, Goldstein says, it is inadmissible that one part is capable of a reaction without having the other parts participate in it. There is no such thing as primitive functions, on the one hand, and higher functions, on the other. Every gesture, every function, presumes the collaboration of the entire individual.

---

[98][This refusal of a psychic pathogeny and the definition of the domain of psychiatry as one without relation to freedom are at the core of Fanon's thought and the points at which he is closest to Ey's position. But we will see that for him there can also be a sociogenesis of mental illness.]

[99]Volume 4 of Ey's *Études psychiatriques* is to be titled *Les Processus somatiques générateurs*. [This volume 4, which was announced at the start of the second part of *Études psychiatriques* in 1950, was ultimately never to appear.] The psychoses present a pathological originality in that they constitute 'anomalies of evolution of psychic life under the influence of a "somatosis", anomalies implying the coming into play of psychic forces that organize the "mental disorders", the "mental illnesses", the "pyschoses", the "neuroses", according to laws specific to the level of dissolution corresponding to the action of the pathogenic organic process' (Henri Ey, *Études psychiatriques*, vol. 1, p. 44.)

[100][On Ey's critique of '*La théorie psychogénétique des états psychopathologiques*' (the psychogenetic theory of psychopathological states) that is to say of Freudianism, see *Études psychiatriques*, no. 6, 'Freud et la psychanalyse'. On Fanon's doubts concerning the notion of inferiority complex, see chapter 4 of *Peau noir, masques blancs*, 'The so-called Dependency Complex of the Colonized'.]

[101][See *above*, p. 51, note 40.]

[102][A step-by-step reaction to a local physical stimulation of the nervous system.]

Patient Sch., suffering an occipital lesion, had both calcarines[103] destroyed. Goldstein and his collaborator Gelb, after making meticulous observations, showed that this case by no means presented any occurrence of aphasia – a word too easily advanced – but instead an inability to put oneself in a certain attitude: they refer this disorder to a collapse of categorial symbolism.[104]

When the core of the problem that splits contemporary neurologists is analysed, the only real point of contention remains cerebral localizations. But beyond the desire to localize or not, it is imperative to recognize the deeper question of mind-body relations.

To a superficial mind, it might seem that the mass of publications and systems that have been updated over the last fifty years indicate an avowal of impotence more than of effective progress. Similarly, scepticism in therapy towards the great number of 'inoffensive' specialities for diseases, is taking hold of more and more doctors and, by induction, of the general public. It must be said that, beyond all discouragement, only impassioned and often ardent research will allow us to raise some hope around the organization of madness, hope for what Lacan has called a 'logic of madness'.

Goldstein took up Monakow and Mourgue's work and tried to give it a scientific value. The success of *Gestalt*-theory around the world shows that he did not fail. Let us quickly go over the various points that the authors developed in *Introduction biologique à l'étude de la neurologie et de la psychopathologie*[105] – I will also make use of isolated works by C. V. Monakow that situate the system philosophically. Monakow considers that, at the risk of using a-scientific reasoning, one cannot speak of cerebral localization: 'A psychic phenomenon cannot admit a spatial localization'. He places humanity's biological and psychological evolution in the curve of

---

[103][A deep groove of the occipital cortex surrounded by the areas in the brain that deal with visual information.]
[104][In the criticism of Henri Ey that Fanon presents in the following section, Lacan comments in detail on Goldstein and Gelb's experiment with this patient who, following an occipital lesion, displayed a great number of neuropsychiatric problems: tactile and above all visual agnosia – an inability to grasp purely visual representations – a loss of a sense of calculation and of abstract reasoning, problems with the body schema and the vision of movement (Bonnafé et al., *Le Problème de la psychogenèse*, p. 25 *sq.*).]
[105][Von Monakow and Mourgue, *Introduction biologique à l'étude de la neurologie et de la psychopathologie*, 1928]

time. Thus the soul has no seat, and extension is not opposed to thought any more than the soul is opposed to the body. On the contrary, any focal alteration can determine disorders in very distant regions (*diaschisis*). Moreover, the body is not left to itself; it is taken up again and valorized by a first principle: the *hormè*. May the reader pardon this leap, but we cannot pass in silence over the kinship between Monakow and Bergson. The Monakowian *hormè* can in some respects be referred back to Bergson's *élan vital*.[106] For Monakow, the human being is fusion with nature to the extent that the *hormè* predominates.

One thing ties us to Monakow's doctrine: the human is human to the extent that he is totally turned towards the future. The occasion will arise, in a work that I have been undertaking for a long time, to tackle the problem of history from a psychoanalytic and ontological angle. In it, I will show that history is only the systematic valorization of collective complexes.[107]

C. v. Monakow's biology is genetic and chronogenic. With Monakow, the world of instincts takes priority over the world of orientation: instincts are at the service of the *hormè*. Pathology results

---

[106][Owing to its critique of spatialism, its reflections on temporality in the processes of psychic and psychopathological development, Monakow and Mourgue's book (especially its introduction) had an important influence on the philosophical thought of the period. Accordingly, Merleau-Ponty adopts the concept of 'kinetic melody' to explain the body schema in *La Structure du comportement* (Paris: PUF, [1942] 1963, p. 168) [*The structure of behaviour*, trans. Alden L. Fisher with a Foreword by John Wild, Boston, MA: Beacon Press, 1967, p. 163]: 'The organism is also distinguished from the systems of classical physics because it does not admit of division in space and time. Nerve functioning is not punctually localizable; a kinetic melody is present in totality at its beginning and the movements in which it is progressively realized can be foreseen only in terms of the whole'. In *Différence et répétition* (Paris: PUF, 1968, p. 372; *Difference and Repetition*, trans. Paul Patton, New York, NY: Columbia University Press, 1994, p. 333, n. 8), Gilles Deleuze comments on this text – and returns to it with Félix Guattari in *L'Anti-Œdipe* (Paris: Minuit, 1975, p. 48; *Anti-Oedipus*, trans. Robert Hurley, Mark Seem and Helen R. Lane, Minneapolis, MN: University of Minnesota Press, 1983, p. 40) – concerning the Monakowian theory of decomposition into spatially unlocalizable psychic bricks and the 'chronogenous localization' of the function. Monakow and Mourgue introduce these concepts through their remarkable analysis of the metaphor of a music box (cf. *Introduction biologique*, p. 20 and pp. 184–5). On the history of holism in German psychiatry, see Anne Harrington, *Reenchanted Science: Holism in German Culture from Wilhelm II to Hitler*, Princeton, NJ: Princeton University Press, 1999.]

[107][This topic is in part tackled in chapter 6 of *Peau noir, masques blancs*.]

from the inversion of this relation. In case of injury, *syneidesis*[108] comes into play and attempts to restore calm. For Monakow, not one but several souls exist. Each cell is endowed with consciousness, with a differential of consciousness. Each vital phenomenon is considered to have a soul assigned to it: the opposition between soul and body is overcome. Soul and life are identical.

With Goldstein, the question takes a gigantic step forward. Evolution and dissolution, Jacksonian integration and disintegration, Monakowian *syneidesis* and compensation, are all rejected. For Goldstein, no absolute, local symptom exists. Every organic manifestation is endowed with a special tonality, which is the fruit of global mechanisms. For him, the organism acts as a whole. An aphasic is not a man who no longer talks, or whose language is altered. He is a new man. Aphasia is the dominant process, but it is essential to consider the background process of the aphasic individual.

In France Ajuriaguerra and Hécaen developed these notions in their critical study of Ey's doctrinal position.[109] By attaching too much importance to the symptom, Ey has falsified the problem. By no means ought the symptom to be valorized. Guillain and Barré have shown, for example, that a patient in the dorsal position can present a plantar reflex in extension: the same patient presents this reflex in flexion once placed in ventral decubitus, with the legs bent towards the thigh. This means that the symptom must be divested of all fixity. Life, which, in Ey's work, is found in undifferentiated state, takes on, in Goldstein's, an organizational value.[110] In his

---

[108][In Monakow's work, *syneidesis* is the vital intelligence enabling the brain to recuperate its functions or at least to adapt to a neurological disturbance (*diaschisis* in his vocabulary).]

[109][Julian de Ajuriaguerra and Henri Hécaen, 'Dissolution générale et dissolution locale des fonctions nerveuses', in Henri Ey, *Les Rapports de la neurologie et de la psychiatrie. Rapport présenté lors des débats des 14 et 15 septembre 1943* (New edition, 1998, pp. 15–95).]

[110][de Ajuriaguerra and Hécaen cite the Guillain-Barré phenomenon on page 84 *sq.* – Fanon has copied their description. They add: 'Simple osteotendinous reflexes vary depending on whether attention is fixed or relaxed, as external excitations can modify them. The studies of Goldstein and Weizsäcker have shown that if the reflex is not an abstraction, it is nonetheless not a physical but a biological reality; it is a form of

The Wisdom of the Body,[111] Cannon has shown us the occasionally abrupt struggles that the organism engages in to maintain health. Goldstein comes somewhat close to this view with his notion of vigilance, which, moreover, he borrows from Head.[112] For him, nervous energy is a constant. As soon as one function is affected, the others come to its rescue. The studies done on the spontaneous correction of hemianopsia are highly demonstrative.[113]

Ajuriaguerra and Hécaen contest the reality of elementary functions and of the functions of synthesis. They remind us that we ought not

---

response obtained in experimental conditions. All this experimental study is carried out by isolating certain regions, with a view to simplification. But the physiological study does not prevent Magnus from saying "the spinal marrow is different at each instant; it is the reflection of the situation and of the activity of diverse parts of the body and of its entirety". Physiology has brought to light the variability of responses at the level of the cortex, the instability of cortical points to an excitation depending upon its state at the moment of excitation.' De Ajuriaguerra and Hécaen had already taken their distance from Gestaltism by the time their 1943 report was published, in 1947. This Gestaltist influence is also to be found in Merleau-Ponty's criticism of behaviourism in *La Structure du comportement* (Paris: Presses Universitaires de France, 1942), which Fanon cites hereafter.

[111][Walter Bradford Cannon, *The Wisdom of the Body*, New, NY W.W. Norton & Company, 1932. Translated as *La Sagesse du corps*, Paris: Éditions de la *Nouvelle revue critique*, 1946.]

[112][Maurice Merleau-Ponty notes the usefulness of the theory of vigilance by British neurologist Henry Head (1861-1940) for understanding 'reflex deficiencies in infection, fatigue, and hypnosis' (*The Structure of Behaviour*, p. 18).]

[113][Hemianopsia is decreased vision or blindness in half the visual field in one or both eyes.] 'If the retinal sectors which remain capable of evoking luminous sensations in a person with hemianopsia are determined by measuring the perimeter of vision, it is observed that he now has the use of only two half retinas; consequently, one would expect that his field of vision would correspond to half of the normal field of vision, right or left according to the case, with a zone of clear peripheral vision. In reality this is not the case at all: the subject has the impression of seeing poorly, but not of being reduced to half a visual field. The organism has adapted itself to the situation created by the illness by reorganizing the functions of the eye. The eyeballs have oscillated in such a way as to present an intact part of the retina to the luminous excitations, whether they come from the right or the left; in other words, the preserved retinal sector has established itself in a central position in the orbit instead of remaining affected, as before the illness, by the reception of light rays coming from one half of the field. [...] If we adhere to the classical conceptions that relate the perceptual functions of each point of the retina to its anatomical structure – for example, to the proportion of cones and rods which are located there – the functional reorganization in hemianopsia is not comprehensible. It becomes so only if the properties of each retinal point are assigned to it, not according to established local devices, but according to a flexible process of distribution comparable to the division of forces in a drop of oil suspended in water' (*Structure of Behaviour*, pp. 40-1).

to confound lesion and function: 'If we argue on the lesional plane, supposedly only quantitative differences exist between the so-called elementary disorders and the disturbances of energetic functions. ... Why give different values to those processes which are distinguished only by a greater lesional extent'?[114] No opposition arises between an elementary phenomenon and an apparatus of synthesis: 'It is the organism in its organization that gives them a more or less important value'.[115]

For Ey, the focal is the neurological, while the global is the psychiatric. Hécaen and Ajuriaguerra, on the contrary, strive to prove that a neurological disturbance is a global disturbance. Here are some of the numerous cases reported by these authors.

Obs. I. A young woman of twenty-eight developed a hemiplegia owing to a cerebral tumour. She denied her menstruation, not recognizing the streaks of blood as her own, and ignored how the stains on the bed sheets got there. She had no other mental disorders: she later developed ideas of negation wherein she claimed her entire body had decayed and she later declared that her body had completely vanished.

Obs. II. A woman of thirty-three developed a left hemiplegia: she also denied her menstruation, behaved childishly and spoke about herself only in the third person.

So much for Ey's first position.[116] As to the problem of the psychogenesis of psychoneuroses, what is the stance of the *gestalt theorists*? They say that the mental state can reveal or create algias [pains], or paresthesias, by itself. Without contending that a trigeminal neuralgia can be purely psychogenic, Wexberg[117] accepts that a special psychic state can by its presence complete the necessary series of conditions for hatching this facial algia; and this occurs, he thinks, through the intermediary of the neurovegetative system. Here we again come across the conclusions of Professor Dechaume, who recently wrote: 'It is at the very least paradoxical that it is not the

---

[114][de Ajuriaguerra and Hécaen, 'Dissolution générale et dissolution locale des fonctions nerveuses', p. 89.]
[115][Ibid., pp. 91–2.]
[116][Valorization of the symptom.]
[117][Erwin Wexberg (1889–1957), an American psychiatrist of Austrian origin and a student and follower of Alfred Adler, was a theoretician of the so-called school of 'individual psychology'. A neurologist as well, he took an interest in periodical neurological disorders and in psychosomatic medicine.]

cerebrospinal system, said to be that of relational life, that is its main instrument. The neurovegetative system, that of animal life, which for ancient authors was charged with getting the viscera to agree with one another, is in fact that which ensures the unity of the human person'.[118]

Pain, add Ajuriaguerra and Hécaen, is a psychic fact. It is a whole. It has meaning only in accordance with the individual who suffers it. How could we not recall Professor Leriche's beautiful book on pain and above all his most recent works, *Chirurgie discipline de la connaissance* and *Philosophie de la chirurgie*?[119] Besides, the surgeon of pain took up this notion of totality, for, he says, 'the patient for us remains a puppet each string of which produces a particular movement, whereas in fact, in the acts of life, the whole is in the whole'.[120]

For Gestaltists, the neurological and the psychiatric go hand-in-hand. There is an intertwining of neurological disturbance and psychiatric disorder. The repercussions of a neurological fact are not 'limited'; they are no longer a simple aureole, but instead an upheaval of the personality; what we get is an individual who is profoundly modified in his ego.

When all is said and done, Ajuriaguerra and Hécaen in my view commit a serious extrapolation: beginning with phenomenological research, they undertake to perform a clinical analysis. I subscribe to Ey's viewpoint. As he says, 'What defines their position [most accurately] seems to me less the manifest concern to conceive the neurological phenomenon as a global disorder than the real tendency to "return" psychiatric disorder to neurological disturbance'.[121] To the extent that Hécaen and Ajuriaguerra ground their doctrine on

---

[118] *Traité de médecine*, vol. 16, p. 1075 [André Lemierre *et al.* (ed.), *Traité de médecine*, vol. 16, pp. 1063–75].

[119] [René Leriche, *La Chirurgie de la douleur*, Paris: Masson & Cie, 1940; *La Chirurgie, discipline de la connaissance*, Nice: La Diane française, 1949; *La Philosophie de la chirurgie*, Paris: Flammarion, 1951.]

[120] [René Leriche, *La Chirurgie, discipline de la connaissance*, p. 337.]

[121] [Ey, *Neurologie et psychiatrie*, p. 100. Ey describes thus his counter argumentation to Ajuriaguerra's and Hécaen's *rapport*: 'It comes down therefore to presenting the distinction that I propose [between neurology and psychiatry] as the expression of a natural difference between two modalities of cerebral pathology. The one being heterogeneous to the other in the sense (1) that neurological phenomena do not "pass" in themselves and by themselves through a simple increase in intensity into mental disorders and that they present themselves in relative contrast with them; and (2) that mental disorders, if they often "contain" neurological syndromes, do not "reduce" to them. It is therefore quite evident that if the mental disorder can envelop

the body schema and its alterations,[122] they leave aside the properly psychogenetic aspect of the question. Before ending this rapid survey, I would like to discuss the work of another theoretician, Jacques Lacan, who, in a minimum of articles, has made a really vigorous attempt [at solving?] the problem of the psychogenesis of mental disorders.[123]

Jacques Lacan's Position

So rather than resulting from a contingent fact – the frailties of man's organism – madness is the permanent virtuality of a gap opened up in his essence. And far from being an 'insult' to freedom, madness is freedom's most faithful companion, following its every move like a shadow. Not only can man's being not be understood without madness, but it would not be man's being if it did not bear madness within itself as the limit of his freedom. ... A weak organism, a deranged imagination, and conflicts beyond one's capacities do not suffice to cause madness.

(Jacques Lacan, 'The essential causality of madness'.)[124]

---

the neurological disturbance, the neurological disturbance cannot envelop the mental disorder' (Ey, *Neurologie et psychiatrie*, p. 116). This distinction is evidently at the core of Fanon's dissertation. At the end of this long comparison of various theoretical viewpoints liable to explain the crucial problem of Friedreich's ataxia, a choice is made in favour of Ey's phenomenological perspective and against mechanistic materialism. One finds an echo of it in Fanon's thinking on history and politics, which pays some attention to Marxism in its theory of exploitation but ultimately gives it rather little credence in its theory of liberation.]

[122][In a section on 'Troubles du schéma corporel et états de dépersonnalisation' (de Ajuriaguerra and Hécaen, 'Dissolution générale et dissolution locale des fonctions nerveuses', pp. 63–71), de Ajuriaguerra and Hécaen remain prudent and describe a complex causality in the relations between psychotic disorders and those of the body schema and of the awareness of one's own body. The importance of the notion of the body schema in the analysis of the 'Lived Experience of the Black Man' in *Peau noir, masques blancs*, is well known, but the causal relation in it is more complex, since if depersonalization has a negative impact on the body schema, this depersonalization itself is entailed by the socio-historical constraint imposed on a being reduced to the facticity of a skin colour.]

[123][After providing this inventory of all the perspectives, and deciding, after many hesitations, in favour of Ey's, Fanon presents Lacan's perspective, which is apt to put into question the distinction between psychiatry and neurology, no longer through the flattening of the psychic onto the neurological, but through a refusal of the organogenesis of mental illness and, as a result, through the inscription of the pathological within the very heart of the psychic.]

[124][This passage is taken from the first *rapport* submitted by Lacan to the third colloquium organized by Henri Ey in Bonneval, in 1946 (In English, *The essential causality of madness*, 1946, in *Ecrits: The First Complete Edition in English*, trans. Bruce Fink, New York, NY, and London: W.W. Norton & Company, 2002, p. 144). The first

Few men are as contested as Jacques Lacan. Parodying the expression, it might be said that, among psychiatrists, Lacan has supporters and he has adversaries. It would be further necessary to add that the adversaries by far outweigh the supporters ... The 'logician of madness' does not seem specially bothered by this.[125] 'Logician of madness': although semantically unacceptable, this coupling expresses a certain reality. Personally, were I to define Lacan's position, I would call it an unremitting defence of the nobility rights of madness.

In trying to determine the site of Lacanian thinking, it seemed interesting to me, first, to gather the governing ideas of his dissertation.[126] Two elements appear important in Lacan's analysis

---

colloquium on 'L'histoire naturelle de la folie' took place in 1942, and the second on 'Neurologie et psychiatrie' was held in 1943. The format was the same: an introduction by Henri Ey, presentation of a long critical report by an opponent, followed by a reply from Ey and a discussion. On the sessions of 28, 29 and 30 September 1946, three reports were presented in response to Ey's introduction on 'Les limites de la psychiatrie, le problème de la psychogenèse': (1) Jacques Lacan, 'Propos sur la causalité psychique'; (2) Julien Rouart, 'Y a-t-il des maladies mentales d'origine psychique?'; and (3) Sven Follin and Lucien Bonnafé, 'À propos de la psychogenèse'. The citation retained here by Fanon comes from the second part of Lacan's report titled 'La causalité essentielle de la folie' (Bonnafé et al., *Le Problème de la psychogenèse*, p. 42).

The question of the psychogenesis (in opposition to the organogenesis) of mental illnesses is crucial for Fanon, since if madness is a pathology of freedom and if its genesis is psychic, then alienation is at the core of human essence. Later he would resolve the question by means of a sociogenesis of mental illness.]

[125][Recalling his years of study with Lacan, Ey notes in his reply: 'I was at an uncertain age and quite close to throwing myself body and all into a metaphysical adventure along which I would have met, behind Heidegger and Husserl, Hegel and beyond Hegel *the logic of madness*. This path, which is perhaps the one that he [Lacan] has taken, I nonetheless deliberately didn't take. And I oriented myself towards a *natural history of madness*, refusing to make light of "naturalism", "somatism", "medicalism", or "rationalism", all of which, while implied in the mechanicism that I set out to combat, nonetheless exceed it and make it possible to escape from its harmful embrace' (Bonnafé *et al.*, *Le Problème de la psychogenèse*, p. 55). See also Lucien Bonnafé and Jacques Chazaud, *La Folie au naturel, Le Premier Colloque de Bonneval comme moment décisif de l'Histoire de la Psychiatrie*, Paris: l'Harmattan, 2006.]

[126][Jacques Lacan, *De la psychose paranoïaque dans ses rapports avec la personnalite*, dissertation, 1931, Paris: Seuil, 1980: p. 39 *sq*. Lacan introduces the topic of his dissertation as follows: 'A symptom – mental or physical – is psychogenic if its causes are expressed as a function of the complex mechanisms of the personality, the manifestation of which reflects them and whose treatment may depend upon them. This is the case: – when the causal event is determining only as a function of the lived history of the subject, of his self-conception and that of his vital situation in relation to society; – when the symptom reflects in its form an event or a state of psychic history, when it expresses the possible contents of the imagination, of desire, or of the subject's volition, when it has a demonstrative value that aims at another

of personality. These are: a) the relations of comprehension that he inherits from Jaspers; and b) intentionality.

a) *Relations of comprehension* – as criteria of psychological and psychopathological analysis, [these relations] represent the common measure of human feelings and acts liable to being grasped with reference to a participationist interpretation.

b) *Intentionality* – rendered through intentional phenomena, intentionality discloses the development of the person in each of its manifestations.

What is important in Lacan's dissertation is the subsumption of the characteristics that he includes in his definition: a) the biographical development and relations of comprehension to be read in them (*Erlebnis*); b) a conception of oneself (ego ideal); c) a certain tension pertaining to social relations (ego-other). Lacan, we shall see, has held to this general framework.

It seems to me that the essential value of Lacan's work resides in the definition he gives of desire. He turns desire into a cycle of behaviour characterized by certain general organic oscillations, which are qualified as affective, a more or less directed motor agitation, and fantasies whose objective intentionality will be more or less adequate depending upon the case.

When a vital experience – given, active or endured – determines affective equilibrium, motor rest and vanishing of fantasies, we say by definition that desire has been satisfied and that this experience was the end and object of the desire. In the detailed analysis that he gives

---

person; – when the treatment may depend upon a modification of the corresponding vital situation, whether this modification occurs in the facts themselves, in the affective reaction of the subject in their regard or in the objective representation that he has of them. The symptom at issue here nonetheless rests on organic bases, always physiological ones, most often pathological, and sometimes on marked lesions. It is another thing, however, to study its organic causality, whether lesional or functional, and its psychogenic causality.'

'In effect a delusion is not the same kind of object as a physical lesion, a painful spot or a motor disturbance. It expresses an elective problem of the patient's highest behaviours: of his mental attitudes, of his judgement, of his social behaviour. Further, delusion does not express this disturbance directly; it signifies it using social symbolism. This symbolism is not univocal and must be interpreted' (Jacques Lacan, *De la psychose paranoïaque dans ses rapports avec la personnalité*, pp. 45–46 and p. 100). As Fanon himself goes on to stress, the relational or social character of these parameters is crucial.]

of the case of Aimé[e], Lacan appears to conceive psychosis as a cycle of behaviour, such that the point is not to undertake a symptomatic study of psychosis like Kraepelin and Bleuler, but instead, on the basis of Jaspers' relations of comprehension, to grasp the organizing mechanism of desire and its satisfaction.

To my mind, Lacan's thought bears the influence of Paulhan's work *Socialisation des tendances*, which, moreover, he does not cite.[127] In effect, the vital experience in which the end of desire is recognized is essentially social in its origin, exercise and meaning. So, 'to recognize in morbid symptoms one or several *cycles of behaviour* that, as anomalous as they are, show a concrete tendency that may be defined as *relations of comprehension*, such is the viewpoint that we take to the study of the psychoses'.[128]

I mentioned earlier the considerable importance that Lacan attributes to the social instance. Indeed he expresses this in the three functions that he recognizes in the personality under the attributes of the comprehensibility of development, the idealism of one's self-conception, and lastly, as the very function of the social tension of personality, in which the first two attributes of the phenomenon are actually engendered.[129]

Lacan places the postulate of psychogenetic determinism at the basis of his doctrine. This postulate makes possible a science of personality; the object of this science is the genetic study of the intentional functions into which human relations of a social type are integrated. This is what he calls the phenomenology of personality.[130]

Applying his method to the paranoid psychosis of self-punishment, Lacan reveals its status as a phenomenon of the personality in a development of the delusion coherent with the lived history of the subject, in the character of manifestation, at once conscious (delusion) and unconscious (self-punishing tendencies) of the Ego Ideal, by its dependency on psychic tensions specific to social relations (tensions expressed immediately both in the phenomena[131] [and] contents of delusion and in its etiology and reactive outcome).

---

[127][Frédéric Paulhan, *Les Transformations sociales des sentiments*, Paris: Flammarion, 1920. First part, 'Organisation, spiritualisation et socialisation des tendances'. In his dissertation, Lacan cites other texts by Paulhan.]
[128][Lacan, *De la psychose paranoïaque dans ses rapports avec la personnalité*, p. 312.]
[129][Lacan, *De la psychose paranoïaque dans ses rapports avec la personnalité*, p. 314.]
[130][Ibid., p. 315.]
[131][This sentence is a paraphrase of a paragraph from p. 317 of Lacan's book. Instead of 'phenomena' Lacan wrote 'symptoms'.]

Alongside this phenomenological manifestation of psychosis, we can, with Lacan, single out three sub-characters, which are, moreover, very important: 1) a humanly comprehensible meaning; 2) virtualities of dialectical progress, the cure being catharsis – a cure that for the subject represents the liberation from a conception of oneself and the world, illusory in that it depends on unknown affective drives, and this liberation is accomplished through a shock with reality. One noteworthy fact being that spontaneous catharsis is not entirely conscious; and 3) its opening onto social participation.

The social category of human reality, to which I personally attach so much importance, is one to which Lacan has been attentive. He reprises the discoveries of the ethno-sociology of projection, as illustrated by Mauss and Lévy-Bruhl,[132] and describes the phenomenon of representation (*mandatement*). Some images, he says[133] (stars in film, newspapers, sports) represent the necessities of dramatic space (*espace spectaculaire*) and of moral communion specific to the human personality; they are liable to compensate for the orgiastic or universalist, religious or purely social rites that have represented these necessities hitherto.

After giving the lie to the notion of constitution, which he considers absolutely mythical, Lacan tackles the restrictive point of view of his work. Delusion becomes the intentional equivalent of an insufficiently socialized, aggressive drive. But it is interesting to discover here the *concrete tendency* subjacent to the intentional phenomenon of delusion. Calling on Jaspers,[134] Lacan distinguishes between: a) the delusion that is manifest as the development of a personality; and b) the delusion that is presented as an irruptive psychic process, that disrupts and rearranges the personality. Only an examination of the personality's genetic and structural continuity will shed light on cases of delusion in which a psychic process and not a developmental process is at issue; that is to say, the cases in which one ought to recognize the intentional manifestation of a drive that is not of infantile origin, but instead is of recent acquisition and exogenous, and is such that, in effect, certain affections such as

---

[132][Lacan, *De la psychose paranoïaque dans ses rapports avec la personnalité*, p. 288.]
[133][Ibid., p. 317.]
[134][Ibid., p. 335.]

lethargic encephalitis make its existence seen by demonstrating to us the primitive phenomenon.

After dismissing the Tainian parallelist solution of the personality, Lacan proposes a definition of delusion: 'It is the expression, within forms of language formed for understandable relations in a group, of concrete tendencies, of which the subject misjudges (*méconnait*) their insufficient conformism to the necessities of the group'.[135] As we will see this phenomenon of misjudging (*méconnaissance*) subtends the Lacanian edifice. In his critical argument concerning organo-dynamism, Lacan raises this question: does the originality of our object (madness) pertain to social practice or to scientific reason?[136] Lacan seeks out the response on both these planes.

Ey encountered delusion as part of his structural analysis of madness. He views the latter as the sort of deficiency that the English call 'loss of control'.[137] There is a 'delusional intuition' (Dublineau[138]) on the basis of which the delusional belief takes effect. For Lacan, delusional belief is ignorance. In my view, we can situate Lacan's logical reversal of the scientific attitude at this level. By tackling the human value of madness,[139] Lacan moves from the plane of causality

---

[135]['Of delusional knowledge, on the contrary, this conception makes it possible to provide the most general formula, if one defines delusion as the expression, in the forms of *language* forged for understandable relations in a group, of concrete tendencies whose insufficient conformism to the group's necessities is unknown by the subject. This very definition of delusion makes it possible to conceive, on the one hand, the affinities noted by psychologists between the forms of delusional thinking and the primitive forms of thinking and, on the other, the radical difference that separates them, based on the sole fact that some are in harmony with the conceptions of the group, while the others are not' (Lacan, *De la psychose paranoïaque dans ses rapports avec la personnalité*, p. 337 *sq.*). Such a text is important for understanding the way in which Fanon will reject the ethnopsychiatry of the Algiers School, which is founded on the ideas of psychic *constitution*.]

[136]['To put it in concrete terms, is there nothing that distinguishes the alienated individual from other patients, bar the fact that one is confined to an asylum, while the others are hospitalized? Or again, is the originality of our object a question of social practice – or of scientific reason' (Bonnafé *et al.*, *Le Problème de la psychogenèse*, p. 25).]

[137][Ey, *Études psychiatriques*, *Étude* 7, p. 170.]

[138][René Targowla and Jean Dublineau, *L'Intuition délirante*, Paris: Norbert Maloine, 1931.]

[139]A psychiatrist from Lyon, M. Balvet, has also considered this problem. Let us note, moreover, that their respective arguments are far from overlapping. [Paul Balvet, 'La valeur humaine de la folie', *Esprit*, p. 137, September 1947.]

to that of motivation. Setting out from knowledge [*connaissance*] and belief, he considers madness from an intersubjectivist perspective. 'Madness', he says, 'is lived within the register of meaning. And ... its metaphysical impact is revealed in that the phenomenon of madness is not separable from the problem of meaning for being in general, that is to say, of language for human beings'.[140]

I would have like to have written at length here about the Lacanian theory of language,[141] but this would risk taking us further away from the topic. Nevertheless, upon reflection, we ought to recognize that every delusional phenomenon is ultimately expressed, that is to say, spoken. Thus, the best way of analysing a delusion or an abnormal psychic process is still to squarely face the making explicit of that delusion.

Drawing a parallel between Ey and Lacan is difficult for the good reason that the latter aims above all to produce a logic of the delusional fact. 'Madness', Lacan says, is neither more nor less than a 'stasis of being'.[142] The madman, facing the disorder of the world (which is a disorder of his own consciousness, transitivism), wants to establish the law of his heart.[143] So, two solutions remain possible: either he breaks the circle through outward violence or else he strikes a blow to himself by way of social after-effect.

Such is the general formula of madness. It applies to 'any one of those phrases whereby is accomplished, more or less in each destiny, the dialectical development of the human being, and it is always accomplished as a stasis of being'.[144] The law of the heart that the

---

[140][Bonnafé et al., *Le Problème de la psychogenèse*, p. 34.]

[141][Lacan's text continues with a reflection on language.]

[142][Bonnafé et al., *Le Problème de la psychogenèse*, p. 39.] Levinas, on an ontological plane, recognizes that inauthenticity is introduced into existence under cover of a *stasis of being* (Emmanuel Levinas, *De l'existence à l'existant* [Paris: J. Vrin, 1947, p. 139 *sq.*]).

[143][In his presentation, Lacan uses the section on the 'The law of the heart, and the frenzy of self-conceit' in Hegel's *Phänomenologie des Geistes* to analyse Alceste's madness in Molière's *Le Misanthrope*.]

[144][Such is the general formula for madness that we find in Hegel, since you shouldn't think that I am innovating, even though I thought I had to take the care to present it to you in a figurative form. I say: general formula of madness, in the sense that it can be seen applied in a particular way to any one of those phases whereby is accomplished, more or less in each destiny, the dialectical development of the human being, and that madness is always carried out in it as a stasis of being; as an ideal identification which characterizes this point of a particular destiny.

(Bonnafé et al., *Le Problème de la psychogenèse*, p. 39).]

madman wants to impose is the price of freedom. The madman is no longer an insane person, but one who has accepted to inventory all the abysses that freedom offers. By making delusion the contingent effect of a lack of control, of a deficit, Ey goes right by the problem and, correlatively, its solution. The perpetrator of a crime of passion is not deficient since he is adjudged responsible. The act has a meaning that medical jurisprudence will clarify through its practice. Therefore, phenomenologically, the deficiency is unacceptable.

In closing, I would like to recall the broad outline of psychogenesis as Lacan conceives it. Invoking an implicit Jungian position, Lacan goes beyond the concept of imago, turning the phenomenon of projection, which Lévy-Bruhl presents as an index of a primitive mentality, into the cornerstone of his system. He ties the unhappy consciousness to the magic consciousness. Internally, then, Lacan seems to be the point of encounter between Hegel and Lévy-Bruhl.

Where with Jung the image was the projection in the object of a conflictual subjective state or the second side of an ideal, with Lacan it becomes the fellow human in its human generality, for the adult, and in its intoxicated ingenuity, for the child. The author grounds the history of psychic life in the mirror phase. Within this phase, two instances join up: the primordial Ego, which is ontologically unstable, and the existential complex engaged in a struggle, in which Freud perfectly distinguished the death instinct. 'At the start of psychic development, the primordial Ego as essentially alienated is tied with the primitive sacrifice as essentially suicidal'.[145] Thus, Lacan says: 'there is an essential discordance within human reality. And even if the organic conditions of intoxication are prevalent, the consent of freedom would still be necessary. The fact that madness manifests itself among humans only after the "age of reason" clearly verifies the Pascalian intuition that "a child is not a man".[146]

---

[145][Bonnafé et al., Le Problème de la psychogenèse, p. 50.]

[146][Here Fanon paraphrases the text that follows the preceding citation: 'Hence that primordial discordance between the Ego and being would be the fundamental note, which would resound in an entire harmonic scale through the phases of psychic history, the function of which would be to resolve this discordance by developing it. All resolution of this discordance by means of an illusory coincidence of reality with the ideal would resonate right down to the depths of the imaginary node of narcissistic suicidal aggression. But this mirage of appearances in which the organic conditions of intoxication, for instance, can play their role, demands the ungraspable consent of freedom, as it appears in this, that madness only manifests among humans and after the 'age of reason', which verifies the Pascalian intuition that 'a child is not a man'.]

What are we to conclude from these few considerations? And besides, is it even necessary to do so? Would it not be better to leave open a discussion that involves the very limits of freedom, that is to say of humanity's responsibility? In closing, I would like to speak about the new tendency in the human sciences: psychosomatic medicine.[147]

This science, bolstered by the fundamental ubiquity existing within the nervous system, convinced that the sympathetic [system] in fact represents the real frontier, that is to say the effective plan of action between the organic and the functional, proposes to go beyond the opposition lesional disorders/functional disorders towards a unitary perspective of the ill person. Defenders of this theory base themselves on anatomophysiological and particularly physiopathological data.

'*Functional impairment* is a transitory disturbance, a temporary anatomical modification, detectable with histochemical techniques, reversible, liable to *restitutio ad integrum*, but it is also capable, through its repetition and through multiple transitions, of leading to a lesion. The *organic lesion* is the definitive alteration; it is in constant evolution, often irreversible and maintains itself in a sort of vicious circle. Functional disturbance is liable to lead to a lesion; there is no illness of an organ, but of the entire organism: it is the morbid unity in the somatic unity'. From these first elements, the following observations can be made: '1) the most localized visceral diseases can have a psychic impact; 2) mental diseases can have visceral or somatic repercussions and manifestations; and 3) lastly, psychic causes can trigger and foster alone the most authentic visceral diseases'.[148]

We see what such facts imply, but the authors clarify their position to the utmost. From the gastric ulcer of psychic origin to emotional impotence, including diencephalic schizophrenias, the progression is continuous. One of the unquestionable interests of this new orientation in medicine is its resolute bearing on the very core of the

---

[147][Fanon had probably been expected to broach this topic, as it was the speciality of his doctoral supervisor. It nevertheless remains that this interest in the articulation of the functional and the organic remains constant throughout his work, and is evident in both *Peau noir, masques blancs* and in *Les Damnés de la terre*, which contains a section on 'psychosomatic symptoms' (pp. 217–19).]

[148][Dechaume, 'Affections du sympathique', pp. 1070–1.]

human conflict. Developing Jungian conclusions to the extreme, this current is proof of the possibility of a medicine of the person.

This doctrine could be reproached for its esoteric character. Likewise, with psychoanalysis, the 'singular' colloquium risks taking the aspect of a confession. But is not every consultation inevitably a confession? Is it not therefore a call, as Professor P. Savy has said?[149] And is the appeasement that the doctor brings to ulcerous pain by prescribing bismuth very different from that which he brings to muddled and dazed minds, as only our civilization can produce them, by strengthening the very bases of psychic synthesis?

One ought above all not believe that this is a modified psychoanalysis. The authors are resolutely opposed to psychoanalysts. To the work of analytical dissection, they contrast the more aesthetic work of synthesis.[150] Psychoanalysis entails a pessimistic view of humanity. The medicine of the person presents itself as a deliberate choice for optimism in the face of human reality.

Conclusions

1) The mental disorders described in spinocerebellar heredodegeneration are, in their order of frequency, the following: a) mental retardation in all its forms; b) character disorders with their instinctive perversions; and c) certain delusions, notably of persecution. Here I have presented a case

---

[149][Fanon's library, probably not unlike those of most medical students at the time, contained two works by Paul Savy: *Précis de pratique médicale* (Paris: Doin & Cie, 1942) and *Traité de thérapeutique clinique* (Paris: Masson, 1948).]

[150][Toward the end of his article Dechaume quotes an article from 1946 by Hécaen and Duchêne on psychosomatic medicine: 'Psychosomatic medicine is thus revealed,' say Hécaen and Duchêne, 'not as the pure and simple application of psychiatry or psychoanalysis to general medicine, but as an original synthesis able to recognize the multiple causality of morbid phenomena. It presents an effort to apprehend the individual in its biological totality and not to neglect in the therapeutic act any of the factors involved' (p. 1072). The orientation of Dechaume's 'medicine of the person' is ultimately Christian. When Fanon returns to the question of psychosomatic medicine in the important chapter 5 of *Les Damnés de la terre*, 'Colonial War and Mental Disorders' (series D), he claims to adopt the viewpoint of the Soviet psychiatrists so as to disentangle himself from the risk of 'idealism' inherent in the psychosomatic conception.]

of delusion of possession involving a hysterical structure. I have been unable to find any similar cases in the literature.

2) The single problem raised here was that of the relations between neurological and psychiatric disorder, without the solution having been provided. But this work has put into question the hypotheses of mechanism and of dynamism in neurology.

3) Saquet presents three hypotheses: a) that medullary/cerebellar lesions are the cause of mental disorders; b) that there is a merely simple coincidence between these two orders of phenomena; and c) that among these patients an evident predisposition exists and the lesions of the cerebral cortex result from an associated process.

The study of this observation permits of two conclusions. Mental disturbances, mental retardation, and psychological immaturation observed in spinocerebellar heredodegeneration, are related to the diffuse anatomical lesions of this clinical cluster. By contrast, systematized delusions, hysterical manifestations and neurotic behaviours must be considered reactional conducts of an ego at odds with intersocial relations. However, from an organo-dynamist viewpoint, it would be necessary to account for disorders of proprioceptive sensibility that, in the course of delusional experiences,[151] are able to draw the delusion to this or that structure.

Bibliography[152]

Adano E., *Maladie de Friedreich*, dissertation, Buenos Aires, 1904.
Bagh K. V., 'Friedreich's disease with progressive dementia; a typical case', *Annals of Internal Medicine*, 1946, pp. 241–253.
Barú, 'Sur la maladie de Friedreich', *Archives uruguayennes de médecine*, vol. 10, Chirurgie et spécialités, 1937.

---

[151]Lacan might say 'fecund moments'. ['Moments féconds du délire', *in* Bonnafé *et al.*, *Le Problème de la psychogenèse*, p. 37.]
[152]For a complete bibliography of Friedreich's ataxia and of the group of spinocerebellar heredodegeneration, see Pierre Mollaret's dissertation, Paris, 1929. [The bibliography of Fanon's dissertation is reprinted here. We have completed the references and corrected some typos.]

Benon R., and Lerat G., 'Hérédo-ataxie cérébelleuse et délire', *Gazette médicale de Nantes*, 1st June 1920.[153]

Birkmayer W., and Lenz H., 'Friedreich's ataxia in patient with dementia praecox case', *Wiener Klinische Wochenschrift*, vol. 52, 14 July 1939, pp. 667–669.

Bleuler M., and Walder H., 'Mental disorders in Friedreich's ataxia and their classification among basic forms of mental diseases' ['Die geistigen Storungen bei der hereditaren Friedreich'schen Ataxie und ihre Einordnung in die Auffassung von Grundformen seelischen Krankseins'], *Schweizer Archiv für Neurologie und Psychiatrie*, vol. 58, 1946, pp. 44–59.

Van Bogaert L., 'Les atrophies cérébelleuses avec troubles mentaux', *Compte rendu du 32ᵉ congrès des médecins aliénistes et neurologues*, Anvers, 1928, pp. 277–286.

Van Bogaert L., and Bertrand I., 'Une variété d'atrophie olivo-pontine à évolution subaigüe avec troubles démentiels', *Revue neurologique*, vol. 1, 1929, p. 165.

Van Bogaert L., and Borremans P., 'Cortical cerebellar atrophy with beginning of axial sclerosis and involvement of central grey nuclei, mental disorders and symmetric lipomatosis', *Journal belge de neurologie et de psychiatrie*, vol. 47, May 1947, pp. 249–267.

Van Bogaert L., and Moreau M., 'Combinaison de l'amyotrophie de Charcot-Marie-Tooth et de la maladie de Friedreich chez plusieurs membres de la même famille', *L'Encéphale*, vol. 34, 1939, pp. 312–320.

Van Bogaert L., 'Les maladies systématisées', *in* André Lemierre et al. (ed.), *Traité de médecine*, volume 16, Paris: Masson et Cie, 1947.

Bonnus G., *Contribution à l'étude de la maladie de Friedreich à début tardif*, dissertation, Paris, 1898.

Del Cañizo A., d'Ors J. H., and Álvarez Sala J. L., 'Contribución al estudio de la enfermedad de Friedreich', *Archivos de neurobiologia*, vol. 13, no. 46, 1933, pp. 1025–1052.

Claude H., 'À propos de l'atrophie cérébelleuse dans la démence précoce', *L'Encéphale*, vol. 1, 1909, p. 361.

Combes P., *Maladie de Friedreich: essai historique anatomo-clinique et physiologique*, dissertation, Montpellier, 1902.

Darre H., Mollaret P., and Landowski M., 'La maladie de Roussy-Lévy n'est-elle qu'une forme fruste ou une forme abortive de la maladie de Friedreich?', *Revue neurologique*, December 1933.

---

[153] [We have been unable to find a record of this text under this reference. But it can be found in *L'Encéphale* (vol. 15, 1920, pp. 565–72), as indicated in the body of the dissertation.]

Davies D. L., 'Psychiatric changes associated with Friedreich's ataxia', *Journal of Neurology, Neurosurgery and Psychiatry*, vol. 12, August 1949, pp. 246–250.

De Smedt E., De Wulf A., Dyckmans J., and van Borgaert L., 'Quatre cas de maladie de Friedreich avec troubles mentaux dont trois dans la même famille', *Journal belge de neurologie et de psychiatrie*, vol. 37, 1937, p. 155.

Dufour H., 'Démence précoce simple. Ensemble de signes associés à des troubles cérébelleux, démence précoce de type cérébelleux', *L'Encéphale*, vol. 1, 1909, pp. 155–158.

Dupré J., and Logre E., 'Maladie de Friedreich et débilité mentale avec perversions instinctives', *L'Encéphale*, vol. 2, 1913, pp. 557–559.

Ey H., Bonafé L., Follin S., Lacan J., and Rouart J., *Le Problème de la psychogenèse des névroses et des psychoses* [1946], Paris: Desclée de Brouwer, 1950.

Ey H., *Études psychiatriques*, vols. 1 and 3, Paris: Desclée de Brouwer, 1950.

Ey H., de Ajuriguerra J., and Hécaen H., *Les Rapports de la neurologie et de la psychiatrie*, Paris: Hermann et Cie, 1947.

Fouque P., *Maladies mentales familiales*, dissertation, Paris, 1899.

Gareiso A., and Vijnovsky B., 'Developmental stages of Friedreich's disease in three brothers and sister. Aetiology, symptomatology, diagnosis, prognosis, therapy and evolution', *Archivos argentinos de pediatría*, vol. 23, May 1945, pp. 363–369.

Götze W., 'Neural muscular atrophy and heredo-ataxia as manifestations of same disease, with marked vegetative disorders and mental changes [Neurale Muskelatrophie und Heredoataxie als Erscheinungsformen einer einheitlichen Erkrankung]', *Archiv für Psychiatrie*, vol. 113, 1941, pp. 550–573.

Guillain G., 'Le mode de début de la maladie de Friedreich', *Revue neurologique*, vol. 53, 1930, p. 248.

Guiraud P., and (de) Ajuriaguerra J., 'Aréflexie, pieds creux, amyotrophie accentuée signe d'Argyll et troubles mentaux', *Annales médico-psychologiques*, vol. 92, 1, 1934, pp. 229–234.

Guiraud P., and Derombies M., 'Un cas de maladie familiale de Roussy-Lévy avec troubles mentaux', *Annales médico-psychologiques*, vol. 92, no. 1, 1934, pp. 224–229.

Hiller F., 'A study of speech disorders in Friedreich's ataxia', *Archives of Neurology and Psychiatry*, vol. 22, 1929, pp. 75–90.

Klein D., 'Recherches familiales, corporelles et psychopathologiques dans une famille de Friedreich [Familienkundliche, körperliche und psychopathologische Untersuchungen über eine Friedreich-Familie]', *Schweizer Archiv für Neurologie und Psychiatrie*, vol. 39, 1937, pp. 89–116 and pp. 320–329.

Knoepfel H. K., and Macken J., 'Le syndrome psycho-organique dans les hérédo-ataxies', *Journal belge de neurologie et de psychiatrie*, vol. 47, May 1947, pp. 314–323.

Lhermite J., and Klippel M., 'Anatomie pathologique de la démence précoce', *L'Encéphale*, vol. 2, 1908, p. 656.

Lhermite J., and Klippel M., 'De l'atrophie du cervelet dans la démence précoce', *L'Encéphale*, vol. 1, 1909, pp. 154–161.

Lloyd J. H., 'Friedreich's ataxia in two colored boys – brothers', *Journal of Nervous and mental Disease*, vol. 51, 1920, p. 537.

Long E., 'Débilité mentale et maladie de Friedreich', *L'Encéphale*, vol. 2, 1912, p. 486.

Maere M., and Muyle G., 'Un syndrome d'ataxie cérébelleuse progressive avec oligophrénie chez deux jeunes israélites polonais', *Journal belge de neurologie et de psychiatrie*, vol. 38, 1938, pp. 96–108.

Mollaret P., *La Maladie de Friedreich. Étude physio-clinique*, dissertation, Paris, 1929.

Monakow C. V., and Mourgue R., *Introduction biologique à l'étude de la neurologie et de la psychopathologie*, Paris: Felix Alcan, 1928.

Nolan M. J., 'Three cases of Friedreich's ataxia associated with genitous idiocy', *Dublin Journal of Medical Science*, vol. 99, 1895, p. 369.

Paulian D., and Tudor M., 'Clinical study of two cases of Friedreich's disease', *Bucuresti Med.*, vol. 11, April 1939, pp. 21–24.

Pellizi G. B., 'Paraplégie spasmodique familiale et démence précoce', *Rivista sperimentale di freniatra*, vol. 31, no. 1, 1906, p. s1.

Persch R., 'Heredo-degenerative schizophrenia with combined systematic disease (Friedreich's ataxia and progressive muscular dystrophy); case' ['Heredodegenerative Schizophrenie bei kombinierter Systemerkrankung'. *Psychiatria Neurologia. Wochnsehr, no. 40, July. 1939*, pp. 311–313].

Pienkowski M., 'Syndrome d'ataxie cérébelleuse précoce proche de l'hérédo-ataxie cérébelleuse de Pierre-Marie', *Revue neurologique*, vol. 2, no. 2, 1932, pp. 246–247.

Refsum S., 'Heredopathia atactica polyneuritiformis; familial syndrome not hitherto described; contribution to clinical study of hereditary diseases of nervous system', *Acta psychiatrica et neurologica*, vol. 38, 1946, p. 1303.

Saquet, *Des troubles mentaux dans la maladie de Friedreich et dans l'hérédo-ataxie cérébelleuse*, dissertation, Paris, 1919.

Scripture E. W., 'Studies in speech neurology', *Journal of Neurology and Psychopathology*, vol. 11, no. 42, 1930, pp. 156–162.

Taddei G., 'Le forme di passaggio tra atassia ereditaria di Friedreich et eredo atassia cerebellare di Parie', *Rivista critica di clinica medica*, vol. 22, 1921, pp. 169–178.

Trelles J. O., 'À propos d'un cas anatomo-clinique de maladie de Friedreich avec troubles mentaux. Les lésions cérébelleuses dans la maladie de Friedreich, les atrophies cérébelleuses avec troubles mentaux', *Annales médico-psychologiques*, vol. 2, 1934, pp. 760–786.

Valente A., 'Transitional form between Friedreich's disease and cerebellar heredo-ataxia; progressive muscular dystrophy with congenital abnormality of heart', *Revista de neurologia e psychiatria de São Paulo*, no. 4, April–June 1938, pp. 63–74. [original reference: Valente A., 'Forma de transição entie a doença de Friedreich e a heredo-ataxia cerebellar: associação de uma dystrophia muscular progressiva e de um vicio congenito do coração'.]

Vincelet J., *Étude sur l'anatomie pathologique de la malade de Friedreich*, dissertation, Paris, 1900.

De Vries E., 'Two cases of congenital cerebellar ataxia and mental weakness so-called imbecillitas cérébello-atactical', *Nederlands Tijdschrift voor Geneeskunde*, vol. 67, 1923, p. 849.

Winckler C., and Jacobi J. W., 'Appréciations sur l'état mental d'un patient atteint d'ataxie héréditaire', *Psychiatrische en Neurologische Bladen*, vol. 2, 1898, p. 36.

2 LETTER TO MAURICE DESPINOY

Frantz Fanon, June 1953[1]

My dear Despinoy,

A win – a rather slight one, but a win all the same – I am an HP [psychiatric hospitals] doctor and a few hours after the result I applied for a position in Guadeloupe. The position is not available until December. As for Martinique, there can be no question of it. There has been no news from Mme Blanchard. So I am rather annoyed. The minister sent me the list of available positions: Blida, Pontorson, Aurillac, Lannemezan, Aix-en-Provence, Auch, Rennes.

I am rather annoyed, since I will have to delay the studies I have begun. I have met someone named Dell, who passed the competitive exam. He is the brother of your Dell. I handed him your letter. He will write to you. In any case, if a second position cannot be created in Martinique, at least there is Guadeloupe. Neuve-Église passed the exam and wants to go there. I am at a slight disadvantage. I placed thirteenth out of twenty-three. At least eight people, if we except

[1]Undated letter (IMEC Fonds Fanon, FNN 2.4), probably from June 1953, to Maurice Despinoy, a psychiatrist for whom Fanon interned at Saint-Alban in 1952 and who was to establish the Colson psychiatric hospital in Martinique (since 2014 named the Centre hospitalier Maurice-Despinoy) in December 1953. On Fanon's interest in his experiments with lithium salts in the treatment of psychoses and his relations with Despinoy in general, see Jacques Tosquellas, 'Entretien avec Maurice Despinoy', *Sud/Nord. Folies et culture*, vol. 22, 2007, pp. 104–14, https://doi.org/10.3917/sn.022.0105. Letter transcribed in *Sans Frontière*, special issue on Frantz Fanon, February 1982, and corrected in line with the manuscript conserved at IMEC.

those who will not take up a position, will choose ahead of me. That is obviously depressing.

This morning Josie is taking her Latin philology exam and I am taking my psycho-sociology exam this afternoon. I haven't gone into the curriculum, incidentally, but I paid the enrolment fee, so ….

I will return to Saint-Alban tomorrow morning.
Sincerely,

Figure 2 Saint-Alban Psychiatric Hospital at the time Fanon practiced there. Courtesy: SACPI (Saint-Alban arts culture psychothérapie institutionnelle).

3 TRAIT D'UNION[1]

Frantz Fanon, editorials from the ward journal, Trait d'Union, *of Saint-Alban psychiatric hospital, December 1952–March 1953*[2]

19 December 1952, no. 127. *Weariness*

The slightest conversation with a patient, often provokes sentences or expressions such as, 'I am tired, I have no taste for anything, I am weary, I am lazy ... If I listened to myself, I would stay all the time in bed. Talking tires me. I wish I could stay in a corner without moving.'

At other times, none of this is expressed, but in each department, do we not know women and men always isolated, not speaking to anyone, who seem to be examples of people for whom any effort, any speech, every gesture is a mountain to climb?

A contemporary philosopher, fortunately not a psychiatrist, has voiced a sentence which I believe is of some interest to us: 'If you want to go deeper into the structure of a particular country, you have to visit its psychiatric hospitals.'

And certainly, it must be admitted, is there not in the world of today a wave of carelessness, of indifference, of letting go? When we talk to people, do we not discover exhaustion quickly enough?

---

[1] [Translator's note: *Trait d'union* literally means hyphen in English, but in French can also serve as a metaphor to designate a person who serves as an intermediator, as a bridge between two beings or objects.]
[2] Here we republish recently discovered editorials by Fanon written for the ward newspaper of the Saint-Alban psychiatric hospital, where he was François Tosquelles' intern.

JOURNAL Intérieur de l'Hôpital Psychiatrique de St-Alban
ABONNEMENT 3 MOIS 120 FRS PRIX: I ET 10 FRS
—CE JOURNAL NE DOIT PAS SORTIR DE L'HOPITAL—

N° 127
VENDREDI
19
DECEMBRE
1952

Trait d'Union

LASSITUDE

La moindre conversation avec un malade, provoque souvent des phrases ou des expressions comme, " Je suis fatigué, je n'ai plus goût à rien, je suis las, je suis paresseux.. Si je m'écoutais, je resterais tout le temps au lit. Parler, me fatigue.

Je voudrais pouvoir rester dans un coin sans bouger."

D'autres fois, rien de cela n'est exprimé mais dans chaque service, ne connaît-on pas, des femmes et des hommes toujours isolés, ne parlant à personne qui semblent bien être des exemples de gens pour qui tout effort, toute parole, tout geste est une montagne à soulever ?

Un Philosophe contemporain, heureusement non psychiatre a prononcé une phrase qui, je crois, présente pour nous un certain intérêt : "Si vous voulez approfondir la structure d'un pays déterminé, il faut visiter ses hopitaux psychiatriques".

Et certes, il faut l'avouer, n'y a-t-il pas dans le monde d'aujourd'hui une vague de laisser aller, de laisser dire, de laisser faire. Quand on discute avec les gens, ne découvre-t-on pas assez rapidement une certaine fatigue ?

Si nous nous interrogeons, nous voyons que tout cela répond à une démission.

Quand un chef de gouvernement considère que l'opposition est trop forte ou qu'il ne résoud pas selon les vœux du pays les problèmes actuels qu'il n'est plus enfin à la hauteur de la vie, il démissionne, se sent las, fatigué, désabusé, désespéré.

Vivre, ce n'est pas seulement manger et boire, ou du moins, c'est manger et boire, et puis après beaucoup d'autres choses. Celui qui démissionne ne veut plus que manger et boire ; celui qui démissionne totalement, ne veut même plus manger ni boire. Être las, être fatigué, ce n'est pas seulement être las et fatigué des autres mais surtout de soi-même.

Dr. Fanon

(à suivre)

Figure 3 Ward Journal, Saint-Alban Psychiatric Hospital. Courtesy: SACPI (Saint-Alban arts culture psychothérapie institutionnnelle).

They were kindly provided by Association SACPI (Saint-Alban, Art, Culture, Psychiatrie Institutionnelle). We have corrected some obvious punctuation errors. The reader will note how present the theme of vigilance is in these texts from the start. It forms a central point of Fanon's thinking on commitment – on engagement with the present – and it underlies his distrust of all institutionalization See Figure 3.

If we question ourselves, we see that all this corresponds to a renunciation. When a head of government finds that the opposition is too strong or that he cannot solve, according to the wishes of the country, current problems, that he is no longer at the summit of life, he resigns, feels weary, tired, disillusioned, desperate.

Living is not just eating and drinking, or it is at least eating and drinking and then after that a lot of other things. Whoever gives up wants only food and drink; he who gives up totally, does not even want to eat or drink. To be tired, to be weary, is not only to be tired and weary of others but above all of oneself.

Dr. Fanon

[Part Two, 26 December 1952]

We must not confuse 'weariness' with 'rest'. No more 'weariness' with 'idleness'. Weariness is the refusal to continue; we have been able to start, we have even gone quite far towards carrying out the act, but there now arises this immense weight in the arms, this unusual heaviness in the legs, this unusual void in the head and above all this anguish that harrows your breast.

'We must try to live' said Valéry,[3] let us say, we must try to continue. If at forty, and it must be said, it is especially at forty that it appears, this desire is born in me to do nothing anymore, or more exactly if at forty, I realize when I wake up one morning that I no longer have the taste for anything, what must be understood?

I do not want to give an explanation that is valid for everyone but often I think that it looks this way. For ten or fifteen years, I lived like that, without worry; without worry because I was convinced that something was going to happen. Perhaps I will be told that I was at least worried about that. But I was not even waiting for it and I was expecting a lot of things from it, I did not do anything to know what it was.

I did not do anything to provoke or facilitate what I was waiting for. Like the little Indian in the Buñuel film *Los Olvidados* who waits for his father for a whole day in the face of all evidence that his father has deliberately forgotten him.

---

3 [Paul Valéry, 'Le Cimetière marin', 1920, line 139.]

Well! At forty, I am a forgotten person: the world has not responded to my expectations, the world has not come to kiss me on the forehead or caress my cheek. Is that it?

Alas no! I have not been forgotten, it is I who have forgotten, and when I say at forty that I am weary of working or suffering or being unhappy, on the contrary, I must understand that I am tired of having waited like those friends whom one expects, one day, two days, three days, and then dammit! you don't wait for them anymore.

In one sense, being weary at forty, is saying damn to the world, to others, to life, to oneself, damn, damn, damn, to everyone, damn to those who want to be nice to me, damn to those who don't like me, damn! Besides, I am weary, I am tired.

Doctor Fanon

(to be continued)[4]

30 January 1953, no. 133. *The human being faced with things*

In the world, there are objects, trees, fields, cars, planes. In the world, there are things. The individual who looks at these objects, these things, can remain indifferent to them. He can also desire them. To want or to desire a car is to want to have the desire for a car no longer. To desire something is to want to desire it no longer. It is usually said that desire sees further than the thing desired: the desired thing is always a limit.

A change of plane transpires when a person is put in place of a thing. Every person belongs to an institution, is embodied in a framework. If he's a military man, he'll be an officer or a private. He can be a stonemason, an entrepreneur or a peasant. Such a man is married or single; he has children or does not, likes reading or cinema or dominos. When you meet a person, a certain timidity nearly always arises. A new farmer comes to a farm: others look at him from afar at first, before drawing nearer to him: someone then says good day to him … At noon, the social act of eating and drinking, you might say, works to untie tongues. But at the start, they respect each other, take each other's measure by looking.

4[No sequel or conclusion was printed in later issues of Trait d'Union. – ed. These two editorials on weariness were translated by Robert J.C. Young.]

Whenever you meet a new person, you speak, you can only speak. Language is what breaks the silence and the silences. Then you can communicate or commune *with* this person. The neighbour in the Christian sense is always an accomplice. An accomplice who can betray, as with any accomplice. To fall out with someone is to realize that you have nothing in common. To commune with means to commune when facing something.

An intention forms the basis of all communication, but this intention must be sincere. In order to discover and desire that sincerity, a distinction must be made between the world and the sum of objects to be found on the earth. Faced with objects, we act differently than when we are faced with other people. We eat in order to eat; we breathe in order to breathe. This doing, we live. And we eat or breathe sincerely. To live is a kind of sincerity. It ought not be said that eating or drinking or smoking is not living. We must not scorn what is referred to as the 'every day'. There is no need always to be on a search for the unusual. Creative intentions can emerge from out of the common. But I will come back to this another day ...

On Saturday morning at the newspaper meeting, we talked a bit about sleep. And Doctor Tosquelles reminded us that many patients ask for sleeping medication. This difficulty in getting to sleep is called insomnia. What is insomnia? Insomnia is a way of living that likes to think it is justified. You stay awake when there is a reason to stay awake. The ordinary man is able to suspend his wakefulness. His sincerity is such that he possesses the freedom to be suspended. The insomniac does not have this freedom to sleep, to relax, to doze. The insomniac does not stay awake: it's the night that stays awake. It stays awake.

6 March 1953, no 138. *Yesterday, today and tomorrow*

For a person and a country alike, one of the most difficult things is to keep all three constituents of time in view: past, present and future. Bearing these three constituents in mind amounts to recognizing a great importance in waiting, in hope, in the future; it means knowing that the acts we performed yesterday can have consequences in ten years' time and that we might therefore have to justify these acts. Memory is therefore required to achieve this union of past, present and future.

However, memory ought not to get the upper hand with humans. Memory is often the mother of tradition. Now, if it is good to have a tradition, it is also agreeable to be able to go beyond that tradition and invent a new mode of living. Someone who considers that the present is worthless and that our sole interest lies with the past is, in a sense, a person who is lacking two dimensions and on whom you cannot count. Someone who deems that you must live with all your might in the here and now and that you do not have to worry about tomorrow or yesterday can be dangerous, since he believes that each minute is severed from the minutes that follow or precede it, and that he is the only person on this planet. Someone who turns away from the past and the present, who dreams of a distant future, both desirable and desired, is also deprived of the opposite everyday terrain on which one must act to accomplish the future sought-for. You thus see that a person always has to take into account the present, past and future.

If we ask someone in hospital: 'When did you become ill?' and he tells us: 'I cannot recall', we say that this person is trying to forget bad memories – illness, being without his parents – and behaves as if the past were dead. If we ask someone, a patient: 'What day is it today?', and he replies: 'I know neither the day, the month nor the year', we should say to ourselves that this patient has lost all interest in the world and acts as if he were dead. Similarly, if the patient takes leave of himself and makes no effort to get better, to understand his troubles, to fight against his [the] illness affecting him; if this patient makes no attempt to criticize his own attitude, his own ideas, we should think that this patient is no longer interested in the true life that is in society, and that he has already accepted that he is going to remain ill his entire life.

The past, present and future must comprise human beings' three predominant interests; it is impossible to see and achieve anything positive, valid and lasting without taking all three elements into account.

27 March 1953, no 141. *The therapeutic role of engagement*
One thing is very important in the domain of psychiatry; I mean here the constant concern to refer a patient's every word, every act and every facial expression to the illness affecting him or her. Each gesture, each word, each facial expression must be referred to the affection from which the patient is suffering, to the current stage

of the illness, to the emergence (or not) of chronicity. But if this is important in psychiatry, a second question then arises: who is apt to register these modifications, these fluctuations, these changes, these mutations? *A priori*, it must be said that the patient is rarely in a position to undertake this self-observation on his own, given that he suffers from his disease as much as he lives it. However, were it possible for him, materially and organically possible, he would like to say to his doctor or orderly: 'I am going to become agitated, my hallucinations are going to start up again, my insomnia is coming back; I'm beginning to feel anxious'.

Just as someone who has a stomach ulcer in spring will go to see his doctor to resume his diet, the catatonic, upon feeling the return of his inertia, his disinterest, his mutism, would, if he could – if he was not abominably united (*faire corps*) with the rigidity of the body we call catatonia, with that substantialized body, with that body that strives only to be a body – of course say to us: 'Do something so that I do not become catatonic again'. But then, if neither the doctor nor the orderly stands in this role as vigilant guardian for the patient, then it may happen that, in his vigilance against catatonia, this patient's angry act comes to be labelled by the orderly as a nasty reaction, the patient as irksome, disagreeable.

I often get an orderly to tell me about this or that patient. The replies she gives are always vague. I get the impression that the orderly does not ever consider the patient that is to be looked after and treated; there is no psychotherapeutic tension, you might say. I am not addressing a reproach to the ward orderlies here; instead, since I am in fact in charge of first-stage professional training, I am suggesting a technique for performing the job well. If you want to carry out your job perfectly as an orderly, you must try to take note of two things in your ward: the signs indicating that this patient is getting better; and the signs indicating that this other patient will relapse or develop towards chronicity. But above all, a piece of advice: never concede that a patient is definitively chronic, for by considering a patient to be a chronic case, you are no longer heeding the activity of psychotherapy. I even think, but this issue exceeds my prerogatives, that orderlies ought not to be left too long in a hospital's so-called chronic services, since they lose the vigilance that is the fundamental feature of the modern orderly.

4 ON SOME CASES TREATED WITH THE BINI METHOD[1]

François Tosquelles and Frantz Fanon (Saint-Alban), July 1953[2]

We would like to put up for your consideration and criticism some concrete cases of psychiatric therapy in which organotherapy and psychotherapy, with everything that is most antithetical and most complementary about them, together combine in a coherent and effective ensemble.

The point here is to situate annihilation therapy through repeated shocks within an institutional therapeutic performance. Our experiment involves cases of serious neurosis or of chronic delusional psychosis with a strong pathoplastic charge. Setting out from some favourable facts, the theoretical orientation of which remains highly debatable, the intention here is to go beyond the stereotyped framework of what, in the psychiatric literature, has

---

[1][The Bini method, or electroconvulsive shock therapy, is named after Professor Lucio Bini, who delivered the first ever report on the first use of electricity to induce a seizure for therapeutic purposes in psychotic patients delivered at the 3rd International Neurological Congress in Copenhagen in August 1939 – translator's note.]

[2]*Comptes rendus du Congrès des médecins aliénistes et neurologues de France et des pays de langue française (51st session, Pau, 20–26 July 1953)*, Paris: Masson, 1953, pp. 539–44. [In this text, Tosquelles and Fanon explain how electroconvulsive therapy, insulin shock therapy and narcotherapy can be used to produce a revival or reprogramming of the personality, thus opening up the way to psychotherapy.]

become a commonplace devoid of practical significance: namely the imprecise appeal that is made to so-called complementary psychotherapies or ergotherapies, which are to be established either consecutively or in parallel with classical organotherapies: electric shock, insulin, leucotomy, etc.

Among the nine cases that we have treated using electroconvulsive therapy over the last three years, all with some efficacy, if not total success, we will dwell on a more elaborate description of an 'exemplary' case, and reserve another paper for the problem of the legitimacy of the very limited indications of the annihilation method within the framework of institutional therapies.

The case that concerns us here was not the first in date among those making up our experience [with electroconvulsive therapy]. One of the present authors, after a series of attempts at trial and error, was able to work through to completion with Millon[3] on the therapy of two 'desperate' cases. However, here is the first case in which the coherent set of therapeutic conducts that we are suggesting was applied in complete knowledge of the fact and in line with a preconceived plan. The other cases are largely superposable onto it.

Doctor Valat of Limoges entrusted us with a patient of forty-five years of age, a nun, who for several months had presented – he says –

> serious mental disorders, characterized by some delusional ideas of persecution, serious behavioural problems manifested in raucous cries, screaming at any time and in any place (in the house, outside, at church). She presents alternate and intermittent diurnal or nocturnal psychomotor agitation, sometimes with completely incoherent but short-lived delusions. In addition, she is readily aggressive to persons of her entourage. Her mental disorders, already longstanding and evolving, make her retention in a psychiatric hospital indispensable, etc.

This sister arrived in our unit accompanied by only one of her companions. At the first meeting, we had to foil the well-meaning ruse that her community had devised. The patient, lucid, sthenic and unwilling, had not the slightest awareness of her disease, and refused all psychological-psychiatric examinations, which she deemed

---

[3] [Robert Millon (1923–2009) became one of Tosquelles' interns at St Alban in 1947, at the same time as Jean Oury.]

incompatible with the respect owed to her condition as a nun and to her personality. The plan was thus to trick her, by putting her in the ward for acute sufferers, monitoring her closely to prevent her escape and divesting her of her religious habit during her sleep. Her companion was to wait until night time before leaving. At the risk of being misunderstood, and making the most of the voluntary character of the placement, we refused to admit the patient without a first explanatory session together with the accompanying sister. During this interview, it was partially possible to overcome the patient's reluctance and to get her to recognize the appropriateness of her placement in an observational clinic (*service libre*), thus facilitating her turning up in the ward dressed in civilian clothes from the outset. That naturally included the right to go on extra-hospital outings outside of examination and treatment hours and the observance of the ward rules and regulations. However, the patient took up our offer more because 'she does not argue against the orders of her superiors' (*sic*) than out of a real understanding of her situation. The first interviews confirmed our initial impression of a strong paranoid personality, but we were unable to conquer her absolute sthenic reticence. Proper verbal contact was possible when she was asked about practical questions concerning life at the hospital. However, the most total silence surrounded any attempt to get information about her personal, familial or community life. During this period, we were unable to obtain any delusional confession from her, or any indication that would explain her strange behaviour: she showed no resistance to physical examination, which, it goes without saying, did not reveal any disorder. She spent her days walking in the garden or outside the hospital in the chapel; she read a lot. She did not make any friends, and fled from the other patients: 'I refuse to have anything to do with those girls from up there', she told us frankly. However, with much patience, we gleaned from her that she was busy 'in her room making dresses for dolls'. She was nevertheless courteous in greeting the club committee members, who in this ward always come to visit the new arrivals. She accepted their gift and wishes, but avoided all collaboration, though not without excusing herself.

Her demeanour reflects the psychorigidity and hypertonia of the ego. Real screams developed from simple scrapings of the throat, exaggerated and repeated with gradually increasing intensity. They peppered her speech or interrupted her silence. They did not seem to represent an anti-hallucinatory defence or respond to a delusional attitude. They emerged without any external manifestation of anxiety, but also without her considering them as foreign to her ego. She attempted successfully to minimize the pathological meaning of this behaviour. However, it was not difficult to observe the character of these screams as scornful for her neighbours, for the people she came across or for the doctor, above all when she was faced with the awkward questions that he may ask her. The acumen of the sister orderlies came up against the same symptomatology involving refusal.

During this period, we received some complementary pieces of information, the most important of which were: a brother of hers had committed suicide, probably close to the onset of a schizophrenic process; her father died with a syndrome of mental weakness involving indeterminate neurological disturbances; a sister of hers had comitiality or convulsive hysteria. The patient always maintained a very proud character. Self-taught and very close to her dead brother, she then entered a convent where she always proved 'very difficult to handle'. Sent on a mission in Libreville, she had to be removed by her superiors shortly afterward because of her violent and scornful behaviour towards indigenous people and especially towards the children. When speaking to her about these difficulties, she spoke evasively of the aridity of the climate, while letting it slip that the negroes 'were naked', and 'that she never lowered herself to their level and their dirty way of living'.

We then formed our opinion: we were dealing with genuine paranoia, the development of a personality in which hysterical conversion disorders were established secondarily. Some narco-analysis sessions, in which we adopted a passive attitude, provoked neither further change nor did they open onto other psychotherapies. Once we had verified the social impossibility of readaptation outside the convent in her family, we decided to submit the patient to electroconvulsive therapy, in line with the following design.

First stage: one of us quickly undertook some active intervention psychotherapy, which aimed at unveiling to the patient the meanings of her conduct and the psychological interpretation of her behaviour as a whole. The psychotherapist converted the narcosis sessions into frank discussions, almost aggressive ones, about her character and her life. Her defences wore down in part and, though she protested about the violation of her personality ('my soul or my subconscious belong to God only') she admitted her poor character and her arrogance, as well as her decision to live in isolation, to be self-sufficient. As was to be anticipated after some days of relative improvement, the conversion syndromes increased. Then the second stage began.

Second stage: during narcoanalysis, an injection was dosed for deep sleep. The patient was moved to a different setting and transferred to another section where she was to be given electroconvulsive therapy without any new contact with the former psychotherapist. To arrive at the confusional stage as quickly as possible, the first period's 'mental home' milieu with separate room was substituted for the 'set' in which many other patients were around and which was very hospital-like. Practically speaking, if she had some bright intervals of consciousness during these first days, she cannot have failed to note the vague notion of 'disease', as well as the very reassuring one of 'attentive care'.

Third stage: once the amnesiac confusional stage had been obtained, the patient was given insulin shock therapy, the aim of which was to put her, upon the start of her recovery of consciousness, in the very primitive situation of mother-child relations: spoon-feeding (*nourriture à la bouche*), hygiene care (*soins de propreté*), first words. The 'awareness' ('*connaissance*') of the orderly's face upon waking from the insulin, is, in these conditions, objectively set on the same plane of maternal confusion in which 'one comes into the world'. The primary and secondary identification processes had to be closely monitored by the new psychotherapist who, moreover, acted indirectly this time, essentially through the means of the institution, on a mode akin to that in which the infant lives the presence of the father within the family. For that matter, these inter-human identifications are not unique. A 'social' process is involved: the learning of names and identification of objects through the intermediary of others.

Our patient experienced her return to consciousness around several complexual 'nodes', which her objective and verbal conduct made explicit each time. And each time she 'went beyond' the stage with the direct collaboration of the ward matron and with the psychotherapist, who was at once distant and present. There was naturally a period of infantile amazement, in which all was beautiful and a game, in which she obeyed out of duty, a period in which personal inquiry faced with the world is undertaken with the help of one's friends and accomplices (the other patients, the staff ....), then ..., she was seven years old, 'and her mother was pregnant'. She stated she had no need of another brother (the one, precisely, who committed suicide). 'I would love my father more (she said to Miss X., a childhood friend – false recognition of an orderly, it seemed) had he not put so many children into the world'. Then her ideas of marriage revived: 'I am twenty ..., what are all those girls there doing? ... they ought to get married like me'. She integrated quite smoothly into the collective life of the workshop; she did not yet know that she was a 'sister'; when, finally, she came to realize this, it did not stop her from accepting to take part in a play on the hospital stage with her ward. The role she chose was nonetheless very significant, namely, she worked as a typist just as she did upon entering the convent ... She had been fired owing to her character, pride, etc. but was rehired in spite of her character because no one better could be found and because she'd learnt to behave differently.

Little by little, the rectifications and her awareness of the situation became complete.

I am sorry, I really was ill, the other day, I spoke to you as if you were Miss X., from twenty years ago ..., when my brother was born ..., we had no need of him. Now, I should not be having the same ideas. This conversation I had had with her. We spoiled him so much that he was poorly brought up ... I am embarrassed. I was indeed told that I was ill, but I didn't believe it ... It's very good here ... If I relapse one day – it is hereditary in our family – I wouldn't hesitate to return for a second ...

She spoke and busied herself with the concrete problems of her community, above all with our sister-orderly ... and sometimes with us ...; her behaviour became entirely normal and no signs of deterioration remained. She returned to her community and quickly adapted to it. Her hospitalization with us lasted a total of three months. During the five days of annihilation treatment, she had seventeen electroshocks. She underwent forty sessions of insulin shock therapy, or forty days of managed institutional therapy.

5 INDICATIONS OF ELECTROCONVULSIVE THERAPY WITHIN INSTITUTIONAL THERAPIES

François Tosquelles and Frantz Fanon (Saint-Alban), July 1953[1]

Nowadays it seems that our extensive shared experience means we do not need to hold back against the taboo surrounding electroconvulsive therapies. Not holding back does not mean not hesitating, not weighing up the pros and cons on each occasion. Electroconvulsive therapy can be legitimated only in terms of efficacy. Henceforth, the simultaneously scientific and human problem consists in specifying the indications as carefully as possible as well as the technical conditions of putting them into action. This is what we aim to do as regards the annihilation method. Shock therapies have doubtless been abused, so before there can be any suggestion of engaging in treatment using many frequent electroshocks with little interruption, the level of vigilant prudence and self-criticism must be especially high; prudence

---

[1]*Comptes rendus du Congrès des médecins aliénistes et neurologues de France et des pays de langue française (51ᵉ session, Pau, 20–26 July 1953), pp. 545–52.*

and vigilance are already essential for simple electroshocks, which are as an exception able, but able they are, to provoke irreversible lesions and death.[2]

The utility of annihilation treatment for agitation is often spoken about, and yet agitation has been insufficiently specified or described from the semiological point of view. A common impression, unfortunately all too correct, is that repeated electroshocks are sometimes performed out of convenience or, in the best cases, as a symptomatic medication for agitation, as if agitation was a behaviour with a univocal cause. It appears, however, that these states can be overcome with less dangerous and perhaps more effective therapeutic conducts.

In its negative aspects, the history of Bini annihilation overlaps with that of leucotomy. And this parallel has been taken as far as to suggest an identity as regards efficacy, indications and even curative or lesional mechanisms. However, it is well known that Sargant has contested this claim. Notwithstanding, the comparison is useful in allowing us to note some common dangerous or negative aspects: in the first place, the possibility of establishing, using each of these methods, a state that Bordonner considered as a Pötzl frontal syndrome, sometimes definitive; secondly, for each method the problem with indications extends between two poles that do nothing to lessen our astonishment or our hesitation: on the one hand, there is a claim as to the usefulness of leucotomy and annihilation for a series of disorders, minor, as it were, but persistent ones, such as obsessive disorders, whose psychogenetic aetiology is easily admitted. We see this especially in the works of Bini and Cerletti and such was Egaz Moniz's initial opinion of leucotomy. However, Stengel, Muller, Jones, etc. all argue against this position. Mario, Barbi, and Goldenberg elaborate a more nuanced opposition, believing in the efficacy of annihilation for serious neuroses that 'begin in middle age', and in its dangerous inefficacy in neuroses of puberty.

On the other hand, however, these 'major' therapies are always presented as an ultimate remedy in chronic, desperate or complicated cases in which post-therapeutic deficient disorders are deemed

---

[2][According to Tosquelles and Fanon, doubts about annihilation therapies often derive from a 'fixist' view of personality (see *below*, p. 133). They propose to incorporate these techniques into a psycho-therapeutic practice that exceeds them and gives them meaning.]

a minor trouble as compared with the development of the illness towards 'vesania' or dementia.

Granting that both types of indications are founded, is it possible to decide logically in each concrete case? How can these two extreme poles be related: a therapy for simple and acute cases and a therapy for desperate ones? In our view, the only possible link is essentially constituted by the notion of personality development, or, if you will, of neurotic content being manifest as a leading syndrome, whether in the framework of classic neurosis, or in that of certain psychoses. This is how, in many clinical pictures of psychoses, the structure of the new personality, which is conditioned by diverse processes, is filled with human, psychological and neurotic manifestations. The language, the engagement or compensatory behaviour or stereotypy are often authentically neurotic, although psychosis can have conditioned them. We know that many 'chronic cases' owe that 'chronicity' precisely only to their own personalities and not to their illnesses. This is the case with 'façade psychoses', that of 'morbid mental persistence'; it is also the case with most delusional stabilizations. This is the problem of 'attitudes' or of strongly fixed and conditioned reactional behaviours. But at this point, precisely, the majority of authors advise caution. And we ask whether that caution does not reflect a very frequent theoretical bias concerning the 'fixity' of character, the 'fixity' of so-called constitutions, the implacable progress of pathological developments in the personality, of which the notion of paranoia is the extreme example. According to the authors, the issue concerns the classic contraindications of annihilation therapy: one is urged to 'beware', since, for example, 'will the patient not undertake new dissenting moves faced with possible memory disorders?' In a word, does this attitude not hide an ignorance about the dynamism of personality, such as psychoanalysis has revealed it to us, and also a material inability to apply these therapies within a hospital setting specially set up to reconstruct the personality?

We know of only one attempt to propose electroconvulsive therapy as part of a more general psychotherapy, namely Barbi and Goldenberg's. In a paper delivered at the 1950 Congress, they detail the ward's organization, the precaution taken to isolate and the technical details of the psychotherapy aided by recordings of the patient's statements: this seems to us of highest importance.

Our method – different in the detail – nonetheless connects with their foremost intention; otherwise said, electroconvulsive theory can be effective within an institutional and psychotherapeutic framework. We did not adopt the recording practice, although this psychotherapeutic method is very good in the psychagogy of many hysterical behaviours, as Mira[3] has shown through the use of films. In addition, it is a method that connects with 'explicative' psychagogies, which are of utmost usefulness at the end of the procedure or in certain dementias in the process of encapsulating themselves. However, this psychagogical method, applied after repeated shocks, does not take account of the process of dissolution-reconstruction of the personality, which takes place in broad stages, as we saw in the example we reported earlier. It can be used in a complementary, not an essential, fashion. In this case, what appears essential are the inter-human encounters and the practical activities in which the patient gets involved during the process of rediscovery of the ego and the world – including naturally the fantasmatic stages that the milieu enables him or her to cling to. Now, these fantasies have the same structure as psychoanalytic fantasies, but, as Daumézon so well put it in the field of institutional therapy, it is the real of the hospital that incarnates, supports and resolves them. The doctor and the material and human plasticity of the 'ward' must be adapted to these investments and must facilitate their overcoming. This is why the organization of the life group in which the patient is placed must be ready to evolve in parallel with the 'reconstruction' of the patient's ego and world. This is only possible by integrating the workshop together with the collective and spontaneous life of the hospital. Hence, 'the ergotherapy-factory' and gymnastic-motor ergotherapy are ill-suited to facilitate these curative investments.

Our nine cases attest that the major indications for annihilation – which we are not far from taking to be unique indications – are precisely serious neuroses, in particular those that have stabilized from middle age, an age when analytic elementary psychotherapeutic deconditioning is no longer possible. But, among these 'neuroses', we must include a large number of arrested delusional developments, indeed genuine paranoias, because the disorders' mechanism and

---

[3] [Emilio Mira y Lopez (1896–1964), Catalan psychiatrist of Cuban origin.]

meaning are identical in both cases. We thus treated a delusion of jealousy, two erotomanias, a paranoid hypochrondria and improved or cured socially some hallucinatory psychoses – to the extent that the most apparent disorders corresponded to the reaction of the morbid personality.

Some of these delusions, it is claimed, quickly relapse. One of our patients, who, besides, had not had the benefit of preparatory psychotherapy except in the 'erroneous' form of the psychodrama, has been out for more than two years and has returned to her position as a public servant in the central administration. Concerning a case of delusional, passionate, hallucinatory states, the hallucinations returned, but not the delusions. The patient works and occupies herself at home. In the course of one of our visits, the husband, who had believed she was totally cured, showed surprise at this unexpected avowal of her hallucinations.

Three years of experimentation evidently seem insufficient; but this experimentation is encouraging, especially as no complications have arisen: in all patients the 'psycho-organic' syndrome totally regressed. As a case in point, we thought that the delusional disorders of a sixty-year old patient, an erotomaniac, presented traits of presenile deterioration. What is more, the tests confirmed the deterioration. Well, after the annihilation treatment, this patient took to the stage and played roles 'from memory', whereas prior to the treatment she had only performed by constantly consulting a prompt book.

Treating patients using this approach, we insist, necessitates granting the greatest importance simultaneously to hospital arrangements, to the classification and grouping of patients, as well as to the concomitant establishment of group therapy programs. The co-existence of the workshop, the wards and the social life of the entire hospital is just as essential as the stage of *active*, interventionist *analysis* preceding the treatment. *Outside the possibility of such therapeutic linkages, the Bini cure appears to us a complete nonsense.*

If simple electroshock can be interpreted, as Cerletti believes, as a defence process, as a process of 'diencephalic reactivation' or as a 'stress', his collaborators, G. Martinotti first and foremost, has shown that this is not the case with repeated electroshocks. Not even the biological syndrome any longer corresponds to Selye's 'alarm' syndrome. On the contrary, the biological syndrome of the Bini cure corresponds to the 'exhaustion' syndrome of the same author, a syndrome that Martinotti compares, moreover, to De Morsier's 'confusional-amnesic' syndrome, with mesencephalic or pontobulbar impact. Henceforth, Delmas-Marsalet's opinion on dissolution-reconstruction – on the proviso that it is understood in its concrete content as comprising lived events within which psychological life is dramatized and appears – seems the most valid to us. Thus understood 'dissolution-reconstruction', while explaining the fortunate evolution of our cases, allows us to delimit the indications of electroconvulsive therapy in the framework of institutional therapy.

Discussion

Dr. Cossa. – I would be glad if the author would explain what precisely is meant by the expression 'institutional therapy'.

Dr. Tosquelles. – There is indeed an annoying confusion around the terms of ergotherapy, social therapy, group therapies and institutional therapies. Our general secretary is absolutely right to ask us to specify the meaning of the words. From the US Daumézon took the expression 'institutional therapies' to qualify the form of group therapy that is established – oftentimes – unbeknownst to doctors in psychiatric hospitals on account of the material arrangements, the psychological and social interactions between patients, and between patients and staff. It is clear that therapy – if therapy exists – inasmuch as it is carried out unbeknownst to the doctor and without his directives, cannot be a true therapy. Institutional therapy only rightly exists at the level of that awareness, and I would say, at the level of the acquisition of power and mastery in the medical handling of the 'institution' through all that it contains of a material and living nature. In this respect, institutional therapy distinguishes itself from the group therapies – psychodramas, courses, and so on – in that the latter are established through 'sessions' that are, as it were, detached from the patient's daily life. In 'group psychotherapies' the doctor has to lead the patient through artificial and short-lived conditions with the aim of deeply affecting the patient's lived experience. In institutional therapies, the point of departure is a spontaneous, everyday lived experience and the psychotherapist is at once materially absent and present in the hospital institution, which, in fact, represents him. In our paper we gave a concrete example of the dialectic of that presence and of its role in the treatment process.

I refer notably to the works of Daumézon-Kœchlin (*Archives portugaises de neurologie et de psychiatrie*, January 1953), to issue 3 of *L'Évolution psychiatrique*, 1952, on the occasion of the colloquium in Bonneval, and to the corresponding chapters of *L'Encyclopédie médico-chirurgicale*, which is forthcoming. In this last work, Requet shows that ergo-therapeutic techniques, magnificently developed in Anglo-Saxon countries, have scant relation to the conception of an institutional therapy.

In institutional therapy, ergotherapy can and often must take a role, as do insulin shocks or Bini therapy. The same can be said of certain group psychotherapies. But Daumézon is quite right to repeatedly insist on the fact that in most French hospitals the practice of what is called ergotherapy is much closer to an 'unconscious' institutional therapy on the part of the doctor than to some genuine Anglo-Saxon ergotherapy.

Were we pushed to draw consequences from our fourteen-year long experience of 'institutional' trials and errors at Saint-Alban, the therapeutic demands of hospital organization from an institutional perspective could be defined as follows:

1) Make possible the arrangement of 'life communities and heterogeneous treatments', involving between ten to twelve patients, maximum. These communities ought, on the one hand, to be linked at the level of the ward (three groups or four maximum) and, on the other, at the level of the entire hospital by means of the centralization of the hospital's shared social life. This group life must give the patient a permanent possibility of 'expression' and the possibility of the therapeutic, psychagogic or psychoanalytic use of his/her initiative.

2) The integration of ergotherapy at the level of the life community, to be used as part of group psychotherapies and institutional therapy.

3) The doctor's psychological preparation of the 'group' and, above all, of the nursing staff relative to the concrete 'case' being treated or helped with. Ward meetings and regular

meetings between orderly '*cadres*' are the essential 'organs' of that preparation.

4) The objective limitation of 'active' in-treatment patients in each group and in each ward: the material possibilities of a ward of forty to fifty patients does not allow for the 'active' treatment or therapeutic assimilation of a large number of new arrivals – five patients per month and per ward seems to us the desired optimum. In certain cases, this number can be exceeded and reach a total of eight. The hospital's overall construction must take this major requirement into account. The admissions ward is a therapeutic heresy. It's a traffic jam.

5) The classification of patients by 'elective' affinities, age, culture, etc., or by evolutive, syndromic or therapeutic similarities, prevents any possibility of progress in the dialectic of identifications and mythical transfers established by the patient with the milieu. In that case, the 'milieu' cannot be 'handled' as an 'institution' of treatment. On the contrary, the ward or the milieu 'sets' the patient at levels that are most often pathological.

6) All therapeutic, psychiatric work necessitates medical team work …. Two or three doctors at least must collaborate with one another closely as part of the same 'life milieu' in order to enable the dialectical game of most paths toward cure. A lone doctor cannot provide for any rapid solution to most of the Oedipal or pre-Oedipal conflicts that patients project or embody in the course of their illnesses.

7) All – the hospital's – activities must enable the patient to maintain, and even to explore, his or her utmost 'awareness of the illness'. Gradually demystifying the 'approximative' conceptions that the patient forms of the morbid event and of his-/herself, the psychiatric hospital must be an institution of disalienation.

6 ON AN ATTEMPT TO REHABILITATE A PATIENT SUFFERING FROM MORPHEIC EPILEPSY AND SERIOUS CHARACTER DISORDERS

François Tosquelles and Frantz Fanon (Saint-Alban), July 1953[1]

In September 1952, a young woman of twenty-eight years was transferred to us from Le Vinatier hospital, where she was admitted in August 1944.[2] She had been found at Perrache station, disoriented and confused. The admission certificate reported a recent affective shock: the deaths of her mother and father in her presence during an aerial bombardment at Saint-Lô. She was then given a series of electroshocks. The clinical picture is described as follows:

---

[1] *Comptes rendus du Congrès des médecins aliénistes et neurologues de France et des pays de langue française (51st session, Pau, 20–26 July 1953)*, pp. 363–8.

[2] [At issue here is a serious case of trauma inducing a psychiatric illness. In this case, shock therapies (electroconvulsive and insulin) also serve as a preliminary to treatment. Tosquelles and Fanon cautiously emphasize that even in such a case the therapeutic milieu seems crucial. They note that the prior use of hypnotics has aggravated the illness. At this time, then, pharmaceuticals in and of themselves did not seem to them to be of therapeutic use.]

'Periodically presents discordant psychic and motor agitation, calling for tying up, cries, laughs when the death of her parents is brought up with her, has intermittent affective siderations, with disinterest. She currently presents no problems in the flow of her thinking, nor catatonia; the patient is suspected to have dementia praecox and has suffered a considerable affective trauma. Dr Gallavardin.'

The 24-hour assessment states the following: 'melancholic state including ideas of, and attempts at, suicide. Longstanding comitiality. Not to be discharged. Dr Rochaix.'

The patient stated that she had had epileptic crises over the last three years at a rate of one a month. A sister of hers is allegedly also epileptic and a brother died of tuberculous meningitis.

We were supplied with two more assessments, the content of which read:

'Suffers convulsive and psychic epilepsy, serious character and behavioural disorders; instability; impulsiveness, phases of rage and depression, has ideas of suicide and has attempted it. This is a particularly dangerous patient who cannot be transferred unless kept obligatorily in an establishment for the mentally ill in accordance with the Law of 1838;[3] satisfaction is denied to a request to be placed in an open-door hospital. Not to be discharged. Dr Christy (10 May 1952).'

'Suffers convulsive and psychic epilepsy; serious character and behavioural disorders; instability; impulsiveness; phases of rage and depression, suicide attempts; dangerous reactions.

Can be transferred to any psychiatric hospital, i.e., to any mental institution subject to the Law of 1838, with special monitoring conditions during the transfer. But, in my view, the transfer will bring no improvement to the mental state; the patient is beyond the reach of psychotherapy. Dr Christy (9 July 1952).'

---

[3]The basic law organizing care in psychiatric institutions in France, in particular sectioning or involuntary commitment, until 1990.

Doctor Christy's pessimistic opinion was justified by the facts. His reluctance to meet the request for transfer is understandable, a request made by his former student, Doctor Despinoy, who, as it happens, practices at Saint-Alban. Kept in the secure ward at Le Vinatier, she had made several suicide attempts, whether by hanging, slitting her wrists, etc., and had committed several attacks against her neighbours, the staff and on various objects. For a period of eight years, she had had to be kept almost permanently confined in a cell and straightjacketed. She had become the privileged object and most enterprising subject of playing out the sado-masochistic myths so often incarnated in our psychiatric establishments. Despinoy's initiative was to submit our social therapeutic organization to a test that we feared would be too dissolutive, and which probably would have been without some fortuitous circumstances, which, on their own, justify our paper.

Our presentation is divided into three parts: first, a brief summary of the social therapy approaches of a first period, which, as was to be expected, ended in semi-failure; then, we put forward some therapeutic considerations corresponding to a second term, which did not end in failure; and, in finishing, we will present what we believe are some very modest conclusions.

The patient's introduction and adaptation into the ward were difficult. Placed (under the Law of 1938) in a ward of incoming patients – a revamped and transformed ex-ward of agitated patients, in which an extremely fertile atmosphere prevails in terms of social relations – on the first evening the patient refused to eat and take her 'phenobarbitone' without a reaction from our orderlies, who stood alert. Over the first days, no convulsive crisis appeared, she complained of not sleeping, tried to obtain a special meal plan owing to a supposed longstanding condition of nephritis, and was administered – wrongly we now believe – 30 cg. of phenobarbitone during the day, 2 g. of chloral hydrate and a vial of phenergan in the evening. 'Studying the situation', said the report of the head ward orderly. Upon examination, she presented no focal neurologic signs, nor distinctive physical disease. Her WR is negative. Her CSF, normal: cells: 3; albumin: 0.30 g.; chloride: 7 g.; sugar: 0.52 g.; benzoin: 00000.22110.00000.

Oriented and lucid. Her affective state was remarkably tiresome, smarmy, bradypsychic, unrelenting, inappropriate, temperamental, disgruntled, sullen, sometimes ironic.

She insistently testified to her good will and put her impulsions down to her illness and to being unaccustomed to living in an ordered social milieu. She wrote to an orderly at Vinatier, 'I am dazzled and disoriented, I need some time in order to adapt, I was not quite myself, I was intoxicated with the emotion. Here it is cheerful, there is no coarseness, no straightjacket; what would you say, if one fine day, instead of a hundred agitated lunatics, you found yourself in a group of sixteen patients and a family life'. This did not prevent her from exploding, from throwing drink in the middle of the dormitory or from getting up and making a wall-to-wall racket at night, breaking a few glass panes if need be. At the end of a twenty-day period, including a wrist injury incurred with broken glass and a two-day hunger strike sometimes accompanied by cries and chants, she busied herself in bed with sewing jobs, for which she required scissors. Our medical attitude derives from biological studies and examinations, conspicuously disregarding behavioural disturbances. The taking on and examination of such are reserved solely for the collective psychotherapy sessions, either on the occasion of the meeting of the ward ergotherapy group, or during the newspaper articles to which she spontaneously committed herself. Little by little the patient became 'livable', with minor dysthymia, although it was often necessary to thwart her attempts at starting conflicts with other patients and with staff. Two months later, in a memorable session in which her companions did not spare her from criticism, nor their desire to help her, she was named ward delegate, meaning she was free to leave the ward to do her work at the club canteen. However, the general atmosphere of the ward was profoundly altered by her presence. Everyone lived in a permanent state of tension, clashes opposed patients to one another, patients to orderlies and orderlies to patients, and orderlies to other orderlies. Bouts of rage and jealousy broke out, and for a whole month her attempt at fitting into the club canteen failed owing to her 'manual clumsiness', which resulted in what the canteen committee deemed an excessive breaking of utensils. This last episode seemed to coincide with an increase in the number of fits, which remained nocturnal, despite our adding six tablets of solantyl to her treatment.

It must be admitted that we were not directly able to observe these fits. Hyperventilation and light stimulation did not elicit significant modifications in her electroencephalographic recordings, which were taken on several occasions. In the recordings, which are hard to interpret, one observes at most a slow dysrhythmia of 5 c/s, without peaks, in the right temporoparietal area, unresponsive to exercise; arrest reaction is rather poor. In fact, the patient presented more and more paratonic troubles, and a sullen mood interspersed with spurts of aggressive vivacity.

At this point we decided to perform electroconvulsive therapy followed by insulin shock therapy and *transfer the patient to the hospital's open-door service*. After twenty-five comas, the patient spontaneously presented a series of tonic crises, which were arrested by means of intravenous Somnifene. Despite improvements in her behaviour and increased adaptation in the observational clinic, nocturnal crises continued to be registered and the Rorschach test confirmed the comitial structure of her characterological disorders; we considered the likelihood of morpheic epilepsy. Little by little we substituted Ortedrine (five tablets) for the anticonvulsants.

This patient had become used to taking anticonvulsants and hypnotics over a period of many years and barely got any sleep, but she began to sleep once all the sedative medication was stopped. Now she has to be woken up three times during the night to take her Ortedrine. She falls asleep again afterward without difficulty and the character problems have disappeared. She may still occasionally present some nocturnal absences (?), since she has wet herself during the night without noticing. She busies herself at the workshop of the observational clinic and in the club canteen without much problem and willingly helps her colleagues.

The comparative study of tests undertaken at diverse periods is of some interest. We don't have the space to develop it at length here. So we shall cite these facts by way of example: Rorschach given on 16 September 1952: 2 hours and 20 minutes for twenty-four responses. Rorschach given on 24 February, 1953: 1 hour and 10 minutes for twenty responses. Rorschach given on 4 May 1953: 40 minutes.

Progressive inversions of the type of succession over the three tests. Example:

1) 16.9.52 *Card V*	2) 24.2.53 *Card V*	3) 4.5.53 *Card V*
1) Horns.................Dd 2) Legs................... Dd 3) Bats.............. ....G	Cockchafer......... ....G However that seems to me.. There are indeed... (signals horns without naming them) ....Dd	Cockchafer...... ....G The two sides are not symmetrical.
Card III 1) Shoes.................Dd 2) That may be puppets...................G	*Card III* Where, that, fellows and their feet......................G As well....................... Dd	*Card III* That, human figures looking at each other...... ....G
Card IV - Crabs (by pincer.......... sup.)....................ddD - They look like eyes.....................dd	*Card IV* A rug, it's not ....G the same on each side, looks like it has eyes, that's why (scratches with the finger a printing mistake), there, too, there is something that....in the glass mount.......................dd	*Card IV* Looks like a bear skin..........G Look like eyes............. ....dd
Card II Don't know.......what that represents. There is something like blood. The two sides are not the same.	*Card II* In any case a drawing brr, not much, don't know...... let's put there, let's put spilt blood. The black blots can represent an animal.In short, which is crushed there, with some blood.	*Card II* I don't know.... the red...I don't know what that may represent.
Card VIII Looks like a bear, it only has two legs, no, three, the fourth is lost. There, a vertebra, might be some flowers. That blue, my goodness, in any case if it is an animal, it does not have legs all alike, it only has three legs, which is disturbing.	*Card VIII* That changes everything. There are some vertebrae and right there, take this, if you look like this (indicates the animals but the word does not come out).....take this.....that changes colour, but the legs....you wouldn't say it's a lion. I said to you vertebrae. Chromatic choice: blue	*Card VIII* Animals, lions. I don't see anything else. The other blots are not even solid. Chromatic choice: red

The Szondi test still continued to present much variation. Overt reactions, notably concerning the paroxysmal vector, were present and were at most substituted for the negative choice at the start. Diffuse anxiety and affective accumulation with difficulties in their manifestation, as indicated by the negative choice, disappeared in favour of an aggressive liberation, which was, as it were, more socialized. By contrast, the patient's most recent choices showed the persistence of a strong tension or positive charge in the pair of the contact vector. Oral dependency continued to remain very high, whereas factor D (anal), formerly positive and charged, became ambivalent.

In light of this curious case, we would like to conclude simply by drawing attention to two problems:

1) The transfer of a certain number of patients ought to be envisaged as part of therapeutic policy, on the same level as ward changes. This issue is one on which Parchappe greatly insisted. We ought to recall also that some 'morbid mental persistence' (*persistances mentales morbides*) and 'façade psychoses' are kept up by the 'persistence' of the milieu. Gruhle showed, for example, how some paranoiac delusions or even stabilized and sthenic paranoid delusions practically subsided, were encapsulated, or even rendered to the 'bygone past', when the transferred patient was able to regard the acute period of his or her illness a past affliction.

2) The file on characterological disorders perpetuated by the use of hypnotics, of which the patient fights the depressive and confusional action – must be reopened. And we are entitled to ask whether barbiturate use did not exacerbate this patient's state, although we are not blind to the possibility that a patient can attempt to convert the current stimulant treatment into a new toxicomaniac substitute.

7 NOTE ON SLEEP THERAPY TECHNIQUES USING CONDITIONING AND ECTROENCEPHALO- GRAPHIC MONITORING

Maurice Despinoy, Frantz Fanon, Walter Zenner (Saint-Alban), July 1953[1]

Publications by Soviet authors have renewed interest in sleep therapies. But the novelty that they have contributed to this therapy, a much-researched topic prior to the advent of insulin, seems largely to have been neglected by most authors. The difficulties encountered in creating the conditioning process discourage them all the more easily that they doubt the effectiveness of the recommended methods. A further contributing factor to this neglect of the most original element in the Russian works appears to have been the introduction into therapy of a remarkable potentiator in the domain of anaesthetics. In recent publications it is frequently

[1]*Comptes rendus du Congrès des médecins aliénistes et neurologues de France et des pays de langue française (51st session, Pau, 20–26 July 1953)*, pp. 617–20.

to be read that the use of 4560 RP renders conditioning, and even soundproofing, superfluous.[2]

Our study's goal was to bring into focus a sleeping therapy technique that makes conditioning possible, and to establish whether this technique permits a reduction in sleeping medications. We performed these sleep therapies in two rooms of the Saint-Alban hospital, one of which could accommodate two patients, in 1951 and 1952. The conditional stimulus was luminous and sonorous, synchronous, and a water mill worked to light up a low-intensity lamp placed above the head of the patient at regular intervals and to trigger an electric metronome. The usual rhythm was 70 per minute. Noise insulation was attempted by an additional partition separating both rooms from the rest of the ward and by wall hangings. The medications used were: a Cloetta type mixture, administered in suppositories, intramuscular Somnifene, potions of chloral-bromide, Eunoctal, then mixtures of 4560 and Dolosal, combined or not with the foregoing.

We accepted that the creation of conditioned sleeping reflexes requires the coincidence, on the one hand, of sleep brought on by the medication, and, on the other, by the activation of the sound-and-light system. A considerable difficulty involved not waking the patient while the conditional stimulus was active at the start of the treatment prior to establishing the reflex. For in that condition, the stimulus induced loses all its efficacy.

Now, it is difficult to determine the precise moment at which a person is awakened. The technique, formerly admitted by German authors, had consisted in setting oneself at a certain distance from the patient and calling her by name in hushed tones; this runs the risk of shortening the sleep and gives only an imperfect idea of the degree of sleep. The reading of an article by [Charles Horace] Mayo on the automatic adjustment of general anesthetics by an electro-encephalograph led us to think that it was possible to monitor the sleeping state of our subjects at a distance.

---

[2][This refers to chlorpromazine, a molecule synthetized by Rhône-Poulenc at the end of 1950 under the name '4560 RP'. Initially it was used as an antihistamine and then as an anesthetic by Henri Laborit and was soon to be experimented within a psychiatric milieu: the first works undertaken at the initiative of Laborit at Val-de-Grâce tried out the molecule as a part of sleep therapy (it is highly likely that this paper is alluding to these works). In 1952, two psychiatrists from Val-de-Grâce, Pierre Deniker and Jean Delay, observed that this molecule had spectacular 'neuroleptic' effects in the treatment of certain psychoses (such as schizophrenia).]

Designing a satisfactory system required much trial and error. For the electrodes we were obliged to use an arrangement of very fine intradermic needles, and a removable central socket was connected to wires hanging above the patient's head. The needles were well tolerated, but their position often had to be rectified during periods of waking. The machine itself was placed in an adjacent room, the wires routed through a dividing wall. Recordings were taken at regular intervals. Although the electro-encephalographic characteristics of the waking phase were less stable than those of the sleeping phase, by taking a recording of about three minutes it was easy to assess the depth of sleep. We will not detail here the lessons these recordings provided, nevertheless we indicate that this method has the advantage of determining the limits of intoxication at each moment. It shows that, after several days of treatment, slow waves persisted during sleep in all cases in which the doses administered were too strong. Thanks to this system, we were able to determine the moment at which either triggering the waking-up or else the soporific medication ought to intervene.

Results. – We will not insist on the therapeutic results properly speaking. Once again we found the traditionally indicated mood enhancement, the attenuation of delusional concerns, barely improved hebephrenic-catatonic states, a seemingly favourable influencing of acute psychoses, and erratic results for neuroses. In a general manner, we believe to have observed that the sleep therapy was an effective 'primer' ('*mordançage*'), by preparing the way for other therapies.

Owing to the large number of products used, the twenty utilizable sleep therapies that we performed do not enable us to establish quantitatively exact comparisons of efficacy with certainty. We might nonetheless say that the use of 4560 made it possible to reduce considerably the quantities of medications used. Above all it made it possible, with the addition of Dolosal, to extend the length of a whole sleep to six hours after medicinal introduction, whereas previously the duration was only around four hours in length.

Although we rarely used this procedure, the continuous, intravenous slow drip of serum enabling 'upon demand' the addition – depending on the electroencephalographic recordings – of potentiator or of Eunoctal seemed best to us. The use of anaesthetic enemas, which often result in 'incidents' detrimental to conditioning, as well as the dangers of intoxication from sleeping medication, have already been noted. Let us point out the disadvantage resulting from the incompatibility by precipitation of a 4560-barbiturates mixture. Some febrile reactions following the use of this potentiator were observed with a slightly greater frequency than in other cases.

The most important factors that determine the quantity of sleeping drugs to use are the number of awakenings provoked and the isolation of parasite excitations. It seemed to us inaccurate to claim that the potentiate makes it possible to neglect the factors of the surrounding milieu. With 4560 as with any other sleeping drug, the number of spontaneous awakenings increased whenever the patient was disturbed by outside noises.

The number of awakenings provoked must not be increased with the goal of accelerating the conditioning; two awakenings per 24 hours are a maximum.

The creation of a conditioned sleeping reflex appeared very fragile to us – nonstop spontaneous awakenings of the rhythmic systems were enough to make it disappear. A perfect technique is essential if one is to benefit from the acquisition of this reflex. The current state of our research has not allowed us to come to an entirely satisfying result, as the difference is only weak between a sleeping treatment in a well-insulated milieu and a treatment with conditioning. This difference becomes noticeable around only the sixth day of treatment, through the fact that the necessary doses do not have the same increase. (It is certainly better to perform a treatment without conditional stimulus but with very good insulation conditions, than it is an approximately conditioned treatment.) The technique of electroencephalographic monitoring should make possible the precise codifying of sleeping therapies with a conditioned reflex. Only then will it be possible to make a value judgement on this new technique. In the current state of things, we did not study the therapeutic effect of the sleep, but only that of the sleeping drugs used.

8 OUR JOURNAL

Frantz Fanon, editorials of the weekly ward journal of the Blida-Joinville Psychiatric Hospital, December 1953–December 1956[1]

Introduction: du côté de chez Fanon

Amina Azza Bekkat, April 2015

When the Blida-Joinville Psychiatric Hospital was created in 1933, it was located on the fringes of the city, as per the custom of the day, according to which patients were located far from urban centres so as

---

[1]We republish here Fanon's editorials in the rediscovered issues of *Notre Journal (Our Journal)*, kindly given to us by Amina Azza Bekkat, professor of comparative literature and African literature at the university of Blida, who was happy to introduce them, something for which we are greatly appreciative. Paul Marquis also passed on some missing issues to us. For 1954, the issues that we were not able to check are 9–12; for 1955, 1, 3–5, 7, 9–12, 24, 40–41, 44, 46–47, 50; for 1956, 3, 7, 8, 11, 12, 14, 24. The editorial was written by several doctors. We have only reprinted those that Fanon himself wrote except in cases where he refers explicitly to a preceding editorial. Each issue was originally published with the following heading: '*Our Journal*: Blida-Joinville Psychiatric Hospital, an internal weekly journal published Thursdays. This journal must not be taken outside the establishment'. Apart from the editorials, the journal contained announcements from different associations (music, sports, recreational) and columns written by patients. These columns alone would warrant a study, for they are signed and attest to a social diversification among contributors over a period of years. The patients' medical files are not yet available. We have corrected a certain number of obvious punctuation errors. Our corrections to the vocabulary are placed in square brackets.

not to disrupt the social order. A vast complex surrounded with fields and prairies, the hospital provided, so it was thought, the necessary security measures. Today, more than eighty years later, the city has spread in sometimes uncontrolled ramifications. Everywhere, the name of Fanon is present. On businesses, on buses and, of course, at the entry to the hospital that henceforth bears his name and where photos of him continue to keep his memory alive.

When he came to this place in November 1953, a young, recently graduated doctor, full of ardour and enthusiasm, he undertook to reform the approach to psychiatric illness in accordance with the 'disalienist' teaching of the Saint-Alban asylum and Professor Tosquelles. The fifth division, which he created and with which he was entrusted, comprised three wards of Muslim men and one ward of European women.[2] Fanon's project was to make accessible to patients the creative, cultural and manual activities that might enable them to become human beings again with personal aspirations. Socialization constitutes an important approach. With this goal in mind, Fanon created basketwork and pottery workshops, celebrated religious feasts, both Muslim and Christian, organized a film club, sports events and excursions, and above all founded a small weekly publication called Notre Journal, which was launched in December 1953 – an 'on-board journal, as he defined it himself – which marked the evolution and progress made in treating patients and which 'livens up the boat'.

In the first issues, Fanon set the journal's guidelines: 'To write is to communicate with others, even if absent' (no. 1). The first thing to note is the simplicity of the language used. Known for his richness of style, honed with ancestral wounds, Fanon expresses himself here in a simple manner to facilitate understanding. In the following issues he provides some directives for the correct application of his method: call patients by their name (no. 2); organize a time schedule in order to break with indifference and inertia (15 April 1954); prevent orderlies

---

[2][On the work Fanon carried out at the psychiatric hospital of Blida-Joinville, the reader can usefully refer to: Alice Cherki, *Frantz Fanon: A Portrait*, p. 38; Macey, *Frantz Fanon*, chapter 6, p. 199 *sq.*, as well as Paul Marquis, 'Frantz Fanon and the nursing staff at the psychiatric hospital of Blida-Joinville', *Le Carnet des Glycines*, 25 March 2015, <https://glycines.hypotheses.org/301>.]

Figure 4 Wards at Blida-Joinville Hospital. Credit: Fonds Frantz Fanon/IMEC.

from becoming a disruptive element (22 April 1954); apply the rule of three times eight – work, recreation, rest (6 May 1954); maintain the patients' relations with the outside and the necessity of writing (27 May 1954); live fully by celebrating religious feast days (3 June 1954); allow recreation (10 June 1954) … The June 24 issue calls for particular attention. Its first text is by a Muslim patient, Ahmed Noui, who registers his surprise that all the roles of the Bourgeois gentilhomme were played by women. And he asks the essential question: why make things abnormal through this separation; why do we always have to have this gap? In his careful reply, Doctor Fanon agrees with Ahmed Noui, but explains this state of affairs as stemming from not having an auditorium large enough to bring everyone, women and men, together.

In a subsequent issue, we are informed that a Moorish café was set up on 1 July 1954. Fanon wrote about it on July 15, emphasizing its importance. His next article appears in issue no. 35 of 19 August 1954, and the title is significant: 'Towards a Living Journal'. In it, he emphasizes the need for the boarders to express themselves clearly and to 'think in measured ideas' so that they can be better understood – some statements, it is true, were somewhat exalted. Fanon put his name to the editorial of issue no. 42, in which he expresses concern that the journal is no longer having an impact but merely encounters the very indifference they were trying to combat.

The journal's presentation improved as of August 1954 (no. 35): just as with the first issue of December 1953 (which was printed, whereas later issues were only mimeographed), the heading was written in French and in Arabic, and a drawing depicting a mosque – a local symbol without religious connotation, as the doctor himself explains – henceforth decorated it. The publication grew, going from one sheet to two, but texts by Fanon would appear more seldom. From issue no. 49 on, Fanon gives an account of the reports drawn up at the request of the OMS and raises concerns about costs, wastage and useless purchases. On 30 December 1954, he further makes clear that the act of writing is itself a higher act. The act of reading, too.

For the duration of his stay in Blida, we know that Fanon endeavoured to train his orderlies. Attesting to this are the notebooks left behind by the orderlies, who took notes assiduously during the doctor's lectures. Also to be found in the 4 August 1955 issue of Our Journal are extracts from a psychiatric handbook (Paul Bernard), as if the lectures began to spill over into the journal. Similarly, in another article written for the orderlies and in order to improve the monitoring of their behaviour, Fanon admits the occasional usefulness of punishment (no. 48). However, in the editorial of 13 December 1956 (no. 51), he qualifies this judgement. To prevent patients from being transformed into 'child boarders' and made to tremble before 'orderly parents' – behaviours which, despite the progress made in psychiatry, reappear from time to time – Fanon issues a warning: 'Each time we disregard our profession, each time that we give up our attitude of understanding and adopt an attitude of punishment, we are mistaken'. This is a stance that he expresses even more clearly in his editorial of 20 December 1956, in which he pleads that the idea of formulating a series of disciplinary rules must be abandoned once and for all. That was his last contribution.

All the editorials that Fanon wrote present and further his ideas for a hospital that conforms to the lessons he learnt at Saint-Alban. The patients themselves take up the reins and endeavour to express themselves, especially the women of the fifth ward. We see some names crop up frequently, such as Cécile Nouad, a patient who often expresses her happiness and also wrote poems. In the later issues, the names of

Muslim men start to appear, especially on topics concerning sport, football or bowls competitions.

A change occurs in the very last of Doctor Fanon's editorials, especially in the December 1956 issue, a change that is impossible not to notice. In the articles written in the years prior, he addressed both patients and the nursing staff, while the last three editorials revolve around the orderlies and their training, as if Fanon were now handing over the reins. In March 1955, according to Pierre Chaulet (Fanon colloquium, Algiers, July 2009), Algerian officials, including Chaulet himself, met with the young psychiatrist who from then on committed to the Algerian revolution. This parallel activity, to which he devoted himself with characteristic passion, probably explains the somewhat distant tone notable in his last texts. In December 1956, Fanon sent a letter of resignation to minister Robert Lacoste, refusing to participate any longer in the enterprise of 'dehumanization' that France was carrying out in Algeria. His expulsion order came in the first week of January.

24 December 1953, no. 1. *Memory and journal*

At the previous pavilion meeting at De Clérambault, we made the decision to publish a journal. We also pondered about the name we would give it: the question was raised and no one found it obvious. After a while, however, some titles were timidly put forward. I recall one of them: namely, *Journal de bord*.[3] I would like to dwell a little on this title and try to clarify the journal's importance.

On a ship, it is commonplace to say that one is between sky and water; that one is cut off from the world; that one is alone. This journal, precisely, is to fight against the possibility of letting oneself go, against that solitude. Every day a news-sheet comes out, often poorly printed, without photos and bland. But every day, that news-sheet works to liven up the boat. In it, you are informed about the 'on-board' news: recreation, cinema, concerts, the next ports of call. You also learn, of course, about the news on land. The boat, though isolated, keeps contact with the outside, that is to say, with the world. Why? Because in two or three days, the passengers will meet up again with their parents and friends, and return to their homes.

---

[3][Fanon himself wrote an 'on-board journal' ('*journal de bord*', lit. ship's log or journal) during his reconnaissance mission to Mali during the summer of 1960 (*Œuvres*, pp. 860–71).]

Note that every traveller has a journal. The tourist sends cards or long letters to his friends in which he tells of his encounters. Storytelling is a very difficult discipline to acquire. I remember a young boy of eight years of age who never managed to tell *Little Red Riding Hood* properly, jumbling up all the different parts of the story.

The discovery of writing is certainly the most beautiful one, since it allows you to recall yourself, to present things that have happened in order and above all to communicate with others, even when they are absent.

7 January 1954, no. 3. *Memory and action*[4]

Some days ago, I drew a very abrupt reply. I asked a patient from Reynaud[5] what the date was. 'How do you expect me to know the date? Every morning, I am told to get up. To eat. To go to the courtyard. At noon, I am told to eat. To go to the courtyard and afterward to go to sleep. Nobody tells me the date. How do you expect that I should know what day it is?'

The patient was clearly right. In the Middle Ages, a town crier was specially employed to announce the days and the hours. It was very useful. In modern times, we have calendars. But we don't know where to put a calendar in a ward. And also, where do we get this calendar from? It's a very difficult problem to resolve.

Mrs Mina, for example, has to organize a recreational session for January 7. For this she will have to draw up a timetable. She has to know that there are only a few days left to her. She has to get her companions and work with them. For Mrs Mina's team, January 7 is an important date. Mrs Mina's entire team is working toward January 7. The rest of the ward, however, is waiting for January 7. For the whole ward wants some entertainment.

Similarly, Miss Donnadieu is preparing a recreational session for January 21. For Miss Donnadieu, this is a very important date. She and her team will have much to do. As I was told by a patient after asking whether the choir was working: 'Doctor, between the rehearsals, the walks and the workshop, we barely have time to eat.'

'Tomorrow is the Christmas performance'. 'Next Sunday, we will set out on the path of Medea'. 'Today I wrote an article for the journal'.

---

[4][From this issue onwards the journal is subtitled '*Hebdomadaire intérieur du pavillon De Clérambault*' (Internal Weekly of the De Clérambault ward).]
[5][One of the wards.]

'Next Monday, during the meeting, I want to ask you a question, doctor.' Such phrases show precisely that it is possible to live in time. Days are not similar to one another, for each day demands a new plan of action. The calendar is a schedule of action. To rediscover the calendar, that is to say, time, is to rediscover a work schedule.

The patient from Reynaud was right. Who was in the wrong? Nobody. Everybody. Me, Mr Gil, Mr Dussauge. And then perhaps, if one looks closely, one or two 'housekeepers'. Well everybody! De Clérambault has given us a lesson, we must examine it without special consideration for others but also impartially.

21 January 1954, no. 5. *Hospitalization or lockers?*[6]

Yesterday, Friday, De Clérambault received a visit from Mr Lempereur, the hospital's treasurer, accompanied by Mr Nedjimi, the Works Manager, and Mr Rabet, the Head Builder. This visit was motivated, because only De Clérambault, we were told, has had no renovations done since it opened.

After a first inspection, Mrs [*illegible*] presented the requirements of the ward: 1) one locker per patient; 2) one locker per orderly; 3) a space where Mrs [*illegible*], head of the ward, can write. I was present. We looked at all the possible options. After two hours of looking into things we were indeed obliged to recognize that none of the three requests could be met.

Mr Lempereur, after stating the first point, asked us very nicely if the night tables did not suffice. Then the observation was made that there aren't any. It is from him that I take the title of this article. 'Your patients cannot settle in. They must surely have the feeling of being in transit'. And that is strictly accurate. I would go even further: the patients do not have the feeling of being anywhere.

It is an establishment in which the patient's quality of being a spouse or a mother is contested. This quality is contested as their marriage is deliberately ignored. It is an establishment in which they have nothing of their own. Not even their face, since there are no mirrors at De Clérambault. The patients are obliged to carry small bags containing: toothless combs, bread crusts, ripped handkerchiefs and lollies left by the latest visitor! These bags are objects that others covet. Not an uncommon desire: 'I want your

---

[6][On the copy we were given the word is barely legible.]

comb'. Whence, upon attempts at visual break-ins, the macular reactions, the motor discharges, the overall explosive behaviours that our orderlies so naively call: agitation.

But no modifications will be able to make the ward into a pleasant place. Every inch of space is already used up. And the beds are all piled on top of one another. The patients obviously as well. The truth is that De Clérambault was built to accommodate ninety beds. Today we have one hundred-and-sixty-eight beds in it.[7]

1 April 1954, no. 15.

A ministerial circular has asked for psychiatric hospitals to desist with the attitude of calling hospitalized women by their maiden names. In terms of innovation, this circular stipulated that it was good to allow the patients to hold onto their personal clothes and their wedding rings. These small modifications seem unimportant, but it is always necessary to remember that mental illness is often manifest through an alteration in the notion of the 'I'. To call a married woman, a mother of two or three children, by her maiden name, means obliging her to take a step backward. One of my friends, I recall, had a *nom de guerre* during the war, and found it troublesome to be called by this name again in 1949. The point being that, ever since the end of the war, he had regained another personality, one with different reactions, thoughts and concerns. In 1950, he was no longer a member of the resistance, he had again adopted his official name, his normal life in a country that had regained its normal state.

At each major shake-up of one's life, one needs to rediscover one's dimensions, one needs to stabilize one's positions. We ought not to collaborate in the destruction of these positions. How many times have I felt that training needs to be carried out in certain hospitals? Staff are sometimes not content to call patients by their maiden names and would instead use a first name or a nickname. Some do not take care to pause, such as, for example, the orderly who called a patient suffering hallucinations 'Joan of Arc'.

---

[7][Fanon's skepticism toward the notion of agitation is stated in several articles. The sorts of behaviour subsumed under this term do not result directly or only from some endogenous causality, but also from structures imposed on the conditions of existence. Concerning Algeria, Fanon would draw up an inventory of them with his colleagues, from 1955 on, in 'Current Aspects of Mental Care in Algeria' (see *below*, p. 239).]

8 April 1954, no. 16.

Future generations will ask themselves with interest why we were persuaded to build psychiatric hospitals remote from any centre. Several patients have already asked me: 'Doctor, will we hear the Easter bells ring? – I don't know'. I didn't want to answer the question, because, though I was only new in this hospital, I felt responsible for the fact that we are unable to hear the bells from here.

Regardless of which religious attitudes you adopt, daily life is cadenced by a certain number of noises and the church bells represent an important element of that symphony. In France there is a poetry of the Angelus that the peasant close to the land lives in a very profound way. It is very likely that in small urban areas in Algeria this sonorous melody also exists.

Easter is coming. But the bells will not die to be born again because they have never existed at the Blida Psychiatric Hospital. The Blida Psychiatric Hospital will continue to live in silence. A silence without bells.

15 April 1954, no. 17.

In one of the first articles that I wrote, I alluded to those patients who, once hospitalized, erect between the outside world and themselves a very opaque screen behind which they immobilize themselves. These patients surrender, let themselves be won over by inertia. Some get to the point of no longer knowing how to stand upright. They are the ones you see crouching down, lying, sitting, in what is called the 'asylum yard'.

I also said that this letting-go often manifests itself by a total forgetting of one's previous life, an indifference concerning time. These patients are no longer interested in knowing whether it is the month of January or December, the beginning or the end of the month, Thursday or Sunday. This is why I suggest that a psychiatric institution's first goal should be to establish, against this background of inertia and indifference, some tasks, occupations and timetables, including everything from integrating patients into the 'duty' of helping the orderlies to bring in soup, to actively participating in the ward's recreational sessions, including walks outside the hospital.

This ideal is very difficult to achieve, since it has to contend with two forces that are opposed to it: the nursing staff and the patients. We will consider each of these two forces in upcoming issues.

22 April 1954, no. 18.

At De Clérambault, a certain patient took walks in the park with a group of other patients each afternoon. One day that patient had an attack mid-walk. The doctors altered her treatment to reduce the frequency of the attacks, but a new indication presented itself: it was necessary to wait some days before allowing the patient out again, so to enforce this the doctor advised the orderlies not to take the patient out on walks. Well, imagine the doctor's surprise the following day when he was literally taken to task by the patient: 'In fact, you gave the order that I was not allowed to go out, you left orders for the nurses and you said: "Prevent her from leaving".'

Otherwise said, an instruction that started off as medical was erroneously turned into a police prohibition. The truth is that it is easier to say, in blanket fashion, 'It's an order from the doctor' than to make two efforts: 1) to understand the medical interest of such prescriptions; and 2) to explain to the patient the reason for a temporary measure.

In this way, rather than being what he should be – an element of equilibrium enabling a patient not to have to contend with insurmountable forces or incomprehensible prohibitions; rather than becoming the filter enabling the patient to expel from his mind the unusual fragments emergent during his illness, rather than being the doctor's immediate and essential collaborator, the orderly becomes, on the contrary, through the intervention of his errors, a disruptive element that the doctor will have to combat every day. Uniting with the doctor so that the patients in the ward find balance and a homogenous atmosphere turns out to be one of the nursing staff's most fundamental tasks.

27 May 1954, no. 23. *Patients' relations with the outside world*[8]

You can never say enough about the painful feeling that patients endure when, from one day to the next, they are deprived of their home, their parents, their friends, and are hospitalized in an

---

[8][On this date, the subtitle 'Hebdomadaire intérieur du pavillon De Clérambault' is replaced with 'Hebdomadaire intérieur' ('Internal weekly').]

establishment that is sometimes four to five hundred kilometres away from their usual places of residence. When hospitalization is deemed essential due to the state of the patient's health, this is not anything very serious as such. Yet the patient often gets the genuine impression that he is being interned, and we know that in people's mind this word is synonymous with imprisonment.

This is why the staff's attitude must be to help the patient get rid as quickly as possible of this mistrustful feeling toward the hospital establishment. The patient ought not to endure hospitalization as a kind of imprisonment, but instead as the only possible way to receive the maximum amount of treatment in a minimum amount of time. And for the entire duration of hospitalization, we must strive to keep intact the links that unite the patient with the outside world. We must insist that the patients write to their family and friends as often as possible. We must insist that the patients receive visits as often as possible.

The patient's place in society, in his or her family, must be maintained. This is why the patient has to have a social attitude: writing, receiving news and narrating are some of the most important social activities. It must be seen to that the incoming patient is not desocialized. This is why the congested atmosphere of a hospital ward is detrimental to such a reeducation of the personality. If possible, each patient needs to write at least once a week.

3 June 1954, no. 24.

In human communities a perpetual temptation arises and it is important to know how to counter this perpetual temptation with an attitude of refusal. Ramadan was celebrated and then came the end of Ramadan. Normally the end of Ramadan is celebrated with joy, with enthusiasm. Well, as someone matter-of-factly put it, in this hospital 'the occasion was not marked'.

I have always liked the expression '*prise en charge*' (care, nursing). To care for someone is not only to give him or her the possibility not to die, it is above all to give him or her the chance to live. Well, for a Muslim, to live also means to have the chance to celebrate the end of Ramadan. Each year, it seems this has been done; this year, nothing was done. May we see, for the next Muslim celebration, a veritable fireworks of rejoicing!

10 June 1954, no. 25. *Celebrations and recreation*

Ten days ago the open service[9] very successfully put on a celebration for the patients. This celebration had everything: skill, effort, play … And crucially it had many spectators, a very pleasant setting and a very appreciable silence. On this day in the open service the atmosphere was thus important, profound, human. On this day in the open service, we had the material proof of what must be done.

The open service thus provided the material proof that a hundred patients of various divisions can all come together as if in an auditorium. Collective life. The chance to put on a play for others, to see people putting on a play for others. The necessity for some to follow the play, to respect the play. The necessity for the others to play the game, to take the game to its maximum of truth, balance or accuracy. The necessity, for all, to make possible at hospital, balance, poetry and order in aesthetic demonstrations. The open service has shown us the possibility of all that; it has shown us its richness.

For the open service, what would be good now is not to stop there, not to believe that the proof can be given in one go. What the open service needs to do is invite us again in fifteen days' time.

24 June 1954, no. 27.

[Letter from Ahmed Noui to] M. médecin-chef de service, 5th division.

Last evening, during the feast day arrangements at De Clérambault, 'Un homme est un homme'[10] was played. I say, in turn, that 'A woman's a woman', because, apart from the song that charmed the ears of the audience with those soft feminine voices, some scenes from Le Bourgeois

---

[9][A day service for psychiatric treatment, without internment. On Porot's innovations to the conception of the psychiatric hospital, see René Collignon, 'La psychiatrie coloniale française en Algérie et au Sénégal', *Tiers Monde*, vol. 47, no. 187, 2006, pp. 527–46; Saïd Chebili, 'La théorie évolutionniste de l'école d'Alger: une idéologie scientifique exemplaire', *L'Information psychiatrique*, vol. 91, no. 2, February 2015, pp. 163-8. Fanon provides a comprehensive description of the open service of the day hospital that he founded in Tunis in 'Day hospitalization in psychiatry: Value and limits' (see *below*, p. 325). He also heavily criticizes Porot's primitivism in '*Ethnopsychiatric considerations*' (see *below*, p. 251].

[10][Oscar Brand's popular song 'A Guy is a Guy', a French version of which was first released by Yvette Giraud in 1953.]

gentilhomme *were played in which M. Jourdain and his valet were portrayed by women. This meant that the sound and the articulation were missing. Nor was there any charm or attraction.*

Why, then, doctor, are male patients not called upon to participate insofar as they are able to perform a role in performances such as this? Why, then, are the men removed from the women? You reproached me one day for being distrustful, but what then do you call that? You will tell me that these were 'precautions', but the patients were never left alone. Why, then, is there this gap that creates timidity in some and fear in others? Why, then, make things abnormal through such separation, while many patients are reproached for not being sociable? Why avoid bringing people together in a way to end the spirit of longing driving them, some for the others, when they see each other from afar and which even works over one's mind?

Where, then, is your society, doctors of the PHB? In short, it doesn't exist. You are in favour of individualism, there is no mistaking it. With your lucidity, I hope that all this will soon end, doctor, at least concerning our ward.

Doctor's note. Mr. Noui's article is very important. The author indicates certain things that he deems anomalous in a hospital whose self-declared goal is the organization of a social life for its boarders. Mr. Noui is therefore right to ask why the male patients and the female patients are separated from one another. He is right to emphasize that it would be good if the theatre performances offered more of a chance for different boarders to meet with each other and not to have male roles played by women and vice versa. But the author of that article forgets or ignores certain things: first, in the open service men and women do rehearse together and perform plays together, which therefore proves, contrary to what Mr. Noui thinks, that mistrust is not the issue here. The truth is that we have no common theatre space in the hospital in which we can gather all the patients together. The day that this theatre exists, I think that there will be no difficulty in having men and women of the hospital come together, but as things currently stand, it is hard to see how this ideal could be realized. So, Mr. Noui, do not speak of mistrust and do not say that the society of which we speak is only a dream; on the contrary, it is very real, but demands to be built with calmness, prudence and measure.

15 July 1954, no. 30. *From the Moorish café to social life*

There was quite an uproar in that room filled with multicoloured streamers and unusual tables ... The uproar has died down. It is a good thing. But the room remains. And some precious lessons have come out of that continuation.

The Moorish café is a social reality. In France, according to recent statistics, there is one café for every seventy-eight inhabitants – children, women and the aged included. That means that the café is not an exception in social life but that it predominates on all street corners. So the café has a necessity about it. The café corresponds to a need. A social need. The café is a social institution. In France the café is frequented by women. In France the café is a society. In the sense in which one says: 'I'm going out to socialize' ('*Je vais en société*').

In Algeria, the café also exists. Algerians are accustomed to going to the café. Yet there is an essential difference between it and the European café. In Algeria, the café is frequented exclusively by men. It is a society of men. It is the men's living room. The women visit each other at home. The men meet each other at the café. The café is the property of those who go there. That is to say, the consumers behave at the café a little as if they were at home.

The Moorish café at Reynaud introduces into the hospital an embryo of social life that ought to be taken to its fullest.

22 July 1954, no. 31.

At this time, the Blida-Joinville psychiatric hospital is part of the twenty psychiatric hospitals involved in developing constellations of socially structured activities for the hospitalized patient. As Doctor Lacaton said recently, these activities are to be intensified daily. Now, who is to carry out that intensification? It is the various hospital teams in question that will make this progressive enrichment possible. If the hospital receptionist is unwelcoming to visitors, these visitors may not want to come back.

We must never forget that our patients are not merely from the region but also sometimes from Ghardaïa and even from Tunisia. You are aware that, for many people, mental illness is a chronic illness and that [as the saying goes] 'when you come here, you never ever leave'. If the visitor's contact with us is disagreeable, he may use it as a reason not come back, and who is going to suffer from this?

The patients, the parents. But if, on the contrary, the receptionist is friendly, courteous, if he is not seen as a sentinel but rather as someone who is there to put patients within the reach of visitors, well, then this is one reef less.

I was struck, and those who read the second last issue of *Our Journal* must have been as well, by the recognition that most of our patients felt toward the driver. All of them said that the driver drove at an average speed. An appropriate speed for an excursion. There would have been two ways to drive: to go from the hospital to the designated place and return again in the manner of a chore; or drive forty boarders at a pleasant speed enabling them to appreciate and savour the excursion. The driver took the latter option. And he did well. More: he did the right thing.

5 August 1954, no. 33.

This issue deals somewhat with the question of Aïd-el-Kébir. Next week's will deal even more with this question. The Mufti of Blida has accepted to come and visit the Muslim boarders of our hospital for the occasion at 10 am and if possible to preside over a mass at the mosque.

We hope that this first encounter between official Muslim religion and our patients is the prelude to regular, and therefore more edifying, events. When we speak about putting at the patient's disposal a multiplicity of frameworks, a[n infinite] variety of tasks, great attention must be paid to not forgetting to reach out to the majority of the hospital's patients.

Aïd-el-Kébir's celebration is proof that we are trying hard to take them into account.

19 August 1954, no. 35. *Towards a living journal*

Important things were at stake at the Journal Committee Meeting on Saturday July 31. Serious things. The Committee took to making a pronouncement on the value of vague and imprecise texts. The question was asked as to why these articles are so woolly, so obscure, so incomprehensible. One of the authors, I believe, supplied the answer to the problem: the patient knows what he or she puts into his or her text, and that is enough for him or her. Others don't matter!

However, who does not see that, grasped in this way, the journal thus becomes the accomplice of what it claims to be combatting? The journal's mission is not to make public so-and-so's fictional or irrelevant fantasies. The weekly ward journal aims to make public the community's efforts and accomplishments.

We at the hospital do not require any internal dramas, any 'immanent enthusiasm'. What we need is to speak a simple, direct, topical, true language. We need to think in a way that is reflective, not fragmented but instead pulled together. We need dialogues, precisely because dialogue renders us present to our comrades and to the committee.

The journal helps us to think things through and communicate our impressions with the entire hospital. To write means to want to be read. In the same stroke it means to want to be understood. In the act of writing there is an effort being made; muddled and vague things are combatted, surpassed. It is about not enclosing yourself in woolly dreams.

It is not about imitating oneself. On the contrary, owing to the large number of texts that appear in it, the journal serves as a place of getting to know oneself. If two boarders relate the same outing, you will see that the tone of each of the articles changes. Not because the style is the person, but because the tone changes.

The complainer who always has something to criticize recognizes himself, since for him everything is bad. It is by writing and by reading what the others write that the complainer perceives that he does not think exactly like the others. Then an effort to think with measured ideas can arise in him.

2 September 1954, no. 37.

Some weeks ago, the patients of De Clérambault assembled to elect the members of the Record Collection Committee. This Committee is tasked with procuring the records that the boarders request the most and with organizing a fortnightly listening session. Once a sufficient number of records have been collected, the committee members will go to the various wards and hear their comrades' requests. The most sought-after records are the ones that will be played on the day of the listening session. So, it may be that dance numbers, melodies and symphonic music all get played on one and the same day.

We ask all those with musical training to present themselves on the day of the event in question as technical advisors. These technicians will be able to make comments about the records. Along the same lines, the hope is that, at Reynaud, a Record Collection Committee will be created for playing Arab records to Muslim patients.

Everything that facilitates meetings and contacts is a good thing. Let's hope that the first listening session will be arranged as soon as possible.

7 October 1954, no. 42.

During the last Journal Committee Meeting, a delegate from the first division surprised a large number of us. He told us that most of his comrades were in fact unaware of the journal's existence. He himself, he told us, had thought that a mere two or three issues had appeared. Up against such a situation, two explanations can be put forward.

1) The boarders are indifferent to manifestations of collective life: the journal, soirées, outings, cinema, are thus to be interpreted as distracting elements, valueless, meaningless, dead ends and not as possibilities for meeting. And we must no longer endeavour to link together, to socialize. On the contrary, we must recognize that all these things appear in an atmosphere of total indifference, so that the reasonable attitude is to interrupt them.

2) There could be a second explanation. So that a group triggers the involvement of particular individuals, it must provide the different personalities with what might be called fields of action. Do all these groups, all these committees, really allow for such involvement? Does that elementary, primordial, commonplace palpitation arise that is the hearth itself of civility? Mr. Cohen's bitter observation is in reality the most severe criticism that can be directed at us. But it is productive, because ultimately Mr. Cohen is on the Committee and he has promised to 'open up' Our Journal.

14 October 1954, no. 43.

Everything had a beginning. People who are certainly well-intentioned but poorly informed, or who have a short memory, seem to believe and want to spread the notion that a social life was first organized for patients at HPB[11] only some months ago. Well, it is enough to throw a look backwards to observe that:

1) The arranging of work activities dates practically from the birth of the hospital nearly twenty years ago, both on the farm as well as in the workshops or sewing rooms. For several years already, the products made in sewing rooms have been used to improve the lot of patients, and in particular the workers, the aged and the children.

2) Recreation has been arranged for patients for several years already. All the wards have been supplied with radio sets. Films are screened each week. The library loans books to all patients. Feast days have been organized several times each year. Sports fields have been created.

3) Contacts with the outside were not been neglected: many patients have been into town with their families, orderlies and even by themselves. A group of women has regularly attended the cinema club sessions at Blida. Men regularly went to football matches. Other patients have been to the travelling circuses.

4) Each year, the doctors' report has asked that further improvements be made, some of which, decided long ago, only saw the light of day in 1954: outings to the seaside, and setting up an open service as well as a nursing school.

All this is the result of patient and quietly undertaken work, performed in friendly cooperation among all the various doctors who have followed one another in succession here at HPB ever since its creation. To add a pavilion to a building and have it repainted does not mean that it has been entirely built. The strictest steadfastness is the essential condition of correct social relations. This is why this short historical reminder appears essential.

Doctors: Micucci, Fanon, Ramée, Lacaton, Dequeker.

21 October 1954, no. 44.

Mr. Cohen's article certainly made an impression on the Journal Committee. Hence the suggestion that it be published in full.

---

[11] [Psychiatric hospital of Blida-Joinville.]

However, it is important to be careful not to render the elements of social life at HPB abstract. The idea that the Committee is a 'small parliament' is not true. Nor are the doctors, ministers. But the article does have some generous ideas expressed in it.

A Little Parliament

This week's October 14 journal provides us with a large list of social organizations in the clinic. I am however surprised not to find one line concerning Our Journal, *whose creation extends back more than a year and whose activity proves more interesting with each passing week.*

If, among all the planned or already operational projects, it was permitted to state a preference, I would point out the creation of Our Journal, *which has turned out to be an organ of the highest value. It provokes the boarders' personalities and gives them back their souls. It is a powerful link between us all; it is also a vehicle of understanding and a remarkably effective agent of connection.*

For those who have attended a Journal Committee Meeting, you would say it looks like a small parliament sitting opposite a council of ministers, where one side states its wishes and argues for them, and the other sides notes them down, examining and subjecting everything to scrutiny! With a little imagination, do we not see these male and female delegates, coming out of the meeting and returning to their comrades, conveying to all what has been said and done, as a report of their mandate! Is this not a small institution and is the institution not the basis of all social life!

Mr. Cohen (1st division).

18 November 1954, no. 48.

Mrs Kaf Zora, on the occasion of her article, raises a most important question about the elaboration of a social life at the hospital: a festivities room? You must come to De Clérambault, Régis, Magnan, on the evenings when a theatre play is being put on to see the fever that reigns there; the patients are obliged to eat quickly. The washing up, cleaning, polishing must be done; then the decorating, the adorning. The place in which the theatrical and artistic performances are to unfold must be made pleasant, enjoyable.

Soon dozens and dozens of men and women boarders, and of invited guests, will be arriving; everything must be clean, everything must be beautiful. In haste the stage has had to be arranged with the help of tables, and the electricians have come to install everything quickly ... Would it not be infinitely more enjoyable to have a real

Figure 5 The kitchens at Blida-Joinville Hospital. Credit: Fonds Frantz Fanon/ IMEC.

festival hall with the whole arrangement at the very core of the hospital, both independent and grandiose ...

25 November 1954, no. 49.

In 1953, a series of reports appeared in the world; some were elaborated at the behest of the World Health Organization by a committee of experts. *Our Journal* published some extracts of the report devoted to the public psychiatric hospital. Once again, it seems to me important to recall one of the fundamental givens of this report. The committee considers that no psychiatric hospital ought to exceed one thousand beds. Of course, adds the committee, some hospitals exceed these dimensions, but everything must nonetheless be done to discourage this sort of hospital from being built. But let's hear what the committee has to say.

The arguments raised are in general based on the per patient and per day cost reductions that a larger establishment is able to accomplish. However, the widespread opinion according to which the very large hospitals are more economic turns out to be baseless.

Recent studies have shown that from the point of view of financial economy, the optimum capacity of hospitals is probably situated between two-hundred-and-fifty and four-hundred beds.

Smaller establishments are onerous owing to their weak coefficient of occupation and the difficulties in amortizing technical equipment that is not fully utilized. Above four hundred beds, the cost per bed increases slowly and reaches excessive values with 800 beds; the causes probably reside in the uncontrollable wastage, the lack of a spirit of responsibility on the part of a very numerous staff, the useless purchases and the industrial-type of mechanization that is inevitable in large establishments.

30 December 1954, second year, no. 2.

The special issue of *Our Journal* was devoted to the New Year celebrations. Also celebrated was, in a sense, the first anniversary of the establishment's weekly journal. The boarders have written some very beautiful things on this topic. These articles express an earnestness of great worth. It is paradoxical to note, incidentally, the distance that exists between those who write and those who read.

If it's true that such earnestness does not always manage to reach the reader, it seems that an average can be attained fairly easily. However, many of *Our Journal's* readers do not seem to gauge the entire importance of the texts that appear in it. Thus, in no. 51, Mr Muller made some gentle reproaches to the organizers of the Magnan celebration. No. 52 contains a reply to that criticism: 'We'll do better the next time'. But the criticism was not stupid or disagreeable. It was, in a sense, a piece of advice to ensure that 'our celebrations for all' turn out better …

The boarders who write in the journal do not do it for the sake of doing something. They each express something that prevails for them. The act of writing is already a higher act. The act of reading as well.

13 January 1955, second year, no. 4. *Regarding a visit*[12]

The transfer of a patient to the hospital that I had treated in Lyon afforded me the occasion to spend a day with you all. I visited the

---

[12][Here we have transcribed the editorial of Doctor Albert Gambs, because Fanon refers to it in the following issue of *Our Journal*. In addition, he provides a good description of the projects accomplished since Fanon's arrival and of the style of the hospital's operations. It was not unusual for the editorial to be written not by one of Blida's doctors but instead by a visitor, or for it to consist in extracts of texts published by psychiatric periodicals. The hospital journal was therefore also a permanent instrument for the professional training of the hospital's nursing staff. We might note,

wards and I would like to make use of your journal in order to tell you the impression it has made on me.

A modern hospital, new wards, well-kept and well-arranged – that's what strikes one from the first. But that is not the most important thing. A visitor used to psychiatric hospitals is less sensitive to the décor, as beautiful as it may be, than he is to the atmosphere that prevails in it, and in your establishment that atmosphere struck me. No sterile restlessness, no throng of people around the doctor as he passed through a ward: each person is busy with his or her work and interested in it. Your nurses do not monitor you, but really 'live' among you, side by side, participating in the same activities as you.

I saw your Moorish café. It's a genuine café with genuine customers, an excellent terrain for relearning gestures of the outside world. I saw your stadium, the result of your work. You can be proud of it. It will serve well. I saw your raffia workshop, your printing facilities, your journal. I liked the arrangement of your treatment rooms and the competency of your nurses.

Of course many things are still left to be done. There are many of you and there ought to be work for all of you and not only for the most resourceful. You live alongside one another, and you often don't know each other. The group activities, the occupations that you are offered, must become an occasion for getting to know one another, for getting you re-accustomed to living with one another.

I take my leave with your journal in hand, and I hope that it will form an active link and be a source of fruitful exchanges between Blida and Lyon.

Doctor Gambs.

25 January 1955, second year, no. 6.

In the article that he kindly wrote for *Our Journal*, Doctor Gambs wrote: 'I saw your Moorish café, a genuine café with genuine customers, an excellent terrain for relearning gestures of the outside world.'

---

in addition, that Gambs had just published a work about psychiatric experiments conducted with chlorpromazine, a work that could not have failed to interest Fanon: Albert Gambs, *Essai d'application de la chlorpromazine en cures prolongées au traitement de diverses affections mentales. À propos de 58 observations*, Lyon: Bosc, 1954.]

To relearn. I find this expression very beautiful. Let's understand by it that what is at issue is not to give to the boarder a stock of movements, attitudes and words. At issue is not to add onto an inexistent personality a sum of behaviours. At issue is not to create, to produce, to refine, to finish.[13]

It is a matter of enabling the boarder to reprise, to begin again by helping him or her to understand better, to grasp things better, that is to say, to grasp him- or herself better again.

The point cannot be to say: that is all worthless, it must all be destroyed. At issue, once again, is to provide the boarder with frames, groups and occasions within which it becomes possible for him or her to *rediscover* what has existed. It is necessary to induce the boarder to rediscover the meaning of freedom, which is the first milestone on the way to responsibility.

The quest for the personality of the one who is entrusted to us has to be our continual concern.

17 March 1955, second year, no. 13.

Are there no other topics for meditation than those forming the focus of this issue? Such are the questions I have heard this week. Do the male and female boarders of this establishment not have different preoccupations, different concerns, ones that are less immediate, less down to earth, more elevated? And it could be felt from the tone of these diverse reflections that the considerations and criticisms to do with food in this issue were adjudged inappropriate and valueless.

For my part, I do not think that such attitudes, with their extremism, play a role in the concrete and daily preoccupations of this hospital. Eating is not a chore for humans. Eating is not inferior to thinking, and I don't see why considerations about food should yield to aesthetic concerns. The person who is concerned with what he or she eats, who requests that the dishes, though less abundant, be better prepared, who points out that the food is being served cold, that the fish is always covered in sauce, that the vinaigrette is often only vinegar, who bemoans that dessert is such a rare event, who

---

[13][Fanon was aware of Merleau-Ponty's critique of behaviourism. In the copy of *La Structure du comportement* held in his library, the following phrase is underlined: 'To learn is thus never about becoming able to repeat the same gesture, but to provide an adapted response to the situation by different means' (see *Frantz Fanon's Library*, p. 413.]

notes that some dishes are repugnant by virtue of their polymorphous character (ravioli), and for reasons that are given (possible presence of pork for Muslim boarders)…

The boarder who asks for food that caresses the palate and who therefore aspires to turn soup into a meal: I don't see that this patient is doing anything else other than developing the sense of a taste for nuance. This striving to take an interest, concretely, on a daily basis and with accuracy, is a highly elevated form of sociability and we ought to congratulate the boarders who have produced this issue.

24 March 1955, second year, no. 14.

The orderlies from our establishment went to France to take further professional training courses. Their professors' major concern, it seems, was to present a programme concerning what is currently known as social therapy.

The orderlies were struck by the effort that the speakers put in to show just how indispensable it is to have a cordial understanding among themselves. The orderlies were obliged to arrange evening gatherings every day in order to demonstrate clearly the necessity for such perfect cordiality. Let's take some of the phrases uttered by the professors.

The patient's life must be as close as possible to ours, including his or her washing, clothing, meals, occupations, affection and consideration: people need love, affection and poetry in order to live. Patients show this privation in their illnesses by closing up inside themselves.

In the near future, the orderlies who have participated in the course will write a summary of their impressions for *Our Journal*.

7 April 1955, second year, no. 16.[14]

The sports meetings now scheduled on our football field each Thursday attract a considerable 'crowd' that seems to be taking a growing interest in the *game* itself and in the exploits of its favourites players; it must be noted that, hitherto, the most enthusiastic spectators (and the noisiest ones) are the orderlies present at the stadium. This is not a bad thing, however, as sporting 'passion' is communicative.

---

[14][We reprint here an editorial by Raymond Lacaton because Fanon refers directly to it in his important editorial on the notion of institution in the subsequent issue.]

Even better, the number of boarders *playing* is actually growing, for three *teams* have now officially been created. Besides, even for the uninitiated, their technical level and skills are on display insofar as the players regularly go to *training* sessions. Equipment (jerseys, socks, balls) was recently procured through the product of the boarders' *work* to contribute to our hospital football.

The preceding contains words that all hang upon one another: game, team, training, work. Training for a team game is at the same time a training for work because work enables, favours, justifies the game. That whole must remain a solid *institution*.

Doctor Lacaton.

14 April 1955, second year, no. 17.[15]

The 'institution' was the central issue of the previous editorial; and the great merit of the definition put forward of it was the importance granted to movement. The equilibrium between the team game, regular training, and ordered and creative work confers on the institution both its solidity and its plasticity.

From there, the following question must be asked and is asked: is every institution not in constant danger of vitiation? Or again: does not every attempt to give body to an institution risk taking directions that are fundamentally opposed to the open, fecund, global and nevertheless qualified character of the institution?

You have to place yourself at the heart of the institution and interrogate it. If it is a generous source, it must enable multiple personalities to be manifest in it. It has to make possible interminable and fruitful encounters. It has to be multiplied constantly. It has to be at the disposal of its members, at their service.

---

[15][This editorial reprises the preceding one, which Lacaton addressed essentially to the patients, in order to address the orderlies. Here we clearly read about the fundamental principles of social therapy: mistrust toward routine and institutional fragmentation, causes of pathologies produced by the asylum, but at the same time the conviction that a good conception and *constant* reactivation (temporality is at the core of this reflection) of the *movement* of the institution are key to re-socializing the mentally ill. Now Fanon's political thought, his later warnings about neocolonialism, his doubts – attested by many close associates – on the direction taken by the revolution, and finally his interest in Sartre's *Critique de la raison dialectique* upon its publication, a book on which he reportedly gave courses to ALN cadres at the borders, can be reread in the light of this reflection on the permanent danger of 'vitiation' incurred by every institution. This concern can be seen to grow as the editorials progress.]

If it does not radiate, if it fails to achieve its essential duty, which is constant dialogue between its members, if it permits 'collective monologue,'[16] and if, lastly, it does not foster its members' responsibility, then its time is up.

One is on the wrong path.

14 July 1955, second year, no. 30.

Last month, juries constituted by members of the *Académie des sciences, belles-lettres et arts* at Clermont-Ferrand, as well as members from the *Société des artistes* in Auvergne, awarded works by boarders at establishments in France and in its overseas territories. The Blida-Joinville Psychiatric Hospital committed to participating in this major national competition by sending two works along.

A painting by Mr. Domby in the first division and a miniature by Mr. Ranem in the second. A letter from the general secretary of the *Sociétés de croix-marine* informed us that the miniature received joint first prize. By contrast, Mr. Domby's painting, likely held up by the customs services, arrived after the jury's deliberation. In spite of this delay, the secretariat decided to award this work, *Le Méhariste*[17] – the theme of this boarder's work – an hors-jury prize.

What lesson ought we to draw from this competition? It is a very clear one, as we see, namely, that it is necessary to go on. It is absolutely necessary that we be part of the network of avant-garde establishments, in which such events, both manifold and diverse, facilitate social relations, call for comparison, develop a feel for trials and the concern to accomplish.

28 July 1955, second year, no. 32.

One year ago, the Moorish café opened its doors in Reynaud. This anniversary is an interesting one to mark. Be that as it may, how can we not singularly delight in noticing that the Moorish café, which once upon a time represented the only meeting place for boarders, has now lost its central character, its character as an exception. Indeed, we've seen many other meeting places pop up, here and

---

[16][A concept developed by Piaget to describe the egocentrism of the child in its use of language until around seven years of age, when it is not yet fully socialized (see Jean Piaget, *The Language and Thought of the Child*, trans. Majorie and Ruth Gabain, New York, NY, and London: Routledge, 2002 (French original, 1923)).]

[17][Translator's note: the portrait of a mehari, or dromedary, rider.]

there: the oriental salon for Muslim women at Fairet, and *guinguette* at Magnan Park.[18]

We are pleased to observe the ever-widening social relations at our establishment. And we hope that these efforts will continue and enable us always to forge further ahead.

11 August 1955, second year, no. 34.

Not so long ago, a few decades, heroes proved themselves on the battle field. The specificity of heroes was to struggle against death and, most of the time, to bring about the death of the other. Not so long ago, heroes distinguished themselves through exceptional acts, through uncommon attitudes – the hero was different in kind.

It is one of the merits of the contemporary era to have shown the banal, everyday aspect of the modern hero, one lacking in splendour. The famous expression of one of our novelists is not a mere wisecrack: marriage is the tragedy of modern times. Very precisely, this author is alluding to the sort of repetition that is bound to result in enrichment, to the apparent immobility that is internal fecundity. The hero is not one who performs a dazzling feat and goes to bed considering he's done enough. The hero is rather one who gets through his or her task with conscientiousness and love. Every day, without haste but also unremittingly, he weaves his work with precise order.

For the worst mistake is to believe that the work undertaken, if it is abandoned even for a moment, remains intact. Section after section, it falls apart. A person makes or unmakes him or herself every day. Every day the task has to be conducted with tenacity.

25 August 1955, second year, no. 36.

In a few days, the boarders' journal will undergo a major event. In fact, the idea of having a genuine printing facility has taken shape and the matter is now to acquire it. Naturally several problems will emerge.

And the first is the location. At De Clérambault, a small room was made available to *Our Journal,* with the machine's small dimensions

---

[18][Translator's note – A *guinguette* is an old term first used for the open-air cafés, which also served as dance halls, notably located in the suburbs of Paris.]

in mind. Now the new printer is going to be far larger and so a real workshop must be found for it. The bursar will make the cellar of Rogues de Fursac available to us. But this operation depends upon the evacuation of the mosque's ergotherapy annex, which itself depends upon … We are going to have to wait a while. In any case, a tent will be provisionally assigned to the printer.

Then there is the staff. Up to now, the women boarders of De Clérambault have seen to the printing of the journal. But it is clear that they will not be able any longer to ensure the operation of a machine like the one we have decided to buy; it would be good if male boarders could step up and take care of the printing.

Lastly, the third problem and not the least of them: the quantity of articles. It has often transpired that a lack of space prevented some articles from being published, but very often, all too often, the articles were actually too few. Now that the journal hopes to come out with a total of four pages, the instruction is formal: everyone must write. The hospital, as the sociologists say, has gone from the oral phase to the written phase.

27 October 1955, second year, no. 45.

Mr. Boulez's last article, written on the occasion of his leaving, proved, if it were needed, the necessity and the interest of the various committees. His advice was not to give up on the committees. Those who have taken it upon themselves to be present each time perhaps know the internal and external difficulties that must be overcome in order, for example, to be at the Journal Committee Meeting on Friday at 9.30 am. How many times have only six or seven of us shown up out of the 2,000 boarders in the establishment? Boulez knows this. That is why his article has value for us as a testimony.

Accomplish the plans issued by the committees. And naturally how can we not think about the float of flowers. Or about July 14. Come to the committees, work to accomplish the plans made, and little by little you will get back into the activity of social life. Mr. Boulez's article is one of the most important of the year.

17 November 1955, second year, no. 48.

Why do we want at all costs to have a journal within a psychiatric establishment? Why might the idea of a journal at Mustapha or

Marengo hospital seem absurd? Why is it that, for ten years now, so many journals have appeared in psychiatric hospitals? What is the real importance of these journals? What use is a journal in a hospital and, more precisely, in a psychiatric hospital?

By way of an editorial, I would like to submit this questionnaire to the establishment's boarders and staff. The responses should be passed on to *Our Journal's* editorial board. On the occasion of the anniversary of *Our Journal*, such a survey can be significant. The hope is that large numbers of replies will be forthcoming.

28 March 1956, third year, no. 13.

One of the difficulties encountered in the exercise of a profession is doubtless habit. The moment arrives fairly quickly when gestures follow other gestures without novelty. A big effort of imagination is required to discover, or in any case to allow, the appearance of an atmosphere in constant movement.

In a hospital such as ours, a large effort must be made to avoid automatisms from settling in – days ought not to be like other days, hours not like other hours.

When we work on trees or on stones, the modifications alone, the changes alone, the novelties alone, are the deed of our personal histories. In the hospital where we work with human beings, things proceed entirely differently. We really are working with people. So if people are what constitute the goal, that is, the goal of our daily action, then it becomes clear, it becomes necessary, that no dose of habit, of habituation, of automatism can intervene. For people have the extraordinary quality of being in constant renewal.

Meeting the obligation to understand, day-in day-out, the people with whom we come face-to-face and who, more precisely, are entrusted to us, is one of the most important elements of the profession of nursing.

28 June 1956, third year, no. 27.

Following an error, a letter from the boarders at Jean Lépine about the chapel and the mosque was conveyed to *Our Journal*, laying out a difficult problem. But in fact there is no problem at all and it is enough to explain how the image of the mosque came to be in the journal header to prevent anyone from assigning it a meaning other than it has.

During the summer of 1954, a decision was made to improve the somewhat ordinary header of *Our Journal* by adding a drawing with local character. Several proposals were put forward and examined, and the one accepted was the depiction of a mosque, not as a symbol of Muslim religion but as a monument of typically Algerian architecture: had someone thought of it, the palm tree and kiosk at the *Place d'Armes* in Blida could equally have been chosen.

With this clarified, it is very evident that no one has any reason to create a polemic around the journal. Above all, it must be highlighted that we should avoid all occasions to create division or opposition. The arranging of social life within the hospital is based on the existence of friendly relations between boarders, regardless of their origin, their religion. This is why the meeting-points and occasions for meeting have been increased.

The day that people endeavour to make a big deal out of what separates us from each other, we will see a myriad of committees and sub-committees appear: Arabs, Kabyles, Mozabites, Algerian French (with sub-committees for the regions of Oran, Alger and Constantine), metropolitan French (with sub-committees per region ...). And we ought not to forget the group of the non-grouped for those who are unable to find a place in the preceding groups ... The day it comes to this, there will be no need to dissolve all the current organizations that tend toward the improvement of life in common – they will have dissolved of themselves.

So, since life obliges us to spend some weeks or months together, is it not better to seek out occasions for friendly relations? On this point, the football teams provide a remarkable example, and all the outside spectators stated upon leaving the stadium: 'Your matches are far friendlier and more decent that those played by teams outside'. Good examples do not always come from the outside. This is true, and in all domains it is necessary that this spirit of sportive loyalty and of friendly co-existence becomes the hospital's rule of living.

Médecins-chefs of the wards.

19 July 1956, third year, nos. 29–30.

In some wards, competitions take place in the dining halls, rooms, corridors and living rooms. What is judged, evaluated, rewarded are not things like cleanliness, beds with hospital corners, etc. The jury does make pronouncements on the accidental aspects, as seen on the occasion of inspections and official visits. The basis of the jury, its system of reference, has more to do with the general outlook of the ward, its open, non-coercive character. What the jury members are looking for is life in movement, the involvement of the boarders, their commitment, their engagement.[19] What is judged is the value of relations: boarders-staff, boarders-boarders, staff-staff.

At this level everything clearly takes on an importance. That is, insofar as it is true that the ward is and remains the essential therapeutic arm. To say about a ward that it has to be therapeutic in its structure is tantamount to reiterating that the boarder's day, from waking to sleeping, necessitates a rational organization. It is within spontaneous or institutionalized groups that the boarders, through the play of preferences and wishes, respond and commit.

As members of the group, the staff never adopt the aspect of observers or censors. Quite to the contrary, a staff member's nuanced and balanced engagement enables the group to become organized and a source of life.

4 October 1956, third year, no. 41.

We must pay tribute, as is proper, to the near completion of the stadium. We can already say that the construction of the sports block of the hospital will be finished in three years' time. Now the important thing in this little story is less the thickness of the walls or the solidity of the seats than the progressive thriving of the establishment's sporty atmosphere.

Additional teams, the inclusion of training staff in the teams, an official calendar, membership cards, the homogeneity of unanimously adopted training programmes, a real Sports Committee – all these advances of importance, and therefore of style, indicate what still needs doing. And of course all is not yet finished. A column, it may be seen, is not necessarily an institution.

---

[19][Many aspects of this reflection on engagement and 'life in movement' within groups, which subsequent editorials pursue further, echo Sartre's thinking.]

The psychiatric hospital, like every collective, demands two directions of evolution – one horizontal, the other vertical. This means that adding more committees on top of the others is one thing. And infusing life into each committee, transforming each committee into words of truth and enrichment, is another. There is nothing immediately obvious about this. For the lie is not the fact of an isolated individual. Each impairment to truth has something complicitous about it. Last year's teams 'A' and 'B' were somewhat meaningless. Likewise, the open service team backed up by Reynaud. You must always ask, 'What is the question here?'

Is it to offer boarders a type of motor commitment to possibilities of rapid integration that open onto a shared existence, or else to enable a pseudo-ludic identification with a strong exhibitionist charge for the staff? There is no doubting the reply today, but it may have been necessary to pass through this self-criticism, which is the criterion of the true. The staff as a whole, through the gravity that presides over the current committees, has displayed a radical awareness. Let's go, it's time for work.

8 November 1956, third year, no. 46.

When two people meet and decide to live together, they come to agreement on a certain number of points. Between them some things are permitted and some things are prohibited. The advised things pertain to morality and the prohibited things to the law. Every social group implies and requires, among other things, moral authorities and legal authorities. It therefore seems that the concern of the Sports Committee with elaborating general disciplinary regulations – with sanctions, penalties – is proceeding in a customary way. In the first part we will publish the Committee's draft proposal for a list of regulations, and in the second, present some reflections on it.

Rules and regulations. Measures of order.

Art. 1. – Measures of order will be applied to players whose conduct was the subject of an incident or of disorder before, during or after the match, and notably for any improper attitude toward the referee, officials or spectators.

Art. 2. – The following scale has been established:

1) impropriety toward spectators and assaulting a spectator;

2) impropriety toward an adversary (insults or threats), assaulting an adversary, or mutual assaults;

3) wrongs committed against a referee, against a line judge or an obligatory referee: a) offensive remarks; b) insults; c) provocative acts or threats; d) assaults:

a suspension of one to three matches.

Art. 3. – A player sent from the field upon the decision of the referee has 24 hours to address a detailed and written account of the incidents or reasons that led to his or her being sent off.

Art. 4. – The disciplinary committee must meet within six days. It is made up of players-trainers (six). It is presided by a member of the management committee. All persons, whether leaders or players, who are singled out by the referee are obliged to front up to the disciplinary committee. The referee is also obliged to file a complaint for the matters they have singled out.

Art. 5. – Notification of the measures to be taken will be provided by the disciplinary committee to the interested party after the latter has been heard and supplied all explanations.

Art. 6. – A reprieve may be granted following a request to the médecin-chef.

15 November 1956, third year, no. 47.

'Punishments, court, inquiry, filing, reprieve': the draft of the 'rules and regulations' uses these words with astonishing ease. Is it standard for a committee with therapeutic pretentions to employ such words in this way? Yes, it seems. If the aim is in fact to care for someone, ought the emergence of normal, ordered, socialized behaviours not be facilitated? And then, is it not important to single out, penalize and sanction disorderly, asocial and improper attitudes? Let us see where this leads.

If sport is therapeutic, it must serve to cure. To register abnormal behaviour (offensive words, insults, provocative gestures, assaults: paragraph a, b, c, art. 2 of the Regulations), to penalize it, to make sure its authors are thwarted and shamed, this is to force them to account for their actions, to give them a sense of responsibility, to facilitate their aptitude to defend their point of view, to present it in front of the group of their fellow patients.

From that point of view, penalizing a player is neither more nor less than adopting within the establishment ways of proceeding that are common outside it. So, it seems once again that having rules and regulations is the true and fair path to follow. These sanctions prepare the boarder for life on the outside. The process of readapting the boarder cannot be understood otherwise. For an adapted behaviour is one that respects established customs.

We will see in a subsequent editorial that this position remains peripheral to the problem. In actual fact, things are far more complicated. And for starters, where does the desire to penalize come from?[20]

22 November 1956, third year, no. 48.

At the community level, punishment is referred to a written code. The citizen knows the things that are prohibited. He or she knows that all violations will be sanctioned. At the family level, which is tasked with education, it is the parents, as custodians of tradition, who teach morality and good manners to children. These parents are sometimes strict, sometimes soft.

When parents are strict, the children will often be emotional, anxious, inhibited (that is to say, not daring to move). Or else the children are serious, calm, only nine years old and 'already like grown ups'. Parents are proud of these children. They indeed work well in the classroom. They are interested in serious questions. They do not play with people their age. They like to reflect. They are only ever well-mannered.

Children with lax parents will often be turbulent, noisy, and never remain in place. In the classroom, they are average students, sometimes poor ones.

And, well, as a rule we see that strict parents themselves had strict parents. Their parents ruled them with an iron fist from the earliest years. Once adults, they thanked their mothers and fathers. They came to have a position in life because they were ruled strictly. Continuing on the tradition, they are strict with their own children. Besides, they tell them: 'It's for your own good. You will thank me later'. Punishment in the familial milieu heralds all other punishments. If we want to understand why an adult punished by the law several times in a row recommences; if we want to understand why he or she is, as it were, impossible to intimidate, we must find out how he or she reacted to the punishments of his or her father.

---

[20][Fanon had read Nietzsche closely. See *Frantz Fanon's Library,* p. 415.]

But, you will say to me, what relation does this have with the Sports Committee? In our next editorial we will tackle an important question: does the orderly not have a tendency to consider him- or herself a father in relation to the boarders? Or, if you will, does the boarder not often have the tendency to consider the orderly as his or her father?

29 November 1956, third year, no. 49.

Here are the main passages of the letter addressed by Doctor Fanon to Mr. Ader, president of the boarders' Sports Committee, on the occasion of the inaugural discussion about the draft constitution.

'As I mentioned at the start, the Sports Committee is not a society; the mother society is the Algerian Society of Mental Health. This Committee's activities may only be understood under the auspices of the Mental Health Society, which is tasked with organizing events of all sorts apt to facilitate the readjustment of the boarders.

'It is absolutely absurd to want to constitute, outside of the Mental Health Society, another society, a sports society, which has no relation of reciprocity with that society. To do so, would be to run the risk of creating autonomous societies with no point of convergence, societies that would operate in a closed milieu and would interfere with the instilling of a collective atmosphere. Whence the necessity of this Committee, qua emanation of the Algerian Mental Health Society, adhering to the latter's statutes. The Committee has a certain administrative and financial autonomy, but must report to the Society on these matters at least once a year.

'The Committee's integration into the Society ought to be done in a progressive and concerted fashion. The sports committee must not be isolated from the other activities, whether we are talking about the Canteen, Film or Journal Committees. The Sports Committee must form part of the general patients' club. This is why, Mr President, I urge you to study as quickly as can be the possibility of creating other sections within this Committee. A football section, a volley-ball section, a basketball section, a bowls section, a ping pong section, an athletics section. The Sports Committee is tasked with organizing and bringing these activities forth and should form subcommittees to manage each of these diverse activities.

'Outside these statutes, I also ask you to strengthen the ties between your Committee and the other committees, for example, to ask the Film Committee to order some films for you on sports and, by appointing some reporters, to make sure reports are written of all your various sporting events and published in *Our Journal*. *Our Journal* ought not to remain isolated from your Committee. *Our Journal* ought to reflect the social life within the establishment and, as you know, sporting life is fundamental on more than one score'.

6 December 1956, third year, no. 50.

A patient is first of all someone who suffers and who asks for some relief to be given. Suffering provokes compassion, tenderness. Because the patient suffers, he or she acts a little like he or she did in childhood. It is mainly to the mother that a child turns when, for example, he or she falls over and hurts him- or herself. A caress, a kiss and the child takes off again, all better.

In hours of great suffering, the adult again has need of a consoling mother. Besides, it is very often the case that, after an accident or an operation, the first person that a patient calls for is his or her mother. A mother is someone who has protected us from suffering, from troubles. It was one's mother that resolved all the little matters. Whenever things are not going well, a desire arises to confide in one's mother. There thus seems to be a habit, a constant in our way of reacting to suffering: to call for one's mother. Incidentally, the father also plays a role. The mother consoles, caresses. The father, by contrast, settles difficult matters.

Illness more or less induces the patient suffering from it to behave a little like a child. Since this patient is obliged to depend upon others – for food, to keep him or her company, for shopping, for the smallest details – he or she is a little in the position of a child that depends on its parents for everything.

13 December 1956, third year, no. 51.

Just as the patient turns to someone caring, in an attitude reminiscent of childhood, it happens that the orderly behaves somewhat like a father. This attitude can be seen even with injuries, stomach ulcers, etc.; however, such a patient does not remain at the hospital for long, rather the patients come and go often, and in a general medical clinic it is seldom the case that a patient has to stay for a long time, such as for three, six, or eight months. And yet, if you look closely, you notice that, even in these cases, the patient respects and fears the orderly.

In a psychiatric clinic, where boarders may stay for periods of up to several years, things become very pronounced. Orderlies may adopt the habit of ordering the boarder around, and all of us, we have all heard orderlies say, for example: 'Who gives the orders around here?' It is as if the orderly has a tendency, in responding to the boarder's own child-like attitude, to behave like a parent. He will do everything that parents do; he will scold, he will punish. This is why the orderlies in some old hospitals may say to boarders: 'You will not go to the cinema tomorrow'; or: 'You will not be allowed go on the walk'; or: 'You will get no dessert'. In other old hospitals, too, orderlies may be heard saying: 'If you continue, you'll be sent to live with the lunatics and senile patients'.

Otherwise said, if care is not taken, the hospital establishment, which is above all a curative establishment, a therapeutic establishment, is gradually transformed into a barracks in which children-boarders tremble before parent-orderlies.

Of course, this state of mind has completely disappeared from psychiatric hospitals. But it is necessary to be vigilant, since, on occasion, memories from these older times come back. When parents bring their patients for a consultation with a psychiatric doctor and tell one of us that they were obliged to mete out punishment to get the patient in question to remain calm, we are not surprised, because parents always believe that patients may be cured through punishment. Because a patient comes to hospital, others change their attitudes toward him or her, which means that outside, people, who do not understand him or her, mete out punishment in order to induce fear.

Here, at the hospital, all this changes. Because we are therapists, we know that for punishment to be valid, it must rely on a whole host of other things. We do not punish our patients; we are obliged to understand each one of their attitudes. Each time we disregard our profession, each time that we give up our attitude of understanding and adopt an attitude of punishment, we are mistaken.

(To be continued.)

20 December 1956, third year, no 52.

At the beginning of civilization, and still in some regions of the earth today, the gods are called to the rescue when a person is ill.

Elsewhere, however, it is the doctor who is called. But the doctor is not a god, not a magician and does not seek to ask the gods to leave the patient in peace. The doctor makes a diagnosis and provides treatment. If the doctor starts to implore the gods or to make magic to get rid of the illness, he or she is no longer a doctor.

So what? The orderly who forgets that our duty is to understand the patient entrusted to our care and who has the tendency to punish the patient in order to, as is commonly said, 'to teach him or her a lesson' – well, this orderly, it may be said, has forgotten this duty.

The link between these aforementioned, disastrous attitudes and the concern of the boarder Sports Committee to elaborate a code, a discipline, is not an obvious one. It may be seen, however, that creating a disciplinary section risks, from the outset, both interfering with the disappearing of disastrous attitudes, and also fostering their re-emergence if they have disappeared.

It already appears that an arbiter at the psychiatric hospital does not have the same sanctions as a referee on the F.B. stadium or the Saint-Eugène stadium. I have to admit that I am bothered when I observe the refereeing of some orderlies. They act as though they were not orderlies, as if the whistle in their mouth removed from them the quality of being an orderly. They forget sometimes that their function is to be a nurse referee, not an official referee. There are thus several ways of being a referee, but there is only one way to be a good referee at the psychiatric hospital where sport is offered as a therapeutic element within the general atmosphere of the establishment. Of course, the nurse referee may well not know how to referee as a nurse; it is not his fault, which is why the Sports Committee has to ask the establishment's doctors to help it to clarify its ideas. We see, then, that the Sports Committee's role is not so much to organize sports at the hospital as it is to organize these sports within a therapeutic perspective that is part of a more general perspective.

Outside the hospital, when a decision is made to organize a group, laws are created. These laws take absolutely no account of individualities, otherwise said, the preoccupation is with generality and no account is taken of the particular case. At the psychiatric hospital, a general law cannot be established because we are not dealing with an anonymous population. We are dealing with very determinate persons and as therapists we have to take these persons, in all their nuances, into consideration; we must necessarily adapt to each boarder. At the psychiatric hospital, we cannot be hearing phrases such as: 'I do not want to know, just do as everyone else'. Because, precisely, the boarder has to relearn to be like everyone else; it is often because he or she was unable 'to do as everyone else' that he or she was entrusted to us. It is first necessary to see how he or she behaves, to help the patient to understand him or herself better and for this we must very exactly understand him or her in totality.

We may now see that formulating disciplinary rules and regulations at a psychiatric hospital is a therapeutic absurdity and that this idea must be abandoned once and for all.

9 LETTER TO MAURICE DESPINOY

Frantz Fanon, 26 March 1954[1]

My dear friend,

I received your letter long ago, but the harsh necessities of the clinic have scarcely left me the leisure to write to you in peace.

I arrived at Blida at the start of December, in this immense hospital with 2,500 beds which should only have 1,200, where the doctors are exhausted from work and the staff, after a strike that you have heard about, became mistrustful of the administration and by extension the medical body.[2] This makes every attempt at organizing collective psychotherapy extremely difficult, I would even say impossible. I have one hundred and sixty-eight European women in a ward of chronic and senile patients that I am trying to restore a little. When I tell you that these are long-term patients who've spent seven or eight years in the asylum, you'll understand the difficulties I must contend with daily. Imagine 'Providence'[3] transformed into admissions. Next to this ward – which is a manner of speaking, because it is in actual fact 1.2 km away – I have two hundred and twenty-five Muslim men, a ward of epileptics (exactly what I needed!) and one hundred and sixty-eight chronic patients.

I perform insulin therapy with the European women (twelve to fourteen courses of treatment), as I do with the men. Otherwise

---

[1]IMEC Fonds Fanon, FNN 2.5.
[2][On that strike, see Paul Marquis, 'Frantz Fanon et le personnel soignant à l'hôpital psychiatrique de Blida-Joinville'.]
[3][He is referring here to the Hospice de la Providence for women, situated in Lyon.]

put, in two or three months, I will have thirty patients under insulin shock therapy in continuous fashion.[4]

Relations with the doctors here are inexistent, above all outside relations. At Saint-Alban, what was excellent was that, independently of individual attitudes, agreement prevailed on a certain number of things, among others on a certain understanding of psychiatry and the mental life of the patients entrusted to us. Here, you have the impression that each doctor endeavours to form a cell, a block, an absolute. Contacts are external, I tell you, which means that even when we come together to discuss things, a general problem never arises. Here is an example: since arriving, I have asked that we get together once every fifteen days. Thus far, we have talked only about vegetable patches and relations with the judiciary administration. No overall project, no collaboration, no cooperation; and the worst is that at the start of meetings everyone is already tired as if all dialogue was simply in vain. It would seem that this is something specifically North-African and that I, too, will be knackered before too long.

I regret to be barely able to meet your desires to work with you these days for, you know, the problem of North African mental pathology appears more and more as a kernel that, I would not say has been badly explored, but is still unexplored. You recall Aubin's book of which I spoke to you previously and about which I wanted to publish a critique.[5] The reasons I had at the time were of a purely rational order, but it could obviously be objected that I had no concrete experience. After four months of being in North Africa, I can say that I was absolutely right and that the experience of 'systematic denial' just adds to the mass of syncretic terms by which some imagine it is possible to embrace and explain certain

---

[4][On Sakel's insulin shock therapy, see *supra*, p. see *above*, p. 18.]

[5][Henri Aubin, *L'Homme et la Magie*, Paris: Desclée de Brouwer, 1952. Aubin, influenced by psychoanalysis, speaks here of the 'systematic disowning of mental troubles among blacks [le Noir]', and develops a theory of the therapeutic value of denial. See also, 'Conduites de refus et psychothérapie,' *L'Évolution psychiatrique*, no. 4, 1950 and 'Refus, reniement, répression, discussion,' *L'Évolution psychiatrique*, no. 1, 1951, issues which Fanon possessed. On Aubin, see Alice Bullard, 'Late colonial French West African psychiatry', in Warwick Anderson, Deborah Jenson and Richard C. Keller (eds.), *Unconscious Dominions*, Durham, NC, and London: Duke University Press, 2011.]

constellations of collective attitudes.[6] The 'prelogical mentality' of sociologists of the beginning of the century,[7] the basic personality structure of contemporary American anthropologists[8] and Aubin's 'systematic denial' attempt to subsume under an empty category of thought bio-socio-psychological realities with multiple coordinates. I think that one day or another, I will have to return to this to see how what we may call the mental structures of the West Indian are evolving. But for the moment I would like in your next letter for you to tell me about homosexuality there. During my last voyage, I noticed its emergence and would like to know if it is assuming the classical psychoanalytical role or type, or if it remains [linked] to economic motivations.[9]

I have begun a ward journal here, a copy of which I'm sending you. It's poor, but it's a start. The other doctors do not budge and cast a dreamy eye on my restlessness. You spoke to me of *L'Espoir* and ought to send me a copy, so I can pass it around this establishment. Have you kept the same style as *Trait d'union*?[10]

I learnt with a dread mixed with irony about the incarceration of the president of your surveillance committee. I want to believe that you have not taken exception to this news, because it's a very common thing in the tropics.

I've received a letter that I am sending on to you. As you see, it's from a man who wants to return to the hospital. I don't know.

No, Josie is not practicing in Blida; she is still continuing in Algiers. And is Nelly content with her work? Did she have a lot of success with the *baccalauréat*? Does she get on well with her colleagues?

---

[6] [On Fanon's epistemological nominalism in matters of psychiatric nosography, see our 'Fanon, revolutionary psychiatrist'. He returns again to this in his letter to Despinoy of January 1956 (see *below*, p. 267).]

[7] [See Lucien Lévy-Bruhl, *La Mentalité primitive*, Paris: Alcan, 1922. Toward the end of his life, Lévy-Bruhl rejected the idea of a primitivism of mystical and 'prelogical' mentalities.]

[8] [Abraham Kardiner, in particular. Melville J. Herskovits, cited at the end of this letter, described his theory in a chapter titled 'La culture et la société' from his book *Les Bases de l'anthropologie culturelle*, Paris: Payot, 1952, a translation of his book *Man and his Works: The Science of Cultural Anthropology*, New York, NY: A.A. Knopf, 1947.]

[9] [On homosexuality in the West Indies, see the note curiously inserted in a discussion of the analysis of 'anti-Semitic psychoses' by Henri Baruk, in *Black Skin, White Masks*, p. 157.]

[10] [Ward newspaper of Saint-Alban.]

Give our best wishes to your children.

I take my leave of you in the hope of hearing from you again soon. Amicably yours. Josie sends Nelly her greetings.

P.S. I recommend a book that I am reading, *Psychologie de la superstition* from the same series as *Les Bases culturelles de l'anthropologie.*[11]

---

[11][Konrad Zucker, *Psychologie de la superstition*, Paris: Payot, 1952 (*Psychologie des Aberglaubens*, Heidelberg: Scherer, 1948); Melville J. Herskovits, *Les Bases de l'anthropologie culturelle*. Fanon's slip on the title of Herskovits' classic, whose reflections on culture ought to have interested him, perhaps echoes his doubts about anthropology.]

10 SOCIAL THERAPY IN A WARD OF MUSLIM MEN: METHODOLOGICAL DIFFICULTIES

Frantz Fanon and Jacques Azoulay (Blida-Joinville Psychiatric Hospital), October 1954[1]

We have just completed a fruitful experiment in our attempt to organize, from a social therapeutic perspective, a psychiatric ward of Muslim men. We offer this experiment to the reflection of our readers. We will baldly present the difficulties that we stumbled upon

---

[1]*L'Information psychiatrique*, vol. 30, 4th series, no. 9, October 1954, pp. 349–61. [This article comprises a modified version of the second section of Jacques Azoulay's medical doctorate, *Contribution à l'étude de la socialthérapie dans un service d'aliénés musulmans*, which Fanon supervised and which was defended in Algiers in December 1954. The dissertation is dedicated to Fanon in the following terms: 'To Doctor Fanon, médecin-chef of the ward at the psychiatric hospital of Blida-Joinville. He welcomed me with benevolence into his service. He inspired me to write this dissertation, which reflects the accomplishments of his penetrating and always alert mind. I hope to be able to continue to benefit from his teaching.' The first section of the dissertation is a historical and theoretical presentation of social therapy. The first name of Jacques Azoulay on the title page of his dissertation is spelt 'Jack', which is his legal first name. His family has made it known to us, however, that he preferred 'Jacques', the spelling he also used in other works. We have adopted his spelling throughout the present edition.]

and will show that these errors were possible only through an attitude devoid of objectivity.[2]

And the awareness of the twofold alienation resulting from this tyranny of subjectivity and from what Piaget calls sociocentricity, has enabled us to orient our research in a wholly other direction. We have adopted greater modesty faced with the culture presented to us. We took some steps towards it, fearful and attentive.[3] And, the extraordinary thing is that the few indistinct notes that, at the start, awoke our interest, little by little came to form a coherent whole.

The experiment that we relate herein was made possible because our only division included both Europeans and Muslims. What comprises the value of this exception is that the Muslims and Europeans were not mixed together: on the one hand, there were one hundred and sixty five European women, and, on the other, two hundred and twenty Muslim men.[4]

Let's call to mind some particularities of the Blida Psychiatric Hospital. Upon our arrival, our four colleagues were in charge of the medical surveillance of more than six hundred patients each. So any attempt to orient their services around a social therapeutic perspective was impossible for them. The arrival of a fifth doctor, however, relieved these four colleagues of four hundred patients and only then did the possibility of performing real social therapy arise.

At Saint-Alban we had observed a type of organization that, overall and in detail, we thought measured up to a maximal type of sociotherapy in the current conditions of psychiatric care in France. So we took our ward as a point of departure that would in a sense serve as an experimental milieu. We sought to implement bi-weekly ward meetings,[5] as well as staff meetings, newspaper meetings, and bi-monthly celebrations. In our ward of European women results appeared before long.

---

[2][To take into consideration the cultural dimension in the expression of mental illness (a construction following a biological event, an important point in Azoulay's dissertation) is an essential part of scientific explanation. This is why Azoulay spoke of 'methodological error'.]

[3][Azoulay: 'attentive and understanding'.]

[4][Azoulay: 'So this mixed division, containing at once European women and Muslim men, in a sense served as an experimental milieu' (p. 19). See figure 3.]

[5]At Saint-Alban, the collective psychotherapy meetings mostly take place within the club meetings or the journal committee meetings. But as we were at the experimental stage, we were obliged to group everything in the pavilion.

Already in the first month, the meetings became an integral part of the life of the ward. They took place at a set hour and day, and, by means of our strict punctuality in showing up there, we insisted[6] on clearly marking the importance we granted them. In attendance were not only patients and doctors, but also, above all at the start, the nursing staff, who needed fully to understand the sense of our approach. After a brief period of hesitation, we quickly succeeded in getting peoples' general attention and, overall, the requisite atmosphere was created, with interventions following one after another without too much 'dead time' in between. At the start, we simply commented upon minor incidents in the ward, but the more organized the social architecture became, the more the possibilities of meeting on concrete topics multiplied.

Christmas, with its tenaciously ingrained traditional character, gave us the occasion to instil within the ward a series of specific behaviours.[7] Indeed, a vast dorm of sixty-five beds was emptied in toto. Male and female patients from the different services, male and female nurses, flowed in. The medical staff and the administrative services thronged to attend this first experiment. Religious songs, choirs, carols, a nativity scene delicately decorated by hands trembling with emotion, a pine tree – everything was done to ensure the utmost solemnity for this celebration.

And when, after two days, during a meeting of the ward, we proposed to the patients to organize celebrations on a regular basis, we encountered practically no resistance. Certainly, at the start it was very difficult, but the multiple small incidents have all practically disappeared today: after a period of weariness on the part of the patients and also the nurses – for the point was not for the same delusional patients always to come forward, but also to integrate such and such a catatonic, or such and such a senile individual or sitiophobe – we no longer[8] have to concern ourselves with them directly. The celebration is readied, the invitations are sent out, the stage is arranged by the patients with the help of one or two nurses,

---

[6][Azoulay: 'the doctor commits'.]
[7][Not in the sense of behaviour dear to the behaviourists, a complex sequence of mechanical movements, but in the sense of an integrated and meaningful 'conduct', such as studied by Merleau-Ponty in *The Structure of Behaviour* (p. 161 and passim).]
[8][Azoulay: 'the doctor no longer'.]

and we attend it as simple spectators. The celebration thus takes on its veritable therapeutic character. Anecdotally, we ought to report the scene in which the paranoid patient in charge of the sung part – *Sombreros et mantilles*[9] – monitored from the corner of her eye the catatonic who tended to lose the thread, pinching her when needed, so that she would come back into the movement.

Alongside the Celebrations Committee tasked with organizing the recreational evenings, there is a Film Committee and a Record Collection Committee. Film ought not to be a mere succession of images with a sound accompaniment: it must become the unfolding of a life, of a story. So, the Film Committee, by choosing the films,[10] by commenting on them in a special film column of the newspaper, gave real meaning to the cinematographic fact. Similarly, the Record Collection Committee arranges musical sessions during which one could listen to various records, such as by Luis Mariano, but also the *Unfinished Symphony*, the latter incidentally being accompanied by a patient's commentary.

Our Journal, a weekly publication, is run by two committees: the Newspaper Committee, which selects the texts proffered, and the Printing Committee. The editorial, written by one of the members of the medical staff, elaborates on this or that point and provokes in the staff and patients the need to think about the hospital in its totality.[11] The part written by patients was fairly monotonous at the start: 'I thank the doctor for his good care', 'I would like to get out soon'. Today, if, as was mentioned in a recent editorial, we continue to see the same names reappearing in it too often, the journal nonetheless reflects the progress accomplished: invitations for new celebrations, for music evenings; accounts and announcements of outings, walks, the films of the week and, more generally, all events with a collective value.

Ergotherapy has an important place in the life of the clinic, and we seek to integrate it harmoniously in with the other activities: outside the housework jobs, a knitting workshop led by a nurse in which

---

[9][By Luis Mariano, a very popular singer at the time.]
[10]The Film Committee is not presently selecting films, since the programme has finished for the year.
[11][Indeed, most of Fanon's interventions in the Ward Newspaper of Blida, as well as those of the interns close to him, consist in recalling the meaning of each activity with regard to its global therapeutic function (see *above*, p. 151 *sq.*, Fanon's editorials in *Our Journal*).]

several patients are working together on making a single article. Other patients are making and embroidering serviettes, tablecloths and curtains. More recently, we were able to create a dressmaking workshop tasked with making frocks, the fabric having been bought with money taken from the individual stipend.[12] For patients settled at the hospital for five or six years, one senses the importance of such events: fabrics with flowers or stripes, light or dark depending on each person's taste, contrast with the monotony of the hospital gown. And think about the fitting ceremony at which the women had to remain perfectly still while in the expert hands of the dressmaker. The institution, then, becomes too strong not to modify the patient's attitude vis-à-vis the milieu: the patient can no longer live [her] madness without dealing with all that which surrounds her.

The various activities we have just quickly outlined thus constitute the framework of an increasingly enriched social life. Social life could be organized without too much difficulty since we had already had a probative experience of it. So, from the very first months, we felt a rapid and fecund coming together as a group in our ward of European women: the very atmosphere of the ward had changed, and we were able to return all the restraint equipment without needing to fear any major difficulties. Not only had asylum life become less distressing for many, but the rhythm of discharges had already markedly increased.

These rapid and relatively easy successes only underscored the total failure of the same methods when employed in our service of Muslim men. Recapitulating the various attempts in the very order of our efforts, we can observe their successive failure. We knew that group psychotherapy with the Muslims would prove more difficult for us, and after several seminars with the nursing staff, we met with the patients.[13]

The meeting was carefully prepared. The table in the big refectory was covered with a cloth and decorated with flowers. The doctor was surrounded by an intern, a supervisor and some nurses, in order

---

[12][Psychiatric hospitals sometimes ran their own currency to incentivize patients in ergotherapy.]

[13][Azoulay: 'The doctor indeed felt that group psychotherapy was going to be more difficult with the Muslims, and it was only after several seminars with the nursing staff that he organized meetings with the patients'.]

to increase the ceremonial value. The most agitated patients were left in the courtyard. Right away, contact was difficult to establish because we did not speak the same language. We thought we could overcome the obstacle by selecting from among the Muslim nurses an intelligent, voluble interpreter, to whom we took care to explain in detail what we were looking to achieve.

During the hour that the meeting lasted, we tried to take an interest in each of the patients, to transform that abstract and impersonal multitude into a coherent group driven by collective preoccupations. We spoke about celebrations, films and the journal. Rarely did we command silence. Unaware of our existence, this patient kept on with his motor stereotypy, another with his hallucinatory conversation; two others argued loudly; another one went off to go back and lie down in the courtyard. Very few realized the importance of our presence and accepted the dialogue. The only engaged, indeed somewhat too engaged, patient, who suffered from persecutory paranoia, spoke French well and, far from pulling his companions into a group reaction, sought more or less consciously to distance himself from them. Confronted with this general disinterest, we did not know what topics to draw on. The silences grew longer, accentuating the sense of unease.

After a few weeks, the meetings, which were originally supposed to last an hour, had to be progressively shortened. They constituted only a ceremonial devoid of meaning, absurd and, after some hesitation, we decided to break them off. So we went searching for something else: we asked the nurses each to choose ten patients and to get them to meet for an hour in the evening, to get them interested through discussions, games or songs. We gave them precise directives, since in our minds, the point was to create some cooperation, a team spirit apt to revive their feelings of sociability.[14]

On the session reports written each evening by the nurses in charge, the first two days' notes read: 'We all met together and played hide and seek, cards and dominos. The atmosphere was good, but this or that patient was not interested in the games'. Further on: 'the game of *pelote cavalière* was played by the patients whose names follow: ..., assisted by servant K. The game initially appeared complicated, but they learnt the rules and it went well'.

---

[14][Azoulay: 'reawaken'.]

In the days following, the share of time devoted to collective games reduced increasingly, and the reports became more pessimistic: 'At the start, there were ten patients, but ten minutes later only six patients remained. M., N., B. and B. are eager players (cards). B. and L. went to bed, on the pretext that they were tired from work'. Or else: 'Patients O., M., SNP,[15] I. refused to take part in our meeting; the reason being they were too tired. The patients opted to play a round of dominos, they were very content to play a round quietly and without discussion'. The evening narrowed down to a session of listening to Oriental music on the radio. The patients remained indifferent, while the nurses interpreted these meetings as a chore. After some time had passed, and despite our repeated encouragement, they frankly expressed their lack of enthusiasm: 'There are no ways to get the patients interested, as soon as they've eaten they want to go to bed, and we have to lock the dormitories to prevent them from doing so'.

Concurrently with these 'evening conversations', we sought to arrange a ward party. We gave ourselves some time, because we knew it would present difficulties. The party was to comprise two parts: choir and theatre. But we ran into problems in finding two nurses who really wanted to take on the organization. After two weeks of rehearsals, only one old PG[16] mumbled while shaking his head, where the other remained silent. The nurses themselves did not make too much effort and, irritated by their lack of will, we said to them that they were not doing all that they could, since what was possible in the ward of Europeans should also be possible in the Muslims Muslims' ward. So they were not upset when we replaced them with others, who equally failed. Still others were no more successful; and let us say that a last orderly when approached to do the same work asked to change ward, leading us to think that it was perhaps not a matter of simple laziness.

Our attempts to get Muslim patients to arrange recreational or theatrical evenings for themselves having lamentably failed, we thought we could resolve the problem by 'providing' them with some entertainment. Thus, many of them attended the recreational

---

[15][SNP: *sans nom patronymique*, or without patronymic name, the colonial administration's usual term to designate the 'natives', whose names were not ordered in a way that corresponded to its normative criteria (name, first name).]
[16][*Paralysie générale* (general paralysis).]

evenings of the European women. Similarly, they went regularly to the films. But we noted that if the head of the ward forgot to send them to the celebrations, nobody stepped forward to ask to go. And when watching a film, they would leave the chapel[17] while it was still screening and go outside to have a smoke.

So, whether it was a matter of ward meetings, collective recreational evenings or small groups, we were obliged to recognize our failure. As for the newspaper, which was supposed to serve as a veritable social cement, it remained foreign to the patients: in six months only a single article by a Muslim patient had been published; as it happens, it was the same paranoiac who regretted that the male roles had been played by women.[18] And in the wards only a few orderlies read the journal.

If from the recreational and cultural point of view we failed to develop a viable activity, neither did we succeed at the ergotherapy level. Certainly, the hospital mosque there already had a workshop for making mats, baskets and hats, which kept a certain number of patients in our wards occupied. Other patients worked inside the ward or in the general services. But we could not consider these activities as having a properly therapeutic value: the tasks were distributed without any precise choice; the patients accepted them above all for their value as a distraction, as a way of escaping the ward courtyard and oftentimes after having done enough work to procure cakes or cigarettes, they refused to continue, if necessary on the pretext of some stomach or leg pain.[19]

This is why we thought we would create an ergotherapy workshop within our very wards. With this in mind, we placed a nurse on full-time secondment for one and a half months to learn in detail the technique of raffia. Back at the ward this nurse was entrusted solely with patients (about fifteen) undergoing insulin shock therapy, patients whom he had to get working for a part of the morning and for the entire afternoon. But each time we dropped by the workshop, we observed that most of the patients remained unoccupied, completely indifferent to the accomplishment of shared work. As soon as the

---

[17]The film screenings took place in the chapel.
[18][See Ahmed Noui's letter in *Our Journal*, 24 June 1954, *above*, p. 162]
[19]Concerning 'worker patients', the same criticisms can be made in the majority of psychiatric hospitals: the patients leave early and only return at the end of the morning or in the evening. They are more or less excluded from therapeutic activity.

monitor turned his back, they left their work stations, moreover opting to go help their comrades who, using spades and pickaxes, were developing the outside areas. Despite our repeated prompts, no more than three baskets were made, and we quickly sensed that it was vain to expect any more.

Thus, not only were we unable, after three months, and despite much effort, to get the Muslim patients interested in the beginnings of collective life that was being organized in the European sector, but the ward atmosphere remained oppressive, stifling. A considerable proportion of senile patients remained and, at day's end, rarely was enough linen left to keep them somewhat clean. During mealtime, the racket in the refectory, which is too cramped for the high number of patients, was deafening. It seems that these patients took pleasure in throwing food on the table or to the ground, in bending their iron plates or in breaking their spoons.[20] And it is understandable why, in these conditions, cleaning care took up a considerable part of the staff's activity.

Frequent arguments between patients, whom the nurses had to separate with the risk of receiving blows themselves, always kept up the climate of mistrust. Nurses were afraid of the patients, and the hairdresser demanded that the patients were tied up before being shaved. Out of fear of patients, or in order to punish them, the patients were left in secure units, sometimes shirtless, without mattresses, or without sheets on account of this one's being a 'lacerator'. The eternal 'chronics' were often tied up with a belt even before acting out, as a preventative measure. As Paumelle showed so well, the same rhythm, the same vicious circle – agitation, restraint, agitation – always kept up a veritably concentration-camp mindset.[21]

And each new attempt on our part to relax the punitive structure of our service was greeted with the inertia of the staff, sometimes even by a clear hostility dressed up with irony: 'This patient became agitated, he hit someone or broke some tiles. What do we do? Tie him up or let him continue?' We felt powerless in front of the arguments

---

[20]The patients broke their spoons because their handles could be used as a 'master key' to open the doors. At the end of one month, the number of broken spoons was impressive.
[21]Philippe Paumelle, 'Le mythe de l'agitation' ['Le mythe de l'agitation des malades mentaux', in Henri Ey (ed.), *Entretiens psychiatriques* (1953), Paris: L'Arche, 1954, pp. 181–93. See our introduction pp. 22 and 34]

of this 'seasoned' staff, sanctioned by several years of asylum life: 'You've only freshly arrived in Algeria, you do not know them, when you've been in the hospital for fifteen years like us, then you will understand!'

So, after a few months, the contrast was striking: on the European side, the journal was published weekly, theatrical evenings were held regularly and agitation had disappeared. The climate had become therapeutic. By contrast, in the ward of Muslim men we came up against the same difficulties: a considerable number of patients were still tied-up, and despite multiple attempts no improvement had come about. And little by little, it became clear that it was not a matter of coincidence, laziness or bad will: we had taken the wrong course and needed to research the profound reasons for our failure in order to exit the deadlock.

In the meantime, we had studied our ward in-depth, the character of the patients who resided there and, on the outside, their background. We had naively taken our division as a whole and believed we had adapted to this Muslim society the frames of a particular Western society at a determinate period of its technological evolution. We had wanted to create institutions and we had forgotten that all such approaches must be preceded with a tenacious, real and concrete interrogation into the organic bases of the indigenous society.

By virtue of what impairment of judgement had we believed it possible to undertake a western-inspired social therapy in a ward of mentally ill Muslim men? How was a structural analysis possible if the geographical, historical, cultural and social frames were bracketed? Two explanations could be put forward.

1) First, North Africa is French and, when one does not look, one really cannot see how the attitude has to be different from one ward to another. The psychiatrist, reflexively, adopts the policy of assimilation. The natives do not need to be understood in their cultural originality. It is the 'natives' who must make the effort and who have every interest in being like the type of men suggested to them. Assimilation here does not presuppose a reciprocity of perspectives. It is up to one entire culture to disappear in favour of another.

In our Muslim ward, leaving aside the need for an interpreter, our behaviour was completely unsuited. In fact, a revolutionary attitude was essential, because it was necessary to go from a position in which the supremacy of Western culture was evident, to one of cultural relativism. And again it was necessary to return to Piaget: the notions of adaptation and assimilation are very important and far from having been fully developed.[22]

2) Lastly and above all, it must be said that those who preceded us in trying to divulge the North African psychiatric fact remained somewhat too focused on motor, neurovegetative, and so on, phenomena. While the works of the Algiers school revealed certain particularities, they did not, to our knowledge, proceed to the functional analysis, which nevertheless appeared to be indispensable. It was necessary to change perspectives or at least supplement the initial ones. It was necessary to try to grasp the North African social fact. It was necessary to demand that 'totality' in which [Marcel] Mauss saw the guarantee of an authentic sociological study. A leap had to be performed, a transmutation of values to be achieved. Let's say it: it was essential to go from the biological level to the institutional one, from natural existence to cultural existence.

The biological, the psychological and the sociological were separated only by an aberration of the mind. In fact, they were tied indistinctly together. It is for want of not having integrated the notion of *Gestalt* and the elements of contemporary anthropology into our daily practice that our failures were so harsh.

For a period of six months, the Muslim women had regularly attended the celebrations held in the European wards. For a period of six months, they applauded in the European way. And then one day, a Muslim orchestra came to the hospital, played and sang, and our astonishment in hearing the applause of the Muslim women was great: short, acute and repeated modulations.[23] Thus they reacted to the configuration of the ensemble, in line with its specific demands. It became evident that we had to try to find ensembles that would

---

[22]As Gusdorf showed so well in his *Traité de l'existence morale* [Georges Gusdorf, *Traité de l'existence morale*, Paris: Armand Colin, 1949].
[23]Called 'you-yous'.

facilitate reactions already inscribed in a definitively elaborated personality. Socio-therapy would only be possible to the extent that social morphology and forms of sociability were taken into consideration.

What were the biological, moral, aesthetic, cognitive and religious values of Muslim society? How did the native react from the affective, emotional point of view? What were the forms of sociability that rendered possible the multiple attitude of this Muslim? We were faced with certain institutions that astonished us. To what did they correspond? It was necessary to carry out a functional analysis that ought to facilitate the task. In a work in preparation, one of us intends to show the complexity of North African society, which is currently undergoing extremely deep structural modifications. Here we limit ourselves to recalling a few characteristic elements of this society.[24]

Traditional Muslim society is theocratic in spirit. The Muslim religion is in effect, apart from a philosophical belief, a rule of life that strictly regulates the individual and the group. In Muslim countries, religion impregnates social life and gives no consideration to secularity. Rights, morality, science, philosophy – all mingle with it. Alongside the properly religious, Islamic imperative, tradition forcefully intervenes, as bequeathed from the ancient Berber customs, and this is what explains the rigidity of the social frames.

It is also a gerontocratic society. The father is the one that steers the life of the family and he – or in his absence the eldest brother or even the uncle – must be consulted for all decisions of some importance. The family is incidentally very ramified, and sometimes an entire douar shares the same patronymic name! It tends to be identified with the clan, which is the true natural group of Muslim Algeria. Decisions are taken by the *djemaâ*, a sort of municipal council at the head of which there is a president – and whose importance the civil service has, incidentally, recently recognized. There did not in fact exist, at least not until in recent years, a veritable national community, but instead a familial, clan community.

---

[24][The following pages take up long passages from a book by André Leroi-Gourhan and Jean Poirier, subtly modifying them toward an indictment of colonialism: *Ethnologie de l'Union française*, vol. 1, *Afrique*, Paris: PUF, 1953, p. 121 (see our introduction above, p. 196).]

It is also necessary to emphasize the regions' ethnic complexity, since the Kabyles form a large minority among the rest of the Arab population. If both groups [are] united by the Muslim religion, their separation is clearly marked by differences of language, tradition and culture. The Kabyle, of Berber origin, inhabit the mountainous regions. Their villages, perched on the hilltops, constitute the elements in which the tribal organization remains the most solid. The Arabs rather live in the plains and the cities. Farmers are to be found there, but so also are traders and petty artisans. We can obviously not expand upon the other local particularisms: nomads, Arabs of the South, Mozabites, Chaouis – of much less importance for our aims. So it is that in our ward, out of two hundred and twenty patients we had one hundred and forty-eight Arabs, sixty-six Kabyles and six Chaouis, Moroccans and Mozabites.

Lastly, we ought to say a word about the Muslim patients' usual living conditions, which by and large explain their state of ignorance, their traditional primitivism. Prior to French conquest, land was the property of the collective and the notion of wealth was linked to the notion of useful land, arable land, and as a result to the possession of a yoke or a plough; people who owned such things were the real property owners.

French settlement lead to the transformation of land ownership and a redistribution of wealth. The old collective property was subdivided between owners, and then private proprietors. The members of the old tribe led a poor life, but it knew no proletarians. Today there exists, outside of a minority of large land owners, whether European or Muslim, a mass of small proprietors, of fellahs, who find it hard to live from farming a small patch of land with primitive techniques, however much such patches are still an object of envy for those who did not benefit from the carve up. These latter people became destitute, their sociological bond with tribal collective personality loosens daily and they began trying to hire out their labour as *khammès*[25] or day labourers. There is, thus, a movement of dissociation of that once homogeneous society, between on the one hand small proprietors and on the other shepherds, sharecroppers or day labourers.

---

[25]*Khammès*: sharecroppers who work for a fifth of the crop. ['A kind of sharecropper who received only a very small share of the crop, usually a fifth', Pierre Bourdieu, *The Logic of Practice*, Stanford, CA: Stanford University Press, 1990, p. 127.]

Furthermore, as a result of the extension of modern farming techniques to large properties today we see taking shape a mass of unemployed farm workers, whose hunger draws them to the towns, but the absence of industrialization forces them into the condition of the proletariat – and even the subproletariat – further heightening the social disequilibrium. And it must be underscored that, above all among the population of Berber origin, many go to France for an indeterminate period, to seek either a job that they cannot find at home or a supplement to their meagre harvests.

This development among sedentary peoples results in the group's splintering, and in this sense merges with the development of nomads. Today, we struggle to picture the importance of ancient nomadism in North Africa: the tribes of the South went as far as the littoral edge, like a periodic tide rising up from the steppes and the sands, surging up through the high plateaus. But the French occupation naturally led to a constant regression of this nomadism, resolving it into two terms: sedentarization, and renting of labour. But the seasonal workers remain outside the sedentary grouping that they come to support. Ancient nomadism strictly maintained traditional forms of authority and group cohesion; the individual movements that can be seen now proceed outside of any tribal rule and greatly contribute to hastening a dangerous detribalization: the decline of nomadism is ineluctable, but it is being replaced by proletarianization.

These factors, which foster the dissolution of the groups, whether sedentaries or nomads, explains the formation of sizeable shanty towns at the entrances to large cities, thus constituting not only a challenge to aesthetics or even to simple urbanism, but also a serious danger from a health and moral point of view.

By way of example, we studied the social composition of our ward of Muslim men. Out of two hundred and twenty patients, we had: thirty-five fellahs, that is to say individuals with a piece of land that they cultivate themselves; seventy-six agricultural workers, sharecroppers or day labourers; seventy-eight workers (bakers, painters, etc.); five intellectuals; twenty-six without profession. But these figures call for interpretation. It might be thought that there is a relatively high number of workers: seventy-eight out of two hundred and twenty. In actual fact, we were most often dealing with precisely those elements that had been torn from and who had managed to find some manual labour in the city, of whatever kind. Ultimately, out of seventy-eight 'workers', only twenty had at least some form of job specialization. Concerning the five 'intellectuals', let's note that they are indigenous primary school teachers with something like the equivalent of a school leaving certificate.

These problems have considerable resonances: the individuals who escaped traditional society on their own are too numerous to count, but their number is constantly growing. These elements are the forces, still poorly analyzed, that are in the process of breaking the domestic, economic and political frameworks. This society, which is said to be rigid, is fermenting from the base.[26] These few notions, although all too brief and each being in need of a lengthy elaboration, are enough to explain the specificity of Muslim Algerian society that we had to take into consideration in our efforts to create the fundaments for social therapy among Muslims.

We can now understand the reasons for our failure. We said that the ward meetings had turned out not to be productive. This is essentially because we did not speak Arabic and had to make use of two interpreters (for Kabylian and Arabic). This need to have an interpreter fundamentally vitiated doctor-patient relations.

In normal circumstances, a patient may have encountered the image of the interpreter in his relations with the administration or the justice system. Within the hospital, the same need for an interpreter spontaneously triggers a distrust that makes all 'communication' difficult. Incidentally, when the patient's trust had been won, his speech was filled with enthusiasm, such as when explaining vehemently that he was cured and had to leave quickly, often forgetting the presence of the third person and addressing us directly: he felt that the other could not say all that he wanted to express with the same 'warmth'. It is not hard to see the extent to which a study of this three-way dialogue would reveal a disruption of the phenomenon of the encounter.

---

[26][The initial dilemma of this paper will thus be solved by understanding 'indigenous' patients against the historical backdrop of the progressive colonial destruction of traditional structures. Here again Fanon replaces a substantialist approach, that of the Algiers school of psychiatry and of the hospital nurses, with a temporal perspective, as he had done in his analysis of the relationship of the neurological and the psychiatric. See *above*, p. 10 and 27.]

The interpreter does not only bother the patient. The doctor, especially the psychiatrist, makes his diagnostic through language. Well, here the gestural and verbal components of language cannot be perceived in synchronous fashion. While the face is expressive and the gestures profuse, it is necessary to wait until the patient has stopped talking in order to grasp the meaning. At which point, the interpreter sums up in two words what the patient has related in detail for ten minutes: 'He says that someone took his land, or that his wife cheated on him'. Often, the interpreter 'interprets' in his own way the patient's thinking according to some stereotyped formula, depriving it of all its richness: 'He says that he hears *djnoun*' – indeed, one no longer knows if the delusion is real or inferred.

Going through an interpreter is perhaps valid when it comes to explaining something simple or transmiting an order, but it no longer is when it is necessary to begin a dialogue, a dialectical exchange of questions and replies, alone able to overcome reticence and bring to light abnormal, pathological behaviour. But as Merleau-Ponty said, 'to speak a language is to bear the weight of a culture'.[27] Unable to speak Arabic, we did not know the elements of affective or cultural patrimony apt to awaken interest. Among the European women, it was easy to engage a conversation about a record by Tino Rossi or a film with Fernandel. With the Muslim men, meetings soon came to an abrupt end because one no longer knew what to talk about.

Similarly, with a little hindsight, our first attempts at organizing celebrations appeared rather naïve. The very notion of having a celebration outside of family or religious events appears rather abstract to a Muslim. Moreover, the content of collective festivities seems to us to be essentially different from western festivities. It was difficult to form a choir, because the Muslim loathes to sing in a group. In the house, one does not sing because one respects the father or the eldest brother. And among the Muslim nurses of our ward, we could get no one to consent to sing or to perform on a stage. In the same way, putting on a theatre play is impossible, firstly because the theatre

---

[27][In *Peau noire, masques blancs*, Fanon simply wrote, without the reference to Merleau-Ponty: 'To speak a language is to take on a world, a culture' *Black Skin, White Masks*, p. 25).]

as we understand it does not exist among Muslims, and secondly because one does not play a role in front of others. It is true that an Arab theatre does exist today, but its existence is a recent thing and it only reaches the populations of the big cities. The actor or the singer is a professional who remains outside the group. In the villages, in the douars, this figure will be an itinerant 'storyteller' who goes from place to place spreading news and tells folktales accompanied by a rudimentary lute or a darbuka, thus evoking the troubadours of the Middle Ages.

Abandoning our plan to have a celebration, the brief evening meetings had no further success. Going through the reports of these sessions, we see that initial accounts mentioned the games of hide and seek or *pelote cavalière*. Indeed, we had strongly impressed upon the nurses, whom we chose randomly from among the Europeans and the Muslims, that they should find activities apt to awaken a team spirit: the games of *pelote cavalière* and hide-and-seek in effect require each person to act by taking into account the reactions of his companions. One cannot ignore them.

But Muslims rarely play such games. At school is where you learn to play hide and seek or cops and robbers, where you acquire a team spirit. But at ten or twelve years of age, the young Arab boy is a shepherd or else he helps his father with small jobs. If we had wanted to have daily evening meetings, it would have been necessary to take inspiration from reality: after work, the Muslim gathers together with other men at the Moorish café. He remains seated around a table playing cards or dominos, or else lies down on a mat to discuss daily events or listen to music for hours while drinking a cup of coffee or a glass of tea. And this is indeed what experience has shown us: after some weeks, the nurses in charge of the evening sessions had lost all sense of initiative, and the few patients who still consented not to go to bed did nothing but listen to the radio.

Outside of these attempts at active resocialization, the entertainments organized by the hospital were not for the Muslim patients a practically 'vital' need as they were for the Europeans. Thus, apropos of the cinema, most of the films able to be seen did not generate any emotional engagement in the Muslim patient. We list here some of the titles of recently screened films: *Little Women, King Solomon's Mines, Les Noces de sable, La Duchesse de Langeais, Crisis,*

Rio Grande, Teresa, etc. Obviously, the only films that were somewhat followed were the action films without great psychological or sentimental complications. But more than to a certain 'primitivism', this disinterest can be probably attributed to its not being possible for the Muslim to understand the western characters' reactions, which are completely foreign to him. The example of the film by Jean Cocteau, *Les Noces de sable*, is particularly telling. The film relates the adventures of an Arab prince who goes to find his fiancée among the nomads of the Sahara. Although the costumes and the setting were in principle specific to North Africa, the psychological framework remained western. It did not interest the Muslims, because they were unable to participate fully in the action or identify with the personages. And what are we to say concerning the other films? The schema in 'action films' is simple, the picture speaks for itself, language is unnecessary.

Similarly, for the celebrations in the European wards: if a fashionable tune was sung, if one played *Les Précieuses ridicules*, *Le Médecin malgré lui*, *Cyrano de Bergerac*, put on a play by Courteline or by Colette, then a whole section of the audience in the room would remain completely unmoved: at most it would indistinctly emerge from its torpor on the occasion that an actor threw a glass of water into someone's face or struck someone with sticks.

As for the journal, the failure was even more pronounced: as the journal only reflected more or less faithfully the social life at the hospital, it was rather uninteresting for those who remained excluded from it in practice. This is why even the few patients who knew how to read and write never sent any articles. However, the failure is due above all to the fact that most of our Muslim patients are illiterate. More exactly, out of the two hundred and twenty patients in our unit, only five knew how to read and write in Arabic and two, how to read and write in French. The others were illiterate. And again, let's say that out of the seven 'literate' patients, only six had passed the level of school certificate.

At the start we considered the possibility of having the articles written by a nurse, as we did with the Europeans when they did not know how or want to write. But the uniform use of this procedure is practically useless. In actual fact, it can be said that in the conditions of illiteracy prevailing currently in Algeria, culture is more oral than it is written: teaching is essentially carried out through speech. Each group in general has one or several literate individuals tasked with reading and writing for the rest of the group: this is why we were easily able to recognize the writing of the same *taleb* or public writer in the letters that we received from the parents of all patients that hailed from the same douar. We have already noted the important role of the itinerant 'storyteller', who goes from village to village spreading news and stories from folklore, that is, sorts of epic poems relating the events of previous centuries, and thereby ensures a cultural liaison between the different regions.

To end this explanation of our first failures, we must speak about ergotherapy. In a heavily industrialized western country, it is easy to organize a patient's readaptation on the basis of already existing possibilities. On the contrary, for the Algerian Muslim, who lives in a framework that is still feudal in many respects, this readaptation is much more difficult. A man works the land, he has no specialization. He is sometimes able to perform rather rudimentary handicraft work outside of the major urban centres, but he loathes to work with wool or raffia, because that is feminine work: baskets and mats are produced by women.

In a psychiatric hospital, one might seek to organize workshops for raffia, weaving or pottery. But it would be better, it seems to us, to entrust this work to women patients. For the men, you must set out from the most general dispositions and from those most strongly rooted in the patient's personality: we conducted this experiment with delusional patients and even catatonic ones. All you need to do is give them a shovel or a pickaxe to get them to work and start digging up earth and hoeing without having to push them to do so in the slightest. These peasants are close to the land; they are one with it. And if you succeed in getting them hooked on a particular patch of land, in getting them interested in the yield gained from farming, then work will genuinely be a factor of re-equilibration; such ergotherapy can be embedded within a specific social activity.

Ultimately, we see why our first attempts at undertaking social therapy among Muslim patients ended in failure. We nonetheless believe that this failure was not worthless, to the extent that we have understood its reasons. Since then we have altered the direction of our efforts and have seen certain accomplishments crystallize. The establishing of a Moorish café in the hospital, the regular celebration of traditional Muslim feasts, of periodical meetings around a professional 'storyteller', are already concrete facts. With each new event, the number of patients engaged in these activities increases. This social life is only in its beginnings, but already we believe that we have eliminated the methodological errors.

11 DAILY LIFE IN THE DOUARS

Frantz Fanon and Jacques Azoulay,
1954 or 1955[1]

At the dawn of psychopathological research in Algeria, it seemed singularly important to us to clarify certain privileged behaviours that we can agree to call primitive. We will not raise the problem of the value of these attitudes. We will not try to judge them on the basis of a supposed arithmetic of civilization. Certainly, we are not saying that, in this domain, every position is valid and defensible, but neither do we want, under the cover of the latest tendency, cultural relativism, to minimize the tasks that present themselves to the psychiatrist, as Henri Damaye claimed in a somewhat utopian fashion.[2]

---

[1][This manuscript text, featuring in the Fanon archives at IMEC under FNN 1.1, is not signed or dated. But it is clearly part of the research that Fanon and Azoulay were undertaking on the perception of mental illness within a given culture from 1954 onwards. The manuscript is crossed out toward the end and some words are illegible. It seems to have been carefully recopied from a previous manuscript containing notes on the context, to which the final pages, which carry the stakes of the text, were added or heavily reworked. The writing of the first page seems to be Azoulay's, the rest was probably copied and/or written by Fanon. In many respects this text could be read as a critique and response to Suzanne Taïeb's pioneering doctoral dissertation, *Les Idées d'influence dans la pathologie mentale de l'indigène nord-africain*. Taïeb had been an intern in Blida before the War and defended her dissertation in June 1939. She wrote it under the supervision of Antoine Porot, the head of the Algiers school of psychiatry, which Fanon proceeded to criticize violently.]

[2][Fanon's library contains a copy of *Psychiatrie et civilisation* by the French neuropsychiatrist Henri Damaye (1876–1952) (Paris: Félix Alcan, 1934).]

It is traditional to say – as we will show in developing our remarks – that the Maghreb is the land of genies. Such hagiographic givens can only interest the specialist of religions. For the psychiatrist, the thrilling and generous reality of genies is such that he experiences, here and there, the desire to put some order in it.[3] Not so as to classify, but instead in order to discover amidst this cluster of facts the general line according to which all takes shape and can be explained. Some of the data that we will yield might have been explainable on the basis of other constellations. Here the progression is not linear. An attempt to render in their ordered articulation the elements of a doctrine would have been valid were it not for the necessity, which imposed itself on us, to render the mental world of the Algerian Muslim in all its exuberant aridity.

From the start, there is a fact that dominates absolutely everything: the vast majority of the Maghrebi population is distributed into douars.[4] The individuals who live there constitute human communities whose organization varies little from one extremity of the Maghreb to the other. If it is added that in general the Maghrebi remains fixed to his douar for life, it becomes clear that the douar constitutes an essential geographical and human unity. With the decline of nomadism and the progressive sedentarization of semi-nomadism,[5] the importance of the douar is strengthened. It is within this almost immutable framework, with its highly stable form and structure, that the life of the Maghrebs has unfolded for centuries.

---

[3][The aim Fanon sets himself is to reconcile the scientific analysis of a real object, mental illness, with the grasping of a living culture, invariably described in its corporeal feeling. This constant aiming for the significance underlying classification was the starting point of his medical dissertation, just as it is in his injunctions to the nurses of Blida to reinject, each day anew, more life into the social therapy committees, which all too quickly become bureaucratized and lose their meaning. This is the ambition of the subject who declares at the start of the chapter on the lived experience of the Black man in *Black Skin, White Masks*: 'I came into this world anxious to uncover the meaning of things' (p. 80).]

[4]Several adjoining douars can stem from a same tribe. The tribe tends to engender a larger human community than that of the douar and certain beliefs are specific to it. Nevertheless, on the level of everyday life, it does not contribute any new elements. [Fanon's research persuaded him that the Algerian demographic reality was essentially rural. This is one of the sources of his conviction that the revolution there could only be a peasant revolution.]

[5]On nomadism and semi-nomadism in North Africa, see André Leroi-Gourhan and Jean Poirier, *Ethnologie de l'Union française*, vol. 1, *Afrique*, Paris: PUF, 1953, p. 121 *sq*. [Fanon's library contains a copy of this work. See *above*, p. 206, note 24.]

Although the majority of its inhabitants remain definitively attached to it, we nevertheless ought to mention that there are exceptions to this rule. Of the rare nomads and semi-nomads who are called to live far from a douar, there are those that military service removes from their places of birth.[6] Another case concerns those who live in economically deprived regions. In such instances, it is common to see the men seek out work regularly in the towns or in large agricultural regions.[7]

When life in the douars is studied closely, one is struck by the violent contrast between that life and what can be observed in the towns of the Maghreb. In these towns, where a population of European origin largely dominates, the type of life is western, that is to say dominated by modern technology with moving and complex forms. In the douars, on the contrary, the style of life is natural and characterized by its simplicity and its fidelity to a secular tradition that has remained practically unchanged to this very day. It is especially in the Muslim quarters of the towns that we see contact between the two cultures, the two civilizations, that we have evoked, western and Maghrebin. Instead of observing their mutual interpenetration, resulting in a perfect and harmonious interbreeding [*métissage*], one observes their simple coexistence, with the Muslim city-dweller remaining often at the margins of western civilization, despite certain vague desires to go beyond a traditional way of life. The city-dweller, of course, is not the rural-dweller, as his condition is not modelled on the same economic determinants and his life is less rustic; nevertheless, both these Muslims spontaneously recognize each other as belonging to one and the same cultural community; they share the same beliefs, they are brothers. Another observation can be made: if one compares the villages whose populations are essentially of European origin to the Muslim douars, which form geographically comparable human localities, the same dissimilarity

---

[6]The relatively considerable number of individuals who are exempt from military service in Algeria must be noted.

[7]When he emigrates to a town, the douar inhabitant remains uprooted there, most often unable to adapt to his new milieu and lives there in rudimentary conditions before finally returning to his native land when he considers he has gathered enough money to support his own for a certain period. The case of Kabylian douars, in which emigration to France has been common for some decades, is quite remarkable in this respect. After one or several more or less extended stays abroad, the Kabylian always returns for good to the land of his fathers.

that we have indicated stands out. Of a very different and far more complex structure, in their appearance they are very reminiscent of villages in France: they are not typically Muslim.[8]

Such comparisons today make the douar appear like an anachronistic grouping, perpetuating a past that would *a priori* seem impossible to discover in regions in which the offspring of so-called western civilization are prospering with great vitality. Ultimately, powerful reasons thus justify the study of populations that remained fixed to the douars.

The douar constitutes a stable and geographically limited space; it is the permanently unfolding site of the barely changing life of a collectivity that does not become agitated and does not incline to any upheaval of its deep structure, except during largely sporadic paroxysms over the course of the history of the Maghreb. From the human point of view, it is worth describing the society of men separately from that of women, with the former leading an essentially public life, where the latter lead a largely cloistered existence. The man lives little at the familial domicile, which he leaves mostly under the woman's dominion. The feminine element remains attached to it, occupied with obscure and eternal household tasks that are not made complex by the almost complete absence of furniture, the monotony of culinary preparations and the rusticness of a cramped dwelling. It goes without saying that a numerous progeny and very modest revenues, as is the norm, are significant factors that tend to render still more natural the conditions of family life and thus also of women's lives.

In certain regions, the woman can also engage at home in handicrafts (weaving, pottery, following a rudimentary technique in use for centuries). Some domestic chores can take the women out of the dwellings, but then they leave veiled,[9] thus remaining to a certain extent in the margins of public life. However, the women participate

---

[8][The urban Muslims are closer to the rural Muslims than to the urban Europeans. This chiasmus suggests that a purely structural consideration or a simply socio-economic explanation (weakly Marxist) is not enough: it is necessary to bring in the element of culture, with its inertia, but also its specific resistance, its mechanisms of alienation and of liberation.]

[9]Upon reaching nubility, the woman must hide her face; she cannot unveil it except to men closely related to her. However, in some regions such as Kabylia the women often do not veil their features; it must nonetheless be pointed out that even in this eventuality, such women cannot meet a man in public, not even one of her relatives.

in their very own social life. We speak here of that which takes shape during meetings, which are very frequent, among women. Traditional visits from parents and female friends form the main basis of this life.[10] To be added to this are collective Friday visits to the cemeteries, and regular pilgrimages to the marabouts dedicated to worshiping local saints. The large religious celebrations, births, boys' circumcision, marriages, and deaths also comprise part of the various solemnities on the occasion of which women gather together in separation from the men.

Women live in a closed society that remains in the shadows of the men's society, as men alone are able to participate in a really public society, open to the world. Indeed, contrary to his companion, a man can meet with his fellow men freely and in broad daylight after his daily work is done, that is, if the work itself does not already enable him to do so when undertaking jobs in the countryside, as a craftsman, or small businessman, or even as a factory worker in certain cases.[11] The public square and the Moorish café[12] are places at which men come together with other men.[13] Though the men's social life is richer and more elaborate than the women's, it is nevertheless no less natural and serene. If during work some sort of hierarchy becomes evident, subordinating, for example, the landless farmer to the sharecropper who employs him,[14] in the public life of the douar things are not the same. Masculine relations in it rest on deeply democratic bases and

---

[10]These visits are long and generally last a whole day. They are always faithfully returned and are frequently repeated.

[11]The men of some douars are sometimes employed in the industries or enterprises developing not far from their place of origin; similarly, they may happen to go and work in the closest village or town. Most often, lacking possession of a professional 'qualification' that would elevate them, these individuals are reduced to carrying out the simplest tasks. Such facts are important since they create a new spirit in the douar; this is something that must be considered in the future.

[12]The Moorish café has already existed for centuries in the Maghreb. For a long time, it remained located only in the towns; in recent years, this institution has come to be established in the douars, where it is now an important element of social life, even though it sometimes arouses opposition from elders.

[13]It would also be necessary to talk about the markets that offer the individual the possibility to leave his usual frame and to meet in the village or the town some people born under different skies.

[14]Hierarchy between the inhabitants of a douar is never very pronounced in work, since the conditions of life are hardly different. The Muslim large landowners and industrial proprietors do not participate in the life of the douar, since they do not reside there.

the only ones who are set apart from the collectivity are those set in relief by saintliness or personal influence. These latter contribute to making up the *djemaa*, a sort of assembly of notables that animates and directs the life of the douar, by settling individual disputes in it, upholding morality and customs, and ensuring that order prevails.[15] The great religious celebrations of Islam are also an occasion for men to have large meetings in which the followers of one and the same faith come together fraternally. Meetings such as those occasioned by marriages, circumcisions, etc., further provide men with the possibility to fraternize. Solidarity among believers is given a concrete expression and is a remarkable social cement.[16]

When the man joins his wife in her house, it is to occupy the place that the wife has destined and prepared for him, that of a master who is respected for his virility and God-given authority.[17] In a patriarchal type of society, the elders dominate; within the family, the husband, the father, takes precedence. The wife is the servant whom one appreciates and the mother whom one consults. The wife is also the being who is originally foreign and whom one has brought in under one's roof. She is the being who represents the world, others, the unknown. Her situation is ambiguous: on the one hand, her position is a subjugated one and, on the other, it stymies the power of the man. The wife participates in the occult, she stands in relation to a world that baffles the man, she knows a lot of secrets; she must therefore be taken good care of. The man fears his servant; the wife thus gets her revenge.

Religious life in the douars is facilitated by the relative simplicity of Islam's major religious rules and the practices that ensue from them. Belief in an all-powerful God and in the mission of his Prophet Muhammad is absolutely general and always formulated with a very strong conviction. Prayer is quite commonly practiced,

---

[15] The *djemaa* continues to be highly respected and listened to. Today it has officially been replaced by administrative and judiciary authority, by that of the military governor (*caïd*) in particular, who has the mission of maintaining order. This is sometimes a source of conflicts that are difficult to resolve when custom and the law are opposed.
[16] This public mutual aid is practiced very regularly; it is very effective: it is a real institution.
[17] It is necessary to say a word about the polygamy authorized by divine law: it turns out to be increasingly seldom practiced in the Maghreb. The influence of western civilization and economic factors have determined such a phenomenon. Polygamy is a luxury and the douar dweller knows no luxury.

above all by men when they reach middle age. The fasting ritual of the month of Ramadan is always respected by adults and assumes a great importance, modifying for a time the rhythm of group life, as the reverence and abstinence observed during the day contrast with nocturnal liveliness and jubilation. For the child, who begins to fast as puberty approaches, it marks one of the very first contacts with the father's religion. As for charity and mutual aid, these are spontaneously carried out: the neighbour's, the traveller's or the wanderer's request always receives a favourable reply. This is how the life of the Muslim is externalized and his adherence to Islam is concretized. As followers of the same religion, believers thus have the clear conscience of being part of a real, living community.[18] Maraboutism, which we have discussed at length, further adds its mark to religious life, suffusing it with a local character, as expressed in an entire series of popular beliefs and practices shared by the group as a whole.

The life that we have just evoked appears overall simple, rustic, natural, lacking in extraordinary events. This enables us to understand why these populations do not have an experience of duration as universal and as abstract as that of the westerner. The only remarkable givens that permit them to perceive and share a notion of time valid for all are the great natural rhythms that produce cosmic phenomena. The evolution of the sun, the moon, the succession of seasons, permit each person to form a sufficiently objective idea of duration. Added to this are the great religious festivals that recur at set dates, constituting salient events that punctuate community life. We thus have a fairly exact overview of all that constitutes the natural calendar of the illiterate, rural populations, which have remained outside western culture. It is clear that our conception of time and our calendar, imbued with a learned culture and a history that is foreign to them, are too abstract in their symbolism for those that a centuries-old tradition sustains, one popular in origin and oral in transmission. Resulting from this is a major lack of precision in the evaluation of duration, which always astonishes the observer. The rural dweller often has only a rather woolly notion of his age, his

---

[18][In *L'An V de la révolution algérienne*, the motif of a *living* culture or community will be crucial in Fanon's analysis of the impact of colonialism, which tends to reify the culture of the other.]

history and that of the douar. He proceeds via broad approximations and appeals to group-specific temporal markers. The death of a notable, an inundation, a frost, a famine or a superabundant harvest: these elements are already valid for an entire society, as small as it may be. Not to mention someone who has recourse to facts that are of interest only to his own person or those close to him: birth, illness, etc.

However, if the man is placed back in his milieu, our astonishment no longer serves, for the douar inhabitant moves with ease among his own, among his fellows.[19] Throughout his entire life, he remains closely adapted to the framework in which he came into the world and to which his past and his daily experience attach him ever more. His fathers are in his image; they possess the same patrimony, the same certitudes, the same system of reference. Among them an uninterrupted language develops from the outset, one that can do without words, and that gesture or even silence can be enough to maintain, but that the spoken word makes it possible to extend by drawing from the springs of a tradition living in everyone's heart.

The case of the foreigner who arrives at the douar presents, it seems to us, interesting features that ought to be specified. Because he is Muslim, sustained by the same beliefs, an inheritor of the same faith, the foreigner is a brother. His outward appearance, his behaviour, his language, make him all the more familiar. The hospitality reserved for him is always very generous; it has become proverbial in the west, such is its perfection. However, if the stranger is sacred and respectable, he is also the Other, one who comes from elsewhere, who has lived under other skies. This is why the presence of the traveller who gives himself defenseless to his host engenders a feeling of uneasiness: he represents the unknown, mystery. Even if he divulges his thoughts and opens up his heart directly, he cannot prevent anxiety from emerging all around him. If various systems of signals make him familiar to us, to all intents and purposes he represents a system of reference that escapes us. He is one whose

---

[19][This argument is clearly important for the critique of colonial ethnopsychiatry's 'constitutionalism', according to which cultural traits, such as a different awareness of time, comprise racial differences or deficiencies. The first chapter of Suzanne Taïeb's dissertation is titled: 'Dominant features of the indigenous mentality: primitivism, fatalism and predestination. Mental debility', p. 19 *sq.*]

powers are perhaps great, but whose limits and origin one is unaware of. Is one to expect from him a baleful influence or a beneficent blessing (*baraka*)? He is, in a word, someone that must be treated with consideration because the power of his word, of his gaze is unknown, because he perhaps has some secret relation with these Other People.[20]

Ultimately, life in the douars is peaceful and each person's existence is part of a universe of profound serenity; it is, you might say, without history, as the accidental appears absent from it. Regulated by an ancient tradition, authenticated by a common religion, it expresses an intimate and profound adherence of the members of the collectivity to a well-defined, shock-free style of life. The inalterable and unanimous belief in a perfect and all-powerful God, the relative simplicity of the very forms of religious life facilitates the thriving of a life close to nature with its regular rhythms, making all individual hysteria impossible. Man has absolute confidence in God and in his Creation, with the individual, pliant as a reed, bowing and self-effacing before the will of Allah. Man has confidence in his fellow men, who share with him a common vision of the world, in which each thing occupies the place reserved for it in a definitively established order that, being the divine order, it is crucial not to upset. This order is what the collective effort strives to keep going by a production of each instant in which each person is linked with his brothers. Nothing can arise that was not expected in advance; as for the rest, the unforeseen, that is also of the order of God, whose designs are inscrutable to humans.

Much has been said about the carelessness and nonchalance of the Maghrebi, his supposedly characteristic lack of concern about tomorrow; in a word, much has been said about his fatalism. Such an opinion, it seems to us, considers only the secondary, negative aspect of a style of life that in actual fact proceeds from a fundamental certainty and security: man finds himself, wholly, in a stable world that is in fact the heir to a past and to a present whose continuity is recognized and valorized by the individual's total adherence. I know that tomorrow will be made up of yesterday and today, to the extent that God allows me to glimpse his designs; anyhow, whatever may

---

[20][The manuscript contains a footnote reference here but no note is given.]

happen, tomorrow will be unable to signify anything other than the all-powerfulness of God. What escapes me about my future, is nevertheless destined to me by God, in all justice. The accidental, by surprising me, proves just how weak and powerless I am within the Universe; it allows me to make out better Allah's generosity – he is the source of all certainty. Nature, with its reassuring rhythms, constitutes for me a faithful world desired by God – with, for every change, the weight added to it by time with the successive generations that it produces and renders familiar to me, by virtue of our common faith.

As we have just described it, the life of the douar appears to be without history, just like the life of its inhabitants. The advent of history begins with adversity. But there are several forms of adversity. There is the one that strikes the collectivity as a whole or in its quasi-totality; one linked to economic crises, to meteorological cataclysms, to natural catastrophes. The life of the douar, its security, its quiet, are then in danger. The individual never comes to be isolated. Whether he decides to fight or to submit without resistance to the difficulties that arise, he feels his brothers at his side, all of them hit by the same tragic event. The misfortune of each person merges with that of all, the individual feels less alone, his lot being linked to that of the group. This is how he is led to think and to act in accordance with the attitude and decisions of the douar, which, when all is said and done, can call on the resources that God offers to men. The history of each person, in this case, is still that of the community.

But the properly personal history enters into existence and begins at the moment when illness cuts an individual off from others and isolates him without any possible involvement from the entourage. A deep furrow is dug that separates the man from the world, leaving him powerless, alone with an evil that is strictly his. This is when the man that no initiation has fortified, turns spontaneously toward the privileged beings who can help him and cure him, to the extent that God renders such aid effective. Indeed, God's more or less direct action is essential: if one is ill, it is because God has allowed it; if a cure remains possible, it is again with his permission. Whether God is testing me through illness, whether he favours me by thus securing for me the rewards of the beyond in a surer and more rapid manner or whether he is [punishing] me for acts that have offended him, all this escapes me, the ways of God being foreign to me; there is no common measure between his perfection and his power and the humble believer that I am. God plumbs my heart, judges me and I can only adore him. However, he does not forbid me from having recourse to those he allows some hold over sickness, some power of cure. So I will consult those privileged beings able to help me; and this with all the more hope as I know man is able to affect me in my health, to the extent that God permits such an action. Thus the illness that man may have contributed to inflicting upon me, he can also take part in removing.[21]

In the society that surrounds me, several categories of individuals may come to my aid. First, the women, who often participate in the secrets of the world of genies and know the power of the word and of desire; women may perhaps remove the weight of the illness that is harming me. They pass mysterious recipes among themselves that are very often effective. More powerful than the women, and more knowledgeable than them, are the *iqqachs*: versed in knowledge of the Book's words, they know how to wield them against all forms of illness in order to protect and cure. Their science is secretly transmitted, but it is no less official and public in its applications; it is entirely subject to God, for its lettered persons can do nothing without divine intervention. Above the *iqqachs*, there are, lastly, the saints, the [friends] of God, who remain or are destined to remain next to God, the source of all fortune.

The power of the saints is great and their benediction inexhaustible. To prevent or cure the illness that genies, perfidious words or [envy] can cause me, it is enough to ask the marabout to invoke his holy luck. The man has further recourse to sorcerers, though seldom does one maintain relations with such individuals, few of whom exist today and who live removed from the group. Their action does not refer to God's authority, although God is actually the only master governing them and tolerating them having some power, and who thus has them participate in the accomplishment of his designs. The sorcerer, heir to a secret science transmitted through a purely personal initiation, is cut off from the mass of believers. It is shameful to consult him and it is dangerous to do so owing to [his] relations with the forces of Evil.

---

[21][Just as in the phenomenology of *Peau noire, masques blancs*, it is a matter here of reconstructing a first-person thought process, on the basis of an interaction between an incident, an external event, and a consciousness whose history, structures and expectations have been analyzed in advance in relationship to social situations.]

The infirmity that he cures, he may actually also have helped to bring out. Likewise, he may also help it to reappear later.

Such, in its simplicity, is the natural life of the douars. We believe that such a description is fundamental: it brings to light a technical and cultural backwardness that, as we've already said, is characteristic of the populations of Algeria in general and appeared to us nowhere so manifest as in the douars, where its magnitude can be accurately gauged. This backwardness is rendered more palpable by the existence on Algerian soil of a fraction of the population who lives a western lifestyle and possesses a broad experience of modern technologies. This coexistence and contrast is not without interest for the sociologist concerned to establish the exact determinism of phenomena as astonishing as this, and to discern, under the apparent stability of the life of the douar, the signs of a possible transformation that would come about progressively or in the form of a sudden mutation.

But such is not our aim. We have wanted only to indicate that our description, insofar as it is valid, nevertheless remains tied to a given period of Algeria's history. Modern technologies, even if they continue to be unfamiliar to populations still oriented around the exploration and explanation of nature, according to a relatively rudimentary and primitive mode – a bygone one to our eyes as westerners – will nevertheless be the likely source of new problems. Stability, the past, tradition will not be able to explain everything in the future. Tomorrow a new description will be necessary, one that will have to bear above all on research into all that which, in this already less natural life, will signal a break with the past. Without asking why they have remained so important to this day, let's simply say that all the elements we have highlighted explain the still current extent and vivacity of highly ancestral and traditional beliefs.

Stemming from this data is an important notion: some conducts, some reactions can appear 'primitive' to us, but that is only a value judgement, one that is both questionable and bears on poorly defined characteristics, which scarcely helps us progress in our knowledge of the Algerian Muslim man. In actual fact, it must be said that these beliefs, conducts or reactions *ought not to astonish us*, for they are not the sign of the abnormal, the accidental or the paradoxical, as would be the case if we were to find them among populations on the European continent, for example. Were a Parisian to tell us: 'The genies are what produce madness', this statement would not have the same value if we gathered it on the lips of a Maghrebi Muslim, because in Algeria such belief is normal and adapted, and we find it in the mentally ill patient and in a healthy man. It is not the same in Paris, where nothing justifies it, where it does not agree with standard ideas. *In Algeria, it is normal to believe in genies.*

We said that in Algeria the material conditions of populations appear on the verge of being modified. Concerning popular beliefs, this is less apparent: they continue to remain very deeply rooted in individual and collective consciousness, perhaps lagging behind the vital, economic and technological conditions of existence.

12 INTRODUCTION TO SEXUALITY DISORDERS AMONG NORTH AFRICANS

Jacques Azoulay, François Sanchez, Frantz Fanon, 1955[1]

Over the course of our psychiatric practice in Algeria, our attention was drawn to the frequency of disorders that are attributed or tied to sexuality. The fundamental modalities of these disorders are circumscribed by the different types of impotence among men and of vaginismus among women. The importance of this theme within delusions incited us to research the extent to which it had its origin in normal consciousness. It was necessary, then, to investigate normal consciousness, the nodes of belief …

A rapid survey enabled us to observe that sexual impotence was an especially preoccupying problem, since Muslim society is founded on the authority of men. Any deficit of virile potency is felt as a major alteration of the personality, as if the man rendered

---

[1][IMEC Fonds Fanon, typescript FNN 1.4. This is a previously unseen, undated text, probably written at the end of 1954 or in 1955 since it seems to have been written after Jacques Azoulay's dissertation. The typescript is available at IMEC and was initially titled 'Introduction aux troubles de la sexualité chez les Nord-Africains' (the plural of this latter term is crossed out). This text has *djouns* instead of *djnoun* as the plural forms of *djinn* (genie).]

impotent has been targeted in his essential attribute. And impotence appeared proportionally far more frequently in the Muslim milieu than in the European milieu. Several Muslim practitioners were questioned and stated to us that two or three cases of impotence were detected in the course of the same consultation. However, the doctor here is generally the last one to be consulted. One has first recourse to the marabout, the *taleb*,[2] because, as we shall see, these disorders are almost never attributed to an organic origin. They are most often seen to be in relation with magical practices and have to be treated as such.[3] On this view, we can likewise understand the existence of closely related phenomena pertaining to feminine sexuality, which we will also come to study. An attempt at a psychopathological understanding of sexuality disorders can be sketched.

Clinically speaking, it is roughly possible to distinguish between three major groups of impotence: impotence through hormonal deficiency; impotence of nervous origin tied to organic alterations of the lumbosacral cord; and psychic or central nervous system impotence.

We find these distinctions in part in the beliefs of Muslims. We were able to question a *taleb*, S. A., settled in Castiglione not far from Algiers and well-reputed in the region. It could be said that he even specialized in treating impotence. In truth, his explanations seemed somewhat confused to us, but he took his inspiration from a book that we were able to find in which impotence was meticulously studied from a clinical, etiological and above all therapeutic point of view. We are talking about the *Book of Clemency on Medicine and Wisdom* by Al-Suyuti, an Arab writer from the Middle Ages known above all as a commentator of the Koran.[4] For Al-Suyuti, impotence can stem from three causes: malformation of the genitals, the breath of demons and magic.

---

[2]*Taleb*: one who writes. The *taleb* is a sort of healer whose essential attribute is knowing how to read and write old Koranic, which is especially effective as the majority of the population is illiterate.
[3]See Desparmet, *Le Mal magique*, Jules Carbonel, Algiers, 1932. [Joseph Desparmet, *Le Mal magique. Ethnographie traditionnelle de la Mettidja*, Publications de la Faculté des lettres d'Alger, Ancien bulletin de correspondance africaine, 1st series, vol. 63.]
[4]*Book of Clemency on Medicine and Wisdom* by Jalal al-Din al-Suyuti edited at Tanta (Cairo), by Mustapha Tadj El-Koutoubi. We have taken the care to translate these passages. [The British Library record for this edition of Suyuti's book is: Suyūṭī 1445–1505, *al-Raḥmah fī al-ṭibb wa-al-ḥikmah*.[al-Qāhirah]: ʿĪsā al-Bābī al-Ḥalabī [n.d.].]

a) The first group comprises all forms of impotence caused by an obvious malformation of the genital organs: lack of development, testicular atrophy, etc. This disorder is in general accompanied by a weakness or absence of sexual desire. Here impotence is attributed to an infirmity and is in principle beyond the *taleb*'s therapeutic means. It is in this case it seems that the patient is in fact most willingly or even systematically addressed to the doctor. At most said Suyuti, one could try to feed the patient the male organ of a wild donkey, which is to be taken from the animal before it expires and mixed with certain spices that he details expertly.

b) The sort of impotence ascribable to the *djinns*[5] has a different character: 'The man made impotent by the breath of demons is recognized by his ejaculating prior to having had relations with a woman', says Suyuti. The issue here, as we see, is the phenomenon of premature ejaculation.

---

[5]The *djinns* or demons play an important role in North African mental pathology. This influence of the *djinns* has been studied in-depth in Suzanne Taieb's dissertation, which was inspired by Professor Porot. One of us intends to consider in his dissertation the relations between belief in genies and the different levels of destructuration of consciousness. [In his dissertation, Jacques Azoulay refers to Suzanne Taïeb's dissertation in the same terms: 'Here we hit upon an extremely interesting aspect of North African psychiatry. Mental illness is external to the individual. It is sent and can be taken back by God. For some, it is ascribable to *djinns* or spirits, which you can try to capture in sessions of exorcism led by a marabout (see Suzanne Taieb, *Les Idées d'influence dans la pathologie mentale nord-africaine. Le rôle des superstitions*, Med. thesis: Algiers, 1939).' Doctoral dissertation in medicine, presented and defended publicly on June 24, 1939 by Ms Suzanne Taïeb, intern at the psychiatric hospital of Blida, born on August 17, 1907, University of Algiers. The dissertation supervisor and president of the jury was Antoine Porot. In her conclusion to her dissertation Suzanne Taïeb wrote: 'Ideas of influence occur very frequently in the mental pathology of North African natives. They are the expression of very widespread and deeply rooted beliefs and superstitions in their culture. Indeed, what characterizes these natives from the psychological point of view is a rather special "primitivism" into which enters a large store of mysticism and of religious credulity, in the sense that Lévy-Bruhl and Blondel have established in their studies on the "primitive mentality". Rational and scientific explanations do not exist for them; there are only ever affective values, supernatural and mystical acts that are not up for debate, cannot be controlled, to which one is subject and against which means of protection must be found, when they are baleful. ... All these beliefs are found in the various manifestations of indigenous mental pathology. All the abnormal sensations that he experiences (synesthetic disorders, hallucinations), all his behavioural disorders will be ascribed to these magical influences' (p. 147 *sq.*). On Suzanne Taïeb, see Laura Faranda, *La signora di Blida. Suzanne Taïeb e il presagio dell'etnopsichiatria*, Rome: Armando, 2012.]

As that impotence is interpreted as a punishment from the *djinns*, who the man must have annoyed in a more or less distant past, and as these demons are known to be particularly sensitive, then engaging in propitiatory rites to ward off their wrath is an ongoing necessity: 'It is recommended to hold one's hand over the mouth and to pronounce the *bismillah* before spitting, for fear of the ground spirits, so that, if one happens to be in that place, it is advised to move away. ... Micturating has its rite of prior warning, of orientation, of attitude, etc., to which country-dwellers remain faithful. Children are watched to make sure that they do not urinate in the street, in the inner courtyard, in the garden, on the rubbish, or in many places reputed to be haunted, particularly at night. Those who lack respect for genies, those who, according to the Arab expression, "dent their prestige", are almost invariably punished with pathological afflictions such as cutaneous affections, the privation of a sense, nervous diseases, madness.'[6] And we will cite the case of one of our patients who attributed his impotence to the fact that he once accidentally walked in the blood of a sheep with its throat freshly cut on the occasion of the feast of *mawlid*.[7]

The man made impotent on account of offending the *djinns* has to have recourse to the *taleb*, who will seek to appease the *djinns* in various ways: invocations, the making of amulets that must be worn permanently on the body and on which various magical formulae are inscribed in a leather sachet, or the ingestion of specified products. And the marabout that we consulted stated that the results are mostly positive.

    c) Cases of impotence attributed to a magical practice, to some act of sorcery, appear to be the most frequent and the most complex. Impotence here is marked by the inability to achieve an erection, or the loss of erection at the moment of intromission. The man is then said to be bewitched or bound (*marbout*).

The bewitching is in general performed by the spouse who wants to make her husband impotent, unless, deeming herself not to be

---

[6] Joseph Desparmet, *Le Mal magique*, p. 194.
[7] Spilt blood and milk must not be soiled; they are destined for the spirits of the soil. Some fantasist commentators of the Koran think that the prohibition on consuming blood has to be interpreted via this perspective. (Surat of the Table, Verse 4.)

expert enough, she has recourse to another woman reputed for her knowledge of these magical practices. Impotence is then most often selective. Thus a woman who has been cheated on can bind her husband, who becomes impotent for all women other than herself. This bewitching is more or less licit; it is fairly well accepted by the collective morality. It is part of what can be called white magic.

But the binding can be global, such that the man becomes totally impotent. This, for example, is the case of a jealous or abandoned woman who wants to take revenge on her husband. Here we are dealing with a malevolent action accomplished under the influence of the chitan [Satan], one roundly condemned by society as akin to black magic, since, if, on the one hand, this is about the protection of a unity, the promotion of a value, on the other, it is no more than the destruction, the annihilation of the man.

The procedures employed are multiple. We will relate some of the most typical ones. The woman who wants to bind her husband measures the size of his erect organ with the help of a string of wool. She ties a knot at each end and hides the cord. The man becomes impotent.

Or else she can place a totally new, round mirror under the footsteps of her husband, who has to step over it unknowingly. Or the woman may put an open foldable knife under the feet of her husband and then close it again. Some procedures are even more colourful: thus, somewhere close to Algiers, a woman who wants to bind her husband is advised to gather some drops of his sperm and to mix them with a whitish earth found in a specific place, which is then formed into a small statuette in human form. This statuette is then hidden in a place known only to the woman, in general in an abandoned tomb in a cemetery. Lastly, certain magical formulae can be written on the horn of a goat that is then thrown into a cemetery, progressively reducing the man to impotence.

This enumeration is not exhaustive, the methods vary depending on the place and particular customs, but all those listed have certain common features. First is the essential value of speech: in bewitching, there is always an invocation, an incantation that accompanies and authenticates the act. This is why it is necessary to know the lineage of the man that one is binding, in particular his mother's maiden name. In the magic ritual, the act of binding is accompanied with verbal prescriptions, instructions, an actual final notice.

It is also necessary to note the importance of knots and bonds in these practices of binding, which are incidentally to be found in all phenomena of a magico-religious order: 'It is significant that knots and strings are used in the nuptial rites to protect the young couple, though at the same time, as we know, knots are thought to imperil the consummation of marriage. But ambivalence of this sort is to be found in all the magico-religious uses of knots and bonds. ... In sum, what is essential in all these magical and magico-medical rites, is the orientation that they give to the power that resides in any kind of bond, in every act of binding.[8]

The man thus made impotent may heal if the women renounces the bewitching by destroying the knot or statuette-substitute. But the woman is not always so merciful, whence again the indispensable intervention of the *taleb*. As in the preceding case, the *taleb* summons magical formulae, amulets and various preparations that he has the patient swallow. But the formulae and products differ depending on whether the impotence results from bewitching or from the acts of *djinns*. More precisely, the formulae and products are adapted to each particular case and the systems, the real keys that make it possible to determine the nature of the impotence to be treated, are complicated. In these systems such things are introduced as the patient's name, where each letter conventionally represents a certain number, the mother's maiden name, the day of the treatment, the duration of the illness, and so on.

Whence a rather complex classification that, though very detailed, remains confused in Al-Suyuti's work, and which no doubt permits each *taleb* to add his personal note to it. Here are the few formulae that we thought interesting to take from Al-Suyuti: the man made impotent by magical practices is cured by ingesting diverse Indian spices (ginger, pepper, cloves), if his impotence has lasted for barely a year. If it is older, the patient must be made to eat the penis of a fox or of a wild donkey prepared with the aforementioned spices for a period of seven days. The impotence can also be cured by writing

---

[8]Mircea Eliade, 'The "God who Binds"', in *Images and Symbols*, trans. Philip Mairet, New York: Sheed & Ward, 1961, p. 112. (French original: Gallimard, 1952, p. 147) ['The "God who binds" and the Symbolism of Knots', chapter 3 of *Images and Symbols, Studies in Religious Symbolism*; this essay was previously published in the *Revue de l'histoire des religions*, vol. 134, nos. 1–3, 1947, pp. 5–36.]

certain formulae and signs on an axe[9] that is heated up and then cooled again in some water placed under the patient.[10]

It is also possible to write some Koranic verses on a saucer on which the man's and woman's names are also mentioned, together with the plea: 'O my God, I ask you to unite this man and this woman'. Or else the following Koranic expression may be written under the patient's navel: 'Those who have moved away from God and from the Prophet will be destroyed like their predecessors'.

Here is yet another way to cure impotence: the writing of a series of Cabalistic formulae on a vase filled with oil with which the man and woman coat their genitalia. On other occasions, a cabalistic grid with nine squares, in which are inscribed specific letters and numbers is drawn on an egg, and on each side of the grid, in the margins, the following qualifying adjectives are written: violent, strong, hard, powerful. The patient with impotence is made to eat the egg. The shell is enclosed in the small cloth bag that was used to cook the egg and is hung from the woman's neck.

Ultimately, we see that the *taleb* combats the bewitching with a sort of counter-magic: on the one hand, he seeks to replace the penis with the genitals of an animal serving as a product of substitution. On the other hand, he answers the magic formulae of sorcery with incantatory formulae, in which one often finds the words key, open, picket, staff of Moses, etc. And the marabout of Castiglione cited the case of a man from Tiaret who was bound for ten years and whom he succeeded in unbinding with such practices in seven days.

We have just seen that impotence in men is most often attributed to an act of bewitching, to a binding. But the binding can also be directed at women.

a) Indeed, young women are often bound by their parents. At issue in this instance is the protection of their virginity. We know in fact that virginity, in its properly anatomical sense, must be preserved in absolute fashion in the young woman prior to marriage. To give as a virgin a girl who is not one would be a grave insult and a swindle[11] on the part of the parents vis-à-vis the husband and, the day of the marriage, the parents of

---

[9]The axe cuts the bond.
[10]The patient breathes in the steam thus produced.
[11]Indeed, the dowry for a virgin is a lot higher than that asked for a deflowered woman.

the married woman await impatiently the moment when the husband comes out of the bridal room to present to the entire family the blood-stained sheet, peremptory evidence of the virginity of his young spouse. If this virginity cannot be proven in this fashion, the husband has the right to send the girl back to her parents, and the girl is then doomed to shame and celibacy, when for the woman marriage is the only human and social consecration.

In principle, prior to marriage, the young girl does not leave the house unless accompanied by her mother or an old relative, but sometimes, above all in the countryside, that rule cannot be observed because it is necessary to tend the goats and the sheep, gather in the fields of cereals or fetch some water from the spring. This is why the parents take care to bind their daughter to avoid any 'accidents'. At issue here is a protection of the family as a whole and the binding does not assume an occult character: it is done in the knowledge of the one bound, who plays a role in the ritual.

Here again, the techniques are multiple and vary depending upon local and familial traditions. One of those that seemed to us especially frequently carried out was related to us by a female Muslim nurse in our unit who had been bound by her parents before her marriage: the young girl is placed on a brand new trunk with a key lock.[12] The mother then closes the trunk in pronouncing an established formula: the young girl is bound. At the moment of marriage, these gestures are repeated in the inverse order: the young girl is placed on the trunk, the mother opens it and the bind is lifted.

In these rituals ties, knots and padlocks are often used, the symbolic value of which is clear cut, but in all cases the result is the same: the girl is protected against all breaches of her virginity, accepted or not. The mechanism of this protection is not always clearly clarified: it seems that it works in a general fashion by making the potential deflowerer impotent. And this protection is so absolute that it sometimes results in unforeseen consequences.

We were told of the case of a woman who was bound in her youth and whose mother died before she was able to unbind her. This woman, although married several times, was each time sent back

---

[12] According to some, it is better to buy this trunk in a boutique facing Mecca.

by the husband because he could not succeed in having intercourse with her. Let us also relate the anecdote where a young woman's uncle complained to the mother about having seen her daughter seek out the presence of boys a little too much, fearing for her good reputation; it was retorted that there was nothing to fear since she had been bound.

b) Young girls are not the only ones who get bound. Thus the parents of a repudiated woman can bind her so as to be sure that she will respect her transitory celibacy. And one says sometimes that parents wait a few days until after the marriage before they unbind their daughter, to show pointedly to the husband that she has remained responsible since her divorce.

c) Sometimes the husband is brought to bind his own wife, especially when he has reason to doubt her fidelity. Binding can then occur in two ways: in general by making impotent any man other than the husband who wants to have relations with the woman. We again see here the notion of selective binding that we observed in binding-impotence. But it also happens that the bewitching determines in the spouse a vanishing of every desire and even the taste for living, resulting in a veritable affective death, which is indeed effective in eliminating all risk of conjugal infidelity.

d) Lastly, a woman can be bound by another woman, by a stranger: this is usually the case of a woman who, for example, has been cheated on or left for another, and who binds this latter to prevent her from remaining with her husband. But while, in the preceding cases, the bind of the young girl or the woman was a normal and licit practice, one accepted by the collective morality, here it assumes a character of vengeance and malevolence, which society condemns as such. We thus encounter the same distinction between black and white magic that was seen in the binding of men.

13 CURRENT ASPECTS OF MENTAL CARE IN ALGERIA

Jean Dequeker, Frantz Fanon,
Raymond Lacaton, M. Micucci,
F. Ramée (Blida-Joinville Psychiatric
Hospital), January 1955[1]

L'Information [psychiatrique]'s initiative to devote an issue to the institutions in French overseas *départements* seems particularly topical at a time when Algeria is enduring a shortage of several thousands of beds for mental patients who require urgent treatment, as well as for Muslim patients hospitalized in France who have requested repatriation, while the Orléansville[2] earthquake has just deprived it of two hundred vital beds.

The problem of psychiatric care in the colonies was raised in its entirety by Reboul and Régis' report to the 22nd *Congrès des*

---

[1]*L'Information psychiatrique*, vol. 31, no. 1, January 1955, pp. 11–18.
[2][September 9, 1954. According to sources at the time, there were 1,500 dead, 1,200 wounded and 60,000 homeless. Jacques Ladsous, then director of the Ceméa community of children (an establishment of the Red Cross) at Chréa, located at 1,800 metres of altitude above Blida, described Fanon's involvement: 'The earthquake in what was then called Orléansville increased threefold the number of my residents. (120 × 3). To treat the suffering, not to leave suffering those who were entrusted to us was obviously our first concern. While Frantz Fanon helped our team to understand the traumas the children were enduring, we helped him transform the asylum, assisting his

aliénistes et neurologues in 1912. The members of the congress passed a resolution stipulating the conditions of fulfilment of suitable care. Not until 1932 in Algeria did active concern begin to be taken in the performing of psychiatric assistance, at the instigation of the Médecin Général [and general inspector of colonial health services in Ministère des Colonies] Lasnet and Professor A. Porot. A decree of 14 March 1933 governs the recruitment of doctors for psychiatric units in Algeria, doctors from the metropolitan civil service. Two directives from 10 August 1934 govern the operation of psychiatric units in Algeria: the front-line [*première ligne*] units of Algiers, Oran and Constantine, and the psychiatric hospital of Blida.

As for the front-line units, the formula adopted was for open observation units, whereas the psychiatric hospital of Blida was to operate under the conditions prescribed by the law of 30 June 1838. The construction phase was then begun and in July 1935 the intended measures were in place, with the opening of Constantine's open unit.

In 1938, in his report to the *Congrès des médecins aliénistes et neurologues* [*de France et des pays de langue française*] in Algiers, Aubin drew up an assessment of the resources in Algeria, according to which, for the 'first line' units: Algiers, forty-three beds; Oran, fifty-five beds; Constantine, sixty-two beds. At that time, the hospital of Blida had a population of 1,000 patients (already in excess of planned capacity).

From that time on, Professor Porot, a technical advisor in psychiatry [to the General Government of Algeria], insistently asked for an increase in bed numbers: he estimated the need to be 5,000 beds and recommended building psychiatric hospitals in the *départements* of Oran and Constantine. Unfortunately, his advice was not heeded and the solution implemented, the creation of psychiatric outbuildings in Aumale and Orléansville, was unsatisfactory from a psychiatric viewpoint and did not supply the number of beds required. Since 1938, building work has been negligible and the situation in 1954 is as follows.

---

efforts in building and setting up a football field' (Jacques Ladsous, 'Fanon: du soin à l'affranchissement', *Vie sociale et traitements*, no. 89, 2006, pp. 25–9). He confirmed to us Fanon's constant commitment to training nurses and educators of the community of children in Chréa in treating traumas, and their regular contact during Fanon's entire Blida period (conversation held on 10 January 2015).]

Figure 6 Fanon among colleagues at Blida-Joinville Hospital. Credit: Fonds Frantz Fanon/IMEC.

Algeria is a country of 10 million inhabitants, comprising 8,500,000 Muslims and 1,500,000 Europeans. Psychiatry in Algeria is founded on the following principle: in each *département*, there is a 'front-line' service and a 'second-line' service. In the *département* of Algiers the front-line service is located at Mustapha hospital, a faculty hospital in which there are eighty-one beds. The psychiatric hospital of Blida-Joinville, with 2,200 beds, and the annexes of Aumale and of Orléansville, with three hundred and two hundred beds respectively, represent the second line.

The *département* of Oran, whose first line is located at the hospital of Oran, has 545 beds in all. For the *département* of Constantine, its first-line facility is the hospital of Constantine, with seventy-six beds. Secure Units, sixteen in total, represent the second-line at Bougie, Philippeville, Guelma and Bordj-Bou-Arreridj.

These psychiatry clinics are ensured by one psychiatric doctor for the *département* of Oran, by one psychiatric doctor for the *département* of Constantine, by five psychiatric doctors for Blida hospital and by one psychiatric doctor for Mustapha hospital. The faculty clinic is overseen by professor Manceaux and his assistants. Otherwise put, for 10 million inhabitants, there are eight psychiatrists and 2,500 beds.

Moreover, in 1952, 536 mentally ill Muslims were treated in metropolitan hospitals. One thus sees that there is almost one bed per 4,000 inhabitants. But if you consider – and this consideration must be taken into account – that the hospital of Blida-Joinville has been planned for 1,200 patients, with the gradual overcrowding of the service slowly eliminating its effectiveness, then we reach barely one bed for 7,000 inhabitants.

We can easily imagine the number of problems that such a situation raises for a psychiatrist who wants to work. In this study we set out to show how on the three planes of admissions, stays and discharges, psychiatric practice today proves very difficult.

Admissions

Although in the metropole, patients who come to hospital endowed with a placement certificate and an application for admission must be accepted as a matter of obligation, it is not the same in Algeria, where admission takes place only within the limits of existing vacancies (that is, discharges and deaths). As of 23 September 1954, 850 files are pending at the admissions office of Blida; they are divided as follows: European women, thirty-three; indigenous women, one hundred and forty one; European men, eighty seven; indigenous men, five hundred and eighty three. These files came from the three Algerian *départements* and their number grows regularly. Many were opened several months ago, sometimes more than an entire year. (It can therefore arise that a patient has already been cured by the time it is his or her turn to be admitted to hospital …).

These extended delays bring about various incidents: a) aggressive reactions from individuals placed late; b) aggressive reactions from the family toward the patient whose reactions cannot be gauged; c) aggravation of the condition owing to the lateness of treatment; d) minor scandals: it happens that patients driven as a matter of urgency to the hospital are refused and stay for a long time outside the gates before they go back to their families.

Patients who react by committing misdemeanours have their cases dismissed and are nevertheless kept in prison while waiting for a place. The prefect recently issued a formal demand to receive these cases of 'medical jurisprudence' as a priority within a maximum period of one month. It goes without saying that such a measure can only be applied to the detriment of individuals presenting disorders that are perhaps more acute and more characteristic.

The mode of placement for the hospital as a whole is roughly uniform: it is almost always a matter of a PO[3] since for the 2,101 patients present on 22 September, only thirty-six PVs can be noted (fifteen of which are paying clients). The request for free voluntary placement is in fact submitted to a complex administrative inquiry into 'the mental patient's financial and familial situation', which is at best completed in two or three months. It is nevertheless notable that the number of PVGs is tending to increase: with a PO having first been issued, but admission being impossible, a request for a PVG can be made and is often successfully completed prior to internment.

Lastly, a difficulty of an essentially administrative order often arises for a certain number of patients without precise identity (mostly from Morocco or the Territories of the South). These Xs or SNPs (without patronymic name) are later recognized through a reference number and a photograph.

The stay

As the wards cannot be extended, even the smallest spaces were soon used up. And the massive overcrowding of units became such that the planned regulation capacity nearly doubled everywhere: a tuberculosis ward designed for thirty-two patients hosts seventy-four. A ward of 'agitated patients'[4] planned for forty-four contains one hundred and six. A ward planned to host eighty difficult patients contains one hundred and sixty-five, etc. Moreover, the hospital, which at the time of building was planned for 971 patients, currently has more than 2,000. Nearly all the refectories, bathrooms, etc.,

---

[3][PO: *placement d'office*, or involuntary commitment, that is, one ordered by a doctor in case of disruption to the public order or the endangering of a patient; PV: *placement volontaire*, voluntary placement, that is, the one most often requested by the family or entourage; PVG: *placement volontaire gratuit*, or free voluntary placement.]

[4][The brackets indicate the doubts expressed by Fanon and many other psychiatrists at the time, such as Paumelle, about the pertinence of the notion of agitation as a psychiatric condition. On this see the article below by Fanon and Asselah on 'The phenomenon of agitation in the psychiatric milieu' *below*, p. 289 and our introduction p. 33.]

have been transformed into dormitories and, further, some of the refectories no longer prove adequate.

What hope can there be to perform therapeutic activity in a ward of one hundred and seventy beds? For fourteen years, the doctors have been asking the administration to build workshops, day rooms. The chapel, built twenty years ago, is not only used for worship (a priest comes once a month): it has also been transformed into an ergotherapy workshop, into a classroom for the orderlies, into a film theatre, etc. Similarly, the mosque is also used as a basket and wickerwork workshop; in addition, a mufti comes to lead prayer here twice a month.

In the wards, many patients (those who do not attend ergotherapy) have no other choice: they are thrown out into the courtyard after breakfast; there is no day room. Patients have few options for sitting down, unless on the ground, and the sun in Algeria is very harsh in the summertime ...

Staff numbers in the housekeeping services have had to be considerably increased. In the kitchen, there are thirty employees; for the electricity, eight; the linen room, twenty-six; painting, nineteen; masonry, nineteen; laundry, twenty. This clearly enables the hospital to ensure its own maintenance without external help. In the offices, we see the same high numbers: twenty-six employees. Between the housekeeping and the administrative services, there are more than two-hundred and eighty employees.[5]

By contrast, no parallel growth has occurred in the facilities of the general services: the overloaded electrical installations regularly break down, an especially regrettable situation as electricity is used to heat the wards. Insufficient water conveyance only permits distribution for three hours a day in summer despite the serious difficulties that result from this situation in the units, especially the senile unit.

However, the medical equipment is quite satisfactory. All the requests are quite rapidly fulfilled and the audit committee has practically never questioned any expenditure of medical interest. The medical personnel are relatively large in number. Almost in line

---

[5][Figure 4 and 5 give an idea of the size of the kichen and buildings at Hôpital Psychiatrique de Blida-Joinville in Fanon's time.]

with the official norms: one per fifteen in the calm wards, one per ten in the admission wards or in the wards for agitated individuals (the number of medical agents totals 820). Lastly, this year saw the creation of a nursing school. One hundred and twenty agents are now taking these courses and the qualifying exams will take place in December.

As recruitment is carried out in conditions that are sometimes rather exceptional, it unfortunately transpires too often that the agents are illiterate or only know how to write their names. Fortunately, there is no lack of good will, as one says; each time that we have asked the staff for an extra effort, our calls have been answered with perfect spontaneity. Little by little, even those who are most lacking from an intellectual viewpoint, come to be of precious help in a clinic in which there is a lot to do.

All the same it has been necessary to try and regulate the recruitment. Currently school-completion certificates are required or else an equivalent exam has to have been passed. These measures were adopted very quickly, as the medico-administrative team is becoming increasingly aware of the importance of collective problems on the local level. The patients' living conditions are gradually improving.

Only thanks to this collaboration has it been possible to carry out certain things. Thus, a weekly journal was set up for which the administration provided the print shop. Having no room for events, we are obliged to have our recreational evenings in the wards and electricians and joiners are made available to the patients to arrange the stage, lighting, microphones, etc. Similarly, on the occasion of the major feasts that give rhythm to the Muslim religion, traditional dishes are served to the patients. More than a material contribution, the administrative and economic services have taken a great interest in the social and collective events that the patients have arranged and the director and doctors a came together to inaugurate the Moorish café.

Clearly, it will be difficult to continue if no decision is made to build the function room that has been sought after for fifteen years by the institution's successive doctors. Weekly film screenings take place in the chapel, the character and acoustics of which are hardly suitable for such events. Lastly, it has recently been possible to organize weekly outings by coach to the seaside.

Discharges

The problem of discharging patients is particularly serious, especially concerning the Muslim patients. This problem, already made difficult owing to some realities of a geographical order, becomes almost insurmountable in the absence of any policy for local mental care and assistance. Year in year out, in a hospital population that continues unfailingly to grow with the addition of new beds, the number of discharges is reducing or remains the same. To take up the terms of the 1951 report: the hospital is moving slowly but surely toward total paralysis.

The causes of this state of affairs are multiple: 1) the patients discharged from the front-line services are carefully selected in accordance with a scale of notable resistance to cure; for the front-line services, the HPB[6] is an asylum for incurables; 2) the Muslim mental patients arrive at HPB only after a long evolution through to the stage of scandal and public danger; 3) Muslims are reticent about having their wives treated in hospital.

If all these factors have a woeful effect on the therapeutic options, others work to impede the smooth operation of discharge when it is possible.

1) The Muslim wife's status, which allows the husband instant remarriage, is an insurmountable source of difficulties. After repudiation, cured women remain in hospital for several months before being able to reintegrate into a family household, which, in the absence of any precise information, it is necessary to find without any available help from a medico-social service.

2) Discharges into foreign milieus are nearly all doomed to failure. Apart from being impossible in the Muslim milieu, they are so difficult in the European milieu that it is better not to consider them.

3) Contacts with families living several hundreds of kilometres away are difficult; they are carried out through the intermediary

---

[6] [Psychiatric hospital of Blida-Joinville.]

of administrators or superintendants in the absence of any local medical or paramedical facilities.

4) Placement in hospices for the aged, the mentally handicapped or stabilized epileptics is difficult to obtain and often doomed to failure. In Algeria, mental illness is doubled with its old traditional and sacred aspect.[7]

5) Among the Muslims, probationary discharge is an illusion given the impossibility, for want of a community mental health body, to monitor and guide social readaptation. Even guided by the doctor, a probationary discharge is often impossible due to the distance of the responsible parents and their material impossibility to come and collect their patient.

6) These difficulties are multiplied two- or threefold for patients from the *départements* of Oran and Constantine. There is no pathway back for [a] cured patient to the service that first admitted him and which would be better placed, geographically speaking, to resolve all the problems of a discharge.

As long ago as 1940, Professor Sutter, in a report to the prefect, Mr. Gaubert, asked the higher civil service for: (1) clinics of mental prevention and aftercare; (2) a social service to be annexed to the HPB; (3) the appointment of a social worker; and (4) a patronage society able to help discharged patients or those being discharged. The first steps in this direction did not take place until 1954.

The psychiatric annexes

Two psychiatric annexes exist, one in Aumale (120 km from Blida), the other in Orléansville (180 km from Blida). The urgent pressure of the demand and the HPB's progressive overcrowding by patients, more or less proven incurable, have made it possible for this makeshift and easy solution in the absence of buildings suited to active therapy.

Set up in a rudimentary fashion in a general hospital that it has almost entirely swallowed up, these annexes are directly answerable

---

[7][See on this point Fanon's articles written with Azoulay and Sanchez, p. 230 and p. 271.]

to the centre at Blida, which oversees them medically, at a drive of more than three hours away. The HPB's médecins-chefs are obliged to visit them once per month, which, in the absence of any doctor and even of any fixed intern, obliges them to take full responsibility. In practice, they are left to the professional competence of former heads of wards from the HPB, who steer them with a locally-recruited staff that has very basic psychiatric training.

After the Orléansville earthquake, the two hundred patients of this annex were evacuated to the Blida Hospital where they were in part accommodated in tents. To provide them with real shelters before the onset of winter, the general government's health director is considering distributing them among the several new annexes of the civilian hospitals in towns of the region (that is, while waiting for the psychiatric hospitals of Oran and Constantine to be built …). It will probably be necessary to wait a long time, notably due to the financial cost.

Lastly, on the administrative level, some clauses distinguish this hospital from a metropolitan hospital. Examples: 1) the director is chosen from among the executive of the civil hospitals; he does not enjoy the same statutes as the directors of metropolitan psychiatric hospitals and his lack of 'specialization' is a drawback; while we can only be pleased with the current director's competency and understanding, in case of change, a period of hesitation and adjustment is to be feared; 2) during the director's annual leave, or in case of his absence, the administrative service is not entrusted to one of the médecins-chefs but to the bursar; 3) a médecin-chef in the clinic is a member of the audit committee, etc. Experience has shown that these anomalies do not always come without disadvantages. We have decided to fight so that, on the above questions, this hospital becomes as close as it can to a metropolitan psychiatric hospital.

Conclusions

This study shows that we cannot claim to be satisfied with the local conditions of psychiatric practice provided to us – and even less with the current organization of mental assistance in the three Algerian *départements*.

On the local level, we hope that the administration will firmly consider our grievances, which have been regularly expressed for over ten years, and that it will further gauge the importance of the psychiatric hospital as part of general hospital facilities. We wish to have our facilities completed, to have reduced overcrowding and thus to restore the therapeutic efficacy of our establishment. On the general level, it is necessary to speed up the creation of local mental health clinics and aftercare organizations.

It is above all necessary that work is begun to create psychiatric hospitals with sufficient capacity and of rational conception in Oran and Constantine. Clearly, the key to the problem lies there and the doctors have long been saying so. The doctors are naturally aware of the difficulties, of the various sorts of resistances, especially of a local nature, that the administration often faces, but, it seems, the situation has become too serious for any far-off or piecemeal solutions to satisfy us any longer.

14 ETHNOPSYCHIATRIC CONSIDERATIONS

Frantz Fanon, summer 1955[1]

Based on a fait divers, a Parisian lawyer provided us with some reflections not on the 'Algerian problems' that he denies knowledge of, but on a phenomenon that forced itself upon his attention. This racism, which people living in the Maghreb know well because they are the victims or silent witnesses of it, or else participants in it, insinuates itself even into reputedly 'scientific' minds. The simple juxtaposition of medical texts or publications on the psychiatry of North Africans constitutes an arresting condensation of racism with scientific pretentions. In this relation it pays to note some facts that give us food for thought about psychiatric practices in the Maghreb: 1) there is no indigenous psychiatry; 2) the essential weapon of psychiatry is psychotherapy, which is to say a dialogue between the mental patient and the doctor; in Algeria, most psychiatric doctors do not know the local language; 3) the psychological tests used are the ones used in European countries

---

[1]Consciences Maghribines, no. 5, summer 1955. [This text was published as part of a small dossier in this issue titled 'Aperçus sur le racisme: un fait divers ... un article médical', preceded by an unsigned introductory paragraph (that we have reprinted here in italics), that is most certainly by André Mandouze, the editor of the journal, then published in Algiers. The first text is by Claude Dennery, Mandouze's friend, a progressive lawyer and member of the *Mouvement national judiciaire* (which gathered former resistance fighters). The second text is not signed, but Pierre Chaulet and Alice Cherki have attributed it to Fanon. Mandouze's introduction, which clearly reflects Fanon's concerns, confirms this.]

and take no account of the culture, sociology and living conditions of the Algerian masses.

For some years, there has been much talk of ethnopsychiatry. Important monographs have been written, reports have been presented. The World Health Organization has just made this research official with J. C. Carothers' report.[2] Current achievements seem to be sufficiently solid to permit an attempt at systemization.

In 1918, Professor Porot, in Algiers, became the first person to sketch a tentative psychiatric approach to the *Muslim*.[3] In these 'Notes on Muslim psychiatry', he recalls, in a vigorous diagram, the main characteristics of the North African native: none or hardly any emotivity; credulous and suggestible to the utmost; tenacious obstinacy; mental puerilism without the curiosity of mind of the western child; a propensity for accidents and pithiatic reactions.[4] In his work on the criminal impulsiveness of the native North African, written with Arrii in 1932,[5] Porot did not introduce any serious modifications into his way of seeing. He recalled simply that the Kabyle is 'intelligent, educated, hard-working, thrifty and, owing to this, escapes mental debility, the fundamental flaw of the Algerian' (p. 590).

This fertile idea was proposed, notably, in 1935, at the *Congrès des médecins aliénistes et neurologues de [France et des pays de] langue francaise*, held in Brussels, Discussing Baruk's report on hysteria[6] and considering the particular case of the North African, Professor Porot

---

[2]John Colin Carothers, *The African Mind in Health and Disease: A Study in Ethnopsychiatry*, Geneva: World Health Organization, 1954. [This work is available on the WHO's website: https://apps.who.int/iris/handle/10665/41138. Director at the time of Nairobi Hospital, the South African John Colin Carothers (1903–1989) was qualified by French psychiatrist Bernard Doray as a 'pseudo-psychiatrist and an author of extravagant racist theories' (see a detailed portrait of him: Bernard Doray, 'Mais de quoi Fanon est-il le contraire?', *Frantz Fanon International*, 25 January 2012, http://www.frantzfanoninternational.org/Mais-de-quoi-Fanon-est-il-le-contraire).

[3][Antoine Porot, 'Notes de psychiatrie musulmane',] *Annales médico-psychologiques*, May 1918, vol. 74, pp. 377–84.]

[4]That is to say, hysterical.

[5][Antoine Porot and Come Arrii, 'L'impulsivité criminelle chez l'indigène algérien. Ses facteurs], *Annales médico-psychologiques*, vol. 90, December 1932, pp. 588–611.]

[6][Henri Baruk, 'L'hystérie et les fonctions psychomotrices. Étude psycho-physiologique', *in Comptes rendus du Congrès des médecins aliénistes et neurologues de France et des pays de langue française (Brussels, 1935)*, Paris: Masson, 1935.]

came to say that the native, a big mental retard, whose higher and cortical activities are little developed, is above all a primitive being whose essentially vegetative and instinctive life is above all regulated by his diencephalon. And the slightest psychic shock results mainly in diencephalic demonstrations rather than in differentiated and psychomotor reactions.[7]

In April 1939, Professor Porot returned to the question in a paper written with doctor [Jean] Sutter and published in Sud médical et chirurgical.[8] Studying the problem of epilepsy,[9] these authors concluded: 'Primitivism is not a lack of maturity, a pronounced cessation in the development of the individual psyche, it is a social condition that has reached the end of its evolution; it is adapted in a logical fashion to a life that is different from ours. It is not only a way of being resulting from a special education: it has far deeper foundations and we even think that it must have its substratum in a particular disposition of the architectonics, at least of the dynamic hierarchizing of the nervous centres'.

Thus, for the Algiers School, the North African displays a subcortical dominance, more precisely a diencephalic dominance. Psychomotor functions, when they are cortically integrated, are very fragile, labile and depend, in fact, on the diencephalon. Several works led by [Pierre] Gallais[10] are then used to lend a scientific root to these hypotheses. Studying EEG recordings in Blacks, the authors concluded as to a neuronal immaturity with tendencies toward paroxystic manifestations, on the one hand, thus proving, on the other, the predominance of basal ganglia. This is how the hypothesis of the Algiers School came to be verified: on the psychophysiological level, the Black African greatly resembles the North African – the African is a unity.

---

[7][Comptes rendus du Congrès des médecins aliénistes et neurologues de France et des pays de langue française (Brussels, 1935), in Baruk, 'L'hystérie et les fonctions psychomotrices', p. 264, www.biusante.parisdescartes.fr/histmed/medica/cote?110817x1935]
[8][Antoine Porot and Jean Sutter,] 'Le "primitivisme" des indigènes nord-africains. Ses incidences en pathologie mentale' [Sud médical et chirurgical, 15 April 1939, Imprimerie marseillaise, Marseille, pp. 11–12.]
[9]Algérie médicale, March 1938, p. 135.
[10][On Pierre Gallais, Médecin colonel du corps de santé colonial, see Floriane Blanc, 'Trypanothérapie, contribution à l'histoire de la psychiatrie biologique', PSN, vol. 10, no. 1, 2012, pp. 77–94; Guillaume Lachenal, Le Médicament qui devait sauver l'Afrique: Un scandale pharmaceutique aux colonies, Paris: La Découverte, 2014.]

In 1954, the World Health Organization put doctor J. C. Carothers in charge of the ethnopsychiatric study of the Black African.[11] His report, which, however, was limited to English Africa, was found to be in conformity with the conclusions of the French authors. Lobotomy, now familiar to us through neurosurgery, has given the author a better understanding of the African, as, he says, 'the resemblance of the leucotomized European patient to the primitive African is, in many cases, complete'. 'The African, with his total lack of synthesis, must therefore use his frontal lobes but little, and all the particularities of African psychiatry can be envisaged in terms of frontal idleness'.[12] 'These are the data of the cases that do not fit the European categories. They are culled from several parts of Africa – East, West and South – and, on the whole, the writers had little or no knowledge of each other's work. Their essential similarity is therefore quite remarkable'.[13]

---

[11]John Colin Carothers, *The African Mind in Health and Disease: A Study in Ethnopsychiatry*.
[12]John Colin Carothers, *The African Mind in Health and Disease: A Study in Ethnopsychiatry*, p. 157.
[13]Ibid., p. 158.

15 CONDUCTS OF CONFESSION IN NORTH AFRICA (1)

Frantz Fanon and Raymond Lacaton, September 1955[1]

If he is to answer the question asked him – 'Was the accused in a state of insanity at the moment of the act?' – the doctor tasked with writing a mental assessment is obliged to rediscover or at least to research

---

[1] *Comptes rendus du Congrès des médecins aliénistes et neurologues de France et des pays de langue française (53rd Session, Nice, 5–11 September 1955)*, Paris: Masson, 1955, pp. 657–60. [*Conduites d'aveu en Afrique du Nord.* In the Fanon archive at the IMEC is a five-page typescript (FNN 1.15) 'including the summary of Fanon's talk' to this congress, but which is in fact noticeably different from the published version. We thus reprint it here following this, the published version. The reader will find in it philosophical considerations that form the foundations of Fanon's thinking on this subject. At the 1955 Congress, the sessions devoted to medical jurisprudence had confession as their topic. The published proceedings, which contain many significant theoretical texts on this issue, were an important milestone. In both these texts, Fanon strongly claims the need to take into consideration the 'lived experience of the act ... otherwise said the facts as seen by the accused', when determining criminal responsibility. The values or mental attitudes that form the horizon of the act, beyond its immediate causes, therefore determine the meaning of the penal and judicial process, its *'dénouement'*, which is conceived by Fanon in the dramatic sense. But these values are determined by culture. Ignoring this led colonial psychiatry to hypostatize a cultural difference into a biological difference, namely a 'racial' incapacity to take responsibility. Fanon thus attacks here – from the surprising angle of confession in medical jurisprudence – the Algiers psychiatric school, which viewed in 'primitivism' the source of psychiatric troubles affecting action as much as cognition and therefore, in certain cases, the consciousness of responsibility. This text can be compared with another critical article on colonial psychiatry also published in 1955 ('Ethnopsychiatric considerations'; see *above*, p. 251).]

with the accused the ideas, values and mental attitudes on the basis of which that act was decided and carried out. In the practice of medical jurisprudence, the lived experience of the act, its justifications, the conflict that this act attempts to go beyond – otherwise said the facts as seen by the accused – are always of utmost importance. The expert therefore has to try to discover the truth of the act that will be the foundation of the truth of its author. Since, for this perpetrator, to deny his act, to dismiss it, can be lived by him as a fundamental alienation of his being. To lay claim to his act, on the contrary, to assume it in full (like Hugo, one of Sartre's protagonists, who said that only his act remains to him[2]), is to escape from the absurd and to give his life a meaning.

The internal coherence of the criminal act having been established, the fault having provoked in the conscience a self-condemnation and having led, according to the word of the rapporteur,[3] to a veritable segregation, confession becomes for its perpetrator the price of his reinsertion into the group. But how can it not be noticed that this favourable dénouement cannot take place without the prior reciprocal recognition of the group by the individual and of the individual by the group?

This is the point at which it may seem interesting briefly to insert the observations provided by medico-legal experience in Algeria. The assessments given of Algerian Muslims make it possible to appreciate in an instant the particular complexity of the problem of confession. In fact, if the rapporteur says that, as a general rule, the accused had confessed prior to the assessment, then the expert, in Algeria, often finds himself face to face with a defendant who categorically denies having done anything; in the extreme case, he does not even account for his detention.

---

[2][Hugo, ordered by his proletarian party to assassinate a leader in favour of an agreement with the bourgeois liberal parties, is himself sentenced to death when Moscow changes its line and endorses such an agreement. It is possible that Fanon, a great theatre lover, saw Les Mains sales at the Théâtre des Célestins in Lyon, which put on the play during the 1948–1949 and 1950–1951 seasons. See The Plays from Alienation and Freedom, p. 2 note 3, and p. 49.]

[3][In each section of these congresses, papers were preceded by and responding to a 'rapport' covering the field in question. The theme of the Therapeutics section in 1955 was 'l'aveu' (confession). Gabriel Deshaies presented the opening rapport, which in itself is a rich historical and theoretical essay on confession that Fanon has clearly read carefully.]

In the case of crimes committed by Kabyles and which are closely related with customary Berber law, in which the traditional rules, including immobilism and strictness, have barely been disturbed (for example: murders or attempted murders brought about by affairs of inheritance, the sale or exchanges of lands, or again a spouse's betrayal, etc.), in these cases, then, the proportion of deniers is sometimes very high (as many as sixteen out of twenty).

However, in many cases, the information in the case file speaks volumes. Sometimes the denial is made straightaway, but most often the initial investigators receive an integral confession, including the motives, the unfolding of the act, a concurring reconstruction of the facts. During the investigation, the attitude barely changes. Then, from a certain moment on (in principle, after one or two months of detention), the accused goes back on his declarations, he denies them utterly (in the majority of cases, he claims that he confessed under coercion). As this total retraction becomes definitive and unshakeable, the accused does not actively try to prove his innocence. He states his innocence. He has been placed in the hands of the law; if it is so decided, then let him be punished. He accepts all in the name of Allah … (We will come back to this submission, which is not false).

It can well be imagined that such conditions make the expert uneasy. He is genuinely unable to answer the fundamental question, since he is deprived of the diagnostic value of the confession that has been related by the rapporteur, who showed the great difficulties incurred by a retraction. The defendant no longer appropriates the act; the act is revealed to be without perpetrator and a criminological understanding proves impossible. All that remains, then, is the case file. Now, the charges contained in it are, as we've seen, often very serious ones for the defendant. The accused has reconstructed the crime, has revealed the weapon's hiding place and several witnesses claim to have seen him strike (in addition, these witnesses may also happen to retract their declarations).

Thus, at the moment of the examination, the expert is in the presence of a lucid, coherent man who professes his innocence. Responsibility for the act is not taken but totally lacking, as is thus any subjective assent to the sanction, any embracing of the sentence or even any guilt. The expert cannot discover the truth of the criminal. Perhaps we could come closer to this ontological system, which escapes us, by asking whether the Muslim native has in fact established a commitment toward this social group, in whose power he is now held. Does he feel bound by a social contract? Does he feel excluded on account of his wrongdoing? And then, from which group? The European group? The Muslim group? What meaning does his crime, the investigation and lastly the sanction now take on?

Of course, a question can be raised in order to avoid answering it. It can also be said that the North African is a liar. This notion is commonly accepted as true. Any magistrate, any police officer, any employer will give several convincing examples of it (the North African, moreover, is also lazy, sly, etc.). But does such a simplification allow us to discover the elusive truth? This orchestration of the lie, which we have rapidly described, necessarily requires a more in-depth understanding.

In any case, the liar himself is a being for whom the problem of the truth is constantly posed. To claim that the race suffers from a propensity to lie, to deliberate dissimulations of the truth, or that this race is unable to make out true from false, or even that it does not integrate the data of experience owing to a supposed phylogenetic weakness, is only to dispense with the problem without resolving it. The path toward the solution may go via the notions mentioned at the start of this presentation.

Let us indeed recall that the criminal's reintegration via the confession of his act depends upon the recognition of the group by the individual. In short, there can thus be no reintegration if there has been no integration. Whenever several social or ethico-social bodies (according to the words of the rapporteur) co-exist, the group is not homogeneous, harmony is absent. The criminal's subjective assent, which founds the sanction and gives it its value, will not be granted in these conditions. Elementary adherence presupposes a coherent group, collective attitudes, an ethical universe.

For the criminal to recognize his act before a judge is to disapprove of it, to legitimize the irruption of the public into the private. By denying, by retracting, does the North African not refuse this? What we probably see concretized in this way is the total separation between two social groups that co-exist – alas, tragically! – but where the integration of one by the other has not begun. The accused Muslim's refusal to authenticate, by confessing his act, the social contract proposed to him, means that his often profound submission to the powers-that-be (in this instance, the power of the judiciary), which we have noted, cannot be confounded with an acceptance of this power.

These few remarks naturally merit a far more in-depth study. They can nonetheless show the incidence of a vast and serious problem affecting the task of the doctor-expert in Algeria, and this is why we thought to present it to you.

16 CONDUCTS OF CONFESSION IN NORTH AFRICA (2)

Frantz Fanon, September 1955[1]

In the practice of medical jurisprudence, the lived experience of the act, its justifications, the conflict which this act was the attempt to surpass, otherwise said, the facts as seen by the accused, assumes a crucial importance. If we want to answer the precise question: was the accused insane at the moment of the act? – then, with the defendant, we have to rediscover the ideas, values and mental attitudes on the basis of which this act was decided and carried out. It is therefore necessary to seek out the truth of the act, itself the foundation of the truth of its perpetrator. Sartre's Hugo said that his act is all that is left to him.[2] To deny that act, to reject it, not to 'claim responsibility' for it, is lived by him as a fundamental alienation of his being. On the contrary, to accept responsibility for that act is to deny the incoherence, it is to escape the world of the absurd and discontinuity; it is lastly to give his life a meaning. Let's add that an existential approach irrefutably condemns such a neurotic contracture of consciousness.

---

[1]'Talk on medical jurisprudence. Summary of Frantz Fanon's talk at the 53rd session of the *Congrès des médecins aliénistes et neurologues de France et des pays de langue française*, Nice, 5–11 September 1955' (typescript IMEC FNN 1.15). [This text is noticeably different to the published version, reprinted above.]
[2][See note 2, previous text, p. 256.]

However, this consideration clearly raises the problem of the internal coherence of the criminal act. The experience of wrongdoing, says Nabert,[3] provokes in the consciousness a self-condemnation of an absolute and eternal sort. And it is because the wrongdoing is lived as an irreversible vitiation of existence, of one's own existence, that Bergson saw in Raskolnikow's confession the price for his reintegration into the group.[4]

But how can we not remark that these different attitudes postulate a reciprocal and prior recognition of the group by the individual and of the individual by the group? Such attitudes presuppose concrete and everyday relations with a dialectical foundation.[5] The structuring encounter within the group enables the crystallization of collective values. Based on such values, which are marginally dynamic, the sociological definition of crime first becomes possible.

All this once again presupposes the group's homogeneity. And the sanction has value only as ratified by the ego. Subjective assent founds and gives the sanction a meaning. It can be easily surmised that such a harmony is absent each time that several instances of authority coexist. Moral pluralism is unthinkable within one and the same group. The existence of the group presupposes a coherent ensemble, collective attitudes, a fundamental compliance and an ethical universe.

The point is naturally not to founder in the poetry of the 'law of the jungle' so dear to novelists. Not because the sado-masochistic structure of these criminal milieus is devoid of normative attitude, but essentially because some recognition of the true law always obtains. It is not an attempt to establish a better society alongside of another adjudged inadequate. It is an attempt to sustain the reign of terror by recreating the system of the unipolar group that was the horde. However, in the case of gangs, confession is already difficult, if not impossible. This non-condemnation of oneself is interpreted

---

[3][Jean Nabert, Éléments pour une éthique, Paris: PUF, 1943. This volume featured in Fanon's library.]

[4][Henri Bergson, Les Deux Sources de la morale et de la religion, Paris: Felix Alcan, 1932 and Paris: PUF, 1941, 11; (The Two Sources of Morality and Religion, trans. R. Ashley Audra and Cloudesley Brereton, Notre Dame, IN: University of Notre Dame) Press, 1991, p.18: 'He [the criminal] could reinstate himself in society by confessing his crime: he would then be treated as he merits it, but society would then be speaking to his real self.')]

[5][In section B of chapter seven of Peau noire, masques blancs Fanon notes that racism renders the Hegelian dialectic of reciprocal recognition impossible.]

as an act of aggression vis-à-vis the superego. Such an interpretation tranquillizes the 'collective conscience'. Indeed, it is believed impossible that such an act is not totally and utterly condemned internally. The manifest hostility, the spectacular aggressivity, is said to hide a latent moral defeat. We trust in the cultural, educational, religious and ethical givens that, according to the same ceremony, were supposedly deposited in consciousness.

To recognize an act before judges is already to avow that one disapproves it. Even when attenuating circumstances happen to reduce, and even abolish, personal responsibility, it remains that this particular act is illegal, vitiated in its materiality. However, justice cannot intervene unless the act has been recognized by the accused. The accused is allowed to defend himself. He is even obliged to do so. But prior to this the act has to have been claimed. It is because he confesses and thus recognizes he is in the wrong that the defendant can be sanctioned. The sanction seeks to address a freedom, a conscience. This conscience must nevertheless be *true*. Ambiguity is excluded here.

Confession has a moral pole that might be referred to as sincerity. But it also has a civic pole, a position, as is well known, that is dear to Hobbes and philosophers of the social contract. I confess as a man and I am sincere. I also confess as a citizen and I validate the social contract. Certainly, this duplicity is forgotten in everyday existence, but in specific circumstances, it is necessary to know how to lay it bare.[6]

In the particular case of the Algerian Arab, does no such duplicity exist? Has the native contracted a commitment? Does he feel bound? Does he feel excluded by the misdemeanour? What is the lived meaning of the crime? Of the investigation? Of the sanction? The North African, it is commonly stated, is a liar; and every magistrate, every police officer, every employer will give you significant examples. Such a simplification, it may be surmised, dispenses with the truth.

---

[6]['Confession' ('*aveu*') has taken two meanings: (signed) consent and recognition of wrongdoing. Speaking of the social contract, Rousseau wrote: 'each man being born free and master of himself, no one, under any pretext at all, may subject him without his consent [*sans son aveu*]' (*The Social Contract*, trans. Christopher Betts, Oxford: Oxford University Press, 1994, p. 137 [French original, 1762]). Fanon ties both senses together again. All taking of responsibility, all confession, presupposes one's subscription to a social contract, that is to say, to adhere to the social whole of one's own accord (*aveu*).]

Figure 7 Fanon among colleagues at Blida-Joinville Hospital. Credit: Fonds Frantz Fanon/IMEC.

This orchestration of lying requires a less simplistic, subtler, more in-depth understanding.

Several assessments carried out in Algeria have enabled me to appreciate the complexity of the problem. Eight times out of ten, the accused absolutely denies any wrongdoing. In the extreme case, he will not explain his detention. On each occasion, however, he has admitted his guilt during the course of the investigation. Then from a certain moment, in principle after three months in detention, he goes back on his declarations. He does not try to prove his innocence. He claims his innocence. If the court decides it, then let it kill him. He accepts everything, 'Allah is great'. The expert, as one easily surmises, is rather uneasy here. He is unable to answer the fundamental question. There is no appropriation of the act by the defendant. The act now appears to be without perpetrator and a criminological understanding proves impossible.

Sometimes, however, the charges contained in the case file are, according to the expression, extremely hefty. The accused has reconstructed the crime. He has revealed the weapon's hiding place. Witnesses claim to have seen him strike.[7] Yet, at the time of the

---

[7]Similarly, it is not a rare occurrence to have all the witnesses revoke their declarations.

assessment, we find ourselves in the presence of a lucid, coherent man, whose judgement is unimpaired and who claims his innocence. The taking of responsibility for the act, subjective assent to the sanction, or compliance with the sentencing, are lacking. The truth of the criminal is not discovered. We gravitate around a system that, ontologically, escapes us.

17 LETTER TO MAURICE DESPINOY

Frantz Fanon, January 1956[1]

My dear friend,

Above all things, since you are also the most exiled, I think that you should alert me each time that the government funds you for a 'study trip'. On the local level, I believe I can arrange things.

Some brief news from Algeria. Everything's going very well. This evening Mollet took office.[2] Soustelle has announced his departure for Thursday.[3] Big things are brewing here and I am happy to witness them.

Let's talk about the Antilles. Needless to say, I am delighted about the creation of a third position. I assure you, Despinoy, that I am currently unable to make the least promise. There are more than 10 million people to treat here. Colonialist psychiatry as a whole has to be disalienated.[4] I know that this problem has

---

[1]Undated letter, probably from 31 January 1956 in view of the events related. This is a transcription of a facsimile of the manuscript published in *Sud/Nord*, no. 22, 2007, pp. 115–18.

[2][Swearing-in on Tuesday 31 January 1956. Guy Mollet became president of the Council. At the time no one suspected the sort of policy that he would pursue in Algeria.]

[3][Jacques Soustelle, general governor of Algeria from January 1955 until his stormy return to the metropole on Thursday 2 February 1956.]

[4][In an interview conducted by Adams Kwateh, and which was published in *France-Antilles* on 7 December 2011, Maurice Despinoy stated:

My period of work in Martinique was one of the richest and happiest of my career. Some years after my arrival, I obtained the creation of a position. Fanon had the necessary credentials and I appealed to him to join me in Fort-de-France. But then he was caught up in the enthusiasm of his commitment to Algeria and he answered that he had an obligation to pursue it.

arisen in Martinique as well. And, in his critical analysis of your article,[5] I was very grateful to [Émile] Monnerot for having very subtly indicated that you and no one but you had finally *situated* the problem. What you say about [Tosq?] is spot on. [Tosq] must be fought. Being more impertinent than you, less timid (I call timidity the absolute respect of the other's subjectivity), struggle arises more quickly for me. We get to what is essential more quickly. Or we do not. It remains, however, that this often proves trying.

Daumézon and Le Guillant are coming to Blida at the month's end (nursing internship) accompanied by Koechlin.[6]

I will have two dissertations defended this year: one on lithium salts in psychiatry and another on the structure of delusions among Arabs. The second work is likely to be useful to us for an analysis of how that mind-numbing perspective called ethno-psychiatry conceives schizophrenics. I've sent a short article to *La Raison* that takes this up.

I am absolutely enthralled by your determination to tackle the problem at the International Congress in 1957. In a first phase, I think we must determine or delimit our aim in a nosographical fashion.

I suggest to you, then, that we work on the following in the months ahead:

- schizophrenia as a form of existence (Binswanger);
- schizophrenia as an extensible clinical entity (Bleuler/ Minkowski);
- Claudian dualism (DP/schizo – with Kretschmerian subgroups);[7]
- Guiraud/Dide type fuzzy diencephalic hebephrenia [dementia praecox] revamped by Delay;[8]

---

[5][Probably 'Les débuts de l'hôpital psychiatrique de la Martinique', *L'Information psychiatrique*, October 1955, pp. 401–10.]

[6][Philippe Koechlin, psychiatrist, student of Daumézon, and co-author with him of a milestone-setting article: 'La psychothérapie institutionnelle française contemporaine', *Anais Portugueses de Psiquiatria*, vol. 4, no. 4, December 1952, pp. 271–312.]

[7][Henri Claude (1869–1945) distinguished between dementia praecox (DP), which is linked to organic lesions, and schizoid disorders, with a psychogenetic etiology.]

[8][Maurice Dide (1874–1944) was the author, with Paul Guiraud (1882–1974) of the classic *Psychiatrie du médecin praticien*, Paris: Martin, 1922. They assigned hebephrenia an organic source (mainly the diencephalon). Jean Delay (1907–1987), a psychiatrist and neurologist, was known for his research on the first neuroleptics. Fanon's library contains the proceedings of the international conference on chlorpromazine and the use of neuroleptic medications in psychiatric therapy organized by Delay in Paris in October 1955.]

– and then Schneider, Mayer-Gross, and why not Solanes.[9]

First of all, I want to clarify this question: schizophrenia is I think (not I do not think). Things must first be seen clearly. Everything can be validated after that. If you want to lay the foundations for overall psychiatric care, think of me. I will have plenty of work here. And believe you me, it's very difficult.[10]

About myself I shall say nothing. Things are fine. Josie is wholly devoted to her son and from time to time even calls me Olivier.

[*New page*] Starting again, slowly.

Certainly, Nelly must deplore the distance from Fort-de-France. The most unacceptable thing is the gratuitousness of the fatigue. It makes no sense at all.

Concerning my uncle, I thank you for having taken care of him. I think that you met his psychological expectations: thanks to your sufficiently important demeanour, he was able to see a difference from 'our small doctors' and yet you had the familiar touch that made him feel you are 'my nephew's friend' …

Do not blame yourself too much for your silence. In fact, we are both too remote from ourselves, all too adrift in things. Things must allow us to meet again and rediscover ourselves. We will meet and rediscover ourselves within things, in the object. So there is necessarily a vague period, one of detachment, of infidelity, or even of indifference.

All three to you five.

---

[9][Kurt Schneider (1887–1967) and Willy Mayer-Gross (1889–1961) were members of the Heidelberg School, founded with Jaspers. Josep Solanes (1909–1991), a Venezuelan psychiatrist of Spanish origin, was exiled in France until 1949; he worked with Eugène Minkowski toward a phenomenological psychiatry.]

[10][This letter is essential to understanding Fanon's thinking at this time. The articulation of the neurological and the psychiatric continued to be an important question for him and he certainly intended to keep working on it. Indeed he pursued his interest in neuroleptics, whether in the form of Laborit and Delay's chlorpromazine or Despinoy's lithium salts. The picture he presents of the various schools of thought about schizophrenia and its origins (organogenetic or psychogenetic) clearly shows that he kept abreast of the question. But we simultaneously see his two other domains of interest develop: colonial psychiatry, ethnopsychiatry and alienation, and the questions of '*hygiène mentale*', which is to say of public health policy ('more than 10 million people to treat').]

18 MAGHREBI MUSLIMS AND THEIR ATTITUDE TO MADNESS

Frantz Fanon and François Sanchez, 1956[1]

In the chapters that textbooks devote to the history of psychiatry, the creation of establishments for mentally ill people in Muslim countries is constantly dated as prior to the Middle Ages, a time when the creation of such institutions was still very rare. The Muslim's attitude toward madness thus takes on great importance for us. In the present work, we stick to studying the position of Maghrebi Muslims towards mental illness in view of our experience in North Africa, and more particularly in Algeria.

It is common to speak of the Muslim crowds as having a respect and veneration for mentally ill people, who, it is said, are in intimate connection with the mysterious world of the genies: the occult is said to incite respect, engender veneration. Concerning the Maghreb, that statement does not appear to us to be entirely correct. Let us attempt to interpret the facts by clarifying them from the inside, by paying attention to the gaze that a Maghrebi individual projects onto the world. How does he behave toward those in his entourage who he considers to be suffering from mental illness?

---

[1]*Revue pratique de psychologie de la vie sociale et d'hygiène mentale*, no. 1, 1956, pp. 24–7.

Before answering this question, we attempt to state what the ordinary westerner's attitude is in such circumstances. In general, the westerner believes that mental illness alienates the person, that the patient's behaviour cannot be understood without taking this illness into account. However, in practice that belief does not always entail a logical attitude and often everything transpires as if the westerner has forgotten about the illness: the mental patient appears to the westerner as indulging in morbidity and taking advantage of it to some extent in order to exploit those around him. The patient is held to be somewhat responsible for his words and his acts, his will, to be committed to them. If he is aggressive, this aggressivity is not believed to be entirely of the domain of the pathological; it is in part ambiguous, mixed in with a conscious intention to harm – the blows bear and entail retorts that do not aim solely to gain control but to punish at the same time. Or a patient remains constantly inactive, motionless in a corner, becoming active only to have meals or return to bed. The temptation is then to think that he or she has chosen to live as a social parasite, decided to let himself die from hunger were he ever abandoned. The collectivity comes to think of the patient's servitude as a moral coercion that he exerts on it. At the psychiatric hospital comparable interpretations on the part of the medical staff are not uncommonly noted. Such and such a nurse may feel hurt by a megalomaniac's insulting haughtiness and come to bear a grudge that, from time to time, is manifest in the deprivation of a snack or a walk.[2] The mother who receives a poor welcome from her son whom she's come to visit then leaves, her heart churned up. She is certainly well aware that her son is ill, but she does not acknowledge his 'right' to behave in this fashion, to disregard her age, her affection, her solicitude.

If one certainty may be established, it is that which the Maghrebi possesses on the topic of madness and its determinism: the mentally ill patient is absolutely alienated, he is not responsible for his

---

[2]We are recalling here the case of an epileptic whose mood swings, accompanied with unkind remarks toward the staff of his ward, had 'driven' the nurses to complain to the médecin-chef going so far as to ask [him] to 'turn the screw' on this patient who exploited everyone's kindness. We are also thinking of certain newspaper articles that speak of the 'blood-thirsty madness', the murderous madpersons who are veritable 'filthy beasts' and who often manage to take advantage of the 'credulity' of mental health experts.

disorder; the genies alone bear full responsibility for it. The patient is an innocent victim of the genie or genies that possess him. It is not his fault if he is rude and threatening, or if he persists in complete apragmatism. The mother insulted or hit by her ill son will never dream of accusing him of disrespect or murderous desires. She knows that her son would in all liberty be unable to want to do her any harm. There can be no question of attributing to him acts that do not arise from his will, which is itself thoroughly in thrall to the genies. The collectivity never adopts a distrustful or aggressive attitude toward the patient himself. He is not in principle excluded from the group. The entourage may, however, have recourse to means of restraint. For is it not a wise thing in certain cases to constrain momentarily the genies that seem to want to harm the patient's or the group's security? The genies are alone involved in these outbursts. The group agrees not to attribute to the patient the intention to harm. At stake is the exclusive wickedness and duplicity of morbid genies.

The patient's conduct is 'interpreted' in accordance with general beliefs. His credit remains intact. Esteem and social consideration are conserved for a troubled personality. The illness-genie is an accidental illness; more or less long lasting, it remains contingent, affecting only the appearance, never damaging the underlying EGO.[3] This is why there is always hope of cure, which remains the entourage's major concern. All are of the opinion that a pilgrimage to the sanctuaries must be undertaken. Such therapeutic visits are repeated if needed. If the cure does not follow, it has to incite the pursuit of a therapy that presents itself as the most effective on the condition of not giving up prematurely. If improvement is evident, this goes to show the utility of completing a treatment that has already chased away one or several genies. If the patient is restored to health, he can then go back to his place in society without dreading any mistrust or any ambivalence on the part of the group. He will be able to talk about this past illness without a hint of reticence. What use is there in concealing a state that has not concerned you directly? If we question a Maghrebin about his ancestors, he will talk without

---

[3][In such a perspective, the idea of chronicity is meaningless. Indeed, at the time that Fanon was writing up this article, it had become one of the targets of the movements for psychiatric reform, about which Fanon had been well informed since his time in Saint-Alban.]

the slightest embarrassment about any cases of madness of which he may be aware: the genies do not work through lines of heredity. Cases are cited in which the marriage contract stipulates that the husband has the duty to take his wife periodically to a specific marabout; it is required to carry out scrupulously a promise made to the saint who permitted the cure of the young wife.

When all is said and done, we see a harmonious articulation of beliefs in the Maghreb,[4] enabling the creation and implementation of 'mental care'.[5] This care is of course fairly rudimentary and cannot claim to have solved the problem of madness except in a piecemeal way, by bringing into play the good will of individuals and families who are personally affected by such and such a case. On the social level, there can be no talk of a satisfying 'yield' of the system from the quantitative point of view. Relying solidly on its cultural bases, at the human level it possesses a great value that cannot be limited to the mere efficacy of Maghrebi therapy. This natural mode of care is marked by a profoundly holistic mindset that preserves intact the image of a person's normality despite the existence of the illness. Whether the illness represents divine punishment or grace escapes the group, God's designs being foreign to it: its attitude is guided by a concern to respect the human in the person. Someone who is considered mentally ill is protected, fed, maintained, looked after by his own within the realm of possibility. Madness itself does not command respect, patience, indulgence; instead, it is the human being impaired by madness, by the genies; the human being as such. Do attentive treatments given to someone with tuberculosis imply a particular feeling toward tuberculosis itself? Respect is given to a mentally ill person because he remains a human being in spite of it all; care is afforded the madman because he is prey to

---

[4][Harmonious when compared to the two dominant conflicts in western psychiatry: between psychogenesis and organogenesis, and that between moral attitudes and therapeutic attitudes in relation to the patient. This is serendipity from Fanon, not pragmatism: that harmony has to inspire a reflection on the organization of mental care provision, but it does not constitute a true understanding of the illness, as is underscored at the end of the article.]

[5]['*Assistance mentale*', by local psychotherapeutic practices rather than confinement in asylums, is thus the suggestion. For Fanon, madness is not just the product of a determinate social structure, since it arises everywhere. But social attitudes in its relation vary in accordance with cultural structures and make its treatment more or less easy.]

powerful enemies. The issue is never to respect the mad and much less still to venerate them.[6]

Nevertheless, certain facts must not be shrouded in silence. Although rather infrequent, in certain douars one may happen to find mental patients who really are the object of respect and veneration on the part of the collectivity, or at least of some persons, who do not consider the patient to be mad (*mahboul*) and possessed by genies (*majnoun*). They consider him a saint and believe in his *baraka*, or beneficent power. His spirit is thought to have been drawn toward God (*majdzoub*), his brain no longer to be inhabited by human thought. Whether at stake is mental retardation or psychosis, the patient's fantasies, his oddities, his disorders are in general tolerable and compatible with the opinion of the milieu.[7] We know cases of patients who have been interned at the asylum against the will of their families, who take them to be saints, exempt from any illness. Some families, whose resources are stretched to breaking point, have even come to ask for 'their' patient to be discharged, as they hold him to be a marabout, so that they may take advantage of the piety of other faithful.

Such is, ultimately, the attitude of the Maghrebi towards madness. This important point merited some development. It seemed interesting to us to say how the North African lives the problem of madness.

If Europe received from Muslim countries the first rudiments of care for the mentally ill, it has in return contributed to the latter a rational understanding of mental affections![8]

---

[6][Fanon distinguishes himself once again from Jacques Lacan, but also from Paul Balvet, whose important article on 'La valeur humaine de la folie' (*Esprit*, no. 137, September 1947) he cites in his dissertation, though already with a certain distance. It is therefore paradoxically through an analysis of the traditional popular relations to madness that he breaks from any modern idea of a sacralization of the mad.]

[7]Émile Dermenghem, *Vie des saints musulmans*, Alger: Baconnier, 1943, p. 283 *sq.*; [Edmond] Doutté, *Les Marabouts. Notes sur l'islam maghribin*, Paris: [Ernest] Leroux, 1900, p. 77.

[8][In the original edition, that last phrase is set out below the text, in bold, and with a box drawn around it.]

19 TAT IN MUSLIM WOMEN: SOCIOLOGY OF PERCEPTION AND IMAGINATION

Frantz Fanon and Charles Geronimi (Blida-Joinville), September 1956[1]

A projective test, the TAT[2] consists in presenting an individual with a series of situations, of perceptive panoramas within which lines of composition spontaneously emerge, enabling a restructuration of this field for the ego. The polymorphism of the formal contents, the progressive complexity of the situations, the rich and diverse

---

[1] *Comptes rendus du Congrès des médecins aliénistes et neurologues de France et des pays de langue française (54th session, Bordeaux, 30 August-4 September 1956)*, Paris: Masson, 1956, pp. 364–8. [In this text, standardized psychological tests – which now form part of the arsenal of global psychiatry –reveal *a contrario*, through their failures, that perception and imagination ought to be a topic for sociology. This is another corroboration of the new ethnopsychiatric perspective that Fanon defends.]

[2] [The *Thematic Apperception Test* (TAT) is a 'projective personality test' used by psychologists and psychiatrists to diagnose alterations of personality, in general in association with the Rorschach test. It involves the interpretation of ambiguous images; but, in contrast with the Rorschach test, the patient is asked to interpret *figurative* standardized cards representing diverse social situations. Fanon's library contains a complete set of them. This test obviously raised the question of the cultural determination of the content and connotations of the images. The standard TAT picture cards referred to here are easily visible on the internet.]

constellation of possible identifications all permit the emergence, at the level of interpretation, of ambiguous meanings.

Few studies have been carried out on the TAT, in stark contrast with the bibliographic abundance on the Rorschach test. At the international psychiatry congress in 1950, Guera presented an exhaustive and doctrinal study on methods of projection, placing particular emphasis on the TAT. Guera's factorial perspective remains contestable, but it was the first time that phenomenological, gestalt or anthropological data had been gathered: for example, by making mention of the encounter between man and his circumstances. In any case, Guera's work contains one position worth bearing in mind: 'As a test of projection, the TAT presents inherited characteristics reflective of an era and a determinate social structure.'[3] In the context of western civilizations with more or less equivalent technological levels, but with sometimes specific cultural characteristics, people were therefore asked to take into account the rhythms of life, customs, social truth.

In a recent talk to the Royal Belgian Society of ethnography, Ombredane took up the question again. Validating Guera's doctrinal position, he developed a modality of the TAT designed for Blacks of the Belgian Congo.[4] For our part, we would like to report the rather original experiment that we have conducted in North Africa.[5]

---

[3]Alfredo Guera, 'Le TAT comme modèle des méthodes projectives', in Henri Ey, P. Marty and J. Dublineau (eds.), *Congrès mondial de psychiatrie, Psychiatrie clinique*, Paris: Hermann Éditeurs, 1950, p.56 *sq*.

[4]Ombredane, Exploration de la mentalité des Noirs congolais au moyen d'une épreuve projective. Le Congo TAT. [*L'Exploration de la mentalité des Noirs congolais au moyen d'une épreuve projective: le Congo TAT*, by Dr André Ombredane, professor at Université libre de Bruxelles, member of the Belgian Royal Colonial Institute, publication of the Belgian Royal Colonial Institute, Brussels, 1954. A copy is in Fanon's library and bears the stamp of the Blida psychiatric hospital.]

[5][In her interesting article 'The critical impact of Frantz Fanon and Henri Collomb: Race, gender and personality testing of North and West Africans', *Journal of the History of the Behavioral Sciences*, vol. 41, no. 3, 2005, pp. 225–48, Alice Bullard compares the work of Fanon and Geronimi with that of the psychiatrist Henri Collomb (1913–1979), who delivered a talk at the same congress on the adaptation of the TAT in western Africa. She situates them in the context of a larger reflection on the history of psychological tests in colonial environments.]

We gave the standard TAT to a rather large number of hospitalized Muslim women in the open service of the Blida psychiatric hospital. We have retained a dozen observations. The patients included minor hypochondriacs with touches of anxiousness, others who suffered from emotional disorders that had developed against a family background involving no serious behavioural problems, and another with a cured juvenile mania presenting no post-treatment after-effects.[6] What general attitude did we discover? How does the Muslim woman react to the TAT? How does she experience the test? How does she understand it?

With the European woman, perception is fulfilled totally and immediately. The European woman enters immediately into the picture card. By contrast, the Muslim woman adopts a radically different attitude. She can thus be seen to engage in a patient, laborious and tenacious effort to decipher, to analyze. Here are some examples.

Card 3 BM (obs. 4): 'I don't know if it's a boy or a girl. I think it's a girl. I don't know what she's doing. I am not sure what to say. I don't understand. Perhaps he is sick. He has a headache. I'm tired (*she sighs*).'

Card 11 (obs. 7) (Rit.): 'You'd say it's the sea, but it is blue or green, and there it is black. It's not the sea, perhaps it's a village (turns the card around and back), it looks like a plane, a boat, but it is none of these things. I don't understand. You'd say it's a serpent? It looks like a person (*the stones*). (*The card is the right way up.*) It looks like persons, but you cannot make them out properly (*the stones*).'

This unusual approach transforms the test into a test of intellectual performance. The impression is that the patients strive to discover in the card the largest number of known things. Paradoxically, however, the answers given are unorganized, poor and do not cohere. Most often we obtain only a dry enumeration. No guiding line is extracted. No structure emerges. Narrative is inexistent. There is no stage, no drama. All we are given is a jumble of diverse elements taken at random from the card. What Dana calls perceptual organization cannot be discerned

---

[6]From an ethnic point of view, we find three Kabyles and nine Arabs. The average age is twenty-three years old. The rural milieu is predominant. None of the patients can read.

here.[7] Despite our precise instructions, the Muslim patients did not tell us about what was happening in the cards but instead what was in them.

Let us also note some defective identifications: thus the violin of card 1 was described as a 'coffin', a 'cradle'; the crosses of the cemetery (card 15) are described as couch grass brushes, as dog houses. 'Blindingly obvious' elements,[8] such as the sun of card 17 GF, the gun of card 8 BM, are not perceived.

At the level of the test's organization, where situations that appear to be conflicting and the character's ambiguous attitudes generally arouse the involvement of the ego, we obtained poor, indigent replies of no significance. The perceptual modalities analysis shows that the test is not understood and is transformed into a test of decipherment, of interpretation. This intellectual, rational, punctilious, out of kilter attitude is, if we refer to Murray's intentions, paradoxically understandable. It stems from the situation in which the patients are placed. Indeed, by asking them to describe, to live a scene elaborated by westerners and for westerners, we immerse them in a different, foreign, heterogeneous and non-appropriable world. Their first reactions are, moreover, reactions of surprise and perplexity before the unknown: 'My God, what is that!' These Muslim women seek out identifiable elements on the cards, but the key elements organizing perception are missing: the patients 'spell out' the card without ever living it. It can thus be appreciated that despite the considerable, laborious intellectual effort, we only obtained disorganized replies that did not go beyond

---

[7][Richard H. Dana, *A Manual for Objective TAT Scoring*, Saint Louis State Hospital, 1956, https://pdxscholar.library.pdx.edu/rri_facpubs/34/. Dana starts by defining the category of perceptual organization in the TAT system as reflecting the 'subject's ability to follow the standard directions to "tell a story"' upon presentation of the test cards. Here again, the issue is to measure the cognitive capacity to generate some sense of a situation in accordance with cultural parameters.]

[8][To really measure these discrepancies, it is necessary to read them in relation to the card images, which would have been familiar to the readers of this article, and are now easily available through an internet search. As in the previous articles on methodological inadequacies resulting in misunderstandings, such as the difficulties of social therapy in Blida, those of legal expertise concerning confession behaviour, the understanding of the experience of sexuality or that of madness, the conclusion of these reflections on the failure of psychotherapeutic tools is the necessity to denaturalize what had been taken as self-evident, and to relate it to a specific culture. For Fanon this epistemological shift is a precondition to an authentic understanding and a successful clinical practice.]

the stage of enumeration, of the 'there is'. It is similarly easy to explain the perceptual mistakes and unperceived elements. What accounts for these mistakes is the absence of correlation between the 'perceptual stimuli' offered to our subjects, to their personality, for investigation, and the expectations of a precise, demanding, and in a sense spasmed, cultural world.[9]

The incoherent, inappropriate, vague and disjointed replies; the apparently caricatural perceptions – all indicate that our method has something wrong with it. The dynamisms flowing within Maghrebin society, the lived experience of the surrounding European world, the Muslim's marginalized existence, which leads to a scotomization, a distinterest, the cultural truth, ought to have been thematized. Our patient's inadaptation is the correlate of the method's inadequacy.

Exploring the imagination of our patients brought us up against analogous difficulties. The instruction: 'What happened according to you? What is going to happen?' obtained few accounts, all devoid of psychoanalytic value. Short, disorganized replies were a constant banality. No inventiveness was generated. If the TAT test proposes to stimulate literary creativity, we can say that among our patients this goal was never reached. Other patients refused, moreover, to make anything up. They confronted us with their total lack of knowledge: 'I don't know what happened before … I only say things that I know.'

Others justified their refusal in accordance with specific Koranic demands: 'I cannot lie, because that's a sin. Only God knows what is going to happen'. In this perspective, to appropriate the future comes down to taking the place of God, something unimaginable for a Muslim. Indeed, we have to look for what is concealed behind that absence of imagination, that refusal of fiction. To say that the Muslim is unable to invent, by invoking a particular genetic constitution, one subsumed within the more general framework of some primitivism, seems a difficult position to defend in our view. Similarly, the explanation put forward by the Muslim woman, the necessity for her to appeal to Koranic prohibitions, is an attitude that

---

[9][This physical metaphor of a cultural convulsion or spasm (*un monde culturel précis, exigeant, en un certain sens spasmé*) appears in Fanon's books each time he analyses the colonial relation to culture and its real effects.]

demands we seek what lies beyond it.[10] In actual fact, that attitude can be explained by the very logic of the imaginary. Imaginary life cannot be isolated from real life: the concrete, objective world is what constantly fuels, enables, legitimates and founds the imaginary. Imaginary consciousness is certainly unreal, but it drinks from the concrete world. The imagination, the imaginary, are only possible to the extent that the real belongs to us. The image card here constitutes the matrix. Now, in our analysis of the perceptual modalities of the patients tested, we have indicated that the card did not supply any of the specific schemas and cultural patterns. No homogeneity exists between what the patient is presented with and what is known to her: the world presented to her is already an unknown world, foreign and heteroclite. Faced with unusual objects, with unidentifiable situations, rejected by hostile because heterogeneous viewpoints, the Muslim woman is unable to elaborate any imaginary existence. The rare stories gathered did not restore us a world.[11]

We should like to point out an interesting element of this test. The imagination was able to develop when in the presence of the white card, since it was no longer impeded by foreign cultural fetters. Not running up against a world that excluded them, our patients formed rich and varied stories.

Though it was sanctioned by a systematized failure, we thought it timely to report this experiment. On the basis of a cultural survey

---

[10][The critique of Porot's colonialist constitutionalism is repeated here and as in the texts on *djinns* and mental illness, local rationalizations must be surpassed by a scientific outlook. However, this is not a dialectical movement, for if a certain understanding of mental health care can be preserved in the local conceptions of madness, nothing is to be retained of the patient's religious justification for her inability to imagine, or of the essentialism of the Algiers School. That school was content with hypostatizing what it could not or would not explain into categories of 'primitivism' – a major methodological error. See herein, *above*, p. 9.]

[11][This article is another example of Fanon's constant concern to identify the conditions of meaning creation as well as its obstacles for a consciousness engaged in constituting a world. His library contains a worn copy, marked throughout, of Sartre's *The Imaginary*. In it the expression 'against the background of a world' [*sur fond de monde*] in the following sentence is signaled in the margin: 'All imaginary appears "against the background of a world," but reciprocally all apprehension of the real as world implies a hidden surpassing towards the imaginary' (p. 188).]

we have done, we are currently developing a projection test with Maghrebi Muslims in mind. The few trials undertaken confirm our conclusion: the apparent indetermination of projection tests must be inscribed within a spatio-temporal framework, animated by cultural dynamisms that are homogeneous to the psycho-affective forces under examination.[12]

---

[12][This type of interpretation test therefore only has purchase within a cultural framework that is only indeterminate and thus universal in appearance, which is paradoxically revealed by the white image card. This is how Charles Geronimi related his memories of the works undertaken with Fanon on the TAT: 'Other works were to be undertaken: the production of a projection test, the TAT (*Thematic apperception test*, a test in which the subject is asked to relate a story on the basis of a picture that he is presented), adapted for Algerian society, as a preliminary study had shown that the classic image cards were ineffective in the Algerian milieu. Photos were taken with this in mind, but the making of the test, its sampling, etc., was put off again until after independence. We can nevertheless affirm that Fanon was very committed to carrying this out' (Geronimi, *Fanon à Blida*).]

20 LETTER TO THE RESIDENT MINISTER

Frantz Fanon, December 1956[1]

Doctor Frantz Fanon, Doctor of Psychiatric Hospitals
Médecin-chef de service at the Blida-Joinville Psychiatric Hospital
To M. the Resident Minister,
Governor General of Algeria
Algiers

Dear Minister,
Upon my request and by decree dated 22 October 1953, M. the Minister for Public Health and Population was willing to place me at the disposal of the Governor General of Algeria to be assigned to a psychiatric hospital of Algeria. Placed at the psychiatric hospital of Blida-Joinville on 23 November 1953, since that date I have performed the duties of medical director there.

Although the objective conditions of psychiatric practice in Algeria were already a challenge to common sense, it seemed to me

---

[1]This letter was reprinted in *Pour la révolution africaine*, a posthumous collection of Fanon's texts, originally published in French in 1964 by François Maspero (In English trans., pp. 52–4). It was sent by Fanon to Robert Lacoste in December 1956 – which led to his expulsion from Algeria in January. A first version of this letter was written in the summer of 1956, as the formulation 'For close to three years' suggests, and the detailed allusion to the repression of strikers (comprising Algerian workers and shopkeepers who had responded to the Algerian National Movement's call to strike) on 5 July 1956, whereas more notable acts of repression had taken place since, thus seeming to confirm one of the letter's last sentences: 'For long months, my conscience has been the seat of unpardonable debates'.

that efforts should be undertaken to render less vicious a system whose doctrinal bases stood opposed daily to an authentic human perspective.[2]

For nearly three years, I put myself wholly at the service of this country and the people who inhabit it. I have spared neither my efforts nor my enthusiasm. There is not an ounce of my activity that has not demanded as its horizon the unanimously desired emergence of an acceptable world.

But what are a man's enthusiasm and care if daily reality is woven with lies, acts of cowardice and scorn for humankind? What are intentions if their embodiment is made impossible by an indigence of heart, sterility of spirit and hatred for this country's natives? Madness is one of the ways that humans have of losing their freedom. And I can say that, placed at this junction, I have measured with terror the extent of the alienation of this country's inhabitants.

If psychiatry is the medical technique that sets out to enable individuals no longer to be foreign to their environment, I owe it to myself to state that the Arab, permanently alienated in his own country, lives in a state of absolute depersonalization.

What is the status of Algeria? A systematic dehumanization. Now, the absurd wager was to want at whatever price to ensure the existence of some values whereas lawlessness, inequality, and multiple daily murder of humanness were erected as legislative principles. The extant social structure in Algeria stood opposed to any attempt to put the individual back in his or her place.

Monsieur le Ministre, there comes a time when tenacity becomes morbid perseveration. Hope is then no longer the open door onto the future, but the illogical maintenance of a subjective attitude in a systematic break with reality.

Monsieur le Ministre, to the observer's eyes, the current troubles and bloodshed in Algeria do not constitute a scandal. This is neither an accident nor a breakdown in the mechanism. The troubles in Algeria are the logical consequence of an abortive attempt to decerebralize a people.

---

[2][The doctrinal bases of this system are those of colonial ethnopsychiatry, the foundations of which all of Fanon's ethnopsychiatric texts written during his time in Blida criticize.]

It was hardly necessary to be a psychologist to divine that under the apparent affability of the Algerian, behind his bare humility, there lies a fundamental demand for dignity. And nothing is to be gained, upon the occasion of demonstrations that could not be plainer, by appealing to some sort of civic-mindedness.

The function of a social structure is to set up institutions that are traversed by a concern for humankind. A society that forces its members into desperate solutions is a non-viable society, a society that needs replacing. The citizen's duty is to say so. No professional morality, no class solidarity, no desire to refrain from washing the dirty laundry in public, can have a prior claim. No pseudo-national mystification finds grace when up against the demand to think.

Monsieur le Ministre the decision to punish the strikers of 5 July 1956 is a measure that appears literally irrational to me. Either the strikers were terrorized in their flesh and that of their family, and then it was necessary to understand their attitude, to judge it normal, in consideration of the atmosphere. Or else their abstention expressed a unanimous current of opinion, an unshakeable conviction, and then all punitive attitudes were superfluous, gratuitous, ineffective.

I owe it to the truth to say that the dominant trait of the strikers seemed not to be fear. Much more than this, there was an ineluctable wish to bring forth in calmness and silence a wholly new era of peace and dignity.

The workers in the city must collaborate with the social phenomenon. But they must be convinced of the excellence of that lived society. There comes a time when silence becomes a lie. The key intentions of personal existence adapt poorly to permanent infringements upon the most basic everyday values.

For long months, my conscience has been the seat of unpardonable debates. And their conclusion is the will not to lose hope in man, that is to say in myself. My decision is not to bear a responsibility, at whatever cost, on the false pretext that nothing else is to be done.

For all these reasons, I have the honour, Monsieur le Ministre, of asking you to accept my resignation and put my mission in Algeria to an end.

Yours sincerely

[Frantz Fanon]

21 THE PHENOMENON OF AGITATION IN THE PSYCHIATRIC MILIEU: GENERAL CONSIDERATIONS, PSYCHOPATHOLOGICAL MEANING

Frantz Fanon and Slimane Asselah (Blida-Joinville Psychiatric Hospital), January 1957[1]

In a lecture given at a meeting of *L'Évolution psychiatrique*, Doctor Tosquelles distinguished between two types of agitation: he opposed the percepto-reactive type to the expressive type.[2] Such a distinction, which is interesting from a heuristic – or at least from a didactic perspective – seems to us unacceptable from a doctrinal viewpoint. Likewise, with the opposition between reactive and non-reactive agitation.

---

[1] *Maroc médical*, vol. 36, no. 380, January 1957, pp. 21–4.
[2] [François Tosquelles, 'Introduction à une sémiologie de l'agitation', *L'Évolution psychiatrique*, no. 1, 1954. In this paper, Tosquelles takes his distance from the critique of the notion of 'agitation' made by Philippe Paumelle (in a text published by Henri Ey in the 1952 *Entretiens psychiatriques*). In particular, he advocates the necessity of analyzing different types of agitation, thus considering agitation a legitimate object of

In fact, if we except the profoundly toxic agitations with a serious impairment of consciousness, the agitated expression almost constantly accords with a percepto-reactive mode. Or, if you will, besides typically neurological agitations with an automatic physiognomy, made possible by brutal alterations of consciousness (in epilepsy for example), agitated behaviour is at once expressive and perceptive-reactive. Clinically, it is possible to distinguish between a predominantly motor agitation, a predominantly verbal agitation and a type of verbal motor agitation.

Idiots and imbeciles, on the one hand, the senile, on the other, provide a rather impressive contingent of clinical pictures of pure motor agitation. From this we have of course excluded the paranoid's choleric outburst, hebephrenic impulsion or the circumscribed agitation of the catatonic. Here we are aiming at agitation as a state. And we realize that the two poles that favour the birth of motor agitation are characterized by an impairment of neurological appearance.

These empty anideational [*anideique*] agitations border on stereotypy (the pseudo-anxious meandering of the aged or the oligophrenic's laceration of clothing).

Predominantly verbal agitation appears less neurological, more comprehensible. In fact, the incoherent soliloquy of the imbecile, the verbigeration in shreds of the presbyophrenic, strike us on account of their automatic, archaic, disintegrated, somatic character.

Lastly, perhaps the most studied types of agitated behaviour is verbo-motor agitation, precisely because it reveals the basic melody of the existing man. Saying and doing, combined in the spatio-temporal structure, seem to maintain the organism in the grasped

---

research: 'If it is often correct to say that "agitation" boils down to the fear of the mad, the fear he experiences and that he communicates, it is no less true that the problem of agitation exceeds these "psychological" positions. The simple truth is that we have all, more or less, been confronted with agitated patients, of whom we have had to grasp the semiology, of whom we have constantly had to establish a therapy and a prognostic; that this therapy often consists in not letting oneself blindly be taken in by the patients' "mythical" behaviours and to set up an institutional therapy in which agitation sheds its mask; that is not, *a priori*, a major objection to establishing a semiology of agitation' (p. 75). The two types of agitation mentioned by Fanon and Asselah are described by Tosquelles as endogenous and relational:

'A) Those whose spontaneous agitation appears to result from endogenous processes, even if they may be elicited by exterior motives.

B) The occasional (but sometimes no less spectacular) agitations, which have a conflictual meaning' (p. 88).]

world.[3] This is perhaps why frank mania is the most-studied clinical form of that form of agitation. In actual fact, verbal motor agitations exceed the frame of mania. Hysterical manifestations, acute phases of an active delusion with multiple themes adopting the physiognomy of a confuse-choleric agitation, and Schneider anxious-ecstatic seizures all evoke the clinical picture of mania in more than one way.

The mixed and increasingly enlarged states on which Beringer insisted suggest to us, at least for clinical observation, a certain liberty with respect to the traditional equation agitation = mania. Consequently, we are quite at ease in claiming that a patient's behaviour must be understood within the clinic in question and its possibilities regarding assimilation. If the hospital environment is a therapeutic instrument, if above all else the concern has been to institute a general framework for de-alienating encounters, if a will exists to treat the agitated living organism, then the question about authentic discrimination can be raised.

The notions of 'façade psychosis', of 'morbid mental persistence' (*persistance mentale morbide*[4]), as well as spectacular reactions of posture, provocations with a strongly aggressive charge such as those encountered in concentration-camp environments, the sadomasochistic nodes so easily brought about in the asylum framework – all these things demand veritable vigilance. 'Benevolent neutrality' has to be discovered here in all its purity. To view a service as a therapeutic instrument is to organize it, to lead to its being lived by the patient as that which 'understands at last', and not as that which amputates, that which castrates. Clastic aggression, the 'wilful malice' of the patient, as they are endured by the staff, are evidently responses to a type of concentration-camp structure of an essentially repressive character. Certainly, the service must be able to absorb

---

[3][On the notions of basic melody and understanding of the body, see the third section of the first part of Merleau-Ponty's *Phénoménologie de la perception*, 'The spatiality of one's own body and motricity' (*Phenomenology of Perception*, trans. Donald A. Landes, London and New York, NY: Routledge, 2012).]

[4][Under this name, French authors described the condition of patients who were admitted to the mental hospital with, say, depression or a hypomanic condition, and who, although the condition has receded, maintain a number of the attitudes that they had shown during the acute phase of the illness proper. In modern terminology, these patient adopt the 'role' of their initial illness. Sometimes the 'role' is enforced on them by the attitude of the staff or the clinical demonstrations given to students or visitors – translator's note.]

pathological manifestations. An outbreak of agitation ought not to provoke the collapse or breakdown of institutional balance.

Rather, agitation tests the service's degree of resistance, simultaneously probing its plasticity and its solidity. And as the agitated patient is not rejected, excluded, isolated, placed in an isolation unit, one strives to understand him. The point is not at all to decree the abolition of all coercive means out of humanity or hetero-imitation. Fairly quickly, this runs the risk of setbacks and the reuptake of physical restraints indulges in passionate overstatement.

Putting an agitated patient in an isolation unit most often produces unwelcome effects. Isolating a mentally ill person within a psychiatric hospital means carrying out a second internment. The patient has already been expelled by the social milieu, which has requested his sectioning under the 1838 law. But the social milieu's demands are rigid. The external equilibrium has to be monolithic as regards certain behaviours. As for the hospital milieu, in most cases it presents no organizational plan. The lines of force that contribute to constructing the phenomenal field are disastrously poor.[5] Setting aside the biological rhythm of three meals a day and sleeping times, most of the time, the day of the mental patient who is not bed-ridden, spent in the asylum courtyard, suggests the expression of Brownian motion. It can quickly be seen that physionomically repressive means of immobilization are used at the staff's instigation. And oftentimes a doctor may suspect sadistic behaviour from this personnel. The chain reactions – a prohibition on 'tying up the patient'; 'Doctor, this patient has broken everything'; 'Doctor, this patient has injured three staff members'; 'So, doctor, can this patient be tied up'? – appear and vitiate relations between the doctor and his collaborators. In fact, the service itself is sadistic, repressive, rigid, non-socialized, and has castrative aspects. Consequently, the issue is less to advocate or command the suppression of straightjackets or isolation units, than to foster in the milieu the circulation of productive, de-alienating, and functional lines of force with a strong potential for differentiated demands.[6]

---

[5][The point of sociotherapy is to constitute a horizon of perception and life for the patient.]

[6][This vocabulary anticipates some antipsychiatry themes of the following decade. Merleau-Ponty's influence is again noticeable. Merleau-Ponty wrote in the third section of the first part of *Phénoménologie de la perception*, about the difficulties of some

Internment brings about a first dis-adaptation. Isolation, with the fantasies (dark cell, punishment) that it awakens (fantasies that are, moreover, encouraged by the literal explanations of staff members – 'if you persist, you will be put in isolation or put with the agitated') fails in its pseudo-concern: to calm the patient's anxiety.

In addition, due to the isolation, due to the solitude imposed, due also to the motor concentration (we know about the force of verbal-kinetic melody and the body schema disorders that can appear along with a disjunction),[7] we bear witness to the outbreak of new elements. Verbo-motor agitation may become choleric, predatory, elastic or furious due to isolation. It may also happen that a delusion of a hyposthenic type that was isolated on the occasion of a burst of temper linked to the real, and that entertained comprehensible relations with the environment, comes to be complicated with hallucinations.

A study ought perhaps to be done on these provoked hallucinations. On the one hand, the dissolution, and on the other, the organism's reaction, entail the regression to an archaic type of thinking, more massive, more dependent on motricity, less discriminative concerning sensory data. The psychoanalysts think that onirism, pseudo-hallucinations, and the importance of games and mime essentially appear at the oral stage. Logorrhea, the whirlwind emergence of an atmospheric festivity, the being there deployed simultaneously at both poles of temporality, express a vertiginous orality. But so too does an

---

patients: 'This is because all of these operations require the same power of marking out borders and directions in the given world, of establishing lines of force, of arranging perspectives, of organizing the given world according to the projects of the moment, and of constructing upon the geographical surroundings a milieu of behaviour and a system of significations that express, on the outside, the internal activity of the subject. The world no longer exists for these patients except as a ready-made or fixed world, whereas the normal person's projects polarize the world, causing a thousand signs to appear there, as if by magic, that guide action, as signs in a museum guide the visitor' (Merleau-Ponty, *Phenomenology of perception*, p. 115).]
[7][The notion of 'kinetic melody', developed by the psychiatrist and psychoanalyst Paul Schilder (1886–1940) is reprised by Merleau-Ponty in the *Phénoménologie de la perception* (Merleau-Ponty, *Phenomenology of perception*, p. 135). The Fanonian analysis of the rigidity that colonialism introduced in the culture and field of action of the colonized, and of the violence that it causes in return, echoes this critique of an 'agitation' that is perceived as natural only due to the ignorance of the structural causality of the institution. At stake again is to reveal the blindness of a certain pseudo-scientific objectivity.]

aggressive, vehement existence of protest, replete with anxieties linked to infantile frustrations.

The ease with which a classical type of agitated patient develops hallucinations has not been sufficiently born in mind. In fact, the flight of ideas sets the stage for the hallucinatory phenomenon (verbal motor hallucinations) and de Clérambault saw this correctly when he linked mental automatism with intuitions, anticipated thoughts, echos of thoughts, nonsense, explosive words, kyrielles of words and syllabic plays.[8] With the hallucinatory process, we witness the breakdown of the world = a system of reference. Hallucinatory time as well as hallucinatory space do not make any claims to reality. We must, on the contrary, say with Sartre that hallucination coincides with an abrupt annihilation of perceived reality.[9] Hallucinatory time is in permanent flight. The spatio-temporal frame of hallucinatory activity is without order, unreal, fictive. And the phenomenon of belief, on which psychiatrists have insisted so much, is what legitimates in the eyes of the hallucinatory subject the pseudo-import of his disorders. In practical terms, then, isolation, immobilization, and the use of coercive methods through the sadistic instruments brought into play, provoke, or at least precipitate, and deepen the regression. Thought in flight is caught in the flow of images without any possibility for it to escape

---

[8] [Gaëtan de Clérambault, 'Psychoses à base d'automatisme et syndrome d'automatisme', *Annales médico-psychologiques*, vol. 85, February 1927, pp. 193–236.]

[9] [See Jean-Paul Sartre, *The Imaginary*, fourth part, chapter 3, 'Pathology of the imagination'. For Sartre, hallucination is of the order of the image and not of perception and, in this capacity, it is creation. The following passage is marked in the copy to be found in Fanon's library and underlined in places: 'the object of the image differs from the object of perception: (1) in that *it has its own space*, instead of there being an infinite space common to all perceived objects; (2) in that it immediately gives itself as unreal, whereas the object of perception originally puts up, as Husserl says, *a claim to reality* (*Seinsanspruch*). This unreality of the imaged object is correlative of an immediate intuition of spontaneity. Consciousness has a *non-thetic* consciousness of itself as a creative activity. ... The question is posed therefore in the following way: how do we abandon our consciousness of spontaneity, how do we feel ourselves passive before the images that in fact we form; is it true that we confer *reality*, which is to say a presence in flesh, on these objects that are given to a healthy consciousness as absent?' (p. 149). Merleau-Ponty deals with hallucination in similar terms: 'Hallucination disintegrates the real before our eyes and substitutes for the real a quasi-reality' (*Phenomenology of Perception*, p. 349).]

through the benevolent and realistic (*actualisant*) help of another (*autrui*). Shutting the patient in a cell, isolating him, fixing him to the bed – this amounts to creating the conditions of existence for hallucinatory activity.

Starting with anxiety, solitude and the feeling of psychobiological catastrophe that features in nearly all mental illness, and is here fuelled by the aggression typical of rejection, of casting aside, an evident 'complication' of the clinical treatment of hallucinations arises. But hallucination is not the product of cerebral excitation or the result of a specific encephalic, nutritional problem. Instead, hallucination is a global behaviour, a type of reaction, a response of the organism. Of course, the hallucinatory response presupposes a dissolution, an organic impairment, a metabolic disorder. But the alterations are never unequivocal. If we must continually refer to the works of [McFarland] and Goldstein on the level of metabolic stability in relation with levels of emotional stability and those of Hoskins[10] on the chronic deficit in oxygen that occurs with perturbations of enzyme catalysis in schizophrenia, it ought to be kept in mind that hallucination eludes a mechanistic explanation. Something else is required for a hallucination to appear, critically a breakdown of the real world. The phase within chronic hallucinatory delusions termed rumination by ancient authors is very eloquent. We know that, after an initial phase characterized by hypochondriac preoccupations, by unusual bodily manifestations, or by strange visceral sensations, the patient undergoes a phase of anxious rumination, exacerbated ideational concentration, interpretative distrust and aggressive solitude: this is the pre-hallucinatory period, a phase of so-called interpretation.

In actual fact, a rejection of the real world is enabled by the emergence of a pseudo-world based on new relations and meanings.

---

[10][*Étude psychiatrique* no. 22 by Ey, on melancholy, also cites these works incorrectly: 'Mac Ferland [*sic*] and Goldstein, "Biochemistry of M. D.", *American Journal of Psychiatry*, 1939, vol. 96, pp. 21–58)' (p. 138, n. 1). *Étude* 25, which bears on manic-depressive psychoses, cites Hoskins: 'The essential documentation is to be found in the main works of hormonal pathology applied to psychiatry. On this topic let us refer to the book by R. G. Hoskins, *Psychoses and the Internal Secretions*, Cyclopedia of Medicine, Piersol, ed., Philadelphia, 1934' (p. 459, n. 1). In the 1930s, R.A. McFarland, H. Goldstein and R.G. Hoskins published a series of studies linking metabolic abnormalities (in particular of the absorption of lipid and oxygen) with psychoses.]

This rejection requires continued confirmation.[11] The solemn decision (phase of brutal invasion) needs confirming, has to be sustained. And the migrating mentally ill[12] are precisely those who do not manage to neutralize or distance the existence of the surrounding world. Isolation in this perspective can thus operate as an authorization to hallucinate.

Clinical services have a tendency to reject agitated patients without taking note of the reciprocal foundation that exists between each of the sides. Agitation thus appears within a human framework – the clinical service itself. Agitation must be understood not mechanically but dialectically. The same people who refuse any such interpretation of the phenomenon admit and recognize that agitation diminishes in accordance with staff training and the environment's dis-alienation, even superficial. A fitting expression is agitation as asylum putrefaction.[13] Parchappe himself wrote: 'long and extensive experience shows that far from being effective in bringing about the calming of agitation among insane individuals, permanent stays in an isolation unit have, to the contrary, the effect of augmenting and maintaining the agitation.'[14]

---

[11][Chronicity is therefore not a fact of nature and in hallucination an activity of meaning-building occurs.]

[12][In the nineteenth century mentally ill individuals who travelled as a result of a hallucinatory delusion of persecution were categorized as *aliénés migrateurs*. For a history of this notion see Caro Federico, 'Déplacement pathologique: historique et diagnostics différentiels', *L'information psychiatrique*, vol. 82, no. 5, 2006, pp. 405–14.]

[13][In an important article, Bonnafé and Le Guillant derive this expression, *pourriture d'asile*, from *pourriture d'hôpital* (hospital putrefaction) to name the nosocomial diseases common before the invention of asepsy. By analogy they propose 'asylum putrefaction' to designate the aggravation of the disease and the degradation of the patients' personality when interned in an overcrowded environment. Louis Le Guillant, Lucien Bonnafé, 'La condition du malade à l'hôpital psychiatrique', *Esprit*, special issue 'Misère de la psychiatrie', 20 December 1952. Fanon often referred to this issue of *Esprit*, a milestone in the history of asylum reform in France.]

[14][Fanon here cites a passage from the article 'Aliénés (asiles)', in Amédée Dechambre (ed.), *Dictionnaire encyclopédique des sciences médicales*, 1865. In *Des principes à suivre dans la fondation et la construction des asiles d'aliénés* from 1853, page 150, Parchappe wrote:

The material constitution of the agitated patient's cell is where reside the difficulties linked with the appropriation of living conditions to the needs of someone in a state of mental alienation … In no case can the agitated individual's cell be today conceived as a permanent dwelling for nighttime and daytime, which, for a more or less lengthy period of time, the patient must not leave.

If the hospital setting forms a knot of social relations, of ambiguous encounters, then agitation loses its resonance as an entity,[15] as irresponsible behaviour, as something incomprehensible. From a dialectical viewpoint, agitation then enters into the primordial cycle of the reflecting-reflected mirror: you give to me, I receive, I assimilate, I transform, I render to you. It is certainly not the case that all catastrophic reactions, of which agitation is only a modality, will disappear. But these attempts at explanation of the organism regain their value as significations. The second internment that isolation represents is dispensed with once and for all.

The service gets transformed in a lucid and conscious manner into a rolling mill, into a purifier. This notion of rigorous skill, of armed suppleness, of fully articulated institutions, breaks from the outset the vicious circle in which the patient tends to settle. What was once imitation of self, self-intoxication, is reset in an open-institutional framework. And it is one's insertion in these institutions that frees consciousness of all vertigo.

It remains that the pathological reality, the primary symptoms, collide with the institutions. And there can be no question of curing a case of hebephrenia or hyperesthenic paranoia through the play of affective-emotional investments enabled by the clinic's organization. Moreover, holding an agitated individual in this environment fatigues the entourage owing to the tiresome stimulations of which he is the agent. In his *Médications psychologiques*, Janet specially emphasized the harmfulness of such conduct.

Inspired by Paumelle's recent publication of a series of Parchappe's texts, the reference by Fanon and Asselah to Parchappe, against those who believe in a chronic and *sui generis* agitation, is rhetorically important because Parchappe was one of the main organizers of the asylum qua institution in France. See here, *above*, p. 22.]

[15][A type of psychiatry that only worked to hypostasize its working categories into substantial entities had denied itself both understanding and treatment. Each attempt at explanation must be specific to a given situation, and such epistemological rigour entails a transformation of the clinic. Fanon's constant criticism of substantialist attitudes in psychiatric nosology might be deemed contradictory with his interest in North African popular culture's understanding of mental illness through the figure of the *djinn*. But what Fanon and Sanchez describe in their paper is the mental care practice that such beliefs entail, not at all their explanatory value, as they stress in their conclusion. See here, *above*, p. 275.]

The organized service highlights the residual picture and diminishes, to use Ey's terms, the organo-clinical gap.[16] The first task of the service is to reduce this gap to a bare minimum. The pre- and para-therapeutic task. Here, it does not seem useless to recall that understanding the need to organize the ward, to institutionalize it, to make social conducts possible within it, ought not generate any mystification grounded in reference to the outside world. This is how you can understand notions such as 'the village-hospital', 'the hospital, a reflection of the outside world', 'inside the hospital is like outside', 'the patient should feel at home', and so on. Such expressions, you will surmise, are an attempt to mask the reality beneath falsely psychotherapeutic humanitarian concerns. And Le Guillant is absolutely right to condemn these unreal attitudes.[17] Moreover, if the

---

[16][The residual picture is made up of symptoms that are not produced by the institution. This is why a (properly) organized service, constantly vigilant to the variations between and within patients, and engaging them in a social life, will aim to reduce the gap between the organically and the psychologically produced symptoms. Ey defines as follows his concept of an *organo-clinical gap* (*écart organo-clinique*): 'We call thus this margin of indetermination, of elasticity that intercedes between the direct and impoverishing action of encephalitic, or more generally somatic, processes, and their clinical expression. This situates our position at the polar opposite from the mechanicist explanation and constitutes the foundation of our essentially dynamist organicism in that it implies a series of reactions, of evolving movements, certainly ones conditioned by the mechanism of dissolution but ones that also put into play the "dynamics" of subsisting psychic instances'. (*Étude psychiatrique*, no. 7, 'Conception organo-dynamique', p. 167; see also p. XI and pp. 76–7).]

[17][Louis Le Guillant, a Marxist psychiatrist, one of the founders of '*psychiatrie de secteur*' ('community psychiatry'), published a long 'Introduction à une psychopathologie sociale' in the issue of *L'Évolution psychiatrique* in which Tosquelles' text on agitation is to be found (1954, 1, pp. 1–52, text of a talk given in December 1952). Le Guillant quotes Stalin on the nature of dialectics in a way that could have interested Fanon: 'Contrary to metaphysics, dialectics regards nature not as an accidental accumulation of objects, of phenomena that are detached from one another, isolated and independent of one another, but as a united, coherent whole in which the objects, the phenomena, are organically linked among themselves, dependent upon one another, and mutually condition each other. That is why the dialectical method considers that no phenomenon of nature can be understood if envisaged in isolated fashion outside of the surrounding phenomena'. Le Guillant adds: 'Thus, the *indissoluble unity of the individual and the milieu*, which is of course a historical unity, a dialectical one, is the fundamental law, the law from which the normal or ill psyche, the patient *in toto* is unable to escape' (p.19). Fanon's library contained several copies of the review founded and edited by Le Guillant, *La Raison*, one of the goals of which was to introduce a Pavlovian perspective into psychiatry.]

hospital is the outside milieu, the tendency to legitimate it, to provide it with systems of equilibrium reminiscent of the outside, is very strong. Without warning the police office of the doctor unexpectedly meets with the head of ward's decision to cut dessert or the orderly's threat to transfer a patient to the ward of agitated or senile patients.[18]

Agitation is a foreign body, but the insane person is, as well. A clinic ought to enable a reconciliation between the existing being and his manifestations. It ought not to refuse anything from the patient. Outside of the clinic, the patient cannot knock on any doors. The hospital setting is paradoxically the last chance for the social group that wants to rid itself of a mad person and for the mentally ill person seeking his or her lost meaning. Consequently, the point can never be purely and simply to calm down an agitation. Telephone consultations – administer Sedol or Largactil – attest to a total ignorance of the pathological mechanisms involved.

Agitation is not merely an excrescence, a 'psycho-motor' cancer. It is also and above all a modality of existence, a type of actualization, an expressive style. Agitation disarms, since it is what reunites the structures. It can appear at all levels of dissolution. Any such ambiguity is indeed apt to provoke catastrophic reactions. This is why the 'madman-who-knows-what-he-is-doing' meets in the isolation unit with 'the madman-who-does-not-know-what-he-is-doing'. In actual fact, the agitated individual at once does and does not know what he is doing. Or if you will, he does not know what he is doing but he is trying to find out. These are the attempts that clarify here and there the scene, leaving the observer with the disagreeable impression of being fooled. Thus, even at the bottom of these disordered, anarchic behaviours, which are stamped with the seal of nonsense, the fundamental ambiguity of existence is integrally assumed.[19]

---

[18][See *above*, p. 187, the last editorial of *Our Journal*, which rejects all disciplinary regulations.]

[19][Ambiguity of organic life and psychic life, also of an alienated consciousness and its attempts at liberation. In this text, at issue is naturally therapy, to understand the genesis of violence in the asylum, but, finally, as always with Fanon, a thought is opened on alienation in social existence. Here again, his psychiatry and political thought develop in parallel.]

22 BIOLOGICAL STUDY OF THE ACTION OF LITHIUM CITRATE ON BOUTS OF MANIA

J. Sourdoire and Frantz Fanon, 1957[1]

This study was carried out with and at the instigation of Doctor Fanon at Blida Psychiatric Hospital in 1955–1957. Owing to the departure of Frantz Fanon at the start of February 1957 the article was not published. (J. S.)

After fine-tuning the dosing techniques of sodium, potassium and lithium by flame spectrophotometry and of calcium and magnesium by complexometry, we followed the variations of movements of these cathions in the plasma, the cerebrospinal fluid and the urine of seven patients treated with lithium citrate.

Sodium Variations.

In plasma: overall, the rates of sodium increased over the course of treatment before stabilizing.

---

[1]IMEC Fonds Fanon, typescript FNN 1.5. [J. Sourdoire was the pharmacist of the Blida psychiatric hospital. This previously unpublished text confirms Fanon's interest in lithium salts and early trials of pharmacotherapy in psychiatry, an interest emphasized by Charles Geronimi and Maurice Despinoy (see our introduction, *above*, p. 6 and Fanon's letter to Despinoy of January 1956, *above*, p. 267).]

In the CSF [*cerebrospinal fluid*]: an on-average decrease.

In the urine: an increase in elimination with a tendency toward stabilization.

Potassium Variations.

As the doses of potassium were administered on an empty stomach in the morning, with the patients at rest, an approximation is given of the variations throughout the 24 hours during which the patient can go from being calm to a state of agitation.

In plasma: the levels of potassium tend to decrease and then to stabilize.

In CSF: an increase of potassium levels is notable with a tendency toward stabilization.

In urine: we were able to illustrate a reduction of elimination with stabilization occurring in a variable period after the start of the treatment.

Calcium Variations.

In plasma: the calcium showed only a little variation and in general remained near normal.

In CSF: levels remained rather constant.

In urine: in general elimination tended to reduce throughout the treatment and to stabilize at a lower level.

Magnesium Variations.

In plasma: relatively considerable variations were noted with a tendency toward stabilization. (It must be indicated that the methods used for dosing the magnesium in the plasma were not as precise as they are today.)

In CSF: the level remained stable.

In urine: elimination tended to reduce and to stabilize at a lower level, as with calcium.

Lithium Variations.

In plasma: the level remained always very low (2 mg/1,000) even when the daily dosage reached 3 gr of lithium citrate (which is 240 mg of Li [*lithium*] in three doses of 1 gr. each). The maximum level was 5 mg/1,000 one day after a dose of 1 gr of citrate, the minimum level was 0.7 mg/1,000.

In CSL: levels varied from 0.25 to 1.3 mg/1,000.

In urine: average elimination after 24 hours among our patients was between 51 mg and a maximum of 118 mg. This elimination also tended to stabilize after a certain period of treatment.

Diuresis Variations

This stabilized and returned to normal through reduction or increase of the volume starting around 24 hours.

Attempt at interpreting the results

Given that the elimination of elimination of ion lithium was far lower than the absorbed quantities (taking into consideration the increase in doses and rejected or refused capsules) and lithiemia very low, it can be concluded that, as some authors have already foreseen, lithium is retained in the tissues. Boissier and Hazard's works on the effects of lithium on an isolated frog heart[2] and on an isolated rat intestine[3] have shown that ion lithium produces roughly the same effects as ion sodium, but at levels about one third lower. Contrary to the results obtained with sodium, the frog heart stopped by lithium did not start again until after washing, and the isolated rat intestine, the tonus of which was suddenly diminished by the lithium, immediately recouped its tonus after washing.

The result of these works seems to be that: 1) ion lithium has an analogous effect to sodium, but at lower doses corresponding to the difference of atomic weight; 2) lithium seems to leave the cells less rapidly than sodium, since the organ must be washed in order to obtain the cessation of its effect.

---

[2]René Hazard, Jacques R. Boissier and Paule Mouille, 'Action du chlorure de lithium sur le cœur isolé de grenouille', *C.R. Société de biologie*, session of February 12, 1955, pp. 245–9.
[3]Jacques R. Boissier and Paule Mouille, 'Action du chlorure de lithium sur l'intestin isolé de rat', *C.R. Société de biologie*, session of June 11, 1955, pp. 1130–2.

We therefore examined the physico-chemical properties of lithium and we observed that, thanks to the smallness of its radius, lithium has a high capacity for solvation in a solution or in a crystalline form, from which follows a high solubility for halide ions, which is without analogy in the series of other alkali. Ion lithium shares these properties with ion magnesium, of which the greater ionic radius is offset by its double charge. It would seem that ion lithium penetrates more easily into the cell than ion sodium, that it displaces, and leads more water molecules than ion sodium into the cell, which could modify intracellular reactions.

Our attention was also attracted by the weak solubility of lithium phosphates and carbonates, as well as of the same magnesium salts. The poor solubility of these anions might explain the slow-down of the lithium release[4] in comparison with sodium and might therefore modify certain intercellular reactions, as phosphates and carbonates are the major anions of this milieu. This partial replacement of sodium by lithium can perhaps explain its effect on mania owing to the modifications that it ought to contribute to metabolic reactions and to ionic movements, tending toward regulation.

For a bibliography on lithium, see: Mogens Schou, 'Biology and Pharmacology of the Lithium ion', *Pharmacological Reviews*, vol. 9, 1957, pp. 17–58. For this study, we have checked all the works done on lithium since 1949. Details concerning the physico-chemical properties of lithium were taken from Pascal's *Traité de chimie minérale*.[5]

---

[4]Hazard, Boissier and Mouille; Boissier and Mouille.
[5][Paul Pascal, *Nouveau Traité de chimie minérale*, Paris: Masson, 1956.]

23 ON A CASE OF TORSION SPASM

Frantz Fanon and Lucien Lévy, 1958[1]

We present you here today with a case of torsion spasm or Schwalbe-Ziehen-Oppenheim's disease, also called *dysbasia lordotica*.

Patient history

Antoine F. was born prematurely at seven months on 3 September 1936. He was the seventh of ten living brothers and sisters.

The mother is supposed to have endured a significant lumbar spine trauma, which is said to have been the cause of the premature birth. He was born blue and had to be resuscitated; a significant icterus seems to have appeared during the first days. On the third day convulsions appeared. The mother noted that the infant displayed pendular eye movements during his first months.

Antoine's development gradually drew the attention of his entourage, on account of his serious motor retardation. He began to walk at four and formed his first words at five. Schooling was attempted at seven years of age but torsions and puppet movements provoked remorseless irony from his class mates. After two months, Antoine was taken out of school. At that time, his head was alive with tonic movements and had a tendency to go into hyperextension.

---

[1]*La Tunisie médicale*, vol. 36, no. 9, 1958, pp. 506–23.

At thirteen years of age, his parents' attention was drawn to his protruding large stomach, an accentuated lumbar lordosis and the progressive incapacitating of the right arm. At fourteen, the disorders progressed markedly, making all movement extremely difficult. During this period, the dilated fundus examination [DFE] displayed a pupil pallor without other symptoms; the EEG was roughly normal.

At twenty, he suddenly underwent a *grand mal epileptic seizure* with tongue biting and urine emission. An EEG taken at the time showed disorganized recordings without focalization, but with a major electrical delay. In subsequent months, *typical absences* were noted in the family environment which required the addition of some epidione to the barbiturates. In September 1958, a second fit broke out identical to the first. He was admitted to the clinic on 29 October 1958.

His parents had no significant pathological antecedents. However, two miscarriages prior to Antoine's birth and another one several pregnancies later can be reported.

Patient presentation

Antoine F., twenty-one years of age, 1.48 metres in height, presents the typical picture of torsion spasm. His heavily and grotesquely contorted *gait* was reminiscent of a Laocoon, of a 'macabre clown', according to the now classic expression of [August] Wimmer. Bearing an abnormally enlarged support polygon, the foot attacks the ground through the sole mainly to the left. At the level of the lower limbs, there is a permanent hypertonia of the extensor muscles of the thigh and leg. The pelvis is markedly tilted to the rear, its upper canal protrudes above and below through a rotation around the cotyloid axis, with it riding up toward the back. The pelvis digs into the kidneys, displaces the stomach to the front, exaggerating to a maximum the posterior concavity lordosis.

There is no hypotonia in the anterior abdominal muscles, however there is a constant hypertonia at the level of the antigravity muscles, spasmodically reinforced, thus accentuating the lordosis even further. The head is literally tilted to the left and back, the occiput appearing to go contrary to the pelvis. While walking, the right arm is animated by rocker-arm type tonic movements, where the left arm remains stuck to the side of the body. Anarchic, intempestive spasms, involving the head, the trunk and the right arm determine a twisted, undulating, mannered, jolting walk in the manner of a dislocated puppet.

With Antoine, as with most described cases of torsion spasm, there seems to be an inverse relation between the amount of muscular effort required and the uncoordinated movements. This is how the torsion spasm properly speaking diminishes considerably in intensity whenever the organism in its totality finds itself engaged in an important task, such as carrying a heavy object or running at a brisk pace.

The upright position is unstable. There is a veritable torsion of the trunk at the left concavity with lordosis. The head fixed in hyperextension, deviated laterally to the left, is shaken with spasms. As a result, Antoine seeks for favourable positions that limit the amplitude of these movements, most often by leaning against a wall. In this position, the cephalic spasm is certainly restricted, but is not altogether eliminated. The wall, which forms a really active support, gets pounded on by the posterior aspect of the cranium. This spasmodic pressure of the head against the wall would explain our patient's scalp alterations and the exostosis of the outer table of the occipital bone.

In the dorsal decubitus, disorders are reduced to a minimum, the attitude appears normal, but it is far from an attitude of real rest. A muscular resolution at the limit of the normal is notable without any tonic disturbance: neither extrapyramidal hypertonia nor hypotonia. At most the privileged attitude of the head with left lateral and slightly forward deviation, the trunk bent to a curve on the left. Spontaneously, the extremities are not animated by any involuntary movement; however, from time to time, some hand and finger movements arise that evoke sub-athetosic movements.

Moreover, at the slightest incitation, without aura, spasms appear that follow one another in an avalanche. In this instance, the hypertonia of the neck muscles is slowly, powerfully exaggerated, then the trunk curves inward on the left, the upper limbs go into hyperextension, the hand bent over the forearm, the fingers over the palm. The tonic phase then reaches the lower limbs. The hypertonia is at once maxima, but never affects the facial muscles. This tonic seizure lasts between thirty seconds and a minute and disappears without any clonic manifestations and without affecting consciousness. In a general way, the spasms are influenced neither by the forced head flexion nor by the ocular occlusion.

The seated position is possible when Antoine is strongly held by the posterior aspect of the head. If this support diminishes, the trunk gradually curves inward and from a certain angle a large spasm emerges that will thrust the subject suddenly and invincibly backward. The spasms intensify with emotion, fatigue, and disappear during sleep and under narcosis, as we have been able to observe.

Paradoxically, this great motor disorder evolves without any neurological signs. Pyramidal signs are absent, the pyramidal bundles are intact, the tendinous reflexes are normal, there is no clonus, no Babinski response. The cutaneous reflexes are present. All modes of sensibility are unharmed.

Study of the muscular tonus is made difficult by the existence of waves of spasmodic contracture. Nevertheless, no lasting hypertonia appears to exist. There are no fibrillations, and the stretching out and drawing in of the limbs does not cause hypertonia to appear. There is no myotatic reflex. The cranial nerve pairs are unharmed. Speech is disturbed, encumbered, explosive, spasmodic, contorted. Muscular trophicity is not altered; muscular strength is intact and we were able to note that Antoine F. even has a very developed musculature.

There are no visceral disturbances; the liver, the spleen are not palpable; heart sounds are normal, pulse is 70, the AT [*arterial tension*] is 12/8. There are no pigmentation problems, hairiness is normal as are the secondary sexual features. We must signal a considerable prevailing hyperhidrosis on the upper limbs without further vegetative disorders.

Mental examination

The patient has some mental retardation, with a certain degree of puerilism. He has had no schooling. His IQ is at the level of a six-/ seven-year old. He has a good understanding of words and gestures. Affectivity is unimpaired, instead there is a state of sub-anxiety each time that Antoine finds himself alone, such as when the time comes to leave the CNPJ[2] and he is waiting for his brother.

---

[2][Neuropsychiatric daycare centre (*Centre Neuropsychiatrique de Jour*).]

There are no mnestic troubles. His humour, without being jovial, remains generally gay in tone. The praxia are intact; there are no visual or tactile agnosias.

Paraclinical tests

[They] are roughly normal:

Azotemia	0.23	CSF: elements	2.8
Glycemia	0.90	Albumin	0.25
Calcemia	59.99	Glucose	0.55
Cholesterol	1.81	WR	0
Bilirubin	16 mg/100	K	0
The WR is negative		Benjoin coll. normal	

The DFE shows a papilla with a large and deep physiological sort of excavation, there is no macular or peripheral degeneration. There are no Kayser Flechner rings. Cranial x-rays show an exostosis of the external table of the occipital, probably due to the spasmodic bumps of the head against the wall in the favoured upright position that we described above.

The EEG, despite repeated recordings, does not demonstrate any signs of epilepsy. The only thing recorded is the right unilateral muscular artefacts. The rest of the tracings are illegible. It was not possible to undertake a recording of sleep patterns.

Summary

We are dealing with a patient born premature at seven months who during his first days of life had convulsions and an icterus. He is clearly retarded on the psychomotor level, and the torsion spasm appeared as of seventeen years of age. He has had three grand mal epileptic seizures since 1956.

There are several reasons for presenting this patient. First, because cases of torsion spasm are rare. In 1936, Zador was able to count a mere sixty-five of them in the literature.[3] Second, because the torsion

---

[3][Jules Zador, 'Le spasme de torsion', *Revue neurologique*, no. 4, Masson & Cie, October 1936.]

spasm has been the focus of several pathogenic discussions, which were further clarified by the last international neurology congress in Brussels in 1957. Lastly, because the proposed therapies have been overturned by the contributions of neurosurgery.

Schwalbe described the first case of torsion spasm in 1908.[4] One year later, Ziehen[5] followed notably by Oppenheim in 1911[6] came to specify the general physiognomy of this syndrome. These authors described torsion spasm as a familial cryptogenetic illness appearing in Jewish individuals, Polish or Russian. The various authors since then have been classified as either unicists or autonomists.

Unicists. Thévenard describes torsion spasm as a simple particular case of dystonias of posture. Indeed, for Thévenard, the dystonias of posture group together 'non-paralytic motor disorders and those of dystonic nature, the shared characteristic of which is their involving electively the antigravity muscles, achieving their maximum development in the upright standing position, and disappearing in decubitus'. Thus, in addition to these unilateral posture dystonias, there are generalized posture dystonias that twist backward, or torsion spasms.

For Froment, falling backward from a standing position is essentially due to an insufficiency of action of the trunk and pelvis flexors on the thigh. Also a unicist, Hall sought to classify torsion spasm as a hepato-lenticular degeneration. Lastly, we ought to flag the opinions of Marchand and Ajuriaguerra, who include torsion spasm among the tonic epilepsies.

Autonomists. Next to this tendency, others think that the torsion spasm is a syndrome in its own right, an individualized clinical entity in the group of illnesses of the extrapyramidal system.

4[Marcus Walter Schwalbe, *Eine eigentümliche tonische Krampfform mit hysterischen Symptomen*, dissertation, Berlin, 1908.]

5[More likely in 1911: Theodor Ziehen, 'Fall von tonischer Torsionsneurose', *Neurologisches Centralblatt*, vol. 30, 1911, pp. 109–10.]

6[Hermann Oppenheim, 'Über eine eigenartige Krampfkrankheit des kindlichen und jugendlichen Alters (*Dysbasia lordotica progressiva, Dystonia musculorum deformans*)', *Neurologisches Centralblatt*, vol. 30, 1911, pp. 1090–107.

Positive diagnosis of Ziehen-Oppenheim disease

Clinically, [this diagnosis] is based on the gradual onset that usually occurs at the level of the distal extremity of the limbs, predominantly unilateral, with the spasms spreading in a gradual fashion. In the acute phase of the clinical picture specific to the macabre clown, spasms are variable: maximal when in the standing position, diminishing when in decubitus. The problems have extrapyramidal characteristics: they exaggerate with emotion, tiredness, and are not under volitional control. There are few neurological signs and the pyramidal bundle is not impaired.

Besides this pure case, numerous clinical forms exist and descriptions have been provided of cases with a rigidity reminiscent of decerebrate rigidity, with abnormal movements typical of athetosis, with oculocephalogyric crises and with epileptic seizures.

Anatomically. In torsion spasm, there is a diffuse impairment of the basal ganglia with a clear impairment to the extrapyramidal centres of the striatum, to the pallidum, to Luys' body, and often also to the thalamus and the hypothalamus. Moreover, also discovered was an impairment to the dentate nucleus of the cerebellum, to the pontocerebellar system, and to the hippocampus. The pyramidal tracts are intact.

Etiologically. Outside the three main etiological types – familial cryptogenetic torsion spasm, torsion spasm of postencephalitic syndromes, torsion spasm of hepato-lenticular degeneration – other infectious, toxic or degenerative etiological factors were named. Discussions surrounding certain patients focussed on the role of obstetrical trauma in provoking discrete lesions that show relatively late; at a pinch Wimmer was given to considering the existence of predispositions.

In his report on 'the anatomopathology of the extrapyramidal system' given at the Congress of Brussels in 1957, Greenfield seems to have contributed a new note, one full of promise. In this report, Greenfield endeavoured to show the importance of the nuclear icterus in the genesis of these problems. Despite awareness of the rhesus factor and the exchange transfusion, which has reduced infant mortality from hemolytic disease, kernicterus nevertheless remains, whether it appears discretely prior to the transfusion or in premature babies without Rh incompatibility, or, lastly, perhaps the icterus was masked by skin coloration. The indirect accumulation of bilirubin in the blood, overcharging the immature liver, is the supposed cause of the disease.

Thus, out of four hundred spastic infants, he found blood incompatibility in one hundred and nineteen. Out of fifty-five cases of athetosis, thirty-one had jaundice at birth. In short, Greenfield's statistics show that 65% of all the athetosics and 9% of all the spastics had kernicterus.

With Greenfield, we should underscore the fact that in kernicterus lesions prevail in Luys' body, the *globus pallidus* and the hippocampus. The putamen can be invaded and the dentate nucleus, the olivae and the flocculus usually have a brilliant yellow colour. From the histological point of view, we find lesions characteristic of kernicterus.

Let us compare Greenfield's hypothesis with the observation of Jervis G.A. (Thielles), who, in an encephalopathy expressed by dystonic movements, rigidity and dysarthria beginning in infancy, found an indirect bilirubinemia at 15/20 mg%. The anatomical examination showed kernicterus lesions.

Differential diagnosis

We will not insist on the diagnosis that arises with some forms of Wilson's disease, of Westphall-Strumpfell pseudosclerosis, or with some varieties of Parkinsonian syndrome. Pure athetosis presents points of resemblance with torsion spasm; Jakob, moreover, tends to place torsion spams in the symptomatic table of athetosis.

By contrast, decerebrate rigidity can appear similar to a torsion spasm: see the published cases of encephalopathies, of certain cerebral tumours of hydrocephalies. But the following must be observed if one is to claim that someone has decerebrate rigidity: myotatic reflexes, Magnus and Klein reflex and proprioceptive reinforcements of hypertonia – none of which are found in torsion spasms.

Epilepsy can co-exist with torsion spasm, which thus raises the problem of dyskinetic epilepsies and tonic epilepsies. Dyskinetic epilepsies are characterized by the size of abnormal involuntary, isolated movements bearing no relation to the clonuses of classical seizures. They arise in a more paroxystic way, most often preceded by an aura, generally a hallucination, which is what distinguishes them from torsion spasms.

Tonic epilepsy is characterized by a very considerable tonic wave, which rigidifies such and such a segment, or the whole body in such and such a posture during a brief lapse of time. Tonus is normal in the intercritical period. Let us also note that partial continuous epilepsy of a Kojewnikoff or Unverricht-Lundborg type may have arisen in some cases.

Pathogeny

Our pathogenic knowledge is still uncertain and subject to frequent reorganization just as the entire conception of the pyramidal and extrapyramidal systems. We will make do with citing the hypotheses of Bino, Mourgue, and Wimmer, all of whom first considered that torsion spasm expressed the simple hypertonia of a muscular group, and those of Thévenard, who attributes it to a problem with the tonus regulation. Foerster considers torsion spasm to be a partial athetosis with predominant trunk impairment. Marinesco and Jonesco bring a peripheral factor into the mix. For these later authors, the lesion in the upper extrapyramidal centres determines modifications in the excitability of the medullar neurons placed under their dependency. From this fact, peripheral excitations, upon meeting with abnormal physiological conditions at the level of the cord, become deregulated in their functioning.

Lastly, we must cite Bucy's hypotheses about circuits controlling the parapyramidal and pyramidal systems. A lesion in any point at all of these circuits liberates the subcortical formations and provokes a trembling, a hypertonia.

As for Greenfield, in order to explain the topography of lesions, he introduces the notion of maturation from within a Jacksonian perspective. The more precocious the maturation, the greater the vulnerability of the cells. This is why the hippocampus is more affected than the cortex, the Luys' body, and the *globus pallidus* more than the striatum. Understanding abnormal movements still remains difficult; that is to say, none of the theories put forward are entirely satisfactory.

In the case of Antoine F., it seems, after an in-depth study of the history and dynamism of his disease, that the most attractive hypothesis verges on Greenfield's. He was a premature baby with jaundice at birth. The problems appeared with the third, fourth month, settling in progressively, especially after the fourth year. Indirect bilirubinemia was at 16 mg %, similar to the case Jervis reported. The grand mal type of epileptic seizures only appeared very recently (one year ago) and occur rarely – comprising three in total. They cannot be explained by cortical impairment, in fact there are no signs of neurological localization, no aura, no signs of focalizations on the EEG. They can only be understood in terms of a subcortical induction.

For all these reasons, we claim that this is a pure case of Ziehen-Oppenheim disease, even though Antoine is neither Jewish, nor Polish nor Russian. Antoine thus comes close to the cases described by Zador.

What is the treatment for torsion spasm?

Classical treatment has recourse to scopolamine, eserine, atropine and even morphine. For some, the most active medications are datura stramonium powder at 50/60 cg per day and a 5% preparation using the Bulgarian method of belladonna root wine. Recently, synthetic antiparkinsonian drugs have been suggested and have allegedly had some effect.

As for neurosurgery, it has come to be based on pathogenic conceptions. Barré and Fontaine have operated on the peripheral nervous system, whereas others prefer the pyramidotomies or operations at the level of the posterior limb of the internal capsule and of the ansa lenticularus. Let us note David and Talairach's unpublished observation of a serious case of torsion spasm that was much improved by a coaculation of the prerubral field of the red nucleus.

(Work undertaken at the Neuropsychiatry Day Centre, Hôpital Charles-Nicolle, Tunis).

Bibliography

Actes du Congrès international de neurologie, Brussels, 1957.

Barré J. A., and Fontaine R., 'Heureux effets de l'intervention chirurgicale sur le système nerveux périphérique dans le spasme de torsion: la contracture en extension du M.I. de certains cas de sclérose en plaques', *Revue neurologique*, vol. 79, no. 10, 1949, pp. 775–6.

Talairach J., David M., Tournaux P., Corredor M., and Kvasina T., *Atlas d'anatomie stéréotaxique*, Paris: Masson, 1957.

Thévenard, A., *Les Dystonies d'attitude*, dissertation, Paris, 1926.

Wimmer A., 'Le spasme de torsion', Réunion neurologique internationale 3–6 June 1929, *Revue neurologique*, vol. 2, 1929, pp. 904–5.

24 FIRST TESTS USING INJECTABLE MEPROBAMATE FOR HYPOCHONDRIAC STATES

Frantz Fanon and Lucien Lévy, 1959[1]

As part of our semeiological and therapeutic research into 'hypochondriac states', we were able to test the effects of of meprobamate on them.[2] These preliminary attempts are the topic of this talk.

Meprobamate, which corresponds to the chemical formula $C_9H_{18}O_4N_2 = 281.2$ methyl-2-n-propyl-1-3-propanediol dicarbamate, has been studied ever since it was synthesized in the Berger Laboratories by Ludwig and Piech in 1950. It underwent lengthy animal testing in many different countries, in particular in the United States, under the name of Miltow, and also in Germany. Its pharmocodynamic properties are outdone by its almost total absence of toxicity. Thus, in rats, DL 50 is established at around 500 mg/kg intravenously; 800 mg/kg by peritoneal route; 1,700 mg/kg orally.

---

[1] *La Tunisie médicale*, vol. 37, no. 10, 1959, pp. 175–91. [Here the point is again to measure the efficacy of organic therapies and to fix their limits.]
[2] We are grateful to Clin-Byla laboratories, which supplied us with an injectable form of meprobamate, which is not yet commercialized and goes by the name of Equanil.

Very satisfactory results were also obtained from the study of its chronic toxicity, since a series of rats subject to an ingestion of between 250 mg/kg to 500 mg/kg for more than six months at the end of the experiment did not present any modification to the blood formula, any growth disorder, or any visceral alteration, whether micro- or macroscopic, comparatively to a reference group.

From the point of view of its effect on the central nervous system, it is first possible to observe a loss of postural reflexes, then from about 250 mg/kg a relaxation of the musculature that can go as far as suppressing all voluntary movement. Approaching DL 50, the animal remains motionless in the position in which it has been placed, a state that is reversible and without after-effects of any sort. We should also underscore its anti-convulsant effect examined in relation to a strychnic intoxication.

The EEG examination of individuals subject to the action of meprobamate showed a non-modified recording with regular doses of 400 mg/24 h. The recordings are remarkable for the EEG's abundance, its regularity, its amplitude with the onset of sporadic bilateral flashes, synchronous with distinctly higher doses, recordings that have been interpreted as a 'functional effect of placing the reticular system at rest'. Lastly, we must emphasize the effect of meprobamate on the functions of vegetative life, as meprobamate modifies neither arterial pressure, nor cardiac rhythm, nor the frequency or amplitude of the respiratory movements.

As the experiment showed that the nervous centres responsible for the responses of the sympathetic nervous system are more sensitive to the action of meprobamate than those that command vagal reactions, the very considerations that led Marcel Perrault to say that meprobamate is probably the least toxic and safest tranquillizer around, encouraged us to use it with our patients. The various researchers to have worked with meprobamate in psychiatry have all shown its usefulness in hypochondriac syndromes.

Faced with the large number of these syndromes that we have to treat, faced also with the injectable formula placed at our disposal (phials dosed at 160 mg), we set about using it in these cases, with up to as many as six and seven phials per day, or 1,180 mg. This injectable form was the object of an experiment by Bouquerel, Naviau and Lavoine, a report of which was produced in the [*Annales médico-*

psychologiques] (vol. 6, 1958). The meprobamate was used with cases of emotionally disturbed forms of senile psychopathology.

There can be no question here of recalling the painstaking work of nosographic precision that has been carried out around hypochondria. Today, the old illness of hypochondria has been dislocated and its constitutive elements have re-emerged in totally distinct nosological entities. With the 'hypochondriac forms' of melancholia, of epilepsy, of schizophrenia, etc., one tends more and more, with López-Ibor, to note the mostly hypochrondriac attitud. Psychosomatic medicine appears to have revived studies on hypochondria, but the current return is to the first theories, whether purely Freudian, or else those of Stekel on the phenomenological and anthropological tendency with Schneider, Strauss, Uexküll, Weizsäcker.[3]

All our patients have come to us from community clinics or hospital services. They have been monitored through external consultations for several months, or even several years. The decision is made for hospitalization because the clinical setting tends to assume a certain gravity: patients adopt the sudden habit of coming back every day for the consultation, they lament, they become prolix when presenting their disorders, they ask for a 'more energetic treatment' and then firmly demand hospitalization.

Oftentimes the men will leave the building site and the women seriously neglect the housework. These are the conditions under which the patients are admitted to the neuropsychiatric day centre.

Observations

First series

Obs. no 1. – Mohamed B., twenty-six years old, married, two children. Unemployed since 1954. Once in a while earns a bit of money from the black-market selling of vegetables. He has been arrested once or twice by the municipal police. He has never been sentenced. In 1958, after Ramadan, a bout of vomiting obliged

---

[3][On the rejection of essentialism in medical nosology, which Fanon's dissertation upheld from the start and which opens onto phenomenological, anthropological, psychosomatic and ecological perspectives, see our introduction, *above*, p. 10 *sq.* Fanon comes back to this issue in several of his psychiatric papers, see, for instance *above*, p. 297.]

the patient to desist from all activity. He was treated successively at Hospital E. Conseil, Habib Thameur and Sadiki. He came for a neuropsychiatry consultation on 8 September 1958.

The symptomatology is extremely mobile. What is striking above all is the patient's plaintive and desperate attitude. Heat flashes, subcontinuous cephalalgiae with heaviness, paresthesia in the upper left limb and lastly a significant asthenia causing the patient's voice to break up.

Negative clinical examination. WRO, calcemia: 92; urea: 0.34; glucose: 0.96; TA: 11/7. Normal gastroduodenal x-ray.

The patient was placed on three phials of Equanil per day for twelve days. Significant improvement was observed from day three. He left fifteen days later, practically cured. However, it must be noted that the patient returned three weeks after discharge, as he was unable to find work, and because the same social difficulties subsisted, the hypochondriac procession recurred.

Obs. no 2. – Hedi Ben M., forty-five years old, married. He was monitored via external consultations from January 1952 for hypochondriac disorders that were localized in the left side of the body and with a cephalic onset. All the tests, DFE, EEG, PL, were negative. In November 1958, the clinical picture seriously deteriorated, including dizzy spells, syncopal and cephalalgic episodes. Various neuroleptics were used without result. The patient was put on three phials of Equanil per day.

At the end of fifteen days, the observed improvement was such that the daily dosage was increased to five phials. This posology was maintained for one week, after which the patient was put on five tablets of Equanil per day. The patient was discharged after having considerably improved at the end of December.

Obs. no 3. – Saïda Bent S., twenty-three years old. From the age of sixteen, she was monitored through external consultation. She complained of articulation pains in her hands, and legs, as well as of palpitations, cephalalgia, dizzy spells. She came for regular consultations every month or two. All types of nervine sedatives were utilized.

In October 1958, the clinical picture became considerably more complicated. The cephalalgia intensified, with intermittent vomiting and problems in the affective sphere. Three times she got engaged and broke off the engagement. She was treated in the weeks prior by phenobarbital in fractionated doses and by Largactil. Upon admission, diffuse pains spread throughout the body, cephalalgia, dizzy spells, gastric, erratic and mobile pains, stiffness, irritability. From 14 November 1958, the patient was placed on two phials of Equanil per day, until 3 December 1958. From 3 December 1958, two tablets of Equanil were added to these two phials of Equanil, and from 9 December 1958 the phials were cut and the patient was put on six tablets.

The first improvement that the Equanil phials brought about was sleep normalization: her nightmares disappeared and the fatigue of awakening, which had been common for several years, was replaced by an impression of relaxation and good humour. But the headaches persisted as did the pains. From 19 November 1958, the young Saïda began to busy herself with her upcoming marriage and timidly went about preparing her wedding trousseau. Her appetite had been mediocre but returned. Until 18 December 1958, continued to complain, but, in the last week, the patient's contact with the clinic started to change and the cenesthopathic disorders practically disappeared. Discharged on 25 December 1958.

Obs. no 4. – Ali Ben Hadj B., docker, forty-eight years old, married, three children, has not worked for five years. In 1943, subsequent to an altercation with military personnel, he was imprisoned for five years. Recounts that these military personnel were Jews who wanted to harm him. Attributes his illness to the blows received. Out of prison, he resumed his work from 1949 to 1953, at which time he fell ill. The clinical picture began with cephalalgia including vomiting, insomnia with nightmares. These manifestations are interpreted as the consequences of a poisoning, the author of which was additionally identified: allegedly a female neighbour, a friend of the Jews, who wanted to marry Ali.

For five years, the illness progressed. On top of the vomiting, diffuse, erratic pains arose, as well as asthenia and episodic anorexia, all this set against a background of anxiety. Impotence completed the clinical picture and it reinforced the patient's delusional conviction of having been poisoned.

He entered the clinic on 27 September 1958. The clinical and paraclinical examinations were normal. Treatment: three phials of Equanil per day. Improvement occurred gradually and quite markedly. The asthenia, anorexia and insomnia totally stopped, while his headaches and pains diminished, as did the impotence. After a month, the subdelusional ideas were criticized. The patient left with plans of social reinsertion.

Second series

Obs. no 1. – Zohra Bent S. Since 1958 monitored through external consultation for dizziness, humming in the ears, cephalalgia. All the tests, EEG, x-rays, were negative. Was treated with Belladenal, Largactil. State unchanged.

Entered the clinic on 1 November 1958. Upon entry: headaches, paresthesia in the left leg, humming in the ears, pseudo-hallucinations: she would see her daughter, who is dead, asleep on her lap, insomnia, anxiety. Placed on three phials of Equanil on 27 November 1958 until 11 December 1958. No notable improvement.

Obs. no 2. – Saïda Bent B., twenty years of age. Monitored for hysterical neurosis via external consultation over a period of several months. Previously treated with Largactil, Nozinan. Several prior hospitalizations in a general medical clinic. Cardiac neurosis, with left lateral-sternal systolic murmur that was not radiating and disappeared in the seated position. Inorganic murmur, anxiety attacks, continuous nightmares with polymorphous themes. Currently engaged, refuses marriage. Has notions of a previous engagement with a cousin who apparently preferred another.

First hospitalization from 10 July 1958 to 3 October 1958. Was treated with Sedo-carena, Plegicil, Theophylline, Gardenal in fractionated doses. No improvement. Re-hospitalization on 1 December 1958: was put on Equanil on 2 December 1958, with a dosage of five injections daily for nine days and, from 12 December 1958, of three tablets daily. No result as of 27 December 1958.

Obs. no 3. – Habiba Bent S. Patient of twenty-five years of age, monitored through external consultation in neuropsychiatry for six months, married, no child. Had a caesarean two years previous. Some months later, had a nocturnal crisis, probably of a hysterical nature. Upon entry: cephalalgia and dizzy spells, episodic hysteriform crises. An interview with the patient very quickly brought to light a rejection of her husband and an investment in her brother-in-law mixed with feelings of guilt since the death of her sister-in-law.

Placed on injectable Equanil, three phials daily, from 24 November 1958 to 28 November 1958, then on six phials and two tablets per day from 9 December 1958. The illness disorders – insomnia, cephalalgia, dizzy spells, trembling – all remained unchanged for the entire duration of the treatment.

It is possible to describe a basic syndrome complex among our patients. Complaints of pain are what defines them. The alleged disorders are clearly very proteiform. None of the predominantly abdominal characteristics of old hypochondria were to be found. Everything is to be found here: cephalalgia, humming in the ears, lumps in the throat, electrical currents in the limbs, heaviness in the stomach, crushing sensations in the muscles, constipation, etc.

The voice was usually weak, without fullness or emphasis. No underlying aggressiveness is evident in contrast with paranoiac hypocondrias, nor anxiety such as is manifest, among others, in body schema alterations or in serious cenestopathy. No delusions or obsessional or phobic manifestations were involved. Consciousness was not impaired.

We are essentially dealing with diffuse algiae, of a protopathic sort with cephalalgia, humming in the ears and above all a considerable susceptibility to fatigue: moroseness, escape from everyday tasks or the abandoning of projects, impotence and frigidity, and insomnia without oniroid phenomena complete the clinical picture.

Conclusions

It is evident that our experimentation is not sufficiently extensive to be able to draw a therapeutic conclusion. In any case, two things are clear.

1) Administrated Equanil in extremely considerable doses does not alter the patients' activity, judgement or affectivity. Arterial tensions, pulse and temperature, all of which were regularly monitored and several times per day, showed no modification. The patients thus showed a perfect tolerance to Equanil in the sizeable doses that we administered.

2) This experimentation was performed in a neuropsychiatric day clinic where the patients enter in the morning and spend the day semi-confined to bed. Then around 2 pm the patients start to return to their homes. The centre closes at 6 pm. The Equanil course of treatment can thus practically be likened

with ambulatory therapy. The conclusion is that the general practitioner can use sizeable doses.

3) Indications for Equanil must obviously be further specified. It is remarkable, for example, that the patients of the second series, who in addition to their hypochondriac preoccupations manifested either some conversion hysteria (observations 2 and 3, second series), or else oneirophrenia in the sense of Mayer-Gross (observation 1, second series), were not improved by the Equanil.

The interest of injectable phials of Equanil, in the doses that we utilized, seems to be its action on minor depressions devoid of major anxiety, but including susceptibility to fatigue, feelings of bodily malaise, insomnia, cephalalgia and humming in the ears. This minor form of hypochondria, which evokes the old neurasthenia, seems to be a good indication for injectable Equanil in daily doses of between four to six phials in intramuscular injections.

Let us note, by contrast, that sismotherapy is absolutely ineffective here and oftentimes, after one or two ESTs, produces real anxiety while maintaining the hypochondriac background intact. It sometimes happened that we administered six phials in three injections and we did not observe any problems there either. It seems to us that treatment must extend for over twenty days and that for the period of one month the observed improvement must be consolidated by Equanil orally (three to five tablets per day).

(Work undertaken at the Neuropsychiatry Day Centre, Charles-Nicolle Hospital, Tunis).

Bibliography

For the bibliography up until 1957, the reader may consult:

Guilleman P., 'Le méprobamate. Nouveau médicament ataraxique et tranquillisant', *Gazette des hôpitaux*, vol. 13, 1957.

Racamier P. C., Blanchard M., and Faucret M., 'Le méprobamate en thérapeutique psychiatrique: essais préliminaires', *Annales médico-psychologiques*, vol. 115, 1957, p. 123.

Bouquerel J., and Naviau Lavoine, 'Effets du méprobamate chez les psychopathes séniles', *Annales médico-psychologiques*, vol. 116, 1958, p. 121.

25 DAY HOSPITALIZATION IN PSYCHIATRY: VALUE AND LIMITS

Frantz Fanon, 1959[1]

General introduction

After the Second World War, problems with psychiatric assistance were presented with acuity to practitioners in various countries. We know that before 1938 priority was given, on the one hand, to the prevention and early detection of mental disorders and, on the other, to the simplification of the administrative formalities surrounding the hospitalization of the mentally ill.[2]

The 1938 Law adopted in France, to cite only this example, aimed precisely to take the carceral character out of psychiatric asylums.[3]

---

[1]*La Tunisie médicale*, vol. 37, no. 10, 1959, pp. 689–712.
[2][France is now only an example, Fanon indicates that he is working within a larger perspective.]
[3][Fanon is probably referring here to the *Ministerial Circular* of 5 February 1938, which proposed a model for reorganizing the internal regulations of psychiatric hospitals, in order to give greater weight to medical treatment. It is based on 'the idea that the treatment of mental illnesses does not only consist in defined medical measures but extends to the entire regime of life, and that eating, working, the right to spend earnings, reading, writing, and so on, are all circumstances liable to have an influence, whether good or bad, on illness, and, as such, fall under the competency of the medical doctor'. Available at https://www.ascodocpsy.org/wp-content/uploads/textes_officiels/Circulaire_5fevrier1938.pdf, p. 39.]

During the war, the recrudescence of mental illnesses and above all their sudden blooming led doctors in English-speaking countries to increase *open-door* practices at psychiatric hospitals. This open-door approach, inaugurated by Duncan Macmillan[4] at Nottingham and taken up in several other countries, enables the patients to develop freely within the hospital, thus permitting a maximum of contacts between the patients and the social milieu, including: visits from parents, leave of absence, holidays, early discharges, trial discharges.

Certainly, the first patients to benefit from the *open-door* initiative were neuropaths and prepsychotics, but an examination of so-called chronic patients had shown that for a long time the majority of symptoms were of a neurotic order and that the asylum paradoxically exacerbated the illness, fostering psychotization.[5] A further step was taken and the principle of the *day hospital* was inaugurated. The most convincing experiments were those conducted in England, in Denmark and in Canada.

What are the principles of the day hospital? 1) First, the patient is not removed from his or her family milieu and sometimes even continues to be part of his or her professional setting. 2) The psychiatric symptomatology that patients present does not disappear because of internment since, precisely, the elements of conflict, the conflictual configuration, remain present and enduring in the family, social and professional settings. No magical disappearance of the tension occurs, as is usual with internment, and patients' reactions can be continuously studied from within the natural setting of their existence.

In the old type of psychiatric hospital, the patient is subtracted from his conflictual milieu and very often the impression was that the neurotic symptoms would suddenly disappear as soon as the asylum doors closed up around him. This is the sense in which it can be said that internment effects some relaxation. But the neurotic

---

4[Duncan Macmillan (1902–1969), director of Mapperley hospital in Nottingham and theoretician of the open psychiatric hospital. Well known to French psychiatrists of the period as the *Open door* approach. Several studies published in their main professional journal, *L'Évolution psychiatrique*, mentioned it in the 1950s.]

5[On agitation and the psychoses triggered by the asylum, see *above*, the article with Slimane Asselah, p. 293.]

attitudes remain present and their abreaction could be expected upon the wife's or husband's first visit, or at the slightest evocation of former difficulties. The asylum extended a protective coat around the patient, but it was a false protection, since it fostered the patient's lethargy, a sort of wakeful sleep in which the patient led a vegetative life. And the doctor's attention there was drawn only to the patient's behavioural problems, those emerging most often from the asylum's living conditions.

The attempt of doctors to create a neo-society within the hospital (this is the attempt of social therapy) aimed precisely to present the patient with situations akin to the outside world, in which the patient could repeat the neurotic attitudes such as they were to have existed before.

So, the day hospital can be seen to respond to two needs: 1) early diagnosis and treatment of behavioural problems; 2) to maintain the content of patient contact with the outside environment to a maximum, so that no neurotic attitude, no conflictual situation, magically disappears. The point is thus not to remove patients from the circuitry of social life, but to set in place a therapy that is part of the setting of social life. From the viewpoint of psychiatric assistance, this amounts to an attempt to disengage from the apparently secure atmosphere bestowed by the existence of the asylum.

Day hospital experiments have been seldom performed. At most twenty day hospitals exist in the world. All of them are to be found in technologically advanced countries; never before has a day hospital experiment been tried in an underdeveloped country. From a methodological point of view, it became important, first, to ask whether the day hospital is possible in a country with low-levels of industrialization. If it actually is, then a question of doctrine might arise: can the day hospital take on board all types of psychiatric affection?

The Tunisian government's decision to create a neuropsychiatric day centre – the only government on the African continent to attempt this experiment – must be fully appreciated. Here I discuss the results of this experiment. I argue for the validity of the principle behind the day centre, even in underdeveloped countries. My conviction is that, henceforth, it has become medically important and socially beneficial to develop neuropsychiatric day centres in underdeveloped countries.

In eighteen months of activity, as I report, the neuropsychiatric day centre in Tunis received and treated more than 1,000 patients and less than 0.88 % of these patients required internment.

The neuropsychiatric day centre in Tunis

The neuropsychiatric service at Charles-Nicolle General Hospital was originally established more than forty years ago. In practical terms, this service was almost entirely subject to the 1838 Law.[6] Its only difference concerned the relative priority given to so-called voluntary patients who were eligible for the open service method. The surveillance measures ceded nothing to those of ordinary psychiatric hospitals in which the worst methods are used: straightjackets, isolation cells, closed doors and above all the institution's complacently punitive attitude. Ministerial offices had asked the Psychiatric Assistance in Tunisia for an overall plan, so Tunisian psychiatrists, in joint agreement, replied that it appeared important to them not to increase the number of large-hospital type psychiatric establishments, which sooner or later get turned into asylums. They insisted more on the necessity of attaching low capacity neuropsychiatric clinics to already existing hospitals, but clinics whose therapeutic efficacy could be rationally studied and augmented. As an overall reorganization of the Charles-Nicolle Hospital was on the cards, they proposed to the authorities to attempt the experiment immediately and transform this hospital's neuropsychiatry service into a day clinic.

The architectural modifications were minimal and essentially involved putting handles on doors, removing the gratings, demoting means of constraint such as straightjackets and handcuffs, and a team of patients was tasked with demolishing the isolation units. The building was repainted and the hospital capacity was set at eighty beds: forty for men, forty for women. In the women's ward, a small space with six beds was reserved for children.

---

[6][The law that organized the involuntary commitment of mentally ill individuals in France.]

Acute problems arose with the personnel. The old personnel had adopted certain habits in which a repressive attitude was prevalent. As in a great number of asylums of the contemporary period, they considered the patients a source of bother and inconvenience in the clinic. As is usual, the original aim thus gets inverted: the patients, far from being the ultimate end of the clinics, were transformed into the enemies of the staff's tranquillity. These considerations are not specific, since the key critique that, for twenty years now, has been made against the asylum has precisely to do with the sadomasochistic relations that get gradually established between the orderlies and the patients.

The personnel, including five women and six men, were placed under the authority of a monitor. Courses were set up straightaway with the aim of eliminating old attitudes and suggesting behaviours in line with the new conception of the clinic. Early on some of the orderlies (male and female) revealed an inability to adjust quickly. In agreement with the doctors of the service, these staff members asked to be transferred and were replaced by young individuals who had received more extensive general training and who had first and foremost never come into contact with mentally ill patients. These new orderlies adopted a natural attitude toward the patients.

Daytime at the centre

Patients arrive from 7 am onwards. They come alone or accompanied by their family. Upon their arrival, the orderlies are already at their stations to welcome them. Each orderly is responsible for between six to eight patients. It never happens that patients change their orderly. The role of the latter is, first, to repeat certain technical gestures on a daily basis (taking the temperature, pulse, arterial tension), but above all to talk with each of his or her patients and to get informed about the patient's activities and thoughts between leaving the centre the previous day and returning. More specifically, orderlies are asked to inform themselves about the patient's sleep, about spouse relations in cases of marriage and about nightmares and dreams. Each morning upon the doctor's arrival, a report must be drawn up. The orderlies are asked to take a benevolent attitude, especially when the oneiric material provided is spectacularly anguishing. In such cases, the doctor is to be notified upon arriving at the service.

In principle, three days are devoted to the men's clinic, three days to the women's.[7] But very often, when the doctor is notified about an anxious patient, or if difficulties attained an unaccustomed acuity in the family setting the previous day, an intervention is immediately undertaken.

Two categories of psychotherapies take place in the service: the most numerous are the psychoanalytically inspired therapies; but there are also psychotherapies of support and explanation that mostly take their inspiration from Pavlovian theories of the second-signal system. In the latter case, the agent assigned to the patient generally attends the interview. As a rule, the agent must avoid interrogating the family in the patient's presence and must precisely avoid the parents' clumsiness – the agent is even asked not to question the parents about the patient's behaviour at all. Sometimes the patient is so inhibited that it is not possible to obtain any information about his or her activities outside the centre. In this case, we inquire with the parents.

The meal is served at the centre at the same hours as in the other hospital services, that is between 11:30 am and 12:30 pm. The afternoon is devoted to collective activities. This can involve dramatization, in which case the patients are assembled by their respective orderlies, who tell them a story while noting their projections or identifications; or a particular patient is solicited and asked to talk about his or her difficulties and in this case the other patients' reactions to these stated difficulties are noted (we will return to the interest of this method in the chapter on 'Psychotherapy'). Or it may involve making objects with the men or knitting, sewing, ironing or cooking with the women. Or it may involve initiation sessions during which patients are taught about care for babies, about using sewing machines and ironing.

At 5 pm the evening meal is served and at 5:30 the patients begin to leave the service. At 6 pm the service is closed. The centre is also closed on Sundays.

---

[7]The dearth of medical personnel considerably restricts the therapeutic activity of the service. For more than a year, eighty patients were without interns or assistants. The lone head of the unit has to take responsibility for the entire therapy.

Part-time hospitalization

It often happens that a patient is in a state requiring care, but that his or her material condition makes it impossible to leave a job or interrupt an activity. This is the case, for example, with cleaning ladies, students and travelling salesmen. In such cases, the patient may leave the service once treatment is finished. In this way, the problems seen in occupational therapy in asylums are resolved in the best possible fashion, since patients keep their contact with the milieu of their praxis and since the professional mechanisms are not liable to deteriorate. It seems not unrealistic to us to raise a second-order and seemingly important problem: could we not, as already exists in some countries, organize a night service from 6 pm onwards, one in which patients who are in specific social conditions (e.g. civil servants, primary school teachers, artisans) are able to receive treatment without thus having to interrupt their professional activities?

[Year 1958]

As stated above, the Neuropsychiatric Day Centre in Tunis opened its doors in May 1958. From May 1958 to December 1958, 345 patients were admitted, distributed as follows.[8] (Graphs 1 and 2).

Following the curve of the average period of stay (Graph 1), it can be noted that for the first month the average duration was fifty-three days, a figure that will not be reached again. The month of December, for example, saw the average duration of hospitalization reduced to twenty-six days. Both figures clearly indicate that the service's organization progressively improved.

Men are by far the most numerous patients and the low number of children pertains solely to the fact that at the start we wanted to concentrate on the adult segment of the patient population. We were gradually able to set up a space for children. As of 1959, children will be admissible in considerable numbers. The three hundred and forty-five hospitalized patients at the CNPJ during the

---

[8]The patients are admitted through outpatient consultation in neuropsychiatry at Charles-Nicolle Hospital. A neuropsychiatrist is on hand every day to ensure the consultation service.

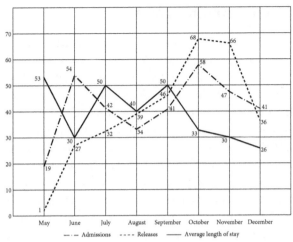

Graph 1 Movement of patients of the CNPJ (1958).

first six months of 1958 included: twelve Jews (six men, six women), nine Europeans (eight men, one woman), twenty-eight Algerian refugees (twenty men, eight women) and two hundred and ninety-six Tunisians.

Average patient age

Examining the diagram (Graph 2) we see that the majority of patients are between fifteen and thirty-five years of age, a peak of twenty and twenty-five years of age for men and women respectively. This curve is interesting, since it indicates that mental illnesses hatch during the period that internist doctors usually consider to be the least exposed to illnesses. Psychiatrists, for their part, mark this period as the time that an individual blossoms and during which a profession is chosen, a home created and children born. To be noted is the remarkable rareness of diseases pertaining to the postmenopausal period and the quasi-absence of senility disorders.

Family status

By taking into account the situations of patients depending upon whether they are single, married with children or married without children, certain observations can be made.So it is, for example, that

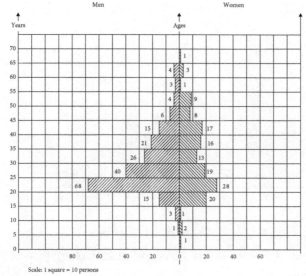

Men | Ages | Women

Graph 2 Patient age pyramid (1958).*

* Two hundred and two men, one hundred and thirty-five women, eight children (four boys, four girls), which is an average of 57.5 patients per month.

out of three hundred and forty-five patients, one hundred and sixty-two are single (one hundred and fifteen men, forty-seven women). The married patients with children are more numerous than the married patients without children. Thus we have one hundred and five married patients with children (fifty-four men, fifty-one women) and only twenty-eight married patients without children (fourteen men, fourteen women).

It is easy to see that the one hundred and fifteen single men are of marrying age, but do not have any work or else earn a salary that is so meagre that it is practically impossible for them to establish a home (Graph 3). Similarly, very often the married patients with children come into extremely difficult material conditions, which makes the problem of keeping and educating the children dramatic.Out of the two hundred and two men hospitalized during the six months of 1958, the petty artisans (weavers, sweets sellers, travelling vegetable sellers, etc.) number forty-one, the unemployed, thirty-nine. These comprise the graph's two peaks. The figures obtained corroborate a constant in the problematic of mental illness, namely that tomorrow's uncertainty

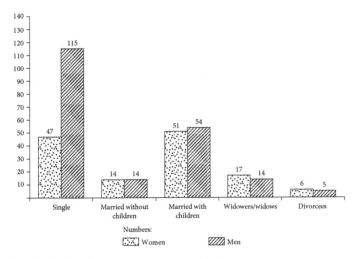

Graph 3 Family status comparative bar chart men-women (1958).

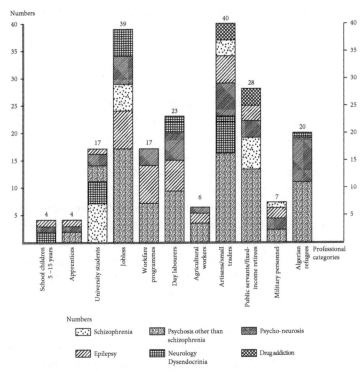

Graph 4 Economic status, men (diagnostics) (1958).

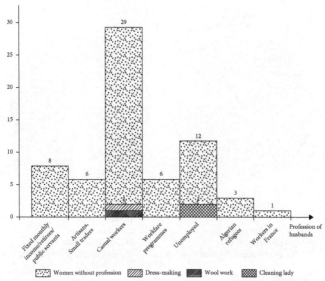

Graph 5 Economic status of female patients (husband's profession, or profession exercised by patient) (1958).

and material negligence foster the hatching of disruptions to an individual's equilibrium, and thus problems with harmonious group insertion. It is not inappropriate here to indicate that Algerian refugees were among the group. Their number, we shall see, increases considerably in 1959.

Economic situation of female patients

Very few of the women work. Out of thirty-five women, four work (two cleaning ladies, two homeworkers). Among the sixty-five married women, the majority are wives of day labourers and unemployed men (Graph 5).

Geographical situation

One hundred and ninety-five patients are originally from the town of Tunis, fifty-three from its surrounding suburbs and fifty-one from the shanty towns (Djebel Lahmar: sixteen; Ras Tabia: six; Melassine, Saïda-Manoubia: twenty-one; La Cagna: three; Le Borgel: five) (Graph 6).

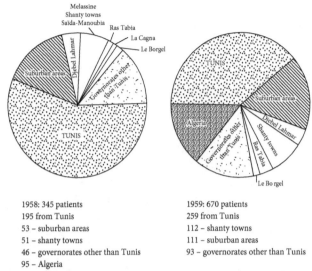

1958: 345 patients
195 from Tunis
53 – suburban areas
51 – shanty towns
46 – governorates other than Tunis
95 – Algeria

1959: 670 patients
259 from Tunis
112 – shanty towns
111 – suburban areas
93 – governorates other than Tunis

Graph 6 Geographical situation of patients (1958 and 1959).

It is occasionally possible for patients who live in other governorates to be housed with parents living in Tunis. There are forty-six in this category. Among the patients who live in Tunis, it would have been interesting to know whether they were born in Tunis or for how long they have been there; if they are there permanently or occasionally; if they come to work there or else to rest there. These details are very difficult to obtain and the question is one that we intend to take up at a later stage.

Diagnosis

Contrary to what might be thought, psychoses (schizophrenias, chronic hallucinatory psychoses, manias, melancolias, paranoias) are not the exception at the CNPJ. In fact, out of three-hundred-and-thirty-seven patients, we find one hundred and twenty-nine psychoses other than schizophrenia and thirty-four schizophrenias. Cases of psychoneurosis, conversion neurosis, anxiety hysteria, obsessional neurosis, sexual perversion, etc., amount to seventy-four. The relatively high number of epilepsies – forty-seven (see Graphs 4 and 7) – is notable.

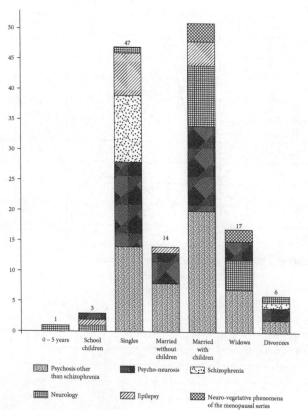

Graph 7 Diagnosis (women, 1958).

Legend:
- Psychosis other than schizophrenia
- Psycho-neurosis
- Schizophrenia
- Neurology
- Epilepsy
- Neuro-vegetative phenomena of the menopausal series

Year 1959

During the eleven months of 1959, 670 patients were admitted to the CNPJ. Progress in reducing the average duration of stay kept apace. We thus find an exceptional duration of fifteen days in the month of November. The same proportions that were measured in 1958 are to be found again this year. For two hundred and thirty-two women there were three hundred and twenty-two men. The large number of children hospitalized in 1959 is notable: one hundred and sixteen (sixty-nine boys and forty-seven young girls). The children are often sent by their schools or family owing to infantile encephalopathy, intellectual retardation, stammering, enuresis, etc. (Graph 8).

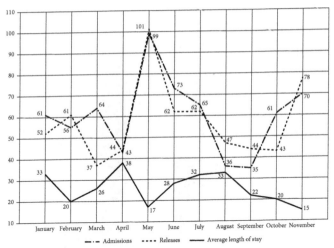

Graph 8 Patient movement, CNPJ (1959).

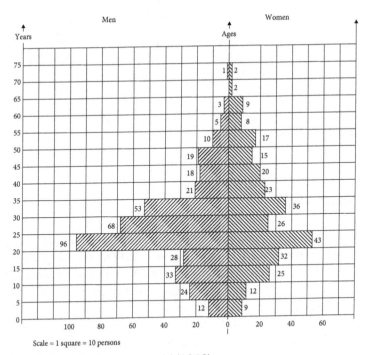

Scale = 1 square = 10 persons

Graph 9 Patient age pyramid (1959).

Average age

In 1959 we again find the same characteristics concerning the patients' ages: mental disorders appear between twenty and thirty-five years of age. The more one ages, the better one carries oneself. Perhaps this ought to be expressed differently: the older one becomes, the better able one is to put up with oneself (Graph 9).

Family status

In 1959, there were 274 single patients and 213 married patients with children. Married individuals without children, widows and divorcees comprised a small fraction of the clinic's population (Graph 10).

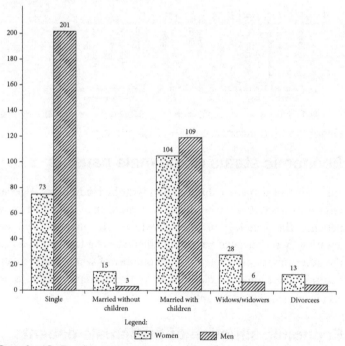

Graph 10 Family status, comparative bar chart men-women (1959).

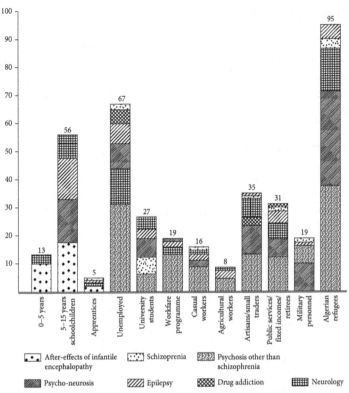

Graph 11 Economic status, men (diagnostics) (1959).

Economic status of the male patients

An important element of this bar chart is the high number of Algerian refugees (ninety-five), who comprised more than one sixth of all patients. The pathology of refugees, which is highly polyvalent and always very serious, will have to be the focus of a later work. As for the other rubrics, let's note the high number of school children and naturally the significant place taken by the unemployed and those exercising 'small jobs' (Graph 11).

Economic situation of the female patients

It can be observed that in general the women do not work. For obvious reasons, the only ones who do are widows and divorcees. Moreover, wives of unemployed men represent the largest proportion of hospitalized women (Graph 12).

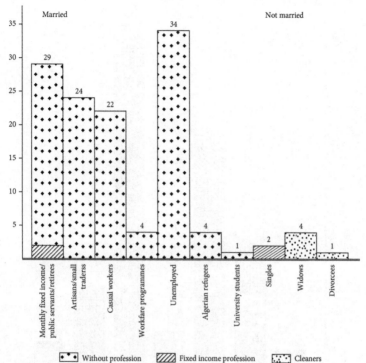

Graph 12 Economic status of female patients (profession of husband, or profession exercised by patient) (1959).

Geographical situation

The majority of hospitalized patients in the day service usually live in the town. Note, however, that contrary to what might be thought patients from the centre of Tunis are greater in number than those from the shanty towns. We also ought to note the large number in 1959 of Algerian refugees impaired with mental illness, a number that exceeds that of Tunisians from governorates other than Tunis (ninety-five as compared with ninety-three) (Graph 6).

Diagnosis

Let us remark the consistently high number of psychoneuroses and psychoses. In 1959, the service also saw numerous infantile encephalopathies and many neurological cases (Graphs 11 and 13).

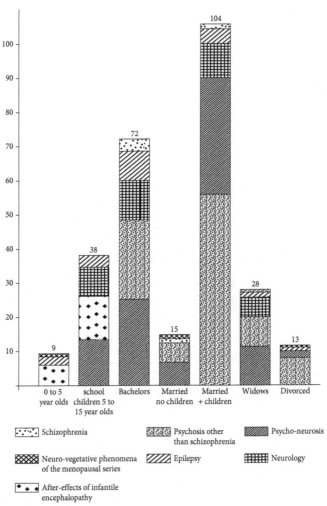

Graph 13 Diagnosis (women, 1959).

Therapeutic activity of the unit

Insulin therapy

Over the past seventeen months, one hundred and seventy-one patients were treated with insulin shock therapy: eighty-four sub-comas [(*choc humide*) modified insulin therapy)] and eighty-seven classic insulin coma therapies. The patients had an average of forty-five comas and thirty-five sub-comas.

From the practical viewpoint, insulin coma therapy in the day hospital presents some difficulties. For example, it is necessary to be extremely watchful at the start, since the patients often neglect to come on an empty stomach and consequently prove resistant to significant doses of insulin.[9] Sometimes, whereas the apportioned insulin dose was already very high, a patient might happen to come on an empty stomach one day, and such an incident must obviously be foreseen, whence the particular vigilance that must prevail among the staff in charge of this therapy. The patient must recover consciousness in all its clarity to enable him or her to leave the service alone and to return home when the time comes.

Another problem concerns coma relapses outside the hospital service. It must be said that these incidents were generally rare and always minor: four coma relapses occurred in 1958 and one in the eleven months of 1959. Parents were given instructions and no doctor had to be called. Patients are immediately administered sugar by the family's own care. In 1958, we had a rather serious incident, namely a cerebral oedema, which led us to keep the patient in the service overnight.

A key concern was the spectre of the month of Ramadan, during which patients were likely both to stay up too late, thus fatiguing the cortex, and to accumulate such sugar reserves that hypoglycaemic coma effectively became unattainable. In actual fact, we observed the following: the importance of the evening was such that the emotional factors and affectivity invested in evening gatherings largely made up for the aforementioned minor drawbacks.

Let's also note that the phenomenon of agitated awakenings with a high discharge of aggression, one classically observed in psychiatric hospitals, was never observed in the centre. In actual fact, it does not seem unrealistic to assert that patients were constantly aware of the 5.30 pm leaving time. In the atmosphere of the hospital, the personality cannot be abandoned, instead the concern to maintain control of

---

[9]This is a matter of genuine insulin shock therapy. As a guide, we push to the fifth degree the South American nomenclature. It is not rare among longstanding insulin-resistance schizophrenias to reach a dose of between 400 and 500 units of insulin.

oneself is constant. The lethargic, sluggish, obtuse and idle patients so commonly found in insulin shock therapies undertaken in asylums are nowhere to be found in day hospital settings.

Sleep and relaxation therapy

In each service, five individual rooms were allocated for sleep therapy. Upon arrival, the patient is served a copious meal totalling more than 1,200 calories. Once the meal is finished, the medication is taken. In principle, the patient then sleeps until 4:30 pm. Sleep therapy, then, lasts from 8:30 am to 4:30 pm with a quarter of an hour break at 12:30 pm. Between 4:30 and 5:30 the patient is taken in hand and woken up. A variable dose of neuroleptics is given to the patient for the night.

A psychotherapeutic interview is conducted with the doctor once or twice a week, immediately after the morning meal and before sleeping. This therapy lasts from two to three weeks. In less serious cases, relaxation therapy is introduced, predominantly with the aid of neuroleptics. Here again, the same principle is observed and the duration of the therapy is roughly the same as for sleep therapy.

Neurology

As Charles-Nicolle Hospital has no neurology service, all the patients impaired by nervous system affections were treated at the Neuropsychiatric Day Centre: multiple sclerosis, general paresis, tumours, etc. We performed – and we think this an extremely interesting experiment – more than seventy gas encephalographies.[10] All the patients left the service in the afternoon and then returned the following day. This method of investigation was used on men, women and children.

Since we were able to perform pneumoencephalographies, we clearly also managed to perform a considerable number of lumbar punctures without incident. In this way, several cases of cerebral tumor (thirteen) were diagnosed at the centre.

---

[10][A heavy and complicated technique that was abandoned in the 1970s. From the outset Fanon wanted to perform all the treatments then available at the CNPJ.]

Seismotherapy

Out of the 1,000 patients admitted to the centre over these seventeen months, seventy-two were treated via seismotherapy. In general, we used simple electroshocks exclusively to unblock patients or to break an anxiogenic circuit that proved too painful. The overall average of sessions never exceeded three. Few incidents are to be reported; among others, a shoulder dislocation.

Psychotherapy

The main guideline of our therapeutic interventions is that consciousness is to be affected as little as possible. Whence the rarity of narcoanalysis or amphetamine shocks. We do not believe in the curative value of dissolutions of consciousness. The service is oriented toward awareness, verbalization, explanation and strengthening the ego.

Dramatization sessions: a story is told in which a patient presents his or her difficulties and each patient in the group studied is urged to give his or her opinion. Very often a criticism arises, which, in cases of mirror identification, can sometimes take on the appearance of a maniacal accusation.

This brings to mind the term social drama,[11] with the difference that we strive to avoid fictional situations. In this way priority is given to the patients' biographies as presented by those concerned. This presentation during which the patient shows, comments upon and takes up his or her responses to conflicts, provokes the listeners to take a stance, make criticisms and express reservations. Correlatively, the patient tries to justify him- or herself through his or her behaviour, which reintroduces the priority of reason over fantasmatic and imaginary attitudes.

We also use the psychoanalytic method at the Neuropsychiatric Day Centre. Its applications are not original: anxiety-hysteria, neurotic depression, sexuality disorders (impotence, vaginism, homosexuality), etc. As the patients do not pay the doctor, the transference neurosis is especially atypical. Also, we often intervened to activate a counter-transference dynamism. The rhythm is the

---

[11][In the sense of the psychodrama techniques of Romanian-born American psychiatrist Jacob L. Moreno (1889–1974), whom Merleau-Ponty cites.]

same: one session daily, except Sunday. The length of a session is forty minutes.

The Neuropsychiatric Day Centre in Tunis, established sixteen months ago, is the only institution of this sort on the African continent. For a hospital capacity of eighty beds, more than 1,000 patients have been admitted. Less than one percent of the patients were directed to the psychiatric hospital of La Manouba. Though the majority of the patients are prepsychotics, a relatively high number of authentic psychoses was observed. No medical or medico-legal accidents were reported.

26 DAY HOSPITALIZATION IN PSYCHIATRY: VALUE AND LIMITS. PART TWO: DOCTRINAL CONSIDERATIONS

Frantz Fanon and Charles Geronimi, 1959[1]

The Neuropsychiatric Day Centre of Tunis (CNPJ)

In the history of psychiatry, the doctrine of assistance to the mentally ill, as well as the conception of illness in its causality and in its dynamism, has changed as our knowledge about mental disease has simultaneously become clearer. Assistance was first conceived as protection: protection of society against the patient through internment; and protection of the mad person against himself by means of the asylum, which offered the patient a calming setting, closed on itself and in which a life could unfold without crises, without dramas – which offered a calmer existence, but also a less and less socialized one. Assistance then aimed at being therapeutic

---

[1]*La Tunisie médicale*, vol. 37, no 10, 1959, pp. 713–32.

and preventative. Legislation was modernized, biological methods were introduced, open clinics were established and local clinics multiplied in number.

Still, one modality of assisting and providing therapy to people with mental illness emerged a few years ago and appeared sufficiently encouraging to us to implement an experiment in Tunisia. This concerns the day hospital method as inaugurated by the Anglo-Saxon school.

The Neuropsychiatric Day Centre of Tunis was established as part of the Charles-Nicolle General Hospital. The patients are able to enter from 7 am on, receive their treatments and return to their homes at 6 pm. Two characteristics thus distinguish the Neuropsychiatric Day Hospital (CNPJ) from other psychiatric establishments: on the one hand, its annexation to a general hospital, on the other, its concept of day hospitalization.

On the level of doctrine, and given the radically biological and physico-chemical orientation of studies on the nervous system, we think it essential that psychiatric services be attached to a general hospital. The psychiatrist is no longer isolated, he is no longer the alienist and relatively alienated doctor of psychiatric prehistory. The psychiatric doctor benefits in the exercise of his speciality from the material infrastructure of the general hospital, including: radiology services, biochemical and anatomo-pathology laboratories … Similarly, the psychiatrist maintains frequent contacts with other colleagues in internal medicine or surgery. As he is no longer shut away in the asylum with the 'insane', the psychiatrist ceases to sport, in the eyes of his colleagues, that fantasmatic, mysterious and overall slightly disquieting demeanour.

In the eyes of the patients too – and this point appears important to us – he remains a doctor like any other. Hospitalization in the neuropsychiatry service of the general hospital loses the major part of its dramatic aspect. The reintroduction of psychiatry into medicine strongly corrects deeply ingrained prejudices in public opinion and transforms the mad into a patient.

However, the major aspect of the day hospital consists in its giving total freedom to the patient. It breaks resoundingly with the relative and sometimes absolute coercion that internment comes to have. It is true that the open service option also provides the patient with this freedom (the possibility of leaving the hospital). But it should be recognized that this freedom is most often formal. All the doctors working in an open service have been tempted (and have succumbed to the temptation) to refuse to discharge a patient who, while clearly not cured and intolerant of hospitalization, had demanded his freedom.[2]

It is clear, and our experience confirms it every day, that for a mental patient semi-hospitalization, which involves the possibility to return of an evening to one's parents, one's friends, one's world of relations, is more easily accepted than complete hospitalization.

We see that all these attitudes involve the ever so crucial problem of the awareness of the illness in psychiatry. Internment signifies more or less explicitly to the patient that he must give up the fight, that he must leave it up to us, that the struggle has become unequal and that he requires, literally, tutelage and protection. Day hospitalization, on the contrary, is offered as a transient support, as a momentary reinforcement of the personality or extended visit to the therapist. Relations between the patient and therapist are normalized. The blackmail that the medical body and orderlies bring to bear on the patient, wittingly or not, no longer occurs and can no longer occur.

The patient no longer experiences his possible discharge as the product of the doctor's benevolence. The *a minima* master/slave, prisoner/gaoler dialectic created in internment, or in the threat thereof, is radically broken. In the setting of the day hospital, the doctor-patient encounter forever remains an encounter between two freedoms. That condition is necessary for all therapy, but especially in psychiatry.

In any phenomenology in which the major alterations of consciousness are left aside, mental illness is presented as a veritable pathology of freedom. Illness situates the patient in a world in which his or her freedom, will and desires are constantly broken by obsessions, inhibitions, countermands, anxieties. Classical hospitalization considerably limits the patient's field of activity, prohibits all compensations, all movement, restrains him within the closed field of the hospital and condemns him to exercise his freedom in the unreal world of fantasy. So it is not surprising that the patient feels free only in his opposition to the doctor who has withheld him.

---

[2]One of the authors opened the only open service in Algeria and headed it for two years. French legislation applied to Algeria does allow, on medical decision, the transformation of an open placement into a closed placement.

All psychiatrists know that the most difficult patients to treat, that is to say, to maintain at hospital, are those at the beginning of their illness, those who think they can get through it themselves, who have not given up. Objectively speaking, patients who do not readily accept hospitalization are precisely the least disorganized ones – the neurotics, the small paranoiacs, those with minor delusions. By contrast, the day approach is generally rejected by patients with an inactive ego, by those who are completely submerged in delusion and who demand total care with insistence.[3]

Keeping to the plane of the patient's lived experience, day hospitalization presents some original features. In a normal psychiatric service, the therapeutic action never goes beyond 6 pm. Once the medicines are administered, once the afternoon collective psychotherapy sessions are terminated, the patient is left to his own devices. This feeling of being left alone is acute in the evening after the follow-up inspection of the assistant or the interns, right as the orderlies, who are already in their civilian clothing, quickly give their instructions to the night watchmen. Outside life filters into the hospitals along with the staff's plans: a film in the evening, an evening gathering at a friends' place, a rendez-vous at a café. Outside life assumes an increased density in the patient's eyes, who remains confined in the silence and the boredom of large rooms. This experience is already painful enough for a patient immobilized by a fracture, typhoid or asystole. For the mental patient, who literally only feels immobilized by the coercion of the establishment, protest, an attitude of revolt against hospitalization, arises several times a day.

The social-therapy experiment was attempted in order to diminish this enormous tension and maintain a certain degree of sociability in the patient. The creation of a neo-society within the psychiatric hospital, the transformation of the hospital into a society with a multiplicity of ties, duties and possibilities so that patients can take on roles and functions, constitutes, it should not be doubted, a decisive turn in our understanding of madness. We used this method with a particular intensity at Blida.[4] Within the newly established society,

---

[3][In his dissertation Fanon distinguished between the positions of Ey and Lacan in the following manner: delusion is not creativity but the absolute passivity of the ego.]
[4]See [Jacques] Azoulay's dissertation, *La Socialthérapie en milieu nord-africain*, Algiers, 1956.

we see a mutation of the old symptomatology in its pure, desocialized state, and progressively invaded by the motor sphere (stereotypies, subintrant agitations, catatonization …), such as we see in asylums. On the contrary, the patient has a need to verbalize, to explain, to explain himself, to take a position. He maintains an investment in an objectal world, which acquires a new density. Social therapy wrests patients from their fantasies and obliges them to confront reality on a new register.

Certainly, that confrontation remains pathological since it is developed most often on the plane of the imaginary or the symbolic. But the doctor can study, with benefits for the treatment's dynamics, mechanisms of projection, identifications, instinctual inhibitions … The doctor can witness and follow the ego in its efforts to maintain its unity and its coherence, which have already heavily regressed.

It is necessary, however, to acknowledge that with institutional-therapy [sic], we create fixed institutions, strict and rigid settings, and schemas that are rapidly stereotyped. In the neo-society, there are no inventions; there is no creative, innovative dynamic. There is no veritable shake-up, no crises. The institution remains that 'corpse-like cement' of which Mauss speaks.[5]

---

[5][Mauss is an always significant reference in Fanon's work. This can already be seen in the 1954 article written with Jacques Azoulay on 'Social therapy in a ward of Muslim men: Methodological difficulties' (see *above*, p. 205). This article is clearly influenced by *Essai sur le don*, which stamps the entire Fanonian analysis of culture, whether dynamic or dead. It is likely that Fanon discovered Mauss through Gurvitch, several of whose books Fanon had in his library. Mauss wrote: 'Thus these are more than themes, more than the bare bones of institutions, more than complex institutions, even more than systems of institutions divided, for example, into religion, law, economy, etc. They are whole 'entities', entire social systems, the functioning of which we have attempted to describe. We have looked at societies in their dynamic or physiological state. We have not studied them as if they were motionless, in a static state, or as if they were corpses. Even less have we decomposed and dissected them, producing rules of law, myths, values, and prices. It is by considering the whole entity that we could perceive what is essential, the way everything moves, the living aspect, the fleeting moment when society, or men, become sentimentally aware of themselves and of their situation in relation to others. In this concrete observation of social life lies the means of discovering new facts, which we are only beginning dimly to perceive. In our opinion, nothing is more urgent or more fruitful than this study of total social facts'. (Marcel Mauss, *The Gift: The form and reason for exchange in archaic societies*, trans. W.D. Halls, with a Foreword by Mary Douglas, London and New York, NY: Routledge, 2002, p. 102.)]

Of course institutional-therapy is far from being useless. In a large psychiatric complex like Blida (close to 1,800 patients) or like Razi Hospital (Tunis), which has a population of 1,300 patients, social therapy fights efficaciously against the progressive disaggregation of the personality. In the asylum milieu social therapy is indispensable, for it has the advantage of preserving the patients' socialized dimension. It contributes actively to avoiding chronicization, asylum putrefaction[6] and patient decline. But it rarely cures. It reactivates delusional and hallucinatory processes. It provokes new dramatizations and enables the doctor to understand better what may have 'happened outside'. But the inert character of this pseudo-society, its strict spatial limitation, the restricted number of cogs and – why hide it – the lived experience of internment-imprisonment, considerably limits the curative and disalienating value of social therapy.

This is why we think today that the veritable social-therapeutic milieu is and remains concrete society itself.[7]

Patients and their illnesses in the day hospital

On the level of professional relations, the patient hospitalized in a day centre can be likened to an employee off work. On a practical level, the patient returns home at the typical hours at which the workshop or factory closes. On the way home the patient may also happen to meet fellow workers returning home from the building site on the bus or suburban train. These encounters are obviously fruitful, since the call of the professional milieu, once the patient has been taken in hand by the psychiatric institution, always proves to be stronger than its negative valence in the pre-hospital period.[8] The life of the building

---

[6][On the history of the expression 'asylum putrefaction', see *above*, p. 296.]

[7][As in the article written with Asselah on agitation, *above*, p. 289, Fanon here takes a distance from the position of Tosquelles.]

[8][The notions of emotional valence and, below, of dynamic or ambivalent relations vis-a-vis the milieu stems from the work of American psychologist Kurt Lewin (1890–1947), who was introduced into France by his French colleague Paul Guillaume (1878–1962), several of whose works Fanon had in his library. In *L'Être et le Néant*, Sartre refers in detail to the Lewinian concept of 'hodological space': 'The space which is

site, the proximity to co-workers which the patient experienced as threatening prior to the psychiatrist's intervention, progressively lose their traumatizing character; and the professional milieu no longer becomes an arena in which liberty is perpetually trampled, but instead a place for exercising and deepening freedom: one understands that with Ey the French school came to define madness as a pathology of freedom.[9]

The patient who leaves the day centre reassumes his automatisms at the hospital door. Thus he continues to be present at periodical meetings at the café, mosque or political cell. After 6 pm the patient is taken in the complex game of sociopersonal coordinates, which delimit his insertion in the world. He thus takes his place in the card game twice weekly, or plays his role in the political cell. The mother of a family remains in constant relation to her sites of activity. On the way back home, she sees, in turn, the grocer, the butcher, the newspaper seller. She continues to occupy her place. Her home does not present itself as fundamentally overturned, but as provisionally shaken.

On Sunday, family reunions are kept up and outings to the countryside to see the grandparents are continued. Cinema, theatre, sports events – all continue to inform the patient's personality by inciting in it affective reactions, options and dynamic relations.

As we see, no cut occurs here. The therapist does not find himself face to face with someone who is excluded, isolated. On the contrary, the psychiatrist is confronted with a personality whose relations with the world are ongoing and active. The patient continues to be engaged with society, family and a professional milieu. No longer is the patient a patient with severed antennas. We know that, in many psychiatric institutions, patients are confined to a ward and legally

---

originally revealed to me is hodological space; it is furrowed with paths and highways; it is instrumental and it is the *site* of tools. Thus the world from the moment of the upsurge of my For-itself is revealed as the indication of acts to be performed; these acts refer to other acts, and those to others, and so on' (trans. Hazel E. Barnes, New York, NY: Washington Square Press, 1992, p. 322). The idea of a world as a space of acts to be accomplished is essential to the phenomenology of *Peau noire, masques blancs*.]

[9][In the fourth *Étude psychiatrique*, on 'The notion of "mental illness"' Ey writes precisely: 'Psychiatry is a pathology of freedom; it is medicine applied to diminutions of freedom. All psychosis, all neurosis is essentially a somatosis, which alters the activity of personal integration (consciousness and personality)' (p. 77)].

deprived of visits for fifteen days, being solely required to present their symptoms to the psychiatrist.

At the day hospital, the psychiatrist is confronted with an illness as lived by a patient, a personality in crisis within a present environment. This makes for a concrete, dynamic, in vivo examination of the illness. Ambivalence is, then, not only a disorder of affectivity *in abstracto*, isolated as a symptom in a delusion or in the course of an interview. Instead, it is a manifest and perceptible ambivalence that tears to shreds the synthetic unity of the person and the milieu every day.

Symptomatology presents itself dialectically and the psychiatrist acts and thinks only dialectically. Descriptive semiology, so crucial in the asylum period, moves into the background, thus fostering an existential and no longer nosological approach.[10] We see the patient live through his illness, develop reactional formations, inhibitions, and identifications in his natural setting. And on the basis of these ego conducts we can come to a dynamic understanding of the structure involved, the indigence of the ego, the assaults it has to contend with; in short, on the basis of this pathological existence we can decide on the place and the type of our action. But what we decide dialectically includes all the elements of the situation. There is no pointillist approach to different symptoms, but a global tackling of a form of existence, a structure, a personality engaged in current conflicts.

At the psychiatric hospital, we can permit the patient to hold onto his personal clothing, his tie, his belt; in some cases, we can allow him his safety razor, some money, his wedding ring … At the day hospital, the problem is inverted. The institution, in fact, has no hold over the patient's freedom, over his immediate appearing. Through the simple confrontation between the patient and the institution,

---

[10][This analysis echoes many of Fanon's other clinical and theoretical notes over this period, further attesting to which is an interesting hand-written page, without date (1955? 1956?), which figures in the Fanon archives at IMEC (FNN 1.6), in which the following four fragments can be read, each separated by a line: 'Mental disorders, far from being akin to common clinical entities, instead move away from normal thinking.' 'There is an evolution of nervous functions: those of the instinctivo-affective unconscious, those of the functions of the real/form [illegible term].' 'If the *djinn* in its aggressive form appears in the course of mental illness, this is due to an ambivalence toward it.' 'A patient's delusional ideas are this patient. They express his beliefs and his personality.']

there is no calling into question of forms of being. There is, by contrast, a progressive calling into question of forms of existence, of existential contents. The patient hospitalized at the CNPJ shaves every morning in his kitchen or bathroom with his razor, chooses his tie, comes close to a precipice, crosses streets, skirts the lake … The woman hospitalized at the CNPJ, washes herself, brushes her hair, makes herself up in her shack (*gourbi*) and among her family each morning … The fact that the patients can take things into their own hands, whether through dressing, hairstyling or, above all, the secrecy of an entire part of the day spent outside the hospital setting, reinforces and in any case maintains their personalities, in contrast with the process of dissolutive integration that occurs in a psychiatric hospital and that opens the way to phantasms of bodily fragmentation or the crumbling of the ego.[11]

M. Klein and S. Ferenczi, among others, have sufficiently indicated to us the importance of the care for one's own body as a mechanism for avoiding anxiety. Internment breaks the patient's narcissism, crucifies him in his hedonistic attempts and engages him in traumatizing fashion on the path of regression, danger and anguish.

From another perspective, day hospitalization enables us to analyse the particular attitude of the family group as regards the patient and mental illness. With the psychiatric hospital, the family has a strong tendency to disengage,[12]and to exclude the patient. And though the familial rejection is more about the pathology, the illness, does the patient not nonetheless experience this decision as an authentic condemnation of his essence, of his truth? By rejecting the pathology, by disowning the illness, the family declares its non-recognition of that excrescence. The family decides to misjudge one of its members and interns him. Family unity is thus broken. Well, is not the question that the illness supports one about the foundation of being qua subject? Who am I, ultimately? Is that not the nagging question that the mental patient repeats to us at multiple levels and on different registers? And if the family, in its decisive response, signifies to the patient that it no longer identifies him,

---

[11][This passage can be likened to the famous analyses on bodily fragmentation under the clinical gaze of the racist in *Black Skin, White Masks*, p. 90.]
[12]This proves, on the phenomenological level, that if the patient flees society, then from a certain stage of evolution on this society will no longer try to hold on to him.

that it no longer recognizes him, that it participates in an essence fundamentally different to his, how many disintegrations become possible and what numberless bridges then open up to fantasies and regressions!

Day hospitalization enables the family to continue the battle of unity. It provides the family with the means to avoid amputation. It enables the patient to remain in the familial body, to take his or her place in it and to be ever a bearer of meanings, a pole of activities, a dynamic element within the familial unit. Day hospitalization makes it possible for the therapist to experience the family concretely as a normative value. And the therapist, each day, really does rely on the family, as the site of all mediations.

'The vertiginous phenomena of being discharged', the spectacular relapses, the difficulties with adaptation are, as one sees, avoided; since not only has the patient not broken with his milieu but the therapy has unfolded precisely by taking into account the multi-relational reality of the ill individual.

The conflict's presence

The day hospital approach presumes and renders explicit a general theory of the dynamics of mental illness. If the psychiatric symptom attests to the submersion of the ego by instinctual, abnormally vehement forces; if the illness is the manifestation of a conflictual existence without hope, then the tendency is strong to remove the patients from the conflict's conditions of birth and activity. The conflict's pathogenic character is privileged. With internment, we witness a genuine thingification of the conflict. And therefore of the patient. By raising the asylum wall between the patient and the outside condition, one of the most essential elements in the genesis of a personality, which postulates that the conflict is the patient, is magically denied. It is impossible to scotomize for a long time the fact that the conflictual situation is the conclusion of the uninterrupted dialectic of the subject and the world. The event is thus systematically insisted upon and history minimized. At issue is clearly not biography, or anamnesis, but instead the subject's history insofar as at the level of successive integrations it contains the conflict and the elements of its overcoming.

An ill brain cannot return to health by denying reality. Internment diminishes the violence of the conflict, the toxicity of reality. But the cure – the ordered calling into question of the established pathological structures – must proceed precisely at the core of the syncopated dialogue established between the overall personality and its environment. Action upon reality – and the patient is one of the elements of reality – is unifying. It cannot proceed satisfactorily in a scattered, disorderly manner. The patient hospitalized in a psychiatric establishment sees the symptoms disappear, witnesses their attenuation, but these symptoms remain foreign, poorly understood, scandalous. They are not appropriated and thematized. We remain indefinitely on the level of magic.

But, it will be said: are we not essentially dealing here with a description of psychiatric therapy in a private practice? Is the day hospital, in neuropsychiatry, not simply a modality of out-patient therapies?

We reply resoundingly in the negative. In actual fact, day hospital patients maintain limited contact with the conditions of the conflict. The therapist controls the action of the conflict, interposing between the pathogenic social messages or the fantasmatic substrates the stamp of day hospitalization. The duration of the conflict's action is diminished and the ego is reinforced with a view towards imminent and daily confrontations. Nearly all the hospitalized patients were treated previously, whether as private clients, or in the various neuropsychiatry local clinics. With day hospitalization, the neurotic kernel can be tackled on the existential level and at the same time the personality effectuates its restructurations, its updating.

The Tunis centre

Our experience in Tunis confirmed these theoretical claims and enabled us to specify the very broad limits in which the day hospitals can have real efficacy. The Tunis centre was created nearly two years ago. More than 1,200 patients were hospitalized in it over the course of that period. The facility is distributed into two sections: forty men and forty women. We admit all nosological categories, from stammering to delusional erotomania, including schizophrenia and attempted suicides.

The absence of a neurological clinic at Charles-Nicolle Hospital meant that, going on the same principle, we were obliged to admit neurological patients: multiple sclerosis in the early stages; early-onset multiple sclerosis, suddenly emergent epilepsy where the etiology required specifying, aggravated or poorly monitored cases of Parkinson's all have come through the CNPJ. Each time a tumoral process was suspected, a pneumoencephalography was performed. Close to seventy patients were injected with gas, either for a likely tumor or for pneumo-shock. In this way, twenty tumors were diagnosed, and a case of pantophobic anxiety and one of secondary delusion with dementia abated spectacularly. No incident was reported and patients who received between 100 to 150 cm^3 of air in the morning were able to leave calmly at 5 pm.

The admitted cases of schizophrenia, a majority of them paranoid, were treated through classical insulin therapy. In these cases we did not perform subcoma, but instead genuine comas which in certain cases attained the fifth degree of the South American school. Treatment started at 7:30 am and patients were woken up at 12 pm, in accordance with the usual technique. They remained under medical surveillance throughout the afternoon, participated in collective activities and in psychotherapy sessions. In the evening, they returned home. Their families received all the necessary instructions in case a coma might resume and were given a telephone number to use in case of emergencies.[13] Though more than one hundred patients were treated with insulin shock therapy, only one schizophrenic, who proved resistant to insulin, suffered two resumptions of nocturnal coma but they were complication free.

At the CNJP all the various psychiatric therapies are generally practiced. We insist particularly on group or individual psychotherapies. Hence, we formed groups of between six to eight patients who assembled in the afternoon. Each patient presents his or her difficulties in turn and each member of the group is asked to give an opinion on the attitudes adopted by that patient

---

[13]The family is told of the reasoning behind the therapeutic decision, the operational mechanism of the treatment, and its role in the treatment. This explaining seems to us to play an important role insofar as it introduces the familial constellation into the therapy dynamic. Similarly, a care card is given to the patient for the time of the treatment that indicates the daily insulin doses he will be administered. This care card is similar to those diabetics have.

toward these difficulties. Thus for each patient, and on the basis of always concrete and lived experiences, the different mechanisms of projection, of identification, and so on, are studied.

Along with these group psychotherapies, individual psychotherapies were carried out daily, including everything from commonplace so-called support psychotherapy to the psychoanalytic cure, as well as psychotherapies of psychoanalytic inspiration. In the psychoanalytic treatment, we practice appeasement, we foster fantasy reconstruction and, as a rule, adopt an active attitude in Ferenczi's sense.

While the day hospital may comprise a remarkable therapeutic instrument, cases still arise in which this option proves insufficient or inapplicable. These are the cases in which organic involvement in the mental illness is massive, dominant, cases in which serious therapeutic problems arise. At stake here are primarily acute, maniacal or confusional psychoses, which require a veritable emergency therapy and constant medical monitoring.[14] Besides, thanks to the progress of chemotherapy, the time spent in complete hospitalization can be considerably reduced and very shortly thereafter the patient can be taken into care by the day hospital.

This is also the case with the acute flashes marking the onset of serious psychosis, as for instance with schizophrenia; *delirium tremens* with its biological disturbance also eludes the day hospital, as do organic dementias. Lastly, the day hospital is not suitable for patients whose active delusions lead to dangerous aggressive reactions and of course for patients who are subject to police measures, medical-legal cases.

In this way, a whole sector of psychiatry escapes the day hospital, a quite considerable sector that commonly supplies a sizeable contingent of the psychiatric hospital's clientele. If we put aside the problem of dementias, which despite all efforts still can only be dealt with in asylum-type assistance, it can be said that all the other cases that are *a priori* excluded from the day hospital can easily undergo diurnal hospitalization after the disappearance of acute symptoms. In addition, the day hospital option raises another problem, namely that of patients who live too far from the hospital complex and are unable to make the

---

[14]However, several colibacillary confusional or postpartum psychoses were also treated at the CNPJ.

trip there and back every day. Similarly, it is important to note that economic or physiological poverty prohibits this type of hospitalization given the trips it involves.

So if the aim is to increase the number of psychiatric or neuropsychiatric services within general hospitals – and this is the aim toward which every plan to combat mental illness must tend – a solution ought to be found that overcomes the drawbacks of the day hospital while conserving this method, which we consider ideal. Many arrangements are possible by taking into account including everything from: for example, the *département* psychiatric hospitals can be transformed into psychiatric clinics, able to accommodate acute psychiatric cases. A mixed method or option could also be envisioned, wherein a certain proportion of beds in the psychiatric clinic were reserved for day hospitalization, with the other proportion going to full-time hospitalization. In this case, to avoid transforming the day hospital into an ordinary open service, strict legislation may need to be envisaged, limiting, for instance, fulltime hospitalization to geographically remote patients and restricting the duration of hospitalization of acute cases. These are only some examples and others can easily be imagined. In any case, it is at all costs necessary to avoid the creation of those monsters that are traditional psychiatric hospitals.

Conclusion

Our Tunisian experiment, which has been ongoing for more than twenty months now, has enabled us to verify the well-foundedness of the theoretical tenets of day hospitalization in psychiatry. Both on the therapeutic level as well as on the prophylactic one, the CNPJ of the Charles-Nicolle Hospital has proven its efficacy: the high number of patients treated (more than 1,200) and the shortened average duration of stay (twenty-five days) speak for themselves and require no commentary.

Moreover, our experiment proves that this technique, which first emerged in countries with high economic development, could be transplanted in a so-called underdeveloped country and lose nothing of its value. Day hospitalization is by far the most adequate form of psychiatric assistance for mental illness, the one best adapted to modern discoveries on the etiology of mental disorders. The multiplication of small psychiatric clinics annexed to general hospitals, in which the largest part ought to be reserved for day hospitalization, seems to us the basis for any plan to build a country's psychiatric amenities.[15] A few rare autonomous psychiatric hospitals can be established on the proviso of being reserved for a specific category of mental patients who are absolutely unable to receive psychiatric treatment under the open clinic or day hospital model. In any case, these hospitals ought to be limited in number and reduced in terms of capacity; it seems presently absurd to create psychiatric complexes of more than two hundred beds.

Lastly, very strict legislation must be established, guaranteeing the patient a maximum of freedom by removing all the carceral and coercive aspects of internment.

---

[15][Beyond a mere report and assessment of the CNPJ, this text already lays the foundations for a public health policy for mental illnesses.]

27 THE MEETING BETWEEN SOCIETY AND PSYCHIATRY

Frantz Fanon's course on social psychopathology at the Institut des hautes études in Tunis. Notes taken by Lilia Ben Salem, Tunis, 1959–1960[1]

Introduction

By Lilia Ben Salem

This course of lectures was given by Doctor Frantz Fanon for students enrolled in the bachelor programme in sociology and psychology as part of a social psychology diploma during the academic year 1959–1960. At the time I was a first-year student doing a bachelor of sociology. Keenly interested in Fanon's work and this course, I kept the notes that I had taken without rereading them. Years later, as a homage to Fanon was being prepared which I could not attend, I spoke of this text to a colleague and friend from the University of Oran, Abdelkader Djeghloul,

---

[1][A first edition of this text was published by the University of Oran, as part of a series titled 'Études et recherches sur la psychologie en Algérie', CRIDSSH (undertaken with the cooperation of the ONRS and APW in Oran), 1984. It was revised in September 2013 by Lilia Ben Salem, professor of sociology at the University of Tunis, who kindly offered to write a new introduction to her notes, for which we are very grateful (she unfortunately passed away on 28 January 2015). Prof. Frej Stambouli, who also attended Fanon's lectures and knew Prof. Ben Salem very well, confirmed the accuracy

and sent him my notes after having reread them and typed them up.[2] I was rather reluctant, no longer knowing whether they were complete, truly faithful to Frantz Fanon's discourse, whether I had missed some lectures ... I nevertheless recalled that I had been very attentive and that Frantz Fanon had expressed himself clearly, making a clear distinction between the course properly speaking, which I had transcribed, and his commentaries; I had not thought that they would be published and did not know that Oran University had already done so. Here I will try to evoke the context in which, in the wake of the country's independence, the Institute of Social Sciences chose to focus on the problems of Tunisia, and to some extent of the Maghreb, in its process of construction.

Tunisia regained its independence in March 1956. During the years 1956 and 1957, it consolidated its sovereignty in a majority of domains: it set up a Constituent Assembly; formed a government led by Habib Bourguiba; Tunisified the interior and exterior security apparatus (18 April 1956); reinstated the Foreign Affairs Ministry (3 May 1956); created a new administrative apparatus with fourteen appointed regional governors; Tunisified the administration; instituted a Tunisian army (1 July 1956); reformed the judiciary system around the principles of secularization, unification and Tunisification (3 August, 17 August and 25 September 1956); and handed over radio transmission to the Tunisian, civil status code (18 July 1957) ... A vast

---

of these notes. He remarked, as several other witnesses did, that in addition to the students enrolled in the course, the whole of Tunis came to listen to Fanon, including some well-known Algerian militants who were in Tunis at the time (correspondence of February 2016).]

[2][Here is the foreword to the 1984 edition, by Abdelkader Djeghloul:

The publication of these notes from Frantz Fanon's lectures, which Mrs Lilia Ben Salem was so kind to entrust to us, presents a threefold interest. (1) It constitutes a modest contribution by the CRIDSSH to the 'homages' and 'rereadings' of Fanon which accompanied the twentieth anniversary of his death. (2) On the documentary level, this text is useful insofar as it reveals an aspect of Fanon's social practice, one that is often unsung: his teaching. If Fanon was a psychiatrist, a political man, a journalist and an essayist, he was also a teacher. During his Tunisian period, and in parallel with his other activities, he lectured at the University of Tunis. (3) At the level of Fanonian thought, embryos of analysis are naturally to be found that were to be developed in *Les Damnés de la terre*. But its interest resides above all in the explicit definition, probably made necessary by pedagogical practice, of his relationship to the categories of psychiatry, sociotherapy and psychoanalysis, categories that fully determine, if implicitly, the writing of his central work.]

educational reform was begun in 1958 (Law of 4 November 1958), concerning middle and upper school.

Tunis University was born later, with the decree of 31 March 1960. An École normale supérieure had been created to train secondary teachers in October 1956. But higher education, or rather an embryo of higher education, was still carried out by the Institut des hautes études, which depended on the French universities. Students would begin their studies at the Institut des hautes études, and complete them at a French university. This was the context in which a bachelor degree in sociology was established in 1959. Students in the humanities prepared their general literary studies in Tunis (foundation year); some first bachelor degrees were created after 1956, notably in Arabic, history and geography. In 1958, the first diploma for a philosophy bachelor was set up, the ethics and sociology diploma. This initiative corresponded less to a desire to give students the chance to do a bachelor of philosophy in Tunis than to the availability of teaching fellows who, for several years, had taught this discipline in upper school and at the Institut des hautes études. Two of them had begun a doctoral dissertation, Jean Cuisenier[3] and Carmel Camilleri.[4] Georges Granai, who was a former student of Georges Gurvitch, was appointed to teach sociology.

It pays to recall that sociology aroused interest in Tunisia in the context of a policy aimed at development. Since the Spring of 1951, the Institut des hautes études had initiated a sociological, ethnological and geographical study group, of which the aim was to undertake several specific studies. In October 1955, the Institut had organized a colloquium on living standards in Tunisia in which Paul Sebag, who was teaching at the Lycée Carnot at the time, participated. Shortly thereafter he was appointed research fellow at the Institut des hautes études. With some colleagues he began work on some monographs on wage earners from the Tunis region and on the outlying districts of the capital.[5]

---

[3]Jean Cuisenier, *Économie et Parenté. Essai sur les affinités de structure entre système économique et système de parenté*, Paris: Mouton, 1971.

[4]Carmel Camilleri, *Jeunesse, famille et développement. Essai sur le changement socioculturel dans un pays du tiers monde*, Aix-en-Provence: CRESM/CNRS, 1973.

[5]Paul Sebag (1919–2004) published a monograph on Tunisia with Éditions sociales [the French Communist Party's publishing house], in 1951, right in the midst of the national struggle. This was the first work to cast a critical gaze on colonization.

In this context, a decision was made with the backing of Jacques Berque to establish a bachelor of sociology, at the same time as that established at the Sorbonne in 1959 and to create the Centre d'études sociales under Georges Granai. During the first year, the students were few. During the first year, these students were few, and included students who had first taken an ethics and sociology diploma as part of a degree of philosophy but then withdrew from philosophy, as well as some new bachelor students of Tunisian, Algerian, French and other nationalities, who, for the most part, had already entered active life. This was the time of the Algerian war and Tunis welcomed refugees and many militants of the Algerian cause. The majority of these students considered that knowledge of our societies, notably those of Tunisia and Algeria, was essential to the shared project of ours to contribute with solid scientific analyses to their independence and their development. Did Jacques Berque not endlessly reiterate that 'there are no underdeveloped countries, there are only under-analyzed countries'?

The bachelor of sociology included four diplomas, one in general sociology, one in social psychology, one in social and political economy; the student was given a choice for the fourth; those who remained at Tunis had to complete the diploma of human geography (part of the bachelor of geography); others left to France where they notably enrolled in a diploma of ethnology.

In the context of the social psychology diploma, which bachelor of psychology students also took, Frantz Fanon, a psychiatrist in Tunis since 1957, after having left Algeria from where he had been expelled,[6] offered – probably at the suggestion of Claudine Chaulet, who was also a refugee with her husband, doctor Chaulet, in Tunis and researcher at the Institut des hautes études – to teach a semester course on social psychopathology. This course, which took place in the late afternoon, was attended not just by the few students of both bachelors, but also by a composite audience

---

[6]Frantz Fanon resigned from his functions as a psychiatrist at the Blida Hospital and addressed an open letter to Robert Lacoste (see *above*, p. 285) saying that it was not possible for him to want at any price to disalienate individuals, 'to put them back in their place in a country in which non-right, inequality and murder are erected into legislative principles, where the native, who is permanently alienated in his own country, lives in a state of absolute depersonalization'. In reply to this resignation letter, Fanon received an expulsion order.

made up of medical doctors, academics, Algerian militants, politicians ...
To the point that it assumed a social character unusual within the Tunisian
university milieu.

The course properly speaking was the core of his interventions,
but the digressions were just as important and enthralling to us. He
talked about his experience as a psychiatrist at the hospital in Blida,
about his conflicts with his colleagues over the methods of psychiatric
intervention; he defended the new methods that he advocated, social
therapy and institutional psychotherapy, which were revolutionary in
this domain at the time. He also evoked relations between Blacks and
Whites – in 1952 he had published Peau noire, masques blancs. He
also told us about colonial oppression and violence, about the racism
he had experienced from his youth on, notably in the French Army,
which he joined toward the end of the Second World War,[7] or again at
the university in Lyon where he was 'dévisagé, remarqué, isolé',[8] about
racism against Blacks, against colonized peoples, and more particularly
the Algerians whose cause he had identified with,[9] about the racism
that was ingrained in the culture of the society that produced it.[10] He
mentioned the Algiers school of psychiatry, as characterized by its
medical body's racist attitude toward north-African patients, which
it took to be 'primitive men whose cerebral evolution is anatomically
defective'.[11] His was a project to combat all forms of alienation. His
analyses and the passion that drove him impressed us. He was in the
process of writing L'An V de la révolution algérienne. We admired in
him the militant of decolonization and of Algerian independence, his

---

[7]'Upon liberation, Fanon and his West Indian comrades were demobilized and
repatriated on a boat set up as a slave ship, with the feeling of having believed they'd
engaged in war for the equality of races and human fraternity, whereas in fact, given
the behaviour of the crowds toward the French soldiers, both the allies and them,
they found themselves alone, ignored and sometimes even scorned; (interview with
Mahmoud Maamouri, former ambassador and friend of Fanon, reported during a
lecture he gave in 2008).

[8]See L'Action, Tunis, December 1963 (on the occasion of the second anniversary of
Fanon's death).

[9]In the resignation letter he wrote when quitting the hospital of Blida, he said: 'If
psychiatry is the medical technique that endeavours to enable individuals to cease being
foreign to their environment, I owe it to myself to state that the Arab, permanently
alienated in his own country, lives in a state of absolute depersonalization.'

[10]Alice Cherki, Frantz Fanon: A Portrait.

[11]Fanon, 'The North African Syndrome', Esprit, February 1952.

refusal of all forms of subjugation and inequality. He taught us a lot. It corresponded to our questioning at the time.

He invited some of us CES students in social psychology to come and attend his consultations on Thursday mornings at the psychiatry day centre at Charles-Nicolle Hospital in Tunis. Upon his arrival in Tunis, he was first appointed to the psychiatric hospital of La Manouba; but, confronted with the reluctance of his colleagues to accept his 'sociological' interpretation of mental illness, he obtained a transfer from the Deputy Minister for Health and Social Affairs to the neuropsychiatric clinic at Charles-Nicolle Hospital, where he was freer to adhere to his principles. Once there he had the good fortune to be able to create a neuropsychiatric day centre, 'Fanon's place in Tunis', according to Alice Cherki, with a young team.

During his medical studies, Fanon simultaneously took courses in philosophy at the Faculty of Letters in Lyon (he was a student of Merleau-Ponty, among others), as well as of sociology, ethnology and psychology. During an internship at Saint-Alban Hospital in Lozère, he also had the occasion to work with Doctor François Tosquelles, a psychiatrist of Spanish origin and an anti-Franco militant who pioneered institutional psychotherapy.[12] His collaboration with Tosquelles, writes Alice Cherki in her introduction to Les Damnés de la terre, *was for him a decisive training, both in terms of psychiatry and of his future militancy.*

Appointed médecin-chef de service at Blida Hospital in November 1953, he endeavoured to practice social therapy with his colleagues. Thrown by the stance of many psychiatrists, who tended to consider illness only in its outward signs, he paid special attention to the patients' social milieu. He was drawn to rejecting the carceral milieu of the psychiatric hospital.

The Neuropsychiatry Day Centre had the particular feature of being part of a general hospital; the mental patient there was a patient like any other, less stigmatized than in a psychiatric hospital; the psychiatric doctor there had the material infrastructure of the general hospital at his disposal and was in daily contact with his internist and surgeon colleagues. But what is most important is that the patient there has total freedom; he spends the day at the hospital but returns home

---

[12]Alice Cherki, *Frantz Fanon: A Portrait.*

after 6 pm, just as any other worker would, going back to civilian life every evening, taking public transport, going to the café, frequenting the mosque, enjoying a family life …. Recourse to social therapy entails that the patient should not be a passive being, but must 'verbalize, explain, explain himself, take a stance': 'Social therapy wrests the patient from his fantasies and obliges him to confront reality'.[13]

Among the psychiatric therapies practised, Fanon emphasized individual and psychoanalytic psychotherapies, but above all group psychotherapies: patients, in groups of between six to eight, each introduced their problems, which became topics of discussion and an exchange of experiences – he was clear that this therapy cannot be applied to really serious pathologies.

During the sessions I attended, Doctor Fanon received many patients. He found it difficult to tolerate the rhythm imposed on him by the hospital: there was always friction with the orderlies, who simultaneously played the role of interpreters; he often realized that he had receive only a brief summary of what the patient had said, though he considered that all the patient's words assumed an importance; he often took the time to inquire among the members of their families and had home surveys done by a young social assistant who worked with him. His consultations began between 8:30 and 9 am and never finished before 1:30, 2 or sometimes 3 o'clock in the afternoon. He commented at length with his team on the cases that he had been presented with, inquiring always less into the symptoms of the illness than into the patient's social and familial milieu.

Many of the patients were Algerian – some from the maquis. He also received former Tunisian fellaghas. He liked to talk about these cases of militants who had been confronted with violence and who turned out to be unable to readapt to a normal civilian and family life. Far from making an apology for violence, he adjudged it unavoidable as a response to the violence of colonization, of domination, of man's exploitation of man. Some of his remarks appeared to us too cynical …. I confess that his personage fascinated us. He was imperious all the while being ready to listen to others, distant, passionate and

---

[13]Frantz Fanon and Charles Geronimi, 'Day hospitalization in psychiatry. Part two: doctrinal considerations). The Neuropsychiatric Day Center in Tunis (CNPJ)' (see *above*, p. 347).

fascinating; we asked him questions; but he rather tended to give monologues, to reflect on things out loud. His expressions were not only those of the doctor, but above all the philosopher, the psychologist, the sociologist …

The mad person is one who is 'foreign' to society. And society decides to rid itself of this anarchic element. Internment is the rejection, the side-lining of the patient. Society asks the psychiatrist to render the patient able again to reintegrate into society. The psychiatrist is the auxiliary of the police, the protector of society against … The social group decides to protect itself and shuts the patient away. When the patient leaves the psychiatric establishment without the doctor's consent, a whole series of consequences ensues. Psychiatrists have reacted violently against this role; they have asked the authorities to allow a certain margin of spontaneity with respect to the family and to the patient. This new way of seeing has borne fruit. We will see below how by practicing self-placement, the mental patient can be conscious of his illness.

The problem of the awareness of the illness has raised dilemmas. There is no method for observing whether a mental illness has disappeared; from what moment can we say that the patient is cured? As of 1930, sociologists supplied psychiatry with some interesting data. Since the patient has effectively lost the sense of the social, he must be resocialized; for some, the socialized being is one who lives without giving anyone else cause for concern. Only, which group does one adapt to? It has been seen that some people could be received into the family group and had troubles being received into the work group and vice versa. We see sexual perverts who have succeeded at the social level. In catatonia, the schizophrenic evidences a withdrawal. There are moral masochists: are they abnormal? Is the aim of a human being never to present a group with problems?

The normal individual, it is also said, is someone who does not make a fuss. But, then, the trade unionists who protest and make demands, are they not normal? What are the criteria of normality? For some, the criterion is work. But a prostitute works! Well, she can nonetheless be a neurotic. Similarly, is an unemployed person ill? Many unemployed people become ill, but is that because they are unemployed? The doctor occupies a position between society and patient. For example, concerning correspondence, the doctor reads the letters sent in from the society to the patient. And society strives to control the psychiatrist's work practice. The patient often seems cured and relapses the moment he leaves, sometimes in a serious way (suicide attempts, for example). Whence the effort to create a society inside the hospital itself, or what we call sociotherapy.

Previously, life at the hospital was disorganized: divisions into wards, into rooms, into isolation units; the essential instrument was the key. Certain principles lie at the basis of sociotherapy:

1) *Madness is prohibited at the hospital.* Up to now, when a patient began to cry out, it was said that he was fulfilling his function as a mad person. Every pathological manifestation must be tackled; reason must be set against the unreason of the patient. This is an extremely rich experience for the person engaged in this practice. One cannot be sick with a healthy brain, with clear neuronal connections; through the connexions, there is a sort of open pathway through which the doctor has to *introduce himself with innovative principles,* so *madness is permitted.*

2) *Modification of the daily rhythm.* The privileged itineraries of the patient were arranged by category up to now. A rhythm has been imposed. Dining rooms were created, forks and serviettes, and patients were asked to have normal attitudes. The patient must work and earn some pay. Competitions were organized, as were meetings which the patient had to attend in the doctor's presence. The problem of the group's tolerance toward the patient is very important.

Difficulties of Sociotherapy: tolerance toward the patient can be at the origin of important material damage; Anglo-Saxon doctors created the police room with a village police officer.

It is said that sociotherapy creates a false society. Can the social milieu be domesticated or harnessed like the natural milieu?

Socialization as a function of cerebral matter

We shall leave aside the classical sociological perspective for neurophysiology. The upright posture straightened up the body, swung up the head, shaped the face, increased the capacity of the cranial box: this hominization deserves our attention:

- growing complexity of the nervous system, of the brain, which reaches its terminal phase in the brain of humankind, with the exaggerated development of the hemispheres;
- two sorts of integration: subcortical integration (in many animals, the cortex is poorly developed): with humankind, sort of development of a cerebral cloak. The subcortical integrations give way to the cerebral cloak. The human brain is not only larger, but also more complicated. A maximum of neurons are accompanied by a maximum of faculties. There is a large number of bundles of associations; there is no point of the brain that is not linked to all the others.

How does the brain function? It behaves just like the protoplasm of the most ordinary animal (phenomenon of depolarization and repolarization). Is the human brain given once and for all? Is the infant born with a brain that develops along an endogenous phenomenon (Cuvier's thesis)? Or is the brain a social product (at the origin there is nothing) as Lamarck would suggest we see it?

There is a hemispherical dominance: the language centre is found in the left hemisphere; children with a right hemiplegia speak. When the left hemisphere is impaired, there is an inversion and the right brain takes the place of the left brain. The deaf are not born mute: since they do not hear themselves, the originary speech movements are gradually abandoned: one becomes mute because one is deaf.

The human brain has enormous potentialities, but these potentialities must be able to develop in a coherent milieu. The messages sent to the brain must be able to be received.

Being able to be socialized is first about having a normally constituted brain. But if this is a necessary condition, other elements intervene. Piaget grants language a major importance, but, before language, there is a preliminary stage.

At the level of the brain, there is a consubstantiality of the we and the I: it cannot be said that the child is egocentric and does not see the outside world. Otto Rank has described his 'famous' trauma of birth. In the practice of painless childbirth, it is noticeable that childbirth is a physiological act and not a pathological one.

Let's ground ourselves in some facts: 1) a six-month old baby cannot sleep without light: he has always slept with the light on, there is a sort of intoxication of the cerebral cells; 2) a three-month old baby suffers a dermatosis resistant to all treatment: the mother breastfed the child as though an object of repulsion; 3) a two-and-a-half month old baby does not sleep, does not eat, then comes around to eating but loses weight: the parents did not sleep either; then, placed in the care of the grandmother, the child took to eating food again and started sleeping again; 4) a baby of fourteen months does not sleep, is aggressive: the father, who was unemployed, beats his wife; 5) a baby of fourteen months has uncontrollable vomiting; it proves to be due to the parents' attitude toward the infant: the father doubts his paternity; 6) a child does not smile: the mother has a double facial paralysis.

Stereotypes exist from the first weeks of life. The social milieu is a constant presence; from the first minutes of its life, the infant is taken in hand by the social milieu. If some children speak late, it is generally because they have to overcome inhibitions that were established in early infancy. Cases of dyslexia can be treated.

Ego formation

The neurological point of view converges with the psychoanalytic point of view, which has it that, during the latency stage, everything is put in order. Lacan says that the child, when it is born, is 'divided up' (associations are not yet established). At six months of age, a mutation occurs which is the child's recognition of the mother's image and the child's acquired certainty that the other is equal to the 'ego'; Lacan calls this stage the mirror stage: if a child is placed in front of a mirror at the age of four months, nothing happens; at seven months, there is extraordinary jubilation: recognition that it ties to the maternal image. The fact that I am me is haunted by the existence of the other. For human beings, the mirror stage is a common stage; the child reacts to the human face from very early on; this is a matter of a conditioned reflex.

The child is very sensitive to modifications to the atmosphere. The brain is not constitutionally weak. To be socializable is to be able to maintain a constant tension between the ego and society.

With language, this get complicated: the word becomes the signal of a signal. If the milieu does not authorize me to reply, I will clearly atrophy, I will be halted, clamped down on, I will not be able to have a normal rhythm; if the milieu grabs me tightly, a conflict occurs; there is no perspective open to the brain's fractional complexity. To be socialized is to respond to the social milieu, to accept that the social milieu influences me.

Control and surveillance

Modern times, it has been said, are characterized by the individual's being put on file. The psychiatrist intervenes when the individual is part of a work scheme, of a technique; the individual working in a team, on the assembly line, needs to be controlled.

Up to now, what was controlled was an object, the work put into a material object; control was qualitative. Now, with the development of the market, a certain quantification has been brought in. The question became one of the number of working hours, of the number of active hours on a production line. This was at the origin of the system of clocking in and out.

The time clock has its nicknames, the 'bargainer', the 'grand-father'. The boss calls it the 'antitheft device'. Being a good worker means you have had no trouble with the time clock. The workers' relations with the apparatus are strict, timed. For the worker, to be on time means being at peace with the time clock. The moral notion of guilt is introduced here. The time clock prevents and limits the endemic guilt of the worker. For the boss, the time clock is indispensable. As the time clock is continually present, it introduces a number of specific conducts into the worker. It represents the overall apparatus that employs the worker. Before the time clock, the worker had the possibility to apologize; from now on, the worker is constantly rejected in the solitude with the impossibility of persuading the employer about his good faith.

Hence the pathological conducts observed: nervous tensions, explosive angers, dreams of these workers/nightmares: a train that departs and leaves me, a gate that shuts, a door that does not open, a game that I am not allowed to play, the boss has vanished, leaving the time clock in his place …

But the relation is not the only thing that has reified, the employee has, too. Whence:

- absenteeism: one arrives late, but does not go in for fear of admonition. Instead the worker goes to the doctor and takes a sick day. But there is an inspection. However, the factory worker does not know what lazing around means. He experiences boredom; he has the feeling of being excluded from the group, of being displaced.
- reinforcement of obsessional attitudes: time is no longer [a] thing in which I make my way in an ordered fashion, but something that I must constantly take into account;
- accidents: there are 50% more accidents before work than on the way home, when the worker is nevertheless more tired;
- loss of control of reflexes.

Are there any ways to anticipate these disorders? It would be necessary for bosses and the collective to start taking an interest in it.

Telephonists' neuroses

The milieu studied is the Paris long-distance call service. On the basis of many cases, Le Guillant[14] observed the following phenomena among telephonists: empty-head sensations, impossibility of intellectual work; impossibility to go to bed without pain: loss of control of reflexes; obsessional phenomena; mood disorders that affect the husband and the family milieu; employees are unable to tolerate noise; insomnia; somatic problems: patients do not eat, or are constantly ill. All that takes its toll on conjugal life.

Where do these problems emerge from? Too many calls; the headset must be kept on. Le Guillant also talks about the wiretapping equipment controlled by the supervisor: the employee feels as though she is constantly being spied upon, she must control herself constantly; the body insofar as it is manifest is persecuted with hallucinations by auditory perception. The employee's role consists in

---

[14][Fanon began following the works of communist psychiatrist Louis Le Guillant early. He cites Le Guillant in an article written with S. Asselah on agitation (see *above*, p. 298). See in particular: 'La psychologie du travail', *La Raison*, no 4, 1952, pp. 75–103; 'La névrose des téléphonistes', *La Presse médicale*, no 13, 1956, pp. 274–7. Le Guillant's essays on the psychology of work were republished under the title *Le Drame humain du travail: Essais de psychopathologie du travail* (edition by Yves Clot), Toulouse: Érès, 2010 (first edition, 2006).]

putting into communication, in inserting phone plugs, in abstracting herself.

In the public services, the telephonist is not monitored and so disorders are due only to the mechanized character of the profession and not to wiretapping or to listeners. This is an example of what in psychiatry is called 'the external action syndrome', which deforms and is often at the origin of suicides.[15]

Employees of large stores

Particularly in the United States, cameras function in the large stores without the employee being forewarned about it; perpetual surveillance. This is obviously not only for employees, but above all for thieves; notwithstanding, the employee knows he is constantly being spied upon. Hence the appearance of the same type of syndromes as those of telephonists monitored through wiretapping sets. Within the technological milieu, the tendency is to reduce communications and transform the human being into an automaton.

Problem of racism (United States of America)

In divided societies, a behaviour can be observed characterized by a predominant nervous tension leading quite quickly to exhaustion. Among American Blacks [*les Noirs américains*], control of the self is permanent and at all levels, emotional, affective … This division, which is called the *colour bar*, is a rigid thing, its ongoing presence has something nagging about it. When reading Chester Himes' detective novels (*The Five Cornered Square, The Crazy Kill*,[16] etc.), the

---

[15][At the *XXXth Congrès des aliénistes et neurologistes de France et des pays de langue française* (Blois-Tours, 25–30 July 1927), discussing the reports that had been presented on 'mental automatism', the psychiatrist Henri Claude (1869–1945), insisted on 'the affective mechanism', which he described as "the external action syndrome", on the role of hidden psychical conflicts in these patients, on the interest in studying them from a psychoanalytical point of view and on the possible role of psychotherapy in treating them'. *Revue Neurologique*, 1927, vol. 2, p. 383, www.biusante.parisdescartes. fr/histmed/medica/cote?130135x1927x02]

[16][*The Five Cornered Square or, A Rage in Harlem*, New York, NY: Dell, 1957, published in French as *La Reine des pommes* (Paris: Gallimard, 1958); *The Crazy Kill*, New York: Berkeley Medallion, 1959, published in French as *Couché dans le pain* (Paris: Gallimard, 1959).]

dominant feature of Harlem is seen clearly to be aggression. By a sort of introjection, the Black man's aggression turns back upon the Black man; the condemnation is adopted; the black individual 'assumes' his own condemnation. Note the importance of feelings of guilt with the Black as with the Jew.

The 'negro' [*le nègre*] understandably wants to leave Harlem; but it is to want to be white. Religion is often conceived as a way of 'becoming-white' ('*se blanchifier*'). Sometimes, other tendencies are also observable, such as: that which consists in showing that paradise is black, that Jesus Christ is black (see *Green Pastures*[17]); the theme of evasion, of leaving, of flight in the *negro spirituals;*[18] the desire to become grand, to be a champion somewhere – thus, the historical revenge of the American Black on the occasion of sporting events such as the Olympic Games.

Obsession with suicide: see the blues and Black American music. In some blues music the aggression is pronounced: 'I pray to God that this east-bound train crashes, that the mechanic dies …' The Blacks often have only one resource: killing. When a Black kills a Black, nothing happens; when a Black kills a White, the entire police force is mobilized.

---

[17][In his critique of Mayotte Capécia's novel *Je suis Martiniquaise* (Paris: Corrêa, 1943), Fanon also refers to the film of the Americans Marc Connelly and William Keighley, *Green Pastures* (1936), released in France the same year as *Les Verts paturages*: 'The withdrawal of the ego as a successful defense mechanism is impossible for the black man [or for the Black]. He needs white approval.

In full mystical ecstasy, carried away to another world by the hymns, Mayotte Capécia imagines herself a "pink-cheeked" angel and that she soars away "all pink and white". But there is the film *Green Pastures*, where God and the angels are black, that gave the author a terrible shock: "How can God be conceived with Negro features? That's not my idea of paradise. But, after all, it's only an American film."

How could the good and merciful Lord be black? He is a white man with bright pink cheeks. From black to white that is the way to go. One is white as one is rich, as one is beautiful, as one is intelligent. Meanwhile, André has moved onto other climes, carrying with him the *white message* to other Mayottes: delightful little blue-eyed genes, pedaling down the corridor of chromosomes.' (*Black Skin, White Masks*, p. 34).]

[18][In Lyon Fanon met Louis T. Achille, a major French specialist of *negro spirituals*, on which Achille had published an article in the May 1951 special issue of *Esprit*, titled 'La plainte du Noir'. This issue also contains an article by Fanon, 'L'expérience vécue du Noir', itself later to become a chapter of *Peau noire, masques blancs*.]

Problem of the encounter

In a society that is as divided as American society, to what extent can a Black encounter a White? When a Black American is face to face with a White, stereotypes immediately intervene; it is necessary for him not to be 'true' with the White because the value systems are not the same; at bottom, there is a lie which is the lie of the situation. To confess is to confess that one is part of one's own social group;[19] if the Black is dominated, he cannot be required to engage in human behaviour. When a Black addresses a White, first he has a particular voice, as well as particular demeanour and style. When the white element intervenes in Harlem, racial solidarity is immediately manifest.

Problems of psychopathology

Society intervenes in the development of the personality starting in childhood. In the 'nounous' romances, the theme of negritude: 'Sleep, sleep, my negro, take your good time, because afterwards it's not funny'. This is a sort of conditioning through absurdity. There is a reserved space, with all the prohibition that it implies. There are intense psychological and muscular tensions that will give rise to headaches, to organic ulcers. The anxiety is considerable. Rejection entails inferiority complexes. The difficulty in defending one's self-love devalues that self-love. There is simultaneously a susceptibility, a raw sensitivity.

'Colonized' society

In territories under foreign domination, we see the same attitudes. Algerians enlist in the German Army, hoping that Germany will liberate their country. The *Manifesto* of 31 May 1943 demanded the right for Algerians to self-determination.[20] There was enormous reluctance from Algerians to get involved in the war. It was said: 'The enemies of our enemies are our friends'. In 1939, the conviction of the Algerian people was that the Germans would be victorious; Hitler

---

[19][See *above*, 'Conducts of confession in North Africa', p. 255.]
[20][Ferhat Abbas, *Le Manifeste du peuple algérien*, republished with a Preface by Jean Lacouture, Paris: Orients Éditions, 2014.]

was referred to as 'Hadj Belgacem'. In 1942, territorial militias were established. But politicians aware of Nazi ideology made clear that there must be no illusions about it. The pro-Nazi movements in Iran and in Iraq were above all anti-English or anti-French.

There is a repositioning of values; when independence is acquired, no longer is there any glory for the former combatant.[21] Aimé Césaire said that if the Europeans are anti-Hitler, it is because Hitler tried to do to them what they did to the peoples that they had colonized.[22]

Ethnopsychiatric considerations

Descriptions have been given of the Madagascan's dependency, the Hindu's indolence. In 1918, a neuropsychiatry professor, Professor Porot of the Algiers Faculty,[23] published a treaty on 'Muslim psychiatry' in which he characterized the Muslim as follows: absence or near absence of emotivity; credulity; tenacious stubbornness; propensity to have accidents and have crises of hysteria. However, in 1932 (*Annales médico-psychologiques*), he would say that the Kabyle, who is intelligent, escapes the mental debility observed among other Algerians. In 1935, Porot,[24] during the discussion of a psychiatric report, said that the Algerian is just a big mental retard; a primitive being whose life is essentially vegetative and instinctive; at the slightest psychic shock, he has diencephalic reactions rather than psychomotor ones.

Professor Sutter revisited the question: 'Primitivism is not a lack of maturity, it is a social condition at the end of its evolution';[25]

---

[21]['When they have used violence to achieve national liberation, the masses allow nobody to come forward as "liberator"' (*The Wretched of the Earth*, p. 51).]

[22][Aimé Césaire, *Discourse on Colonialism*, trans. Joan Pinkham, New York, NY, and London: Monthly Review Press, 1972, p. 3. *Discours sur le colonialisme*, Éditions Présence Africaine, 1955. (The first version was published in the review *Réclame*, 1950). See *Œuvres*, Paris: CNRS Éditions/Présence africaine, 2013, pp. 1443–76]

[23][On Porot and Carothers, see *above*, 'Ethnopsychiatric considerations', p. 252.]

[24][See *above*, 'Ethnopsychiatric considerations', p. 251. The original discussion is available on page 264 at www.biusante.parisdescartes.fr/histmed/medica/cote?110817x1935.]

[25]['*For primitivism is not a lack of maturity, a marked arrest in the development of the individual psyche; it is a social condition at the end of its evolution and adapted in a logical fashion to a different life from our own*' ('Le "primitivisme" des indigènes Nord-Africains. Ses incidences en pathologie mentale'. By Professor A. Porot and Doctor J. Sutter (of Algiers), Marseille: extract from 'Sud Médical et Chirurgical' of 15 April 1939).]

therefore, primitivism cannot be explained by domination; this primitivism is applied in a logical fashion to a life that differs from ours, it has far more deeply-rooted bases.

These works by the Algiers School did not remain isolated. Remarks of the same sort were made in Marseille by doctor Gallais about Senegalese infantrymen. In Kenya doctor Carothers did a study on the Mau-Mau revolt and introduced the notion of jealousy (the English had marked their preference for specific tribes): role of the frustration of love for the father as symbolized by the English colonizer. Carothers affirms that the African, with his total lack of aptitude for synthesis, is akin to a lobotomized European. According to him, the African is constitutively lobotomized (see *The African Mind in Health and Disease: A Study in Ethnopsychiatry*, 1954). These works then allowed him to enter the WHO.

Relations between the colonized and work in a colonized society

Examining the relations of collaboration between the colonizer, the autochthonous colonist and the colonized means showing that there is no relation.

The colonized worker and the state: the state presents itself firstly as foreign. The rubber-plantation worker from Indochina or the South-West African miner are not comparable to the metropolitan peasant. The colonist, the boss, has asserted himself through force; the metropolitan flag raised on his territory amounts to a violation. Among miners in the north of France homogeneity exists; even if there are demands, it remains in the circle of the nation, of the national universe. The colonized people cannot conceive any struggle except by foregrounding the radical contestation of the domination of his country by another country.

Before the arrival of foreigners, the colonial country did not exist, at the least it existed in the state of a thing, in the natural state. The action of the metropole is exerted on nature itself and on beings insofar as they are still in the state of nature. Work, insofar as it fecundates man, is the privilege of the colonist; only the settler works both on nature and on beings. Natives and brush, Mitidja and lazy stubbornness are the same thing. Just as tracks must be created, so too must one fight against leprosy and malaria, against the natives;

nature must be changed in spite of itself, violence must be wrought on it; the native must be brutalized, have good done to him despite himself. When the gold of Transvaal is spoken of, the settler's stubbornness comes to mind. But is there any real hostility from the native? Instead there is inertia, avolition, a desire to perpetuate the actual state of things, whence the difficulty of obtaining any action; there is idleness. To study work in the colonies is in some way to study idleness (refer to the article on this topic in *Présence africaine*, 1952, titled 'Terre'[26]).

This notion of non-effort, of the colonized's non-collaboration, is a constant given in relations between the metropole and the colony. If works are to be created, if nature is to be humanized, it is necessary to force things, to have forced labour. Forced labour is the colonist's reply to the idleness of the native; the native is forced to work; he will be fetched at home. Forced labour is a logical consequence of colonial society. Since the native can be forced, the understanding is that he can be hit.

This idleness contends with the rapaciousness of the settler, with his alacrity to earn money. This idleness is lived in the colonial context as a will not to make raising profit easy; this is the behaviour of a pilferer; the colonist does not work as a function of eternity; he works for his own life. This is why, when positioned from the viewpoint of the colonial state, investments are nonsensical; since to invest is to be on one level with the future of that region. In the colonies, private industry can scarcely invest. The settlers are not settled in the colonies in view of a determinate economic development, but instead to amass the biggest possible profit in the shortest possible time.

If we consider the *trade-union problem*, we will see that it arises in very particular terms. First of all, the trade unionism of the metropole was implanted using the same directives as in the metropole; likewise, with the political parties. The problem is not posed in heterogeneous fashion, but in homogeneous fashion. The trade unionist directives were the same in the metropole and in the colonies. Colonized and unionized workers were already specialized workers or civil servants;

---

[26][This probably refers to the section 'Terre africaine' in issue 12 of *Présence africaine* (1952), which was devoted to 'Le Travail en Afrique noire'. This section contains the translation of an article by Rosa Luxemburg, 'L'expropriation des terres et la pénétration capitaliste en Afrique'.]

there was no question of unionizing agricultural workers. Unionized workers were already, on the economic level, 'assimilated' and were not to be expected to acquire a national consciousness, but the 87% of non-unionized workers could not pose the problem in the same terms. But the national consciousness of workers and employees will come.

The notion of the unemployed: in the colonies, these are not workers without work; they are natives whose energy has not yet been claimed by the colonial society. They form a reserve in case the other workers fail to appear: according to Professor Porot, the North African is quick to become senile (thirty-five/forty years of age). Unemployment is not a human problem; it is an everlasting reserve; first, for replacing cases of early senility, or else it is a reserve of blackmail to maintain wages at a paltry level in cases of protest from indigenous employees. The mass of the unemployed does not bother the settlers.

If in a colony, there is no unemployment, if there is schooling, if the universities are open, then it is not a colony. Unemployment must be as endemic as yellow fever or malaria. Statistics show that tropical diseases have considerably diminished in many regions. This involves introducing new relations in a society and introducing new relations means negating the colonial system.

Is the colonized an idler? The colonized's idleness is a protection, a measure of self-defence, foremost on the physiological level. Labour was conceived as forced labour in the colonies, and even if there is no whipping, the colonial situation itself is a whipping; that the colonized does nothing is normal, since labour, for him, leads to nothing.

Labour must be recovered as a humanization of man. Man, when he throws himself into work, fecundates nature, but he fecundates himself also. Fecundating relations of generosity must exist; there is a reform of nature, a modification of nature, but because man shapes himself.

The colonized who resists is right.

FRANTZ FANON'S LIBRARY

List established, presented and commented by Jean Khalfa

Presentation

This list of some four hundred works was drawn up on the basis of the catalogue made by F. Boulkroune and S. Khouider of the library that Olivier Fanon gave to the Centre national de recherches préhistoriques anthropologiques et historiques (CNRPAH) of Algiers.[1] This family library also contained Josie Fanon's books as well as several books published after Fanon's death in December 1961. In the following list only those titles published in his lifetime are given. A certain number of works that were manifestly not his were left out, but others that likely belonged to Josie were kept insofar as they had perhaps elicited their shared interest. It is well known in particular that Fanon read a lot of poetry and theatre.

During this period in France books and journals were not yet all trimmed. In several cases, only some of the pages are cut, and I have indicated which ones. Each volume has been verified. Many of them contain marks in the margins or under certain words or phrases. When they appear to be significant, in particular in relation to the rest of the œuvre, or when they are accompanied by annotation, I indicate them. While it is quite possible that some of these marks or inscriptions were made by other readers, in most of the cases Fanon's interests, style and writing are discernible. This library also contains a certain number of propaganda brochures or classic editions of Marxist works. It is highly likely that Fanon, as a journalist, and Josie, who was herself a journalist

---

[1]The catalogue can be accessed on the site of the CNRPAH, http://www.cnrpah.org/images/catalogues/fanon.pdf.

in Algiers, automatically received a large number of them, as was the case for a good proportion of the intelligentsia in Europe and in Africa up until the 1970s. Most of them do not seem to have been read. I have presented a separate list of them in the interests of clarity. But from that list Fanon has carefully read various works by Marx, Engels, Lenin and Plekhanov. Lastly, he read and contributed to several important journals of the period, in particular *Esprit, Les Temps modernes* and *Présence africaine*, all of which marked his generation, as well as the major Francophone journals on psychiatry and neurology.[2] I have drawn up a separate list of these journals, which are often abundantly annotated and moreover allow us to date his preoccupations at precise moments. The testimonies concur: Fanon read incessantly and very widely. Many books were probably lost during Fanon's various moves, but this library gives us an idea of the range of his interests. By no means are these works to be taken as 'sources' in the sense in which the œuvre might be reduced to them, but instead as encounters or as shocks,[3] or else as toolboxes that enable the work which unhesitatingly appropriates them to deepen its founding questions and intuitions.

In what follows the reader will find a good proportion of the books to which Fanon's published works, in particular *Peau noire, masques blancs*, refer. Naturally, we find among them a large medical and psychiatric literature, as well as classics of existentialist philosophy, including Jaspers, Kierkegaard, Merleau-Ponty and Sartre. However, one also notes Fanon's considerable interest in

---

[2]Charles Geronimi remarks: 'Training the interns was also one of his preoccupations. He took care of the medical library and enriched it considerably. By 1956, it was notably better endowed with works of psychiatry and neurology than its university counterpart in Mustapha. Under his influence, the HPB [Blida Psychiatric Hospital] had subscriptions to all the Francophone journals of neurology and psychiatry' (*Fanon à Blida*, unpublished manuscript, kindly given us by the author). For this reason, though some collections in the personal library stop upon his arrival in Algeria, this does not imply that he had stopped reading these journals (in particular, *L'Évolution psychiatrique*, in which all the debates in that domain at the time were taking place). This is reflected in the editorials of *Our Journal* that were more specifically targeted at the hospital staff.

[3]Or 'dark precursors' in the sense of Gilles Deleuze in *Différence et répétition* (English translation: *Difference and Repetition*, trans. Paul Patton, New York, NY: Columbia University Press, p. 119). Fanon stages the shock of such an encounter in *Peau noire, masques blancs* concerning the revelation of negritude, Sartre's dialectical critique of it, and the communist critique of both of them (in Gabriel d'Arboussier's article, 'Une dangereuse mystification: la théorie de la négritude' ('A dangerous mystification: the theory of negritude'), cited in note 34 of the chapter on 'The Black Man and Psychopathology', p. 150).

other thinkers: Nietzsche, of course, but also Bachelard, Kojève (for his reading of Hegel), Jean Wahl, Emmanuel Levinas, Simone Weil, Nicolas Calas and Michel Carrouges. In literature, theatre and poetry dominate; readers of Fanon's plays will not be surprised to find Aeschylus, Corneille, Racine and Claudel alongside Saint-John Perse and Césaire.

In a text sent to René Hénane,[4] who kindly passed it on to us, Raymond Péju, the great bookseller of Lyon (Librairie La Proue), described Fanon's relation to books in the following terms:

I can still see that man, who, for some time, came more and more regularly to the bookstore. That was in 1948, I was a young bookseller and paid close attention to the clients, to the readers, who came back to the store regularly; he was one of them! I can see him entering again, a smile on his lips as he 'slipped' between the display stands with the elegance and suppleness that only he had. He was rather young (I think we were close in age), rather tall and thin, with a lively and penetrating gaze – he was immediately rather likeable, to me in any case!

He returned increasingly often, sometimes making only a whirlwind stop, at other times lingering more tranquilly, and then he would talk more readily. He didn't open up much and we spoke above all about literature; he was curious about everything, most especially about the human sciences and poetry, which was one of our favourite subjects. I don't have an accurate memory of the poems that I might have introduced him to, but what I do recall is that he allowed me truly to appreciate Aimé Césaire, about whom he spoke with intelligence and sensitivity. We were very quickly on friendly terms with one another and he started speaking to me of himself.

His name was Frantz Fanon, he was from Martinique, he had completed his studies in medicine, specialized in psychiatry; he talked about his country and his profession with the passion that was so characteristic of his personality; a passion that you felt was, beneath a calm and likeable exterior, wholly ready to ignite, to explode.

Our conversations became longer, more personal and, one day, I proposed to him that we continue them in a more

---

[4] A French doctor who specialized in tropical medicine and authored several books on the poetry of Aimé Césaire, with whom he was friends.

comfortable setting at my place; he accepted enthusiastically! On the agreed evening, my wife Marie-Aimée and Fanon got to know each other and spontaneously sympathized with each other; it was a long and cordial evening and on that day a friendship emerged between the three of us that was to last for as long as he was alive.

He returned often; I think that he liked being in a friendly, almost familial atmosphere, with us, which he had probably been missing; and little by little he began to talk about himself in a more intimate way and more precisely about his suffering as an 'excluded man', as a man rejected owing to the colour of his skin! He told us about the rebuffs, the affronts that he had endured: he mentioned the woman who had advertised a room to rent and who, when he showed up, retorted: 'I asked for a student, not a negro!' And also of the man in the train who interpellated him: 'Hey negro, put my suitcase in the rack.' An imbecilic racism that came through at any given opportunity in the most anodine acts of everyday life. We were sickened, cut to the quick! ...

That must have been the time when he began to write *Peau noire, masques blancs*. He spoke with me about it sometimes in the course of our conversations. ... However, if this topic returned frequently to our conversations, it was nonetheless not the essential point ... Poetry, for example, always had pride of place; we always took the greatest pleasure in chatting about Césaire or Char, as well as Aragon, Breton and Éluard or Damas and Senghor.

One evening, he took us to a poetry reading of Aimé Césaire organized by his friend Achille.[5] He had chosen to recite 'Batouque', a poem that he liked and that he read with a remarkable accuracy

---

[5]Louis-Thomas Achille (1909–1994), professor of English for the preparatory classes at the Lycée du Parc in Lyon from 1946 to 1974. He also hailed from Martinique and was a recognized specialist of African American sacred music, on which he published 'Negro Spirituals' in the May 1951 issue of *Esprit*, the same one in which Fanon published 'La plainte du Noir: l'expérience vécue du Noir', which was later to be incorporated into *Peau noire, masques blancs*, and Octave Mannoni, 'La plainte du Noir'. The author of several articles in French and American journals, Achille participated in the first International Congress of Black Writers and Artists held at the Sorbonne from 19 to 22 September 1956. He taught at Howard University in Washington from 1932 to 1943. There he met the African American intelligentsia. His entry in Sister Mary Anthony Scally's *Negro Catholic Writers 1900–1943 A Bio-Bibliography* (1945) describes him as a Catholic writer who had primarily written about racial problems and about the fate of French colonial subjects.

of tone. Frantz was curious about all things and he could be extremely eloquent, he was a born storyteller!

Books

In what follows I have cited some annotated passages (mostly in pencil) in Fanon's library. Underlined passages are indicated in italics, except when otherwise noted. The dates given are dates of publication of the volume in the library.

Abd-el-Ghani, *Le Problème algérien de l'émigration en France*, Paris: Cahiers algériens, 1951.

A. M. Paul Abély and Jean Delay, *L'Anxiété. Limites et bases, diagnostic, thérapeutique, considérations endocrinologiques*, Paris: Masson & Cie, 1947.

Albert Adès and Albert Josipovici, *Le Livre de Goha le simple*, Paris: Calmann-Lévy, 1921.

Alfred Adler, *Connaissance de l'homme. Étude de caractérologie individuelle*, Paris: Payot, 1949 (*Understanding Human Nature*, trans. Walter Béran Woolf, London: George Allen & Unwin, 1928).

[The chapter titled 'The feeling of inferiority and the striving for recognition', a theme that he tackled in *Peau noire, masques blancs*, is marked in the margins in several places. In particular, the following sentences: 'It is the feeling of inferiority, inadequacy, insecurity, which determines the goal of an individual's existence.' 'His goal is so constructed that its achievement promises the possibility either of a sentiment of superiority, or an elevation of the personality to such a degree that life seems worth living' (p. 72).]

Julian Ajuriaguerra and Henry Hécaen, *Le Cortex cérébral. Étude neuro-psycho-pathologique*, Paris: Masson, 1949.

Alain, *Système des Beaux-Arts*, Paris: Gallimard, 1926.

Alain, *Préliminaires à la mythologie*, Paris: P. Hartmann, 1951.

Théophile Alajouanine, *Les Grandes activités du lobe temporal*, Paris: Masson & Cie, 1955.

[In this volume, Warren S. McCulloch's article, 'L'organisation fonctionnelle du système nerveux central en vue du contrôle de la position et du mouvement', was carefully read and underlined in several places.]

Théophile Alajouanine, *La Douleur et les douleurs*, Paris: Masson & Cie, 1957.

Théophile Alajouanine, *Bases physiologiques et aspects cliniques de l'épilepsie*, Paris: Masson & Cie, 1958.

Théophile Alajouanine, *Les Grandes activités du lobe occipital*, Paris: Masson & Cie, 1960.

Jacques Stéphen Alexis, *L'Espace d'un cillement*, Paris: Gallimard, 1959.

Nelson Algren, *La Rue chaude*, Paris: Gallimard, 1960.

Georges Allègre and Robert Vigouroux, *Traitement chirurgical des anévrysmes intracrâniens du système carotidien: anévrysmes supraclinoïdiens*, Paris: Masson & Cie, 1957.

Ferdinand Alquié, *La Nostalgie de l'être*, Paris: PUF, 1950.

Alexis Amoussou, *Synergie vasodilatatrice, nicotinate de sodium, électrochoc dans les psychoses*, Paris: Impr. Bouchet et Lakara, 1951.

Charles Andler, *Nietzsche, sa vie et sa pensée. Le pessimisme esthétique de Nietzsche: sa philosophie à l'époque wagnérienne*, vol. 3, Paris: Bossard, 1921.

[Many passages are underlined. For example, the following sentences: 'The major novelty of Nietzschean thought is that it makes philosophy into a theory of civilization, that is to say of the superior life that men can live'; an annotation in the margin indicates: 'The criterion of progress would be that of relations between men' (p. 25). 'A civilization is a world of immaterial norms to which men submit because they find in them, in joy or in suffering, their purest blossoming. So who has the right to create these norms? In ancient intellectualism too, one asked: who, then, has the quality to constrain us to observe the law? And Fichte replied: "He who demonstrates by the fact that he can." In the immaterial order of norms, Nietzsche similarly affirms a de facto mastery' (p. 377).]

Joseph M. Angel, Francis Peillet and Pierre Wertheimer, *La Thérapeutique par le sommeil. Physiopathologie, technique, indications*, Paris: Masson & Cie, 1953.

Jean Anouilh, *La Valse des toréadors*, Paris: La Table ronde, 1952.

Aristophanes, *Comédies. Les Guêpes, La Paix*, vol. 2, Paris: Les Belles Lettres, 1948.

Aristotle, *Éthique de Nicomaque*, Text, translation, preface and notes by Jean Voilquin, Paris: Garnier frères, 1940.

Artemidore d'Ephèse, *La Clef des songes ou les cinq livres de l'interprétation des songes, rêves et visions*, Paris: Arcanes, 1953.

Miguel Angel Asturias, *Hommes de maïs*, Givors: Imprimerie A. Martel, 1953.

Maurice Aubert, *Vertiges et surdités d'origine vasculaire*, Paris: Masson & Cie, 1958.

André Aubin, *L'Appareil vestibulaire. Anatomie, physiologie, pathologie. Conférences et travaux pratiques publiés*, Paris: PUF, 1957.

Gaston Bachelard, *L'Intuition de l'instant. Étude sur le Siloë de Gaston*

Roupnel, Paris: Stock/Delamain et Boutelleau, 1932. (*The Intuition of the Instant*, trans. Eileen Rizo-Patron, Evanston, IL: Northwestern University Press, 2013.)

Gaston Bachelard, *La Psychanalyse du feu*, Paris: Gallimard, 1938. (The Psychoanalysis of Fire, transl. Alan C.M. Ross, with an introduction by Northrop Frye, London : Routledge & Kegan Paul, 1964)

Gaston Bachelard, *L'Air et les Songes. Essai sur l'imagination du mouvement*, Paris: José Corti, 1943. (*Air and Dreams: An essay on the imagination of movement*, trans. Edith and Frederick Farell, Dallas, TX: Dallas Institute Publications, 2011).

[The following chapters contain numerous markings in the margins; here are some significant passages. The italics are Bachelard's:
'The Wind', p. 227: 'Through *anger*, the world is created as a provocation. *Anger* founds dynamic being. Anger is the commencing act. As prudent as an action may be, as insidious as it promises to be, it must first cross a small threshold of anger. Anger is that acid without which no impression is stamped on our being; it determines the active impression' (translation modified – SC).
'The Silent declamation', p. 245: 'Emerging in the silence and the solitude of being, untied from hearing or vision, so poetry appears to us as the primary phenomenon of the human aesthetic will. … Before all action, the human being needs to say to himself, in the silence of his being, what he *wants* to become; he needs to *prove* and *to sing to himself* his own becoming. That is the voluntary function of poetry. The poetry of *will* must therefore be placed in relation with the tenacity and the courage of silent being.'
'Cinematic philosophy and dynamic philosophy', p. 295: 'We first need to give a value to our own being in order to gauge the value of other beings. And that is why the image of the weigher is so important in Nietzsche's philosophy. *Je pense* (I think) therefore *je pèse* (I weigh) are not for no reason linked by a profound etymology. The ponderal *cogito* is the first dynamic *cogito*. It is to this ponderal *cogito* that all our dynamic values must be referred' (translation modified – SC).
In an unfinished note written on a sheet of paper inserted into the end of this volume, which joins up with Fanon's reflections and readings on existence and time (Jaspers, Lachièze-Rey, Blondel perhaps, Wahl probably, and of course Kierkegaard and Sartre), we see the outline of a fundamental immanentism and skepticism in relation to both religious and dialectical thinking. It has echoes in what is said about Hegel in *Peau noire, masques blancs* and even of Sartre as regards 'Orphée noir': 'Do not seek the Absolute through a relative. Totally illogical. A conversion must be undertaken and the Absolute must not

be considered as a sort of End, [which] could not be conceived given the relativity of the means. I am thinking essentially of knowledge. The conversion therefore consists in transposing the absolute and in considering it a quality of things and in particular of acts (that would eliminate the pseudo-problem of failure, and even that of the *objective* failure). This is tantamount to return to Existence its character of unicity, metaphysical par excellence. Whence follows the notion of the absolute Other. But it would seem that thereby we rejoin the aesthetic level of Kierk[egaard]. But everything stems from a difference of interpretation of the *instant*, whether in considering the instant as something no longer lived on the aesthetic level but on the religious one, the conversion is made without [giving] primacy to that unique instant in which the disciple receives the condition and which in fact appears as an essentialist infiltration that most heavily strains the metaphysical future of man. Every instant [must] as much as possible …'.]

Gaston Bachelard, *Le Nouvel esprit scientifique*, Paris: PUF, 1949. (*The New Scientific Spirit*, trans. Arthur Goldhammer, Boston, MA: Beacon Press, 1984.)

[Here there are a few marks in the margins, for example at this sentence in the introduction, p. 7: 'As Nietzsche says: everything decisive comes into being *in spite of*. This is as true of the sphere of thought as of the sphere of action. Every new truth comes into being in spite of the evidence; every new experience is acquired in spite of immediate experience.' Bachelard's italics; translation modified – SC.]

Georges Balandier, *Sociologie actuelle de l'Afrique noire*, Paris: PUF, 1955.

Gustave Bardy, *Saint Augustin. L'homme et l'œuvre*, Paris: Desclée de Brouwer, 1940.

Maurice Bariéty and George Brouet, *Phtisiologie du médecin praticien*, Paris: Masson & Cie, 1953.

Philippe Barrès, *Charles de Gaulle*, New York, NY: Brentano's, 1941.

Georges Bataille, *La Haine de la poésie*, Paris: Minuit, 1947.

Georges Bataille, *L'Érotisme*, Paris: Minuit, 1957.

Pierre Bayle, *Pensées diverses sur la comète*, Paris: Librairie E. Droz, 1939.

Simone de Beauvoir, *Le Deuxième sexe*. vol. 1, *Les Faits et les Mythes*, Paris: Gallimard, 1949.

Simone de Beauvoir, *Les Mandarins*, Paris: Gallimard, 1954.

Nicolas Berdiaeff, *L'Esprit de Dostoïevski*, Paris: Stock, 1946.

André Berge, *Le Facteur psychique dans l'énurésie*, Paris: Seuil, 1946.

François Berge et al., *Le Destin de l'individu dans le monde actuel. Enquête internationale auprès des étudiants*, Paris: Éditions de Clermont, 1947.

Henri Bergson, *Essai sur les données immédiates de la conscience*, Paris: Félix Alcan, 1929.

Henri Bergson, *L'Évolution créatrice*, Paris: PUF, 1948.

Paul Bernard, *Psychiatrie pratique. Formation, spécialisation et selection des auxiliaires médico-sociaux du psychiatre. Formation psychiatrique générale*, vol. 1, Paris: Desclée de Brouwer, 1947.

[Some sentences are marked in this volume, for instance: 'Behavioural disorders, which are the object of psychiatry, in general have more complex causes than the organic disorders that are studied in the other branches of medicine. Indeed we know that *behaviour is the reaction of the organism as a whole engaged in its effort to adapt to its milieu*, with incessant exchanges occurring between the milieu and the organism' (p. 60).]

Jacques Berque, *Les Arabes d'hier à demain*, Paris: Seuil, 1960.

Auguste Blanqui, *Textes choisis*, Paris: Éditions sociales, 1955.

Jean Bobon, *Introduction historique à l'étude des néologismes et des glossolalies en psychopathologie*, Paris: Masson & Cie, 1952.

Gerhardt V. Bonin, *Essai sur le cortex cérébral*, Paris: Masson & Cie, 1955.

[This volume bears the stamp of Blida-Joinville Psychiatric Hospital (arrival date 24 February 1955).]

Joël Bonnal et al., *Les Abcès encéphaliques à l'ère des antibiotiques. Étude statistique de 547 observations*, Paris: Masson & Cie, 1960.

Jacques Borel, *Le Déséquilibre psychique. Ses psychoses, sa morale*, Paris: PUF, 1947.

Jorge Luis Borges, *Fictions*, Paris: Gallimard, 1956.

Georges Boudin and Bernard Pépin, *Dégénérescence hépato-lenticulaire*, Paris: Masson & Cie, 1959.

L. Bourrat et al., *L'Enfance irrégulière. Psychologie clinique*, Paris: PUF, 1946.

Olivier Brachfeld, *Les Sentiments d'infériorité*, Genève and Annemasse: Éditions du Mont Blanc, 1945.

Bertolt Brecht, *Théâtre complet. Le Cercle de craie caucasien. Homme pour homme. L'Exception et la Règle*, vol. 1, Paris: L'Arche, 1956.

Albert Burloud, *Le Caractère*, Paris: PUF, 1948.

J.J. Frederik Buytendijk, *Attitudes et mouvements. Étude fonctionnelle du mouvement humain*, Paris: Desclée de Brouwer, 1957.

Roland Caillois et al., *L'Homme. Le monde. L'histoire*, Grenoble: Arthaud, 1948.

[The margins of several pages in this small volume are marked. The following passages, for instance, some of whose phrases are underlined with pencil: 'I have chosen this topic "The lived world and history," because it seemed to me that, in the times in which we live, we have an increasingly acute awareness of the historical depth of the world such as it is lived, and also, correlatively, an awareness of participating in history, of making history. … As a result, while being one philosophy among others, a disinterested philosophy in search of the true, *it has, as it were, a revolutionary pretention, since becoming aware of the situation must at the same time be an act*' (pp. 8–9). 'Marx said: "Reason is not lived as reason," reason has its foundations in a lived historical reality' (p. 12). '[P]henomenological also means historical since the history of consciousness contains in its depth the history of the entire world. If Hegel can rediscover in man, such as he describes him, the stages of the world, it is because man really does contain them, because he lives them in some manner. If there was no lived history – and this history extends endlessly into the past – there would be no reflected history' (p. 47).]

Nicolas Calas, *Foyers d'incendie*, Paris: Denoël, 1938.

[Several passages are marked here, in particular in a section on the inferiority complex, but also on evolution and culture. Thus: 'Henceforth, man's adaptation to his milieu is performed in two times, the first proceeds as with all living beings, by a movement of organic adaptation, and the second produces a transformation of the elements of matter into objects of value, which becomes a form of specifically human assimilation and which is, as we have seen, the fundamental principle of civilization' (p. 241).]

Albert Camus, *Les Justes. Pièce en cinq actes*, Paris: Gallimard, 1950.
Mayotte Capécia, *Je suis martiniquaise*, Paris: Corrêa, 1948.
Mayotte Capécia, *La Négresse blanche*, Paris: Corrêa, 1950.

[Two passages are marked in the margin: 'No drop of white blood. With her slave mentality, she [Lucia, who "was the purest type of African"] was devoted heart and soul to Isaure' (p. 36). 'But you are not black, Isaure, you are scarcely mixed blood [*métisse*]; your skin is nearly white. In a few years, when you've earned millions with your bar, you will have a house built on the Didier plateau and pose as creole' (p. 44).]

Fernand Caridroit, *Psychophysiologie des glandes endocrines et du système neuro-végétatif*, Paris: PUF, 1946.

John C. Carothers, *Psychologie normale et pathologique de l'Africain. Étude ethnopsychiatrique* (English title: *The African Mind in Health and Disease: A Study in Ethnopsychiatry*) Geneva: World Health Organization, 1954.

Pierre Carpentier-Fialip and René Lamar, *Les États-Unis. Civilisation*, Paris: Hachette, 1948.

Michel Carrouges, *La Mystique du surhomme*, Paris: Gallimard, 1948.

[Numerous markings and 'yes's' of approval from Fanon's hand in the section on 'The Overman and the Death of God'.]

John Cassels et al., *The Sterling Area. An American Analysis*, London: Economic Cooperation Administration, Special Mission to the United Kingdom, 1951.

Jean Cathala and Pierre Mollaret, *Manuel de pathologie médicale. Physiopathologie et clinique*, Paris: Masson & Cie, 1947.

Aimé Césaire, *Les Armes miraculeuses*, Paris: Gallimard, 1946.

Paul Césari, *Les Déterminismes et la contingence*, Paris: PUF, 1950.

René Char, *Poèmes et prose choisis*, Paris: Gallimard, 1957.

Paul Chauchard, *Mécanismes cérébraux de la prise de conscience. Neurophysiologie, psychanalyse et psychologie animale*, Paris: Masson & Cie, 1956.

Jean Chesneaux, *Contribution à l'histoire de la nation vietnamienne*, Paris: Éditions sociales, 1955.

Maryse Choisy, *L'Anneau de Polycrate. Essai sur la culpabilité collective et recherche d'une éthique psychanalytique*, Paris: Éditions Psyché, 1948.

[This book on the feeling of guilt, to which Fanon refers in *Peau noire, masques blancs* (p. 134, *Black Skin, White Masks*, p. 70), is marked in several places. The flyleaf bears a note: 'To be consulted: Weulersse, *Noirs et Blancs*, Armand Colin.' Jacques Weulersse's book, *Noirs et Blancs: À travers l'Afrique nouvelle de Dakar au Cap*, Paris: Armand Colin, 1931, is not referenced in Fanon's published works, however.

This sentence, notably, is annotated in the margins: 'It is no doubt also possible to conceive at a pinch an ideal, evolved *overman* – perfect, "like a God" – with whom the unconscious has gradually become conscious' (p. 68); an annotation, most likely Fanon's, reads: 'No! That would amount to returning to Valéry: awareness of nothingness on the shores of the "nothing", "power which consumes itself in getting to know itself"' [a recollection of Valéry's 'Cimetière marin']. The following passage is also annotated: 'In his games, the man cub recommences an event, even a disagreeable one, perhaps "so as to be able, through his activity, to master the strong impression he has received of it, instead of confining himself to enduring it by keeping

a purely passive attitude" [note: Freud, *Essais de psychanalyse*, p. 47].
This repetition is sometimes a pleasure. In any case, it is a way of
making oneself a master of reality. Why will we not have two lives, one
of which would serve as a sketch for the other?' (p. 89); annotation:
'*Cf.* Lacan (imago)'.]

Édouard Claparède, *L'Éducation fonctionnelle*, Neuchâtel and Paris:
Delachaux et Niestlé, 1931.

Henri Claude and Stéphen Chauvet, *Sémiologie réelle des sections totales des
nerfs mixtes périphériques. Considérations sur la technique concernant
l'étude des troubles des sensibilités, les modifications des réactions
vasomotrices et sudorales, les altérations trophiques ostéo-articulaires et
cutanées*, Paris: Maloine, 1911.

Paul Claudel, *La Sagesse ou la parabole du festin*, Paris: Gallimard, 1939.

Paul Claudel, *Théâtre (première série). Tête d'or (première et seconde versions)*,
Paris: Mercure de France, 1946.

Paul Claudel, *Théâtre*, Paris: Gallimard, ('Bibliothèque de la Pléiade'), 1947.

Raymond Coirault, *Le Syndrome de Guillain-Barré*, Paris: Masson & Cie,
Paris, 1958.

Auguste Comte, *Cours de philosophie positive: Discours sur l'esprit positif*,
Paris: Garnier frères, 1949.

Constitution de la République Française, 'Statut organique de l'Algérie. Loi
portant fixation des circonscriptions électorales pour la désignation
des membres de l'Assemblée algérienne, décrets portant règlements
d'administration publique pour l'application du statut de l'Algérie', *Journal
officiel de la République française et Journal officiel de l'Algérie*, Algiers,
November 1950.

Pierre Corneille, *Rodogune*, Paris: Larousse, n.d.

Pierre Corneille, *Cinna. Tragédie*, Paris: Hachette, 1935.

Pierre Corneille, *Le Cid*, Paris: Arthème Fayard, 1946.

Auguste Cornu, *Karl Marx et la révolution de 1848*, Paris: PUF, 1948.

Michel Cournot, *Martinique*, Paris: Gallimard, 1949.

André Cresson, *Les Courants de la pensée philosophique française*, Paris:
Armand Colin, 1946.

[Some annotations in this volume. The first sentence of the introduction
('Human reflection has always oscillated between two poles: the
intellectual pole and the moral pole') is notably annotated as follows:
'No, knowledge is not opposed to action. The best knowledge is achieved
through action.']

André Cresson, *Les Courants de la pensée philosophique française*, vol. 1,
Paris: Armand Colin, 1947.

André Cresson, *Les Systèmes philosophiques*, Paris: Armand Colin, 1947.

André Cresson, *Saint Thomas d'Aquin: Sa vie, son œuvre, avec un exposé de sa philosophie*, Paris: PUF, 1947.

Benedetto Croce, *La Poésie: Introduction à la critique et à l'histoire de la poésie et de la littérature*, Paris: PUF, 1951.

Bertrand d'Astorg, *Aspects de la littérature européenne depuis 1945*, Paris: Seuil, 1952.

Henri Damaye, *Psychiatrie et civilisation*, Paris: Félix Alcan, 1934.

Albert Dauzat, *La Philosophie du langage*, Paris: Flammarion, 1912.

Albert Dauzat, *Le Génie de la langue française*, Paris: Payot, 1954.

Jean-Pierre Dehaye, *Contribution à l'étude des états pseudo-démentiels après traumatisme crânien*, Paris, 1955.

Jean Delay, *Colloque international sur la chlorpromazine et les médicaments neuroleptiques en thérapeutique psychiatrique. Paris 20, 21, 22 October 1955, clinique des maladies mentales et de l'encéphale de la Faculté de médecine*, Paris: G. Doin, 1956.

Robert Delavignette, *Les Paysans noirs*, Paris: Stock, 1947.

Victor Delbos, *De Kant aux postkantiens*, Paris: Aubier, 1940.

Jean Delmas and Georges Laux, *Système nerveux sympathique: Étude systématique et macroscopique*, Paris: Masson & Cie, 1952.

Paul Delost and Marthe Bonvallet, *Récents progrès en physiologie*, Paris: PUF, 1956.

Georges Del Vecchio, *La Justice, la vérité: Essais de philosophie juridique et morale*, Paris: Dalloz, 1955.

[In this volume we find a chapter on 'L'obligation juridique de la véracité: Spécialement dans le procès civil'.]

Émile Dermenghem, *Le Culte des saints dans l'islam maghrébin*, Paris: Gallimard, 1954.

[One paragraph is marked with a red cross in the margin; it bears on the Saint of Birmandreis, whose speciality is the 'curing of the mad, neurotics and paralytics' (p. 104).]

René Descartes, *Discours de la méthode pour bien conduire sa raison et chercher la vérité dans les sciences, suivi des Méditations en latin et en français*, Paris: Librairie Delagrave, 1918.

Maurice Despinoy, *Circonstances et signes du début de la schizophrénie*, Lyon: Bosc frères, 1948.

[A dedication from Maurice Despinoy: 'To Doctor Frantz Fanon I offer this dissertation even though it appears to disdain psychology. With best wishes and the hope of soon having the pleasure of being able to work with him again.']

Jean Despois, *L'Afrique blanche française: L'Afrique du Nord*, vol. 1, Paris: PUF, 1949.

Isaac Deutscher, *Staline*, Paris: Gallimard, 1953 (*Stalin: A Political Biography*, Oxford: Oxford University Press, 1949).

Mohammed Dib, *L'Incendie*, Paris: Seuil, 1954.

Denis Diderot, *Textes choisis: Pensées philosophiques, Lettre sur les aveugles, Suite de l'apologie de l'abbé de Prades*, vol. 1, Paris: Éditions sociales, 1952.

Denis Diderot, *Encyclopédie ou dictionnaire raisonné des sciences, des arts et des métiers. Textes choisis, préface et commentaires par Albert Soboul*, vol. 1, Paris: Éditions sociales, 1952.

Denis Diderot, *Textes choisis. De l'interprétation de la nature (Pensées sur l'interprétation de la nature). Articles de l'Encyclopédie (sept premiers tomes)*, vol. 2, Paris: Éditions sociales, 1953.

Denis Diderot, *Les Salons. 1759–1781*, Paris: Éditions sociales, 1955.

Denis Diderot, *Essais sur la peinture. De la manière. Pensées détachées sur la peinture, la sculpture, l'architecture et la poésie. Tableaux de nuit de Skalken*, vol. 5, Paris: Éditions sociales, 1955.

Paul Diel, *Psychologie de la motivation: Théorie et application thérapeutique*, Paris: PUF, 1948.

[Several passages in the introduction to this book are marked, in particular: 'The external world and the internal world are inseparable, they penetrate one another and this interpenetration is called life' (p. 13); 'But psychotherapy perforce exceeds the medical domain. It seeks a meaningful direction of life, a direction toward the meaning of life. A therapy that does not seek to envisage the meaning of life, that seeks to counter the meaning of life, is necessarily meaningless [*insensée*], false. Added to the fundamental difficulty of defining the metaphysical basis is the no less redoubtable difficulty of defining the moral goal' (p. 15); 'With the individual who is unable to valorize his desires in relation to a meaning of life and is only able to satisfy them through the imagination, the separation between the external world and the internal world, the cause of all insufficiency, will become an uncrossable abyss: the suffering will become intolerable' (p. 19).]

John Dos Passos, *Sur toute la terre*, Paris: Gallimard, 1936.

John Dos Passos, *42ᵉ Parallèle*, Paris: Gallimard, 1951.

Fyodor Dostoyevsky, *Mémoires écrits dans un souterrain*, Paris: Gallimard, 1949.

Auguste Dufour, *Paralysies nucléaires des muscles des yeux*, Gand: Impr. Victor van Doosselaere, 1890.

Marc Dufour, *Traité des maladies du nerf optique*, Paris: Doin, 1908.

Mikel Dufrenne and Paul Ricoeur, *Karl Jaspers et la philosophie de l'existence*, Paris: Seuil, 1947.

[Some of the passages in this work are marked. Thus: 'Kierkegaard and Nietzsche knew that the last word of the meditation on existence is neither in the relation of the awareness of being free with objective knowledge, nor even in the relation of existence with itself; the heart of the drama lies in the relation of existence *with some transcendence that it is not but that is nonetheless its reason and its ultimate peace*' (p. 23); 'Well, there is a scandal that can no longer be silenced, in posing the question on being, that is to say the question of the beginning and the end, when the one who questions is neither at the beginning nor at the end, but finds himself caught in a situation between beginning and end, charged with the past, itself mobile, limited by a character, by passions, a birth, a short life, *blinkered information*. The philosopher has to have an awareness of the immensity of his horizon and the precariousness of his perspective: being is only given in profiles, in sketches, which must themselves fail in order to deliver their message' (p. 28).
The whole first page of the chapter on 'La liberté existentielle' (p. 144) is marked in the margin. ('We must therefore see now how it is that freedom is the act of existence, or better how freedom and existence are identified. ... I am the one who choses, and who by his choice decides his own being.')

In this volume, there is a handwritten letter from Pierre Lachièze-Rey (1885–1957), a Kantian philosopher, who had been close to Le Sillon, a left-wing Christian movement, and held now a chair in Lyon. The letter is dated 17 June 1949: 'Dear Monsieur, I regret that circumstances did not allow me yesterday to go further into your concerns and to reply at greater length to your questions. I repeat that I remain at your disposal to the extent that you deem I can be of help to you in your research. I hope that M. Lacroix will equally be able to be of use to you. I am sending you, as I have promised, an article that I have written on the method of Maurice Blondel. I recommend again that you read the first version of this author's *Action*, if you are able to find it. In this work, you will see what a true transcendence is. Concerning the problem of values and of destiny, I refer you to an article that I have published in *Revue de métaphysique et de morale* in July–October 1947. I implore you to accept my faithful wishes.'
Lachièze-Rey's article (*Revue de métaphysique et de morale*, 52nd year, nos. 3–4, July–October 1947, pp. 244–58) is titled 'Esquisse d'une métaphysique de la destinée' ('Sketch of a metaphysics of destiny'). The

book by Maurice Blondel that is recommended is *L'Action: Essai d'une critique de la vie et d'une science de la pratique*, Paris: PUF, 1893. Jean Lacroix (1900–1986), a philosopher from Lyon, himself also on the Christian Left, was close to Emmanuel Mounier and his journal *Esprit*, which was to publish Fanon's first texts. André Mandouze (who later became the founder of *Consciences maghribines* in Algiers, a journal to which Fanon contributed) attended his clandestine seminars at the end of the war. The question of the relations between values, action and transcendence obviously goes to the heart of Fanon's own concerns at the time.]

Georges Dumas, *Le Surnaturel et les dieux d'après les maladies mentales*, Paris: PUF, 1946.

[There are several markings in the chapters on 'Les psychoses et le réel' and on 'L'automatisme, les hallucinations'.]

René Dumont, *Terres vivantes*, Paris: Plon, 1961.

Charles Durand, *L'Écho de la pensée*, Paris: G. Doin & Cie, 1941.

Pierre Duranton, *La Schizophrénie infantile*, Paris: Librairie Arnette, 1956.

M.J. Saintes, Léon Ectors and Jacques Achslogh, *Les Compressions de la moelle cervicale. Lésions intrinsèques et traumatiques exclues*, Paris: 1960.

Erasmus, *Éloge de la folie*, Paris: Éditions de Cluny, 1941.

Aeschylus, *Les Perses*, Paris: Hatier, 1933.

Aeschylus, *Tragédies*, trans. Paul Mazon, Paris: Club français du livre, 1955.

Auguste Etcheverry, *Le Conflit actuel des humanismes*, Paris: PUF, 1955.

Étiemble, *Le Mythe de Rimbaud: Structure du mythe*, Paris: Gallimard, 1952.

Henri Ey, *La Psychiatrie devant le surréalisme*, Paris: Centre d'éditions psychiatriques, 1948.

[Most of the pages of this text, a long talk by Henri Ey, are abundantly marked. On Fanon's interest in surrealism, see David Macey, *Frantz Fanon: A Life*, p. 130).]

Henri Ey, *Études psychiatriques: Aspects séméiologiques*, Paris: 1950.

Henri Ey, *Études psychiatriques. Historique, méthodologie, psychopathologie générale*, Paris: Desclée de Brouwer, 1952.

Henri Ey and Julien Rouart, *Essai d'application des principes de Jackson à une conception dynamique de la neuropsychiatrie*, Paris: Doin, 1938.

[The section dealing with 'The third factor of madness. The speed at which dissolution is carried out (speed of the disappearance of control upon persisting evolutionary levels)' is marked with an asterix. In a note to Jackson's text, Ey points out: 'What Jackson says about the importance of the speed of dissolution is of extreme interest and we have never seen it emphasized.' An inscription in the margin of p. 37 indicates: 'On this matter, see Jaspers (Introduction).' On p. 69 of this chapter on 'Les dissolutions de l'activité psychique' ('The dissolutions of psychic activity'), several passages are marked: 'Hallucinatory activity is contingent with respect to the essential structure of such delusions [delusions of paranoid structure]. As a rule, the hallucinatory form expresses the most unconscious affects: hallucinations, when they exist, are manifestly the expression of the paranoid personality.' This passage is marked with two 'yes's' in the margin. 'We were struck, with Lacan, by the extreme importance of the fertile moments in the evolution of such delusions. Everything happens as if the delusional arrangement came together and fed on *states of delusional experience* with an intuitive or *illusional* form.' Only '*illusional*' is underlined by Fanon. This passage is annotated: 'See Lacan dissertation. Case of Aimée.']

Guy Fageot, *Troubles de l'intelligence et du caractère à la suite de brûlures chez l'enfant*, Lyon: Bosc frères, 1953.

Howard Fast, *La Route de la liberté*, Paris: Gallimard, 1948. (*Freedom Road*, New York : Duell, Sloan and Pearce, 1944)

William Faulkner, *Absalon! Absalon!*, Paris: Gallimard, 1953 (*Absalom! Absalom!, New York, NY*: Random House, 1936).

Philippe Fauré-Frémiet, *La Recréation du réel et l'équivoque*, Paris: Alcan/ Presses universitaires de France, 1940.

Jean-Claude Filloux, *Psychologie des animaux*, Paris: PUF, 1950.

Abou'Lkasim Firdousi, *Le Livre de Feridoun et de Minoutchehr, rois de Perse*, Paris: H. Piazza, 1924.

Victor Fleury and Mohammed Soualah, *L'Arabe pratique et commercial. À l'usage des établissements d'instruction et des hommes d'affaires. Lecture, écriture, grammaire, syntaxe, exercices d'application, textes suivis, conversation, lexiques, dictionnaire commercial*, Algiers: La Typo-litho Jules Carbonel, 1950.

Benjamin Fondane, *Baudelaire et l'expérience du gouffre*, Paris: P. Seghers, 1947.

Louis-René des Forêts, *La Chambre des enfants*, Paris: Gallimard, 1960.

Émile Forgue, *Précis de pathologie externe*, Paris: G. Doin & Cie, 1948.

[A note on the inside of the cover indicates: 'Alan Paton, *Pleure ô pays bien aimé*', the French title of Paton's *Cry, the Beloved Country*.]

Michel Foucault, *Histoire de la folie à l'âge classique*, Paris: Plon, 1961.

H. Fraisse and Abdul-Kader Husseini, 'Dégénérescence cancéreuse de la vésicule lithiasique. À propos d'une statistique médico-chirurgicale de

197 cas recueillis dans les services du docteur M. Girard et du professeur Bertrand', *Journal de médecine de Lyon*, vol. 35, 5 February 1954, pp. 121–9.

Simon Frank, *La Connaissance et l'être*, Paris: Fernand Aubier, 1937.

[There are some marks in the translator's introduction. In particular, p. VI: 'In opposition with all the subjectivist doctrines that think they can deify man by turning him, through his knowledge, into the origin of the world in which he lives, but only end up rendering him a stranger to reality by enclosing him in a superficial and fictive representation, [Simon Frank] expresses and defends his unshakeable conviction that we belong intimately to the real'.]

Sigmund Freud, *Trois Essais sur la théorie de la sexualité*, Paris: Gallimard, 1923.

[Many marks are contained in the chapters on 'Sexual aberrations' and 'Infantile sexuality'.]

Sigmund Freud, *L'Avenir d'une illusion*, Paris: Denoël et Steele, 1932.

Sigmund Freud, *Introduction à la psychanalyse*, Paris: Payot, 1947. (*General Introduction to Psychoanalysis*, trans. and prefaced by G. Stanley Hall, New York, NY: Boni and Liveright, 1920).

[The chapters on dream are marked in several places. Some of the annotations seem to be by Fanon, in particular those expressing doubts about the symbolism of the sexual organs and the idea of an unconscious knowledge of symbolism. Thus, on p. 137: 'We can only say that the dreamer's knowledge of *symbolism is unconscious*, that it is part of his *unconscious psychic life* [expression in italics in the original and underlined]'. This sentence is accompanied in the margin with 'Stop talking nonsense'. The following sentence, p. 138, is marked with 'Bastard': 'the primitive man made work acceptable at the same time as he used it as an equivalent and substitute for sex-activity'.]

Sigmund Freud, *Essais de psychanalyse. I. Au-delà du principe du plaisir. II. Psychologie collective et analyse du moi. III. Le Moi et le Soi. IV. Considérations actuelles sur la guerre et sur la mort*, Paris: Payot, 1948.

Sigmund Freud, *Psychopathologie de la vie quotidienne*, Paris: Payot, 1948.

Sigmund Freud, *Abrégé de psychanalyse*, Paris: PUF, 1955.

Georges Friedmann, *Problèmes humains du machinisme industriel*, Paris: Gallimard, 1946.

Claude Frioux, *Maïakovski par lui-même*, Paris: Seuil, 1961.

Eugène Fromentin, *Dominique*, Paris: Éditions de Cluny, 1938.

[This book bears the stamp of the Blida-Joinville Psychiatric Hospital.]

Peter Fryer and Patricia McGowan Pinheiro, *Oldest Ally: A Portrait of Salazar's Portugal*, Paris: D. Dolson, 1961.

André Galli and Robert Leluc, *L'Analyse biochimique médicale*, Paris: PUF, 1957.

Jean Garamond, *Images de l'homme immobile*, Paris: Éditions de La Baconnière, 1943.

Alexandre Garde, *Les Complications neurologiques des néoplasmes viscéraux. Rapport de neurologie. Congrès de psychiatrie et de neurologie de langue française*, Paris: Masson & Cie, 1958.

Arthur van Gehuchten, *Les Maladies nerveuses*, Louvain: Librairie universitaire, 1945.

Jean Giraudoux, *Simon le pathétique*, Paris: Grasset, 1926.

Édouard Glissant, *Les Indes. Poème de l'une et l'autre terre*, Paris: Falaize, 1956.

[Copy of one of the deluxe editions, perhaps given to Josie Fanon after Fanon's death. It bears the following dedication: 'This epic of the New World – its sufferings, its humanity – for you, dear Houria, on this first day of the grand Algerian state. Hope! Hope! Éd.']

Kurt Goldstein, *La Structure de l'organisme. Introduction à la biologie à partir de la pathologie humaine (Der Aufbau des Organismus)*, Paris: Gallimard, 1951.

[Volume marked in several places, without annotation.]

André Gorz, *Le Traître*, Paris: Seuil, 1958.

Marcel Granet, *La Civilisation chinoise*, Paris: Albin Michel, 1929.

Antoine Grégoire, *Le Bégaiement. Conseils indispensables à sa guérison*, Paris: Éditions Lumières, 1948.

Bernard Groethuysen, *Introduction à la pensée philosophique allemande depuis Nietzsche*, Paris: Stock, 1926.

Romano Guardini, *De la mélancolie*, Paris: Seuil, 1952.

Daniel Guérin, *Où va le peuple américain?*, Paris: Julliard, 1951.

Miller Guerra, *Le Syndrome cérébelleux et le syndrome vestibulaire*, Paris: Masson & Cie, 1954.

Georges Gullain and Ivan Bertrand, *Anatomie topographique du système nerveux central*, Paris: Masson & Cie, 1926.

Jean Guillaume, *Les Accidents circulatoires du cerveau*, Paris: PUF, 1957.

Jean Guillaume, *Les Méningiomes: Étude clinique et chirurgicale*, Paris: PUF, 1957.

Jean Guillaume and Jean Sigwald, *Diagnostic neurochirurgical*, Paris: PUF, 1947.

Jean Guillaume, Gabriel Mazars and Stanislas de Sèze, *Chirurgie cérébro-spinale de la douleur*, Paris: PUF, 1949.

Paul Guillaume, *La Psychologie de la forme*, Paris: Flammarion, 1937.

[Volume carrying the stamp of the medical library of the Psychiatric Hospital of Saint-Alban.]

Paul Guillaume, *La Psychologie animale*, Paris: Armand Colin, 1947.

[The section 'L'emploi des symboles' in the chapter on 'Le problème de l'intelligence' is marked in the margin in several places, in particular the passages on the failure of attempts to teach symbolism to monkeys, or its transmission, in contrast to the human child.]

Gérard Guiot, *Adénomes hypophysaires*, Paris: Masson & Cie, 1958.

Georges Gurvitch, *La Sociologie au XXe siècle. Les études sociologiques dans les différents pays*, vol. 2, Paris: PUF, 1947.

[Contains a number of marks.]

Georges Gurvitch, *La Vocation actuelle de la sociologie. Sociologie différentielle*, vol. 1, Paris: PUF, 1957.

[There are some marginal marks in the section bearing on anthropology and cultural ethnology. In particular: 'However, the idea can be seen to establish itself more and more that the social penetrates as far as the psycho-pathological. So, in Muslim societies, sociologists have observed that the insane do not commit suicide so long as they are under the sway of religious prohibitions against suicide, which remain profoundly implanted in the mentality of the patients' (p. 34). Similarly, concerning the symbol in the living collective consciousness, a theme that Fanon often broached: 'Each time that, in a global type of society (in the state of revolution, of war or of transition), or in a particular grouping (group of economic activity, a brotherhood, a mystico-ecstatic grouping, a social class, etc.), what we see predominate are effervescent, innovative, creative collective behaviours, what we can observe is that, on the one hand, activist and volitional communions are at work and that, on the other, the symbols and models that were valid up to then lose their efficacy and their prestige' (p. 84).]

Georges Gurvitch (ed.), *Traité de sociologie*, vol. 1, Paris: PUF, 1958.

[In this collective volume, the pages of section III of the first chapter are cut. This is the article by Roger Bastide, 'Sociologie et psychologie'.]

Georges Gurvitch (ed.), *Traité de sociologie*, vol. 2, Paris: PUF, 1960.

Aron Gurwitsch, *Théorie du champ de la conscience*, Paris: Desclée de Brouwer, 1957.

Georges Gusdorf, *Traité de l'existence morale*, Paris: Armand Colin, 1946.

Georges Gusdorf, *Mémoire et personne. La Mémoire concrète*, vol. 1, Paris: PUF, 1951.

Georges Gusdorf, *Mémoire et personne. Dialectique de la mémoire*, vol. 2, Paris: PUF, 1951.

Georges Gusdorf, *La Parole*, Paris: PUF, 1953.

Daniel Halévy, *La Vie de Proudhon*, Paris: Stock, 1948.

Hervé Harant and Nguyên Duc, *Pathologie exotique*, Paris: Maloine, 1948.

Georges Hardy, *Portrait de Lyautey*, Paris: Existence du monde, 1949.

Georg W. F. Hegel, *Principes de la philosophie du droit*, Paris: Gallimard, 1940.

Georg W. F. Hegel, *Esthétique*, Paris: Aubier, 1944.

Georg W. F. Hegel, *La Phénoménologie de l'esprit*, vols. 1 and 2, Paris: Aubier-Montaigne, 1947. (French translation by Jean Hyppolite of Hegel's *Phänomenologie des Geistes*.)

[Some of the passages of this work are marked in the margins, in particular in the chapter on 'The truth of self-certainty', the section on 'Mastery and Servitude'. For example: '*And it is solely by staking one's life that freedom is preserved* [passage underlined by Fanon. Susbsequent italics are in the original], that the essence of self-consciousness is proven not to be *being*, not the immediate way self-consciousness first emerges, nor its being absorbed within the expanse of life – but rather, through this risk, it is proven that there is nothing present which, in itself, could not be a vanishing moment for it, that is, that self-consciousness is merely pure *being-for-itself*. The individual who has not put his life at stake may admittedly be recognized as a *person*, but he has not achieved the truth of being recognized as an independant self-consciousness (pp. 168–9).

The unessential consciousness is therein for the master the object which constitutes the *truth* of his certainty of himself. However, it is clear that this object does not correspond to its concept. Rather, in the object in which the master has achieved his mastery he finds something entirely different from an independent consciousness [in the margin: "mirror"]. It is not an independent consciousness which exists for him but rather a dependent consciousness' (p. 173).

In the volume edited by André Leroi-Gourhan, *L'Homme, races et mœurs*, the following handwritten note was inserted, perhaps one from a course or lecture on Hegel: 'On Hegel's logic. According to Hegel, only language is sense and sense of sense. There is no effective sense unless through the unity of the in-itself and the for-itself. Via language, there is a passage from the realm of sensation to sense and an inverse passage from thought to its own alienation. How can we go from phenomenology to absolute knowledge? Hegel defines true thought, the concept, as a thinking that gives the Ego [*au Moi*] the consistency of being in-itself, objective value, and to the thing thought the subjective value of the for-itself of consciousness. Kant, in order to go from the realm of sensation to the understanding, spoke of the imagination as a common source. Absolute knowledge with Hegel presumes an active man, since there is no given signification, necessity, but an engendered signification, signification of self: the absolute is subject. With Hegel, speculative logic replaces dogmatic metaphysics. The *logos* as speculative life is *selbst-bewusst-sein* with its three moments: being as immediate (*sein*), the appearing of being (*bewusst*) and the sense or the self (*selbst*).']

Ernest Hemingway, *L'Adieu aux armes*, Paris: Gallimard, 1948. (*A Farewell to Arms*, New York: Scribner, 1929)

Ernest Hemingway, *Pour qui sonne le glas*, Paris: Gallimard, 1961. (*For Whom the Bell Tolls*, New York: Scribner, 1940).

Angelo Hesnard and René Laforgue, *L'Évolution psychiatrique. Psychanalyse, psychologie clinique*, Paris: Payot, 1927.

[Several passages of the articles making up this historical collection, in which Hesnard did the first history of the psychoanalytic movement in France, are marked:

René Laforgue and Georges Parcheminey, 'Conflits psychiques et troubles organiques': 'Ultimately, psychoanalysis, by broadening the field of consciousness, makes it possible to study in more precise fashion the organo-psychic complexes; as for the intimate explanation of these processes, we can only underline the interest of it here, without claiming to resolve it' (p. 35). 'In the treatment of clinical complexes, with organic involvement, sympathetic and psychic, which have not yielded to the rational treatments used up to now, psychoanalysis appears to us as though it ought to constitue an effective weapon' (p. 44).

Angelo Hesnard, 'Les applications de la psychanalyse à l'étude du mécanisme psychogénétique des psychoses délirantes chroniques': there are several marks here relating to technical points. 'This conception of neurotic symptoms as a morbid solution to the conflict between repressed tendencies and the "conscious ego" which represses is at the basis of the psychoanalytic theory of neuroses' (p. 76, note 1). Eugène Minkowski, 'De la rêverie morbide au délire d'influence': '*To understand* the content of psychosis hardly seems enough. The point is further to *explain it*, to explain the appearance of mental disorders as well as their particular characters' (p. 157); in the margin there is an accolade linking 'Jaspers' and '*Verstehen-Erklären*'.

Édouard Pichon, 'De l'extension légitime du domaine de la psychanalyse': very negative comments, especially on p. 223 where Pichon seems to advocate a 'noumenal' knowledge of the psyche in opposition to the 'Chinese shadows' that supposedly make up the object of psychoanalysis. Thus: 'A teeny bit of phenomenological reflection would reveal, Pichon, the *pre*-personal field of the empirical consciousness and the *transcendence* of the ego.']

Angelo Hesnard, *L'Univers morbide de la faute*, Paris: PUF, 1949.

Thor Heyerdahl, *L'Expédition du* Kon-Tiki. *Sur un radeau à travers le Pacifique*, Paris: Albin Michel, 1951.

Chester Himes, *La Troisième génération*, Paris: Gallimard, 1954.

Homer, *Iliade*, Paris: Garnier, 1945.

Homer, *Odyssée*, Paris: Armand Colin, 1947.

Victor Hugo, *Les Voix intérieures*, Paris: Garnier frères, 1950.

Johan Huizinga, *Le Déclin du Moyen Âge*, Paris: Payot, 1948.

Edmund Husserl, *Idées directrices pour une phénoménologie*, Paris: Gallimard, 1950.

[Some passages are underlined in the introduction of the translator, Paul Ricœur].

Alex Inkeles, *L'Opinion publique en Russie soviétique. Une étude sur la persuasion des masses*, Paris: Les Îles d'or, 1956.

Anatoli Georgievitch Ivanov-Smolenski, 'Essais sur la physiopathologie de l'activité nerveuse supérieure'. La Raison, *Cahiers de psychopathologie scientifique*, nos. 11–12, 4th trimester 1955.

Max Jacob, *Le Cornet à dés*, Paris: Stock, 1923.

Max Jacob, *Lettres de Max Jacob à Jean Cocteau (1919–1944)*, Paris: Gallimard, 1950.

Cyril Lionel Robert James, *Les Jacobins noirs. Toussaint Louverture et la révolution de Saint-Domingue*, Paris: Gallimard, 1949.

Claude Jamet, *Images mêlées*, Paris: Éditions de l'Élan, 1947.

Pierre Janet, *Les Médications psychologiques*, Paris: Félix Alcan, 1919.

Pierre Janet, *De l'angoisse à l'extase. Études sur les croyances et les sentiments*, vol. 1, Paris: Félix Alcan, 1926.

Pierre Janet, *De l'angoisse à l'extase. Les sentiments fondamentaux*, vol. 2, Paris: Félix Alcan, 1928.

[Several passages are marked in the chapter on 'Les béatitudes', notably pp. 500–32, on the relations between schizophrenia, hysteria, autism and inspired, ecstatic states or states of total inaction.]

Auguste Jardé, *La Grèce antique et la vie grecque. Géographie, histoire, littérature, beaux-arts, vie publique, vie privée*, Paris: Delagrave, 1946.

Alfred Jarry, *Gestes et opinions du docteur Faustroll, pataphysicien*, Paris: Stock, 1923.

Karl Jaspers, *Nietzsche et le christianisme*, Paris: Minuit, 1949. (Nietzsche and Christianity, trans. E.B. Ashton, Henry Regnery Company, [1938] 1961.)

[Some passages are marked in this volume. Thus: 'For it was Christianity which, according to Nietzsche, destroyed all the truth by which man had been living in pre-Christian times – above all, the tragic truth of life as understood by the Greeks before Socrates. To counter this, Christianity put up mere fictions: God, moral world-order, immortality, sin, grace, redemption' (p. 15).]

Andreï Jdanov, *Sur la littérature, la philosophie et la musique*, Paris: Éditions de 'La Nouvelle Critique', 1950.

Francis Jeanson, *La Phénoménologie*, Paris: Téqui, 1951.

[This volume has been very carefully read and contains marks throughout.]

Francis Jeanson, *La Vraie vérité: alibi. Suivi de la récrimination: essai*, Paris: Seuil, 1954.

Francis Jeanson, *Sartre par lui-même*, Paris: Seuil, 1955.

Pierre Jean Jouve, *Ode*, Paris: Minuit, 1950.

Claude Julien, *Le Nouveau Nouveau Monde. L'élite au pouvoir, les syndicats ouvriers*, vol. 1, Paris: Julliard, 1960

Carl Gustav Jung, *L'Homme à la découverte de son âme. Structure et fonctionnement de l'inconscient*, Paris: Éditions du Mont-Blanc, 1940.

[A number of annotations are to be found in this volume, in general negative ones. Thus, all that concerns consciousness from p. 77 on, on the mediately accessible contents of consciousness, is judged 'absurd' or 'simplistic' [*simple*]. Subsequent pages, which localize consciousness in the organic (in opposition to the rest of the psyche) and the passages on 'primitives' are marked with violent comments. Thus: 'Shit, and when I think that there exists a psychoanalysis based on this psychology' in the margin of this paragraph: 'Observe a primitive and you will observe that if he is not breathtaken by some event, nothing happens in him; he remains seated for hours, simply there, in total inertia; if you ask him what he's thinking about, he is offended, because in his eyes thinking is the privilege of madmen! So it cannot be presumed that any thought acts through him; however, his state is also far removed from one of absolute rest: the unconscious exerts in him a vivacious activity, whence sudden and interesting ideas can gush out, the primitive being a master at the "art" of letting his unconscious speak and lending it an attentive ear' (p. 84).

Or else: 'Bastard' in the margin of these phrases: 'At the start of my stay in Africa, I was astonished by the brutality with which the indigenous were treated, whipping being a common practice; first, it seemed superfluous to me, but I had to come to the conclusion that it was necessary; since that moment I constantly bore my rhinoceros-hide whip at my side. I learned to simulate affects that I did not feel, to give out full-throated cries and to stamp my feet with anger. It is necessary to make up in this way for the deficient will of the indigenous' (p. 92).]

Carl Gustav Jung, *Aspects du drame contemporain*, Librairie de l'Université, Paris: George & Cie, 1948.

Franz Kafka, *Journal intime*, Paris: Grasset, 1945.

[Some marks feature in Pierre Klossowski's introduction, such as around this passage, which finds an echo in Fanon's reflections on the relations between illness and religion: 'The patient whose health is refused him can find in illness the path leading beyond health toward saintliness. The man who enjoys health may move to the climes of illness; his own good health has prevented him from living the life of God that he finds at last within the illness of others. In both cases, health appears to obstruct the true path. And it seems that the healthy life proceeds against God' (p. 16).]

Franz Kafka, *L'Amérique*, Paris: Gallimard, 1946.

Franz Kafka, *La Métamorphose*, Paris: Gallimard, 1946.

Franz Kafka, *La Muraille de Chine et autres récits*, Paris: Gallimard, 1950.

Immanuel Kant, *Critique de la raison pure*, Paris: Librairie Joseph Gibert, 1943.

Immanuel Kant, *Fondements de la métaphysique des mœurs*, Paris: Delagrave, 1951.

Søren Kierkegaard, *Ou bien … ou bien …*, Paris: Gallimard, 1943.

Søren Kierkegaard, *Vie et règne de l'amour*, Paris: Aubier, 1945.

Søren Kierkegaard, *Crainte et tremblement*, Paris: Aubier, 1946.

Søren Kierkegaard, *Les Miettes philosophiques*, new translation by Paul Petit, Paris: Éditions du Livre français, 1947.

Søren Kierkegaard, *Étapes sur le chemin de la vie*, Paris: Gallimard, 1948. (*Stages on Life's Way*, ed. and trans. with introduction and notes by Howard V. Hong and Edna H. Hong, Princeton, NJ: Princeton University Press, 1988.)

[Some marks in the last section, 'A concluding word'. On pp. 485–6: 'I look at the religious position from all sides, and to that extent I continually have one more side than the sophist, who sees only one side, but what makes me a sophist is that I do not become a religious person. ... Sophists can be grouped in three classes: 1) Those who from the aesthetic reach an immediate relation to the religious. [in the margin: "FF"]. Here, religion becomes poetry, history; ... But the religious consists precisely in being religiously, infinitely concerned about oneself and not about visions [Fr. Tr.: *fantasmagories*], in being infinitely concerned about oneself and not about a positive goal, which is negative and finite because the infinitely negative is the only adequate form for the infinite; in being infinitely concerned about oneself and consequently not deeming oneself finished, which is negative and perdition. This I do know, but I know it with a balance of spirit and therefore am a sophist like the others, for this balance is an offense against the holy passion of the religious.']

Arthur Koestler, *Le Zéro et l'infini*, Paris: Calmann-Lévy, 1938.

Alexandre Kojève, *Introduction à la lecture de Hegel. Leçons sur la phénoménologie de l'esprit*, Paris: Gallimard, 1947.

[Of course, the first section, comprising the famous analysis of chapter 4, section A, of *Phänomenologie des Geistes*, 'Autonomy and dependance of self-consciousness; mastery and servitude', is amply marked in the margins, notably the page on which Kojève comments on the proposition 'Human desire must be directed toward another desire.' The phrase 'human reality can only be social' is underlined. In the last section, in which Kojève returns to the dialectic of recognition, the last sentence of the following paragraph is marked with a line in the margin: 'The man who has engaged in the fight for recognition must remain alive to be able to *live* humanly. But he only lives *humanly* to the extent that he is *recognized* by the other. His adversary must therefore also escape death. The combat must stop short of death, contrary to what Hegel says in his *Lectures* of 1803–1804 (vol. 19, p. 229)' (p. 569).]

Alexandre Koyré, Henri-Charles Puech and André Spaier (eds.), *Recherches philosophiques. 1931–1932*, vol. 1, Paris: Boivin & Cie, 1932.

[There are some annotations on Gaston Bachelard's article on 'Noumène et microphysique'. In particular, this sentence: 'Thus we can no longer see in the description, even painstaking, of an immediate world anything other than a *working phenomenology* in the same sense in which one formerly spoke of a *working hypothesis*' (p. 57).]

Alexandre Koyré, Henri-Charles Puech and André Spaier (eds.), *Recherches philosophiques. 1932–1933*, vol. 2, Paris: Boivin & Cie, 1932.

[Jean Wahl's article on 'Heidegger et Kierkegaard' is marked in several places with added references to Jaspers (pp. 355 and 362) and Husserl (p. 367).]

Alexandre Koyré, Henri-Charles Puech and André Spaier (eds.), *Recherches philosophiques. 1933–1934*, vol. 3, Paris: Boivin & Cie, 1933.

Alexandre Koyré, Henri-Charles Puech and André Spaier (eds.), *Recherches philosophiques. 1934–1935*, vol. 4, Paris: Boivin & Cie, 1935.

[The articles by André Spaier ('Le complexe de l'individualisme') and by Eugène Minkowski ('Esquisses phénoménologiques') are cut and marked in several places.]

Alexandre Koyré, Henri-Charles Puech and André Spaier (eds.), *Recherches philosophiques. 1936–1937*, vol. 6, Paris: Boivin & Cie, 1937.

[Günther Stern (Günther Anders)'s article, 'Pathologie de la liberté: Essai sur la non-identification', is marked in several places. This important volume also contains Sartre's 'La transcendance de l'Ego. Esquisse d'une description phénoménologique' and Jean Wahl's article on 'Le *Nietzsche* de Jaspers'.]

Hugo Krayenbul, *L'Anévrysme de l'artère communicante antérieure*, Paris: Masson & Cie, 1959.

Henri Kréa, *Grand Jour*, Florence: Éditions Spartacus, 1956.

[Dedication dated 20 September 1956: "To Frantz Fanon, who knows my town of birth and whose intelligence pulverizes the monsters. In fraternity."]

Arthur Kreindler, *La Physiologie et la physiopathologie du cervelet*, Paris: Masson & Cie, 1958.

Roland Kuhn, *Phénoménologie du masque. À travers le test de Rorschach*, Paris: Desclée de Brouwer, 1957.

Henri Laborit and Geneviève Laborit, *Excitabilité neuromusculaire et équilibre ionique. Intérêt pratique en chirurgie et en hibernothérapie*, Paris: Masson & Cie, 1955.

Pierre Lachièze-Rey, *Les Idées morales, sociales et politiques de Platon*, Paris: Boivin & Cie, 1938.

Jean Lacroix, *Le Sens du dialogue*, Neuchâtel: Éditions de La Baconnière, 1944.

[There are some marks in the first section, 'Orgueil et vanité' and 'De la duplicité'.]

Jules Larforgue, *Anthologie poétique. Hamlet*, Paris: Club français du livre, 1952.

André Lalande, *Vocabulaire technique et critique de la philosophie*, Paris: PUF, 1951.

Quentin Lauer, *Phénoménologie de Husserl*, Paris: PUF, 1955.

Louis Lavelle, *De l'acte*, Paris: Montaigne, 1946.

[Some marks. In particular, on the section on 'dialectical action': 'This is enough to show that philosophy and life itself only have a serious character on the conditions that the Absolute is not before me and outside of me as an inaccessible goal, but on the contrary in me and that in it I trace my furrow' (p. 49).]

Guy Lazorthes, *Le Système neurovasculaire*, Paris: Masson & Cie, 1949.

Serge Lebovici and Joyce McDougall, *Un cas de psychose infantile. Étude psychanalytique*, Paris: PUF, 1960.

Auguste Lecoeur, *L'Autocritique attendue*, Paris: Girault, 1955.

Henri Lefebvre, *Le Matérialisme dialectique*, Paris: PUF, 1949.

Henri Lefebvre, *Problèmes actuels du marxisme*, Paris: PUF, 1958.

Michel Leiris, *Contacts de civilisations en Martinique et en Guadeloupe*, Paris: Gallimard/Unesco, 1955.

Michel Leiris, *La Règle du jeu. Biffures*, vol. 1, Paris: Gallimard, 1948.

Michel Leiris, *Race et civilisation*, Paris: Unesco, 1951.

[This volume carries the stamp of Blida-Joinville Psychiatric Hospital.]

Jean Lepoire and Bernard Pertuiset, *Les Kystes épidermoïdes cranio-encéphaliques*, Paris: Masson & Cie, 1957.

René Leriche, *La Chirurgie, discipline de la connaissance*, Paris: La Diane française, 1949.

André Leroi-Gourhan, *Ethnologie de l'Union française. Asie, Océanie, Amérique*, Paris: PUF, 1952.

André Leroi-Gourhan (ed.), *L'Homme, races et mœurs*, Paris: Clartés, 1957.

Claude Lévi-Strauss, *Tristes tropiques*, Paris: Plon, 1955.

Emmanuel Levinas, *De l'existence à l'existant*, Paris: Fontaine, 1947. (*Existence and Existents*, trans. Alphonso Lingis, Pittsburgh, PA: Duquesne University Press, 2001.)

[Some marks are contained in the margins pertaining to Levinas' following sentences: 'What was interrupted does not sink into nothingness like a game. This means that the act is inscription in being. And indolence, as a recoil before action, is a hesitation before existence, an indolence about existing' (p. 15); 'Health, the sincere movement of the desiring toward the desirable, that good will that know exactly

what it wants, gauges the reality and the concreteness of a human being'
(p. 32).]

Georges Lévy, *Formulaire vénérologique du praticien*, Paris: Doin & Cie, 1948.

Jean Lhermitte and Julian de Ajuriaguerra, *Psychopathologie de la vision*, Paris: Masson & Cie, 1942.

[Some marks are contained in the first chapter on hemianopsies (pp. 12–14), including one annotation: 'Nice illustration of *gestalt th*'.]

Maurice Loeper and André Lesure, *Formulaire pratique de thérapeutique et de pharmacologie. Ancien formulaire de Dujardin-Beaumetz-Yvon et Gilbert, Michel*, Paris: G. Doin & Cie, 1948.

Juan José Lopez Ibor, *La Angustia vital. Patología general psicosomática*, Madrid: Paz Montalvo, 1950.

Juan José Lopez Ibor, *El Español y su complejo de inferioridad*, Madrid: Rialp, 'Biblioteca del pensamiento actual', 1954.

Malcolm Lowry, *Au-dessous du volcan*, Paris: Corrêa, 1950.

Georg Lukacs, *Existentialisme ou marxisme?*, Paris: Nagel, 1948.

[Writing on the flyleaf reads: 'Fanon Frantz, 29 rue Tupin' (a street in the centre of Lyon). The pages of the chapters 'Sartre contre Marx' (pp. 141–60) and 'La morale de l'ambiguïté et l'ambiguïté de la morale existentialiste' (pp. 160–211) are cut and bear some marks. For example: 'But this opinion [Sartre's suppressing of the objectivity of nature and history, "since in his eyes, only pure interior subjectivity is worthy of this name"] becomes very difficult to defend, when you have the ambition to defend it against Marxism, qua true philosophy of history' (p. 148); 'No compromise is possible either, between the existentialist conception of freedom and the dialectical and historical unity of freedom and necessity, as established by Marxism' (p. 204). Several pages of the chapter 'Signification dialectique de l'approximation dans la théorie de la connaissance' are cut and marked. Most of the annotations concern the relativism in epistemology defended by Lukacs ('Our knowledge is only ever an approximation of the plenitude of reality and, by the same token, it is always relative' (p. 286)). The commentaries in general express disagreement.]

Georg Lukacs, *La Destruction de la raison. Les débuts de l'irrationalisme moderne de Schelling à Nietzsche*, vol. 1, Paris: L'Arche, 1958.

Nicolas Machiavelli, *Les Pages immortelles de Machiavel*, Paris: Corrêa, 1947.

Gabriel Madinier, *Conscience et amour. Essai sur le « nous »*, Paris: PUF, 1947.

[A loose page of the chapter on 'Espace et durée' from Emmanuel Mounier's *Traité du caractère* (1946, p. 319) is inserted here at p. 66. At issue is a reflection on Bergson. The paragraph that begins as follows was probably of interest to Fanon: 'An overly powerful discovery often blocks reflection into exclusive pathways. By restoring the dignity of lived duration, Bergson has, willy nilly, long prevented our looking with justice at regions where duration approaches space through extension and measured time. As Minkowski remarks, after having erred, in speaking of time, through an excess of statism, since Bergson we err through an excess of dynamism. However, everything today leads us to the idea of a spatiotemporal solidarity that is as close as organo-psychic solidarity.']

Claude-Edmonde Magny, *Les Sandales d'Empédocle. Essai sur les limites de la littérature*, Neuchâtel: Éditions de La Baconnière, 1945.

Claude-Edmonde Magny, *Histoire du roman français depuis 1918*, Paris: Seuil, 1950.

André Malraux, *Les Voix du silence*, Paris: Gallimard, 1951.

André Malraux, *Romans*, Paris: Gallimard, 1951.

Clara Malraux, *Journal psychanalytique d'une petite fille*, Paris: Gallimard, 1928.

Thomas Mann, *Mario et le magicien*, Paris: Stock, 1932.

Octave Mannoni, *Psychologie de la colonisation*, Paris: Seuil, 1950.

[Some marks as far as p. 109. No annotation.]

Gabriel Marcel, *Journal métaphysique*, Paris: Gallimard, 1935.

Jules Marouzeau, *La Linguistique ou science du langage*, Paris: P. Geuthner, 1950.

Luis Martín-Santos, *Dilthey, Jaspers y la comprensión del enfermo mental*, Madrid: Paz Montalvo, 1955.

[There is a handwritten note inserted in this volume that translates the start of chapter 9 of the second part of this book: 'Comprehensive psychology and psychopathology in Jaspers. Psychological understanding consists in applying to individual psychic elements, isolated through a descriptive labour, an ideal schema of motivation, which is situated at the level of the mind. The ideal type is an absolute *a priori* truth that cannot be demonstrated. The relation of motivation, for example between autumn melancholy and the decision to commit suicide, constitutes an absolute truth. This psychological work, which consists in the illustrating of typical motivations, constitutes more an interpretation.']

Jules Masserman, *Principes de psychiatrie dynamique*, Paris: PUF, 1959.

François Mauriac, *L'Agneau*, Paris: Flammarion, 1954.

André Maurois, *Olympio ou la vie de Victor Hugo*, Paris: Hachette, 1954.

Marcel Mauss, *Sociologie et anthropologie*, Paris: PUF, 1950.

Heinrich Meng, *Protection de la santé mentale*, Paris: Payot, 1944.

[A copy of the ward journal of Blida-Joinville Psychiatric Hospital is inserted into this volume (no. 39, 16 September 1954) with this editorial by Jacques Azoulay about the earthquake in Orléansville that occurred on 9 September: 'Thursday morning around 1 am, an earthquake shook the entire hospital. Everyone, surprised in their sleep, felt a displeasing anxiety, which was quickly calmed; when it was time to wake up later on, it was only a topic for discussion, and even for jokes. But during the day, we were informed little by little of the extent of the disaster, which in a few seconds devastated an entire region of our beautiful country. Something that threatened to pass to the status of a scarcely salient event in our memories, was in actual fact to affect us for a longtime, and continues to do so. Something that was likely to quickly become a matter of indifference had all the world talking about it: in London, in Rome, in Paris, everyone spared a thought for our country, for our wounded brothers. And in the hospital, too, we ought to gather ourselves to make room for our comrades of Orléansville who are now homeless. This sad event comes to remind us, as if it were needed, that we must stay in relation with the world, that we must hold onto it, that we must think about it as it must think about us.']

Charles Mentha, *Bases physiologiques de la chirurgie neurovasculaire. Énervations sympathiques, assistance mutuelle des territoires vasculaires*, Paris: Masson & Cie, 1956.

Fernand Mercier (ed.), *Les Médicaments du système nerveux cérébrospinal*, Paris: Masson & Cie, 1959.

Maurice Merleau-Ponty, *La Structure du comportement*, Paris: PUF, 1942. (*The Structure of Behavior*, trans. Alden F. Fisher, Boston, MA: Beacon Press, 1963).

[There are several significant marks, which emphasize in particular the following passages: 'To learn is thus never about becoming able to repeat the same gesture, but to provide an adapted response to the situation by different means' (p. 96); 'It [intuition] is one of the possible perspectives upon the structure and immanent meaning of conduct, which constitute the only psychological "reality"' (p. 184); 'The study of reflex has shown us that the nervous system is the place in which an order without anatomical guarantee is realized by means of a continuing organization' (p. 207); 'Higher behaviour retains the subordinated dialectics in the present depths of its existence, from that of the physical system and its topological conditions to that of the organism and its "milieu". They are not recognizable in the whole when it functions correctly, but the disintegration in case of partial lesion attests to their imminence' (pp. 207–8).]

Maurice Merleau-Ponty, *Sens et non-sens*, Paris: Nagel, 1948.

Robert King Merton, *Éléments de méthode sociologique*, Paris: Plon, 1953.

Gaston Milhaud, *Études sur Cournot*, Paris: Librairie philosophique Vrin, 1927.

[In this volume, the pages of chapter 2, 'La définition du hasard de Cournot', are cut. There are some marks in the margins that can be presumed to be Fanon's, since they bear on the idea of a causality that cannot be reduced to a simple determination. Thus, on p. 41: 'Dependency in the largest sense would probably be represented, in Cournot's eyes, by a function or by a set of functions, being expressed only with the aid of constant parameters, containing no variable coefficient, and leading from the precise data in one of the series to precise determinations in the other. Independence, on the contrary – and I hereby arrive at one of the most important and most poorly recognized points of Cournot's thinking – is inseperable from the idea of a multiplicity of possible determinations for one of the series, the other being given.']

Louis Moland, *Théâtre de Marivaux*, Paris: Classiques Garnier, 1951.

Georges Morin, *Physiologie du système nerveux central*, Paris: Masson & Cie, 1948.

Marcel Mouquin, *Manuel de pathologie médicale. Physiopathologie médicale. Cœur-Artères-Veines-Sang*, vol. 1, Paris: Masson & Cie, 1947.

Paul Mousset, *Ce Sahara qui voit le jour*, Paris: Presses de la Cité, 1959.

Henry A. Murray, *Thematic Apperception Test Manual*, Cambridge, MA: Harvard University Press, 1948 (French translation: Centre de psychologie appliquée, 1950).

[This book carries the stamp of Blida-Joinville Psychiatric Hospital.]

Jean Nabert, *Éléments pour une éthique*, Paris: PUF, 1943.

Pierre Naville, *La Psychologie science du comportement. Le behaviorisme de Watson*, Paris: Gallimard, 1942.

[There are some marks in this classic introduction to behaviourism. Some pages are marked along the entire length of the margin. They bear on the articulation of verbal behaviour and physical movement (pp. 182 and 184–5). What may have interested Fanon in this behaviourist theory of language, which was soon to appear obsolete, is the new relation of thought to the world, no longer as representation, but, through language, as a bodily disposition: '[Between words and things an *equivalence of reaction* is established.] It also enables the isolated individual to transport the external world with him, and to manipulate it in solitude. The world, then, is no longer constituted with objects present to the senses, but is stored in the form of a particular bodily organization (including on the front line the throat and the chest with the sensorial organs of the muscles and the nervous system)' (p. 184).]

Friedrich Nietzsche, *Considérations inactuelles, deuxième série*, Paris: Mercure de France, 1922.

[A citation is written in pencil on the title page of the first consideration of this series, 'Schopenhauer as educator': '"Do not let virtue fly away from earthly things and beat against eternal walls with its wings! [...] Like me, guide the virtue that has flown away back to the earth – yes, back to the body and life: so that it may give the earth its meaning, a HUMAN meaning!" F. Nietzsche.' This is an extract from the start of the second section of the sermon 'On the bestowing virtue' at the end of the first part of *Thus Spoke Zarathustra* (The French quote Fanon gives is from Henri Albert's translation of this work: '*Ne laissez pas votre vertu s'envoler des choses terrestre et battre des ailes contre des murs éternels. Ramenez comme moi la vertu égarée sur la terre – afin qu'elle donne un sens à la terre – un sens HUMAIN*' (Paris: Mercure de France, 1903). 'Human' is not in capitals in Nietzsche's text.]

Friedrich Nietzsche, *La Généalogie de la morale*, Paris: Mercure de France, 1943.

[This volume contains some marks. The bulk of the sixth paragraph of the foreword is marked in the margin or underlined. It bears on the critique of moral values and morality as a 'danger *par excellence*'.]

Friedrich Nietzsche, *L'Origine de la tragédie, ou Hellénisme et pessimisme*, Paris: Mercure de France, 1947. (*The Birth of Tragedy*, eds. Ramond Geuss and Ronald Spiers, trans. Ronald Spiers, Cambridge: Cambridge University Press, 1999).

[There are some marks in section 18. For example: 'When Goethe says to Eckermann, speaking of Napoleon, "Yes, my good friend, actions, too, are a form of productivity", he reminds us, with graceful naiveté, that non-theoretical man is something incredible and astonishing to modern man, so that the wisdom of a Goethe is needed to rediscover the fact that even such a surprising form of existence is understandable, indeed forgivable' (p. 85).]

Paul Nizan, *Les Matérialistes de l'Antiquité. Démocrite, Épicure, Lucrèce*, Paris: Éditions sociales internationales, 1936.
Paul Nizan, *Aden Arabie*, Paris: François Maspero, 1960.
Charles-Henry Nodet, *Le Groupe des psychoses hallucinatoires chroniques*, Paris: G. Doin & Cie, 1938.

[There are many marks (up to p. 151) in this volume, which Fanon no doubt read while writing up his dissertation as well as for *Peau noire, masques blancs* (for the chapter 'L'expérience vécue du Noir'). He underlines several passages in the section on Hughlings Jackson's theory of dissolution of functions (applied to psychopathology in Henry Ey's organo-dynamic theory), seeming to accept with a certain reluctance the organic etiology of the psychoses that it implied. In particular, this annotation on p. 105: 'I confess that the problem of psychosomatic interaction found in the neo-Jacksonian organo-dynamism its most elegant compromise.'
After the sentence: 'One can rediscover and reassemble a comprehensible psychological linkage from the concrete event to other situations (objective or subjective) on which it depends', the following phrase is marked with a 'B(ien)' [Good] in the margin: 'But this linkage, reconstituted *après coup*, considered in its historical and lived *outburst*, would appear only to be a realized possibility and not a totally necessary unfolding' (p. 106). 'As close as it holds to the facts, the psychological explanation always comes up against a certain *indetermination*, often reduced, that it will be unable to grasp. ... The most disconcerting unknown is not the total explanation of the content of the psychopathological phenomenon, but the reason for its triggering. As understandable as all the psychological springs of a delusion may appear in the last analysis, the problem remains completely intact if the point is to know why this delusion exists. Otherwise said, in Jacksonian terms, the analysis of the psychopathological structure will never provide the cause of the dissolution. [Italics in the original.]' These sentences are annotated as follows: 'Incommensurability of phenomenology – study of the structures (*necessity*) with psychology – study of the forms (*contingency*)' (p. 107). In the section on 'Les expériences délirantes' (in which one annotation refers to Lacan): 'We understand by this an original disorder of the mind, a fleeting waning of the personality whereby the patient *lives through* a certain morbid episode, more or less conceptualized. This can only be an intuition, a certain state of the soul, a certain delusional humour (*Grundstimmung*). This *Erlebnis* is intensely felt by the patient, who takes a concrete, particular consciousness, a very new one of his Ego, of the outside world, of the relations uniting them. This phenomenological given, fleeting but irresistibly adopted,

leaves a deep impression on the patient's personality, in the form of a special signification, of a henceforth more or less diffuse, conceded belief, or of a definitively inscribed attitude in his behaviour' (p. 143).]

Julien Offray de la Mettrie, *Textes choisis*, Paris: Éditions sociales, 1954.

André Ombredane, *L'Exploration de la mentalité des Noirs congolais au moyen d'une épreuve projective, le Congo TAT*, Brussels: Institut royal colonial belge, 1954.

[Bears the stamp of Blida-Joinville Psychiatric Hospital.]

Marcel Pahmer, *Les Méthodes de choc et autres traitements physio-pharmacologiques dans les maladies mentales. Travaux américains de 1940–1946*, Paris: Hippocrate, 1946.

[Some marks refer to points concerning the methodology of these shock treatments and p. 29: 'Overall, *schizophrenia* remains the indication of choice for hypoglycemic treatment, on the condition that we are dealing with *acute cases* of *recent* origin in *young individiuals*, cases that make up the majority of favourable reports, and whose treatment is preceded and followed by all the adjuvant methods in use and in particular psychotherapeutic ones.']

Blaise Pascal, *Pensées. Extraits*, Paris: Hatier, 1921.

Blaise Pascal, *Les Provinciales. Extraits*, Paris: Hatier, 1938.

Jean Paulhan, *Petite Préface à toute critique*, Paris: Minuit, 1951.

Jean Paulhan, *La Preuve par l'étymologie*, Paris: Minuit, 1953.

Charles Péguy, *Clio*, Paris: Gallimard, 1932.

Charles Péguy, *Victor-Marie, comte Hugo*, Paris: Gallimard, 1934.

Charles Péguy, *Cinq prières dans la cathédrale de Chartres*, Paris: Gallimard, 1947.

Roger Peyrefitte, *Les Clés de Saint-Pierre*, Paris: Flammarion, 1955.

Édouard Pichon, *Le Développement psychique de l'enfant et de l'adolescent. Manuel d'étude*, Paris: Masson & Cie, 1936.

Édouard Pichon and Suzanne Borel-Maisonny, *Le Bégaiement. Sa nature et son traitement*, Paris: Masson & Cie, 1937.

Henri Piéron, *Psychologie expérimentale*, Paris: Armand Colin, 1939.

Roger Pinto, *La Liberté d'opinion et d'information*, Paris: Domat, 1955.

Luigi Pirandello, *Quand j'étais fou. « Novelle per un anno »*, vol. 2, Paris: Les Éditions mondiales, 1950.

Thérèse Plainol, *Diagnostic des lésions intracrâniennes par les radio-isotopes (gammaencéphalographie)*, Paris: Masson & Cie, 1959.

Plato, *Œuvres complètes*, vol. 1, Paris: Garnier frères, 1936.

Plato, *Ménon [Meno]*, trans. Alfred Croiset, Paris: Les Belles Lettres, 1949.

Plato, *La République* [The Republic], Paris: Hatier, 1952.

Plautus, *Amphitryon-Asinaria-Avicularia*, vol. 1, Paris: 1952.

Roger Pluvinage, *Malformations et tumeurs vasculaires du cerveau*, Paris: Masson & Cie, 1954.

Edgar Poe, *Histoires extraordinaires*, Geneva: Au Grand Passage, 1946.

Raymond Polin, *La Création des valeurs. Recherches sur le fondement de l'objectivité axiologique*, Paris: PUF, 1944.

[In this book, the following chapters are marked throughout: ch. 1: 'Le problème d'un fondement des valeurs'; ch. 2: 'Définition du concept d'objectivité'; ch. 3: 'Postulats généraux de toute axiologie objective.' This volume contains a handwritten note on the back of a request form for a police certificate dated 26 September 1947. The request was made by a student from Martinique, Madeleine Lastel, who contributed regularly to *Alizés, revue antillo-guyanaise d'inspiration chrétienne* in the 1950s.[6] The handwritten note states: 'If it is admitted that God is the creator, it must be further admitted that through his creation God has "committed" himself and that henceforth he finds himself partially engaged in a system of relations.']

Raymond Polin, *La Compréhension des valeurs*, Paris: PUF, 1945.

Georges Politzer, *Le Bergsonisme. Une mystification philosophique*, Paris: Éditions sociales, 1949.

[Several pages are marked here, in particular the pages criticizing the Bergsonian theory of freedom: '*To turn freedom into a purely internal matter, a matter of me with myself*, is as abstract as making it a matter between man and nature: in both cases one conjures away *the concrete life of man*' (p. 77). '*Nothing in the order in which man currently lives is adapted to the unicity of his life* [italics in the original]. He is thrown into a social order whose existence is linked to the fact that the large part of humanity is treated with disregard for the singular

---

[6] On this journal, created by students within the *Aumônerie générale des étudiants d'Outre-Mer*, see the interesting article by Andrew M. Daily, 'Race, citizenship, and Antillean student activism in postwar France, 1946–1968', *French Historical Studies*, vol. 37, no. 2, 2014, pp. 331–57. Daily cites an article by Lastel from October to November 1953, p. 21: 'In an article in *Alizés*, Lastel reports an exchange that she had with a student friend from the Antilles: A young man seriously declared to me, with a tone of reproach in his voice, that I had "Europeanized" myself. "How can you see that?", I asked him. And he replied to me in the same serious tone: "Your short hair!"' Lastel attributes this attitude to the indifference and to the hostility of the Metropole and suggests that some students react to this by donning a rigid and fetishist identity, by becoming critical, or even hostile vis-à-vis those who are perceived as having adapted well to life in the Metropole' (p. 340).

life of each of its members, these latter are thus all tossed together in a mass that is no longer human and that one handles like matter; an order that implies at each instant the irreparable devastation and destruction of unique lives, and this stirs no one anymore than the melting of snow. ... But these observations are not the most important thing here, but instead the fact that they are inseperable from action. *Since once one really adopts the human point of view, what strikes one are not the things to be said, but the things to be done'* [italics in the original] (p. 91).]

Antoine Porot and Jean Sutter, *Le 'Primitivisme' des indigènes nord-africains. Ses incidences en pathologie mentale*, Marseille: Imprimerie marseillaise, 1939.

[There are no annotations or marks in this article, which Fanon violently attacked in his 'Ethnopsychiatric considerations' in 1955, but p. 3 is torn along the diagonal. Thus missing is the beginning of the section of 'Séméiologie psychiatrique', which notably contains the following paragraph: 'When approaching the practice of psychiatry in the North African milieu, one first gets an *impression of monotony*: all the patients appear to be alike; one gets the impression of a rather uniform greyness in which the rich variety of mental forms that we have come to learn about among Europeans are not distinguished. This diversity nevertheless exists, but it is masked from us by a set of common traits that surprise us because we do not know about them: we must change perspective, we must replace a value scale that no longer has any currency with another scale, one of primitive values, or more exactly, one that participates in the scale of primitive values to the extent that the native mentality proceeds from primitivism.']

Georges Poulet, *Études sur le temps humain. La distance intérieure*, Paris: Plon, 1952.

Ezra Pound, *Cantos et poèmes choisis*, Paris: Pierre-Jean Oswald, 1958.

Maurice Pradines, *Traité de psychologie générale. Le psychisme élémentaire*, vol. 1, Paris: PUF, 1948.

Maurice Pradines, *Traité de psychologie générale. Le génie humain*, vol. 2, Paris: PUF, 1948.

Marcel Proust, *Un amour de Swann*, Paris: Gallimard, 1919.

Raymond Queneau, *Le Chiendent*, Paris: Gallimard, 1933.

Pierre Quercy, *L'Hallucination. Les philosophes: théorie de la perception, de l'image et de l'hallucination chez Spinoza, Leibniz, Bergson. Les mystiques:*

sainte Thérèse, ses misères, sa perception de Dieu, ses visions, vol. 1, Paris: Félix Alcan, 1930.

[There are some marks in the introduction. For instance, concerning the visions of saints: 'The most certain thing is the *luminous* certainty of he who is no longer the dreamer and the *dazed* individual of our ordinary wakefulness, but who is finally *awakened* to the divine light.' The last two italicized words are italicized in the original.]

François Rabelais, *Gargantua*, Paris: Les Belles Lettres, 1946.

Jean Racine, *Théâtre complet de Racine. Suivi d'un choix de ses épigrammes concernant son théâtre*, Paris: Garnier frères, 1937.

[Contains some marks, for instance around: *Andromachus* – 'I yield blindly to the transport that carries me away / I love: I come to these places to seek Hermione / to sway her, to snatch her, or to die in her eyes.' *Phaedra* – 'The very light of day is not more pure / Than my heart's core. How could Hippolyte be enthralled by an illicit love …' (Act IV, Scene II) A handwritten note is inserted into this volume: 'Lyon, 20 August, Certif. special studies in neuropsych.']

Ramadhan, Algiers: Éditions algériennes Ennahda, 1961.

Charles-Ferdinand Ramuz, *Les Signes parmi nous*, Paris: Grasset, 1931.

Charles-Ferdinand Ramuz, *Besoin de grandeur*, Paris: Grasset, 1938.

John Reed, *Dix jours qui ébranlèrent le monde*, Paris: Éditions sociales, 1958. (*Ten Days that Shook the World*, New York, NY: Boni Liverlight, 1919.)

Martial Rémond, *Djurdjura. Terre de contraste*, Algiers: Baconnière frères, 1940.

Ernest Renan, *Vie de Jésus*, Paris: Calmann-Lévy, 1957.

Joseph Rennard, *Histoire religieuse des Antilles françaises des origines à 1914*, Paris: Société de l'histoire des colonies françaises, 1954.

Retour dans la nuit. Récits par des auteurs chinois contemporains, Beijing: Éditions en langues étrangères, 1957.

Jean Reverzy, *Place des angoisses*, Paris: Julliard, 1956.

Géza Révész, *Origine et préhistoire du langage*, Paris: Payot, 1950.

Louis Revol, *La Thérapeutique par la chlorpromazine en pratique psychiatrique*, Paris: Masson & Cie, 1956.

André Rey, *Étude des insuffisances psychologiques (enfants et adolescents). Méthodes et problèmes*, vol. 1, Neuchâtel and Paris: Delachaux et Niestlé, 1947.

André Rey, *Étude des insuffisances psychologiques (enfants et adolescents). Le Diagnostic psychologique*, vol. 2, Neuchâtel and Paris: Delachaux et Niestlé, 1947.

André de Richaud, *Le Mal de la terre*, Paris: Charlot, 1947.

Walter Riese (with André Réquet), *L'Idée de l'homme dans la neurologie contemporaine*, Paris: Félix Alcan, 1938.

[On the flyleaf, there are two handwritten notes: 'Ba Amadou Hampaté, 51, rue Lauriston, Paris XVIᵉ' (the writing doesn't seem to be Fanon's); '53 *bis*, Quai des Grands-Augustins'. Fanon met Ba at the first International Congress of Black Writers and Artists, held at the Sorbonne between 19 and 22 September 1956.]

Albert Rivaud, *Les Grands Courants de la pensée antique*, Paris: Armand Colin, 1929.

Maxime Rodinson, *Mahomet*, Paris: Seuil, 1961.

Pierre de Ronsard, *Sonnets pour Hélène*, Paris: E. Droz, 1947.

Hermann Rorschach, *Psychodiagnostics. Plates*, New York, NY: Grune and Stratton, 1955.

Hermann Rorschach, *Psychodiagnostic. Méthodes et résultats d'une expérience diagnostique de perception. (Interprétation libre de formes fortuites)*, Paris: PUF, 1947.

[Contains some marks on the technical passages, but no annotations.]

Jacques Roumain, *Gouverneurs de la rosée*, Paris: Les Éditeurs français réunis, 1944.

David Rousset, *Les Jours de notre mort*, Paris: Éditions du Pavois, 1947.

Jean-Jacques Rousseau, *Rêveries du promeneur solitaire*, Geneva: Droz, 1948.

Mario Roustan, *Montesquieu. Morceaux choisis avec une introduction et des notes*, Paris and Toulouse: H. Didier/Éditions Privat, 1921.

Henri Rouvière, *Atlas aide-mémoire d'anatomie*, Paris: Masson & Cie, 1959.

Jean H. Roy, *L'Imagination selon Descartes*, Paris: Gallimard, 1944.

[In this volume, the detached cover of Paul Ricœur's book *Gabriel Marcel et Karl Jaspers* (Paris: Temps présent, 1948) is inserted on p. 112, on which the following sentence is underlined: 'But for Descartes, there is no reasoning of which consciousness is not aware.']

Bertrand Russell, *Histoire de la philosophie occidentale. En relation avec les événements politiques et sociaux de l'Antiquité jusqu'à nos jours*, Paris: Gallimard, 1952. (*A History of Western Philosophy. And its connection with Political and Social Circumstances from the Earliest Times to the Present Day*, London: Allen & Unwin, 1945.)

Raymond Ruyer, *L'Humanité de l'avenir d'après Cournot*, Paris: Félix Alcan, 1930.

Maurice Saillet, *Saint-John Perse. Poète de gloire*, Paris: Mercure de France, 1952.

Antoine de Saint-Exupéry, *Œuvres*, Paris: Gallimard, 1953.

Léonard Sainville, *Dominique. Nègre esclave*, Paris: Fasquelle Éditeurs, 1951.

Henri Salandre and René Cheyssac, *Les Antilles françaises. Histoire et civilisation*, Paris: Fernand Nathan, 1962.

Nathalie Sarraute, *Le Planétarium*, Paris: Gallimard, 1959.

Jean-Paul Sartre, *L'Imaginaire. Psychologie phénoménologique de l'imagination*, Paris: Gallimard, 1940. (*The Imaginary: A phenomenological psychology of the imagination*, revisions and historical introduction by Arlette Elkaim-Sartre, trans. and philosophical introduction by Jonathan Webber, London and New York, NY: Routledge, 2004).

[Most of the pages of this volume contain marks. There are some annotations: 'Roger Stéphane', placed before a quote given by Sartre as follows 'Observation of R. S., student: "I would have liked to convince myself of the idea that every oppressed person or every oppressed group takes from the very oppression they suffer the strength to shake it off"' (p. 119).

The chapter on 'The Imaginary Life' contains a very large number of marks in the margins, such as alongside this passage: 'This is why the dream world, as with that of reading, is given as entirely magical; we are haunted by the adventures of the dreamed people as by those of the heroes of novels. It is not that the nonthetic consciousness of imagining ceases to grasp itself as spontaneity, but that it grasps itself *as a spellbound spontaneity*' (p. 169; translation modified – SC). The words in italics are underlined and annotated: 'It would be interesting to explain the mechanism of spellbinding.'

'Is not the very first condition of the *cogito* doubt, which is to say the constitution of the real as a world at the same time as its nihilation from this same point of view, and does not the reflective grasp of doubt as doubt coincide with the apodictic intuition of freedom?' (p. 186). 'When the imaginary is not posited as a fact, the surpassing and the nihilation of the existent are stuck in the existent, the surpassing and the freedom *are there* but they are not revealed; the person is squashed in the world, transfixed by the real, and is closest to the thing' (p. 187). Annotation in the margin: 'Hegel'.]

Jean-Paul Sartre, *Situations*, vol. 1, Paris: Gallimard, 1947. (*Sartre: Literary and Philosophical Essays*, trans. Annette Michelson, London: Rider and Company, 1955.)

[This volume is fairly worn out and amply marked and annotated in the margins. Many of these passages have echoes in *Peau noire, masques blancs*. For example: 'That is how things are in his

[Giraudoux's] universe: first come truths, first come ideas and meanings that chose their own signs' (p. 43). 'Man's freedom lies less in the contingency of his evolution [*devenir*] than in the exact realization of his essence' (p. 53) [marked with a 'yes' in the margin].

'Kafka is the novelist of impossible transcendence: the universe is, for him, full of signs that we do not understand; there is something behind the scenery' (pp. 36–7). Annotation by Fanon in the margin of p. 116 [of the French]: 'Camus is right; what Sartre does not see is that we are not foundation [*fondement*] by virtue of our founding of meaning – the absurd is there.'

'They [Kafka, Blanchot] have eliminated the angel's gaze and have plunged the reader into the world with K. and Thomas; but they have left, as it were, a *ghost of transcendence*, floating about within this immanence. *The implements, acts and ends are all familiar to us*, and we are on such intimate terms with them that we hardly notice them. But just when we feel shut up with them in a warm atmosphere of organic sympathy, they are presented to us in a cold, strange light' (p. 72).

This entire paragraph is marked in the margin with a 'TB' (very good) along the last sentence: 'We remember Durkheim's famous precept that we should "treat social facts as things". This is what tempts Mr Bataille in Sociology. If only he could treat social facts and human beings and himself as things, if his inexpiable individuality could only appear to him as a certain given quality, then he would be rid of himself. Unfortunately for our author, Durkheim's sociology is dead: social facts are not things; they are meanings and, as such, they refer back to the being through whom meanings come into the world, to man, who cannot both be scientist and object of science at the same time. You might just as well try to lift the chair you are sitting on by grabbing it by its crossbars. Yet Mr Bataille revels in this vain effort. It is not by chance that the world "impossibility" flows frequently from his pen. He belongs, without a doubt, to that spiritual family whose members are susceptible, above all, to the acid, exhausting charm of impossible endeavours. *The myth of Sisyphus would more aptly symbolize his mysticism than it would Camus' humanism.* ... But we *are* projects, [Sartres' italics], despite what our author says. And we are so not out of cowardice or to flee from an anxiety: *we are projects from the first*' [The English translation of this passage is to be found on pp. 81–2 of *We have only this life left to live: Selected Essays of Jean Paul Sartre, 1939–1975*, eds. Roland Aronson and Adrian Van Den Hoven, New York, NY: New York Review Books, 2013 – translator's note].

'The rest is a matter for psychoanalysis. Yet before anyone protests, I do not have in mind the crude, questionable methods of Freud, Adler or Jung; there are other sorts of psychoanalysis.' Annotation in the margin: 'Can Sartre psychoanalyse Bataille?' (*We have only this life left to live*, p. 82).

'Ponge's movement is opposite: for him it is the thing that exists first, in its inhuman solitude; man is the thing that transforms things into instruments. It is enough, then, to gag in itself this social and practical voice for the thing to be unveiled itself in its *eternal and instantaneous truth*.' Annotation in the margin: 'TB' (Very good) (cf. *Situations 1*, p. 258).

'His end goal, however, is the substitution of a veritable human order for the social order that it undoes. Taking the side of things leads us to the "lesson of things".' Annotation: 'Good'. We find a number of similarly approving remarks in this chapter on Ponge (cf. *Situations 1*, p. 268).

The following citation, by Sartre, of the fourth of Descartes' *Méditations métaphysiques*, an essential text on the will, is marked with a 'capital':
'Since, even as it [the will] is incomparably larger in God than in me, … *it does not seem larger, however, if I consider it formally and precisely in itself*' (cf. *Situations 1*, p. 318).]

Jean-Paul Sartre, *Situations*, vol. 2, Paris: Gallimard, 1948. ('*What is Literature?'And other Essays*, introduction by Steven Ungar, Cambridge, MA: Harvard University Press, 1988.)

[This volume is also marked throughout. Here are some significant marked passages from it. 'Presentation of *Les Temps modernes*': 'Thus, by taking part in the singularity of our era, we ultimately make contact with the eternal, and it is our task as writers to allow the eternal values implicit in such social or political debates to be perceived. … Far from being relativists, we proclaim that man is an absolute' (p. 254).

'But it is not, we repeat, simply a question of effecting an advance in the domain of pure knowledge: the more distant goal we are aiming at is a *liberation* [word circled in pencil]. Since man is a totality, it is indeed not enough to grant him the right to vote without dealing with the other factors that constitute him. He must free himself totally – that is, make himself *other*, by acting on his biological constitution as well as on his economic condition, on his sexual complexes as well as on the political terms of his situation' (p. 261).

'Without its future, society is no more than an accumulation of raw material, *but its future is nothing other than the self-projection beyond the status quo of the millions of men composing it*' (p. 264).

Long passages on language and literature are underlined in the section 'What is literature?': 'In fact, the poet has withdrawn from language-instrument in a single movement. *Once and for all he has chosen the poetic attitude which considers words as things and not as signs.* For the ambiguity of the sign implies that one can penetrate it at will like a pane of glass and pursue the thing signified, or turn one's gaze towards its *reality* and consider it as an object.' In the margin: 'Lettrism' (p. 29).

'Thus, regarding language: it is our shell and our antennae; it protects us against others and informs us about them; it is a prolongation of our senses, a third eye which is going to look into our neighbour's heart. We are within language as within our body' (p. 35).

'It must be borne in mind that most critics are men who have not had much luck and who just about the time they were growing desperate, found quiet little jobs as cemetery watchmen. God knows how peaceful cemeteries are; libraries are the more cheerful of them. The dead are there: the only thing they have done is write. They have long since been washed clean of the sin of living, and besides, their lives are known only through other books which other dead men have written about them' (p. 41).

'And the literary object, though realized *through* language, is never given *in* language. On the contrary, it is by nature a silence and an opponent of the word' (Sartre's italics). In the margin: 'Merleau, indirect language' (p. 52).

'For I call a feeling generous which has its origin and its end in freedom' (p. 58). 'The world is *my* task, that is, the essential and freely accepted function of my freedom is to make that unique and absolute object which is the universe come into being in an unconditioned movement' (p. 65).

'If so, I'd like to be shown a single good novel whose express purpose was to serve oppression, a single good novel which has been written against Jews, Blacks, workers, or colonized peoples. "If there is none," it will be said, "there's no reason why one may not be written some day." But you then admit that you are an abstract theoretician. You, not I. For it is in the name of your abstract conception of art that you assert the possibility of a fact which has never come into being, whereas I limit myself to proposing an explanation for a recognized fact' (note 8, p. 335; translation modified – SC). 'the freedom to which the writer invites us is not a pure abstract consciousness of being free. Strictly speaking, it *is not* [Sartre's italics]; *it wins itself in an historical situation* [underlined in pencil]; each book proposes a concrete liberation on the basis of a particular alienation' (p. 72).

Sartre's pages on *Black Boy* by Richard Wright, whom Fanon admired at the time of *Peau noire, masques blancs*, are underlined in several places (p. 126 *sq*.), above all concerning the nature of the readership that Wright aimed at (Black bourgeoisie and White liberals in America): 'Just as one can catch a glimpse of *eternal freedom at the horizon of the historical and concrete freedom which it pursues, so too is the human race at the horizon of the concrete and historical groups of its readers*. ... But, whatever the good will of the white readers may be, for a black author they represent the *Other*. They have not lived through what he has lived through. *They can understand the negro's condition only by an extreme stretch of the imagination and by relying upon analogies which at any moment may deceive them*' (p. 79). 'Thus, each of Wright's works contains what Baudelaire would have called a "double simultaneous postulation"; each word refers to two contexts; two forces are applied simultaneously to each phrase and determine the incomparable tension of his tale. Had he spoken to the Whites alone, he might have turned out to be more prolix, more didactic, and more abusive; to the Blacks alone, still more elliptical, more of a partner, and more elegiac. In the first case, his work might have come close to satire; in the second, to prophetic lamentations. Jeremiah spoke only to the Jews. But Wright, writing for a split public, has been able both to maintain and go beyond this split. He has made it the *prextext for a work of art*' (p. 80).

The passages on religion, classicism, enclosure in the past and situatedness also bears several marks (p. 135 *sq*.): 'since the two great earthly powers, the Church and the Monarchy, aspired only to immutability, *the active element of temporality was the past, which is itself a phenomenal degradation of the Eternal*; the present is a perpetual sin which can find an excuse for itself only if it reflects, with the least possible unfaithfulness, the image of a completed era' (p. 86). '*Literature became confused with negativity*, that is, with doubt, refusal, criticism, and opposition. But as a result of this very fact, it led to the setting up, against the ossified spirituality of the Church, of the rights of *a new spirituality, one in movement*, which was no longer identified with any ideology and which manifested itself as the power of continually surpassing the given, whatever it might be' (p. 98).

'*This impassioned sense of the present saved him [the writer] from idealism*; he did not confine himself to contemplating the eternal ideas of Freedom or Equality. For the first time since the Reformation, writers intervened in public life, protested against an unjust decree, asked for the review of a trial, and, in short, decided that the spiritual was in the street, at the fair, in the market place, at the tribunal and that it was by no means a matter of turning away from the temporal, but, on the contrary, that one had to come back to it incessantly and go beyond it in each particular circumstance' (p. 102).

'In a stable society, which is not yet conscious of the dangers threatening it, which possesses a morality, a scale of values, and a system of explanations to integrate its local changes, which is convinced that it is *beyond all historicity* and that nothing important will ever happen any more, in a *bourgeois* France tilled to the last acre, laid out like a chessboard by its secular walls, congealed in its industrial methods, and resting on the glory of its Revolution, no other fiction technique could be conceivable; the new operations that some writers have attempted to introduce were successful only as curiosities or were not followed up. Neither writers, readers, the structure of the collectivity, nor its myths had any need of them' (p. 129; translation slightly modified – SC).

'*Being situated* is an essential and necessary characteristic of freedom. To describe this situation is not to cast aspersions on freedom' (p. 133).

'The spiritual, moreover, always rests upon an ideology, and ideologies are freedom when they make themselves and oppression when they are made' (p. 138). 'In short, literature is, in essence, *the subjectivity of a society in permanent revolution*' (p. 139).

'Thus, it was not a matter [for the surrealists], as has too often been said, of substituting their unconscious subjectivity for consciousness, but rather of showing *the subject as a flimsy illusion at the heart of an objective universe. But the surrealist's second step was to destroy objectivity in turn*' (p. 152).]

Jean-Paul Sartre, *L'Imagination*, Paris: PUF, 1948.
Jean-Paul Sartre, *Les Mains sales*, Paris: Gallimard, 1948.

[On the flyleaf: 'Even if we should soil our hands, freedom will be brought to triumph. Marat. M. J. Dublé [Josie Fanon's maiden name], 29 July 1948.']

Jean-Paul Sartre, *Les Séquestrés d'Altona*, Paris: Gallimard, 1960.
Lucien Sausy, *Grammaire complète*, Paris: Librairie Fernand Lanore, 1947.
Alfred Sauvy, *Théorie générale de la population. Économie et population*, vol. 1, Paris: PUF, 1952.
Paul Savy, *Précis de pratique médicale*, Paris: G. Doin & Cie, 1942.

[On the flyleaf: 'Dr Fanon Frantz, 19, rue Salomon Reinach, Lyon.' There are many marks in the chapter on extrasystolic arrythmia.]

Paul Savy, *Traité de thérapeutique clinique*, vols. 1 and 3, Paris: Masson, 1948.

Paul Sebag, *La Tunisie. Essai de monographie*, Paris: Éditions sociales, 1951.

Gregorio Selser, *Sandino. General de hombres libres*, vol. 1, Havana: Ediciones especiales, 1960.

Seneca, *Dialogues. De la vie heureuse. De la brièveté de la vie*, vol. 2, Paris: Les Belles Lettres, 1949.

William Shakespeare, *Théâtre. Hamlet, prince de Danemark, Othello ou le Maure de Venise, Macbeth*, Paris: Beziat, 1936.

L. William Shirer, *Le Troisième Reich des origines à la chute*, Paris: Stock, 1960. (*The Rise and Fall of the Third Reich: A History of Nazi Germany*, New York, NY: Simon & Schuster, 1960.)

Miguel Sholojov, *Campos roturados*, vol. 1, Moscow: Ediciones en Lenguas Extranjeras, 1960.

René Silvain, *Rimbaud. Le précurseur*, Paris: Boivin, 1945.

Samuel R. Slavson, *Psychothérapie analytique de groupe. Enfants, adolescents, adultes*, Paris: PUF, 1953.

Edgar Snow, *La Chine en marche*, Paris: Stock, 1961.

Leonid Soboliev, *Alma marinera*, Moscow: Ediciones en lenguas extranjeras, 1955.

Albert Spaier, *La Pensée concrète. Essai sur le symbolisme intellectuel*, Paris: Félix Alcan, 1927.

Oswald Spengler, *Le Déclin de l'Occident. Esquisse d'une morphologie de l'histoire universelle*, Paris: Gallimard, 1948.

Baruch Spinoza, *Éthique. Démontrée suivant l'ordre géométrique et divisée en cinq parties*, vol. 1, Paris: Garnier, 1934.

Baruch Spinoza, *Éthique. Démontrée suivant l'ordre géométrique et divisée en cinq parties*, trans. and notes by C. Appuhn, vol. 2, Paris: Garnier, 1953.

Oliver Spurgeon English, *Problèmes émotionnels de l'existence*, Paris: PUF, 1956.

Stendhal, *Le Rouge et le Noir. Chronique du XIXᵉ siècle*, Paris: Les Belles Éditions, n.d.

Stendhal, *La Chartreuse de Parme*, Paris: Éditions du Dauphin, 1948.

Éric Stern, *Le Test d'aperception thématique de Murray (T.A.T.). Description, interprétation, valeur diagnostique*, Neuchâtel and Paris: Delachaux et Niestlé, 1950.

August Strindberg, *Le Fils de la servante. Fermentation. Histoire d'une âme (1867–1872)*, vol. 2, Paris: Stock, 1927.

August Strindberg, *La Sonate des spectres. Pièce en trois actes*, Paris: Stock/Delamain et Boutelleau, 1949.

August Strindberg, *Le Fils de la servante. Dans la chambre rouge. L'Écrivain*, Paris: Stock/Delamain et Boutelleau, 1949.

Raphaël Tardon, *Le Combat de Schœlcher*, Paris: Fasquelle éditeurs, 1948.

[Some passages of this book by the Martinican novelist Raphaël Tardon on the abolitionist Victor Schœlcher are marked with a stroke in the margin: 'So what is a slave in the nineteenth century? It is perforce a negro, often of mixed blood, never a White, in the colonies. What is a negro slave? It is a commodity, a movable (*meuble*) – in the juridical sense of the term – an animal of a livestock, in the end a monkey' (p. 16). Writing in the margin: 'Object of property law'.

'Art. 46 [of the *Code noir*]: "For slave seizures, the formalities of our edicts and the customs for movables seizures" will be applied.' And, lastly, art. 48: 'Prohibits seizing for debt the slaves of a property or the property independently of each other' (p. 17). Writing in the margin: 'The negro is a statutory immovable'.

'No code has regulated the droit du seigneur. The negress is a female. No more' (p. 20).

'Schœlcher speaks: "M. Virey affirms that the dorsal spine of the negro is more hollow in its length and arched at its base than the White's. The negro's occipital hole (this, as is well-known, is the opening situated at the base of the skull, through which passes the spinal cord, the extension of the brain) is as with the brute far closer to the posterior part of the skull, in such a way that an African would be unable to hold his head perpendicular on his shoulders." "The white man, says the doctor, is perfectly straight, the black man leans forward ..." The size of the cervical nerves, with the negroes as with the beasts dictate that physical nature perforce wins out over moral nature. This is why negroes have more developed and active senses than Whites. They are greedy, drunkards; they have a piercing sight and a sense of smell keen enough "to scent the snakes and follow the tracks of the animals that they hunt". The negro's blood, bilious humours, viscera, bladder, etc., are impregnated with a blackish tint. (Merckel, a Prussian doctor, copying Herodotus and Aristotle, had already written in 1757 that the negroes "are a separate race of men, because their brain and their blood are black"' (p. 40).)]

Lê Thank Khôi, *Histoire de l'Asie du Sud-Est*, Paris: PUF, 1959.

Gérard Thiriet, *Contribution à l'étude des kystes vrais et des pseudo-kystes nécrotiques du pancréas*, Lyon: Bosc frères, 1949.

André Tilquin, *Le Behaviorisme, origine et développement de la psychologie de réaction en Amérique*, Paris: J. Vrin, 1942.

Leo Tolstoy, *Anna Karenine*, Moscow: Imprimeries réunies de Chambéry, 1956.

Palmiro Togliatti, *Le Parti communiste italien*, Paris: François Maspero, 1961.

Joseph de Tonquedec, *Une philosophie existentielle. L'existence d'après Karl Jaspers*, Paris: Beauchesne et ses fils, 1945.

[Several passages are underlined, bearing on the essential relations between freedom and existence in Jaspers. Thus: 'In action and decision, I am the origin (*Ursprung*) of my action and of my being at one and the same time' (p. 23). *'This choice is the decision to be myself in* Dasein ["decision" in italics in the original]. ... [He implies] that by wanting, I can be, properly speaking. ... *Decision as such is above all a leap* (or only consists in a leap: *ist erst im Sprunge*)' (p. 27). Facing the next passage, 'Engagement' is written in the margin: 'But the great source of clarity, which illuminates above all the theatre, in which freedom has to be produced, is what Jaspers calls *Weltorientierung*, orientation in the world. Man explores the universe without letting up, in order to uncover its mystery, to find himself within it and to act within it. He discovers in it, as far as the eye can see, the conditions and possibilities for action; he becomes aware of the motives that can solicit him in diverse senses' (p. 29). The title of the section 'Liberté et nécessité', in the chapter on liberty, is underlined. In this section we find familiar themes from *Peau noire, masques blancs*, in particular concerning the constitutive historicity of all human existence (p. 37).]

Sékou Touré, *L'Action politique du Parti démocratique de Guinée pour l'émancipation africaine*, Conakry: Imprimerie nationale, 1958.

Rodolphe Tourneur and François Contamin, *Dossier de pathologie médicale pour l'internat des hôpitaux de Paris*, Toulouse: Jean Bertrand, 1951.

Arnold J. Toynbee, *La Civilisation à l'épreuve*, Paris: Gallimard, 1951.

Arnold J. Toynbee, *L'Histoire. Un essai d'interprétation*, Paris: Gallimard, 1951.

Tsouen Tsing, *Le Vieux Messager*, Beijing: Éditions en langues étrangères, 1956.

Union of the populations of Angola, *Populations de l'Angola. La lutte pour l'indépendance de l'Angola. Déclaration du comité directeur de l'Union des populations de l'Angola*, 1960.

Paul Valéry, *Poésies*, Paris: Gallimard, 1942.

Paul Valéry, *Souvenirs poétiques*, Paris: Guy Le Prat, 1947.

Paul Valéry, *Traduction en vers des Bucoliques de Virgile*, Paris: Gallimard, 1956.

Gisèle Vallerey, *Contes et légendes de l'Afrique noire*, Paris: Fernand Nathan, 1955.

Joseph Vendryes, *Le Langage. Introduction linguistique à l'histoire*, Paris: Albin Michel, 1950.

Paul Verlaine, *Nos Ardennes. Huit dessins de Paul Verlaine, Ernest Delahaye, Germain Nouveau*, Geneva: P. Cailler, 1948.

Louis Vidal, *Dictionnaire de spécialités pharmaceutiques*, Paris: Office de vulgarisation pharmaceutique, n.d.

Alfred de Vigny, *Poésies complètes*, Paris: Éditions de Cluny, 1937.

Voltaire, *Zadig et autres contes*, Paris: Éditions de Cluny, 1950.

Voltaire, *L'Ingénu. Anecdotes sur Bélisaire*, Paris: Éditions sociales, 1955.

Jean Wahl, *Le Choix, le Monde, l'Existence*, Grenoble: Arthaud, 1947.

Simone Weil, *Intuitions préchrétiennes*, Paris: La Colombe, 1951.

[Pages 92 to 107 are cut. They bear on Aeschylus' *Prometheus* and its Christian posterity.]

Jean Weill and Justine Bernfeld, *Le Syndrome hypothalamique. Synthèse endocrinienne, métabolique, végétative et psychique*, Paris: Masson & Cie, 1954.

Edward Weiss and Olivier Spurgeon English, *Médecine psychosomatique. L'application de la psychopathologie aux problèmes cliniques de la médecine générale*, Neuchâtel and Paris: Delachaux et Niestlé, 1952.

Pierre Wertheimer and René Leriche, *Neurochirurgie fonctionnelle*, Paris: Masson & Cie, 1956.

Walt Whitman, *Feuilles d'herbe*, Paris: Mercure de France, 1955.

Oscar Wilde, *Le Portrait de Dorian Gray*, Paris: Stock, 1947.

[Written on the flyleaf: '26 May 1952. Errance and aberrance'.]

Thomas Wolfe, *Aux sources du fleuve*, Paris: Stock, 1929.

Richard Wright, *Les Enfants de l'oncle Tom*, Paris: Albin Michel, 1946.

Richard Wright, *Black Boy*, Paris: Gallimard, 1947. (*Black Boy (American Hunger)*, New York, NY: Harper Brothers, 1945.)

[Some passages are marked in the margins, in particular: 'Though I had long known that there were people called "white" people, it had never meant anything to me emotionally. I had seen white men and women upon the street a thousand times, but they had never looked particularly "white". To me they were merely people like other people, yet somehow strangely different because I had never come in close touch with any of them; they simply existed somewhere in the background of the city as a whole' (p. 23). 'He asked me questions in a quiet, confidential tone, and quite before I knew it he was not "white" any more' (pp. 31-2).

'And when I brooded upon the cultural barrenness of black life, I wondered if clean, positive tenderness, love, honor, joy, loyalty, and the capacity to remember were native with man. I asked myself if these human qualities were not fostered, won, struggled and suffered for, preserved in ritual form from one generation to another' (p. 37).

'I would stand for hours on the doorsteps of neighbors' houses listening to their talk, learning how a white woman had slapped a black woman, how a white man had killed a black man. It filled me with awe, wonder and fear, and I asked ceaseless questions' (p. 73).

'Like "K" of Kafka's novel, *The Castle*, he tried desperately to persuade the authorities of his true identity right up to the day of his death, and failed' (p. 140).

The first two sentences of this paragraph are marked with a line in the margin: 'Inside of me my world crashed and my body felt heavy. I stood looking down the quiet, sun-filled street. Bob had been caught by the white death, the threat of which hung over every male black in the South. I had heard whispered tales of black boys having sex relations with white prostitutes in the hotels in town, but I had never paid any close attention to them; now those tales came home to me in the form of the death of a man I knew' (p. 172).

'In my dealing with whites I was conscious of the entirety of my relations with them, and they were conscious only of what was happening at a given moment. I had to keep remembering what others took for granted; I had to think out what others felt' (p. 196).

'Here, in this underworld pocket of the building, we munched our lunches and discussed the ways of white folks toward Negroes. When two or more of us were talking, it was impossible for this subject not to come up. Each of us hated and feared the whites, yet had a white man put in a sudden appearance we would have assumed silent, obedient smiles' (p. 229).

'(There are some elusive, profound, recondite things that men find hard to say to other men; but with the Negro it is the little things of life that become hard to say, for these tiny items shape his destiny. A man will seek to express his relation to the stars; but when a man's consciousness has been riveted upon obtaining a loaf of bread, that loaf of bread is as important as the stars.)' (pp. 232–3).]

Joseph Zobel, *La Rue Cases-nègres*, Paris: Jean Froissart, 1950.

Émile Zola, *Les Rougon-Macquart. Histoire naturelle et sociale d'une famille sous le Second Empire*, Paris: Fasquelle éditeurs, 1960.

Marxism and political brochures

Chassons les impérialistes Américains de l'Asie!, Beijing: Éditions en langues étrangères, 1960.

Constitution de la République populaire de Chine. Adoptée le 20 septembre 1954 à la première session de la première Assemblée populaire nationale de la République populaire de Chine, Paris: Éditions en langues étrangères, 1960.

Constitution de la République socialiste tchécoslovaque, Prague: Orbis, 1960.

Ivo Babic, Marijan Filipovic and Mihailo Milosevic, *Les Institutions scientifiques de Yougoslavie*, Belgrade: 1958.

Commission médicale du centre culturel et économique France-USSR, *Orientation des théories médicales en URSS*, Paris: Centre culturel et économique France-URSS, 1951.

Friedrich Engels, *Études sur* Le Capital. *Suivies de deux études de Franz Mehring et de Rosa Luxemburg sur* Le Capital, Paris: Éditions sociales, 1949.

Friedrich Engels, *Anti-Dühring*, Paris: Éditions sociales, 1950.

[Alice Cherki reports that in Tunis 'Rédha Malek, who undertook studies in philosophy before 1955, gave Fanon Engel's *The Role of Force in History* and *Anti-Dühring* to read. Fanon was reserved. He found these texts too removed from the qualitative experience that an individual has of violence' (*Frantz Fanon: A Portrait*, p. 108). Most of the opening of the first chapter *Anti-Dühring* is marked with long lines in the margins. 'We know today that the *reign of reason* was nothing other than the *idealized reign of the bourgeoisie*; that eternal justice found its realization in bourgeois justice; that equality amounted to bourgeois equality before the law; that to be proclaimed as one of the essential rights of man was … bourgeois property' (p. 50). In French translations the traditional title of Engels' essay is *Le Rôle de la violence dans l'histoire*.]

Friedrich Engels, *L'Origine de la famille. De la propriété privée et de l'État. Sur l'histoire des anciens Germains. L'époque franque. La Marche*, Paris: Éditions sociales, 1954.

Ho Chi Minh, *Œuvres choisies. Le procès de la colonisation française*, Hanoi: Éditions en langues étrangères, 1960.

[This volume carries a dedication: 'As a testament to our fraternity in struggle. Boualem and Ali. W[ilaya]4.']

Vladimir Ilitch Lenin, *L'État et la Révolution. La doctrine du marxisme sur l'État et les tâches du prolétariat dans la révolution*, Moscow: Éditions en langues étrangères, 1918.

Vladimir Ilitch Lenin, *La Maladie infantile du communisme (le communisme de gauche), essai de vulgarisation de la stratégie et de la tactique marxistes*, Paris: Éditions sociales internationales, 1930.

Vladimir Ilitch Lenin, *L'Impérialisme, stade suprême du capitalisme*, Paris: Éditions sociales, 1945.

Vladimir Ilitch Lenin, *Deux tactiques de la social-démocratie dans la révolution démocratique*, Moscow: Éditions en langues étrangères, 1949.

Vladimir Ilitch Lenin, *Notes critiques sur la question nationale. Du droit des peuples à disposer d'eux-mêmes*, Paris: Éditions sociales, 1952.

[This volume is marked in several places.]

Vladimir Ilitch Lenin, *L'Alliance de la classe ouvrière et de la paysannerie*, Moscow: Éditions en langues étrangères, 1954.

Vladimir Ilitch Lenin, *La Faillite de la II*e *internationale*, Moscow: Éditions en langues étrangères, 1954.

[This volume is marked in several places.]

Vladimir Ilitch Lenin, *Que faire?*, Moscow: Éditions en langues étrangères, 1958.

Vladimir Ilitch Lenin, *Sur le parti révolutionnaire du prolétariat de type nouveau*, Beijing: Éditions en langues étrangères, 1960.

Vladimir Ilitch Lenin, *L'État et la Révolution. La doctrine du marxisme sur l'état et les tâches du prolétariat dans la révolution*, Moscow: Éditions en langues étrangères, n.d.

Vladimir Ilitch Lenin, *L'Impérialisme, stade suprême du capitalisme. Essai de vulgarisation*, Moscow: Éditions en langues étrangères, n.d.

Liu Shaoqi, *Rapport sur le projet de constitution de la République populaire de Chine. Constitution de la République populaire de Chine*, Beijing: Éditions en langues étrangères, 1954.

Liu Shaoqi, *Le Triomphe du marxisme-léninisme en Chine. Écrit pour la Nouvelle Revue internationale. Problèmes de la paix et du socialisme à l'occasion du X*e *anniversaire de la République populaire de Chine, 14 septembre 1959*, Beijing: Éditions en langues étrangères, 1959.

Mao Zedong, *La Guerre révolutionnaire*, Paris: Union générale d'éditions, 1955.

Mao Zedong, *De la juste solution des contradictions au sein du peuple. Discours prononcé le 27 février 1957 à la onzième session élargie de la Conférence suprême de l'État*, Beijing: Éditions en langues étrangères, 1958.

Mao Zedong, *Analyse des classes de la société chinoise*, Beijing: Éditions en langues étrangères, 1960.

Mao Zedong, *À propos de la pratique*, Beijing: Éditions en langues étrangères, 1960.

Mao Zedong, *Contre le libéralisme*, Beijing: Éditions en langues étrangères, 1960.

Mao Zedong, *De la guerre prolongée*, Beijing: Éditions en langues étrangères, 1960.

Mao Zedong, *Discours prononcé à l'assemblée de la région frontière Chensi-Kansou- Ninghsia*, Beijing: Éditions en langues étrangères, 1960.

Mao Zedong, *Discours prononcé à une conférence des cadres de la région libérée du Chansi-Souei-Yuan*, Beijing: Éditions en langues étrangères, 1960.

Mao Zedong, *Entretien avec la journaliste américaine Anna Louise Strong*, Beijing: Éditions en langues étrangères, 1961.

Mao Zedong, *La Démocratie nouvelle*, Beijing: Éditions en langues étrangères, 1960.

Mao Zedong, *La Dictature démocratique populaire. En commémoration du 28ᵉ anniversaire du Parti communiste chinois*, Beijing: Éditions en langues étrangères, 1960.

Mao Zedong, *La Ligne politique, les mesures et les perspectives de la lutte contre l'offensive japonaise*, Beijing: Éditions en langues étrangères, 1960.

Mao Zedong, *La Révolution chinoise et le Parti communiste chinois*, Beijing: Éditions en langues étrangères, 1960.

Mao Zedong, *La Tactique de la lutte contre l'impérialisme japonais*, Beijing: Éditions en langues étrangères, 1960.

Mao Zedong, *Le Camarade Mao Tsé-toung sur* L'Impérialisme et tous les réactionnaires sont des tigres en papier. *Département de la rédaction du* Renmin Ribao (*27 October 1958*), Beijing: Éditions en langues étrangères, 1960.

Mao Zedong, *L'Impérialisme et tous les réactionnaires sont des tigres en papier*, Beijing: Éditions en langues étrangères, 1960.

Mao Zedong, *Le Rôle du Parti communiste chinois dans la guerre nationale*, Beijing: Éditions en langues étrangères, 1960.

Mao Zedong, *L'Orientation du mouvement de la jeunesse*, Beijing: Éditions en langues étrangères, 1960.

Mao Zedong, *Les Problèmes stratégiques de la guerre révolutionnaire en Chine*, Beijing: Éditions en langues étrangères, 1960.

Mao Zedong, *Les Questions de stratégie dans la guerre de partisans antijaponaise*, Beijing: Éditions en langues étrangères, 1960.

Mao Zedong, *Les Tâches du Parti communiste chinois dans la période de la résistance aux envahisseurs japonais*, Beijing: Éditions en langues étrangères, 1960.

Mao Zedong, *L'Indépendance et l'autonomie au sein du front uni*, Beijing: Éditions en langues étrangères, 1960.

Mao Zedong, *Luttons pour entraîner les masses dans le front national antijaponais uni*, Beijing: Éditions en langues étrangères, 1960.

Mao Zedong, *Luttons pour la mobilisation de toutes les forces pour remporter la victoire dans la guerre antijaponaise*, Beijing: Éditions en langues étrangères, 1960.

Mao Zedong, *Mener la révolution jusqu'au bout*, Beijing: Éditions en langues étrangères, 1960.

Mao Zedong, *Pour la parution de* Le Communiste, Beijing: Éditions en langues étrangères, 1960.

Mao Zedong, *Pourquoi le pouvoir rouge peut-il exister en Chine*, Beijing: Éditions en langues étrangères, 1960.

Mao Zedong, *Pour un gouvernement constitutionnel de démocratie nouvelle*, Beijing: Éditions en langues étrangères, 1960.

Mao Zedong, *Problèmes de la guerre et de la stratégie*, Beijing: Éditions en langues étrangères, 1960.

Mao Zedong *Rapport sur l'enquête menée dans le Hunnan à propos du mouvement paysan*, Beijing: Éditions en langues étrangères, 1960.

Mao Zedong, *Réformons notre étude*, Beijing: Éditions en langues étrangères, 1960.

Mao Zedong, *Soucions-nous davantage des conditions de vie des masses et portons plus d'attention à nos méthodes de travail*, Beijing: Éditions en langues étrangères, 1960.

Mao Zedong, *Sur les dix grands rapports*, Beijing: Éditions en langues étrangères, 1960.

Mao Zedong, *Sur quelques questions importantes de la politique actuelle du Parti*, Beijing: Éditions en langues étrangères, 1960.

Mao Zedong, *Une étincelle peut mettre le feu à toute la plaine*, Beijing: Éditions en langues étrangères, 1960.

Mao Zedong, *À propos des méthodes de direction*, Beijing: Éditions en langues étrangères, 1961.

Mao Zedong, *La Situation et notre politique après la victoire dans la guerre de résistance contre le Japon*, Beijing: Éditions en langues étrangères, 1961.

Mao Zedong, *La Situation actuelle et nos tâches*, Beijing: Éditions en langues étrangères, 1961.

Mao Zedong, *L'Élimination des conceptions erronées dans le Parti*, Beijing: Éditions en langues étrangères, 1961.

Mao Zedong, *L'Enquête à la campagne*, Beijing: Éditions en langues étrangères, 1961.

Mao Zedong, *Poèmes*, Beijing: Éditions en langues étrangères, 1961.

Mao Zedong, *Préface et postface à* L'Enquête à la campagne, Beijing: Éditions en langues étrangères, 1961.

Mao Zedong, *Raffermir le système du comité du Parti*, Beijing: Éditions en langues étrangères, 1961.

Mao Zedong, *Rapport à la deuxième session plénière du Comité central issu du VIIe congrès du Parti communiste chinois*, Beijing: Éditions en langues étrangères, 1961.

Mao Zedong, *Sur le Livre blanc américain*, Beijing: Éditions en langues étrangères, 1961.

Mao Zedong, *Sur le problème de la coopération agricole. Rapport présenté le 31 juillet 1955 à une réunion des secrétaires des comités des provinces, municipalité et régions autonomes du Parti communiste chinois*, Beijing: Éditions en langues étrangères, 1961.

Mao Zedong, *Sur les négociations de Tchongking*, Beijing: Éditions en langues étrangères, 1961.

Mao Zedong, *Sur notre politique*, Beijing: Éditions en langues étrangères, 1961.

Mao Zedong, *Sur quelques questions importantes de la politique actuelle du Parti*, Beijing: Éditions en langues étrangères, 1961.

Karl Marx, *Les Luttes de classes en France (1848–1850). Le 18-Brumaire de Louis Bonaparte*, Paris: Éditions sociales, 1948.

Karl Marx, *La Guerre civile en France, 1871*, Paris: Éditions sociales, 1953.

Karl Marx, *Salaire, prix et profit*, Paris: Éditions sociales, 1955.

Karl Marx, *Le 18-Brumaire de Louis Bonaparte*, Paris: Éditions sociales, 1956.

Karl Marx, *Contribution à la critique de l'économie politique*, Paris: Éditions sociales, 1957.

[There are some markings in the first chapter on the commodity, as well as at the start of the famous passage on the relations of Greek art and Shakespeare's art with our time (p. 174).]

Karl Marx, *Manifeste du Parti communiste*, Paris: Éditions sociales, 1960.

Karl Marx and Friedrich Engels, *Études philosophiques*, Paris: Éditions sociales, 1951.

[There are several markings on the pages on Hegel in the essay on Ludwig Feuerbach. A cut-out of newspapers from 1964 rejecting the idea that torture is still used against the counter-revolutionaries in Algeria is inserted in this volume, a sign that it was perhaps annotated by another reader.]

Georges Plekhanov, *Les Questions fondamentales du marxisme*, Paris: Éditions sociales, 1947.

[The chapters on 'La philosophie de Hegel' (up until p. 123) and 'Dialectique et logique' are marked throughout.]

Georges Plekhanov, *L'Art et la vie sociale*, Paris: Éditions sociales, 1953.

Union international des étudiants, *Réalités économiques martiniquaises*, Prague: 1960.

Récits de l'Armée rouge chinoise, Beijing: Éditions en langues étrangères, 1961.

Ts'ien Siao, *Leur Terre, ils l'ont gagnée*, Paris: Les Éditeurs français réunis, 1954.

Conference proceedings, article offprints, medical brochures

Congrès des médecins aliénistes et neurologues de France et des pays de langue française, 54ᵉ session, Bordeaux, August 30-September 4 1956. Rapport d'assistance, Paris, 1956.

Congrès des médecins aliénistes et neurologistes de France et des pays de langue française, 55ᵉ session, Lyon. Rapport de neurologie (Paul Castaigne and Jean Gambier), *Valeur des examens paracliniques au cours des accidents vasculaires cérébraux*, Paris: Masson & Cie, 1957.

Les Collagénoses. Rapports présentés au XXXIᵉ congrès français de médecine, Paris, 1957, Paris: Masson & Cie, 1957.

Jean Bancaud, Vincent Bloch and Jacques Paillard, 'Contribution EEG à l'étude des potentiels évoqués chez l'homme au niveau du vortex', *Revue neurologique*, vol. 89, no. 5, 1953.

E. Berard and Gabrielle C. Lairy-Bounes, 'Quelques remarques sur l'électro-encéphalogramme au cours de l'hibernation artificielle', *Electroencephalography and Clinical Neurophysiology*, vol. 7, no. 4, November 1955.

Henry Christy, 'Encéphalite psychosique suivie d'un syndrome de démence précoce. Pyrétothérapie. Apparition d'un érythème noueux. Rémission actuelle', *Comptes rendus du congrès des médecins aliénistes et neurologistes*, Brussels, 22–28 July 1935.

Henry Christy, 'Phénomènes de balancement psychosomatique. Expression particulière d'une loi générale dans les localisations viscérales tuberculeuses. Rôle du terrain', *Comptes rendus du congrès des médecins aliénistes et neurologistes*, Nancy, 30 June–3 July 1937.

Henry Christy, 'Discussion du rapport de M. Hans W. Maier sur la thérapeutique des psychoses dites fonctionnelles', *Comptes rendus du congrès des médecins aliénistes et neurologistes*, Bâle-Zurich-Berne-Neuchâtel, 20–25 July 1936.

Georges Daumézon, Yves-Henri Champion and Jacqueline-Louise Champion-Basset, 'Étude démographique et statistique des entrées masculines nord-africaines à l'hôpital psychiatrique Sainte-Anne de 1945 à 1952', *L'Hygiène mentale*, no. 43, 1954, pp. 1–20 and 85–107.

Michelle B. Dell, Colette Dreyfus-Brisac and Gabrielle C. Lairy-Bounes, 'Le problème des complexes pointe-onde dans l'épilepsie', *L'Encéphale*, no. 4, 1953, pp. 353–76.

Michelle B. Dell, 'L'électroencéphalographie dans l'épilepsie', *Encyclopédie médicochirurgicale, Psychiatrie, Méthodes de diagnostic*, 1955.

James Gray, 'Le mécanisme du mouvement ciliaire' [translation of 'The mechanisms of ciliary movement. Photographic and stroboscopic analysis of ciliary movement', *Proceedings of the Royal Society of Biology*, no. 107, 1930, pp. 313–18].

Paul Hazoumé, 'La révolte des prêtres', *Présence africaine*, nos. 8-9-10, June–November 1956, pp. 29–42. Actes du 1ᵉʳ Congrès international des écrivains et artistes noirs, held at the Sorbonne from 19 to 22 September 1956.

[It is hardly surprising that Paul Hazoumé's remarkable article attracted Fanon's attention, since it joins his interests on the relation between religion and madness, popular spirituality and the disalienation of the colonized. The set of events and ceremonies which Hazoumé describes and which amounts to a revolt by the caste of priests in Dahomey upon an individual expressing a sacriligeous opinion (for example, by stubbornly calling a priest by his previous layperson's name), consist in organizing an outbreak of social 'madness', to the point of blocking all economic activity, and reasserting this caste's power over the political authorities. Hazoumé concludes his articles with a comparison with the profanations demanded by atheist as well as falsely religious colonialists and suggests the possibility of future outbursts against the colonial power, henceforth denuded of all spiritual authority. See also the discussion between Hazoumé and Achille (a friend of Fanon's) on the relations between 'animist beliefs and the inevitable spread of the scientific spirit' (p. 79).]

Laboratoires Laroche-Navarron, *Actualités sur le diabète. 5ᵉ partie, 'Le coma diabétique'*, scientific documentation, record no. 25, January 1954.

Laboratoires Laroche-Navarron, 'Le virilisme pilaire de la femme: définition', scientific documentation, record no. 26, January 1955.

Laboratoires Laroche-Navarron, 'Données récentes sur la cortine naturelle Laroche-Navarron', scientific documentation, record no. 40, January 1956.

Gabrielle C. Lairy-Bounes and Joseph Benbanaste, 'Quelques aspects électroencéphalographiques particuliers des syndromes posttraumatiques tardifs', *Annales de médecine légale*, vol. 34, no. 1, 1954.

Jacques Rabemananjara, 'L'Europe et nous', *Présence africaine*, nos. 8-9-10, June–November 1956, pp. 20–8. Proceedings of the 1ᵉʳ Congrès international des écrivains et artistes noirs, held at the Sorbonne from 19 to 22 September, 1956.

[Rabemananjara's famous address expresses a distance to the idea of négritude (nevertheless associated with an admiration for Césaire) that is similar to Fanon's position in many points.]

Léopold Sédar Senghor, 'L'esprit de la civilisation ou les lois de la culture négro-africaine', *Présence africaine*, nos. 8-9-10, June–November 1956, pp. 20–8. Proceedings of the 1er Congrès international des écrivains et artistes noirs, held at the Sorbonne from 19 to 22 September 1956.

Georges Verdeaux and Jacqueline Verdeaux, 'Étude électroencéphalographique d'un groupe important de délinquants primaires ou récidivistes au cours de leur détention', *Annales médicopsychologiques*, 113th year, vol. 2, November 1955, pp. 644–58.

Georges Verdeaux and Gabrielle C. Lairy-Bounes, 'Valeur et limites actuelles de l'électroencéphalographie en criminologie'.

Georges Verdeaux, 'Utilisation de l'électroencéphalographie dans l'expertise médico-légale', *L'Encéphale*, vol. 47, no. 1, February 1958, pp. 1–30.

World Health Organization, 'L'hôpital psychiatrique public', *Troisième rapport du Comité d'experts de la santé mentale, Série de rapports techniques*, no. 73, November 1953.

Periodicals

Bulletin de l'ordre des médecins, 1953: 4; 1956: 2.

Cahiers du communisme, 1950: 12; 1954: 6–7.

Cahiers du Sud, 1948: 291; 1953: 320.

Cahiers internationaux de sociologie, 1952: vol. 12; 1965: vol. 39.

Esprit, 1948: 10; 1952: 5–6; 1953: 2, 4, 5, 8, 9; 1954, 5; 1955: 6, 7, 12; 1956: 6, 9.

L'Évolution psychiatrique. Cahiers de psychologie clinique et de psychopathologie générale, 1929: 1; 1931: 2; 1947: 1–4; 1948: 1, 2; 1949: 2–4; 1950: 1; 1953: 2.

[Some of the texts published in this important journal are not easily accessible. Since they provide the background of the evolution of his psychiatric thought, I give extensive quotes from issues Fanon anotated.

In issue 2 of 1947, the article by Jan Hendrik van Den Berg, 'Bref exposé de la position phénoménologique en psychiatrie', has been attentively read, in particular concerning the distinction, which phenomenology suspends, between the subjective and the objective. Most of the annotations seem to indicate a certain distance. The following phrase is marked and annotated: 'The demand of *the pre-reflexive attitude* (die Vorwissenschaftlichkeit) *is to let speak all that exists in order to give it the possibility to show what it is in reality, that is to say, its essence, its sense.*' Annotation: 'this is only *one* aspect of the phenomenological approach' (p. 30).

In volume 4 of 1947, Sacha Nacht's article, 'Le rôle du moi dans la structure du caractère et du comportement', contains several marks. The passages on the psychoanalysis of masochism, of fear and of failure neurosis are especially underlined (with a reference in the margin to Lacan concerning the primary identification at the oral stage, p. 62).

In issue 2 of 1948, titled 'Neuropsychiatrie', Henri Hécaen's article on 'La notion de schéma corporel et ses applications en psychiatrie' is abundantly underlined and favourably commented. We know that the notion of the body schema, inherited from Lhermitte and from Merleau-Ponty, is crucial in *Peau noire, masques blancs* and *L'An V de la révolution algérienne*, since what the racist gaze produces is conceived in it as a pathology of the body schema.[7] Fanon marks with a *'Bien'* ('Good') and a *'Oui'* ('Yes') the following paragraphs: 'What we said above about the development of the ego images enables us to conceive that the affective disorders are liable to modify the knowledge of our body. It does not appear impossible to admit that the incessant alternate process of construction and of destruction, which gives us our model of posture, no longer works, or at least is abnormally realized, when the *energy* that maintains and directs it, that is to say the emotional processes, is perturbed. [Added: "*Cf.* Janet."]. It will easily be grasped that, in anxious melancholias in which the subject's aggressiveness gets intensely expressed against his own ego, identified, according to the psychoanalysts, with the lost object, knowledge of the physical ego, henceforth deprived of its propulsive element, fades until its disappears from consciousness or is only manifested there in a strange fashion' (p. 97).

In the margin of a reflection on heautoscopy (the perception of one's body as split into two) in its link with introspective habits: '*Cf.* J.P. Sartre's self-observation, related by M. MP in his "phéno de perception"' (p. 110).

The following phrase is marked with a 'most certainly': 'The feeling of the physical ego cannot be separated from that of the moral ego, both being profoundly integrated together by our affective life, which assures their unity; all that tends to dissociate one is reflected in the other. No distinction can be formally made between depersonalization and hemiasomatognosia [affection where the patient does not recognize the paralysed part of his body as his own]' (p. 112).

Significant disagreement is also expressed. Hence, on p. 114, Hécaen designates as a schizophrenic one of his patients 'all of whose activities are now only centered on the search for the ideal ego that he possessed in his younger years' and whose bodily perception is totally deformed.'

---

[7] See Jean Khalfa, 'Fanon, *corps perdu*', *Les Temps modernes*, nos. 635–6, November–December 2005/January 2006).

This observation is annotated in the margin with a: 'No! This is a *psychasthenic* patient.' Psychasthenia, a concept forged by Janet to designate a pathology involving a fundamental inadaptation to social life, was an essential parameter for Fanon.

In issue 1 of 1949, Hubert Mignot's article, 'Étude critique de l'exploration du psychisme sous état hypnagogique provoqué par les barbituriques', was read and marked with care. The point of it was to examine 'narco-analysis'.

Issue 3 of 1949 is important owing to Henri Ey's article on the 'Efficacy of Psychotherapy'. Fanon's annotations reveal his preoccupations at the time, such as the one bearing on these sentences: 'For us, only a dynamist conception of the relations between the physical and the moral, which presumes that the latter is a form of integration of the former, can enable us to overcome these difficulties. By virtue of this hypothesis, which seems to us to conform to the nature of things, mental illness is defined as a *regression of psychic life conditioned by a disorder of its organic infrastructure*.' Concerning this summary of organo-dynamism, which emphasizes the organic aspect, Fanon wrote: 'Beware! [*Alerte!*]' (p. 291).

Similarly, on p. 292, the first part of the following paragraph is marked with a 'yes', whereas the second is marked with a 'Beware!': 'This way of looking at things situates at the centre of every "mental illness" the individual sufferers' psychic life (that is, the totality of relational life), such that this mental illness appears phenomenologically as a way of being inferior as regards adaptation to reality, to society, to events, but all the same as a way of "being-in-the-world", a disturbed "*Dasein*", the object of a structural analysis or of a necessary "*Daseinanalysis*." But it supposes that this abnormal organization of psychic life *depends* on an inherited or acquired disorder of the *organic* infrastructure, the essential object of a physiopathology. It is evident, as a result, that it posulates both the necessity and the limit of psychotherapy.'

On p. 297: the following paragraph is marked with a line in the margins and a cross: 'What we call "psychosis" is hardly an immobile and static structure with rigid nosographical characteristics, but a certain more or less typical form of evolution, which passes via a series of levels of dissolution and secondary organization of the personality – and, during this psychopathological "work", *some phases* are favorable to psychotherapy. The entire *practical* problem consists in accurately evaluating evolutive work and not losing sight of the opportunities for the psychotherapeutic act, which may be decisive.'

We then find some marks on Eugène Minkowski's article on 'Les voies d'accès à l'inconscient', displaying some skepticism concerning the diverse distinctions examined pertaining to the unconscious and consciousness, such as the possibility of explaining the unconscious as a conservation 'in the form of traces of a physiological order' (annotation: 'Slippery terrain!'), and towards all static conceptions. On the other hand, Minkowski's presentation of Janet's conception of things is marked with a line and a cross: 'Here, the unconscious trace, if trace there is, hardly serves in being evoked from time to time, but it is what at a given moment will determine my conduct; far from serving for the simple reproduction of the past, it will bear within it a sort of propulsion toward the future, which at the desired time will enter into action. I recall here the role that Pierre Janet attributed to the *deferred act* in the constitution of the notion of time: he considers it to be the first element' (p. 390). Janet's dynamic ontology indeed has important echoes in Fanon's dissertation.

The following sentences, which might appear Wittgenstinian, define consciousness in the pragmatic terms of 'lived experience'. They are marked with a line in the margin: ['Remorse, hope, prayer, belief] exceed the "field of consciousness", not in the sense that they are situated outside this field, but in the sense that they are associated with an entirely different way of being, which, much larger, overflows the one determined by the couple conscious/subconscious. They pertain to *lived experience (le vécu)*; and consciousness, together with its field, now seems to detach from this lived experience, in part by impoverishing it, and to be only one of its forms, and certainly not the most alive one' (p. 393). Such a conception corresponds to the descriptions that Fanon gives both of the experience of racism (lived experience structuring the alienated consciousness) and of the colonial reification of cultures, transformed into 'forms' of consciousness and into objects of knowledge.

The conception of the unconscious as *depth* of consciousness, underlined in the following sentences, is indeed necessary to an analysis of ideology: 'Besides the conscious, there is the *lived* (vécu), with the features that are proper to it. The latter, which is much larger, embraces the former' (p. 394). 'All that is connected to research, creation, discovery, is in part elaborated outside of the operations of conscious thought to *arise*, or better still *burst out* [*jaillir*], at a given moment, certainly not in the details, but in a condensed view of the whole, in the manner of a ray of light, within consciousness' (p. 395). 'This unconscious is situated in relation to the conscious not under the sign of the "alongside", as is the subconscious in the field of the conscious, but under the sign of *depth*. It constitutes the ground [*fond*] of our life, from which spring the very personal, diverse experiences of this life' (p. 397).

This paragraph on time is marked with a 'Yes': 'Past, present, future are hardly for us simply "cardinal points", slices of time, but instead present, each for itself, as I have attempted to show in previous works, a particular mode of living of time. These differences have also been found here in relation to the unconscious' (p. 399). Concerning a paragraph in which it is stated that, 'the unconscious is not exclusively a deposit of repressed complexes', Fanon notes: 'Good God! Is it so difficult – especially for a philosopher – to "signify" the libido by recognizing it as an *indeterminate* power of "fixation" and of "investment"?' (p. 401). In a page on the need to preserve the relation of consciousness to liberation and therefore to revise the role attributed to the unconscious, Minkowski writes: '*It is consciousness which liberates.*' Fanon underlines the word 'alone' here: 'On the psychological and philosophical level it is thus affirmed – and this seems to me important above all else – that this faculty to liberate and to liquidate is a fundamental trait of consciousness alone' (p. 403). The following paragraph is marked with a 'Yes' ('Oui'): 'Every doctrine relative to the human being must respect the fundamental features that confer on this being the human aspect and that thereby comprise its essence. There thus exists for doctrines of this sort a specific *criterion of the human*. They take a fatally wrong path inasmuch as they move away from it through an *excessive* concern for what it is customary to call a scientific explanation, based on the principles of evolution, causality, determinism and universal ends' (pp. 403–4).

Lastly, p. 404, which raises an important question about the nature of the unconscious and the complex, is amply annotated: 'The opposition between latent and manifest dream content, and, thereafter, between the latent and manifest content of psychosis, leads us to a crossroads. At this point the paths diverge: does the latent content condition the dream state or solely determine its content? [Fanon's annotation: "Why *abstract* the signification from the content?"]. It certainly seems that the answer ought to concur with the second sense. Similarly, for psychosis. But thereupon the generative role of the complex comes to be limited; it only appears to be called to secondarily fill with a precise content the particular form of life, itself determined by other mechanisms. It may well be that the psychogenesis to which psychoanalysis lays claim is in actual fact neither genesis nor "psycho". The annotation in the margin of these last two sentences reads: 'In other terms: *reductibility* of the complex to primary forms of signification, i.e. seek in the complex – as archaic as it may be – the announcement and the first sketch of the human *drama*.'

Issue 3 (1950) carries the stamp of the medical library of the psychiatric hospital of Saint-Ylie (where Fanon had his first position). It is a special issue paying 'Homage to Pierre Janet'. There is no annotation, but it is indicative of Janet's importance for Fanon that he held onto this issue.

In the table of contents of issue 4 (1950), many articles are marked with a cross, which Fanon did to indicate the important sections of a book or of a journal. Alexandre Vexliard's remarkable article on 'Le clochard, les phases de la désocialisation' [The tramp, phases of de-socialization] is marked throughout.[8] Thus in the analysis of the third phase of regressive adaptation of the homeless person to the situation of social destitution, Fanon marks the following paragraph with several lines: 'Consciousness, whose usual role is to be a guide for action, is barely able to keep up with the events that devalorise the ego. However, if the individual effectively had an awareness of his situation, he would have been able to adopt in advance dispositions that would (perhaps) have allowed him to adapt better to the new situation instead of seeking to re-establish the past' (p. 633). The article's conclusion is underlined with a thick line: 'The social contact [*contact social*] is broken, because the needs, the motivations, the values and the mechanisms of behaviour, which enable a normal social life, have almost completely disappeared, under the invading upsurge of an existence in which the old values have lost all signification, all power to inspire' (p. 639).

The second article marked in this issue is Hubert Mignot's analysis of Henri Ey's thought in his *Études psychiatriques*. In it, Fanon underlines everything that concerns the relation to time and memory. Thus, among the numerous passages pointed to, we find this paragraph, which corresponds clearly to Fanon's analysis of the relation to memory in colonial alienation, in which the past has no longer any relation with possible existence: 'And to conclude, H. Ey emphasizes that "memory disorders can be considered as the phenomenological substance of all the symptoms of the neuroses and the psychoses, insofar as they are more or less direct effects of the *dissolution of consciousness*, i.e., of the alteration of the links that unite in time the form of existence currently lived to buried existence and to possible existence"' (p. 647). Notable also are some marks on the relations

---

[8]On Vexliard, pioneer of the psychosociological analysis of social destitution, see Laurent Mucchielli, 'Clochards et sans-abri: actualité de l'œuvre d'Alexandre Vexliard', *Revue française de sociologie*, vol. 39, no. 1, 1998, pp. 105–38.

between the spatial order of cerebral localisations and the temporal order of evolution in psychiatry in the article that Ey devotes to Guiraud's *Psychiatrie générale* (to which Fanon's dissertation refers), in particular p. 653. Elsewhere in this issue, some marks are to be found that underline in particular Fanon's interest in the developments of psychosomatic medicine in the United States, but no annotation is made on the edifying review that Henri Aubin wrote about Sartre's *Orphée noir*. Aubin, one of Porot's former students and a contributor to the sections of colonial ethnography in the *Manuel alphabétique de psychiatrie* (Paris: PUF, 1952), sees Sartre's article as an attempt at a 'sincere comprehension of the black soul'. He notes, however, that 'recent physiological research reveals in the Black of tropical Africa certain electro-encephalographic characteristics that attest to an "incontestable neuronal immaturity" of the cortex'. If Fanon read this article (marked with a cross in the table of contents), perhaps he found in it an opportunity to reflect in parallel on negritude and on contemporary ethnopsychiatry.

There is no mark in issue 1 from 1951, but it contains the second part of Vexliard's article as well as an article, cut, by E.L.K. Zeldenrust, on 'L'art et la folie: étude ontologique et anthropologique' [Art and madness, ontological and anthropological study], which revisits (p. 84) Ey's reflections on art and madness in the study on psychiatry and surrealism, which Fanon cited in his dissertation. Cf, *supra*, p. 20.]

L'Information psychiatrique. Livraisons mensuelles publiées par le Syndicat des médecins des hôpitaux psychiatriques, 1954: 1–10 (3 is missing); 1955: 1–10; 1956: 1–10 (4 is missing).

[No. 1 of 1955 is dedicated to psychiatry in the colonies. This is the issue in which Fanon and his collaborators published 'Current aspects of mental care in Algeria'. The article of Doctor Le Mappian on 'La psychiatrie à l'île de la Réunion' depicts the difficulties of conducting psychotherapies in the local milieu there (see p. 43 in particular).]

La Nouvelle Critique, 1953: 45; 1954: 51, 53; 1955: 66, 67.

[No. 66, from June 1955, is a special issue on the theme of 'Racism, colonialism and civilization'. It contains a famous article by Maxime Rodinson, 'Racisme et civilisation', which targets the 'agnosticism of bourgeois ethnography', which is ignorant of Marxism; the underlined passage in the following sentence is also marked with two lines made with a pen in the margin: 'But it is necessary to see clearly that the attitude that I have just described [the relativism that consists in putting all "cultures" on the same level] serves many ethnologists (I do not say all), whether consciously or not, to support a policy that *locks the "native" within his tribal, archaic life, within his traditional activities* (since all civilizations are equivalent and since "progress does not produce happiness"), whereas the Whites continue to bear their burden, as Kipling cynically said: the government of these sympathetic peoples' (pp. 131–2).]

La Nouvelle Revue française, 1948: 10; 1953: 6; 1954: 16–17; 1955: 25.
La Nouvelle Revue internationale, 1959: 14, 16. *Les Lettres et les Arts*, 1956: 1.

[This issue, edited by Michel Beaugency and Henri Kréa (see the dedication to Fanon in his book *supra*), contains a section titled 'Trois poètes noirs: Charles Calixte, Édouard Glissant, Léopold Sédar Senghor.']

Les Temps modernes, 1948: 29, 31, 32; 1949: 48, 49, 50, 52; 1951: 63, 68, 70, 73, 74; 1952: 75, 76, 78, 79, 81, 82, 83; 1953: 92, 93–4; 1954: 102, 108; 1955: 109, 110, 111, 114, 115; 1956: 121, 122, 126.

[In no. 29 from 1948, the second part of Francis Jeanson's article 'La récrimination' (published in three parts in nos. 28, 29 and 30) is marked right throughout. For example: 'Thus may I recriminate against the evil of living in a world in which my life is stolen from me just as I may against one in which I *wanted my life to be mine fully* [note in the margin: "Fanciful self-possession"] and where I come up against the impossibility to assert myself once and for all. These two forms of recrimination I will now bring to light by addressing, by turns, the diverse aspects of the situation in the sense I have already made clear, that is to say in what in it seems to be *objective and fatal – for a consciousness, all of whose effort consists precisely in admitting that everything already has a meaning, and that this meaning does not depend upon it*' (p. 1420). Annotation in the margin: '*Cf.* Robert Browning (life has a meaning and it is vital for the ego to discover it)'. '"When my meaning is not at stake" I identify myself with my body – and this is why I hold to it so much. However, because in that the "I" will be able to escape itself into an irresponsible gaze, this "me" will become frozen as an "object", as a bundle of characteristics, as a "character," a temperament, a nature; correlatively, my body will receive from this a sort of objectivated, solidified signification. But when a difficulty arises, when I suddenly find myself in immediate peril, then I frankly break with this body and this "me"; *having turned them into objects*, I can become disinterested with them, I can leave them behind to constitute myself as a pure subject – and this is close to what André Breton said, in the wake of Freud: *that in case of a serious scare, the psychic accent is withdrawn from the ego and transferred to the "superego"'* (p. 1422). In *Peau noire, masques blancs*, Fanon notes that such a break is not possible for anyone who is the object of the racist gaze.

Next to a passage on death, we find this annotation in the margin: 'Read the formidable chapter of *L'Être et le Néant*, "My Death"'[9] (p. 1429). 'If the thought of death can spoil my life and prevent me from really living it, then this occurs to the extent to which I persist *childishly* [underlined with a double line] *to think of death* as being for me the supreme peril and the most definitive of catastrophes. [Annotation: "This is indeed a fundamental ineptitude". And we cite merely for our recollection the Spinozist thought according to which *"a free man thinks of death least of all things, and his wisdom is a meditation not of death but of life* [this last word is underlined with a double line]", a thought that ought obviously to be constrasted with the opposite tradition, which leads to Heidegger' [Annotation: 'And his "being-toward death"'] (p. 1430).

'As we see, all these behaviours are understood in reference to some *absolute self-possession.* Whether I abandon myself to the anonymity of a collective destiny or I rise up without respite against any despoliation, wherever it comes from, it is always for having *posited* [underlined with a double line] in principle that *the ideal form of existence and the perfect type of happiness resided in the total satisfaction of my right of propriety over myself.*' Annotation facing '*absolute self-possession*': 'That is, coincidence of self with self–abolition of that distance to the self whose permanence conditions all authentic "lack of being"'[10] (p. 1432).

---

[9]See Jean-Paul Sartre, *Being and Nothingness*, trans. Hazel E. Barnes, London: Methuen 1957, pp. 531–53. It is evident that Fanon also found the previous section interesting, 'My Fellowman', pp. 509–31, in particular pp. 525–31 on the 'total alienation of the person' produced by the racist gaze in the case of anti-Semitism, a theory developed in *Réflexions sur la question juive*, which Fanon mentions several times in *Peau noire, masques blancs*.

[10]On the 'lack of being', see Sartre, *Being and Nothingness*, p. 129 sq. It is well-known just how Fanon was able to commit himself absolutely while always putting into question what had seemed to be of the order of certainties, as his analysis of neo-colonialism also shows. The ending of *Peau noire, masques blancs* is a celebration of the very posture of questioning as an ultimate end.

Facing the following description of an attitude refusing engagement, 'BIEN' ('GOOD') and 'that is the node of the *inauthentic*': 'At issue – in the narrow frame of my life or in its compact vacuity, made of perpetual refusals – not *to give way to the* upheaval of the instant, *to the catastrophic upsurge of an interrogation that would no longer be part of the system, but would put the entire system in question*' (p. 1435). 'All efforts at moralization imply a *practice of the social as a human milieu, a place of ineluctable co-existence* [this last term is underlined twice] for beings *each one of whom possesses inwardly the same power of liberation*, but whose situations differ on the exterior and *none of whom could manage to liberate themselves all alone*' (p. 1445).

In no. 31 (1948), Harold Rosenberg's article, 'The Stages: Geography of Action', translated as '*Du jeu au je. Esquisse d'une géographie de l'action*', an article on the theatre, in particular Shakespeare, is marked in several places, above all at the points concerning the free act, human will, spontaneity and madness (pp. 1740 *sq.*). There are also some marks in the text of Sartre's *Mains sales* (pp. 1773 and 1800).

In no. 50 (1949), Francis Pasche's article, 'Le psychanalyste sans magie', contains several marks. The article aims to reply to Lévi-Strauss' critique, which compares psychoanalysis to chamanism, whose therapeutic successes can be reduced to 'a simple reintegration into the irrational system of beliefs of the group' (p. 961). The following paragraph is marked with an 'Of course!': 'What is left is to examine the most serious accusation that can be made against psychoanalysis: "Perhaps you abolish domestic cults, but to the benefit of a state religion, since by interpreting as a disorder of familial origin that which may result from a conflict of classes, you deliver the patient to the collective myths that alienate him. You cure him by *adapting* him, whatever the cost, to the society of which you are both part, even if it is untenable in reality, which comes down to absolving the objectively privileged oppressor and to getting the oppressed to accept his yolk"' (p. 971). Annotations in the margin: 'Official psychoanalysis can have no other ambition'. Further below, opposite the last sentence: 'Absolute regression in relation to the "previous conflict situation"'. 'Our ambition will there be, to adopt Lévi-Strauss' terminology, to disadapt them [the exploited]: the awakening of their social consciousness and not euthanasia.' In the margin: 'I doubt so' (p. 972).

No. 57 (1950) contains Francis Jeanson's review of Octave Mannoni's book *Psychologie de la colonisation*. It contains no mark or annotation. This subtle and dense analysis ought probably to be related to Fanon's ambivalence toward Mannoni in *Peau noire, masques blancs*.

No. 60 (1950) contains Else Frenkel Brunswik and R. Nevitt Sanford's article 'La personnalité antisémite. Essai sur quelques conditions psychologiques de l'antisémitisme.' The several marks in this text, which undertakes an analysis of the anti-Semitic personality, show that Fanon may have been interested in it not only on account of the topic (in *Peau noire, masques blancs*, he states that Sartre's 1946 book *Réflexions sur la question juive* is essential to his own thought), but also for its use of psychological tests based on the interpretation of images. On the back of no. 81 (July 1952), which contains the first part of Sartre's article 'Les communistes et la paix', there is the following handwritten note: 'Vocabulary of psychiatry, of psychology. Husserl's *Ideas* by Ricœur. Coll. TM'.]

Présence africaine, 1947: 1, 1948: 4, 5; 1949: 7; 1950: 8/9; 1951: 10/11, 12

[In no. 4 of 1948, Horace R. Cayton's article, 'A psychological approach to race relations', is marked right throughout and its title is circled and marked with a cross in the table of contents. Similarly, there are some marks on Paul Niger's long poem, which follows it, 'Je n'aime pas l'Afrique' ['I do not like Africa'].

In no. 7 from 1949, Francis Jeanson's important article on 'Sartre et le monde noir' ['Sartre and the black world'] is heavily marked. The following passage is annotated in the margin with 'yes'. *Oncle Rémus'* (Fanon discusses the tales of Uncle Remus and the film that Disney made of it in 1946 in *Peau noire, masques blancs*): 'The master expects from the slave something in addition to his work: he expects him to perform without any reticence at all, and to present his perfect resignation through a perfectly carefree attitude' (p. 209). A good part of p. 214 is marked, in particular: 'Moreover, the entire question is to know to what extent incomprehension, hostility and bad faith will play here against the black revolutionaries and reject them either on the side of a forgetting of the universal meaning that their project bears, or else on the side of its hijacking for the benefit of some theoretical certainty, some vain arrogance as regards history'.

No. 12 from 1951 is an important issue, edited by Alfred Métraux, and devoted to 'Haïti: poètes noirs'.]

Présences. Revue trimestrielle du 'monde des malades', 1956: 54, 'Le malade mental. Qu'en avons-nous fait?'

[There are no marks, but this issue does include several articles by psychiatrists that Fanon knew, for example Philippe Paumelle ('Folie et conscience de la maladie'), Paul Balvet and Nicole Guillet ('Le malade mental, un malade comme les autres'), Louis Le Guillant and Paul Béquart ('Relations avec les familles et le milieu extérieur'), Paul Sivadon ('La sortie de l'hôpital psychiatrique') and Jean Oury ('Désaliénation en clinique psychiatrique').]

Psyché. Revue internationale des sciences de l'homme et de psychanalyse, 1948: 15; 1949: 27–8.

[No. 15 contains the first part of Octave Mannoni's article, 'Ébauche d'une psychologie coloniale. Le complexe de dépendance et la structure de la personnalité.' It is unmarked.

Nos. 27–8 contain Maryse Choisy's 'Quelques réflexions sur la guerre de la paix', Angelo Hesnard's 'Le drame de l'aveu' and René Laforgue's 'Au-delà du scientisme. Freud et le monothéisme. Psychologie du mérite.' Fanon has amply annotated Choisy's article, whose work on collective guilt *L'Anneau de Polycrate* he cites in *Peau noire, masques blancs*. Some passages are marked, in particular on creation, genius and boredom. Also, we find this citation of Nicolas Berdiaeff: 'If communism threatens the mind with its totalitarianism, socialism threatens it *with its boredom and its mondanity*. The problem of boredom is a serious problem. The virus of boredom exists in all Christian parishes of all confessions as well as in traditional Christian literature, which in this regard is able to compete with the socialist press. The antidote to boredom is creative power or the power of hatred' (p. 71).

On p. 78, there is a half-sheet of paper that serves as a bookmark and has typed and handwritten text on it: '*Éléments pour une éthique* de Nabert', p. 110: 'Well, as humble, as fleeting as it may be, at the first, the feeling of contrast between the *depth of inclination* and the *satisfaction received* after the tendency had in some sense been thrown outside of itself *on the search for the object*, it is the condition of possibility, as much as the indice, of a consciousness in which a desire is born that is no longer to be confounded with object-oriented desire, that is, the desire that depends on the object and only knows itself as such through the interval that separates it out from it, through the resistances it encounters and through the internal tensions accompanying them. This desire that awakens in the depths of desire attests that consciousness, which was only the experience of a certain opposition that simultanesously had to be endured and overcome, does not move back into the night. Since, in order to shed light on the tendency, it makes use of the light it owes to the contraried expansion of the inclination.' The piece of paper is torn here. On the back: 'Since the subjectivity that is produced to appease this opposition can do so only by an appropriation of the inclination for a goal that it is called to serve, although it passes over it. Whereby is discovered that paradox of ethics according to which the roots of the liking ought never be cut, to which the sap of the liking must circulate through the most distant ends of the primary function of the tendency.' This dialectic (which is a religious one in Nabert's work) of a desire that, by reflecting on its very exercise, unties itself progressively from the object, may well have found Hegelian echoes in Fanon. It was to be transformed in one of his contemporaries, Deleuze, into a theory of desire no longer as a lack of object but as creativity.

A handwritten note on another piece of paper is inserted in this issue: 'Grace and merit. Health, said Laforgue (*Psyché*, 27–8, p. 41), is a balance between several illnesses. Eliminate one of them and illness explodes. Laforgue does not conceive of the good without the bad. The moral ghetto.'

Two other articles are marked: Marie-Madeleine Davy, 'Des limites de la psychanalyse à la forme de la mystique', the marked passage is as follows: 'Delusion is characterized by a false interpretation of everyday events, whereas the *mystical sentiment allows common sense to subsist entirely*' (p. 110); François Piazza, 'Sur le *Chien andalou* de Luis Buñuel et Salvador Dalí'. This is a 'psychoanalytic examination of the essential themes of the screenplay'. The parts of the article devoted to the symbolism of the film sequences (pp. 148–54) are underlined in multiple places.]

Revue de la nouvelle médecine, 1953: 1, 2; 1954: 3.

[This was a journal put together by communist doctors and edited by Yves Cachin. There are several articles linked to Pavlov or bearing on medicine in the USSR or in Romania. No. 3 is devoted to painless childbirth.]

Revue française de psychanalyse, 1948; 3, 4; 1949: 2.

[In no. 3 of 1948, there are some marks in the article by Nacht on 'Les manifestations cliniques de l'agressivité et leur rôle dans le traitement psychanalytique'. Lacan's article on 'L'agressivité en psychanalyse' is not marked.

In no. 4 of 1948, Marie Bonaparte's article 'De l'angoisse devant la sexualité (notes du 23 juillet 1935)' is copiously marked. Mostapha Ziwar's article, 'Psychanalyse des principaux syndromes psychosomatiques', which undertakes a systematic analysis of cases of physical disorders (asthma, ulcers, hypertension, etc.) to relate them to neuroses, was carefully read and marked in several places. Many of the bibliographical references are underlined. Fanon took an early interest in psychosomatic medicine, which would later come to play a major role in his understanding of the 'lived experience' of alienation. See, *supra*, p. 8 and 108.

This paragraph, which sheds light on certain psychogenic vision disorders, is marked with two lines in the margin: 'Freud thus distinguishes two categories of functional disorders; one of a physical nature and that essentially consists in physiological alterations brought about by the untimely use of a given function; and another that includes functional disorders with a precise unconscious meaning, disorders that are the expression of fantasies in a bodily language and are directly accessible to psychoanalysis in the same way as dreams. These disorders are evidently "conversions". The former are currently referred to as psychosomatic' (pp. 507–8). The article's conclusion (p. 539) is marked with a cross: 'However, it is necessary to consider these psychological characteristics as etiological factors. The specificity of the psychic picture does not imply psychogenesis, no more, moreover, than the therapeutic successes obtained by psychoanalysis. As Bonger and his collaborators point out, in the current state of our knowledge, we can only consider psychic disorders and somatic disturbances to be two expressions of the fundamental failure of adaptation.'

Fernand Lechat's article, 'De la sublimation', is underlined in several areas. The passages on the difference between sublimation and schizophrenia in relation to mysticism may have found an echo in Fanon's dissertation. Hence, on pp. 580–1, the following paragraph is marked several times in the margins: 'It must be emphasized here, to ward off all confusion, that there is an essential difference between sublimation and the schizophrenic attitude: the exalted individual [*le sublime*] and the schizophrenic [*le schizophrène*] have the same taste for abstraction and tend to place their main interests outside the field of human relations, but that is the only common feature they share. One important factor eliminates any resemblance between their structures, which is social contact. … And that leads me to oppose true sublimation to mysticism, no matter the ideology on which the latter depends. To my mind, mysticism, as I conceive it, is a pathological fact belonging to a schizophrenic constitution: it is an autism externalized in acts and the acts it inspires are marked with the psychotic seal, as is attested by the permanent delusions of the mystics and psychopathological manifestations, from the hallucinations of some to the insane acts of others.'

To be noted here is a question mark in the margin of p. 577 referring to Lechat's mention of the 'Groupe lyonnais d'études médicales, philosophiques et biologiques (1947)'. This group, led by Gustave Thibon, was therefore not known to Fanon.]

Revue pratique de psychologie de la vie sociale et d'hygiène mentale, 1954: 3, 4; 1955: 1, 2; 1956: 1, 2.

KEY DATES OF FANON'S LIFE

Chronology prepared by Robert J.C. Young

1925   20 July: Frantz Marguerite Victor Fanon is born in Fort-de-France, Martinique. Fanon lives in the family home at 33, rue de la République, Fort-de-France. He goes to school at École de la rue Pérrinon, then at the Lycée Schœlcher.

1939   Start of the Second World War. The schools in Fort-de-France are closed. September: the admiral Georges Robert arrives in Martinique. The period of 'Tan Robè' begins on the island.

1940   June: Armistice between France and Germany. Robert announces his support for Pétain and for the Vichy government. November: Frantz and Joby are sent to Le François to stay with Uncle Édouard. The lycée there is still open.

1941   Schools reopen and the boys return to Fort-de-France. Fanon meets Aimé Césaire, then a twenty-six-year-old teacher at the Lycée Schœlcher.

1943   January: on the day of his brother Félix's marriage, Fanon, seventeen years old, makes a clandestine crossing to Dominica to join the Free French Forces.
        June: Admiral Robert is toppled by the Gaullist Henri Tourtet. Fanon, repatriated from Dominica, goes back to the lycée.

1944   Fanon, enlisted in the Free French Forces, is assigned to the 5th Bataillon de marche antillais (BMA5).
        March: the battalion disembarks at Casablanca, from where it is transported to Guercif and then to El Hajeb camp close to Meknès, Morocco.
        May: transfer to Bougie (Béjaïa), in Algeria.
        August: beginning of operation Anvil, launched by the US First Airborne Task Force, in the south of France; liberation of Paris.
        August: Fanon crosses the Mediterranean and alights close to Saint-Tropez. Fanon is reassigned to the 6th regiment of tirailleurs sénégalais. They advance toward the north as far as the Rhone Valley.

September: Lyon is liberated.

November: The French advance in Alsace begins.

15 November: while fighting close to Montbéliard in the Doubs, Fanon is wounded in the chest by shrapnel. He is hospitalized in Nantua and then awarded the Croix de guerre with a bronze star. Recovered, he goes to Paris.

1945   January: he rejoins his regiment on the shores of the Rhine.

May: Germany capitulates.

September: Fanon is sent to Rouen and stationed in the Château du Chapitre.

September: he takes the *San Mateo*, a cargo ship, to Martinique. Fanon returns to the Lycée Schœlcher to finish his baccalauréat.

1946   Autumn: Fanon departs for Le Havre, from where he takes the train to Paris, with the intention of studying dentistry. After some weeks, he leaves Paris to study medicine in Lyon. He takes courses in biology, physics and chemistry.

1947   January: Félix Casimir Fanon, Fanon's father, dies at the age of fifty-six.

Fanon is clubbed by the police at a demonstration for the liberation of Paul Vergès, the head of the Communist Party of Réunion.

1948   February: Fanon publishes a small student magazine, *Tam-Tam*. He begins a relationship with Michelle B.; birth of his daughter Mireille.

1949   Fanon meets Marie-Josèphe Dublé (Josie) at Célestins, a theatre in Lyon. He writes two plays, *L'Oeil se noie* and *Les Mains parallels*.

1949–   He begins his specialization in psychiatry. He follows a course at
1951   the psychiatric hospital of Vinatier, then he decides to study at the Faculty of Medicine at Lyon University under the supervision of Professor Jean Dechaume. He meets Nicole Guillet, who will introduce him to the psychiatrist François Tosquelles (probably in 1952).

1950   December: Fanon is required to give up a temporary, irregular position as an intern at the hospital of Saint-Ylie in Dole (Jura).

1951   April: Fanon's proposal, originally made in November 1950, to submit an early version of what would become *Peau noire, masques blancs* as his dissertation, entitled 'Contribution to the study of the psychological mechanisms likely to hinder a healthy understanding between different members of the French Community', is rejected.

November: viva voce for his dissertation *Altérations mentales, modifications caractérielles, troubles psychiques et déficit intellectuel dans l'hérédo-dégénération spino-cérébelleuse*.

1952   February: he publishes his first article, 'The North African Syndrome', in *Esprit*.
        February-March: a stay in Martinique.
        Returning to France, he visits the psychiatric hospital of Saint-Alban-de-Limagnole (Lozère), where he works as an intern with François Tosquelles.
        April: publication of *Peau noire, masques blancs* by Éditions du Seuil.
        October: Fanon and Josie are married.

1953   June: Fanon passes the medical examinations for psychiatric hospitals, which enables him to take up a position as *médecin-chef*. He applies for a position in Guadeloupe.
        September: he takes up a position as a temporary replacement at Pontorson, La Manche.
        November: Fanon is appointed to a position at Blida-Joinville psychiatric hospital in Algeria. There he begins to reform current practice and establishes an institutional psychotherapy on the model of Saint-Alban. His interns include Jacques Azoulay and, from 1956, Charles Geronimi.

1954   1 November: start of the war in Algeria.

1955   Fanon makes first contact with the FLN. Birth of his son, Olivier.
        February: death of his sister Gabrielle, aged thirty-three.
        April: a state of emergency is declared in Algeria. During the summer, Fanon publishes an unsigned article criticizing the psychiatry of the Algiers School in *Consciences maghribines*.

1956   July:[1] Fanon sends letter of resignation to the Resident Minister in Algiers.
        September: talk at the first World Congress of Black Writers and Artists in Paris, on 'Racism and culture'.

---

[1]This letter is often dated December, but according to the detailed chronology of Fanon's life from 1954 to 1959 prepared for the French secret services, the letter was written in July, a date presumably derived from the actual letter that Fanon had sent to the Resident Minister ('Fonds Foccart' Archives de la Présidence de la République: Secrétariat général des Affaires africaines et malgaches et de la Communauté (1958–1974). Fonds Élysée, Affaires politiques, Afrique « hors champ » 1958–1974. Afrique occidentale britannique 1959–1971. Carton: AG/5(F)/2213 Ghana 1960–1962). Henceforth 'Fonds Foccart'. For internal evidence that suggests an earlier date for the letter, see also p. 433, fn 1, above.

1957   January: expelled from Algeria. Fanon goes to Paris, then, via
        Switzerland and Italy, to Tunis.
        Under the pseudonym of 'Dr Farès', works as psychiatrist at the
        hospital of La Manouba, then creates the Psychiatric Day Clinic
        at Charles-Nicolle General Hospital.
        June: joins the FLN press office.
        5 June: holds an FLN press conference accusing the French of
        the Melouza massacre (now attributed to the FLN).
        September: becomes a member of *El Moudjahid's* editorial
        committee.
        Travels to Rome, returning to Tunis 21 September.

1958   June: General de Gaulle takes power in France, visits Algiers
        and calls for a referendum to be held in September in order to
        establish the 5th Republic. Martinique votes to continue to be
        part of the French Community.
        September: establishment of the Provisional Government of the
        Algerian Republic (GPRA). Travels to Rome.
        December: Fanon is a member of the FLN delegation to the
        All-African People's Congress in Accra. 15 December returns to
        Tunis via Lisbon and Rome.

1959   March: Fanon speaks on 'National Culture and the War of
        Liberation' at the Second Congress of Black Writers and
        Artists in Rome. He calls for a 'literature of combat'.
        April: Travels to India with Ferhat Abbas, then flies to Cairo
        and then Casablanca.[2]

        May: voyage to Rabat, Morocco, passing through Rome and
        Madrid; his destination is the ALN (Algerian National Liberation
        army) military base of Ben M'Hidi located at the border. He is
        injured in a car accident.
        July: he returns to Rome for some hospital treatment;
        he survives an assassination attempt at the hospital by a
        commando of La Main rouge (French secret services).
        August: returns to Tunis for ALN political meetings.
        October: publication of *L'An V de la révolution algérienne* by
        Éditions François Maspero, without Fanon's introduction. Three
        months after publication, the book is seized by the police.

1960   February: named itinerant ambassador of the Provisional
        Government of the Algerian Republic (GPRA) in Africa, based in
        Accra, Ghana.
        April: Fanon gives a talk at the Afro-Asiatic Solidarity
        Conference, in Conakry; then another at the Positive Action
        Conference for Peace and Security in Africa, in Accra.
        June: he speaks at the Conference of Independent African
        States, in Addis Ababa.

---

[2]Fonds Foccart.

September: he takes part in the Pan African Congress in Léopoldville (Kinshasa) in the newly independent Congo Republic. October: takes a flight from Accra to Monrovia; he is informed that the plane for Conakry is full and that he has to take an Air France flight; suspecting a trap, he opts to travel by road to Bamako. He writes a travel diary on the road as he goes to Mopti, Douentza, Gao and then to Tessalit on the Algerian border to identify a possible entry route for the ALN into Algeria via the south.

He returns to Accra and writes 'The Stooges of Imperialism' for the GPRA (published in December in the information bulletin of the Algerian Mission in Ghana).

December: Fanon returns to Tunis for medical tests; he is diagnosed with leukaemia.

1961   January: Assassination of Patrice Lumumba in the Congo. Foundation in Algeria of the Secret Army Organization (OAS). Spring: a stay in Moscow for medical treatment. April: returns to Tunis and writes *Les Damnés de la terre*. He writes to Maspero to ask him to ask Sartre to write a preface. May: his article 'Concerning Violence' is published in *Les Temps modernes*. During the summer: he gives lectures on Sartre's *Critique de la raison dialectique* to the ALN forces stationed at the Tunisian border.

July: Fanon travels to Rome. Simone de Beauvoir and Claude Lanzmann come to meet him at the airport. He meets Sartre with whom he speaks for three days straight. His last meeting with Édouard Glissant, in Rome.

July–September: Sartre writes the preface to *Les Damnés de la terre*.

October: Fanon travels to Rome again, meets Sartre for the last time, and then flies to Washington for medical treatment. He has to wait a week before being admitted to the Clinical Center, National Institute of Health, Bethesda, Maryland (Washington).

October: publication of *Les Damnés de la terre* in Paris by François Maspero.

6 December: Fanon dies.

7 December: the police in Paris seize copies of *Les Damnés de la terre*.

1962   3 July: Declaration of Algeria's independence.

1964   Publication by Maspero of *Pour la révolution africaine*.

INDEX

Doray, Bernard 252 n.2
dosing techniques 301–3
    lithium 303–4
douars 28, 211, 213, 216, 216 n.4,
    226, 275
    celebrations/meetings 220
    cordial to foreigners/strangers
        222–3
    djemaa 206, 220 n.15
    employment of men 219 n.11
    faith on God 223–5
    inhabitant 217, 217 n.7, 219
        n.14, 222
    Kabylian 217 n.7
    religious life in 220–21, 223
    social life of men/women
        218–19
    traditional life 217, 221–2
Duchêne 108 n.150
dysbasia lordotica 305
dyskinetic epilepsies 312

editorials of Fanon 151, 151 n.1,
    154–5
    guidelines 152
    on weariness 117 n.2, 118–24,
        120 n.4
        human and things 120–1
        memory 121–2
        therapeutic role of engage-
            ment 122–4
egocentrism 176 n.16, 372
electroconvulsive therapy 21
    n.41–2, 125 n.2, 126, 128–9,
    131, 133–4, 136, 143. *See also*
    Bini therapy (electroshocks)
electroencephalography 143,
    148–50, 438
Eliade, Mircea, 'The "God who
    Binds"' 234 n.8
elocution disorder 74
energetic functional plane 85

engagement 118, 122–3, 133, 181,
    211, 320, 322, 430, 449
entity (clinical) 10, 12 n.24, 40, 268,
    297, 310, 351 n.5, 354 n.10
epilepsy 20, 290, 309, 319, 336, 358,
    358. *See also specific epilepsies*
    case of 140–5
    Porot's study on 253
    with torsion spasm 312–13
epistemology xii, 8 n.16, 10, 12,
    12 n.25, 193 n.6, 280 n.8, 297
    n.15, 411
Equanil 317 n.2, 320–4
ergotherapy 36 n.70, 126, 134,
    136–7, 142, 178, 198–9, 199
    n.12, 202, 213, 244
ethnology xv, 366, 368, 402
ethnopsychiatry 27, 104 n.135, 252,
    252 n.2, 254, 269 n.10, 277 n.1,
    379–80, 393, 419, 446
    colonial xii, 2, 4 n.7, 9, 12, 24
        n.45, 222 n.19, 286 n.2
    study of Black African 254
Europe/Europeans xiv, 10 n.18,
    24–6, 28, 32–4, 38, 43, 152, 164,
    196, 201, 203–4, 207, 211, 217,
    218 n.8, 226, 230, 241, 246, 251,
    254, 258, 275, 281, 332, 379–80,
    384, 419
    celebrations in ward of 205, 212
    criminals 28
    women (ward) 24–5, 191, 196,
        199, 202, 205, 210, 242, 279
'exhaustion' syndrome 117, 136
existence 8 n.16, 16 n.32, 19–20,
    30–1, 32 n.59, 34 n.65, 41,
    51–2, 54, 72, 89 n.90, 90 n.92,
    104, 105 n.142, 158 n.7, 167,
    180, 182, 200, 205, 211, 218,
    223–4, 226–7, 230, 262–3, 268,
    274, 281–2, 286–7, 294–6, 299,
    299 n.19, 308, 311, 326–7, 347,